S0-BDP-273

ROCK CLIMBING EUROPE

Stewart M. Green

FALCON GUIDE®

GUILFORD, CONNECTICUT
HELENA, MONTANA
AN IMPRINT OF THE GLOBE PEQUOT PRESS

Dedicated to the memories of Earl Wiggins and Billy Westbay.
Friends, climbing partners, and fellow travelers on the vertical path.

A FALCON GUIDE®

All photos by Stewart M. Green
Front cover photo: Chris Fossli on *Catalonia* (5.10a) at Hauktjern crags near Oslo, Norway.
Back cover photos, counterclockwise from top right: Village of Bonnieux near Buoux, France; climbers on Nago at Arco, Spain; climbers on Millstone Edge at Gritstone Edges, Great Britain; Cristos Batalogianis on *Nixenkante* (5.11d) at Meteora, Greece; Ian Spencer-Green on *Tippler Direct* (5.10d) at Gritstone Edges, Great Britain; and Ian Spencer-Green on *Le Rose et Le Vampire* (5.13d) at Buoux, France.
Spine photo © Brand X Pictures
Text design by Casey Shain
Maps by Volker Schniepp Geographisches Institute © 2006 Morris Book Publishing, LLC

Library of Congress Cataloging-in-Publication Data
Green, Stewart M.
    Rock climbing Europe/Stewart M. Green.—1st ed.
        p. cm.—(Falcon guide)
    Includes bibliographical references and index.
    ISBN 0-7627-2717-9 (alk. paper)
    1. Rock climbing—Europe—Guidebooks. 2. Europe—Guidebooks. I. Title. II. Series.
    GV199.44.E8G74 2005
    796.52'23'094—dc22

                                                                        2005010157

Manufactured in the United States of America
First Edition/First Printing

WARNING:

Climbing is a sport where you may be seriously injured or die. Read this before you use this book.

This guidebook is a compilation of unverified information gathered from many different climbers. The author cannot assure the accuracy of any of the information in this book, including the topos and route descriptions, the difficulty ratings, and the protection ratings. These may be incorrect or misleading, as ratings of climbing difficulty and danger are always subjective and depend on the physical characteristics (for example, height), experience, technical ability, confidence, and physical fitness of the climber who supplied the rating. Additionally, climbers who achieve first ascents sometimes underrate the difficulty or danger of the climbing route. Therefore, be warned that you must exercise your own judgment on where a climbing route goes, its difficulty, and your ability to safely protect yourself from the risks of rock climbing. Examples of some of these risks are: falling due to technical difficulty or due to natural hazards such as holds breaking, falling rock, climbing equipment dropped by other climbers, hazards of weather and lightning, your own equipment failure, and failure or absence of fixed protection.

You should not depend on any information gleaned from this book for your personal safety; your safety depends on your own good judgment, based on experience and a realistic assessment of your climbing ability. If you have any doubt as to your ability to safely climb a route described in this book, do not attempt it.

The following are some ways to make your use of this book safer:

1. Consultation: You should consult with other climbers about the difficulty and danger of a particular climb prior to attempting it. Most local climbers are glad to give advice on routes in their area; we suggest that you contact locals to confirm ratings and safety of particular routes and to obtain firsthand information about a route chosen from this book.

2. Instruction: Most climbing areas have local climbing instructors and guides available. We recommend that you engage an instructor or guide to learn safety techniques and to become familiar with the routes and hazards of the areas described in this book. Even after you are proficient in climbing safely, occasional use of a guide is a safe way to raise your climbing standard and learn advanced techniques.

3. Fixed Protection: Some of the routes in this book may use bolts and pitons that are permanently placed in the rock. Because of variances in the manner of placement, weathering, metal fatigue, the quality of the metal used, and many other factors, these fixed protection pieces should always be considered suspect and should always be backed up by equipment that you place yourself. Never depend on a single piece of fixed protection for your safety, because you never can tell whether it will hold weight. In some cases, fixed protection may have been removed or is now missing. However, climbers should not always add new pieces of protection unless existing protection is faulty. Existing protection can be tested by an experienced climber and its strength determined. Climbers are strongly encouraged not to add bolts and drilled pitons to a route. They need to climb the route in the style of the first ascent party (or better) or choose a route within their ability—a route to which they do not have to add additional fixed anchors.

Be aware of the following specific potential hazards that could arise in using this book:

1. Incorrect Descriptions of Routes: If you climb a route and you have a doubt as to where it goes, you should not continue unless you are sure that you can go that way safely. Route descriptions and topos in this book could be inaccurate or misleading.

2. Incorrect Difficulty Rating: A route might be more difficult than the rating indicates. Do not be lulled into a false sense of security by the difficulty rating.

3. Incorrect Protection Rating: If you climb a route and you are unable to arrange adequate protection from the risk of falling through the use of fixed pitons or bolts and by placing your own protection devices, do not assume that there is adequate protection available higher just because the route protection rating indicates the route does not have an X or an R rating. Every route is potentially an X (a fall may be deadly) due to the inherent hazards of climbing—including, for example, failure or absence of fixed protection, your own equipment's failure, or improper use of climbing equipment.

There are no warranties, whether expressed or implied, that this guidebook is accurate or that the information contained in it is reliable. There are no warranties of fitness for a particular purpose or that this guide is merchantable. Your use of this book indicates your assumption of the risk that it may contain errors and is an acknowledgment of your own sole responsibility for your climbing safety.

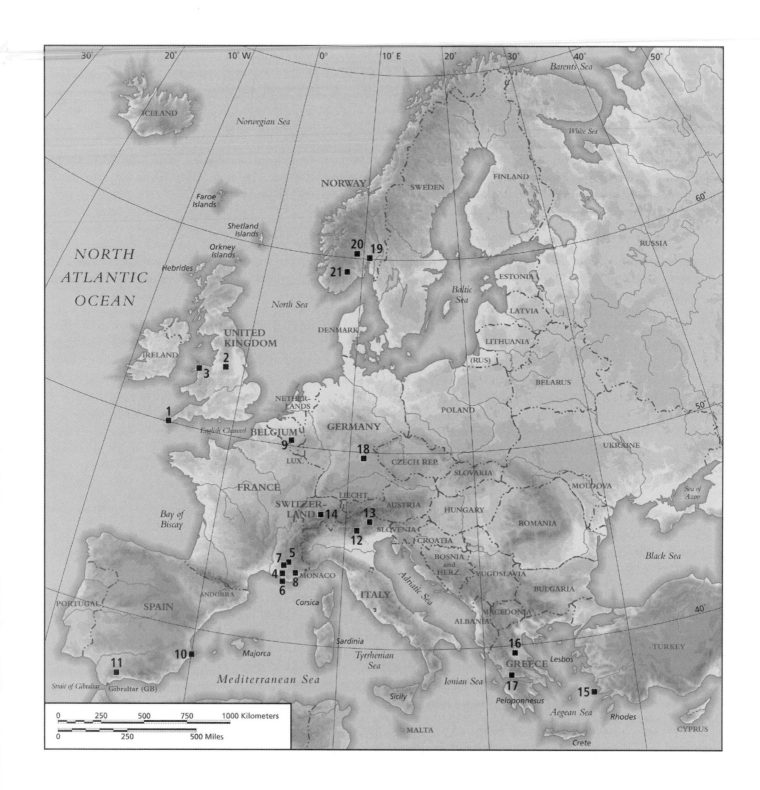

CONTENTS

ACKNOWLEDGMENTS

Rock Climbing Europe is the culmination of my dream to create a guidebook for Americans to discover and explore the best and most famous climbing sites in Europe. Europe offers a stunning array of magnificent and beautiful areas with some of the best rock climbing adventures on planet earth. I'm grateful to The Globe Pequot Press to have faith in my ability to create this book of climbing dreams.

This book took me the better part of five years of work, including traveling across the Atlantic Ocean many times by Air Canada, United, American Airlines, US Airways, Delta, Lufthansa, Olympic, Scandinavian Air, and British Air to all the described areas. It is extremely time-consuming and expensive to do the field research for a comprehensive book like *Rock Climbing Europe*—making photographs for topos; talking to local climbers; shooting action photographs; writing descriptions of roads, trails, cliffs, and routes; and then actually putting hands and feet to rock and climbing routes. The book research also includes camping and other accommodations; shops, stores, and groceries; and rest-day activities and cultural attractions.

It would have been impossible to have created this book without the help, knowledge, and friendship of my many friends both in the United States and Europe. Many thanks, *muchas gracias, tusan takk, merci, efharisto, grazie,* and *danke* to everyone who aided and abetted in making *Rock Climbing Europe* a reality. A special thanks are due to Dennis Jump and Chris Baddams in the Peak District for putting up with me and my idiosyncracies for long periods of time; my good friend Aris Theodoropoulos in Athens for hospitality, climbing adventures, translations, and setting me up with local climbers; my *ami* Jean Bourgeois at Reux Astronomical Station in Belgium for help with Freÿr and Les Calanques; Chris Fossli and Jan Westby at Tyrili Klaterclub and Henrik Bollingmo in Oslo for hospitality, area trips, photo shoots, and lots of information on Norwegian climbing; *min kjære vennen* Elisabeth, Sunniva, and Solrun Rørvik in Tønsberg *og* Andebu for hospitality, real *Norsk* food, language lessons, and for understanding that I'm a Norwegian at heart, and Bjørn, especially for rescuing me from the train station at midnight; Klaus Ruppert and Franzi Schwarz in Frankfurt for much help with the Frankenjura while cooking in the climber's shed or waiting out rainstorms; also Oskar Roshed from Sweden, Shawn and Amanda Brown from Wisconsin, and other Frankenjura climbers; Christos Batalogiannis and Vangelis Batsios, the local hardmen at Metéora, for beta, suggestions, and climbing; George Hatzismalis on Kálymnos; *merci* to the great climber Daniel Dulac for information on his favorite French areas; my friend Matt Robertson, formerly of Europe and now Taiwan, for thoughts, corrections, and editing; Eric Jones at Tremadog, Wales, for camping, tea, and beta; the Dangerous Brothers—John Bates and Dave Ross in Loughborough, UK; John and Christine and the rest of the crew at Finca la Campana at El Chorro; Alan Higham for Kálymnos information; Boulder climber Chris Archer, who tested the Kálymnos chapter and added lots of good information; Paul Drakos and Vibeka Wilberg in Santa Fe for reviewing chapters on Norway; Dennis Jackson in Taos for test-driving the Costa Blanca chapter; my friend Howard Brooks for comments and suggestions; my friends Cindy Hintz and Charles Ganote for hospitality at the New River Gorge; Ed Webster in Maine for info on Norway and connecting me with his friends there; a *verde gracias* to my good *amigos* Eric Hörst in Pennsylvania and Eric McAllister, my friend and Web master in New Hampshire.

Many thanks to the crew at The Globe Pequot Press/FalconGuides, including executive editor Jeff Serena, director of sales Max Phelps, Utah sales rep Larry Siedl, field sales manager Mike Pallesi, John Burbidge for his editing, and Jan Cronan, the book's editor. On all my sojourns across Europe, my two wonderful sons Ian and Brett Green were always with me, if not in body at least in lively spirit. I'm thankful for their love and support. Lastly many thanks to climbing partner, buddy, and fellow planet traveler Martha Morris, who navigated roads, demystified climbing areas, ate baguette and Camembert, and in the end understood the joy of "being French."

Andrea Dorigatti on *Capuvers* (8a) (5.13b) at Pian Schiavaneis near Passo Sella, Dolomites, Italy.

INTRODUCTION

Europe—it's the pulsing heart of the old world. It's the ancestral place for so many Americans, a place of origins and long human history, and the land of parents, grandparents, or long-dead relatives. This is the homeland.

It's a continent of tribes speaking different languages and observing ancient customs. It's a diverse place of communism and democracy, of Mercedes-Benz and Jaguar, of Brigitte Bardot and Hugh Grant, of Bordeaux wine and Greek coffee, of Michelangelo and Dali, of chip butties and *spanakopitta*. It's the place of the ancient Greeks, Romans, Celts, Basques, Bretons, Flemings, Welsh, Walloons, and Catalans. It's the continent of Andorra, England, Russia, Kosovo, Bulgaria, Norway, Monaco, and Portugal. It's the place we admire and mimic for food and drink, for fashion and style, for culture and history. Europe is a place where we're an audience, a respectful pupil sitting at the foot of this wise and wizened continent.

As climbers we look to Europe for immaculate limestone and alpine granite, for sport climbing and strict traditional ethics, for its possibilities and storied climbing history. This is where climbing began when men began scrambling up alps for pleasure. It's where pitons were invented to anchor climbers to rock walls; where ropes were first used for belaying; where smooth-soled shoes were found to grip rock better than Tricouni nails; where vertical paths were named and comparative rating systems devised.

Climbing in Europe is as diverse as its cultures. Climbers in different countries follow different ethics and rate routes with different systems. They also use the same epigrams, prejudices, and stereotypes to describe their climbing areas and climbers as they do to sum up their varying nations, regions, and cities. Even the immense north-south divide of the Alps that splits Europe is noticeable among climbers. The industrious climbers of the north are serious, almost dour, with strong ethics and an almost workaholic attitude at the crags, whereas the indolent sun lovers in the southlands along the Mediterranean approach the sport with a *mañana* sense and fun-in-the-sun attitude. No wonder the Brits like to head south to Spain for winter climbing holidays.

As a visiting climber you travel beyond the usual tourist circuits through the big European cities. You leave Paris, London, and Munich behind and journey into the backcountry, on back roads, to off-the-beaten-track places, villages, valleys, and mountains. As an American you're a rarity. The locals aren't jaded by Americans. They have preconceptions about America and Americans, yes, but they also have little real experience knowing Americans. Traveling around Europe as a climber, you rarely see other American climbers or tourists.

DECIDING TO GO

This is a book of European climbing dreams. A book to leaf through and see what catches your fancy, to find where you want to go, climb, and pay homage. It's not hard to go to Europe these days. Airfares are relatively cheap, and flights are plentiful. It's easy to rent a car and get around. Many people speak English, so language is no excuse. There's no better time than now to plan your European escape.

Just Say Yes!

Taking a monthlong climbing trip to Europe is taking time out from your everyday American life. It's a whole different experience than road-tripping in your own country since you have to overcome lots of barriers and impediments to going. It takes effort. It takes setting a goal and going for it. You have to set aside time. You have to earn money to travel. You have to organize logistics. And the rewards are commensurate with your effort. Your trip to Europe can, if you let it, change you and your outlook on life and the world. Your trip can turn you into a vagabond, a traveler, an explorer, into a person with an interest in possibilities—in other places, in new friends, and in yourself and your attitudes. But it all begins with choice. Your choice to just say yes.

You have to decide to go. Now. Soon. But not later. Don't put it off for some future time when you think you can better afford it or when you think life and relationships will be settled. By buying this book you are setting yourself on the path to going now, not later. You can stay home, tying yourself to house, hearth, career, family, and future, and mortgaging your self and money to some future choice. You can, as the great naturalist Henry David Thoreau wrote in *Walden*, spend "the best part of one's life earning money in order to enjoy a questionable liberty during the least valuable part of it." If you're a climber, you know something about risk taking, you know about putting yourself on the line and going for it. You know about taking control of the moment rather than letting the moment take control of you. If you haven't learned that lesson on the crags, then you haven't worked the moves and finally clipped the anchors on an elusive redpoint project.

The most difficult part of travel is making up your mind to go and working toward that goal. You make the commitment and then make it happen. You can experience a lot of anxiety over travel. How will I get there? Where will I stay? How can I communicate? What if I don't have enough money? What if I get lost? Lots of questions—and the answers? Well, you know they're inside of you. You're a climber. You're resourceful. You make things happen, and you will. There will be a day on your journey—perhaps you'll be standing on the rim of the Verdon Gorge at sunset—and you'll think, "Wow, I'm here. I made it. I saved and scrimped. I quit that good job. And now I'm here and tomorrow I'm going to climb that big wall!" That's part of your inward journey—pride, gratitude, awe.

Climbing in Europe is adventure travel. It's getting off the tried and true tourist routes and into the backcountry, into the places where Americans seldom

Climbers at the base of Stanage Edge's Popular End in the Peak District, England.

go. But consider that word "adventure." It's not only a physical state but a mental one as well. It's venturing into the world to experience it on its own terms, not yours. It's something that you can't pay for. The true adventurer realizes that it is not something that you buy by hiring an adventure travel company, but instead you rely on your own wits and strengths to survive and thrive. It's spiritually satisfying, sort of like reaching the belay after leading a hard pitch. You did it. You earned the right to stand there on the summit through your own hard work and ingenuity, not because you paid some guy to drag your sorry ass up. Adventure is not a commodity that is bought and sold; instead, it's something that is earned.

The Trip Takes You

Okay, you're in Europe on your once-in-a-lifetime climbing trip. You want to go everywhere. You want to see everything.

You want to climb at every area. You have to let those thoughts go. Just whisk them out of your mind. None of that will happen. If you think of it as a once-in-a-lifetime trip, then that is what it will be, and you'll probably be forever disappointed. Instead, think of this trip as just that—a trip. You'll do what you can, see what you can, climb where you can. And you'll be back. Always remember that you can come back. And you will. You will return to climb with new European friends, to visit new areas, to stop by new cathedrals and museums. As you travel about Europe, you sense that many Americans consider their European vacation as a once-in-a-lifetime opportunity. You'll feel good knowing that you've let those thoughts go, that you know this fact: I'll be back.

Travel needs to be simple, simplicity itself. Don't get bogged down in too many details and plans. Live simply on the road. You're carrying your worldly possessions, packed into your climbing sack, and you realize you don't need more than

that. Down the road in the next French village is a campground where you can spread your sleeping bag on the ground. You can walk to a cafe for a meal and after-dinner coffee. Travel helps dispense with fears and opens you to the world and all the good things that happen. Simplicity connects you with community, with friends, with yourself.

One of my keys to travel is to go without a master plan. That doesn't mean you shouldn't have an itinerary, but let yourself go where you want. Don't hold tight to "the plan." Remember the traveler's adage: Wherever you go, there you are. Maybe there is some place you've always wanted to go. The name entrances you, or maybe you saw a picture of it when you were ten years old and it stuck in your mind in the passing years. Go and check it out. Maybe you'll be disappointed, or maybe you'll discover another place or person much more interesting on the way.

While driving to Chamonix after leaving Grimsel Valley in Switzerland, I thought I'd like to see the Matterhorn—that perfect and potent mountain symbol. I threaded the rental car up a twisting valley to Zermatt, stopping for road construction, and reached road's end in the village. Here I discovered that the Matterhorn isn't visible from Zermatt itself. It's around the corner behind a stony ridge. Instead of the stunning mountain, I found a place crammed with tourists, parking lots crowded with tour buses, kitsch shops, and damn expensive coffee. You have to take a bus up the valley, with a paid reservation, just to get within looking distance. This is nuts, I said. I'm out of here. The Matterhorn still waits behind the ridge, but I wasn't disappointed and am content knowing that it's out there.

Every traveler is an optimist. How else do you travel but with an innate sense of optimism, a sense that everything will be fine, that you'll discover something new, that you'll find a place to lay your head at night and a place to feed your stomach and soul. And if it's not fine, then it's an adventure, a note in your journal, and still something that was worth leaving home for. Sometimes it's the fall of sunlight on a leaf, the rain skirling down the gutter, the swoop of a hawk against a gray limestone cliff, the smile of delight on your partner's face as she grabs the last pockets of the pitch below your feet.

John Steinbeck wrote in his great book *Travels with Charley,* "Once a journey is designed, equipped, and put in process, a new factor enters and takes over. A trip, a safari, an exploration, is an entity . . . no two are alike. And all plans, safeguards, policing, and coercion are fruitless. We find after years of struggle that we do not take a trip; a trip takes us." Let this trip take you.

LANGUAGE

One of the biggest obstacles travelers must overcome in Europe is the perceived language barrier. Let's face it, even though most Americans are horribly Anglocentric and think that American culture and language is the center of the world, the rest of the globe doesn't agree with this arrogant assessment.

Part of the whole ugly American stereotype is tied to language. I experienced this firsthand in Delphi, Greece, when an American couple from Pennsylvania approached me on a narrow street and asked slowly and in a loud voice, "DO YOU SPEAK ENGLISH?" I stood there stunned by their rudeness and then, after a pregnant pause, quietly said, "Yes, what are you looking for?" And it was their turn to be stunned. Our linguistic arrogance also leads some Europeans to pretend that they don't understand English, even though they may speak perfect English.

We need to remember that Europe is first and foremost a continent divided into tribes that speak different languages. Even in Scandinavia, with the cultural homogeneity between Norway, Sweden, Denmark, and Finland, each country speaks its own language and sometimes more than one. In Norway alone there are two Norwegian tongues, plus the ancient Sami language in the far north.

As a climber you travel to parts of Europe that are remote and off-the-beaten tourist track. Most tourists hit the cities—London, Paris, Rome, Munich, Amsterdam, and Vienna—but as a climber you spend little time in cities and most of your time in small villages near the crags. In these places the residents speak little or no English. So you have to make an effort to communicate by using the local language and with hand signs. If you're armed with a handful of memorized words and a decent phrasebook, you can get by in places like Provence in France, rural Spain, Germany's Frankenjura, or Greece.

Everyone can learn to speak a different language besides their native tongue. In America we don't have to learn other languages. We get by everywhere with English. We push for referendums and laws for English only. We're afraid of other languages. We're afraid of not understanding, of being ignorant, of being left out. And it's our loss not to communicate with others in their language, of not learning the nuances and beauty of their words. Many Europeans are fluent in languages besides their own. This is especially true in Scandinavia, Netherlands, and Germany, where English is a required school subject.

I met a climber from the Lofoten Islands in northern Norway who was fluent in six languages. He said his father spoke thirteen languages.

Learning a new language is all about attitude. If you haven't studied a language in high school or traveled before, don't worry—you'll do all right with a bit of fortitude and a dose of humility. No matter how badly you mispronounce words, usually to your chagrin, the native is delighted with your efforts and will go out of his way to understand what you need or what you're trying to say. Learning a language requires courage. The courage to sound stupid. The courage to speak like a child. The courage to be a beginner again.

The best way to learn a foreign language is by studying at home and memorizing common words, expressions, and questions like "Hello," "How are you today?", "Where is the toilet?", "How much is this?", and "What route is this?" Try to build a small vocabulary before you leave. Familiarize yourself as best you can with pronunciations and elementary grammar. When you travel, carry a phrase book. A small bilingual dictionary is also helpful. Read and translate signs and billboards. Speak to people as best you can, and don't worry about how you sound. Overcome the thought that you're uttering a string of unintelligible sounds. They mean something to someone, just not you, at least not yet. Use phrases and words that you understand and that mean something to you. Use the words you know to build more comprehension. One of the difficulties in learning languages is that although your own pronunciation is good, hearing and understanding the words when someone speaks to you is lacking.

People learn languages in different ways. We learn information through various senses—seeing, hearing, and touching. Usually we learn by some combination of all our senses, but some learn better by seeing the word written out. Then we know its structure, its letters, its physicality. Others learn by hearing the words and by listening to the cadence and sounds. And still others learn by analysis, by understanding grammar and the underlying

The scenic Verdon Gorge, the "Grand Canyon" of France.

structures of sounds, words, and sentences. Then we piece words together into sentences, into coherent understandable structures.

The best thing is to immerse yourself in the culture and language of wherever you visit. Go into shops and order bread. Stop at a cafe and ask for coffee and cake. Ask climbers at the cliff what routes they recommend. Speak to the family camping next to you. Ask questions. Be inquisitive.

Be brave. Be not an American, but a citizen of the world.

PLANNING YOUR TRIP

Itineraries

Okay, so you've looked through the travel guides to Europe and glanced at suggested itineraries. After reading those suggestions you feel almost as manic as anyone who actually follows those foolish schedules. You know the secret to quality travel, and you know that it isn't following the Yankee speed freaks around Europe with their mindset that yesterday was Paris, today is Milan, and tomorrow is Munich. As a climber you know that the secret is smarter and slower travel. You can't just show up at Céüse and think you're going to send *Carte Blanche* let alone *Realization* without spending some serious time there. Plan your itinerary accordingly.

Itineraries are fine. They're travel plans. They're what you want to do, some of your goals. It's a good idea to commit them to paper long before you leave. Open a European road atlas, and map out your trip. Pencil in where you plan to be on different dates on a calendar, remembering that the best-laid plans are always subject to change. Because they will change. The sunny weather might turn to slanting rain and cold; the mistral might blow with tempestuous ferocity; the sun might appear and shatter southern Europe with a week of record-high temperatures. You want flexibility and the ability to change schedules midstream.

Keep the following items in mind when you plan your European itinerary:

Decide where you want to go. Sounds easy enough, but consider variables like weather, time of year, and your budget. List all your dream climbing areas, as well as what cultural attractions and cities are important for you to visit. Decide how much time you want to climb and how much to sightsee. I usually climb two days and then take off a day to rest, recharge, and look around. If you're working a hard project, you need time to physically recover, which makes it nice to be close to interesting villages or cities.

Make a dateline for your route. First figure out when you arrive in Europe and when you leave, then hammer out day-to-day plans. If you come in summer, plan on visiting the southern areas in Italy or Provence in June, when temperatures will be cooler than July or August. Save the warmer months for cooler areas in Switzerland, the Dolomites, Frankenjura, Belgium, Norway, and Great Britain.

Consider flying open jaw. This means flying into one city and out another. This sometimes saves lots of extra travel time to get back to your point of origin. It usually costs a bit more for airfare and car rental since you'll be dropping the vehicle in a different city or country, but you save lots of time, the traveler's best friend. Fly into London, cross the channel to the continent, explore around, and fly out of Rome or Munich.

Don't be too ambitious. You will never go everywhere you want and climb every route on your tick list. That's the reality of a trip to Europe. Just remember that you will be back. I find it's best to spend at least a few days at each area you visit. If you want to go daily crag hopping, it's best to go to southern France, where you find many cliffs in a relatively compact region. In this case you can set up base camp near Buoux and then make day trips to cliffs like Volx, Sisteron, Sainte Victoire, Oppède-le-Vieux, Cavaillon, Orgon, St. Rémy, Mouries, Fontvieille, Russan, Claret, Seynes, and Dentelles de Montmiral. Likewise, the Peak District in Britain is excellent for the crag jumper, with all its gritstone edges and limestone cliffs.

Sample Itineraries

Consider the following sample itineraries as possibilities for extended road trips around Europe. Some areas and countries, including both Greece and Norway, are hard to combine with others, so you want to plan a climbing trip only to them. Spain is best as a winter trip.

Britain and France Cliff Tour. This trip to some of the continent's best climbing areas requires a minimum of twenty-one days to do it right. You'll need more time if you want to work hard projects. Fly into London, rent a car, drive north up the M1, climb for five days on the Gritstone Edges, drive to North Wales, climb and sightsee for three to five days, and drive south to Dover. Drop off the rental car, take the ferry to Calais in France, and pick up another hire car at the ferry terminal. Drive south to Paris, camp at Fontainebleau, and boulder for a day. Drive the autoroute to Avignon, and set

up base camp in Apt. Climb at Buoux and surrounding cliffs for three to five days. Drive to Orpierre for a day of easy routes and then to Céüse for five to seven days. Finish up at either Les Calanques or Verdon for three more days of climbing. Fly from Marseille to Paris to home.

Northern Europe Summer Tour. An excellent cragging trip to cliffs not often visited by Americans, as well as great sightseeing. Allow a minimum of fourteen days to do this one justice. Fly into Paris, and spend a day at Fontainebleau bouldering and recuperating from jet lag. Drive to Le Freÿr in Belgium, and climb for three days. Drive for a day to the Frankenjura, climb for seven to ten days, and fly home from Munich.

Le Grande Tour du Europe. This trip gives the grand tour of the best climbing areas in continental Europe. To do it right you need at least a month, but two or more months is better. This is an ambitious road trip that is best broken into a couple of separate trips. But if you have the time, fly into Paris, drive south to Fontainebleau, boulder for three or four days, and drive south, stopping for a day at Saussois and a day at Saffres south of Auxerre. Continue south to Avignon, camp in Apt, climb at Buoux for four or five days, and spend another four or five days at nearby crags. Drive to Cassis, and climb at Les Calanques for five to seven days. Drive north, climb at Sainte Victoire, and then set up base camp at Verdon Gorge. Climb at Verdon for five to seven days. Drive to Orpierre, and climb for two days. Drive to Gap, and climb at Céüse for seven to fourteen days. Drive northeast to Chamonix, and climb for three to five days in the French Alps. Drive to Interlaken, and climb at Grimsel Valley and lower elevation limestone cliffs for five days. Drive southeast to Arco, and climb for five days. Drive to the Dolomites, and climb for five to ten days. If you have time, drive southeast to Trieste and then over the Slovenian border to Osp for five days. Drive north through Innsbruck and Munich to the Frankenjura. Climb at the Frank for seven to ten days. Drive west to Belgium, and finish at Le Freÿr. Fly out of Brussels, Amsterdam, or Paris.

GETTING THERE

Getting off your duff and getting on a plane is the major reason why so many folks never end up traveling to Europe. It takes a will and a way to combat the stay-at-home American inertia. Don't convince yourself that it's too much work to make that first step and find an air ticket. It's not.

The air ticket is the single most expensive part of your climbing trip, but with some planning and shopping, you can manage the expense. A great ticket price always sends you packing—for your trip. A high price leaves you frustrated and willing to just forget the whole damn mess. Usually the balance is somewhere in between. The fact is you can't get to Europe for next to nothing, but you can get there for a very good price.

The vast air space over the Atlantic Ocean between North America and Europe is one of the busiest airways in the world. Every day hundreds of flights served by American and European carriers wing across the big pond. Thousands of seats need to be sold every day at a wide range of prices to keep those carriers in business and those planes flying. Your job is to find a couple of those seats at an affordable price.

Shopping for Tickets

You need to answer three basic questions to find that elusive affordable price. First, when do you want to go? Second, how long do you want to stay? Third, how much can you spend? Everything is, of course, contingent on your answers.

The travel seasons with the highest prices are from mid-June to early September and again for a few weeks around Christmas and New Year's. Travel then is expensive. Plan ahead to find affordable tickets. If your travel dates are flexible, you won't have a problem finding good tickets. The spring and fall shoulder seasons are always cheaper than summer, the weather is more tolerable at most climbing venues, and everything is less crowded. Winter is always cheap, except for the Christmas rush. December through

February is ideal for bargain flights to Spain.

Most tickets have minimum and maximum restrictions on the length of your stay. You usually have to book and pay for the flight at least twenty-one days ahead of time, spend at least seven days and not more than three months abroad, and get penalized if you change your ticket or violate the provisions. You might think that the longer you stay, the cheaper the ticket. That's not usually the case. A good scenario is to travel one leg in shoulder season, which drops the overall price. Also try to schedule your travel dates during the week. Airlines are always booked up on weekends.

Decide on your travel dates, the length of your stay, and where you will fly from and to, and then search for fares with flexibility for both dates and length of stay. Figure out how much you can spend for an air ticket, and begin from that point. Usually a quick surf around the Web gives an idea of average fares. Buy tickets when it seems like a good deal. If you wait, the dates will quickly sell out, and you'll be stuck with a higher fare. Usually the airlines publicize cheap fares to popular destinations, but these seats are always limited loss-leaders.

Where to fly from and to is another important question. If you're close to any North American hub cities like New York, Newark, Atlanta, Dallas, Chicago, Los Angeles, San Francisco, or Seattle, then you can find cheap nonstop flights that fly to the European gateway cities of London, Paris, Frankfurt, and Amsterdam. If you're not near the hubs, you will pay more for tickets, so consider finding a cheap flight to one or even driving and leaving your car at a pal's house. Likewise, if you're flying to European cities like Oslo, Athens, or Milan, you pay more for the extra leg. Another way to travel is "open jaw," that is, flying into one city and out another. This makes sense if you're doing a grand climbing tour, starting in Britain and ending in Italy.

The keys to finding a cheap ticket are to hunt for the best fares, be willing to jump immediately for a bargain flight, look for last-minute deals, consider charter flights, ask about discounts, look for fare wars between competing carriers, and be willing to travel by any means to a hub city. Remember that students, anyone younger than twenty-six, and seniors never should pay full price for an air ticket. A rule of thumb is that the cheaper the ticket, the more restrictive and inflexible it will be. Cheap seats are usually non-refundable, and itinerary changes are impossible or expensive.

Internet, Airline, or Agent

Should you use a travel agent, the airlines, or surf the Internet on your own to find those elusive air tickets? There are advantages to all, and it's really just a matter of choice and time.

A good travel agent is a fortunate ally for the intrepid traveler. A travel agent, a travel expert in your own town, is invaluable in your search for the best airfare—but only if he or she understands you and your particular needs. As a climber you're already an independent traveler, and those package tours that they're pushing for agency profits don't fit your scheme. Look for an agent who is knowledgeable about European travel and understands the realities of budget travel. Sometimes a travel agency that specializes in student travel works best for your needs.

Travel agents, if they work for you, are worth their weight in gold. Before the Internet, agents made most fees from the airlines. Now the airlines are pocketing those commissions, so the agent has to charge you a fee for each ticket. Think of travel agents as consultants, and you are paying a fee for their knowledge and services. Agents are your friends; they will look out for your interests and find you the best ticket. They will tell you that by leaving three days earlier, you'll save $200. And right there you've already saved money above their commission. It's best to let the agent only book your flights and perhaps a car rental and the first night's hotel. Beyond that you want to be on your own and free.

Lots of seats are sold on the Internet. Using a mouse, a modem, and time, you can find some unbelievable ticket prices, but you also find a lot of average and high-priced tickets. Do lots of online research at different travel Web sites to understand the plethora of available fares. Only then are you able to purchase seats with confidence. Super last-minute deals regularly crop up. Go to big Internet sites like Travelocity, Orbitz, Expedia, and Sabre to find flights with fewer restrictions and inconveniences than sites like Cheaptickets. You can comparison shop for airfares, car rentals, and hotel reservations using these sites. Look for last-minute specials, sometimes called E-savers, to quickly fill empty seats. These are usually posted early in the week for weekend travel. The downside is they are often restrictive in the length of stay. Lastly, get a paper ticket if at all possible. If you have flight problems in Europe, a paper ticket goes a lot farther to getting on another flight then having a scrap of paper with a vaporous E-ticket number that may or may not be on the agent's computer.

Airlines have jumped on the Internet bandwagon, building their own Web sites and squeezing the travel agent out of the cash pie. But airline Web sites rarely offer the best deals—after the military complex, travel is the second-largest industry on the planet. The airlines are in the business of filling seats for maximum profit, so don't expect much help from them to find lesser-priced tickets. They won't be telling you that if you change plans and fly three days earlier, you'll save $200. The airlines are not out to cut you any breaks. Still, if you regularly check their sites, some good deals can be uncovered. Look online for upcoming promotional fares or special rates. Airlines also offer booking incentives like extra frequent flyer miles, Internet discounts, and even discounted car rentals or free cell phone rentals when you buy an online ticket. Sometimes competition on trans-Atlantic crossings leads to fare wars between carriers.

The usual American airlines that fly to Europe are United, Northwest, Delta, American, Continental, and US Airways. Also consider the foreign carriers, including Air Canada, British Airways, Air France, Scandinavian Airlines (SAS),

Ian Spencer-Green cranks *Les Spécialistes* (5.14a) in the upper Verdon Gorge, France.

Olympic, Iberia, Swissair, Alitalia, and Lufthansa. Many Asian carriers have routes from North America to London.

Passports and Visas

Unless you're a seasoned traveler, you can't just buy a plane ticket and go. You need to get your on-the-road life in order. The first and most important items you need are travel documents—passports and visas.

If you don't have a passport or need to renew, then head over to a U.S. Passport Agency, post office, or federal or state courthouse and pick up a passport application, or download one online. Fill it out, get a couple standard passport photos taken, and ship it to the nearest office. You need to enclose your old passport for a renewal. If all goes well, you will have your new passport within four weeks. If you can't organize your time enough to plan that far ahead and need the passport now, then you can pay an extra $60 to

expedite its processing and delivery in twelve to fifteen days. An adult U.S. passport is good for ten years, whereas an under-sixteen passport is valid for five years. Cost is $85 for a new passport, $70 for a minor's passport, and $55 for a renewal. If your passport is set to expire, renew it before you leave so it doesn't sunset on your trip.

Visa requirements vary from country to country, but the good news is that all the countries in this book do not require visas for U.S. citizens for stays that are shorter than three months. You enter the country, show your passport to immigration authorities, get the passport stamped, and you're on your way.

Your passport, a document owned by the U.S. government, is your overseas identification. It's a hot commodity wherever you travel, so you need to protect it. Keep it on your person. Don't leave it in luggage or hotels, and never lend it to anyone, use it as collateral, or ask someone to hold it for you. It should be safe and

handy because you may be required to show it when using a credit card, changing money, checking into a hotel or campground, or crossing a border. Some campgrounds may ask for your passport to hold as collateral for camp-fee payment. It's best not to relinquish it and pay each day rather than when you leave.

If your passport is lost or stolen, notify the local police and the nearest U.S. embassy or consulate as soon as possible. To get a new passport, you need all your pertinent personal information and must be able to show identification and proof of citizenship. It's best to make a few photocopies of your passport before you go and store them in different safe places like your luggage and your climbing pack. Also leave one at home with relatives so you can call for the info if needed. You should be able to receive a temporary passport or papers within a couple days that will allow you to continue your trip and to reenter the United States.

GETTING AROUND

The 747 touches down, taxis to the terminal, and disgorges you and the rest of the passengers. You cruise through immigration and customs, and step into the round international terminal at Charles de Gaulle Airport in Paris. Ah, at last you're in France, land of the fabled cliff Céüse, which just happens to be located several hundred kilometers to the southeast. You've already made plans to get there though. Over in the next terminal wait the papers and keys for a rental Fiat, ready to transport you down the Autoroute de Soleil to that fabulous limestone rampart.

When you come to climb in Europe, you need a car. It's that simple. Your own wheels spell freedom. The freedom to go where and when you want. The freedom to not be limited by trains, schedules, cities, terminals, buses, your thumb. The freedom to bring lots of climbing and camping stuff that the foot traveler omits. Out there too, on the open road, you will see the real Europe—a continent of small towns, villages, valleys, mountains, and sea coast—and not the usual American tourist vision of immense cities. Also, the reality is that you can only reach most of the climbing areas with your own vehicle. You may eventually be able to get there by train and bus, but a lot of precious climbing time will be wasted.

Car Rentals

Driving your own car with three or four buddies is cost-efficient and convenient. The price of a weekly rental, gas, and highway tolls is still cheaper than several train passes, not to mention the time savings. You conserve also by camping instead of staying in hotels or B&Bs. Gasoline is expensive, as much as $5.00 a gallon in many countries, but your rental, unlike most American cars, gets super mileage, and distances are short.

Renting a car in Europe is just like in the United States. You make a reservation, pick it up, and go your way. Shop around before you go by calling lots of companies with toll-free numbers, asking your travel agent, or surfing the Internet. Prices vary, depending on the time of year, pickup points, current specials, and competition. The best deal is usually a rental for a week or longer with unlimited mileage. Always arrange your rental from the United States; otherwise, it's exorbitantly expensive to hire in Europe. If you're over there and need a car, call home or your travel agent and have them make a stateside reservation for you. Save money by picking up your car at a cheaper downtown office rather than the airport.

An option to renting is to lease a vehicle. Leases can be as short as seventeen days or as long as several months. Renault has a good lease program. Another option that Americans usually don't use is to buy a used vehicle, run it into the ground for a few months, and then sell it back. The best cities to buy a car are London, Frankfurt, and Amsterdam.

Your American driver's license is usually all you need to rent a car in Europe, although some nations require an International Driver's License, which you can purchase for a nominal fee from AAA. It's required to have the license if you're driving in Greece, Austria, Spain, Poland, and Turkey. If you're stopped by police, the international permit usually soothes them. I was driving overseas without the permit and was stopped for speeding. I knew I was street legal with my Colorado driver's license—after all, why would the rental company give me the car without proper licensure?—but he took offense that I had no international license. It turned out he was upset because he had needed an extra license when renting a car on a Disney World trip, but after a long harangue he let me go with a hissed warning. The permit also works as a security deposit and identification at campgrounds, bike rental shops, and hotels.

European Driving

Driving in Europe is not a problem. It's different from driving at home, but most of the rules, regulations, and signage is similar. European drivers tend to be more aggressive but more courteous than American drivers. It's best to remember that you're on vacation, so slow down, yield to the maniacs, and enjoy the drive.

Always keep to the right, especially on highways, since the fast lane is just for passing. If you're pushing that little rental Citroën down the far left lane of the *autoroute* south of Paris, you will quickly become aware of a black Mercedes with lights flashing as it bears down on your rear at 120 mph. In Greece drivers routinely drive on the road shoulders, effectively turning a two-lane highway into a four-lane *autobahn*. Of course Greece has the highest accident rate in Europe. It's important to remember that you drive on the left or the "wrong" side of the road in Britain. Be especially alert at stop signs or when making turns since the traffic is coming from the opposite direction. You'll encounter lots of roundabouts or traffic circles, particularly in Britain.

Most roads and highways are well signed. Signs always direct the way into a town center, saying *Centreville, Centro,* or *Centrum,* and also point toward the local tourist office and even campgrounds. In some countries, like Greece, you need to write down directions, including towns and places along the way, in both Greek and Roman letters. Otherwise, you'll come to a posted junction and be unable to read the signs. Speed limits are posted but not often enforced. Even the famed German *autobahn* has limits based on current driving conditions.

The highway system in western Europe is excellent, especially the toll routes in France, Italy, and Spain. Use them whenever possible as they really are the quickest way to get around. The toll highways are very pricey, but the convenience and speed is worth the expense. To drive from Paris to the Calanques is an easy day drive down the *autoroute,* but plan on paying $40 for the privilege. If you drove the free highways and back roads down, it would be a three-day drive. The French *autoroutes* are excellent, with rest areas, restaurants, hotels, and even showers every 20 or so kilometers. The British motorways are also good, but like the German *autobahns* are usually very busy.

The most important tool to successfully drive around Europe while visiting remote climbing areas and exploring off-the-beaten-track places is a good map. You can buy maps in America, but wait until you get to Europe to purchase them. If you fly to Paris or wherever, ask for a free area map with directions to exit the airport and head in the direction you want. Once you're on the road, stop at an *autoroute* rest area, where you can buy a comprehensive road atlas or detailed regional maps at half the price you pay at home. The Michelin maps are particularly good, with lots of detail as well as layout maps of most cities and towns. It's also imperative to have a good navigator in the passenger seat to read the map, look for road signs, and give directions.

MONEY MATTERS

Money matters to the budget-conscious traveling climber. It's easy to spend loads of cash in Europe, but it's not impossible to travel frugally and still have a great time. It's best to work up a budget before you go. European prices are really not that much different from American ones. Some things are more expensive, whereas others are cheaper. Europe north of the Alps is more expensive than Europe south of the Alps. If you're doing a grand cragging tour, find an economic balance by following a budget in the northern countries and then allowing yourself some luxuries in the south.

Budget Busters

The big budget busters are airfare, ground transportation, accommodations, and food. These essential costs, however, are anything but fixed. Use budget flexibility and self-control as you travel to save your hard-earned bucks for the important stuff, like souvenirs.

Shop for a reasonable air ticket. That's the biggest single expense of any European vacation. Transportation costs a lot of euros too. Keep expenses down by splitting car rental fees, as well as gasoline and road tolls, between two to four people. You can also travel by train and bus, budgeting them as individual expenditures. In that case visit only a couple climbing areas, or stay at popular areas like Céüse or Verdon for a few weeks.

Accommodations and food are big budget breakers, but fortunately you can control those costs. I almost always camp on European climbing trips. Campgrounds are everywhere, relatively inexpensive compared with hotels, and usually close to the crags. France in particular offers excellent value for campers, with every village and town having a campground that almost never costs more than $15 per night for two, and sometimes half that depending on the season. After a week of tenting, you can splurge on a *gîte, pensione,* or bed-and-breakfast inn for a peaceful night between the sheets. Likewise, when you're on the road, you can easily find cheap hotels like the ubiquitous Formule One in France. Here you sleep for as little as $20 per night for three people. Hostels, scattered across Europe, are another cheap sleep.

Control food expenses by eating at your campsite and going out every so often for a great local meal. Food prices in *supermarchés* and markets are roughly the same as the United States, although most real food like vegetables and fruits are downright cheap. Buying in supermarkets not only saves you money, but is an authentic cultural experience that gives insights into how locals live. If you dine out, avoid the tourist traps that declare WE SPEAK ENGLISH. Instead, patronize local restaurants where residents dine. The food, service, and prices are almost always better. You'll blow lots of euros ordering water, which usually comes in a bottle, as well as drinks.

ATMs, Credit Cards, and Cash

Most of western Europe converted from individual national currencies to the euro in 2002, with the only holdouts being Great Britain, Norway, Sweden, Denmark, and Switzerland. The change allows travelers more freedom between countries and makes price comparisons easy.

It's best to travel with ATM cards and credit cards. ATM machines are everywhere in Europe, even in the smallest villages. Withdrawing money is just like at home. You step up to the bilingual machine, enter your card and PIN, punch in the amount, and take the cash. You save time by not having to find open banks and stand in lines, and you get great exchange rates. Usually your bank limits the amount of cash that can be withdrawn daily and adds a transaction fee. It's best to withdraw a large amount so the fees don't add up. Debit cards have lower transaction fees than credit cards. Ask your bank and credit card companies what their fees are to avoid future bill surprises. Likewise, let them know that you will be using the card overseas; otherwise, they may freeze your cards after finding unusual spending activity.

Using credit cards is an ideal way to travel. You don't have to carry loads of cash, you don't get the bill until you get home, and you always get an excellent exchange rate. Some card companies add a foreign transaction fee onto every charge you make. Credit cards are handy for confirming room reservations and car rentals. The best card to take is VISA; after that, MasterCard and American Express.

Travelers checks are good but now passé for the savvy traveler. It's okay to maybe carry a few larger denomination travelers checks, but they can be a pain to cash, and you usually end up paying substantial fees when you cash them.

In the remote places you travel as a climber, most local businesses do not accept credit cards. Backcountry Europe is a strictly cash economy, so use the ATM to keep a ready supply in your wallet. Don't plan on using any American dollars hanging around your wallet. Locals want the local currency. Familiarize yourself with the money, and figure out a rough translation in U.S. dollars. I always carry a small calculator so I can easily convert pounds, euros, or kroner to dollars in the store or restaurant. Also keep an eye on the cashiers so they don't shortchange you. It's surprising how often they take advantage of unsuspecting Americans.

Lastly, keep your cash in a hidden, round-the-waist money belt. A wallet in your back pocket might get lifted, especially in the large cities. One trick I use to avoid pickpockets in busy cities is wrapping a couple large rubber bands around the wallet and then keeping it in a front pocket. No thief will steal that baby without you feeling his hand first.

WHAT TO BRING

What should I bring? That is the age-old question for every prospective traveler. The first bit of advice that every seasoned traveler and every travel guide gives is this: as little as possible. You won't go wrong following the old traveler's adage: Estimate what you need, then take half the clothes and twice the money. Remember too that if your bags are oversize, overweight, and over the limit, then you will pay an extra baggage fee.

Traveling light means taking only essentials, buying what you need along the way, dumping useless items, and bringing multipurpose clothes. The big problem for a traveling climber is that it's darn hard to travel light when you tote a personal kit as well as a rack, rope, and camping gear.

If you haven't traveled overseas, then you probably want to bring everything but the proverbial kitchen sink. I once met a fellow American in Europe who did bring everything. He showed up at a friend's house in England's Peak District with a movie camera, video camera, mountain bicycle, six-man tent, air mattress, climbing gear, and what my English mate called "a whopping big suitcase." He had all his comfort stuff—and then he had to figure out how to haul it around the continent. Yep, that was a big mistake.

Clothing

Clothes are among the most important items you'll need. It's wise to carefully consider your clothes and pack only what you need. If you forget something, you can always buy it over there. Prices are generally comparable to the United States, although styles are different.

Before packing clothes, consider the average European's wardrobe. Most Europeans, particularly in damp countries like Germany and Britain, wear clothes made from synthetic fabrics. The reason? They dry quickly and look smart. Do the same. Cotton shirts and denim jeans look great at home, but when you're on the road they take a long time to dry, easily wrinkle, and take up precious room. Even those stylish cotton climbing clothes that you wear at your home crag are not ideal for distant road trips.

The advantages of synthetics? Polyester fabrics keep you warm when they're wet. They dry quickly, especially in damp climates. Many wick moisture and sweat away from your skin so it evaporates. They're lightweight, compress easily, and hardly wrinkle after being stuffed in a suitcase. People used to complain about lingering body odor on the clothes, but now most fabrics have antimicrobial treatments to reduce fragrant scents.

Go light. Adopt that as your packing mantra. Figure out where you are going, what the climate is like, and what you will be doing. Spread everything you want to take out on your bed and then ruthlessly cut the amount in half. A good rule is to pack enough clean clothes for three or four days. When they get dirty, do laundry. It's that simple. Most campgrounds have laundry sinks. You supply the soap, elbow grease, and a thin cord for a clothesline.

Bring versatile clothes that can be worn for outdoor play, sightseeing, and nightlife. The weather can vary from day to day, so you want clothes that can be used as layers to keep warm or to stay cool. A lightweight fleece or packable down jacket along with a windproof, water-resistant shell make good outer layers. If you're traveling to a cool and damp part of Europe like Norway, Great Britain, Germany, or Switzerland, then you will be grateful that you brought warm, waterproof clothing. Zip-off-leg pants, converting from long trousers to shorts, are ideal. Check out the newer models that are less goofy. Also get them loose so zippers don't chafe your skin.

Plan to wear shorts in summer since temperatures are usually hot. If you plan

to visit cultural or religious sites like cathedrals in France, Italy, and Spain or the monasteries at Meteora, you need to dress respectfully. Many require that men wear long pants and a shirt, while women wear a skirt. You will be denied entry with bare shoulders, exposed midriffs, or barebacked dresses. Casual wear in most European countries and cities is noticeably dressier than in North America. Americans often stand out because they're dressed like slobs in sloppy T-shirts, ragged shorts, and baseball caps.

Shoes are always a difficult decision. It's best to bring a pair of comfortable, broken-in walking shoes for your crag approaches or for trekking around villages. Also in summer bring a sturdy pair of walking sandals like those made by Nike ACG. They're good for hot days, wet approaches, and wearing around the crag base. Bring plenty of socks—five or six pairs is enough—since you'll want a fresh change every day. Ditto for underwear.

Lastly, how do you pack your clothes? The two camps—the folders and the rollers—are vehemently divided on the topic. The folders say clothes aren't meant to be rolled, they're made to be folded; folding takes up less room; they wrinkle less; and they're easier to retrieve. The rollers declare, no, clothes pack tighter if they're rolled; they don't wrinkle; and they compress with rubber bands and fit in stuff sacks. I've done it both ways and see no benefit to either. They all compress, they all wrinkle, and you still wear them.

Luggage

Deciding what luggage to bring is another huge question: pack versus suitcase. If you're renting a car to get around, then a large suitcase works just fine as long as it lives in the trunk of the car. The problem is lugging it around with you.

If you're staying near the crags, camping or overnighting in hostels, huts, or B&Bs, then a spacious backpack is unbeatable. It's liberating to travel about Europe with a pack and all your earthly belongings attached turtle style to your back. You can leave cities, congestion, and cares behind as you board trains, planes, and automobiles. It can free up your hands to sip a double latte or browse through a Carrefour grocery store.

The problem is selecting the right pack for your trip. There is nothing worse than wearing an ill-fitting pack all day. Choose wisely and you'll be fine. Look for comfort and a pack with lots of zippered, easy-to-reach compartments and flaps that allow quick access to your goodies—you will not enjoy digging for your raincoat from a top-loading pack as the downpour begins. Lastly, don't let a pack's good looks or brand name seduce you into buying; instead, let comfort and ease of use determine your final decision.

Try to use all the space when you pack. An ergonomic study shows that heaviest items should go at the top of the load rather than the bottom to reduce muscle strain. Roll or fold your clothes, and then stuff or cram them into various-size stuff sacks or mesh bags. Put underwear in one, socks in another, shirts in a third, and so on. You can buy pack systems from different luggage and pack companies to organize your stuff. Finally, when the pack is packed, you will find that it's always too heavy. Then it's time to get ruthless.

Large soft-sided suitcases with rollers are good for camping and traveling in a car. The case inhabits the trunk of the car at night and your tent during the day. It's easy to fit clothes, shoes, coats, toiletries, and camping gear in a large case. Also bring a medium-size pack for climbing gear, ropes, helmet, and sleeping bag.

Also consider using a small travel bag with zippered compartments and a shoulder strap. Your passport, international driver's license, airline tickets, and other documents are in a quick and easy-to-reach place as well as a notebook, pens, thin book, couple of CDs, address book, and energy bars. Plan on carrying this bag everywhere you go. It fits in the top of your climbing pack, or you can tote it through the grocery store or market.

Other Stuff

You can bring lots of different items and conveniences. Just remember that you have

The famed concrete catwalk El Camino del Rey edges 300 feet above El Chorro's narrow gorge in Spain.

to carry them all. A lot of things are just easier to buy over there, use, and discard before coming home. After all, more than 300 million people live in Europe, and they use everything we do in America.

The following are a few essentials you might want to consider: a handful of ziplock baggies, travel clock with alarm, small day pack or fanny pack, plastic zip ties for locking tents and luggage, first-aid kit, sunglasses, a thin 20-foot cord for a clothesline, small towel, sewing kit, journal or notebook, pens and pencils, flashlight or headlamp, CD player with a couple of CDs or MP3 player, a few envelopes and paper clips, electrical plug adapters, and that traveler's fix-all remedy—duct tape. Don't bring batteries. Remember to economize on weight by buying heavy stuff in Europe.

The toiletries kit is a big deal to most folks. The nice ones have a zipper, fold out, and hang beside the mirror. They also take up a lot of room. I go with the no-frills economy toiletry kit—a medium ziplock baggie. It's compact, crushable, works fine, and is easily replaced. Only bring the minimum: a toothbrush, small tube of toothpaste, travel-size shampoo, minibar of soap, hairbrush, and floss. Fingernail clippers and tweezers are optional. Pack all bottles in a ziplock bag; otherwise, air pressure changes during flying will ooze them all over the inside of your luggage. When you run out of shampoo and toothpaste, buy them at a local market. It's fun and informative to figure out exactly what you're buying. One of the first things you'll want to pick up in Europe is toilet paper. Most toilets are not supplied with toilet paper, so keep a roll or wad of tissues handy.

You don't need to bring your cell phone. It won't work in Europe. You need to rent or buy a Euro phone if you want that convenience. Likewise, you don't need to bring a laptop computer, PDA, or any other high-tech, whiz gadget. Part of going to Europe is to get away from all that damn stuff. Nor do you want to worry about someone helping themselves to your electronics while you're off having fun at the crag. There are lots of cyber cafes if you really need to be connected, but after being out in the wilds climbing your brains out, the newest e-mail in your in-box will be the last thing on your mind. You may want to bring a floppy computer disk with personal data, travel information, and itinerary, and any other relevant information you might need to access.

Climbing Gear

There is no getting around the fact that when you travel to Europe as a climber, you have to bring a lot of extra weight in gear. The good news is that you can get away with a light climbing kit if you're heading to any big sport-climbing area in Germany, Greece, France, Spain, and Italy. For those trips, bring fifteen or so quickdraws, a 200-foot (60-meter) rope, a set of wired nuts, and helmets. It's sometimes good to bring an extra cord for long rappels or to rotate with the other one. That amount of gear is easy to spread between two packs.

If you're planning on trad climbing in Britain or doing a long Dolomite route, then a large rack with sets of wired nuts, TCUs, cams, a couple ropes, and helmets are the bare necessity.

It's no problem in Europe if you have gear problems like a shredded rope, lack of quickdraws, or worn-out shoes. Lots of climbing shops are found near the areas, and most offer great prices, especially on European-made gear and shoes that are usually subject to large import tariffs in America. You can find killer deals on Boreal shoes at Spain's Costa Blanca, where the factory shop is located. Italy offers lots of bargains on gear and shoes, like Cassin, Camp, and La Sportiva. La Sportiva has factory shops in the Dolomites and Arco. France has climbing shops, including the famed Au Vieux Campeur with stores in Geneva, Chamonix, Lyon, and Paris. Petzel gear is always reasonably priced in France. Gear prices in the other countries are not as good. Careful shopping in Britain, Germany, Switzerland, and Belgium can uncover some bargains, but it's expensive in Norway and Greece.

Camping Gear

To camp or not to camp—that is the question. Camping is good. You save lots of money. But the trade-off is that you need to pack camp gear across the pond. If you're used to expeditioneering, then this is not a problem. A small, three-season, lightweight tent is perfect most of the year. Just make sure it is waterproof. Bring a light, compact sleeping bag and a tiny inflatable foam pad, and you're set for some wild nights.

If you don't have luggage room, you can always buy any of this gear over there at reasonable prices. The megastore Decathlon, with locations everywhere in France, has a huge selection and great prices. Buy items like foam pads, use them for a month, and then discard or give them away.

You need a cook kit and stove to save money on food. The best stove is a compact unit that screws into a canister. Bring the stove top but not the canister. It's illegal and dangerous to bring them onto any airplane. Besides, you can buy them in any outdoor shop in Europe. Gas stoves are illegal to bring on airplanes, and you will have a hard time finding the right fuel for them. Bring a nesting cook set along with plastic utensils and a cup, or buy these items in Europe. Fly into Paris, drive to Fountainbleau, and stop at a big Carrefour on the way. You can purchase a couple pans, a couple mugs, plates, bowls, cutting knife, and silverware for less than $20 there. At the end of your trip, give it away to fellow climbers, leave it at the campsite for someone else to use, or toss if it's trashed.

KEEPING IN TOUCH

The ease and speed of modern communication has made the world a smaller and more friendly place. It's easy to be a citizen of the world using e-mail and telephones. It's a great feeling to stand at a telephone booth in a Greek village that is just coming awake in the sunrise light. Birds chirping, shutters being pulled back at the cafe, and you chatting on the phone with a friend back home in the American night.

The hardest thing for many travelers is making the break from instant communication with home and limiting conversation and contact with loved ones. But a big part of a road trip is being disconnected from that world of home. It's good to regularly ring home to check on the dog or what the latest mail brought, but if you drop the regularity you'll soon discover a new rhythm and an awareness of the American addiction to being connected all the time and any place. Break the connection, and you'll be more in the moment, more present in the great eternal show.

Telephones

It's simple in Europe to make local or international telephone calls. The phone systems and phone booths are different in every country: different dial tones, different instructions, different phones. The good news is that multilingual instructions are pasted beside every pay phone. The key is to approach each new phone system without assuming it's like the one back home or the one in the last country you visited. Look at it, read the instructions, and try it. If you have problems, most operators speak enough English to answer your questions. Or you can always ask an amused local for help.

The first problem you encounter is that few pay phones are coin operated. You need a phone card, which is usually sold in magazine kiosks, tobacconists, post offices, and newsstands in convenient denominations. The cheapest is around $5.00, which is often more time than you might need unless you're calling home. If you have time left on your card when you're exiting the country, leave it next to a pay phone for some lucky guy to find. The cards are a snap to use. Just slide it into the marked slot and dial. A digital display on the phone shows how much time and money is left on the card.

The big problem is not having a card when you need it. I once arrived late at night in Athens and took a cab to my friend Aris's home in the suburbs. The taxi dropped me at 2 A.M. among canyons of apartment buildings lining streets with undecipherable Greek names. Ah, I'll ring him and let him know I'm here. I found a phone up the street, but no place was open to buy a phone card. I ended up in my sleeping bag on a patch of grass next to a parking lot under what turned out to be the right building. Next time I bought a phone card at the airport.

Local phones are great for smooth travel. Call ahead to confirm those reservations for the French *gîte* that you made in Colorado, ring the museum in Bolzano to make sure it's open on Monday (it wasn't!), ask directions to the Au Vieux Campeur store in Paris, or double-check the car reservation at the Dover side of the channel. Use the phone as a tool to iron out future difficulties.

The best and cheapest way is to dial direct on all local, national, and international calls. Some countries use area codes like in the United States, where you dial a prefix before the number. Others use direct dial to any number from anywhere in the country. You can also make cheap direct-dial international calls. To call from any European country or the United States and Canada, first dial the international access code 00. Then dial the country code like 1 for the United States and Canada, 44 for Britain, or 33 for France, then dial the area code, if applicable, and local phone number. And voila, it's ringing, and mom answers the phone.

Calling home from Europe is generally expensive no matter what system you use, unless it's someone else's phone and nickel. Without careful planning you can and will spend a small fortune on phone calls. It's best to limit the number and length of your calls home. An easy and controllable way to phone home is to buy a national phone card from whatever country you're in, plug it in, and dial away. That $10 card will expire pretty quickly unless you muster self-control to limit the call length. Calls to the United States are about $1.00 a minute.

Many Americans use the ubiquitous calling card from MCI, AT&T, or Sprint to make international calls. Just don't do it. Hidden fees, connection fees, as well as pricey minute charges will boost your minute charges from $3.00 to $7.00 per minute, which makes you into a nice profit center. If enough callers don't use them, perhaps they'll wise up and offer fair rates. Never use a calling card to make any country-to-country calls within Europe—they are routed through the United States and very expensive. Always use a local phone card for these calls.

Alternative calling cards are available. Surf the Internet to find low-rate, international, prepaid cards, and read all the fine print before signing up. I recommend and use the *ekit* phone service available through Lonely Planet guidebooks for a relatively inexpensive global communication service. The easy-to-use system gives you a private number, a PIN, voice mail, e-mail, and the ability to call from almost any country in the world. Go to www.lonelyplanet.ekit.com for more information.

Some countries, like Greece, have phone offices where you're assigned a cubicle with a phone, you call and talk, and pay on your way out. Ask the price per minute before calling, and make sure that the office is run by the phone company and not an independent. Avoid calling home from hotels or you'll cry when you get the next VISA bill. The fees are exorbitant and a major rip-off.

Some folks buy a mobile (not cell) phone in Europe, use it, and then chuck it, or bring it home to use again on their next European vacation. If you plan on talking a lot, then it makes some economic sense—but not much. You will find lots of places selling mobiles, like department stores or shops on the street corner. Either way it initially sets you back $75 to $100 with some basic minutes. Try to buy from a shop with an English-speaking salesperson so you can understand your contract and how to use their system. Also make sure you get instructions written in English. For an additional fee you can purchase chips, which come with new phone numbers, that allow the phone to work in other countries. You can also rent a phone from car rental companies at the airport.

E-mail

Yes, Europe is totally connected. Cyber cafes and computer kiosks are seemingly everywhere, but you run into problems as an itinerant climber far from the madding crowd. The people in those small villages near the climbing areas really don't care if they're wired to the rest of the known world. Maybe that's a good way to be. You'll probably feel that way too after you've navigated around some foreign Web server for an hour, finally got onto good old AOL, and found that 95 percent of your messages are offers for Viagra, Prozac, and various sexual aids.

Seriously, though, if you want to be wired, it is no problem in most places. Many shops and cafes in cities and towns

Cristos Batalogianis on the classic ridge route *Ostkante* (VI) (5.7) on Doupiani Rock in Metéora, Greece.

offer Internet access. In smaller towns and villages, you will have problems finding access. Check at libraries, copy shops, hostels, hotels, and post offices. Ask at the local tourist office for Internet locations. You can also download possible locales before leaving home by going to Web sites like www.cybercafes.com and www.net cafeguide.com or just Web searching under cyber cafes.

Consider a free e-mail service like Hotmail or Yahoo! Mail to use while traveling. It's easier to access your mail this way than through servers like AOL. You can also send relevant Web site addresses and travel information to yourself before you leave and then either download it or read the information at a Euro cafe rather than bringing reams of printed copy with you. Remember that foreign keyboards are surprisingly different than the ones at home, sometimes forcing you into a hunt-and-peck mode. You can download digital photographs from your storage card and mail them home as e-mail attachments.

Some cafes will also burn them onto a CD for you.

HEALTH, SAFETY, AND INSURANCE

Travel is about risk. And one of the biggest risks is your health. The odds are against it, but sometimes you get sick on a long trip, or worse, have an accident. It happens, and when it does, it's best to be prepared.

Preparation before traveling helps ensure that your health needs are taken care of while you're on the road. Write in your passport the names of anyone at home who needs to be contacted in case of emergency. Also make a list of any medical problems and drug allergies, as well as updated copies of prescriptions from your doctor that list the drug trade name, the maker, the chemical name, and dosages. This is important if you need to fill a prescription while traveling, although it's best to carry all needed medication from home. Also plan on putting together

a traveler's medical kit before leaving home, along with basic first-aid supplies that are always in your climbing pack.

Jet Lag

Jet lag is the bane of every overseas traveler. You've left home in the best climbing shape of your life, and you're ready to rock and roll. But now that you're in Europe, you feel dragged down, lethargic, and out of sorts. Welcome to jet lag—the traveler's hangover.

It's unfortunate, but jet lag has no magic antidote or treatment available. You can only combat its debilitating effects in the days before you fly and when you arrive. Health experts say it takes a day of recovery for each time zone you've crossed. Symptoms include insomnia, headaches, dehydration, exhaustion, anxiety, impaired coordination—not exactly how you want to feel on your first couple days at the crags. Flying east from America to Europe maximizes jet lag, whereas flying back home has minimal jet lag effect. Flying west to east is traveling one long day rather than flying all night through today and tomorrow.

Here are a few suggestions to minimize the effect of jet lag on the first days of your trip:

- Get plenty of rest before departing. Sleep as much as possible at home. Don't leave exhausted on the trip. Don't think you will catch up on shut-eye on the red-eye flight. Preset your watch to your destination time.
- Drink plenty of water on the plane rather than soda, coffee, tea, or alcoholic drinks. Alcohol tends to dehydrate you. Eat lightly on the plane.
- Try to sleep on the plane, as hard as that is. I'm always crammed in a seat with no leg room. If I'm on a half-full plane, I usually move to a row of empty seats in the middle and stretch out. Remove your shoes and get your feet up. Don't watch the in-flight movie. Ask the stewardess not to disturb you. And don't use sleeping pills, which can reduce blood circulation and lead to blood clots in your legs.
- Get moving when you get there. You usually arrive in the early morning with a full day ahead of you. Get in your rental car, and drive to a prebooked hotel where you can relax for the day. Your body's schedule will be screwed up for several days. On a trip to Spain, I drove solo from Madrid to the Costa Blanca, napping at a rest area en route, then found a campsite and passed out until I awoke at 3:00 A.M. I got up and walked along the empty beach, called home, and then crawled back into my sleeping bag and fell asleep.
- Reshift your circadian clock by exposure to bright sunlight along with early-morning and late-afternoon exercise, like a brisk walk. I also take melatonin for a couple days after arrival to help synchronize my internal clock and to fall asleep at night when my body still feels like it's daytime. It does have side effects, so consult a physician before taking it.

- Drink lots of liquids, and take something to replenish electrolytes.
- Lastly get up early in the morning and go to sleep at a reasonable hour so you get lots of sleep. Before you know it you'll be living on French time, eight hours ahead of Eldorado, Vedavoo, and Moab.

Vaccinations

If you're coming from the United States or Canada, then no specific immunizations are necessary for entry to European countries. All the countries north of the Alps are generally free from diseases requiring inoculations. Southern European countries, however, do have outbreaks of cholera, smallpox, typhoid fever, and hepatitis. It's a good idea to make sure all routine vaccinations, including tetanus, diphtheria, and polio, are updated before you go. The tetanus injection is particularly important since as a climber you will be getting cuts and scrapes, and tetanus enters through breaks in the skin.

The U.S. Centers for Disease Control and Prevention offers lots of traveler's health updates and advice. Check out their Web site at www.cdc.gov/travel for information.

Usual Ailments

The worst troubles most travelers have are sore feet, upset stomach, constipation, or diarrhea. All are easily prevented or treated.

You will be on your feet a lot, walking to cliffs and trekking around villages. Bring good shoes, both climbing and walking, that are broken in for your feet and lots of clean socks. A shaker of talcum powder keeps your feet dry.

Plan on drinking lots of fluids to prevent the traveler's usual curse—constipation. It's usual in Europe to drink bottled water, which is available everywhere, rather than tap water. Dehydration is also a problem if you're traveling and climbing in summer, particularly in areas near the Mediterranean where temperatures are hot.

Bring antacids or buy them there to battle upset stomach resulting from strange foods. Diarrhea commonly occurs after drinking untreated water, eating uncooked foods like vegetables, or as a reaction to bacteria in new and different foods. Typical symptoms include bloating, nausea, and the urgency to find a toilet. If you are loose, eat binding foods like rice, keep away from spicy strange dishes, avoid sugary drinks and foods, and drink lots of water to avoid dehydration. Fluid replacement is essential to managing diarrhea, so it's important to drink rehydrating solutions that replace essential minerals and salts. It's good to bring over-the-counter antidiarrheals like Imodium or even prescription ones like Lomotil to combat this traveler's scourge. You can buy antidiarrheal drugs in any European pharmacy. If the symptoms persist for several days, it is wise to see a doctor.

Also remember that with the possible exception of parts of Norway and Sweden, all free-flowing water is unsafe to drink without purification. Various evil microbes, tapeworms, and *Giardia* are found in untreated water. Either boil the water or use chemical or filtration systems to purify it before drinking. A pump-filter unit is very good at removing harmful contaminants. Make sure your unit filters out small pathogens like *Giardia* and is easy to carry and use. The easiest water solution is to buy bottled water and carry it wherever you go.

Tap water, as well as most unpeeled vegetables and fruit, are safe throughout most of Europe, especially the areas described in this book. Most food purity problems are in the Mediterranean countries, with the common culprits being vegetables washed in contaminated water, ice cubes, raw shellfish, or dishes containing raw eggs or unpasteurized milk.

Medical Treatment and Insurance

Europe is as modern as the United States, so excellent medical treatment is available everywhere in hospitals, clinics, and emergency rooms. Health-care costs are expensive, although most countries have some type of socialized medicine that covers their citizens with basic health care. If you need medical treatment for allergies, infections, diarrhea, or minor ailments, you can usually go to a nearby clinic and receive treatment and a prescription. I went to a local clinic in England and received free treatment and antibiotics for a painful eye infection. Emergency treatment is free through the British National Health Service, but further hospital care is not.

Some clinics or hospitals, however, require you to have health insurance since you're not a resident. Before you go overseas, check with your health provider to see if and what they will cover for emergency medical costs. If you aren't covered, purchase some basic health insurance that covers hospital treatment and stays as well as emergency transport. A comprehensive travel policy includes not only medical insurance but also coverage for your personal property.

In case of emergencies you usually need an English-speaking doctor or dentist. The American consulate, local tourist office, police, or even your hotel receptionist can provide names. All countries offer twenty-four-hour emergency medical services, ambulance transport, and rescue. The European Union (EU) uses 112 as its official emergency telephone number. Some countries, however, use other numbers, including the United Kingdom's 999.

If you're going to Europe for several months, get a complete medical checkup from your doctor and an oral exam and cleaning by your dentist. Tend to dental problems like fillings or caps before traveling, because you really don't want to go through a root canal in Spain. Unless you have good medical insurance, you will pay for a dental visit.

First-Aid Kit

A good first-aid kit is essential for on-the-road health. Assemble a kit that is useful but compact enough to carry. It's best to make a basic kit at home and then buy anything additional over there. You can also purchase prepackaged medical kits

from outdoor stores. One member of your party should carry the main first-aid kit, but also make smaller individual ones to stow in packs.

Essential medications are prescription drugs; aspirin or ibuprofen for pain and fever; benadryl or other antihistamines for allergies; an antibiotic like Ciprofloxin (Rx); Imodium or other antidiarrheal drugs; antibiotic ointment and antiseptic for cuts and scrapes; antinausea drugs for motion sickness; calamine lotion or hydrocortisone cream for bug bites and allergic reactions; cold and flu tablets; nasal decongestant; water purification tablets; and an antifungal cream for skin infections.

Essential supplies are adhesive tape; bandages and gauze of various sizes; different-size Band-Aids; gauze swabs; small scissors; tweezers; thermometer; paper stitches; moist towelettes; moleskin for blisters; safety pins; and a first-aid booklet.

Other important and useful items are insect repellent; sunscreen; lip balm; eye drops; multivitamins; Dramamine for motion sickness; and several prescription meds, including Vicodin for pain, Valium or other sleep meds, Compazine for nausea, and Allegra or other allergy meds.

Also carry a spare pair of glasses and contact lenses, as well as a copy of your eye prescription if you need a new pair.

Remember that any item you don't have or forget to purchase you can buy at any pharmacy in Europe. Many medications that require a prescription in the United States are sold over-the-counter in Europe.

Accidents

Climbing is a dangerous sport. That's the truth of the matter. Bad stuff happens, and it can happen anytime and anywhere. As careful as you are climbing, accidents and traumatic injuries occur. If an accident happens, remember that medical care is usually nearby in Europe.

It's a good idea if at least one member of your party is certified in first aid. It's a great idea if everyone takes a Red Cross certified program before traveling anywhere so they're prepared to save

someone's life—it may be your own or your buddy's.

Objective dangers abound at European climbing areas. These include loose rock, falling rocks or other projectiles, worn bolts or lowering anchors, parties climbing above, lightning strikes, and fording rivers and fast streams, as well as minor problems like insect stings and bites. Also remember that driving in Europe is dangerous, and many accidents happen on the road.

Always try to manage emergency situations yourself by self-evacuating. This is not always possible with serious accidents that require quick medical intervention. Europe offers an excellent network of emergency evacuation, transport, and treatment. Call the listed emergency numbers for a quick response.

Major climbing accidents tend to be broken bones, usually legs, ankles, back, and head injuries. Detailed first-aid advice is beyond the scope of this book. That is your responsibility. But if you're involved with a major accident, use the following MASS guidelines:

Make sure that other members of your party and yourself are safe and out of danger.

Assess the injured person's condition.

Stabilize their injuries by performing basic first-aid procedures—controlling bleeding, clearing breathing passages and administering mouth-to-mouth resuscitation or CPR, treating for shock and keeping the person warm, and immobilizing possible fractures.

Seek immediate medical attention by alerting other climbers with cell phones to call emergency services or by moving the victim to a hospital.

Climbing Dangers and Safety

Climbing rocks is inherently dangerous. That's an unadulterated simple fact. You climb high above the ground, tethered to your partner by a slender cord, and you assume the risks of gravity. The perils of rock climbing, however, can be overstated but should never be minimized. The only risks we take are those that we choose to take. If you put yourself in a perilous situation, you better be damn sure you can get out of it or take the consequences of failure, which can be severe injury or death. We climbers choose the risks of our sport, yet do everything possible to mitigate the downward effects of gravity and lessen the great dangers to life and limb. Still, despite our efforts, H. L. Mencken's astute observation of nineteenth-century balloonists holds true for rock climbers: "They have an unsurpassed view of the scenery, but there is always the possibility that it may collide with them."

Rock climbing is a serious business. No matter how much fun you're having on the crags, bad juju can happen. Every route has potential to kill or maim you or your partner, no matter how benign it might appear at first glance. Every climber, experienced or novice, can and will make stupid, thoughtless mistakes.

Remember that every single time that you slip on your rock shoes, buckle up your harness, and tie into the sharp end of the rope, you or your partner might die as a direct result of your actions or by a senseless random act of God. Climbing, despite all the fun, games, conversation, and rushes, is a deadly serious business, and you always need to treat it that way. The fun quickly seeps out of the vertical game when your pal is hauled off on a litter or worse, in a body bag.

It's up to you to minimize the risks of climbing. Always be safety conscious. Always check your knots. Always double-check your belayer's harness, anchor, and belay device. Is the harness doubled back? Is the belayer securely knotted into the anchor? Is the anchor loaded properly? Does the rope run through the belay device properly? It's not only risky, it's just plain dumb not to ask simple questions that you assume you know the answer to. Don't just ask questions, but look. Look at the rope, the anchor, and the harness. Observant eyes catch mistakes.

Inexperienced Climbers

If you're inexperienced, hire a guide to lead you or take a climbing class and learn the ropes. If you're pudgy, weak, and out

Henrik Bollingmo leads the classic *Hollywood* (4+) (5.5) at Kolsås near Oslo, Norway.

of shape, train in a climbing gym or toprope routes to get stronger and more able. Safe rock climbing takes lots of experience and practice. Beginning climbers used to serve an apprenticeship under the watchful eye of more experienced climbers, learning how to set equalized belay anchors, rig rappel lines and anchors, protect leads with natural gear, and protect both the leader and the second. Now with the burgeoning growth of indoor climb-

ing gyms, lots of relatively inexperienced novices with only basic climbing knowledge and a handful of gym routes think that they are rock climbers. But they're not. It's just not true. Don't succumb to this folly. There is no face lost in admitting that you're a beginner.

Climbers who have learned their techniques and gained their experience in an indoor gym should take note of their very real limitations. Climbing in a rock gym is no substitute for actual rock climbing experience outside, on the rock, in real situations. Climbing in a gym is safe. Climbing outside on a cliff is dangerous. Climbing outside requires not only movement skills but also rope handling, placing protection and anchors, setting up belay and rappel points, and doing all the little things all the time that keep both your partner and you safe on the rock.

You Are Responsible

Every climbing route is X-rated. Every route is a serious affair since a fall can have dire consequences. Accidents and fatalities happen because equipment is improperly used, fixed protection and anchors fail, climbers make bad judgments, and shit happens.

This guidebook, as well as all other climbing guides and instruction books, is not a substitute for your own experience and your own good judgment. Do not depend or rely on the information in this book to get you safely to the cliff top and then back to the parking lot. Guidebook writing is by necessity a compilation of information obtained by the author through personal experiences and observations at the climbing areas, along with other information given by experienced area climbers or from existing European climbing guides.

Errors can and do creep into route descriptions, cliff topos, gear recommendations, anchor placements, fixed gear notes, and descent routes and rappels. When using any climbing guidebook, you might find misleading information and errors. Use your own judgment and experience to decide how to safeguard yourself and your partner. Every effort has been made to ensure accuracy in this book, but in the real world of rocks and ropes, things change and fall apart. The fixed pitons protecting that hard crack or the rappel anchors on that lofty ledge may not be there anymore. Rockfall may have obliterated a crucial bolt at the crux move. You must always rely on your own experience, judgment, and wisdom to ensure your personal safety.

Getting Experience

Climbing experience is gained by getting outside on the rocks, in the sun, in bad weather, and doing lots of routes. If you do not have the necessary experience, it is wise to avoid long and dangerous routes. In this case you would be wiser to hire a local guide to help you. If you're at home and training for your trip to Europe, find climbing gyms or local instructors to show you the ropes. Their invaluable services allow you to safely develop the techniques and wise judgment necessary to safely ascend climbing routes. Before committing cash to a guide service, ask about their experience, accident rates, safety procedures, certification, and class or group sizes. If you have any questions about any area or route in this book, by all means seek out local climbers and guides and ask their recommendations and advice. Most, if they speak English, are happy to share information from their local areas with you, including updated ratings, new routes, gear lists, and topos.

Safety on the Rocks

Use common sense to keep safe on the rocks. Most accidents and fatalities happen because of bad judgment and improper decisions by climbers. Most accidents are preventable. Rely on yourself and your experience to evaluate changing conditions and make the best choices for you and your partners. Your safety depends entirely on you. Use the following reminders to be safe and avoid accidents:

- Always protect yourself near the start of a route by placing lots of gear or stick-clipping a high bolt to avoid groundfalls.
- Always double-check your harness and tie-in knot before climbing, as well as check your harness and belay device before rappelling or your tie-in knot before lowering.
- Avoid climbing below other parties. Rockfall can be fatal.
- Wear a helmet for cranial protection from falling or rockfall.

- Gravity kills. Do not solo routes without a rope. Even a 30-foot fall is deadly.
- Do not climb beyond your skill level without proper safety and protection devices.
- Rope up on wet, snowy, or dark descent routes.
- Tie knots in the end of your ropes to avoid rappelling off the ends of the rope.
- Tie in properly after finishing a sport pitch, and double-check your knot and rope before downclimbing or lowering.
- Remember that the belay is a crucial part of the safety link. Your life is entrusted to your belayer.
- Belayers should be alert, competent, and anchored. Expect and remind your belayer to pay attention to you while you climb and not visit with the neighbors or fix lunch or talk on the cell phone.
- Tie a knot in the end of your rope to avoid being dropped by inattentive belayers while they are lowering you.

Objective Dangers

Always remember that bad things can happen to good people. Bad stuff can always happen at the crag. Keep that in mind when you're out climbing for the day, whether it's at your home cliff or across the ocean in Europe. Objective dangers, those that you have absolutely no control over, are found while hiking up to the cliff, climbing your chosen route, descending the backside trail to the base, and trekking back to your car. It's a good rule to never consider your climbing day over until you and your party are safely at the parking lot. Many accidents happen on descents because of rockfall, carelessness, fatigue, bad weather, and darkness. Always rope up on any descent that you are the least bit uneasy about, whether it's loose boulders, rain-slick slabs, or just an intuitive voice. Unlike a madman, you need to listen to those voices. Pay attention to your intuition. It keeps you coming back alive.

Loose rock. The main danger at most cliffs is loose rock. Loose blocks and flakes are found on routes everywhere, whether it's sun-drenched limestone walls in the Provence or glacier-scraped slabs in Norway. Loose rock can be perched on ledges and shelves or wedged in cracks and chimneys. Use extreme caution around any suspect rock. Falling rocks are deadly to your belayer and friends at the cliff base or belay ledge, and rocks can even chop your lead rope. Warn your partners if a block seems unstable so they can be prepared for a possible rockfall. The repeated thaw and freeze cycles of winter and spring loosen flakes and boulders. Use caution early in the summer season, especially in places like Switzerland, the Dolomites, and Norway. Your climbing rope can also dislodge rocks. Use particular care when pulling rappel ropes down. Always wear a helmet while climbing and belaying to reduce the risk of serious head injury or death from falling rocks.

Fixed gear. Use fixed gear with caution. Severe weather in Europe's mountains as well as the corrosive effects of sea air along coastal cliffs can cause unseen deterioration of pitons and bolts. Bolts can shear from the force of a leader fall. Fixed pitons loosen due to rock weathering and expansion caused by freezing and thawing. Metal fatigue, rust, and age affects the useful life of fixed gear. Always back up fixed pieces whenever possible, and always back them up at belay and rappel stations. Never rely on a single piece of gear for your safety, especially when lowering or rappelling and at belays. Always build redundancy into your climbing system so the failure of one piece will not affect the overall safety and security of the system. Never rappel or lower from a single bolt, and don't lean straight out on a bolt. Some European areas like the Frankenjura in Germany have a single large bolt as an anchor. These are glue-in 12-mm stainless steel bolts, and they swear by them. So there you don't have a choice—just lower away. Don't trust your life to questionable anchors or rotten rappel slings. Don't be so cheap that you're unwilling to leave gear to safeguard your life. In Britain climbers use thick wads of slings or "tat"

A climber on *Waldvöglein* (6b) (5.10c) at Settore Felsnelke Frea, Dolomites, Italy.

that the rope is looped through for rappels. Carefully look at the condition, wear, and age of the slings before rappelling. You usually want to tie a piece of your own webbing into the mess for safety's sake.

Noxious plants, bugs, and snakes. In Europe, unlike the United States, you don't have to deal with problems like poison ivy or poisonous snakes. Keep an eye out for bees and wasps, which usually live in hives in the rock. Take note of hives in

summer, and try to avoid them. Flies and mosquitoes can be a nuisance in summer. Mosquitoes are active from dawn to dusk in moist areas. Use repellents to keep them at bay. In Britain, particularly in the Peak District and north into Scotland, there is the bug phenomenon called *midges*. These small biting flies are particularly annoying and are most active on summer evenings. They can drive you absolutely mad. Slather on lots of repellent to keep them away or risk lots of bites on exposed skin. Ticks are found in Europe and can, as in the United States, cause Lyme disease as well as a tick-borne encephalitis. They're found in rural forested regions, just the kind of place you'll be climbing. Few poisonous snakes are found in Europe, and the only one you might see is the shy, secretive adder. These small snakes, occurring from Britain south to Spain, Italy, and Greece, generally only bite if they're handled. My only sighting was in a field of ferns near Bosigran in Cornwall.

Weather. Keep a close eye on the weather, especially in mountainous regions, where it can be fickle and changeable. Thunderstorms, accompanied by lightning, can build and move in quickly, so be prepared to bail off your route if necessary. This occurs most often at places like the Dolomites, Céüse, Verdon Gorge, Grimsel Valley, and North Wales. It can rain suddenly and often in much of northern Europe. Be prepared for wet weather by carrying a good raincoat and extra dry clothes and shoes. Use extreme care on descents during wet weather.

CLIMBING GRADES

Beginners and gym climbers should take special note of climbing ratings. Rated indoor gym routes do not accurately reflect real outdoor ratings. Just because you crank a 5.12 indoors on the gym's steepest wall doesn't mean you can jam a 5.9 crack up a gritstone face. Climbing route ratings are subjective grades and are arrived at by consensus opinion by expert climbers. Use ratings with caution. Many climbing movements are subject to an individual's experience, technique, body size, and strength. Some routes may be harder for you than the rating indicates. Again, use your better judgment, and don't let the rating fool you into thinking a climb is easier than it really is. It might be easier for someone else, but not for you. Every climbing route is serious business, no matter what the grade. Every experienced climber can relate a horror story or accident from a seemingly innocuous "easy" route.

RATING SYSTEM COMPARISON CHART

YDS	British	French	UIAA
5.3	VD 3b	2	II
5.4	HVD 3c	3	III
5.5	MS/S/HS 4a	4a	IV
5.6	HS/S 4a	4b	V-
5.7	HS/VS 4b/4c	4c	V/V+
5.8	HVS 4c/5a	5a	V+
5.9	HVS 5a	5b	VI
5.10a	E1 5a/5b	5c	VI+
5.10b	E1/E2 5b/5c	6a	VI+
5.10c	E2/E3 5b/5c	6a+	VII-
5.10d	E3 5c/6a	6b	VII
5.11a	E3/E4 5c/6a	6b+	VII+
5.11b	E4/E5 6a/6b	6c	VII+
5.11c	E4/E5 6a/6b	6c+	VIII-
5.11d	E4/E5 6a/6b	7a	VIII
5.12a	E5 6b/6c	7a+	VIII+
5.12b	E5/E6 6b/6c	7b	VIII+/IX-
5.12c	E5/E6 6b/6c/7a	7b+	IX-
5.12d	E6/E7 6c/7a	7c	IX
5.13a	E6/E7 6c/7a	7c+	IX+
5.13b	E7 7a	8a	X-
5.13c	E7 7a	8a+	X-/X
5.13d	E8 7a	8b	X
5.14a	E8 7a	8b+	X+
5.14b	E9 7a	8c	XI-
5.14c	E9 7b	8c+	XI
5.24d	E10	9a	XI+

This book makes rough translations of European climbing grades into the American Yosemite Decimal System (YDS) grading system. Take all YDS grades with a grain of salt. It is very difficult to translate many grades, but especially the British ones, which give both an overall grade as well as a technical grade. Use the YDS grades in this book as a ruler, but use the European grades as the actual rating.

Great Britain

Legend:
- Climbing region
- River
- International boundary
- National capital
- Expressway
- Major road

0   50   100   150 Kilometers
0   50   100 Miles

ORKNEY ISLANDS
Mainland · Kirkwall
Hoy
Thurso · Wick

Stornoway
Lewis with Harris

SCOTLAND

North Uist
South Uist · Skye
HEBRIDES · Ft. William
Mull

Inverness
Loch Ness · Aberdeen

NORTH ATLANTIC OCEAN

Perth · Dundee · St. Andrews
Stirling · Kirkcaldy
Glasgow · Edinburgh · Motherwell
Isley
Ayr · Tweed
Arran

North Sea

GREAT BRITAIN

Dumfries · Newcastle upon Tyne · Tynemouth
Stranraer · Sunderland
Londonderry · Stockton-on-Tees · Middlesbrough
Bangor · Scarborough
Northern Ireland · Loch Neagh
Belfast · Isle of Man
Craigavon · Barrow-in-Furness · Lancaster · York · Kingston-upon-Hull
Douglas · Bradford · Leeds · Grimsby
Irish Sea · Blackpool · Preston
Blackburn
IRELAND · Holyhead · **Liverpool** · **Manchester** · **GRITSTONE EDGES**
· **Sheffield** · Lincoln · **ENGLAND**
Caernarfon · Bangor · Chester · Derby · Nottingham · King's Lynn · Norwich
NORTH WALES · Shrewsbury · Walsall · Leicester · Peterborough · Lowestoft
WALES · Wolverhampton · Coventry · Cambridge · Ipswich
Aberystwyth · **Birmingham** · Northampton · Bedford
Severn · Milton Keynes · Luton · Southend-on-Sea
Fishguard · Wye · Gloucester · Oxford · **London** · Basildon
Newport · Thames · Reading · Elmbridge
Swansea · Swindon · Dover
Cardiff · Bristol · Portsmouth · Hastings
Southampton · Brighton
Exeter · Poole · Bournemouth
CORNWALL · Torquay
Penzance · Truro · Plymouth
English Channel
ISLES OF SCILLY · Alderney · **FRANCE**

CORNWALL

■ OVERVIEW

The long peninsula of England's West Country juts into the Atlantic Ocean like a crooked finger on the southwest side of Britain. Surging waves batter its long rocky shore while the passing Gulf Stream keeps it warm and temperate most of the year. The West Country is a land of isolated moors and rugged coastal cliffs, rolling hayfields and cow-filled pastures, cathedral towns and quaint fishing villages. The area is divided into six counties: Wiltshire, Avon, Dorset, Somerset, Devon, and Cornwall.

Cornwall, or *Penwith* to use its Cornish name, is a distinct and unique part of Britain. The county of Cornwall comprises the final joint of the finger, with its very tip, dubbed Land's End, the westernmost point of mainland England.

The long rocky coastline of Cornwall is walled with compact cliffs broken by occasional beaches and secluded bays. "This Cornwall is very primeval," wrote the great British novelist D. H. Lawrence, who lived at Zennor in 1916. "Great, black, jutting cliffs and rocks . . . and a pale sea breaking in . . . It is like the beginning of the world, wonderful: and so free and strong." Climbers make pilgrimages to climb these wave-resistant, granite cliffs to test their strength, ability, and nerve on some of the best sea-cliff climbing in all of Europe.

The sea adds dimensions to the climbing experience. Sea-cliff climbing is atmospheric. Out there you're pinned on the sheer cliff face. The surf crashes onto rocks below, the smell of salt water lingers in the air, and the scenery is boastful and grandiose at this meeting of hard land and ill-tempered water. These aesthetic factors combine with more pragmatic and serious difficulties, such as timing your climbs with the daily tides, to make Cornish sea-cliff climbing a potentially risky but immensely satisfying business.

Climbing here is not like monkeying up a bolted sport route on the south coast at Portland. Instead, Cornwall is a brilliant arena for adventure climbing and a major climbing area that is still free of bolts. Come here and you won't find a bolt every 5 feet or drilled anchors at the end of a pitch, but you will find a natural crag environment with no bolts and few fixed pitons, which corrode anyway in the constant wash of sea air.

Cornwall is a place to find all the thrills and chills of real traditional climbing. It's a place that places a premium on experience, competence, good judgment, and self-reliance. By no means, however, does this mean that the Cornish cliffs are dangerous. Adventure is never equated with danger, but with commitment and resourcefulness in the face of adversity. Most of the routes are well protected with modern gear, and you don't have to climb those that aren't. As at any climbing area, it's up to you to create a safe experience by relying on your own good sense and climbing ability.

The Cornish climber needs to be competent at his rock craft. Successful climbing here is not about busting hard moves up steep stone, but about being aware of all the subtle aspects of climbing. You need to be competent at leading pitches and placing gear. Competent at setting up equalized belays on ledges, small stances, and sloping, grassy cliff tops. Competent at finding the right descent to the cliff base and competent at reading tide tables. You also must be competent at evaluating both objective and subjective dangers, of knowing when to be bold and when to retreat.

Sea Cliff Dangers and Tides

As an American climber the aspect you need to take most seriously is the sea itself. Most Yank climbers have little experience on sea cliffs since few are found in the United States. Climbing on sea cliffs is inherently much more dangerous than

CORNWALL   RF 1 : 256,000

0   Kilometers   5

0   Miles   5

N

Atlantic Ocean

St. Ives

BOSIGRAN

Zennor

B3306

To Redruth

Pendeen

Hayle

A30

A307

Penzance

St. Just

A394

To Falmouth

Newlyn

Mount's Bay

SENNEN CLIFFS

A30

B3283

Mousehole

Sennen

Land's End

B3315

Treen

CHAIR LADDER

inland climbing simply because the sea is fickle and unknown. Always err on the side of caution by using a rope when approaching routes across tidal rock shelves or traversing along the base to the start of your chosen line. Even in low surf, sneak waves can occur, and when they do, you can be swept off the shoreline rock and into deep, treacherous water. The tidal shelf below cliffs like Sennen seems fairly benign. Don't let this fool you. People have been swept off this high shelf into the sea. Chair Ladder shelf is also dangerous since it's just above low-tide level. Bosigran is the safest cliff described here since it rises well above sea level and is nontidal. Always rig a secure anchor at the base of your route so the belayer is safe. Remember too that it is difficult to swim in surging seawater with a rack of gear and rope. Knowledgeable Cornish climbers carry their gear sling over their shoulder so it can be easily jettisoned if they're knocked into the surf. Lastly, always check the daily tide table to know when high and low tides occur so you're not trapped when the tide sweeps in. Tide tables are available from any news shop and are usually published in local newspapers. Take into account the current weather, daily forecast, and the wind speed and direction before heading down to the cliff base.

All the cliffs described here are composed of a roughly weathered, compact granite, flecked with mica, quartz, feldspar, and veins of black tourmaline. The rock surface tends to erode in the salty sea air into sharp edges, knobs, and flakes that are useful as holds. Crack systems tend to be incipient and broken rather than splitters. Corners and dihedrals cleave the walls, forming many obvious lines. The diversity of cracks and seams allows for lots of protection on most routes.

Many sea cliffs line West Penwith, the part of Cornwall that extends on its north coast from St. Ives to Land's End and on its south coast from Penzance to Land's End. The Cornish coast is one of the wealthiest sea-cliff areas in all of Britain. This guide describes the three best and most popular areas: Bosigran, Sennen Cliffs, and Chair Ladder. These crags absorb most visiting

Dennis Jump leads *The Mitre* (VS) (5.8) at Chair Ladder.

climbers, so after a few days at these crags, you should head out to the more remote cliffs. The best of these are The Great Zawn, an intimidating gash just west of Bosigran, with its assortment of difficult classics; the short, impressive, and dramatic cliffs around Land's End itself; and the excellent crack and corner routes on the sharp headland at Carn Barra. Details, descriptions, and directions are found in the comprehensive area guidebook.

Rack, Protection, and Descent

The Cornish cliffs are a superb destination for the traditional climber who enjoys placing gear and scaling routes with no fixed gear and scant evidence of previous ascents. No bolted sport routes are found on West Penwith. If that's your cup of tea, then you are better served by heading east to Portland.

Bring a standard rack that includes a set of wired Stoppers or Rocks, a set of

TCUs, a set of Friends, Camalots, or their equivalents, and an assortment of slings for tying off chockstones and blocks. A large cam is also helpful on some routes, but not a necessity. A set of small wired brass or steel nuts is useful. A 165-foot (50-meter) single, dry rope is adequate for most Cornish climbs, although double-rope technique lessens rope drag on wandering lines. Bring a helmet, and wear it. Rocks are constantly loosening with the sea weather, and the popular routes often have traffic above that can dislodge stones from the cliff.

Descent for most sea-cliff climbs is done before starting the route since they all begin beside the sea. Descent is usually down gullies or easy downclimbs, although a few descents are by rappel.

Seasons and Weather

Cornwall's cliffs, unlike many British areas, are a four-season experience with good year-round climbing weather. The peninsula, jutting into the Gulf Stream, is the country's banana belt. Summer is the best time for climbing, with long days and sunny weather. Unfortunately, the drawback is that the rest of Britain likes the summer here too, so it is busy with tourists and other climbers. In summer Sennen Cliff is the most popular venue, although in a day you'll climb everything.

Autumn is also excellent at Cornwall, with good weather and fewer people. Spring can be dreary and rainy, but it can also be sunny and warm. This is the best place to climb during the damp British winter with spells of warm, clear weather. But, like spring, it can also be absolutely horrendous with rain, wind, and gray skies for weeks. Also remember that winter days are short, and many accommodations and attractions are closed. If you visit in the off-season, the weather is a gamble, but Cornwall has lots of microclimates, which work to your advantage. If it's damp and gloomy at Sennen, it might be gloriously sunny at Chair Ladder.

Climbing History

Cornwall boasts a long and colorful climbing history that began at the start of the twentieth century. The area's first recorded climber was alpinist A. W. Andrews, who, with his sister Elsie, scaled the granite faces at Bosigran, Chair Ladder, and the pillar at Wicca. In 1905 Andrews and J. B. Farmer made the first climb up Bosigran's main face—*Ledge Climb.* In 1922 George Mallory of Everest fame added a direct start. Besides his routes Andrews's other contribution to early climbers stemmed from tennis, his other passion, and traversing. He usually wore tennis shoes for his Cornish adventures. Professor Odell climbed with Andrews at West Penwith before making the first ascent of *Tennis Shoe* on the Idwal Slabs in Wales. Andrews also was passionate for traversing the sea cliffs in "the limbo of no man's land between high and low tide." At one point his ambition was to traverse the entire British coast. Another early pioneer was Donald Romanis, who climbed *Alison Rib* on Bosigran in 1923 but left no records of other ascents.

There was little Cornish climbing action other than repeats of Andrews's routes from the mid-1920s until the end of World War II. Andrews enticed many climbers to visit and sandbagged them on his harder lines. The famous Colin Kirkus came for a couple weeks and added *Black Slab* to Bosigran, and Menlove Edwards visited during the war and did three routes. Royal marine commandos used the Bosigran area for training cliff assault teams, often running up *Commando Ridge,* another of Andrews's climbs. The commandos did several firsts at Sennen, including Joe Barry's ascent of *Demo Route* in 1943. After the war Cortlandt Simpson established *Zig Zag* and *Doorway* at Bosigran and *South Face Direct* up Chair Ladder.

The publication of Andrews's first guidebook to the area began Cornwall's golden climbing age in the 1950s. In 1951 Manchester University students M. J. Ridges and G. F. Lilly established the brilliant *Diocese* on Chair Ladder. The Royal

Marines Cliff Assault Wing, with active climbers John "Zeke" Deacon, Rawdon Goodier, Mac McDermott, and Viv Stevenson, were a driving force on many now-classic routes. Deacon led the way with brilliant first ascents of *Pegasus, Seal Slab, Excelsior, Bishop's Rib,* and *The Mitre* at Chair Ladder.

These exploits, however, were soon overshadowed by gritstone-trained Peter Biven's arrival in 1955. Bevin and others added four routes at Bosigran in a week, including the sensational *Suicide Wall* up the main face center. Later Biven and Trevor Peck added *Little Brown Jug, Anvil Chorus, Paragon,* and *Thin Wall Special* at Bosigran. By the end of the 1950s, most of today's classics at Chair Ladder and Bosigran were climbed, along with routes in the intimidating Great Zawn and at Land's End.

The 1960s initially saw repeats of the great 1950s routes. It also saw sea-cliff climbing become a main course rather than an appetizer. By the late 1960s new climbers—including Frank Cannings, Martin Jones, Mark Springett, Keith Darbyshire, and Pat Littlejohn—pushed standards higher. Strenuous problems like *Vulcan* and *Paradise* were established at Bosigran. New cliffs were discovered and climbed, a trend that continued into the 1970s, and hard lines were opened on existing crags like The Great Zawn. These wild routes included *Desolation Row, Xanadu,* and *The Dream/Liberator,* free-climbed by Ron Fawcett and Peter Livesey in 1976.

By the 1980s and 1990s, all of the classic lines were climbed, so climbers focused on the harder, athletic possibilities. In the late 1980s Rowland Edwards and son Mark established several new areas, including Dutchman's Zawn and Pendower Cove, and worthy routes like *Animated Wall* and *The Tempest* on crags like Chair Ladder. Now almost everything worthwhile has been ascended, so climbers are busy exploring new bouldering areas, trying to repeat old routes in better style, and just getting out in the fresh sea air for a day's cragging on Europe's best sea cliffs.

Getting Around

A hire car is necessary for getting from London to Cornwall and traveling around to the various crags. Pick up a detailed area map from a tourist office or a magazine shop to ensure that you can find your way around. West Penwith is a maze of two-lane highways, roads, and narrow lanes, so a map immensely helps road navigation.

The Cornish back roads, some more than a thousand years old and protected as historic byways, are lined with towering hedges that are so high you cannot see beyond them. Be aware that these soft, fuzzy hedges conceal huge blocks of unyielding granite hidden inches below their innocuous-looking exterior. Make sure that when you pull to the left when yielding to oncoming traffic on these single-lane roads that you do not scrape the hedge growth. Otherwise the side of your rental car will be scratched, dinged, or worse. Also remember that the roads are packed with people, the vast majority accustomed to only driving on London highways. Beware of myopic city drivers and the timid Yankee climber types approaching in the middle of the road on a blind corner.

Camping, Accommodations, and Services

Cornwall, a popular British holiday destination, offers a wealth of accommodation possibilities, including campgrounds, rental caravans or trailers, hotels, hostels, guest houses, and bed-and-breakfast inns. B&Bs are ubiquitous but difficult to find in summer without prebooking a reservation. Lots of good campsites are scattered about the peninsula, particularly along the coast. It's best to pick one place and use it as a base camp for day trips. Look under "Trip Planning Information" and in the Appendix for suggestions. Otherwise, lots of places are found on the Internet or by stopping at the local tourist offices for suggestions, directions, and reservations. Wild camping is discouraged, but the odd overnight bivouac is overlooked if you're discreet.

Gil Male surmounts the dicey crux of *Thin Wall Special* (E1 5b) (5.10a) at Bosigran.

Food and Drink

West Penwith offers lots of restaurants, cafes or *caffs,* and pubs for your dining enjoyment. Must-do Cornish culinary experiences include visiting a real Victorian tea house like Charlotte's in Truro for a proper cream tea. There you will undoubtedly come under scrutiny by locals who still debate whether the strawberry jam goes atop the clotted cream on the scone or vice versa.

You should also sample a Cornish pasty, which are readily available in any respectable takeaway joint, cafe, or bakery. The pasty, originally called "Tehidy Oggies," served as a lunch for Cornish tin miners. The pasty was made with a thick crust on its edges, which served as handles for the hungry miner's dirty hands. After eating he could simply throw the handle crust away. The filling was usually a fish-based mixture at one end and apple at the other, making it both dinner and dessert.

Last, make sure you visit the old pubs scattered about West Penwith after a day of cragging. The locals are friendly, the beer is tasty, the dartboard is busy, and the food is usually cheap and plentiful. A couple of the best are The Logan Rock in Treen and the old Zennor village pub. The Logan Rock, serving Cornish food and ales, is named for a nearby balancing rock that was toppled in the nineteenth century by Her Majesty's drunken sailors. They were forced to restore it to its original position. A series of etchings of the process adorns the pub walls.

Cultural Experiences and Rest Days

Besides climbing and dining, loads of attractions and points of interest are found in Cornwall. The area retains a proud and rich heritage that stretches back thousands of years to the Bronze and Iron Ages. Cornwall was long isolated from the rest of Britain by its rough terrain and the great distance from London to Land's End. Its isolation helped retain the spirit and language of the Cornish, a Celtic people never fully absorbed by any invaders. Their windswept land at the end of Britain was one of the last Celtic refuges from the invading Saxons. Even today the Cornish language, although not spoken, is alive, especially in both family and place names like Praze-an-beeble, Carnkie, Goonvrea, Perranzabuloe, and Ventongimps.

Since the area was inhabited in ancient times, many villages and mega-lithic sites, including standing stones and stone circles, scatter across the hills. One of the best is the nineteen-stone circle dubbed The Merry Maidens near Lamorna. The stones are reputed to be maidens turned to stone as punishment for dancing on a Sunday. Another wonderful site is the ancient Iron Age village ruins at Chysauster north of Penzance.

Other good sights are St. Michael's Mount offshore from Penzance, the natural landmark of Land's End, the artist's town of St. Ives, and the famed village of Mousehole. If you want to hike amid splendid scenery, spend a couple days hiking the Cornish Coastal Footpath, which follows the entire coast of Cornwall and is part of the longest continuous footpath in Britain.

After climbing for a week in Cornwall, spend your last evening sitting on the grassy cliff edge at Land's End. The surf crashes onto boulders below. The sun slowly sinks behind burnished clouds on the western horizon. As you sit with your comrades and feel the night creep across the old and weathered land, remember what the great British climber Pete Biven wrote about Cornish sea-cliff climbing: "[T]here will still remain the wonderful fascination in climbing on beautiful rock with the sharp Atlantic beneath and beyond the crest of the ridge . . . nothing but sea, America, and the night."

Trip Planning Information

General description: Traditional climbing routes on granite sea cliffs at Bosigran, Sennen Cliffs, and Chair Ladder on the rugged and rocky coast of Cornwall.

Location: Cornwall in southwest Britain. There are two ways to get from London, Heathrow Airport, and Gatwick Airport to Cornwall. Head southwest on the M3 motorway, and then exit onto the A303 and head west to Exeter and the M5 and A3. Or drive west on the M4 motorway to the M5 just outside Bristol. Go south on the M5 to its end at Exeter. Continue southwest on the A30 to Penzance. Allow six hours for the drive.

Camping and accommodations: There are lots of campsites and other accommodation possibilities in Cornwall. Some are Trevalor Campsite, Land's End Youth Hostel, Sea View Camping Park, Trevedra Farm Camping Site, Kelynack Camping Park, and Secret Garden Camping Park. Many bed-and-breakfast inns are in Cornwall. Ask at any local tourist office or the main one in Penzance for details. It's best, however, to avoid staying in the fleshpots of Penzance and St. Ives.

Ther, a good campsite in the village of Treen, is close to Chair Ladder and the Minack Theatre—a worthwhile evening diversion. Ask at the village post office for details. The village of Zennor, close to Bosigran, has a good, relatively cheap bunkhouse with breakfast in a converted chapel.

Climbing season: Year-round. Cornwall is the British equivalent of a banana belt, with generally mild temperatures. The best time is May through September, although good weather can be found in the other months. Winters can be cold and dreary, but fine sunny days occur more regularly than elsewhere in the country. The only problem is the short days. Spring is often cool and rainy. Cornwall is famous for its microclimates. If the weather is bad where you are, then take a drive to find sunshine.

Restrictions and access issues: The cliffs are on National Trust land, but access is not a problem. There is no camping or bivying on the land, although climbers do it and keep a low profile.

Guidebooks: *West Cornwall* by The Climber's Club is the updated comprehensive area guide. *Southwest Climbs* by Pat Littlejohn is an excellent select guide to the best routes and the best cliffs in the West Country. Also *Cornish Rock* by Rowland Edwards and Tim Dennel is a topo guide to the main areas.

Services and shops: All services are found in the main towns, including Penzance and St. Ives. The smaller villages offer more limited services, but most have B&Bs, pubs, and a grocer for supplies. Off-season hours might be severely curtailed.

Emergency services: Call 999 for emergencies. If you're at Chair Ladder, go directly to the coast guard station atop the cliff. It's open from Easter until the end of September, and then erratically the rest of the year. The flag will be flying out front if it's manned. Otherwise, public phones are found in Porthgwarra and Sennen Cove. The closest hospital with emergency services is West Cornwall Hospital on St. Clare Street, Penzance, Cornwall TR18 2PF (Tel: 01736 362382).

Nearby climbing areas: Many other climbing areas and cliffs are found in Cornwall. The sea-cliff areas include Carn Gowla, Zennor Head, Gurnard's Head, Carn Gloose, Carn Kenidjack, Land's End cliffs, Carn Les Boel, Carn Barra, Fox Promontory, Lamorna, Vellan Head, and Lizard Point. Up the Devon coast are more excellent crags. These include Lower Sharpnose Point and Baggy Point with its classic route *Kinkyboots*. Inland areas are the limestone cliffs at Chudleigh Rocks and the superb granite routes of Dartmoor, including *Haytor, Low Man, Hound Tor,* and *The Dewerstone.*

Nearby attractions: Lots of historic sites and visitor attractions are in Cornwall. Some highlights are the attractive market town of Penzance; the fishing village of Mousehole, which poet Dylan Thomas called "the loveliest village in England"; The Merry Maidens and The Pipers, ancient standing stone circles; Minack Open Air Theatre overlooking the sea; Land's End, England's westernmost point; Lanyon Quoit, an exposed burial chamber with a large capstone balanced atop three upright ones; Chysauster, the ruins of an Iron Age village; Geevor Tin Mine, the last working tin mine in Penwith; the seaside resort and artist colony of St. Ives and its Tate Museum; and St. Michael's Mount, a granite island topped with a fourteenth-century castle. More information on these and other sights, attractions, and activities can be obtained at the various tourist offices, including Penzance (Tel: 01736 362207) and St. Ives (Tel: 01736 796297). The main Cornwall Tourist Board is at Pydar House, Pydar Street, Truro TR1 2XZ (Tel: 01872 274057).

Finding the area: Specific directions to the described climbing areas are found in the area descriptions. Most of the Cornish roads off the main highway are very narrow and lined with high hedges. It is easy to get lost here, so it's a good idea to obtain a detailed map of Cornwall from one of the tourist offices or a news shop.

Sennen Cliffs

Sennen Cliffs, stretching across the rocky headland just west of the village of Sennen Cove in West Penwith, offers some pleasant and popular climbs on perfect granite in a beautiful coastal setting. Sennen is a great place to come for your first Cornish sea-cliff climbing experience, being more friendly and with easier access than Chair Ladder or other nearby cliffs. The west-facing cliff, easily accessed from the picturesque seaside village, yields a wide range of routes from easy to very hard. Most, however, are steep, juggy, moderate lines on vertical rock with good protection. The routes are also easy to toprope. Many climbers find Sennen a hard, undergraded area, with the climbs being deceptively steep and without the numerous flakes found at Bosigran and Chair Ladder.

This guide describes a selection of the best classic routes here, including *Demo Route,* a Cornish ultraclassic first climbed by J. F. Barry in 1943. Many other routes and variations exist since the granite is blanketed with holds, edges, and cracks, making it possible to climb just about anywhere you want. Many of these routes have traditionally been climbed in two short leads, although most American climbers will want to just do them as single pitches.

Land's End is just south of Sennen Cliffs and offers not only excellent views at this westernmost point of England, but a selection of impressive routes that are generally steep, sustained, and serious. Pick up a local guidebook if you want to go at any of these routes, but be advised that this area is very dangerous with high tides and big waves—not a place for the inexperienced. After you've climbed at Sennen, it's a worthwhile pleasant outing to hike south for a brisk fifteen minutes along a mile-long cliff-top trail to Land's End.

The base of Sennen Cliffs and its routes begin from a wide nontidal platform

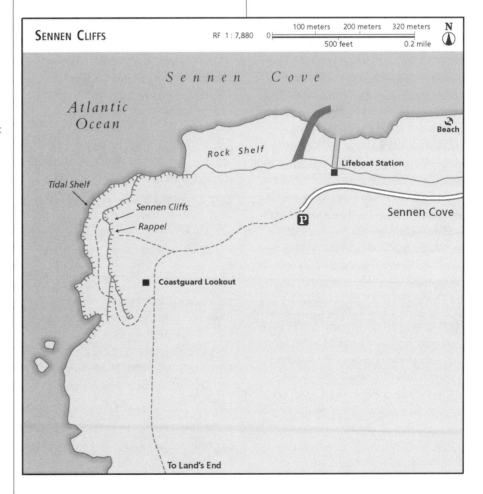

SENNEN CLIFFS   RF 1 : 7,880

Sennen Cove

Atlantic Ocean

Rock Shelf

Beach

Lifeboat Station

Tidal Shelf

Sennen Cliffs

Rappel

P

Sennen Cove

Coastguard Lookout

To Land's End

that rises 25 feet abruptly out of the rough sea. Be extremely careful and alert on the platform, especially if the sea is running high or it's close to high tide. Sneak waves, even in calm seas, can break over the platform and sweep unsuspecting climbers to their deaths.

Bring a standard rack of gear, including sets of Stoppers and Friends. A 165-foot (50-meter) rope is fine since all the pitches are half-a-rope-length long. A helmet is useful to protect your skull from falling rocks if it's busy and lots of people are on the cliff top.

Finding the cliff: Follow the A30 highway west from Penzance toward Land's End. Turn right (from Penzance) at a marked turn, and follow the road down a steep hill to the village of Sennen Cove. Park in the farthest west car park if possible. From this lot walk west and up steps on a path that heads toward a stone lookout point, then left or south along the coast trail to

Land's End. Branch right to the top of the obvious west-facing cliff.

There are three ways to reach the base of the cliffs. The easiest way to the base is by fixing a rope and rappelling down *Griptight Gully*, an obvious gully in the middle of the cliff, or downclimb the gully. Alternatively, you can rappel off other sections of the cliff. Make sure you pad the edge where the rope runs over it, and avoid climbers on the routes below. Last, you can walk past Coastguard Lookout south of the cliff and locate a gully below a split boulder. Scramble down the gully, then work right (north) to the cliff base. Walking time from car to crag is five minutes. (Parking lot GPS: N50°4.669' W5° 42.315'. Elevation: 37 feet.) Routes are described from left to right.

1. Zig Zag (HVS) (5.9) This route ascends an obvious zigzag crack up the farthest left face above the Black Zawn. Jam the

pumpy overhanging crack past a couple large niches to a sloping stance. Climb up right over a roof with good holds. 60 feet. This route has the greatest risk from tides and sneak waves. Be aware.

2. Demo Route (VS 4c) (5.8) Sennen's classic route. First climbed by Joe Barry of the Commando Cliff Assault Wing in 1943. Start below a leaning crack system up the obvious smooth face. Climb the flake crack to an awkward off-width section to a small ledge. Move up left and under the base of the overhanging nose on great holds to airy moves around the nose onto a slab. Grab large holds up the final corner to the top. 80 feet. Use long slings on your gear. The upper crack is notorious for stuck ropes.

3. Corner Climb (D) (5.4) Fun climbing on jugs and jams up the broken corner right of *Demo Route*.

4. Banana Flake (VD) (5.5) A fun easy route on the broken wall right of *Griptight Gully.* Start below the right groove of two left-angling grooves down right below a banana-shaped block. Climb the easy right-hand groove to a spacious ledge. Swing up good holds in either a shallow corner above the right side of the ledge or directly up the face to its left.

5. Staircase (VD) (5.5) Also called *Black Slab.* An excellent easy route with good position. Locate a narrow, south-facing black slab. Climb edges and jugs up the slab to a cliff-top belay. 60 feet.

6. Overhanging Wall (VS 4c) (5.8) More good climbing. Start at *Staircase.* Work up a steep slab right of *Staircase* to a slightly overhanging corner to the right. Step left, and jam two overhanging cracks to a spike. Grab it, and pull onto a stance. Climb easier rock to the top. 65 feet.

7. Africa Route (VS) (5.8) Good route on the next buttress to the right. Start at black water streaks with a prominent hole about 12 feet up. Boulder up to the pocket, and edge to a small ledge. Move left, and climb a rib to a stance. Continue up right, then step left and finish up twin cracks to a good ledge belay. 60 feet.

8. Double Overhang (HS) Another favorite area classic up the buttress right of *Africa Route.* Begin below an obvious quartz vein. Climb up left along the vein to a stance, and step left into a left-leaning groove/crack. Jam the groove to a small pinnacle, move left, and finish up a short, steep corner. 60 feet.

Right of *Double Overhang* is a high step that leads to another platform that leads south to another buttress. This buttress yields several excellent gems. Consult the local guide, or ask other climbers for beta. These hard routes are, from left to right, *Vertical Crack* (HS), *Gillian* (E3 5c), *Golva* (E1 5b), and the spectacular roof crack of *Superjam* (E5 6b).

Bosigran

Bosigran, an impressive granite wall that towers above the sea, is an excellent cliff for classic multipitch routes up to 200 feet long in a wild setting. The cliff, along with the nearby Great Zawn, is one of the major climbing venues in West Penwith. A selection of superb routes of varying grades lace the crag. The west-facing cliff, overlooking Porthmoina Cove, is composed of a rough, compact granite with abundant holds, including jugs, flakes, cracks, edges, and smears. The cliff, although by the sea, is not technically a sea cliff. Almost all of the climbs are high and dry, and unaffected by the tides. The north part of the cliff, called Seaward, offers a sea-cliff experience since it rises out of the crashing surf.

The cliff was first climbed in 1905 by A. W. Andres and Bretland Farmer, who did *Ledge Climb* after traversing halfway up. In 1922 George Mallory added a first pitch. Later, during World War II, the cliff and nearby areas, including the famed *Commando Ridge* route, were used for training by the Commando Cliff Assault Wing stationed at St. Ives. A big year in Bosigran's development was 1955. That year the Biven brothers, Peter and Barrie, along with Trevor Peak, did four new routes in a week, including the classic *Suicide Wall*. *Little Brown Jug*, named for the popular Glenn Miller song, was cleaned and climbed, and it became an instant classic that same year.

The Great Zawn is a yawning chasm west of Porthmoina Cove and Bosigran

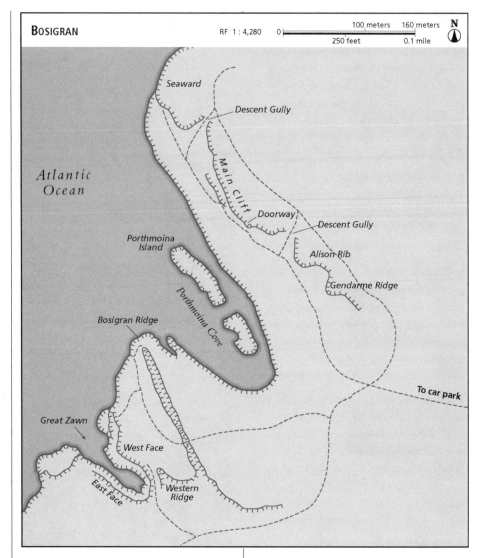

BOSIGRAN   RF 1 : 4,280   0   100 meters   160 meters   N

250 feet   0.1 mile

Atlantic Ocean

Seaward

Descent Gully

Main Cliff

Doorway

Descent Gully

Alison Rib

Gendarme Ridge

Porthmoina Island

Porthmoina Cove

Bosigran Ridge

To car park

Great Zawn

West Face

East Face

Western Ridge

Ridge, the long ridge opposite Bosigran cliff. This intimidating and atmospheric defile offers some of Cornwall's finest hard routes. Some of the best are *The Dream/Liberator* (5.11a); *The West Face* (5.11c/d), a bold technical masterpiece; the sustained *Desolation Row* (5.10c); and the outstanding line of *Xanadu*

(5.10c/d). Consult the comprehensive guide for access details and route descriptions.

Bring a solid rack of gear that includes sets of cams, TCUs, and wired nuts. Double 165-foot (50-meter) ropes are helpful on some routes. Otherwise, a single rope is fine if you use enough slings

Main Cliff

Descent

Seaward Cliff

To parking

Porthmoina Cove

to lessen rope drag on wandering pitches. A helmet is useful for head protection, particularly if the crag is busy.

Descent off all the routes is from the cliff top. Walk south from the top, and descend one of two gullies. The first gully is a bit more tricky, with some down-climbing. The second gully is easier. Be careful in both gullies not to dislodge any rocks as people are below on the access trail or other routes.

Finding the cliff: Bosigran is off the B3306 road between St. Ives and St. Just on the north coast of Cornwall. The area is west of the village of Zennor.

From Zennor, drive west a few miles, and park by the engine tower ruins on the north side of the B3306 road about a mile

past the Gurnard's Head Hotel. The ruins, a National Trust site, are Carn Galver Mine. Nearby is the Count House, a Climber's Club hut with its own parking lot for club members. (Parking lot GPS: N50° 10.305' W5° 36.766'.)

Walk north from the ruins, and descend through several stone-walled pad-docks with grazing sheep and cows to stone ruins at the head of steep slopes above the cove. Keep right on the good but narrow path, and follow it north. Scramble over boulders to the cliff base. This trail is unsafe for young children, with steep grass slopes that drop steeply down to cliffs and into the water. Allow fifteen to twenty minutes to hike from the parking area to the cliff base.

Main Cliff

The Main Cliff is the high, central part of the wall's great sweep. Many excellent routes lace this climbable cliff. Most of the classics on the central section are described here. A good classic on the right side is *Anvil Chorus* (5.9), with a superb layback dihedral at the top. More excellent routes are on the wall's left side. Consult the comprehensive area guide for details on these routes, including *Paragon, Zig-Zag, Raven Wall, Evil Eye,* and *Kafoozalem.*

Descent off the cliff top is by walking south from the summit to an easy descent gully. Watch for loose blocks when down-climbing it.

Routes are described from right to left when facing the cliff.

and over a bulge right of a roof to some tricky face moves (5.8) that lead up right to a ramp. Finish up the wide overhanging crack above to the top. 70 feet.

3. Doorpost (Severe) (5.7+) 3 pitches. 185 feet. This spectacular and excellent route is one of Cornwall's must-do classics. Start off boulders below a loose corner. **Pitch 1:** Climb the easy corner for 30 feet. Work up right along a right-angling crack system with perfect holds and good protection. When the crack ends, climb to a small belay stance. 85 feet. **Pitch 2:** Jam twin cracks above the belay. First up the left-hand crack and then the awkward right-hand crack (5.7+) to a spacious belay ledge. 40 feet. **Pitch 3:** Step left from the belay, and move up exposed cracks on the face (5.7) to a knobby rib to an easy finishing crack and the cliff top.

4. Thin Wall Special (E1 5b) (5.10a) Excellent route. 4 pitches, but many just climb Pitch 1 and then continue up *Doorpost*. This description is only for Pitch 1. Locate a steep slab right of *Doorpost* with an incipient, left-leaning, black crack system. **Pitch 1:** A tricky start with the first protection awkward to arrange. Edge and smear up along the crack, and seam to the top of the *Doorpost* traverse. Finish up right to the first *Doorpost* belay ledge. Continue up *Doorpost* to the summit. If you really enjoy this pitch, then seek out the authentic top pitch, which traverses right around the roof at the top of *Doorway*. **Rack:** Bring small gear—Stoppers, TCUs, and small to medium Friends.

5. Bow Wall (E2 5b) 2 pitches. 175 feet. This excellent route ascends a light-colored wall, then zigzags through the right side of some big roofs. The first pitch can be broken into two shorter pitches. Begin at boulders below a loose corner. Scramble 30 feet up the easy corner (3rd class) to a belay atop a large flake below the steep wall. **Pitch 1:** Diagonal up right across the steep wall to a spike. Face climb directly to an obvious left traverse to a small stance below the big roof. This is the alternate belay. Climb strenuous moves (5.10b/c) up right to the pancake, a jutting blade of rock. Continue along a crack

1. Doorway (S) (5.6) 3 pitches. An old classic with worthwhile climbing and good positions. Begin on the right side of the cliff below a corner and a black slab on its left edge. **Pitch 1:** Climb the slab or corner up left and then over broken rock to a belay stance beneath an overhang. 70 feet. **Pitch 2:** Thread left over blocks, corners, and slabs to a ledge belay below a big dihedral. 40 feet. **Pitch 3:** Climb the wide crack up the dihedral to the roof that caps it. An exposed traverse left leads to a crack and an easier finish. 85 feet.

2. Little Brown Jug (VS) (5.8) 3 pitches. 200 feet. A popular and fun adventure climb on the right side of the wall. Start just right of a short overhanging corner. **Pitch 1:** Climb up right on flakes into a corner system. Follow the corner up left to a small belay ledge shared with *Doorpost*. 70 feet. **Pitch 2:** Move up right on edges across a steep slab toward a hanging block. Climb up right to a small stance beneath the roofs. 60 feet. **Pitch 3:** Climb right and up a short rib to a black sloping ledge with a fixed piton. Step left up right, and make an airy step onto a slab above the overhanging wall. Pull through a break in the roof above, and belay up left at a small stance left of *Doorpost's* upper belay. 80 feet. **Pitch 2:** Make an exposed traverse left above the main roof to a stance below a roof. Work up right along a diagonal wide crack until you reach *Doorpost*. Finish directly up on good holds. 90 feet.

6. The Ghost (E2 5b) (5.10b/c) 3 pitches. 175 feet. Powerful and exposed climbing through the left side of the big overhangs. There are several alternative starts, including the first pitch of *The Phantom,* which climbs directly to the first belay or up the first pitch of *Suicide Wall* to the first belay. Start below a long, right-angling ramp. **Pitch 1:** Climb the ramp up right to the base of the black Coal Face. Edge up the left side of the face (5.8) to a belay stance atop the Pedestal. 65 feet. **Pitch 2:** Step back right from the Pedestal and continue up the Coal Face to the left side of a big roof system. Work past a short corner, move left and pull over a bulge, and climb to the base of the next roof. Do an exposed traverse right below a roof and across the lip of a huge roof below your feet until you can climb up 15 feet to a small belay stance. 80 feet. **Pitch 3:** Climb 35 feet up easy rock to the top.

7. Suicide Wall (E1 5c) (5.10a) 3 pitches. 210 feet. This popular route, the original 1955 line up the central wall, offers good and varied climbing. Start at the same place as *The Ghost* below the ramp. **Pitch 1:** Climb the easy rightward-leaning ramp into a dihedral right of the black Coal Face. Climb the corner, then follow a left-angling crack across the black face. At its top, step down left to a belay stance atop the Pedestal, a hanging block. 130 feet. **Pitch 2:** Move up and hand traverse up left along a series of flakes to a committing mantle (5.9) at a rounded horizontal crack/ledge and belay. 25 feet. **Pitch 3:** Do hard moves off the ledge (5.10a) up a shallow groove/corner. Work up the corner above until you can grapple right to good holds. Continue up easier rock to the cliff top. 60 feet.

Seaward

Seaward, the northernmost section of Bosigran, is a slabby wall that rises out of the sea. The Black Slab is its obvious feature. Several excellent middle-grade routes ascend this wall. The best are *Ding* (5.7); the superb *Black Slab* (5.4) up its namesake; and *Ochre Slab Route 1* (5.8), with delicate slab moves followed by an overhang. Also worthy for the lower-grade climber are the *Autumn Flakes/Nameless* combination and *Zig Zag.* Check out the comprehensive guides for route details. This sector is reached by continuing along the cliff-base path to ledges below the wall.

Chair Ladder

Chair Ladder, a southwest-facing complex of buttresses, faces, and gullies, represents the best of Cornish sea-cliff climbing. This traditional area along the rocky south coast of Cornwall offers superb situations on excellent granite above swelling waves. The routes are steep and exposed, and the rough, knobby rock offers lots of holds. It's a serious, atmospheric place to climb, especially if the seas are rough and the wind is howling off the water. Do not underestimate the cliff or its routes. Every outing at Chair Ladder has the potential for serious disaster, particularly with the short low tide period each day.

Chair Ladder is a tidal cliff, with access to the start of most routes below the high tide level. The ledges below the main faces can be accessed for only three hours at the most each side of low tide, leaving you a narrow margin to descend and start your route. The base ledges of all the faces can be affected by the swell and by rough seas at any time. If the sea is sloshing and rough, the access ledges are not safe. The ledges below Ash Can Gully are the lowest and hence the most dangerous. Get an updated tide table, and carefully check the times before descending to the foot of the cliffs. Be aware of sneaker waves crashing onto the tidal shelf below the cliff. It can easily sweep you off the ledge and into the dangerous offshore water. Avoid this by setting up belay anchors.

In case of emergency go to the Coastguard station above the cliff. It is manned from Easter until the end of September and sporadically the rest of the year. If it is manned, a flag is flown. Otherwise, the nearest telephone is at Porthgwarra.

The main problem for first-time visitors is locating the correct descent gullies to the cliff base. Three descent gullies are used to access the climbs. From left to right when facing out to sea from the cliff top, these are Pinnacle Gully, Ash Can Gully, and Zawn Rinny. The gullies are steep, grassy, and have loose rock. Well-traveled climber paths descend to the seaside terraces where the routes begin. Pinnacle Gully accesses The Pinnacle, Bishop Buttress, and the right side of Wolf Buttress. Ash Can Gully descends the cliff's midsection to Main Cliff, Southeast Buttress, and Wolf Buttress. A path descends grass slopes and then boulders and ledges on the flank of Zawn Rinny, a deep chasm on the west side of the cliffs, to access Bulging Wall. Directions to each of the descent routes is given under the cliff description below.

Chair Ladder, the southernmost point of land in Penwith, was long known by fishermen as Land's End. Sailing along this coast is treacherous, with several underwater granite reefs. Local myth recounts the witch Maggie Figgen, who sat atop the cliff in a tall chair and lured sailors and ships onto the rocks below.

After climbing at Chair Ladder, a good diversion is to stop for a quick climb at Hella Point while hiking back to the car park along the coast path. This rocky headland offers worthwhile shorter climbs, including *Panda* (5.6). A couple other good south coast areas are Cribba Head, a giant, leaning cube of granite with some interesting jam cracks and overhanging corners, and Tater Du near Lamorna. *Martell Slab,* one of Cornwall's best middle-grade routes, ascends three pitches up the middle of Tater Du. It's a very atmospheric place on misty afternoons when the mournful fog sirens wail.

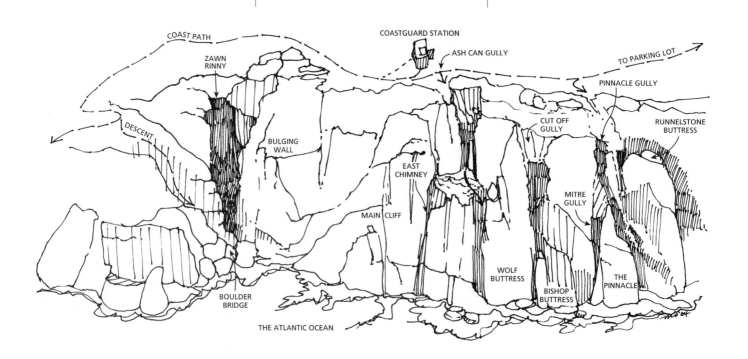

Finding the cliff: It's tricky driving to Chair Ladder. You're navigating typical Cornish back roads—very narrow, lined with high hedges, and busy on weekends. Drive west from Penzance on the A30 to a left turn onto B3283. Drive southwest through St. Buryan to a junction. Keep straight ahead on B3315, pass the quaint village of Treen, and continue to the village of Polgigga. Go left at a very sharp right elbow turn onto a narrow lane (look for a small hedgerow sign for Porthgwarra), which twists down 2 miles to Porthgwarra and the head of a secluded cove. Alternatively, you can drive southeast from Land's End, Sennen, and the A30 on B3315 to Polgigga.

Park at the Porthgwarra car lot at road's end. It's a "pay and display" parking area, and you won't escape a ticket even if you are a visiting Yank! It's very busy in summer from midmorning until late afternoon. (GPS at the parking area: N50° 02.274' W5° 40.389'.) A small cafe and toilets is by the car park. The *caff* has excellent pasties. From the parking, follow a lane that runs uphill past some granite buildings on the left. Look for a path to the cliff from a right turn on the lane. It strikes out left and uphill across the heathland to Gwennap Head Coastguard Lookout, which sits on the highest point above the central cliffs of Chair Ladder.

Only the summits and the tops of the gullies can be seen from the summit of Chair Ladder. There are three main descents to the base of the cliffs. On the west you descend Zawn Rinney to access Bulging Wall and the western section of Main Cliff. Ash Can Gully descends to Main Cliff, Southeast Buttress, and Wolf Buttress. Pinnacle Gully descends to Bishop Buttress and The Pinnacle. The best thing for the newcomer to get his bearings is to first search for and identify Pinnacle Gully. This is the first gully on the left and about 50 yards east of the Coastguard Lookout. It has some stone steps to combat erosion.

The Pinnacle

The Pinnacle is a semidetached pinnacle on the far east or left side of Chair Ladder (if you're facing out to sea at the top). Its lower face rises steeply from a seaside shelf. The top is a jumble of immense blocks culminating in a tabletop summit. Descent off the summit requires easy fifth-class downclimbing on the west side of the summit block. The described route is one of the best of its grade in Cornwall.

Finding the cliff: The cliff face is accessed via Pinnacle Gully. Scramble down a path to the backside of the Tooth, rack up, and stash your packs. Continue down grass and rocks left to a rappel from a sling around a block or scramble (fourth class) down steep rock farther left to the tidal shelf. If you leave a sling for the rappel, it's easy to scramble back down after the climb to retrieve it. Be very careful on the tidal shelf below the route—it's slippery and sometimes washed by waves.

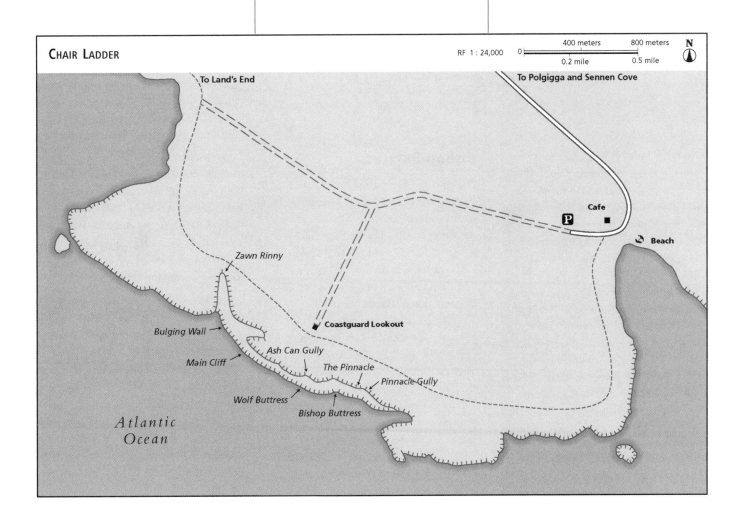

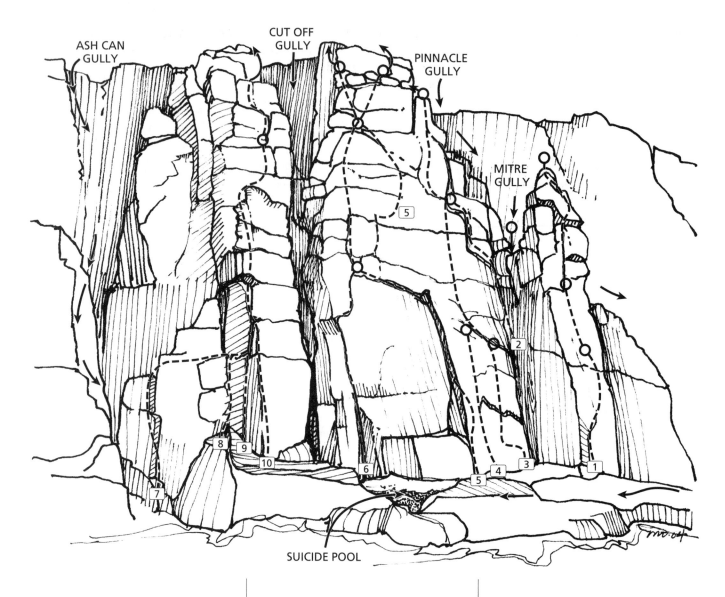

ASH CAN GULLY

CUT OFF GULLY

PINNACLE GULLY

MITRE GULLY

SUICIDE POOL

1. Terrier's Tooth (VD) (5.7) 2 or 3 pitches. A classic climb first done in 1940. The route begins below an obvious left-angling, shallow crack. **Pitch 1:** Climb up left along a quartz vein/seam to a face with good holds. Or start farther right on easier rock to the face. End up left on a spacious belay ledge. 60 feet. **Pitch 2:** Swing up an easy crack above to another big ledge. 30 feet. **Pitch 3:** Scoot up a crack to a roof, and ease right onto a narrow shelf. Pull over the roof via a crack (5.7), and edge up the crack and slab 10 feet to the top of the spire. 40 feet. Pitches 2 and 3 are easily combined. **Descent:** Downclimb off the steep west side of the pinnacle (4th class) into the top of Mitre Gully. It's best to belay the weaker members of your party down, with the strongest climber going last. Protection can be arranged for the descent.

Bishop Buttress

Bishop Buttress, the large buttress on the right side, is Chair Ladder's best sector, with a stunning selection of classic routes on perfect granite. The brilliant *Diocese* follows the cliff's most prominent feature, a large, arching corner capped by a roof. The deep, dark cleft of Mitre Gully marks the right side of Bishop Buttress.

The National Trust, which administers and conserves the West Penwith coastline, is concerned about erosion in the Pinnacle Gully descent route to Bishop Buttress and The Pinnacle. Keep to the existing downhill path to minimize erosion and avoid future access problems. To reach the descent route down Pinnacle Gully, walk east or left when facing out to sea for about 150 feet to a steep grassy gully. Descend the steep climber path here

to the backside of The Pinnacle. Continue carefully down the steep slope to the left until it cliffs off. You can rig a short rappel here from natural anchors and slings. Rappel 60 feet to the cliff base. Retrieve your anchor later after climbing.

Routes are described from right to left when facing the cliff at the base.

2. The Mitre (VS) (5.8) 3 pitches. 195 feet. This superb line ascends the far right margin of Bishop Buttress. The bottom pitch, which is not as good as the rest of the climb, can be eliminated by beginning the route halfway down Mitre Gully. To reach this alternative start, downclimb the gully between Bishop Buttress and The Pinnacle (a couple of tricky traverse moves under a boulder) until the gully cliffs off. Belay here to start Pitch 2. The last two pitches can be combined into one long lead.

Pitch 1: Climb the left side of Mitre Gully (5.8) to the base of the upper gully. This pitch is often wet and slimy. 60 feet. **Pitch 2:** Great climbing! Jam cracks just right of a prow to an obvious knob below a deep crack. Make a traverse with poor footholds and sudden, alarming exposure left from the knob (5.8) to another crack. Jam to a belay ledge. 60 feet. **Pitch 3:** Swing up easier cracks to the top of the crag. 75 feet.

3. Bishop's Rib (E1 5b) (5.10b) 3 pitches. 190 feet. One of Chair Ladder's best routes with sustained, exposed, and interesting face climbing up the right side of the face. Start below the left side of Mitre Gully below the Bishop's Rib. Beware of the rope-munching crevasse at the base, especially if your ropes dangle while belaying at the first stance. If the sea is running, you can easily lose your rope if it knots around boulders and jams in crevices. **Pitch 1:** Face climb up and left (5.10b) to a stance below a small square-cut roof. Pull the overhang on the right, and grab good holds to a belay stance below another roof. 45 feet. **Pitch 2:** Exposed face moves (5.9+) lead up left on the steep wall to a horizontal crack beneath a roof. Traverse up left and over the left side of the roof to a sloped ledge. Move up left to a crack, and face climb the crack up a steep golden face to a belay ledge. 70 feet. **Pitch 3:** Climb the easier, lichen-coated face above to the cliff top. **Rack:** Bring a standard rack plus a good selection of small wired nuts.

4. The Spire (E3 5c) (5.10d) 2 pitches. 170 feet. Good technical climbing up the left side of Bishop's Rib. Start below a thin crack system about 10 feet right of the left edge of the Rib. **Pitch 1:** Climb the faint crack to a slot, and continue up dicey rock (5.10d) to a stance. Move left and work up thin cracks to a thin corner. Belay above on a small shelf. 70 feet. **Pitch 2:** Climb up right, and pass the left side of the roof on *Bishop's Rib*. Jam the vertical crack above to a ledge, and continue up easier rock to the top. 100 feet. **Rack:** Standard rack plus some RPs for the first pitch.

5. Diocese (VS) (5.8+) 4 pitches. 200 feet. One of the cliff's megaclassic, must-do

routes and one of the area's longest lines. First climbed in 1951 by M. J. Ridges and G. F. Lilly. Begin from the wide tidal shelf and just left of the obvious left-facing dihedral. **Pitch 1:** Work up a wide crack or the easier slab to its right for 20 feet to a long narrow ledge. Climb up right, and continue up the dihedral (5.8) to a belay cave under the roof. 65 feet. **Pitch 2:** The short but excellent crux lead. Traverse left below the roof (5.10a) using either jams in a well-protected crack under it or a line of face holds below with your feet smeared on the wall. Either way leads to an exciting move around the final prow and a small belay stance. 35 feet. **Pitch 3:** Step left, and climb the exposed rib above (5.7) to a final slab section. Belay from a block on a large ledge. 75 feet. **Pitch 4:** Finish up right in a shallow corner (5.7). 25 feet.

6. Flannel Avenue (S) (5.6) 4 pitches. Exposed, classic, and reasonable for its moderate grade. Start on the left side of the face below a deep, obvious chimney above Suicide Pool. **Pitch 1:** Stem up the chimney (5.7) for 50 feet, then step left and climb the rib outside the chimney to a good belay. 60 feet. **Pitch 2:** Go right onto the left edge of the buttress, and grab good holds up the steep wall to a niche belay. 30 feet. **Pitch 3:** Excellent climbing with exposed positions on great holds! An exposed traverse edges up right above the *Diocese* roof to a flat-topped block. Climb the steep slabby wall above on good edges (5.7) to a belay from a large block on a ledge. 70 feet. **Pitch 4:** From the top of the block, step right and muscle up the face (5.7) to the summit. 25 feet.

Wolf Buttress

Wolf Buttress, rising in the middle of Chair Ladder, is a narrow sector dominated by a tall, jutting buttress flanked on the east by Cut Off Gully, a sharp cleft that separates the cliff from Bishop Buttress, and on the west by Ash Can Gully. The described routes are the best on the buttress. The moderate *Aerial* winds its way up the face of the buttress, whereas the other three harder lines follow incipient cracks for one pitch before joining *Aerial*.

Finding the cliff: The buttress is accessed via Ash Can Gully on its west side. The gully begins just east of the coast guard-station on the rim. Scramble down the obvious gully in front of you to its base. If the sea is running high, you can traverse left onto the ledges atop the first pitch of *Aerial*.

7. Aerial (VS 4c) (5.8) 4 pitches. A fun climb with a couple short cruxes that follows the path of least resistance up the buttress. It's best to climb the first pitch at low tide; otherwise, traverse across broken ledges from the left to the first belay point. Start 35 feet right of the bottom of Ash Can Gully below a thin crack. **Pitch 1:** Work up the thin crack, and make a step up left onto a ledge. 35 feet. **Pitch 2:** Traverse right to a step, and mantle onto it. Continue traversing right onto the main buttress face to the base of a double crack system. Jam the right crack (4c) to a good belay ledge. 65 feet. **Pitch 3:** Work up a wide crack above the left side of the ledge to a tricky move left under a small roof. Continue up the crack above to a ledge and then right up a steep wall to a spacious belay ledge. 55 feet. **Pitch 4:** An easy lead up broken blocks and shelves to the cliff top.

8. Animated Wall (E5 6a) (5.11d) 1 pitch. This is a direct starting pitch to *Aerial*. To begin, scramble right across the tidal shelf from the bottom of Ash Can Gully until you're below a thin, streaked, right-facing flake. Edge up a steep face to the flake, and work up right along the flake to a groove. Continue left then right to a hidden crack, which leads to *Aerial's* ledges.

9. Caliban (E3 6a) (5.11b) 1 pitch. Another direct pitch. Start right of *Animated Wall* by a pointed flake at the base. Step off the flake, and climb dicey incipient cracks to a groove. Above, jam the left of *Aerial's* twin cracks to its second belay ledge.

10. The Tempest (E5 6b) (5.12a) 1 pitch. A third direct start. Begin just right of *Caliban*. Edge up a steep wall to a flake with a fixed piton. Continue directly up, and join *Aerial* at the twin cracks.

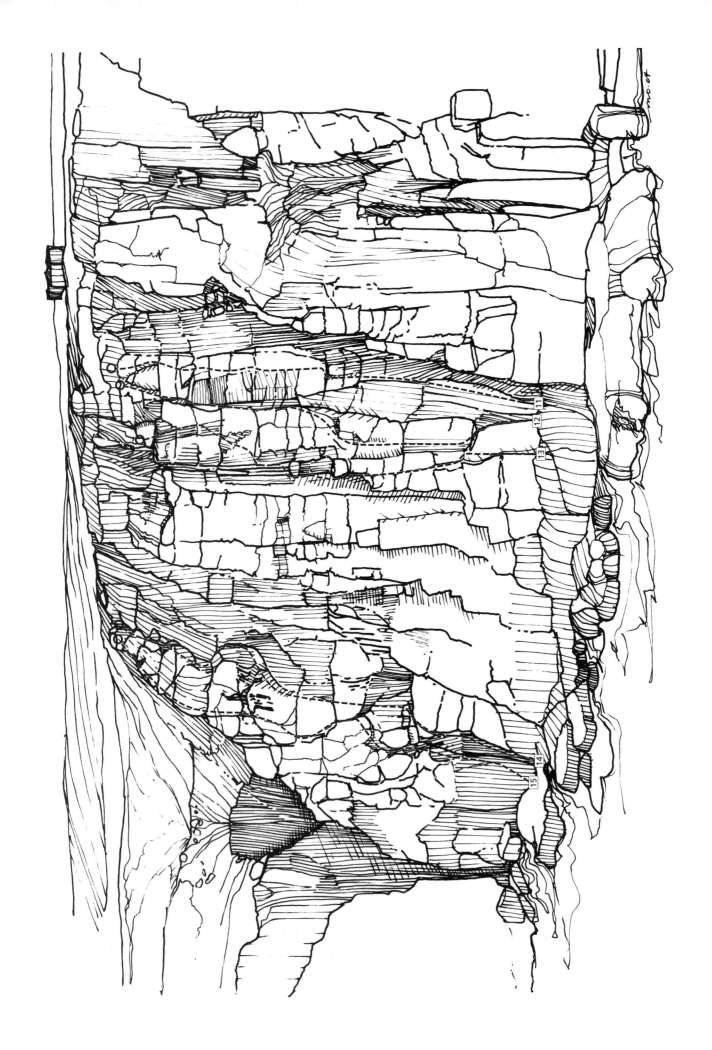

Main Cliff

The Main Cliff is just that—the big bulky cliff broken into three distinct buttresses in the middle of Chair Ladder. This complex cliff yields superb climbing with excellent positions above the sea. The left side is split by *Western Chimneys,* a 1910 line that was the area's first route. As always, pitches can be strung together.

Finding the cliff: Descend Ash Can Gully, which begins just left or east when facing out to sea from the Coastguard station. Scramble down the gully's right side, then down a final steep section to the tidal ledges. At the base go right along the terrace to the base of the routes. First pass a small buttress, a gully, the Southeast Buttress, and then a deep chimney system. The Main Cliff is left of this. All three routes begin on the left side of the chimney/gully system. Routes are described from right to left. All belays not shown on topo.

11. South Face Direct (VS 4c) (5.8) 4 pitches. An outstanding line up exposed cracks on the seaward face of the buttress. Begin below a wide crack just left of the base of the big East Chimney and about 50 feet above the tidal shelf. **Pitch 1:** Climb the wide crack to a square belay ledge. 35 feet. **Pitch 2:** Best pitch. Work up a shallow crack system above the ledge to a niche. Continue up the crack until it's possible to move right, using a chickenhead at a shelf. Finish up a V-crack to a stance. 60 feet. **Pitch 3:** Climb a steep crack above the belay past a roof. An easier open corner leads to a good belay platform. 45 feet. **Pitch 4:** Jam a crack up the right side of the summit slab to the top. 30 feet.

12. Pendulum Chimney (S) (5.6) 4 pitches. A classic outing up the middle of the buttress. Avoid it during bird-nesting season as it's noisy and dirty. Begin left of #11 below a flat-topped pedestal. **Pitch 1:** Climb the face of the pedestal to a belay on its flat top. 25 feet. **Pitch 2:** Work up a V-shaped chimney above, then step up right to a belay stance. 40 feet. **Pitch 3:** Traverse down right to a crack. Follow the crack up a steep face to an easier gully. Belay on blocks. 40 feet. **Pitch 4:** Work up the obvious chimney above to an awkward exit to a stance. The steep but easier wall on the left leads to the summit. 60 feet.

13. Excelsior (E1 5b) (5.10b) 4 pitches. Bits of good climbing with a steep, exciting finish. Begin left of #12 at the left side of the pedestal. **Pitch 1:** Climb easily up a groove/crack to a belay ledge atop the pedestal. **Pitch 2:** Climb double cracks and then a single crack to a belay stance. 40 feet. **Pitch 3:** Easy climbing leads to a recess topped with a big roof. Climb the right wall to the right side of the roof, and move out right onto a belay ledge. 65 feet. **Pitch 4:** A brilliant airy lead. Climb a black groove above the ledge to a horizontal crack. Pull into the undercut groove above (5.10b), and work it to the top. 35 feet.

Bulging Wall

Bulging Wall, the westernmost buttress at Chair Ladder, sits back from the Main Cliff. The wall is a series of slabs, dihedrals, corners, and steep walls seamed with cracks. Several excellent classic routes ascend the 180-foot wall. Be careful along the base. The platforms can be very slippery when wet and dangerous if the tide is coming in. The base of the cliff is accessed for only two to three hours on each side of low tide. Access is limited with heavy surf, even at low tide. Check the tide tables and the sea, and plan accordingly to be safe.

Finding the cliff: The descent route to Bulging Wall is on ledges on the west side of Zawn Rinny, a deep cleft that separates Bulging Wall from Carn Guthensbrâs, a smaller cliff. Walk about 150 feet west from the Coastguard lookout to the grassy slopes above the west side of the zawn. Follow a path down the slopes to the right side of the zawn, and scramble down over boulders and ledges to a large boulder jammed in the mouth of the zawn. Cross the boulder to reach the sea-level terraces below Bulging Wall. Routes are described from left to right.

14. Seal Slab (VS 4c) (5.8) 3 pitches. A fun and enjoyable route up the left side of the wall. Begin below the center of the big slab. **Pitch 1:** Climb the slab, working up right into a big left-facing corner system. Stem the corner to a tricky move left onto a ledge below a left-angling ramp. 75 feet. **Pitch 2:** Layback a crack up the face above the ramp to a steep ramp to a ledge. From the right side of the ledge, climb a short chimney to a good belay ledge. 75 feet. **Pitch 3:** Continue up the chimney to another ledge below a lichen-covered headwall. Finish by climbing up the left side or moving right and climbing an easy slab to the cliff top. 30 feet.

15. Pegasus (HS) (5.7-) 3 pitches. Excellent, sustained, and classic line that wanders up the right side of the face. Start below a crack in a corner just right of *Seal Slab's* left-facing dihedral. **Pitch 1:** Move up the steep corner crack, and exit right to a stance. Continue up and over a roof on jugs to an obvious ledge system. 70 feet. **Pitch 2:** A great pitch. Climb up and right to a black wall that is easily ascended to a small ledge below a right-curving corner. Belay here, or continue up the corner until you edge up a slab to a belay stance by a block. 60 feet. **Pitch 3:** Scale a black headwall up left to a mantle onto a shelf. Continue up left to another ledge and finish up easy slabs. 50 feet.

GRITSTONE EDGES

■ OVERVIEW

Great Britain's most celebrated climbing area lies in the Peak District of central England, the unassuming Midlands region. The Midlands has long been the core of England's industrial heart. This was the seat of the Industrial Revolution in the eighteenth and early nineteenth centuries around Birmingham, Stoke-on-Trent, Coventry, Sheffield, and Manchester. It's a place of factories, foundries, and potteries built near coal mines that fueled their growth. But it's also a place of rolling hills and leafy vales, of grassy pastures and mustard fields, of quaint villages, red-brick houses, and golden stone churches. The Peak District in Derbyshire is a land of startling contrasts between the old industrial centers and the 540-square-mile Peak District National Park. This beguiling upland of moors and valleys is the least populated and most beautiful part of the Midlands. Despite its name, it is not mountainous. Instead, the bucolic Peak District draws its name from the old English *peac,* which referred to any sort of hill.

The high, treeless moorlands of the Peak District lie open to the sky and to vagaries of the weather—rain, sun, and wind. This is an intimate landscape of undulating tablelands blanketed by heather, bracken, and peat and dissected by wooded valleys, fern-green dells, and bleached limestone crags smoothed by creeks and rivers. Sheep, scattered like shards of fallen rock, graze in paddocks hemmed by ancient stone walls. This land is wild and lovely enough to be considered beautiful, but it is also worked, quarried, and engineered in the name of industrial progress. Along the abrupt rims of the moors stretch long, dark necklaces of gritstone cliffs that define the sharp edge between the valleys below and the sky beyond.

The gritstone, yes, the grit. This is the rock that brings the world to climb in England. The intimate cliffs are short, blunt, and rough, seamed with cracks and very human sized. Gritstone is a friendly

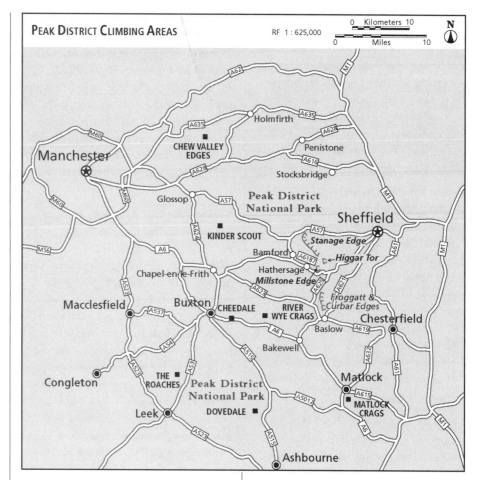

rock, not forbidding like the Welsh sea cliffs, nor atmospheric like the big walls lining the Verdon Gorge. Instead the rock offers a simple, plain geometry. But the smallness of the cliffs and their initial welcoming air are misleading. To successfully climb grit requires a climber's complete attention, a bit of boldness and nerve, and a veritable arsenal of climbing techniques. The first time you touch gritstone, you fall in love. This, you think, is rock made for climbing. Solid to the touch, compact like concrete, it offers some of the best friction for hands and feet anywhere on the planet, and some of the best climbs you'll ever do.

Gritstone is an odd sort of rock, unlike any found in the United States. It's a gritty sandstone formed almost entirely of worn bits of quartz up to a tenth of an inch in diameter with occasional larger pebbles thrown into the mix. Quartz, an erosion-resistant rock, was found in ancient granite mountains that extended across a vanished continent from today's Appalachian Mountains in America into

Scotland and Norway. About 300 million years ago the traces of this range, including the quartz grains, were deposited in large river deltas in today's northern England. The grit strata were buried and compressed into rock by overlying layers of silt, mud, and limestone. Later they emerged from the sea, and erosion began shaping and sculpting the hard rock into today's vertical cliffs cleaved with cracks, sloping ledges and shelves, rounded caves, and overhangs.

The jam cracks have long defined gritstone climbing. It was on the grit in the 1950s that legends Joe Brown and Don Whillans refined the savage art of hand jamming. The ability to jam cracks is an asset that every prospective climber values when confronted with a grit route. If you don't know how to jam, you'll soon learn. Your gritstone days are filled with jams up every kind of fissure imaginable—perfect hand jams, awkward elbow-deep off-widths, thrutches past offset horizontal cracks, and fingerlocks over rounded bulges. And at the end of the day, the backs of your hands are pocked with scrapes, tears, and love bites from coarse crystals.

Besides the cracks other gritstone features are delicate friction slabs, pebble-pinching walls, rounded holdless arêtes, rippled faces, and, of course, the new-wave "hard-grit" lines up dicey routes on dimples, slopers, and smears with sparse protection and serious groundfall consequences. To climb hard gritstone requires a smooth, confident style, the ability to find and place gear, and a bold, necky mindset. Remember that this isn't a sport-climbing area, pardner!

The gritstone is for traditional rockers only. There's always been a strict no-bolts ethic here. You won't see a single piece of fixed protection—no bolts or pitons—on any grit crag. Dennis Jump, a long-time grit man, says, "If anyone placed a bolt on the gritstone, it would be the start of World War III." Although, he adds with a sly grin, "I've always fancied gluing a line of bolt hangers and studs up *Hargreaves's Original* at Stanage on April Fools Day."

The Gritstone Cliffs

Thousands of routes are found on the gritstone cliffs lining the Peak District moors. The routes range from 25 to 100 feet in height, and the vast majority are 5.9 or easier. The cliffs divide into three categories: the popular classic edges like Stanage, Curbar, and Froggatt; the high, remote crags in the central Pennine Range, with long approaches and few climbers; and the quarries, where rock was excavated for millstones, churches, and buildings in surrounding cities. This guide describes three of the Peak's best gritstone areas: Stanage Edge, the queen of the grit cliffs; Higgar Tor, a small fierce outcrop; and Millstone Edge, the best of the quarries.

Stanage Edge is the longest and most impressive of all the cliffs. Visible from the Hope Valley to the south, Stanage rims the moor's edge north of Hathersage. The cliff band, attaining a maximum height of 75 feet, stretches for 3.5 miles along the west side of the moor from its southern end at Cowper Stone to its northern tip at

Brett Green pulls the big roof of *Flying Buttress Direct* (HVS 5b) (5.9) at Stanage Edge.

Stanage End. The west-facing escarpment, at an elevation of 1,400 feet, boasts more than 850 routes up perfect rock. Stanage is a place to spend days, starting with the classic routes at the south end and working northward. On a long midsummer day, it's an easy cliff for a good climber to tick twenty or thirty routes, soloing the easier ones and alternating leads on others.

Higgar Tor, across the moors south of Stanage, is a rambling cliff of buttresses,

smooth faces, and its obvious feature, an immense leaning block. The west-facing crag, open to wind and weather, yields a variety of classic routes up cracks and flakes. Higgar Tor is renowned for its brutish, strenuous routes, including *The Rasp,* a brilliant overhanging flake route that wears your arms out as you sprint for the summit. *On Peak Rock,* the area select guide, calls the crag "a spiritual home for gritstone thugs." The compact crag is quiet, somewhat remote, offers great views, and is rarely busy.

Millstone Edge, the finest gritstone quarry in the Peak, is a sheltered, west-facing quarry tucked into the moor edge east of Hathersage. Millstones, used in nearby factories, were hewn from the quarry in the eighteenth and early nineteenth century. The 5-foot-wide, round wheels, some still scattered about the quarry, were used for grinding needle points, cutlery, and grain into flour. The quarry climbing differs from the natural grit cliffs, with crisp edges, sharp arêtes, splitter cracks, and routes up to 100 feet long. The vertical faces are sudden, smooth, and immaculate. Many routes follow cracks that were aid lines in the 1950s and 1960s. These heavily "pegged" cracks are now climbed free, using piton scars for shallow jams and finger locks, including the unrelenting 5.12 finger crack *London Wall*. Other Millstone classics scale the spectacular, testpiece arêtes of *Masters Edge* and *Edge Lane*. Millstone Edge is often busy, especially on weekends, but rarely crowded.

Other Gritstone and Limestone Areas

After sampling these three gritstone areas, you'll want to taste other grit dishes in the Peak District. Each of the other gritstone sectors offers subtle contrasts in rock quality and texture, as well as distinctly different climbing adventures.

Other good crags in the Eastern Edges sector, besides Stanage Edge, are Burbage North, Burbage South, Lawrencefield Quarry, Froggatt and Curbar Edges, Gardom's Edge, Birchen Edge, and Chatsworth Edge. Burbage North, southeast of Stanage, offers short walls and bouldering, whereas Burbage South is the test site for hard grit routes, including *Parthian Shot, Braille Trail,* and *Equilibrium.* Lawrencefield Quarry, across from Millstone, is a popular venue with warm, sheltered cliffs. The twin edges Froggatt and Curbar rival Stanage in both quality and quantity of routes. The cliffs, overlooking the Derwent Valley and the villages of Froggatt and Curbar, yield some real gems. These include gritstone's best slab route, *Three Pebble Slab;* 60-foot

Froggatt Pinnacle; the airy arête of *Chequers Buttress;* Jonny Woodward's landmark route, *Beau Geste;* the classic *Peapod;* impressive *Elder Crack; Knockin' on Heaven's Door,* a serious 5.14 X route; and the superb line of *Prophet of Doom.* Gardom's Edge offers classic lines up a long cliff, and nearby Birchen Edge is a small crag laced with moderate and beginner routes. Visit Chatsworth Edge for one of gritstone's best cracks—*Sentinel Crack,* another fierce Whillans's jamming test.

More excellent gritstone tors—The Roaches, Hen Cloud, and Ramshaw Rocks—rear above the Staffordshire plain in the Peak's southwest corner between Buxton and Leek. The Roaches, a 100-foot-high outcrop, rivals Stanage for best gritstone crag. The area features big buttresses and steep walls capped with gritstone's largest roofs. The best routes are *Black and Tans* (5.6) and *Saul's Crack* (5.9+), two moderates on the upper tier; the classic *Pedestal Route* and its direct finish; *The Sloth* (5.9), with jugs out a huge roof; and the dicey hanging slab of *The Elegy* (5.10c). Down the road is the hilltop fortress of Hen Cloud, the tallest unquarried gritstone crag. Lots of hard classics ascend steep cracks, faces, and arêtes. Recommended routes are airy *Delstree* (5.9+), *Central Climb* (5.8), *Encouragement* (5.10b), and the delicate and technical *Caricature* (5.11d). Ramshaw Rocks is a prickly ridge of pinnacles and standing buttresses. Expect rough gritty rock, hard jamming (bring tape), and great routes. *Ramshaw Crack* (5.11b) is a must-do, overhanging crack, whereas *Dangerous Crocodile Snogging* (5.13a) is an X-rated delicacy.

Several high crags scatter across the north Peak at Kinder Scout, Bleaklow Moor, and Black Hill, which under the right conditions (read dry and warm) offer superlative gritstone adventures. Laddow Rocks, overlooking the Pennine Way, and excellent Shining Clough, Bleaklow's best crag, yield fine climbing on the high moors. The Kinder Northern Edge's five cliffs are remote, peaceful, and excellent. Kinder Scout Downfall's crags are wild and atmospheric, with few climbers and great routes.

If you exhaust the grit and want to snag some limestone, then the Peak

District hides some of Britain's best limestone in the valleys below the edges. The best is High Tor, a stunning, west-facing outcrop dissected by traditional pocket climbs up an open wall above the River Derwent near Matlock. Most routes are worth doing, but the best are *Debauchery* (5.10b), *Darius* (5.10c), *Flaky Wall* (5.11b), *Bastille* (5.11d), and the *directissima Supersonic* (5.11d). Other good limestone areas include Plum Buttress, with the brilliant nose of *Sirplum* (5.10b); Chee Dale's fingery sport climbs on The Embankment, Long Wall, and The Cornice above the River Wye; Raven Tor, described by British climber Jonny Woodward in *Climbing Magazine* as a "tottering pile of choss," but home to some of Britain's hardest routes, including *Hubble* (5.14c); Beeston Tor, with fun pocket routes; and Wildcat Crags near Matlock.

Consult a comprehensive area guide for details, topos, descriptions, and directions for all the Peak District's gritstone and limestone crags.

Rack, Protection, and Descent

Since natural gritstone is a limited rock resource and protected by stout traditional ethics, you need to be a competent traditional climber to enjoy the finest routes. Remember that no bolts or hammered pitons are ever used for protection. It's that simple. The local guide *On Peak Rock* states: "Gritstone climbing is a religion and infidels will have fingers, or worse, cut off." The gritstone boasts a long, storied history in the annals of rock climbing, and from the beginning, climbers abided by a pure, free climbing ethic. Nuts or artificial chockstones were invented here to avoid damaging fragile cracks with pounded pitons. Some routes, however, are still piton protected, but only ones placed by hand and carefully shimmed in place with pieces of cardboard.

The gritstone climber deals only with what the rock offers for both holds and gear. Protection ranges from sew-'em-up cracks to bold, unprotected solos with the usual topping-out crux. Most are somewhere in between. Almost all the classic routes are protectable with modern gear. The new-wave grit routes are a different story. Gear is often feeble and route specific. Ask around for protection beta before venturing onto any of these risky routes. Carefully size up prospective routes, especially if you're new to the grit medium. Those good-looking cracks can fool you, as they are often flared, bottoming, and impossible to protect.

Gear information is not listed for any routes unless it's a specific oddity needed. It's best to scope out your proposed climb and decide for yourself what you need to safely protect it. Every climber protects routes differently, depending on experience and skill level. An important maxim to remember is that the error is not carrying too much gear, but too little. The piece you leave in your pack may be the piece you need at the crux.

A standard gritstone rack should include sets of TCUs, Stoppers or other wired nuts, and Friends, Camalots, or their equivalents. A large Camalot for the occasional off-width is a nice luxury to carry. Tri-cams, larger micronuts, and Hexentric nuts are also useful. Carry several 2-foot slings for tying off blocks, threading chockstones, and alleviating rope drag.

Most area climbers use traditional British double-rope technique rather than single-rope American style. The reason is that many routes wander across faces rather than beeline it from point A to point B. If you use a single rope on some routes, you may find yourself hampered at a dicey move or a strenuous top-out by rope drag. Consider yourself forewarned—use double ropes or lots of slings. If you use a single rope, preferably a 200-foot (60-meter) cord, double it up to lead the oddball, dogleg route that requires double-rope technique. A couple 9-mm or 8.8-mm, 150-foot (45-meter) ropes are adequate for any Peak gritstone or limestone route.

Descent off all gritstone cliffs is by walking off, descending gullies and chimneys, or downclimbing easy routes. Climbers never rappel since there are no fixed anchors.

Seasons and Weather

The best season to climb gritstone is during the British summer. The long, placid days are usually dry and warm, with occasional bits of blustery weather and rain. June and July days are longer than anywhere in the continental United States, so you can easily stretch your climbing hours until 11:00 P.M.—an hour long after respectable British climbers have retired to the pub for an ale and chip butty. Other good months are May, September, and October.

Hard-grit aficionados climb only on dry winter days when friction is at its optimum. Traveling climbers, however, don't have the luxury of waiting weeks for the sky to clear. Here in central England, it can rain at any time. Fortunately, the gritstone outcrops, open to the sky and wind, dry quickly. But be sure to stow a raincoat in your pack before heading out to the crag.

Climbing History

The gritstone cliffs are not only one of Britain's first technical climbing areas, but one of the first in the world. In the late nineteenth century, young lads from the industrial cities of the Midlands escaped urban squalor and poverty by trekking into the countryside and tackling the fissures and chimneys on the squat cliffs. Early noteworthy ascents include John Laycock's 1909 ascent of *Central Climb* (5.9) at Hen Cloud, Morley Wood's daunting *Kelly's Overhang* (5.10b) on Stanage in 1926, Pete Harding's superlative 1943 ascent of *Goliath's Groove* (5.9) at Stanage, and Harding's superb *Suicide Wall* (5.9) at Cratcliffe Tor in 1946.

In the 1950s Joe Brown and Don Whillans, a pair of 5-foot, 3-inch climbers, arrived at the gritstone and pushed standards to atmospheric heights. Their list of classic routes is too long to be named, but if you're climbing a 5.9 or 5.10 classic, then it's likely that the pair was first. Some of their best lines are *Right Unconquerable* (5.9) at Stanage, *Great Slab* (5.10d X) and *Three Pebble Slab* (5.10a X) on Froggatt Edge, and *The Rasp* (5.10d) at Higgar Tor.

By the 1970s a new generation of free climbers pushed the limits. John Allen, a teenage prodigy, walked all the old lines and then opened his own classics.

These include the stemming groove of *Prophet of Doom* (5.12a) at Curbar Edge, the peg crack of *London Wall* (5.12a) at Millstone Edge, and *White Wand* (5.12a X) on Stanage. Other 1970s climbers include Tom Proctor, Ed Drummond, Pete Livesey, and tall Ron Fawcett. Fawcett grabbed lots of first ascents, like the perfect arête of *Master's Edge* (5.13b R) at Millstone Edge.

The 1980s brought harder climbing and tough climbers who pushed standards higher with bolder routes. Jonny Woodward's outstanding 1984 route *Beau Geste* (5.13a R) required three ropes to lead its dicey arête. Johnny Dawes, the "Stone Monkey," began his career by plucking some last great challenges like *The Braille Trail* (5.13b R) at Burbage South, *Slab and Crack* (5.13c) at Curbar, and the stunning arête of *End of the Affair* (5.13c/d R) at Curbar Edge. Jerry Moffatt also was active, doing the classic arête of *Ulysses* (5.12c X) in 1982, and later the bouldery routes *Renegade Master* (5.13c) and *Samson* (5.14a).

The 1990s and 2000s brought harder routes on holdless arêtes and faces, and bold, dedicated climbers who stretched the envelope of the possible. The new-wave "hard-grit" routes are highball boulder problems. They require delicate climbing movements, combining raw power with tenuous finesse. Some climbers toprope the lines until they're wired, whereas others push for the pure on-sight ascent on the edge of madness. Climbers are injured from falls, and a few have died. Some of the best new-age climbers are the big man John Dunne, Seb Grieve, and Neil Bentley. Dunne's masterpieces include *The New Statesman* (5.14a X) and *Parthian Shot* (5.13c X). Grieve quietly repeated most of the hard-grit classics and then established his own like *Meshuga* (5.13d R), and Bentley did *Equilibrium,* one of grit's hardest lines.

Getting Around

You'll need to hire a car to make the most of your gritstone holiday. Make sure to book your car reservation in America because it's cheaper than just showing up at the airport rental kiosk.

Driving is relatively easy in Britain. All road signs are in English, and most roads and highways are well marked. Yanks initially have problems adjusting to driving on the left (some say the wrong!) side of the road. It's best to pay attention, not get distracted by conversation, have a navigator in the passenger seat reading the map and giving directions, and religiously looking both ways at intersections.

Another problem Americans have is negotiating the huge roundabouts, especially those off the big motorway exits. Some have as many as eight roads exiting to various directions. Pay attention so you know which one to take, and don't stop in the middle. If you miss your turnoff, just continue around and take it on the next lap.

The roads in the Peak District are generally busy but rarely congested, except on sunny weekends and bank holidays, when people from surrounding cities clog the roads. Parking at the crags is no problem, although the lots often fill on busy weekends. In that case look for alternative parking sites, which may entail hiking farther to the cliff. Stanage Edge, perhaps the most heavily used cliff in Britain, has the biggest parking troubles. The Peak Park addressed the problem by instituting measures to control parking, including the creation of formal parking lots at The Popular End and at North Lees Estate. Car crime is also a problem at Stanage and other secluded lots. Break-ins regularly occur in summer, so leave nothing of value in the car. Open the glovebox and leave the trunk cover off so prospective thieves can see that nothing of value is inside the vehicle.

Adequate public bus service runs between the towns and cities in the Peak District, but you usually end up walking, hitching, or bumming rides part of the way. It's best to pool your resources with your climbing partner and rent a car so you can easily sample lots of cliffs. Derbyshire County Council provides a listing of bus service throughout the Peak District, which can be obtained from a tourist office.

Trains regularly run between Sheffield and Manchester, stopping at Grindleford Station. From there a long hike heads up Padley Gorge to the nearest crags, including Burbage South, Millstone Edge, and Lawrencefield Quarry. You can also walk to Froggatt from there.

If you're staying in Sheffield, it's easier to rely on public transport. A dedicated, inexpensive bus service called the Stanage Bus runs from Sheffield to the Stanage Popular End on Tuesday, Wednesday, and Thursday during the summer months. The Sheffield-Castleton bus stops at Surprise View on the A625, allowing access to Millstone Edge, Lawrencefield Quarry, and other nearby crags. The best place to hitchhike into the Peak from Sheffield is the Ecclesall Road area by Hunters Bar.

Camping, Accommodations, and Services

Lots of campgrounds are found in the Peak District. In summer they're busy, but it's always possible to find something. Campground facilities vary greatly, so ask first, or check on the Internet for details and prices. You will find everything from setting up a tent in a farmer's field to a camping area filled with caravans and screaming children. Also, don't forget insect repellent. Check the Appendix for addresses and phone numbers.

Lots of other accommodation choices abound in this popular region, including several youth hostels, some excellent bed-and-breakfast inns, self-catering cottages, and hotels. Ask at one of the tourist information centers scattered around the region for information and booking.

Food and Drink

The English pub and cafe are an important part of the gritstone climbing scene, but now the traditional climber's pub is sadly something of a dinosaur when compared with the boisterous climbing scene of the 1970s and 1980s. Don't fret, though—plenty of pubs still give a warm welcome to climbers, and even a couple original climber pubs are still going strong. The climber's cafes are in a similar decline, especially the "greasy spoon" variety that fortified the tigers of yesteryear.

It's a real delight to visit the local climbing *caffs* and pubs, as well as the various tea rooms and "chippies" or fish-and-chip shops. It's considered essential sustenance for the British soul to sip an afternoon cuppa tea before heading to the crag or campground. However, pick the establishment with care, or you'll endure milky tea, soggy chips, and flaccid fish swimming in grease.

The following pubs and *caffs* are deemed to be the best for climbers. Only two noted climber's cafes are left. Many obscure *caffs* are found around Derbyshire, but they are not the sole domain of the climber anymore.

Lover's Leap Cafe at Stony Middleton, formerly the exclusive realm of the climber, has been refurbished into a smart cafe by morning and an expensive bistro by night. The owners, however, still welcome climbers and cavers. The breakfast is excellent, with home-cured bacon, local sausages, wild mushrooms, and free-range eggs cooked in virgin olive oil. Climbing action photos and portraits on the wall add to the ambience. The cliff above was the scene of a legendary leap by Nora Baddesley, providing the name.

The Grindleford Station Cafe, a basic eatery in the old railway station off the B6001, is the last bastion of the climber and rambler. Expect no frills here. The Grindleford *caff* experience will either shock or thrill you. Be prepared for friendly notices posted around like: PLEASE DO NOT STAND IN FRONT OF THE COAL FIRE—IF YOU WANT TO BE A 'FIRE-GUARD' JOIN THE FIRE BRIGADE! and PLEASE DO NOT ASK FOR CREDIT AS A SMACK IN THE GOB OFTEN OFFENDS! Sample a real pint mug of tea and the biggest chip butties imaginable here. A chip butty is an order of chips (fries to Americans) wrapped inside a large white cob (bread roll).

Many good pubs that cater to the climber and rambler scatter around the Peak District. These are great places for a fine postclimb ale and a basket of chips.

The Grouse Inn is a great pub out in the wild along the road north of Froggatt Edge. Expect good cheap food, friendly service, and a choice of real ales. It's handy for Froggatt Edge, Millstone Edge, and Lawrencefield Quarry.

The Chequers, just below Froggatt Edge, is unfortunately not the climber's mecca it was in the good old days. A TV advert in the 1970s featured two climbers descending from *Valkyrie* on Froggatt Pinnacle to get into the pub ASAP, still in their climbing kit as they walked into the bar. Just try that now!

The Moon at Stony Middleton is probably the last of the great climber's pubs. No frills, good beer, and friendly atmosphere. And it's a stone's throw from Stony Middleton's limestone crag.

The Red Lion at Litton is an absolute pub gem stuffed full of characters. It's a real locals pub with truly excellent beer and food. Get in early to eat because it's usually busy. Camping is handy next door also if you get too drunk. It's close to lots of limestone, but not too far if you're at Froggatt, Curbar, or even Stanage.

The Three Stags Heads, at the foot of the hill between Litton and Stony Middleton and opposite the filling station, is another unusual pub with an original flagstone floor and coal fire. We walked in the wrong door one night and into a room with an old geezer sitting in a tin bath in the middle of the room scrubbing his back! It offers an interesting selection of beers, usually very strong and expensive.

The Little John, another remaining traditional climbers pub, is in Hathersage below Stanage Edge. It's ordinary with simple meals, generous portions, cheap prices, and cheaper beer. It's named, of course, for Robin Hood's compatriot, who's buried in the nearby churchyard. The Hathersage Curry House has tasty Indian meals, and Longlands above Outside, an outdoor shop, is very popular and a good meeting point. There are also many other pubs around Hathersage.

Handy brews and snacks are easily obtained at the roving tea shacks and ice cream vans at every lay-by (pullout) along the busy roads. Likewise, there are lots of eating establishments in area towns and villages. Be sure to try a famed Bakewell tart at Bakewell.

Cultural Experiences and Rest Days

The Peak District is one of Britain's popular holiday spots, with lots of charming villages, lovely countryside, historic sites and buildings, and other cultural and scenic diversions. The Peak District, established as Britain's first national park in 1951, is an easy one-hour drive for seventeen million people or 30 percent of England's population. So it's no surprise that it's very popular, especially in summer, on sunny days, and on bank holidays. It's the second-most-visited national park in the world, with thirty million visitors a year. Still, the Peak is big enough to lose both yourself and most crowds on all but the busiest days.

The interesting town of Hathersage, a corruption of "heather's edge," sits in a sheltered valley below the eastern gritstone outcrops and the panoramic view from Surprise Corner. The town, with historical ties to Robin Hood and the Eyre family, was an industrial center in the early nineteenth century, with several mills that made pins and needles that were ground on millstones. Terrible working conditions and a short life expectancy for mill workers led to factory laws safeguarding workers. Little John, Robin Hood's chubby companion, was born in Hathersage, worked as a nailmaker, and became an outlaw. An 11-foot-long grave in the parish churchyard is his supposed burial spot. Charlotte Brontë stayed here in 1845 and based her novel *Jane Eyre* on the village, which she renamed Morton. The heroine's surname came from a local family. Hathersage is a good walkabout after climbing at Stanage, with restaurants, shops, old hotels and inns, an outdoor swimming pool in summer, and quaint pubs.

Chatsworth House, seat of the Dukes of Devonshire, is down the valley from Hathersage. This grand Tudor manor, overlooking the River Derwent, is worth a visit. The mansion, a maze of stately apartments, balconies, and grand staircases, is one of England's great historic homes. Outside are extensive gardens and the Emperor Fountain, which at 290 feet is the tallest gravity-fed fountain in the world.

Farther away is the medieval manor of Haddon Hall, a living example of building styles from the twelfth to seventeenth centuries. This carefully restored great house includes a chapel, the impressive Long Gallery, and a banquet hall. Its terraced rose gardens are glorious in summer. The house is popular with filmmakers, including Zefferelli, whose movie *Jane Eyre* was filmed here.

Eyam, a picturesque village atop a hillock, is best known as the "plague village." During the bubonic plague of 1665, the village was infected by cloth from London, so the inhabitants isolated themselves to stop the plague's spread. Their only contact with the outside world was to pay for essential supplies. Payment was placed in still-visible pools cut in boulders and filled with vinegar to disinfect the money. The disease killed 259 villagers.

Some Neolithic stone henges and Bronze Age stone circles scatter around the Peak moors. The Neolithic settlers erected stone circles as ceremonial places for the solstices and equinoxes 5,000 years ago. The best are Arbor Low and Nine Ladies. Arbow Low, a circular henge built 4,000 years ago and comparable to Stonehenge, is the largest in the Peak and one of Britain's most important Neolithic sites. The henge sets within a 250-foot-wide circular bank with forty-seven stones lying on the ground and three central stones. The nine standing stones dubbed the Nine Ladies sit atop Stanton Moor, along with other ancient cairns and circles, including the King Stone. The cairns usually mark the burial site of cremated remains in urns and beakers. A Bronze Age stone circle is above Froggatt Edge, and an Iron Age fort is near Higgar Tor.

Bakewell, the largest town in the Peak District, is famed for its Bakewell Pudding dessert. This tasty, almond-flavored sweet was devised here in 1804 at the Rutland Arms Hotel after the cook ruined a dish of strawberry tarts. Founded in 1254, Bakewell is a good rural market town. Check out the 700-year-old bridge over the River Wye and the twelfth-century parish church overlooking the town. Behind the church is the Old House Museum, dating to 1584.

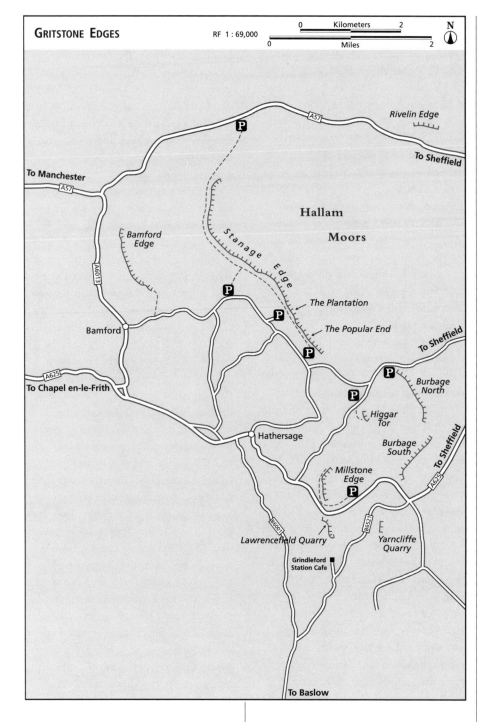

GRITSTONE EDGES

RF 1 : 69,000

Kilometers 0 — 2
Miles 0 — 2

N

Rivelin Edge

To Sheffield

To Manchester

Hallam

Moors

Bamford
Edge

Stanage Edge

The Plantation

The Popular End

To Sheffield

Bamford

Burbage
North

To Sheffield

Higgar
Tor

Hathersage

Burbage
South

To Chapel en-le-Frith

Millstone
Edge

Lawrencefield Quarry

Yarncliffe
Quarry

Grindleford
Station Cafe

To Baslow

Lots of other attractions and activities are found in the Peak District. These include visiting Matlock Bath, a popular tourist spot in the south Peak with promenades, amusement arcades, the Heights of Abraham, and Gullivar's Kingdom. The area offers some of Britain's best caving adventures, including both tourist and wild caves. Many hiking trails thread through the entire Peak. The most famous is the Pennine Way, a long-distance path that begins in Edale and runs 250 miles to Kirk Yetholm in Scotland. Lots of other paths explore the high, harsh moors like Bleaklow and Kinder Scout, the bucolic valleys of the River Derwent and the River Wye, and lots of lovely country in between.

Trip Planning Information

General description: Excellent traditional climbing on numerous gritstone outcrops scattered throughout Peak District National Park.

Location: Central England. In the Peak District between Sheffield and Manchester.

Camping and accommodations: Lots of campsites and youth hostels are found in the national park. These are often marked on area maps and found in local guidebooks. Bed-and-breakfast inns offer a superb value and a warm, dry bed on stormy nights. Primitive camping is generally prohibited. Some suggested campgrounds in the Peak District include Eric Byne Memorial Campsite (near Gardom's Edge), Hardhurst Farm Campsite (east of Wirksworth), North Lees Campsite (the site for Stanage Edge), and Peaklands Caravans (close to Stony Middleton).

If you're on the cheap, bivouac at the cliffs. This is frowned upon by authorities, but it is tolerated as long as you are quiet, tidy, and discreet. Traditional bivy sites are Robin Hood Cave at Stanage Edge, Millstone Edge bivy (secluded and sheltered at the cliff base, but watch for car break-ins), and the usually wet Froggatt Edge Cave.

If you don't camp, then lots of accommodations await you. You can book rooms in bed-and-breakfast inns (B&Bs), hotels, small cottages, and caravans. Good villages to stay in are Hathersage and Bakewell. The larger town of Buxton is close to the cliffs.

Climbing season: Year-round. Grit aficionados will blather on that you just can't climb grit in summer, not enough friction, but tell that to the hordes of Brits and visitors who descend on the cliffs in the summer sun. The best months are May through September. June and July are usually dry and warm. And really, there won't be too many days that it's too warm. Weather influences your choice of crags. The gritstone crags are usually west facing and along high ridgelines, making them prone to wind. It also rains, especially in the off-season. The gritty nature of the rock, however, allows for safe climbing in light rain, and the cliffs usually dry quickly.

Restrictions and access issues: Most cliffs are in Peak District National Park, but some are on private property. Access agreements allow public use of the land and cliffs. Parking is often restricted. Use parking lots, and don't park on the road shoulders unless absolutely necessary. The parking lot at Stanage quickly fills up on summer weekends. Plan on coming early or taking the Stanage Bus. Do not leave valuables in your vehicle. Car crime is a serious problem at remote parking areas.

Guidebooks: The British Mountaineering Club (BMC) publishes six definitive guides to the different gritstone areas. These hefty books detail recorded routes and variations, as well as lots of history and photos. But unless you're planning on spending a lot of time, it's unnecessary to purchase them. *On Peak Rock,* a select BMC guide to the best gritstone and limestone crags in the Peak District, is an excellent guide to the best areas and classic routes. *Peak Gritstone East* by Chris Craggs and Alan James and *Western Grit* by Chris Craggs and Alan James are good topo guides. *Stanage Topo* by Malc Baxter is a topo guide to Stanage Edge.

It's worthwhile to purchase a good area map, although an inexpensive road atlas works fine. The best maps are the Ordnance Survey Landranger map series. Maps #109, #110, #118, and #119 cover the Peak District.

Services and shops: Lots of shops and cafes are in the Peak towns. Outside, a climbing shop, is conveniently located in Hathersage below Stanage and Millstone Edges. Climbing shops are found in Manchester, Sheffield, Buxton, and nearby cities.

Good cafes near the grit include Little John, an old pub in Hathersage serving generous meals; Hathersage Curry House; Stony Cafe aka Lover's Leap Cafe; and Grindleford Station Cafe. Lots of pubs for après-climb brews scatter along the roads. Ask climbers at the crags for their recommendations and then explore.

Nearby climbing walls include The Edge and The Foundry in Sheffield, and The Leeds Wall in Leeds.

Emergency services: Call 999 for emergency services. The nearest hospital is in Sheffield.

Nearby climbing areas: More than 10,000 routes are in the Peak District— enough for several lifetimes. Climb the

described areas, then prowl around to discover other gritstone crags and loads of limestone routes. Although really, if you want to climb limestone, go to France!

Other gritstone crags in the Eastern Edges are Rivelin, Burbage North and South, Bamford Edge, Derwent Edge, Lawrencefield Quarry, Yarncliffe Quarry, Froggatt and Curbar Edges, Baslow Edge, Gardom's Edge, Birchen Edge, and Chatsworth. In the northern Kinder area are Kinder Scout Northern and Southern Edges, Kinder Downfall, and Wormstones. Farther north is excellent Shining Clough, Laddow Rocks, Tintwistle Knarr, Dovestone Quarries and Edges, Ravenstones, and Standing Stones. The Roaches Area in the southwest includes The Roaches, one of the best grit cliffs, as well as Hen Cloud, Ramshaw Rocks, Baldstones, and Newstones.

The White Peak, the limestone areas tucked into valleys below the moors, include some of Britain's best limestone areas. Cliffs at Cheedale include Chee Tor, Nettle Buttress, Long Wall, Moving Buttress, Plum Buttress, The Cornice, The Embankment, and The Sidings. The Lower Wye valley includes Raven Tor, Water-cum-Jolly, and Rubicon Wall. The Matlock area offers High Tor, one of Britain's best crags, Wildcat Crags, Willersley Castle Rocks, and the isolated grit outcrop Black Rocks. Dovedale and Manifold Valley includes Beeston Tor, Raven's Tor, Dove Holes, The Watchblock, Dovedale Church, and Tissington Spires.

Nearby attractions: Hathersage, Little John's Grave, Chatsworth House, Haddon Hall, Eyam, stone circle sites, Surprise View, Tideswell, Hartington (taste the Stilton cheese), Tissington, Peveril Castle at Castleton, Bakewell, Matlock Bath, hiking trails, scenic views, mine tours, caving, and nature study.

For information on the many area attractions, visit or contact one of the Tourist Information Centres in Sheffield, Buxton, Bakewell, Leek, and Chesterfield. More information and other travel tips are on the web at www.travelengland.org.uk and at www.thepeakdistrict.info.

Stanage Edge

Stanage Edge, a 3.5-mile-long gritstone edge, is perhaps the best gritstone cliff and certainly the most famous. The impressive west-facing escarpment, reaching a maximum height of 75 feet, offers more than 850 traditional routes that range in difficulty from fourth class to 5.13. Stanage provides a perfect introduction to gritstone cragging, with the majority of its routes being easy to moderate and relatively short.

Stanage is the most heavily used crag in Britain. Busy weekends bring as many as 1,000 climbers, with huge parking problems and queues for classic routes. In the late 1990s the park began managing traffic and parking at Stanage Edge, creating formal parking areas and roadside mounds to curtail illegal parking, and reducing speed limits. More than 300 parking spaces are available, enough for all but the busiest weekends. The Stanage Bus, operating between mid-April and early September, also alleviates parking worries. The low-cost bus service runs between the main Sheffield Interchange via Hunters Bar, Burbage, and the south end of Stanage. Car break-ins occur at the parking area. Do not leave any valuables in your vehicle, and hide everything else in the boot.

Stanage offers year-round climbing, although it can be iffy in winter with rain or snow. The cliff is open to bad weather from the west, but quickly dries and rarely seeps.

Bring a general rack of gear, including sets of Stoppers, TCUs, and Friends or their equivalent. A single rope is adequate for most routes, although the traditional British style is to climb with double 9-mm ropes. This is a good idea on wandering routes with lots of gear; otherwise, plan on bringing extra slings to ease rope drag.

Descent off all Stanage routes is by descending nearby gullies or downclimbing easy routes.

Finding the cliff: There are several ways to drive to Stanage, depending where you're coming from. The following directions are from Hathersage. Most roads on the east side of town lead to the cliff.

Stanage is 10 miles west of Sheffield. From Sheffield, follow the A625 west, and reach Hathersage after 10 miles. As you enter the village, turn sharply right down a small lane. Drive up the lane in a valley, past a church and houses, and then steeply uphill for about 2 miles. The obvious crag is straight ahead as you reach an intersection. Turn left onto a small road with a long parking strip on the right. Parking is a problem on busy weekends. The parking lot below The Popular End on the south quickly fills up. On busy days plan on arriving early or parking in Hathersage and taking a shuttle to the cliff.

The obvious access trail heads north for five minutes to The Popular End. Alternatively, continue down the narrow road for another mile to another large car park on the right and the start of a ten-minute trail to The Plantation area. Other roads also lead to Stanage. Most minor roads north and east of Hathersage lead to the various parking areas.

The Popular End

The Popular End is exactly that—the popular southern end of the cliff. Since it's easy to access and close to the car park, lots of climbers come just to this sector. Plan on queuing for routes, especially the well-traveled classics, on weekends.

Routes are described from right to left or south to north.

1. Grotto Slab (D) (5.3) An easy line often used as a downclimb for nearby routes. Climb the right edge of a large leaning slab, then up a series of steps.

2. Heather Wall (VS 4c) (5.7+) Up a vertical face left of *Grotto Slab*. Pull past several horizontal cracks to a ledge. Finish up a short headwall to a belay below the big roof.

3. Crack and Corner (HVD 4b) (5.6) An old classic up an obvious crack and corner. Jam and face climb the polished crux start. Work up and left along the crack to an awkward finish over a bulge. Belay below the big roof, or pull over on good holds to a mantle.

4. Manchester Buttress (HS 4b) (5.7) Classically awkward. Climb a flake crack on the outside of a buttress to a horizontal break. Traverse left under a nose, then up right on jugs to a ledge. Finish up the prow. *Manchester Buttress Direct* (5.9) avoids the traverse, taking a direct line up the arête.

5. Gargoyle Buttress (VS 4b) (5.8) Begin right of a big roof. Traverse left above the roof, then up an easy slabby buttress above.

6. Blizzard Chimney (D) (5.3) Begin below an open book. Climb a short, easy corner to a stance below the tight book. Stem up the corner to a left exit below a roof.

7. Black Hawk Hell Crack (S) (5.6) The easy, blocky, and polished crack system left of *Blizzard Chimney.*

8. Black Hawk Traverse (VD) (5.4) Popular and fun. Climb a short crack system, and step left to a shelf. Move straight up a crack system.

9. Castle Crack (HS 4a) (5.7) Up a big right-facing corner. Jam or layback the crack in the corner to a ledge. Step right and finish up a crack in the face, or left and up a crack on the side of a pillar.

10. Eliminator (HVS 5b) (5.9) Airy roof route. Begin below a large double roof. Climb a couple of right-facing corners to the first roof. Hand traverse left a couple moves, and grab edges under the big roof. Pull past and finish up cracks and face.

11. The Tippler (E1 5b) (5.10a) Classic. Start below the right side of a long, narrow roof system. Face climb to the base of the roof, and hand traverse left to a fixed thread in the lip. Strenuous moves above on horizontal cracks lead to face climbing and a spacious ledge.

12. Tippler Direct (E3 6a) (5.10d) A pumpy direct start with good pro. Begin below the thread. Face moves lead up and over a couple roofs to the thread. Pull past the upper roof and edge to the top.

13. The Dangler (E2 5c) (5.10c) A strenuous classic crack. Start below the left side of the long *Tippler* roof. Climb a short corner to the roof, and jam and layback out a pumpy crack. Make tough moves above the roof into the wide crack above.

14. The Unprintable (HVS 5b) (5.10a) What you cry on this desperate crack is unprintable! Climb a crack 3 feet left of

The Dangler to the base of a flared crack. Work up the overhanging crack with strenuous jams and layaways to a finishing groove.

15. Jitter Face (VD) (5.4) No topo. Clamber up boulders left of the *Tippler*

roof to the left side wall of the buttress. Climb up right above the roof on good holds, then up left of the prow above. More direct variations ascend directly up the face.

16. Flying Buttress Direct (HVS 5b) (5.9) No topo. A wild, must-do classic over a big roof. Run up an easy slab to the base of the overhang. Monkey out the roof on jugs with heel hooks, and pull past a couple horizontal cracks. Finish up with exposed but easy rock to a belay ledge.

17. Flying Buttress (VD) (5.4) An old classic. Begin below the left side of the slab. Smear up right to the base of the roof. Traverse left, and step around a corner. Follow a blocky, right-facing corner

to a large roof. Traverse right under the roof, and grab for the top.

18. Leaning Buttress Crack (VD) (5.4) Walk left to the base of a prominent pillar. Climb blocks to the base of a right-facing corner. Follow a crack up the corner to the cliff top.

19. Queersville (HVS 5a) (5.8+) Interesting, varied, and sustained. Begin below a small, jutting rock rib. Swing up the rib, and work up left to a small stance

below a thin roof. Work back right over a series of overlaps to a ledge. Finish straight up.

20. Hollybush Crack (VD) (5.4) Climb an inviting crack system up an open book to a layback finish.

21. Narrow Buttress (VS 4c) (5.8) Begin on the outside face left of *Hollybush Crack*. Work up the narrow face to an exposed, juggy finish out a V-notch in the upper roof.

22. Via Media (VS 4c) (5.8) The prominent left-leaning hand crack is on the right side of a wall with rust-colored encrustations. Jam the crack to a break and then past thin overlaps to the top.

23. Rusty Crack (HVS 5b) (5.9) A thin crack left of *Via Media*. Tough finger jams lead to a horizontal crack. Continue through a notch to the cliff top.

24. Rusty Wall (HVS 5c) (5.9) Crimp thin edges left of the crack to a break, then up overlaps to horizontal cracks.

The next seven routes are on the Black Slab sector.

25. Topaz (E4 6a) (5.11c/d R) A serious arête without much pro. Climb a sharp arête to a bushy break. Continue up the arête. It's possible to move left for an easier finish.

26. Right Hand Trinity (HS 4b) (5.7) Follow a crack up a right-facing corner past a break. Continue on good holds.

27. Central Trinity (VS 4c) (5.8) Jam a short vertical crack for 10 feet, then hand traverse left a few feet and work up a crack that widens and becomes easier.

28. Christmas Crack (HS 4b) (5.7) Begin below a short flared corner. Stem and jam a splitter crack to a stance at a horizontal break. Climb the right-leaning corner above to the cliff top.

29. April Crack (HS 4b) (5.7) Layback and jam a crack up an obvious large, right-facing corner.

30. Hargreaves's Original Route, aka Black Slab (VS 4c) (5.8) First ascent by A. T. Hargreaves in 1926 without pro. Recommended and classic. It's tricky, bold, and runout but not difficult—just keep a cool head. Start between two roofs at the center of the slab. Climb a steep slab up left to the left edge, then wander up past many horizontal cracks. Carry lots of cams.

31. Black Magic (HVS 5b) (5.9) Walk left around Black Slab to the wall left of a low roof. Start below a triangular roof. Climb up and traverse right under the roof to a small stance. Work delicately up the blunt buttress above.

32. The Great Flake (S 5a) (5.6) Begin below a huge flake left of a recess capped by a large balanced boulder. Swing up the crack on the left side of a detached flake to a final finishing wall.

33. Robin Hood's Right Hand Buttress Direct (HS) (5.7) An older classic line on the left side of the broad buttress face. Start below an obvious roof right of a deep V-shaped dihedral. Face climb up a crack to the base of the big roof, and traverse out right under the roof to a shelf below a wide crack. Jam and face climb the awkward crack to the cliff top. Bring some big cams for extra security.

34. Inverted V (VS 4b) (5.8) One of the best VS's at Stanage. The prominent V-shaped open book. Climb the dihedral crack to a large roof. Traverse right under the roof, and finish up another crack.

35. Desperation (E1 5c) (5.10b) A superb face line up a smooth wall. A crimpy bouldery start leads to a horizontal crack. Move left a few feet, and work up a right-leaning finger crack and flake to the top.

36. Robin Hood's Balcony Cave Direct (VD) (5.4) Climb a deep V-shaped groove to a right exit below blocky roofs.

37. Cave Arête (HVS 5a) (5.8+) Up the blunt prow left of the V-groove. Climb good edges up the prow to a ledge. Work through the big roof above at an obvious break.

38. Cave Eliminate (E2 5c) (5.10c) Begin at an obvious pocket below a small roof. Crank pumpy moves past the roof on rounded edges to a stance. Thread through the overlaps above and then back left to a stance. Pull over the final roof at a break.

39. Robin Hood's Cave Innominate (VS 5a) (5.8) Begin on the left side of a buttress below an arête. Make delicate moves to the base of a crack. Climb the thin crack for 10 feet to Balcony Cave, a large cavity. Step to the right side of the cave ledge, and climb right and then left to the top.

40. Cave Gully Wall (HVS 5a) (5.8+) Start off some large boulders in a gully left of #39. Pull pockets to a narrow tongue between two caves. Continue straight up flakes.

41. Robin Hood's Crack (VD) (5.4) On the buttress immediately left of a deep gully. Climb a short, left-facing corner past a small roof onto a big ledge. Continue up easy, slabby rock to the cliff rim.

42. Paucity (HVS 5b) (5.9) Left of the crack system. Climb to the left side of a narrow roof, and exit left. Continue up a tricky, shallow corner to an easy slab finish.

43. Wuthering (E2 5b) (5.10b) A typical English route. Double ropes necessary. Begin below a deep cleft right of an immense, flat roof. Stem up the V-shaped cleft, and place a high piece of gear. Traverse out left past the arête on the left

side of the cleft, and work up left across the exciting, pocketed face above the roof to a shallow corner to a large belay ledge.

44. The Asp (E3 6a) (5.11a) A striking thin-crack testpiece on the sidewall left of

Wuthering. Begin uphill in a breakdown gully. Traverse right along a seam, and climb a thin, vertical crack to a spacious belay ledge below the top.

45. Right Twin Chimney (VD) (5.4) Walk left past a squat, detached pinnacle to the base of an obvious chimney system. Climb a rib right of the chimney until it's possible to step left into the chimney. Continue to a broken ledge.

46. Left Twin Chimney (M) (5.2) Climb the left-hand chimney.

47. Crack and Cave (VD) (5.4) Start left of a blunt prow. Jam a thin crack to the right side of a large scooped cave. Climb right and then straight to the top.

48. Agony Crack (HVS 5a) (5.8+) Excellent short jam problem. Climb a short thin crack, and pull onto a stance below a roof split by a crack. Jam over the roof, and climb past several breaks to a belay ledge.

49. Balcony Buttress (S) (5.6) The slabby right side of the next buttress. Climb a series of cracks and ledges. At the upper roof move left past flakes to the cliff top.

50. Amazon Crack (VD) (5.4) Start left of a recess and below a roof. A tricky start to an overhanging flake leads to corners along a flake to the cliff top.

51. Morrison's Redoubt (E1 5b) (5.9+) The face left of a broken gully. Difficult face moves lead to a horizontal crack and the first gear. Work up the steep wall above to another horizontal crack. Continue face climbing up right, pulling past a roof to a ledge.

52. Stanleyville (E4 5c) (5.11c/d) Serious and interesting. Climb onto a large block, and face climb to a horizontal crack with a poor Friend placement. Make thin face moves up left to a hard mantle shelf. Continue above using rounded face holds.

53. The Mississippi Buttress Direct (VS 4c) (5.8) Excellent route. Climb edges, flakes, and corners along a left-leaning crack system to the cliff top.

54. Congo Corner (HVS 5b) (5.9) Another superb line. Start below a large

roof. Climb a thin crack to the base of the roof, and work out left on big flakes to the left side of the roof. Move back right above the overhang via a hand traverse crack to a small stance. Finish up the right side of the prow above.

55. Mississippi Chimney (VD) (5.4) An easy chimney.

56. Louisiana Rib (VS 4c) (5.8) An interesting line up the outside of a pillar. Climb a thin crack, and make a traverse right. Edge up the rib above.

57. Heaven Crack (VD) (5.5) A perfect little climb. Start below a flake system left of a descent gully. Layback the juggy flake to the top.

58. Hell Crack (VS 4b) (5.8) An awkward jam problem left of *Heaven*. Work over a bulging roof via a crack, then stem up the wide crack above.

59. Styx (VS 4c) (5.8+) Begin right of a deep chimney. Difficult face moves lead into a crack. Jam the crack to a good stance. Move up right, and cruise upward.

60. Devil's Chimney (D) (5.4) A good stemming route up the obvious chimney.

61. Saliva (HVS 5b) (5.9 R) On the slabby face left of *Devil's Chimney*. Climb a short, thin crack to a left-angling traverse with pockets to a flake on the left arête. Finish up the arête.

62. The Scoop (HVS 5a) (5.9) Begin at a large, jutting boulder on the next buttress. Clamber onto a small edge and then up the left side of a rounded scoop. Continue past horizontal cracks to the top.

63. Martello Buttress (HS) (5.7) Mantle onto the left-hand jutting block. Climb up left to a shelf on a prow. Head up rounded bulges to the cliff top.

Walk about 100 feet to Verandah Buttress, the next outcrop.

64. Verandah Buttress (HVD 5b) (5.5) Tricky moves lead into a scoop. Traverse up left, and pull up juggy rock.

65. The Guillotine (E3 5c) (5.10d) Cool but pumpy climbing. Swing up through a tiered roof to an exciting finishing pull-up.

66. BAW's Crawl (HVS 5a) (5.9) Classic, awkward, and fun. Walk farther up the trail past a short wall to a large, flat roof. Climb flakes under the roof to a horizontal crack and shelf. Crawl onto it, and wiggle right to a tricky stand-up move.

The Plantation

The Plantation is the central cliff section above a group of good boulders and small forest. It's easily reached from the parking area directly below the sector or by the cliff-base path from the south.

67. The Right Unconquerable (HVS 5a) (5.10a) The classic gritstone problem—a must-do for any climber. Climb a crack to the base of an awesome overhanging flake. Layback and jam the rounded flake edge up right to the crux, a final committing mantle move onto the rounded summit edge.

68. The Left Unconquerable (E1 5b) (5.10c) Just as good as its twin, but harder. Jam and layback a thin hand crack that angles up left to a small roof. Tricky layback moves and jams lead over the roof to a jug exit.

69. The Little Unconquerable (HVS 5a) (5.9) No topo. A 25-foot route up the far left side of the Unconquerable face. Scramble onto a flat boulder at the base of a crack. Jam the overhanging crack to final pulls over the upper bulges.

70. Calvary (E4 6a) (5.11c/d R/X) Begin below the center of the face. A short hand crack to a horizontal break. Hand traverse left along a crack, and mantle onto handholds. Work up a thin, fragile flake, and move up left and over bulges to the top.

71. Telli (E3 6a) (5.10d) No topo. On a little buttress left of #70. Climb a short blank slab seamed with horizontal cracks.

72. August Arête (HVS 5a) (5.9) No topo. Left of *Telli*. A short blunt arête above a holly tree.

73. Namenlos (E1 5a) (5.10a R) On the right side of the buttress. Climb a thin crack to a small ledge. Work up left, and follow a left-angling groove (bad pro) to some final chimney moves behind a detached block.

74. Wall Buttress (VS 5a) (5.8) Recommended. Jam one of two cracks to a horizontal crack. Jam a wide crack to the left side of a perched block.

Continue along the trail a couple hundred feet to Paradise Wall, the next buttress.

75. Millsom's Minion (E1 5b) (5.10a) Begin off a flat boulder below a roof. Pull past a crack, and climb pockets to double horizontal cracks. Traverse right along a shelf, and pull pockets and cracks to the top.

76. Billiard Buttress (HVS 5a) (5.9) Same start as #75. At the first horizontal crack, climb pockets up left to the left arête. Edge up the face above.

77. Curved Crack (VD) (5.4) No topo. An obvious chimney fissure on the right side of a recess.

78. Silica (E2 5c) (5.10c) Start in the obvious recess. Face climb to a roof, and swing over it. Jam the curving crack above to a slab finish.

79. Comus (E4 6a) (5.11d) Pockets and edges up a steep blank wall.

80. Paradise Wall (VS 4c) (5.8) Good fun! Finger and hand jams up obvious double cracks to the upper wide crack finish.

Follow the trail north for about 400 feet to Tower Face.

81. Nuke the Midges (E1 5c) (5.10a) On the short lower face right of a chimney is this boulder problem route. Start at the right side of the 25-foot-high face. Use good holds to a horizontal break, and hand traverse left. Finish with a mantle onto a ledge.

82. Tower Face (HVS 5a) (5.9) Begin off boulders. Tricky face moves lead up right to a thin, fragile flake. Ease up the flake, and traverse left. Finish up a superb final flake crack.

83. Tower Chimney (HVS 5b) (5.9) No topo. The obvious, flared chimney around the corner from *Tower Face.* Thrutch up the chimney to a good ledge.

84. Tower Crack (HVS 5a) (5.9) No topo. Excellent climb. Scramble onto a ledge below a pretty, left-facing corner. Jam a thin hand crack up the corner to a ledge. Work up right around a detached block to a belay.

85. Cinturato (E1 5b) (5.10a) On a broken-down buttress just left of *Tower Crack.* Begin left of a deep gully on a grassy ledge. Work up the left side of a rounded arête, and finish past some large blocks.

Follow the cliff-base trail for a few hundred feet to the next cliff sector. This area, one of the highest cliffs at Stanage, yields some stunning routes, including a trilogy of hard arêtes and the area's best crack climb.

86. White Wand (E5 6a) (5.12a R)
Heelhooks and desperate laybacks lead up
a blunt arête to a break. Continue up the
easier slabby face above.

87. Ulysses (E6 6b) (5.12b X) The obvious arête right of a dihedral. Layback up
the rounded arête (no pro for 30 feet and
a bad landing) until it's possible to step left
into the corner. Bring crash pads.

88. Goliath's Groove (HVS 5a) (5.9-)
Perhaps the best route on Stanage. A classic corner climb first done in 1943. The
off-width at the bottom defeats many an
aspiring leader. Begin below the obvious
open book flanked by rounded arêtes.
Thrutch up the off-width crack to good
jams, and climb to a stance. Layback the
crack above to a ledge belay just below
the cliff top. A #4 Camelot protects the
initial crack.

89. The Archangel (E3 5b) (5.10d R/X)
The third of the arête routes. Perfect
barn-door layback leads up the sharp
arête (no pro for 25 feet) to a horizontal
crack. Breathe a sigh of relief, and continue up the easier blunt arête above to a
final roof problem. Some put protection
high on *Goliath's Groove* to protect the
opening arête.

90. Helfenstein's Struggle (D) (5.3)
Awkward but interesting. Scramble up to
the base of a deep chimney. Work past
blocks, and struggle through a hole
formed by a wedged chockstone.

91. Holly Tree Crack (HS 4b) (5.7) On the
buttress left of the chimney. Climb a hand
crack to a ramp that goes right to a holly
tree. Climb the left-hand flake to the top.

92. Wall End Crack (S) (5.6) Climb either
of two cracks to start. Edge up the face
left of a wide crack to the flat top.

Millstone Edge

Millstone Edge, overlooking Hathersage and the Derwent Valley, is an impressive quarried crag that offers classic routes that range from shallow piton-scarred cracks to technical arêtes, including the bouldery classic *Master's Edge*. Grit purists scoff that Millstone is merely a quarry and not a real cliff, but this is the *real* thing. Unlike nearby crags, which are rounded and smoothed by rainy English weather, Millstone's abrupt features are sharply defined. Many of the thin cracks were nailed in the 1950s and 1960s as practice aid lines; hence the hardest crack routes jam their shallow peg scars.

All the routes reach the cliff top. It can be difficult to arrange belay anchors, so look around.

Descent off all routes is by walking off. It's easiest to hike south along the edge of the quarry, then drop down to the base at the southern end.

Finding the cliff: The quarry is above the A625 Sheffield-Castleton road east of Hathersage and just past Surprise Corner. Park at the Surprise Corner "pay-and-display" parking area (fee), and hike west on a path from the lot. Pass through two gates, and drop into a small overgrown quarry to a good footpath (old quarry road). Go right, and hike up the road to Millstone. It's a maximum ten-minute walk from car to cliff. Alternatively, you can park at a small pullout at the start of the quarry trail, but it's often crowded and hard to park here. It's also safer to leave your car in the pay lot.

1. Regent Street (E2 5c) (5.10c) Excellent jamming up a peg-scarred crack. Thin finger jams lead to a notched-out roof. A difficult move over the roof and more technical climbing to a roof right of the circular indentation. Step right under the roof to a no-hands rest. Sustained jamming up a right-angling crack leads to the top. 65 feet.

2. Jermyn Street (E5 6a) (5.11d) Just left of #1. Follow a thin, piton-scarred crack to a left-facing corner. Balance up the corner and a rib to the right side of a cave. Work up the curving arête right of the cave, then hand traverse across its lip until you can pull over. Exit up left across the face to the top.

3. Coventry Street (E5 6b) (5.12a) Good route. Most climb just to the cave. Work up the steep thin crack (5.11d) to a final tricky move into the cave. Rappel or continue by swinging over the sandy roof and then up the wall above.

4. Piccadilly Circus (E2 5c) (5.10c/d) Start a few feet left of #3. Jam another thin crack to the cave. Finish out by the left side of the cave to a stance, then up a thin crack.

5. London Wall (E5 6a) (5.12a) A sustained and superlative thin-crack testpiece for the hardman. First free climbed by John Allen in 1975. The route ascends an obvious crack system up the right wall of a huge dihedral. Jam the thin pin-scarred crack up left to a rest. Finish up an unrelenting vertical finger crack to the cliff top.

6. The Mall (VS 4c) (5.8) Good climbing, but it's sometimes sandy and dirty after rain. Jam, pull, and stem up the huge dihedral left of *London Wall.*

7. White Wall (E5 6b) (5.12a/b R) A thin face route left of *The Mall.* Follow a thin crack and pockets to a thin roof. Pull past on pockets to a narrow shelf. Edge left and finish up a thin crack with piton scars.

8. Great Portland Street (HVS 5b) (5.9) Excellent, well-protected climbing up a thin, left-facing corner system. Start off rock ledges. Begin with a tricky mantle to the base of the corner. Stem and layback up the corner to a cliff-top belay. Tie off a couple of the stone fence posts set back from the cliff for anchors.

9. Bond Street (HVS 5a) (5.9) Recommended. An obvious, splitter jam crack left of *Great Portland Street.* Jam the hand crack to a triangular niche. Use finger jams (crux) above the niche to gain a juggy crack and finish on ledges. Scramble up broken rock to the top.

10. Convent Garden (VS 4b) (5.6) 2 pitches. Pitch 2 is often avoided. **Pitch 1:** Clamber over several shelves, then up the left side of a small pillar to a stance atop it. Swing up narrow corners above to a spacious ledge. Belay here, or continue up easy rock to the cliff top. **Pitch 2:** Move left on a narrow ledge to a sharp arête. Climb the airy, mostly unprotected arête on big holds to the top.

4th Class

11. Embankment 4 (E1 5b) (5.10a) This is the right-hand route on the smooth, west-facing wall left of a big dihedral. Jam and layback a sustained thin crack system to a small ledge belay. Scramble up and right (4th class) to the cliff top.

12. Time for Tea (E3 5c) (5.10c/d R) An excellent but committing line for the fearless leader. Begin 5 feet left of *Embankment 4* at the next crack. Jam a finger crack for 35 feet until it ends. Set some good wires, and traverse up left to a good foot shelf. Make a couple committing moves to a tree and a ledge belay. Scramble up and right (4th class) to the cliff top.

13. Embankment 3 (E1 5b) (5.10a) Classic finger crack. Jam piton scars up a steep, thin crack to a belay on the terrace above. Scramble up right (4th class) to the cliff top, or climb a fun second pitch up a short right-facing flake (5.6) to the moor above.

14. Embankment 2 (VS 4c,4b) (5.8+) 2 pitches. Superb jam crack. **Pitch 1:** Jam the obvious double cracks on the left side of the lower wall with right hand in the right finger crack and left hand in the left hand-and-fist crack to a ledge belay. Scramble up right on easy rock to the top, or do **Pitch 2:** Layback up a short right-facing flake (5.6) to the cliff top.

15. Embankment 1 (VS 4c) (5.8) The far left crack on the wall. Work up a short fingery crack, and dogleg up right past a piece of iron (don't use it!) to the terrace above. Scramble right up easy rock to the top.

16. Blind Bat (E4 5c) (5.11c) This is an alternative second pitch to the *Embankment* routes. Start from the left side of the upper terrace, and climb good but thin edges right of the arête past a manky piton. Finish just right of the upper arête.

17. Great North Road (HVS 5a) (5.9) A superb route, one of the longest on gritstone, climbs a prominent left-facing dihedral left of the *Embankment* routes. Nicknamed the "Cenotaph Corner of Millstone." Climb broken flakes to the base of the corner. Layback to an airy ledge below the left-leaning corner. Continue laybacking (crux 5.9) to a roof. Pull past on good holds to a final layback finish.

18. Knightsbridge (E2 5c) (5.10b/c) A fine route with interesting moves and decent wire protection. It traditionally starts up a clean left-facing corner with ferns, but most parties now climb *The Scoop,* an easy slab, to a belay stance below the vertical wall. Climb edges up left, and work up a sustained, tricky finger crack to a tree. Move left to the cliff top. Walk off north to a downclimb descent.

19. The Master's Edge (E7 6c) (5.13a R/X) This stunning, sharp arête is one of the most famous gritstone routes. First climbed by Ron Fawcett, it offers sustained, athletic climbing with virtually no pro—a route only for the calm rock master. Hard bouldery moves lead to triple shot holes 20 feet up (bring #2.5 tri-cams or the rare Amigo for pro). More hard edging and laybacking leads to a juggy finish. Bring crash pads and spotters.

20. Green Death (E5 6b) (5.12a R) A height-dependent climb up an open corner. A tricky start leads to good holds and a fixed piton, then scary edging up the thin corner above.

21. Edge Lane (E5 5c) (5.12a R/X) The immaculate arête left of *Master's Edge* is basically a long, heady boulder problem with serious injury potential. Layback and crimp up the left-hand arête past two distinct cruxes with sloping holds. Finish past a big jug.

22. Great Arête (E5 5c) (5.12a R) The exposed, airy, scary arête above *Master's Edge.* Climb the right side of the arête with scant protection.

23. Great West Road (E2 5b) (5.10c) 2 pitches. Another 3-star Millstone classic.

24. Xanadu (E3 5c) (5.10d) Stem up an impressive left-facing corner to a narrow ledge. Continue up the corner above until it's possible to traverse left to a finishing arête.

25. Crew Cut (VS 4c) (5.8) No topo. A perfect layback left of the shot holes. You

can also climb it as a desperate off-width (5.10).

Hike up and out of the main quarry, and continue left along the cliff-base trail to the following routes. For the first one, #26, walk past a scree slope on the right, and descend slightly past an obvious corner system.

26. Billingsgate (HVS 5b) (5.9) No topo. Climb a fun, obvious corner up left to the cliff top.

The next three routes are about 100 feet left of #26 on the left side of an amphitheater with a cave on its left wall.

27. Twikker (E3 5c) (5.11a) Excellent. Climb the left side of a cave recess, and angle right under a roof. Jam a crack out the right side of the roof, and make pumpy moves to a small niche. Strenuous moves over narrow roofs lead to an easier finish.

28. Erb (E2 5b) (5.10b) Same start as #27, but below the left side of the cave, jam a thin crack over the left roof edge. Make tricky moves above, and finish up a slab.

29. Lyon's Corner House (HVS 5a) (5.9) Same start as #27, but work up left from the left side of the roof, and climb an arête.

Walk around the corner to an obvious smooth slab.

30. The Great Slab (HS 4a) (5.7) Move up a thin crack on the slab to a break. Continue up a crack system above.

31. The Snivelling (E5 6a) (5.12a R) Edge up a line of chipped holds to an overlap. Pull thin edges to the break above, step right, and finish up #30.

32. Svelt (HVS 5a) (5.9) Start on the left side of the slab. Climb a right-angling corner, and pull past an overlap to a shelf. Climb the shallow corner above.

Continue walking along the cliff base past some broken cliffs to a large amphitheater.

33. Eartha (HS 5a) (5.7+) On the right side of the amphitheater. Climb a slab past a small roof to a shelf. Step right, and layback and jam a crack to the cliff top.

34. Close Shave (S 4a) (5.6) On the left side of the amphitheater is a large leaning block called The Cioch. Begin just right of the block. Climb cracks and corners to a ledge. Finish up the dihedral above.

35. Supra Direct (HVS/E1 5c) (5.10a) Climb pin scars up the outside face of The Cioch block to a ledge.

36. Dexterity (HVS 5b) (5.9) Recommended. Jam the pumpy crack left of the block to a crux at the overlaps. Finish up *Close Shave's* upper corner, or step left and climb the obvious *April Arête* (HVS 4c) (5.9).

37. Dextrous Hare (E4 5c) (5.11c) A thin piton-scarred crack left of #36.

More routes, not described here, are around the corner on the diminishing wall. The best one is *Saville Street* (E3 6a) (5.11b), an obvious finger crack up a steep wall with a strenuous finish past a roof.

Higgar Tor

Higgar Tor is a small, west-facing crag at an altitude of 1,410 feet that overlooks the Derwent Valley southeast of Stanage Edge. The 50-foot-high cliff offers fifty-five routes and boulder problems on its sturdy, compact flanks. An immense leaning block is Higgar Tor's main event, with several gritstone testpieces up its overhanging wall. The best is *The Rasp,* a strenuous classic established by Joe Brown in 1956. The thuggish route swings up a steep flake system and features a sustained layback that feels like a sprint before the arms give out. Around the corner is *The File,* a 1956 Don Whillans route up a perfect hand crack. Expect pumpy routes up cracks and flakes with occasional face moves. Most routes are well protected.

The cliff, situated high on the moor's edge, is exposed to the weather. It can be cold and windy. Summer evenings are excellent. The tor is ideal when other edges are midge infested. The crag is rarely crowded, even on weekends, and most traffic is on the easier lines.

Finding the cliff: Higgar Tor is 2 kilometers east of Hathersage and sits above the minor road that goes to Stanage Edge and Ringinglow. A small parking area (SK 256822) is along the road north of the crag. Cross a stile over a fence, and follow a path south around a hillock to the hidden cliff. Hiking time is five minutes. Routes are described left to right.

The first four routes on the left side of the cliff are good introductory warm-ups on a short wall. The base of the left wall offers a long, pumpy bouldering traverse with a soft grass landing.

1. Mighty Atom (E2 5c) (5.10b) On the face left of the obvious recess on the left side of the wall. A good start leads to an underprotected exit on rounded rock.

2. The Riffler (VS 5a) (5.8) Fun climbing. Jam the cracks above the cave niche to an easy finish.

3. The Cotter (HVS 5a) (5.9) Start at the right side of the recess. Work up cracks to the top.

4. The Rat's Tail (VS 4c) (5.8) An obvious crack system. The crux start leads to jams.

The following routes are up the leaning block, a gritstone cube that weighs an estimated 10,000 tons.

5. Surform (HVS 5a) (5.9+) Surprisingly pumpy and stiff for the grade. Follow a right-facing flake on the left side of the block's face up and right until it's possible to exit up left into a triangular niche. Work out the left side, and finish up rounded horizontal cracks.

6. The Rasp (E2 5b) (5.10d) One of grit's best routes—strenuous, steep, and spectacular. There are two starts. The regular start heads up *Surform's* right-angling flakes. Swing up the flake corners to the third roof, and move right. Continue laybacking up flakes and big holds to a niche and a poor rest under the final roof. Shake out and then hand traverse right along a horizontal crack to a notch through the roof.

7. Rasp Direct (E3 6a) (5.11a) The direct other start to *The Rasp.* Jam a thin, strenuous finger crack for 15 feet to a roof. Pull up the widely spaced flakes to the niche rest. Move right a few feet, and make a wild mantle and belly flop over the lip above onto the flat summit.

8. Bat Out of Hell (E5 6a) (5.12a) An exciting line up the right side of the overhanging block. Face climb up rock left of a short corner to a 5-foot crack to a horizontal crack. Layback a flake to cruxy layaways. Finish up sloping holds to *The Rasp's* final cleft.

9. Flute of Hope (E4 6a) (5.11c/d) A wandering excursion up the face first freed by Ron Fawcett in 1977. Start at the bottom right corner of the face. Edge up the corner, and traverse left under a roof. Continue up #8 to the second horizontal crack. Hand traverse left on poor holds to *The Rasp,* and labor up its flakes to the niche. Go left from here onto an airy nose and another sloping exit.

10. The File (VS 4c) (5.8) A megaclassic 1956 Don Whillans route. Jam the perfect hand crack up the south side of the leaning block. Work through the crux bulge at the bottom, then motor up the crack.

11. Paddock (VD) (5.4) Begin off a block right of #10. Jam zigzag cracks for 25 feet to the top.

NORTH WALES

■ OVERVIEW

North Wales is famed for its wild and somber mountain scenery, a stirring landscape of shapely mountains creased by glaciated valleys and the wave-beaten coastal cliffs bordering the Irish Sea. This area embraces an upland region of picturesque mountains huddled around 3,560-foot Snowdon—or in Welsh, *Yr Wyddfa,* "The Great Mound"—the highest peak in England and Wales. This rugged land has long merited the attention of rock climbers, who explore the cliffs that wall its deep valleys, alpine cirques, and battered shoreline. The Snowdonia region is simply one of Britain's best climbing areas and arguably the birthplace of rock climbing.

North Wales is a compact land of extraordinary diversity, a place that packs the best of Britain into a relatively small area. It's a place of stunning natural beauty, as well as a human landscape replete with nostalgic castles erected in the thirteenth century to control the Welsh, cobble-lined streets in old towns, charming cottages, abandoned industrial works and slate quarries, and an incomprehensible ancient dialect that is perhaps Europe's oldest living language.

The Welsh are hardy stock descended from the ancient Celts. Many are bilingual, especially in North Wales, speaking both English and their ancestral Welsh tongue. If you sit in a village pub and sip your pint, you will undoubtedly be amid native speakers, leaving you with the peculiar illusion of being in a distant foreign land. The Welsh are considerate, friendly, courteous, and entertaining, especially when they find out that you're a Yank and not a lout from London! Wales is a place that has been battled over for thousands of years, and the natives still rebel against what some perceive as the English yoke. A Welshman told me that all those castles "are lovely but to us they're symbols of English oppression."

Snowdonia, encompassed by Snowdonia National Park, is not only the natural heartland of North Wales but is also renowned for its cultural heritage. The

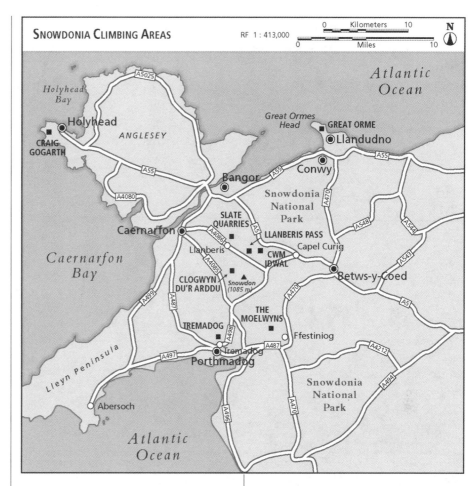

SNOWDONIA CLIMBING AREAS — RF 1 : 413,000

park's boundary is roughly identical to that of the ancient Welsh kingdom of Gwynedd. Celtic tribes settled here more than 3,000 years ago, building villages, growing crops, and finding natural religion. The island of Anglesey was a Druid stronghold. Later the Welsh retreated into Snowdonia from successive English invasions meant to conquer and subdue the Celtic tribes. The conquest was largely completed when King Edward I marched into Wales in 1277 and built massive castles to secure his authority and peace. Snowdonia, however, remained a remote backwater with a population of farmers and herders until the nineteenth century, when miners and workers of the Industrial Revolution came here.

Now North Wales is one of Britain's great natural areas as well as a major tourist attraction. Visitors assemble to trod the numerous trails threading across the mountains, indulge in excellent trout fishing in dashing streams and rivers, trek to the summit of Wales's highest peak, marvel at majestic stone fortresses, and test their

mettle and skills on both classic and cutting-edge rock climbs.

Snowdonia's geology is complex, with its oldest rocks on the Lleyn Peninsula and Isle of Anglesey dating back a billion years to the Precambrian period. Many peaks, including Snowdon and Cader Idris, formed during volcanic episodes in Ordovician times some 450 million years ago. A series of glacial ice advances, the last of which retreated a scant 10,000 years ago, excavated and sculpted the mountains and valleys.

North Wales Crags

North Wales is a compact region. Within a half-hour's drive from anywhere is a startling abundance of cliffs, with climbing from the most traditional gear routes to overhanging limestone clip-ups. Some routes are completely safe and sewn up with gear placements, whereas others have a big-scare factor and serious fall potential. Some crags crowd along the roadside with thirty-second approaches. Others are

Dave Trumbull leads *Suicide Wall* (E2 5c) (5.10c) above Cwm Idwal.

isolated and high in the mountains and reached only by hoofing it uphill for three hours.

Wales offers routes of all grades for climbers of all abilities and tendencies. The area contains thousands of routes, from long fourth-class scrambles up mountain ribs to powerful limestone sport routes. Many well-protected routes are found in the popular grades between 5.7 and 5.11. Most climbers come to North Wales to sample the old classic routes, mostly established in the first half of the twentieth century, which still retain interest, charm, and beauty.

The Welsh climbing areas are roughly sorted by rock type. Along the north coast are limestone routes at Craig y Forwen, Craig Pen Trwyn, Great Orme, and Little Orme. The mountain areas include Ogwen Valley, Llanberis Pass, and Clogwyn Du'r Arddu, one of Britain's biggest rock walls at 800 feet high. The lower part of Llanberis Pass offers man-made slate quarries that locals simply call The Slate. The

south part of Snowdonia includes low crags at Gwynant Valley, The Moelwyns, Tremadog, and small cliffs on the Lleyn Peninsula. The outmost edge of the Isle of Anglesey harbors Gogarth and Britain's most famous sea cliffs.

This guide details the main crags and the best routes at North Wales's major climbing areas, including Ogwen Valley, Llanberis Pass, Tremadog, and Gogarth.

The Ogwen Valley is a glacier-scraped valley lined with superb cliffs that stair-step up steep grassy mountainsides. The cliffs, including Idwal Slabs and Walls, offer a plethora of moderate climbs. Some, like *Tennis Shoe* and *Hope,* are time-worn ancient classics that still attract the faithful to their polished holds. Others, like the famous *Suicide Wall,* were the "tiger" routes of yesteryear and are still serious and bold undertakings. These valley crags are magical places to discover the joys and the roots of rock climbing.

Llanberis Pass, in the heart of Snowdonia, is a high misty valley that

slices through the mountains. Numerous crags scatter along its flanks, including Dinas Cromlech. This famous and popular cliff overlooking the upper valley is steeped in climbing history and legend. The west-facing crag yields a host of multipitch routes up vertical faces and ridges, and the cliff's center is split by the celebrated *Cenotaph Corner,* a sheer 120-foot-high dihedral that is North Wales's best-known route. Across the valley rises Dinas Mot, a pyramid-shaped face with a steep headwall. A handful of excellent multipitch adventures scale its east face.

Tremadog, lying near the coast in southern Snowdonia, is a series of excellent south-facing cliffs and buttresses perched on a wooded brow overlooking a broad valley filled with sheep paddocks. It's one of Britain's best and most popular climbing venues, with numerous perfect moderate routes like *Merlin, One Step in the Clouds,* and *Creagh Dhu Wall;* quick access from the road; and a campground and cafe below the cliffs.

The cliffs of Craig Gogarth, lying on Isle of Anglesey at the northwestern tip of Wales, plunge off Holyhead Mountain into the Irish Sea. These 300-foot-high walls, Britain's most famous sea cliffs, are laced with more than 300 routes. Most are frightening, committing, and difficult climbs with meager protection and big adventure value. The moderate leader finds few routes here. The cliff divides into two main sectors—North Stack and South Stack. This guide details *Dream of White Horses,* the area's most renowned route, on Wen Slab at North Stack. After gaining familiarity with this dramatic area by climbing *Dream* and perhaps a couple other easier lines, you can safely ascend other testpieces within your physical and mental capabilities.

Rack, Protection, and Descent

The described routes in this guide are traditional gear-protected lines up cliffs. No bolts and few fixed pitons are found on the cliffs, and those pitons that irregularly occur are not to be trusted because of rust and age. Most routes are well protected, although you should be skilled at finding and equalizing gear placements and competent at setting up safe belay anchors. Bolted climbs are found at The Slate, limestone crags at Upper and Lower Pen Trwyn, and other north coast areas, including Great and Little Orme. Lower Pen Trwyn boasts a concentrated selection of hard sport routes.

A standard North Wales rack includes sets of Stoppers, TCUs, and Friends, along with a handful of 2-foot slings, a few cords for tying off small spikes, and two ropes. Although many routes can be climbed American style with a single rope, an equal number require double-rope technique to equalize protection and minimize rope drag. Bring RPs or other steel nuts, as well as thin crack trickery to increase your potential for finding gear placements, particularly at serious places like Gogarth.

Descent off most crags is by topping out and hiking off along various descent paths. These are generally well marked and easy to follow. They can be slippery and muddy when wet, so use caution in adverse conditions and rope up inexperi-

enced climbers. Some routes can be rappelled from fixed anchors or slings around trees or boulders. Rappels are required to reach the sea-level base of most of Gogarth's routes. Anchors are often worn and weathered slings, which the English call "tat." It's wise to carry a piece of your own webbing to add to the mass of slings, especially since your rope runs directly through the tat and not a rappel ring.

Getting Around

Your own car gives freedom and flexibility to travel around the region, particularly on bad-weather days, in search of sun for the day's cragging. If you rely on public transportation, hitchhiking, or hiking, then lots of time is wasted on logistics. Car rentals are arranged at all the major airports in Britain, as well as locally, although you pay a premium for that service. Local operators are generally not as reliable or convenient, but sometimes good deals can be negotiated.

Wales is dissected by highways and roads, allowing quick access to all the climbing sites, as well as visitor attractions and towns. Everywhere lies within an hour's drive of wherever you're staying. Some highways are very narrow, and most have no shoulder. The roads are not designed for high-speed travel, even though some drivers treat them as Grand Prix courses. But you're on vacation, so leave speed and recklessness at home to be safe. Remember too that you drive on the left side of the road, so use appropriate caution at intersections, on narrow curves, and when crossing the street. Also remember that distances are measured in miles, not kilometers, and that you yield to the right at roundabouts or traffic circles.

For a cheap adventure, don't hire a car. It's easy to catch a train or bus to North Wales and still get around and have a great time. The best place to stay in this case is in Llanberis, where you can easily walk up the pass or over to quarries. You can hook up with local climbers too and bum rides over to Gogarth or Tremadog. Tremadog is another good place to stay without a car since a campground and cafe are convenient to the cliffs and nearby villages. Trains serve Porthmadog and

Pwllehli on the south and Bangor and Holyhead on the north. Contact British Rail for timetables and ticket prices. Reasonably good bus service also serves the area.

Seasons and Weather

Welsh weather is infamously bad. The best months are in summer—July through September. But that's no guarantee that it will be dry for your whole expedition. Realistically, go prepared for rain any time of the year by packing a good raincoat and rain pants. The prevailing westerly winds sweep unimpeded from the Atlantic Ocean, bringing moisture that rises as it bumps the mountains, forms clouds, and rains. Rainfall increases with altitude, with the top of Snowdon receiving 160 inches of annual precipitation. The weather is extremely localized here. If it's raining at Llanberis Pass, the sun might be out at Tremadog. If you're willing to travel, then you'll probably climb every day that you want. Wales is a place where most visitors are always wondering about the weather and posing important questions. Is it going to rain? Will there be sun? How long will this crap weather last? It's best to check the forecast in the morning. Some cafes post the daily forecast, or you can ring the tourist board in most towns. Also drop by climbing schools or shops and ask the resident experts. The Plas y Brenin bulletin board usually exhibits an updated forecast.

Some areas are better than others if the weather is bad. Tremadog is the best bet as an alternative to the wetter mountains. The area gets plenty of sunshine, even in winter. But it does rain here too, making the surrounding woods a temperate rain forest. Gogarth is another good place to go if the mountains are soaked. These windward cliffs are often dry and sunny. Most North Wales cliffs dry quickly after rain, although some mountain crags will seep for a few days.

If it is raining, there's still lots to do. It's best to be like the Brits and just go climbing on one of the famous wet routes. One of the best is *Lockwood's Chimney* on Clogwyn y Bustach, a broken crag in Gwynant Valley. The route, a thrutching affair that squeezes through a deep chimney, is usually done only in downpours. The Idwal Slab routes are also popular rainy day outings, depending on how much water cascades down the polished crack systems. It's customary to wear heavy socks that slip over your climbing shoes for extra traction on the slippery slabs. Or lace up your GORE-TEX shoes and trek through the mountains. Good hikes are around Cwm Idwal or walking to the summit of Snowdon or Tryfan. If the above adventures aren't your cup of tea, then head into the villages and quaff a few pints or take in a castle or two.

Climbing History

Snowdonia is one of the places that spawned modern rock climbing. This was the craggy epicenter where yesteryear's heroes grappled with vertical rock—learning to climb cracks and faces and developing the ropework needed for safe climbing, belaying, and anchoring. The other place in Britain where climbing developed concurrently was the damp crags in the Lake District. But in North Wales, climbers were able to freely exchange information and ideas and push their explorations of the area's unclimbed cliffs.

It's fitting that the first recorded climb in North Wales took place on the magnificent face of Clogwyn Du'r Arddu, affectionately dubbed "Cloggy," beneath Snowdon's summit. Here in 1798 a couple amateur botanists, Reverends William Bingley and Peter Williams, while searching for plant specimens, scrambled too high on the face to safely retreat. The intrepid duo found, like many novice climbers, that it's easier to press upward than risk downward. Almost 300 feet above the scree, Williams surmounted an overlap. According to *Welsh Rock* by Trevor Jones and Geoff Milburn, Bingley later wrote, "After some difficulty he succeeded . . . and took off his belt, and holding firmly by one end, gave the other to me." The reverend grabbed hold and cranked the roof with "a little aid from the stones."

Another one hundred years passed before technical climbing, without the aid of belts, began in the Welsh highlands. In the 1890s climbers began spending holidays here to hone their alpine skills for the Alps. Foremost among this generation was eloquent Winthrop Young, George Mallory (who later disappeared on Mt. Everest), and James Archer Thomson. These climbers explored the gullies and chimneys of Snowdonia, particularly the friendly cliffs and slabs in Ogwen Valley. During World War I the Idwal Slab routes were ascended, including *Hope, Charity,* and *Faith*. A significant advance in climbing footwear came in 1919 when Professor Noel Odell returned from Cornwall where he climbed in tennis shoes or "rubbers." The professor frictioned his way up *Tennis Shoe* on Idwal's left side, creating a new standard for shoe rubber.

The 1920s and 1930s flourished as the golden age of British climbing. New techniques, new equipment, and a new sense of the possible pushed climbers and standards above the shoulders of their predecessors. Two climbers loom during this era: John Menlove Edwards and Colin Kirkus.

Edwards, a prolific climber and literate climbing author, dominated the age. He loved new routes, bad and vegetated rock, and adventure. He also was tortured by depression, homosexuality, and the death of his brother, who, while coming to see Edwards receive his medical degree, was hit by a train and died in Edwards's arms. He established scores of routes on Idwal Slabs, on the dark Devil's Kitchen buttresses, and on the Upper Cliff of Glyder Fawr, where his *Grey Slab* route, a delicate classic line, is still among Ogwen's best climbs.

In Llanberis Pass Edwards explored new crags and climbed stellar routes, including *Dives, Spiral Stairs,* and *Flying Buttress* (solo) on Dinas Cromlech and *Western Slabs* on Dinas Mot. Edwards pushed up steep rock on Clogwyn y Grochan in the early 1940s with worthy ascents of *Brant, Slape,* and *Nea*. Besides climbing, Edwards was water crazy, going for solitary rowboat journeys in the sea, jumping off sea cliffs at Cornwall, and even swimming down waterfalls and raging rapids. He died in 1957 after his third suicide attempt.

Colin Kirkus certainly wasn't as dark as Edwards, but he also brought ambition and talent, along with an elegant grace, to his climbing. Kirkus made Llanberis Pass his personal playground, pushing new routes and high standards up its cliffs. Even today, if you sample the best Welsh classics, you won't go wrong by only ticking the Kirkus routes. It was the great aerie of Clogwyn D'ur Arddu, however, that lifted Kirkus into the pantheon of Welsh climbing gods. His stunning sequence of first ascents on this immense wall are described as the best series of firsts ever seen on a British cliff. These brilliant pieces of climbing include *Chimney Route* with Edwards in 1931, *Curving Crack, Pedestal Crack,* and the marvelous *Great Slab* done in 1930 when he was barely twenty years old. Kirkus also loved free soloing and doing ropeless first ascents. Unfortunately, his brief climbing flame was extinguished in World War II.

The postwar generation continued pressing standards higher. A significant ascent came in 1945 when Chris Preston, a climbing instructor with the Mountain Commandos, began working a tricky and virtually unprotected route named *Suicide Wall*. The devious line, which had defeated Kirkus and Edwards, was finally led by Preston in two pitches on October 7 after toprope preview. The route, now rated 5.10d or E2/5c, was Britain's hardest route for the next decade, as well as the scene of many serious accidents.

This era, though, was dominated by a single climber: Joe Brown. The mythical Brown, nicknamed the Human Spider, was a working-class lad from Manchester and a climbing genius. Brown, they say, perfected the hand jam. He also used clean climbing techniques by carrying various-size stones in his balaclava hat to wedge in cracks and then thread for protection. Brown was motivated to climb a lot, with a firm desire for first ascents. Coupled with partners such as Don Whillans, Brown was the major activist in North Wales. His crags included Dinas Cromlech in Llanberis Pass, Tremadog, Cloggy, and Gogarth. It's hard to find a crag here that doesn't have a classic Joe Brown route up it.

One of Brown's greatest ascents and epics was on *Cenotaph Corner,* a clean dihedral that cleaves Dinas Cromlech. He first attempted the route, now Britain's most famous rock climb, in 1948 with Wilf White. The eighteen-year-old Brown began the crack, toting a mason's hammer, five soft iron pitons, a few steel carabiners, and slings and cords for tying off spikes and threading chockstones. All went smoothly until he was 90 feet up at the route's crux. He whacked a piton in and grabbed the hammer between his teeth to free his hand while pulling up rope to clip. Brown forgot the hammer as he shouted slack to Wilf. The hammer arced through the air and cracked the belayer's skull, knocking him out. Brown clipped in and lowered hand over hand to White, who quickly recovered and told him to get back up there. He climbed back up, but was a piton short so he retreated. Brown returned two years later after an army stint to fire the first ascent.

By the 1960s another generation of "tigers" were making an impression on the scene. These fellows included Peter Crew, Martin Boysen, Rowland Edwards, Jack Soper, and Barry Ingle. Crew in particular managed many new routes at Cloggy like *Scorpio, West Buttress Eliminate,* and the brilliant *Great Wall* with a few points of aid. Edwards was active on the limestone at Great and Little Ormes, almost single-handedly exploring their potential.

They were also active into the 1970s and 1980s, along with younger climbers who pursued a free climbing ethic. Pete Livesey was one of the best, grabbing major lines like the *Right Wall* on Cromlech and Tremadog's *Cream.* His contemporary Ron Fawcett also shared the spotlight. His difficult crack route *Strawberries* at Tremadog was perhaps the country's first 5.13 route. Another master was John Redhead, who concentrated on serious extreme routes on Gogarth's complex faces.

The sport-climbing revolution visited Wales in the 1980s and 1990s. Climbers discovered a whole new area near Llanberis: The Slate. The old quarries were perfect for delicate and sustained climbs protected by bolts and gear, only gear, and sometimes just a couple of RPs. On the headland Great Orme, climbers found perfect limestone at Craig Pen Trwyn, slammed in bolts, and voila—the area's only sport crags. Some of its hard routes are *Sea of Tranquillity* by Ben Moon and *Liquid Amber* by Jerry Moffatt in 1990. Moon's 1984 route *Statement of Youth* was Britain's first 8c or 5.13b route. Moffatt also did the serious traditional route *Master's Wall* on Cloggy.

One of the great 1980s climbers was Johnny Dawes, who brought a bold grit-stone attitude, traditional values, and burly technique to the Welsh crags. His greatest route is *The Indian Face,* a dramatically unprotected 5.13a line up Clogwyn Du'r Arddu. A fall off this tenuous creation would be fatal. Another nasty was Gogarth's *Hardback Thesaurus,* another underprotected route with serious fall consequences.

By the 1990s local activists were chasing the high numbers and using traditional ethics with no bolts, no fixed pitons, and no toprope previewing. Some deadly climbs were established, including Nick Dixon's *Face Mecca,* a 5.13b Cloggy line with a crux pitch protected by a couple of tied-off RURPs, as well as *Beginner's Mind,* a serious line in Llanberis Pass. Climbers also climbed "microroutes," short bouldery climbs with scant protection and hard movements, and developed problems on the previously undeveloped boulder fields.

Camping, Accommodations, and Services

North Wales is a big holiday center, particularly during summer vacation in July and August, which coincides with the best time to climb. Nevertheless, lots of varied accommodations are found, including campgrounds, bed-and-breakfast inns, huts and cottages, and hotels. During all but the busiest weekends, you'll have no problem finding a roof for your head. Camping is the cheapest way to go, but you need to bring a tent and sleeping bag. A better alternative is to stay in a B&B or a self-catering cottage that supplies crockery, cutlery, sheets, and blankets.

Eric Jones's Cafe below the Tremadog cliffs in southern Snowdonia is a great place for a base camp. You're a five-minute walk from great climbing, and the weather is warmer and sunnier than in the surrounding mountains. It's a good place during extended spells of inconsiderate bad weather. Guests lodge at a level grassy campsite behind the cafe, in a self-catering cottage, or in a couple bunk barns across the highway. The campground is tents only with free parking, showers (50 pence), toilets, and lots of sheep in the surrounding paddocks. The cafe is convenient for an English breakfast and a morning cup of tea. The traditional stone cottage sleeps four to seven and includes television, washing machine, and a kitchen. The two bunk barns are for larger groups, making an inexpensive place to stay for a few days.

Lots of climbers stay in Llanberis because it's not only the hub of the local climbing scene, but also boasts a pub and party scene. All the climbing areas are within a forty-five-minute drive of the town. Ask at the local tourist office for accommodation suggestions and to make reservations. The Heights Hotel is popular with climbers since it has a pub, pool room, and bouldering wall.

In Betws-y-Coed near Llanberis Pass are a couple good bed-and-breakfast inns: Greenbank Bed and Breakfast and Maelgwyn House. Nearby is Plas y Brenin B&B, which has rooms when they're not filled with climbing students. The Dolgam campsite is just outside Capel Curig on the A5. It offers free hot showers and is an easy walk from pubs and a *caff.* It suffers a bit from midges on damp days. A couple of campgrounds are at Nant Peris across the lake east of Llanberis. They're close to the Pass but suffer from high winds and can be wet. A large campground that caters to holidaymakers rather than climbers is a mile north of Beddgelert. It's a bit more expensive than the others, and theft has been a problem here.

It's also common to bivouac in Llanberis Pass itself. The unofficial camping places are below Dinas Cromlech next to the creek or in the field west of the bridge and below Clogwyn y Grochan. Keep a low profile, take all litter, and don't pollute the water. The farmer sometimes stops by to collect a small use fee. You'll find no facilities or pubs within walking distance, but the price and the view are unbeatable.

Food and Drink

Wales is unique in Britain in that here you'll find the true pubs and cafes or *caffs* that welcome and cater to a climber clientele. Climbers are encouraged to visit these establishments to boast about the day's achievements and to part with a few hard-earned quid before trekking back to the campsite.

In Llanberis, where else is there to go but to the legendary Pete's Eats? This is the quintessential British climber's *caff*, where the famous hang out and reminisce about their latest gnarly testpieces or the good old days. It's the place that some locals haughtily call the "center of the climbing universe." The walls are plastered with a priceless collection of action photos of the masters of stone—local hero Joe Brown, Yorkshireman Don Whillans, the late Derek Hersey with wild hair, stone monkey Johnny Dawes, Jimmy Jewell, who died soloing at Tremadog—and the list goes on.

If you spend any time rambling around North Wales and sampling its rock climbs, then you will end up at Pete's, sipping a steaming pint mug of afternoon tea and eating a chip buttie, a white bread roll sliced open and overstuffed with freshly fried chips. The kitchen supposedly makes a ton of chips a week. Pete's Eats has lost a bit of its old character since it was remodeled and enlarged, but still it's the place to be in Llanberis on a Saturday morning before heading to Dinas Cromlech. The upstairs lounge has Internet access, a guidebook library, and maps from around the world. It gets crowded when it rains.

A few cafes are found near Capel Curig just east of Llanberis Pass. The Bryn Glo in Capel Curig is a good morning spot for a "full monty" breakfast, although if you plan to climb in the next hour, it might be best to settle for a normal breakfast. The Capel Post Office Caff in front of Joe Brown's shop in Capel Curig, although not catering to climbers, is a good stop on wet days for a cuppa tea and a cake. The Tyn-y-Coed, a mile east of the village on the A5, is a recognized climber's pub with a stagecoach outside. You get standard pub fare at a reasonable price and wash it down with pints of southern beer. It's usually busy, and they stop serving food at 9:30 P.M. Also good is Plas-y-Brenin. They don't advertise it, but their bar is open for nonresidents, and they serve good pub meals.

Down the highway before Betws-y-Coed is Miner's Bridge Arms, aka Oakfield Hotel. They serve basic food with generous helpings at a cheap price. Another popular pub is Pen-y-Gwryd, near Llanberis Pass at the junction of A4086 and A498.

Climbers at Tremadog experience both roadside cragging and dining at Eric Jones's Cafe, a couple horizontal rope-lengths from the nearest cliff. The cafe, owned by Welsh climbing legend Eric Jones, serves breakfast, lunch, afternoon tea, and evening meals. Eric opened the cafe in an old gas station after realizing the economic potential of owning a *caff* next to a major crag. Most climbers stop in the morning for tea or Eric's special cappuccino and to peruse their guidebook. Later in the day they pop by again for afternoon tea before heading for the day's last route. The popular Climber's Special Breakfast is served all day. Hours are flexible, depending on demand, but during winter it's usually open only on weekends.

If you're camping at Eric's and don't want to cook, then walk down to the village square at Tremadog to eat at the two pubs. Remember, they're closed on Sundays. Or drive over to Porthmadog, where you have more dining choices but lots of tourists milling about.

As you travel get a taste of Wales or *blas ar Gymru* by sampling local products and trying traditional dishes and recipes. Being close to the shoreline and fishing ports, lots of restaurants serve seafood, including king scallops, lobsters, crabs, and whiting. All the sheep roaming the Welsh highlands have long provided a staple of the Welsh diet: fresh lamb, a lean natural meat traditionally served with vinegary mint sauce. The humble leek, a popular ingredient in soups and stews, is an unlikely emblem of Welsh nationalism dating back to medieval battlefields when Welsh soldiers pinned leeks to their chests to identify themselves to their countrymen. If you find a cheese shop, stop in for hunks of famous *Caerphilly*, a mild creamy white cheese; mustard seed- and ale-flavored *Y Fenni* cheddar; and garlic-flavored *Llangloffan*. Buy old-style breads, including Welsh cake and *bara brith*, a tasty fruit cake, in cafes and bakeries.

Cultural Experiences and Rest Days

North Wales is wealthy in cultural, historical, and recreational opportunities. Outdoor pursuits include great hiking trails up mountains, fly fishing in dashing streams, biking along twisting roads, and quietly sitting on a ridge above the restless Irish Sea. Or experience the vibrancy and richness of Welsh culture and its Celtic roots. On rest days roam about the countryside and visit the majestic castles, abbey ruins, and picturesque villages.

Every athletic visitor should hike Snowdon to the roof of Wales. Snowdon, called *Eryri* or "Home of Eagles," is justly popular, with expansive summit views and footpaths from every direction. Tourists take the easy trail but climbers prefer the demanding Horseshoe Route, which traverses knife-edge ridges. If you're bored, be eccentric and scale Snowdon on crutches, roller skates, piggy-back, or stilts. Of course Snowdon Mountain Railway carries the lazy to the green summit.

The marvelous Welsh castles are a must-do attraction. King Edward I built a series of forbidding fortresses in North Wales to subdue the Celtic natives and establish English sovereignty. Caernarfon Castle, the birthplace of Edward II, is one of the best. Beaumaris Castle, on Anglesey Island, is symmetrical and impregnable with a moat and inner and outer walls. The third impressive relic is Conwy Castle on the north shore. South of Porthmadog is Harlech Castle, noted for its massive gatehouse. Near Llanberis is Dolbadarn Castle, a thirteenth-century fortress erected by Llywelyn the Great. This marvelous ruin is less visited than its famous neighbors, allowing a more private visit.

On rest days it's worth driving around and seeing the region's villages and towns. Caernarfon is a busy port town, with medieval streets and the Roman ruins of Segontium built in 78 A.D. Beaumaris on Anglesey offers handsome Victorian buildings, the fun Museum of Childhood, and Ye Olde Bull's Head pub, where Dr. Samuel Johnson and Charles Dickens drank. Llandudro, a Victorian seaside town, was frequented by Lewis Carroll, who wrote *Alice in Wonderland* here. The Lleyn Peninsula, a 24-mile-long finger jutting into the sea, has an untamed beauty and a sense of isolation.

One of Britain's most famous points of interest is in a village west on Anglesey. The village boasts the longest place name in the world—*Llanfairpwllgwyngyllgogerychwyndrobwllllantysiliogogogoch,* otherwise shortened to LlanfairPG. The settlement was originally called Llanfair, but in the nineteenth century it was lengthened to mean "St. Mary's Church in the hollow of white hazel near a rapid whirlpool and the Church of St. Tysilio near the red cave." Most visitors pop by the old railway station to have their photo taken next to the lengthy nameplate.

Trip Planning Information

General description: Superb climbing adventures on classic cliffs scattered across the mountains, cirques, valleys, and coast of North Wales, the birthplace of modern climbing.

Location: North Wales in western Great Britain.

Camping and accommodations: Numerous campgrounds are in Snowdonia and Gogarth. At Tremadog, the Eric Jones's Cafe has an inexpensive campground, a cafe, bunkhouses, and B&B units. Lots of other B&Bs are found. Inquire at local tourist offices for details. Some climbers "rough" camp among the Cromlech boulders below Dinas Cromlech at Llanberis Pass. The local farmer may collect a small fee. Be advised that is not safe to leave your tent and gear unattended here.

Accommodations are plentiful in the Ogwen Valley. Several campsites are in the vicinity, including Gwern y Gof Isaf (Willy's Barn), Gwern y Gof Uchaf, and Dol-gan and Garth Farm at Capel Curig. There are also B&Bs and a hostel at Capel Curig.

Check with the local tourist offices in the various towns for suggestions and reservations for accommodations.

Climbing season: Year-round. May through September are best, although weather is highly variable with frequent rain, especially in the mountains. Warm, sunny periods do occur. Winters are damp and cold, although good days are found at Tremadog and Gogarth.

Restrictions and access issues: The climbing areas and Snowdonia National Park are a combination of private and public land. Some crags like Bwlch y Moch at Tremadog are owned and managed by the British Mountaineering Council for climbers. At all areas it's important to be environmentally respectful to ensure continued access. Observe the following guidelines:

- Park in designated parking areas. Avoid parking on road shoulders or edges—your car creates a safety hazard.
- Use toilet facilities whenever possible. At the crag be discreet, bury all human waste, don't relieve yourself near any streams or lakes, and pack all toilet paper out in plastic bags. Don't leave tissue in the open or under boulders at the cliff base.
- Follow existing trails to the crags and for descents.
- Reduce damage to trees and vegetation by not using trees for belay or rappel anchors, or by running a rappel rope around the tree trunk. Also avoid cutting, trimming, and damaging vegetation.
- Avoid crossing fenced fields with livestock.
- Pick up all your trash and any other trash you find. That should go without saying!

Guidebooks: *Rock Climbing in Snowdonia* by Paul Williams is an excellent select guide to the classic routes in North Wales.

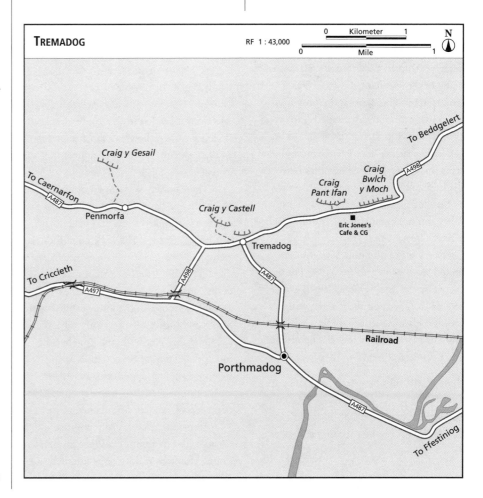

Other guides include *Llanberis Pass, Owgen and Carneddau, Slate: A Climber's Guide, North Wales: 100 Classic Climbs, Scrambles in Snowdonia,* and *North Wales Limestone.*

Nearby mountain shops, guide services, and gyms: Shops include Great Arête in Bangor, Conwy Outdoor Shop in Conwy, Outside on High Street in Llanberis, Joe Brown's in Capel Curig and Llanberis, Ellis Brigham's in Capel Curig, and Climber and Rambler and Cotswold Camping in Betwys-y-Coed. Eric Jones's Cafe at Tremadog also sells some gear and guides.

Services: Services are found in most towns, including groceries, B&Bs, hotels, pubs, and restaurants. A popular climber hangout is Pete's Eats in Llanberis. Eric Jones's Cafe at Tremadog is a good place to sip tea and chat with British climbers on rainy afternoons. Check at the local tourist offices for accommodations, suggestions, and reservations.

Emergency services: Dial 999 for accidents, emergencies, and ambulance services. Clinics and hospitals are found in most towns, including Llangollen, Conwy, Caernarfon, and Bangor.

Nearby climbing areas: Besides the described North Wales areas, there are many other excellent climbing sites. The area around Llandudno and Conwy on the north shore includes superb limestone cliffs. These cliffs facing the Irish Sea are generally warmer and drier than mountain areas since they lie in Snowdon's rain shadow. Craig y Forwen, near the village of Llanddulas, is a fine steep crag with many multipitch affairs. The jutting peninsula of Great Ormes Head, north of Conwy, yields a stunning selection of bolted sport routes up to 5.14+. The area's most popular crag is Craig Pen Trwyn, one of Britain's best sport areas, with sound rock and plentiful bolts. Castell y Gwynt, a large cliff below the lighthouse, yields some real gems on hard rock.

Nearby attractions: Many attractions are found throughout North Wales. Read the "Cultural Experiences and Rest Days" section above for the best recommendations.

Tremadog

Tremadog, one of the best and most popular climbing areas in North Wales, lies at the southwest corner of Snowdonia near the village of the same name. The area offers a tremendous variety of quality climbing and an almost unrivaled concentration of routes on excellent dolerite, a compact volcanic rock. The cliffs, looming above dense forest, gleam in the slanting sunlight with sharp cleaved edges, roofs, dihedrals, and arêtes sharply outlined against the dark woods. The compact cliffs appear small and slabby from a distance and are well hidden by tall trees, but that's a misconception. The cliffs, although broken in places, are bulky, broad, and reach heights of 200 feet.

South of the escarpment are sheep paddocks that spread across a flat sediment plain to a river and tidal estuary. The cliffs were once wave-battered sea cliffs but now sit more than a mile inland.

Tremadog, composed of five south-facing cliffs spread along an east-to-west-trending ridge, offers excellent climbing on three major cliffs—Craig Bwlch y Moch, Craig Pant Ifan, and Craig y Castell. The two less-frequented crags are Carreg Hylldrem and Craig y Gesail. Craig Pant Ifan, composed of several sharp buttresses, is steep and angular, with a selection of crack and slab routes. Craig Bwlch y Moch, the area's most popular and largest cliff, yields marvelous routes on its half-dozen faces.

The climbing is summed up in a single word: excellent. The dolerite rock is studded with sharp edges and flakes that welcome fingertips. The rock underfoot is gritty and grips shoe rubber, especially on the unpolished holds. The routes are wandering affairs, with the lower pitches ascending grooves and chimneys filled with blocks and surrounded by shady foliage and twisting vines. Above the first pitches the routes emerge onto belay stances at the treetop level. The upper leads are superb, with clean perfect rock, friendly moves, lots of protection, and airy situations.

Tremadog is deservedly popular because it's filled with excellent moderate routes, although it does offer tougher climbs for the hardman. Most climbers, though, come to sample the area's brilliant Severe (S) and Very Severe (VS) routes. Expect queues, especially on good weekends, for the classics—and they're all worth the wait. Tremadog is also popular because it's usually sunny and warm, unlike the mountain crags, which are often inundated with rain and clouds.

The focal point of the Tremadog scene is the Eric Jones's Cafe across the highway from the cliffs. Eric himself is a larger-than-life Welsh climber, a fit sixtyish contemporary of Joe Brown and other great Welsh climbers. He was the first Brit to solo the Eiger Nordwand and established lots of first ascents across Snowdonia. Now he's retired from climbing but BASE jumps around the world and runs his humble cafe and bunkhouse for climbers. Climbers park in the *caff* lot in the morning, wander in for a morning "cuppa" tea, scour the area guidebook, visit with other blokes from around Britain, and ask Eric for beta on the crag desperates. It's a friendly place with an atmosphere unlike any American cragging area.

Finding the cliffs: Tremadog, on the southwest side of Snowdonia, is just north of the town of Porthmadog. The cliffs are alongside the A498 highway east of the village of Tremadog. It's easy to reach by a couple different routes: one along the coast and one over the mountains.

If you're approaching North Wales from the Manchester area, drive west on the A55 highway paralleling the Irish Sea.

For the mountain route, exit onto the A470 just before Conwy. Follow the A470 south 15 kilometers to Betws-y-Coed. This point is also reached from the east via M54 from Birmingham and the Midlands and then the A5 highway.

Continue south on the A470 for 10 kilometers to Blaenau Ffestiniog. Go right or west here on the A496, briefly join the A497, and turn right onto the small B4410. Follow this to the A498 at Prenteg. Go left a couple kilometers until you reach the cafe and obvious cliffs.

For the coastal route, follow the A55 to Bangor, exit onto the A487, and follow it to Caernarfon. Continue south and east on the A487 for 18 kilometers to the village of Tremadog. Turn onto the A498, and drive a kilometer to the cliffs.

The main parking is at Eric Jones's Cafe. Go in the cafe after parking and pay a 50-pence fee to park for the day. Except for a small nearby parking bay, avoid parking anywhere along the road; it's not only illegal, but also dangerous with passing traffic.

The cliffs are easily reached by walking from the cafe car park. Walk on the road's shoulder to the signed trailhead for your prospective cliff. Specific directions to access each cliff are given below in the crag's description. Direct any questions about which trail to follow and directions to other climbers or at the cafe.

Craig Bwlch y Moch

Craig Bwlch y Moch, a series of buttresses towering above the highway, is the most popular and best cliff at Tremadog. The long cliff, broken by gullies and forests, offers an assortment of joyful classics as well as harder lines. The cliff's Welsh name means "Crag of the Pass of the Pigs."

Craig Bwlch y Moch divides into several obvious buttresses. The left cliff end, nearest the cafe, is two-tiered Grasper Buttress, followed by smaller broken cliffs and then narrow, elegant Neb Buttress, with a sharp roof and long arête on its right side. To the right is The Fang, named for a rock tooth hanging from a roof. Vector Buttress, a steep buttress filled with square-cut roofs, overhangs, and slabs, is one of the best sectors with many classic hard routes. The dark slabby wall of Shadrach Buttress, stretching east from Vector, is one of Tremadog's busiest faces. A large gap of broken rock and forest lies between Shadrach Buttress and Merlin Buttress, the last major outcrop on the east.

The cliff base is overgrown with dense vegetation and brambles in summer, so finding the start of routes is sometimes difficult. The first pitches of most routes are dark and damp because they are in the woods. The access paths to the cliff bases are well worn and easy to follow. Locate the start of the paths along the highway by looking for gaps in the vegetation and wall of trees.

Descent off the cliff is by a steep path with steps that descend dense forest on the

west side of the cliff, or by descending Belshazzar Gully on the east. When you reach the cliff top, look for a well-used path along the top beside a fence. Follow either east or west to the appropriate descent. Both paths are marked with white paint. Do not climb the fence into the fields north of the crag. It is all private property used for grazing livestock. Updated details about descent routes are often posted on a bulletin board at the parking bay below Vector Buttress. If it is necessary to rappel because of rain or impending darkness, take extreme care not to throw your ropes onto climbers below or dislodge any rocks that might injure climbers on the ground.

Finding the cliff: Park at Eric Jones's Cafe along the A498 just east of Tremadog. The parking is not exclusively for climbers but

for cafe patrons. Go into the cafe after parking and pay a small fee. The cliff base is overgrown, particularly in summer, with lots of brambles. The eastern buttresses are the least overgrown. It's difficult to find your route from the cliff base. Take a look from the parking area to figure out where your route goes. Then walk up the road shoulder, cross the ditch alongside the road, and locate the appropriate path that disappears into the forest.

1. Valerie's Rib (HS) (5.7-) 3 pitches. An esoteric but fun line up the left side of Grasper Buttress on the crag's left end. Start by scrambling up left of broken rock to a belay above and left of the buttress's lowest point and level with a large roof. **Pitch 1:** A short lead. Climb up right to a belay stance on the front side of a nose and above the roof. 20 feet. **Pitch 2:**

Work up a corner for 20 feet, then step left onto a slab. Edge directly up the open slab to a rib. Continue up a slab above to a large belay ledge. 120 feet. **Pitch 3:** Not usually climbed. Easy climbing heads up right to broken blocks on a ledge. Climb a steep crack past a tree, and finish up another crack to the top. 90 feet. **Descent:** Scramble down left from the top of Pitch 2. Atop Pitch 3, walk left (west) along a cliff-top path to the descent. **Rack:** A selection of cams and wired nuts, with a few extra small ones. Bring extra slings to alleviate rope drag.

2. Christmas Curry with Micah Finish

(VS 4c) (5.7+) 2 pitches. Can be done in three or four short pitches. An excellent classic up the left side of The Plum, the buttress right of Neb Buttress. Follow a path through woods to the base of a deep chimney groove. **Pitch 1:** Climb the easy chimney groove to a ledge. Follow broken corners up left (5.5) to a possible belay at a large oak tree. Continue up left across sloping shelves to a short headwall. Climb the right side, then move up left to a good ledge with a tree anchor. 130 feet. **Pitch 2:** A superb lead. Step right from the belay, and follow shelves right to a right-facing corner. Layback the corner to an obvious step left on blocks to the base of a thin crack. (Alternative belay stance here). Face climb a right-angling crack up right to a steep, exposed prow. Pull jugs to the cliff top. **Descent:** Walk left (west) along a cliff-top path to the descent trail. **Rack:** A selection of cams and wired nuts, with a few extra small ones. Bring extra slings to alleviate rope drag.

3. The Plum

(HVS 5b) (5.9) 2 pitches. Another killer route with interesting moves and exciting exposure. One of the crag's best lines, following the arête right of *Christmas Curry*. Scramble to the base of the arête, and start below a steep corner that leads to a roof. **Pitch 1:** Climb a crack up the steep corner to a sloping stance. Step left onto a rib, and pull the airy rib (5.9) to a small ledge below a V-shaped groove. Edge up the groove to a small sloping belay stance by a large flake. 60 feet. **Pitch 2:** Climb a crack formed by a flake to a shelf. Step right, and work up a corner until you can step left (5.9)

onto the upper arête. Tricky moves (keep left) quickly lead to jugs up the exposed arête and the summit. 80 feet. **Descent:** Walk left (west) along a cliff-top trail to the descent trail. **Rack:** A selection of Friends and Stoppers, along with extra slings to alleviate rope drag.

4. Striptease

(VS 5a) (5.8) No topo. 2 pitches. Very different from the usual Tremadog lines, but still worthy—especially since it's dry after rain. It's thuggish, strenuous, sustained, and well pro-

tected. Start by scrambling to the base of the gully between The Fang and Vector Buttress. **Pitch 1:** Work up a chimney to a roof. Turn on the right, and continue stemming up the precarious groove past a couple overhangs to a slightly overhanging face. Move right, and climb to a welcome tree and belay stance. Lots of bomber gear. 120 feet. **Pitch 2:** Step left onto an arête and follow to the top. 40 feet. **Descent:** Walk left (west) along a cliff-top trail to the descent. **Rack:** Bring a generous selection of Friends, TCUs, and Stoppers.

5. One Step in the Clouds (VS 4c) (5.7) 3 pitches. Brilliant climbing, exposed, perfect protection, good belays, and character— simply one of the best in Wales. Up the left side of Vector Buttress. Hike a short trail from parking area right of the house to the toe of the buttress. Begin below a blocky corner. **Pitch 1:** Grab tree roots and big holds up a blocky chimney to a large tree. Move up left to a polished V-groove. Make a tricky move up the groove (5.6), and belay on a stance by a flake. 90 feet. **Pitch 2:** A perfect lead with good pro and airy moves. Step left to a tree, then climb up right above the lip of several stepped overhangs. Pull crisp edges (crux) to a step right and a short crack, or go left to a tree belay. 90 feet. **Pitch 3:** Climb up right on an easy slab past some ledges to the top. **Descent:** Follow a path left to a trail down a descent gully. **Rack:** Sets of Friends and Stoppers.

6. Vector (E2 5c) (5.10c) 4 pitches. Sustained and interesting—a must-do 1960 Joe Brown classic. Perhaps Tremadog's finest climb, this masterpiece threads through beetling overhangs on Vector Buttress. Start at the buttress foot beside a large flake. **Pitch 1:** Climb a short groove and then right onto a slab. Move up left (5.8), and tackle a steep corner. Above, traverse left a few moves to a small belay stance. 50 feet. **Pitch 2:** Spectacular pitch. Awkward moves up right to a thin angling crack. Climb the crack to a jutting spike. From the spike's top make difficult moves left and up an ochre-colored slab (5.10c) to a rest. Work past a fixed piton to an overhang, climb past to a narrow slab, and groove to a large obvious roof. Traverse left under roofs to a niche belay stance. 80 feet. **Pitch 3:** Climb up left to a shelf. Grab a good hold and pull over a roof. Traverse up left across a slab to a crack system. Tricky moves up

the crack lead to easier climbing. **Pitch 4:** Climb the last pitch of route #5. **Descent:** Follow a path left to a trail down a descent gully. **Rack:** Bring a selection of small and medium Friends, some TCUs, and a set of Stoppers. Double ropes alleviate rope drag.

7. Grim Wall (VS 4c) (5.8) 2 pitches. Good route with contrasting pitches up the left side of Shadrach Buttress. Scramble up a worn path to the base of the buttress, and look left for a belay tree below obvious Shadrach Chimney. **Pitch 1:** A rising leftward traverse pitch. Take care to place enough protection to keep your second from taking a big swing. Work up and left to a ledge and then a scoop. Climb the scoop and a shallow corner right to a ledge. Climb to a sharp flake and move left, climb a wall to a spike, and continue up left to a belay ledge below the upper headwall. 110 feet. **Pitch 2:** Steep and intimidating. Angle up right to a small roof, grab holds, and move up left above the roof (5.8) to a narrow shelf. Continue up left to a blunt prow, and pull convenient jugs to the summit. 80 feet. **Descent:** Follow a path left to a trail down a descent gully. **Rack:** Bring small and medium Friends, TCUs, and a set of Stoppers. Double ropes alleviate rope drag.

8. Meshach (HVS 5a) (5.9) 2 pitches. A superb and satisfying line that wanders up the left side of the face. Start same as *Grim Wall* below the chimney. **Pitch 1:** Work up and left to a small ledge and scoop above. Climb the scoop and a groove to a ledge. Move up the wall above for a few moves until you can step down left to a niche. Climb up left past a spike to a belay ledge. 110 feet. **Pitch 2:** Move up right to a small roof, and pull up left past the roof to a shelf (same as *Grim Wall*). Make an airy step right above the roof, and work up the wall above (5.9) past a fixed piton to a narrow shelf. Traverse right, and angle up right to the cliff top. 80 feet.

9. Shadrach (VS 4c) (5.7+) 2 or 3 pitches. A popular classic that attacks the middle of the face. It's usually busy, especially on weekends and holidays. The route humbles many novices, especially the first and last pitches. Begin below an obvious chimney. **Pitch 1:** The leader will undoubtedly entertain you with his antics to get up this pitch! Climb an infamous chimney (5.7)

← To Descent path

to a belay ledge. Climb either the outside, which is easier but sparsely protected (#4 Friend), or thrutch up the damp secure crevice. Or climb a crack to the right to avoid the fun. 50 feet. **Pitch 2:** Step left, and climb a flake and slab to a cramped belay stance left of a prominent hanging block. 40 feet. **Pitch 3:** Pull atop the block and make an exposed bridging move left (5.7+ crux) into a groove. Follow the crack system to a stance on the right, and finish up a fun headwall. 60 feet. **Descent:** Follow a path left to a trail down a descent gully. **Rack:** Bring small and medium Friends, TCUs, and a set of Stoppers.

10. Merlin with Direct Finish (HVS 5a) (5.10a) 2 pitches. Excellent, interesting, steep, and cunningly varied—one of the best of its grade in Wales. The route ascends the farthest right buttress. Follow a path to the base of the face, and start left of a slab and big, right-leaning dihedral and left of a small pillar. **Pitch 1:** Climb cracks up and right (5.7 move) to a V-groove. Work up to an awkward exit around blocks to a narrow belay shelf. 80 feet. **Pitch 2:** One of the area's best pitches! Climb up left to an obvious flake. Jam, layback, and stem up the flake crack to a good rest on a horizontal flake. *The Direct Finish* continues up the crack 10 feet, then traverses left along a thin crack to the base of a steep thin crack up an immaculate wall. Edge up the crack (great wires) to an airy and tricky finish and a spacious belay ledge atop the cliff. 80 feet. **Descent:** Walk off left and down a trail in steep Belshazzar Gully. **Rack:** Set of Friends and Stoppers. Bring extra #2 to #5 Stoppers.

Craig Pant Ifan

Craig Pant Ifan, meaning "Crag of Evan's Hollow," rises above the A498 just west of Craig Bwlch y Moch and Eric Jones's Cafe. The steep cliff is characterized by slabby buttresses, sharp arêtes, steep slabs, and clean roofs. The crag, less popular than Bwlch y Moch, offers a selection of stunning gems. It is quiet and secluded, especially along the wooded base. It's best to scope the cliff and prospective routes from the highway so you can locate the route base in the forest. The first pitches are mostly damp, dirty, and shaded, whereas the contrasting top pitches are open and clean.

Descent off the top is a steep trail with steps down Porker's Gully on the crag's west end. The path is easy to follow, but is a nightmare if wet and muddy.

Finding the cliff: Park at Eric Jones's Cafe, and walk west up the highway shoulder 500 feet to a stile on the right. Cross the stile, and follow a path to the cliff base. Routes are described from left to right.

11. Poor Man's Peuterey (S) (5.6) 2 pitches. A superb and popular classic with a perfect upper pitch. The start is hard to find. Look on the left side of the cliff for a groove/corner with a blocky rib on its right side. The initials PMP are scratched at the rock base. **Pitch 1:** Work up the groove or rib—watch for looseness—to a large tree. Climb the groove above (sometimes damp) to another large tree. Make a fun traverse right for 35 feet to a good belay ledge. Use lots of runners to avoid rope drag. This pitch is traditionally broken into three short leads but is easier as one. 135 feet. **Pitch 2:** Excellent! Climb an easy slab up right to a fixed piton. Hand traverse right, and pull jugs up an airy nose. Jam well-protected cracks up a steep slab to a belay ledge. A block and short chimney is the usual finish above. **Descent:** Scramble to the cliff top, and descend a steep trail just west of the cliff. **Rack:** A selection of Friends and Stoppers.

12. Pincushion (E2 5c) (5.10c) 2 pitches. Popular, well-protected, and brilliant slab climbing. Begin below the slab and line of roofs by a tree with a hanging root. **Pitch 1:** Climb a groove and arête to a step left below a small roof. Climb past a tree root, and traverse up right past a tree in a corner to a tree below a big chimney. Belay here. 50 feet. **Pitch 2:** Work up the chimney to the base of a long roof that divides the face. Sling a spike for extra pro, crank over the roof (5.10c) past a fixed piton, and delicately establish yourself on the slab above. It's 5.9 to aid the roof. Edge and friction along a thin crack until it bends right. Move up right with pockets and edges to another crack, and follow to the uppermost roof. Traverse right, and finish up a crack and corner to the cliff top. 140 feet. **Descent:** Scramble to the cliff top, and descend a steep trail west of the cliff. **Rack:** A selection of small to medium Friends, a good assortment of TCUs, a set of Stoppers with extra small and medium sizes, a few slings. Good with double ropes since Pitch 2 is fairly long.

Descent Path

13. Silly Arête (E3 5c) (5.10d) 2 pitches. Superlative climbing with impressive position, compelling moves, sparse protection, and a good scare factor up a perfect arête. Begin by climbing Pitch 1 of *Pincushion* to its belay at the chimney foot. **Pitch 2:** Step right onto the lower arête, and climb to the base of the roof. Reach left, crank over the roof on tiny edges (5.10d) above the chimney, and establish yourself on the slab. Work up right along a flake to the arête. Layback its sharp edge, and smear on crystals past horizontal cracks for TCUs to a narrow shelf. Finish a short crack to the top. 120 feet. **Descent:** Follow a path to the top, and descend a steep trail west of the cliff. **Rack:** Small to medium Friends, a good assortment of TCUs, a set of Stoppers, and a few slings. Use double ropes since the rope runs over edges on Pitch 2.

14. Barbarian (E1 5b) (5.10a) 2 pitches. A strenuous, intimidating, but well-protected crack climb. Scramble to the base of a big dihedral. **Pitch 1:** Climb the dihedral's right wall (5.7). Step left into the dihedral, and climb to a small belay ledge on the left. 50 feet. **Pitch 2:** Make hard moves past a roof above the belay (5.10a), and work up the corner then up the cracks on the right slab to a niche beneath the big upper roof. Strenuous moves on the left wall lead to a fingerlock in the crack above the roof (5.10a). Crank past the roof, and layback the crack to a stance. Continue up the corner to a tree belay. 110 feet. **Descent:** Follow a path to the top, and descend a steep trail west of the cliff. Alternatively, rappel slings are sometimes on a tree above the route, allowing a 2-rope rappel to the base. **Rack:** A selection of Friends, a set of Stoppers, and a few slings.

15. Scratch Arête (VS 5a) (5.8+) 2 pitches. A fine moderate line up the far right arête. Begin below a rib and corner on the crag's right side. **Pitch 1:** Climb the rib and corner to a ledge. Follow a crack above until you can move right and over a tricky bulge to a belay stance on the left. 100 feet. **Pitch 2:** Edge up the steep slab left of the arête. At the roof, climb right onto the arête (fixed piton around the corner to the right). Reach up left, and make strenuous pulls on small edges over the roof (5.8+). Step up, grab good holds, and climb easily to the cliff top and an airy belay. 110 feet. **Descent:** Follow a path to the top, and descend a steep trail west of the cliff. **Rack:** A selection of Friends, a set of Stoppers, and a few slings.

Craig y Castell

This 175-foot-high, southwest-facing cliff, named "Castle Crag" for its distant view of Criccieth Castle, lies on the steep mountainside west of Tremadog or a couple kilometers west of Eric Jones' Cafe. The sunny cliff dries quickly after rain. Its crystalline dolerite rock is climber friendly with plentiful holds, perfect friction, and lots of protection. The described route is one of the best of its grade in Britain.

Finding the cliff: From the cafe drive west through Tremadog past the junction of the A487 and the A498 in the middle of town. Drive a few blocks, and park on the side of the street or in the Tremadog village square. Walk west to a lane at the village school. Follow the lane past the school, through a fence, and continue up a grassy lane to a broken-down stone wall. Hike north across a grassy field, pass through woods, and scramble up loose talus to the cliff base. Allow fifteen minutes to hike from the village.

16. Creagh Dhu Wall (HS) (5.7) 2 pitches. This 3-star outing ascends the middle of the face of the Tremadog's leftmost crag. Begin at a worn staging area below an obvious corner capped with roofs. **Pitch 1:** Climb easily up blocks to a short corner. Jam and layback a slanting crack, and make an obvious move right around an arête. Foot traverse right along a horizontal crack in a slab, and finish up a dihedral to a spacious belay ledge. 90 feet. **Pitch 2:** Climb down, and make an airy hand traverse left along big flakes to a blunt prow. Work up left along exposed cracks and corners to a final tricky polished groove (5.7). Climb past a small roof, and belay on ledges. 110 feet. **Descent:** Tricky and easy to get lost. Some make a double-rope rappel from a tree to the ground. For the walk-off, scramble to the cliff top and hike off right (east) to an unobvious path that scrambles down through trees and cliff bands to the base. **Rack:** Sets of Friends and Stoppers. Pitch 2 is protected by wired nuts.

Llanberis Pass

Llanberis Pass, or the Pass, as locals call it, is a deep glaciated valley that divides the Snowdon massif on the west from the Glyders on the east. The A4086 highway, traversing the valley floor between Llanberis and Pen-y-Pas hostel, allows easy access to a wealth of excellent crags. These crags, including Dinas Cromlech, Carreg Wastad, Crws y Gwynt, and Craig Ddu on the northeast side of the valley, and Dinas Bach and Dinas Mot on the southwest flank, make up what is arguably Britain's most important climbing area.

These rhyolite cliffs saw the beginnings of roped technical climbing at the turn of the twentieth century, landmark first ascents in the 1930s by John Menlove Edwards and Colin Kirkus, some of the world's most intimidating crack climbs in the 1950s by Joe Brown and Don Whillans, and scary leads by Pete Livesey in the 1970s. Today they're busy with climbers who come to test their mettle and nerve on yesterday's bold testpieces and honest classics of all grades.

Climbing in the Pass is sheer delight, especially on sunny summer days. The climbable rock is hard and compact, laced with cracks, and studded with flakes and edges. It takes lots of protection. The distinctive cliffs offer strong architectural features—square-cut dihedrals, blunt arêtes, castellated ridges, bold vertical cracks, sweeping slabs, and smooth faces.

Besides roped climbing, climbers come to sample the area bouldering. The Cromlech Boulders have easy access, lots of problems, and a beautiful setting. The boulders, directly below Dinas Cromlech, are a good place to warm up and meet local climbers.

Dinas Cromlech

The fortress of Dinas Cromlech, an excellent southwest-facing cliff, perches high on the rugged northeast flank of Llanberis Pass. This imposing cliff, Britain's most famous crag, is split by a huge central dihedral that forms an open book flanked by sheer 125-foot-high walls. The crag, at an elevation of 2,000 feet, is an imposing monolith laced with some seventy routes and variations, including hard rock classics like *Cenotaph Corner* and *Cemetery Gates.* Many extreme routes here were landmark ascents that pushed the standards of the possible. The rock, a solid rhyolite, is seamed with numerous cracks and broken by flakes and occasional pockets. The face dries quickly after rain, although the vertical cracks often seep afterward.

The best descent from the cliff top is the gully on the far right (south) side. Routes that finish on the left side require crossing the summit to reach the gully. The usual descent for routes that finish at The Valley, the large terrace above *Cenotaph Corner,* is a double-rope rappel from anchors. If other climbers are below, it's best to climb to the summit via a diagonal flake from the top of the corner and then descend the gully.

All routes require a good-size rack that includes a set of wired nuts, a selection of small to medium cams, some TCUs, a few slings and free carabiners, and two ropes. It's a good idea to climb English-style with double ropes to avoid rope drag on the wandering lines. Double ropes are also needed to rappel from The Valley. The harder routes are difficult to protect, so bring your best traditional game to find and equalize all the protection.

Finding the cliff: Dinas Cromlech is on the northeast side of Llanberis Pass, Snowdonia's most popular climbing area. The cliff, along the A4086 highway between Llanberis and Pen-y-Pass, rises on the slope directly above the Pont y Cromlech bridge. Park at the lay-by below the cliff, and hike uphill to the base. Hiking time is fifteen to twenty minutes. Parking is limited, so plan to arrive early, or park farther away and walk. Routes are described from left to right.

LLANBERIS PASS   RF 1 : 66,000

Kilometers 0 — 2
Miles 0 — 2
N

Llyn Peris
To Llanberis
A4086
Llanberis Path
Cwm Idwal
Devil's Kitchen
Glyder Fach 994 m
Glyder Fawr 999 m
Clogwyn y Grochan
Craig Nant Peris
Craig Ddu
Dinas Cromlech
PASS OF LLANBERIS
Carreg Wastad
Bryn Du
Pont y Cromlech
Llyn Cwmffynnon
Afon Nant Peris
Cwm Glas Mawr
Dinas Mot
Dinas Bach
Pen-y-Pass
To Capel Curig
ROMAN CAMP
Cyrn Las
Pyg Track
Glaslyn
Llyn Llydaw
Snowdon 1085 m
A498
To Beddgelert

1. Noah's Warning (VS 5a) (5.8) 2 pitches. A 1951 Joe Brown route. Excellent, continuous, and recommended line up the left side. Start by scrambling to the base of an obvious pocketed crack. **Pitch 1:** Climb good holds up the crack to a large hole. Continue over several bulges to an overhang (5.8). Pass on the left, and belay on a ledge above. 130 feet. **Pitch 2:** Work up a chimney above the belay to an overhanging flake. Scoot around the flake's right side (5.8), and move up left to a thin crack. Follow this up left to a dicey finish. **Descent:** Scramble left, and then up to the cliff top. Descend a gully on the far right side. **Rack:** Bring a selection of Stoppers, small to medium Friends, some extra slings, a few quickdraws, and two ropes, although a single rope works fine on this route.

2. Sabre Cut (VS 4c) (5.7+) 2 pitches. A 1935 climb up the first major dihedral left of *Cenotaph Corner*. Locate a vertical corner system below the Forest, a clump of bushes on broken ledges. **Pitch 1:** Climb

the corner until it splits. Go right here (5.7+), and edge up the wall to the bushes. Continue up easy rock to a good belay below a prow left of the dihedral. 100 feet. **Pitch 2:** Traverse left into a crack that leads over a chockstone. Continue up the excellent corner crack (5.7) to a large belay ledge. 80 feet. **Descent:** Scramble left across ledges, then up to the cliff summit. Descend a gully on the far right side. **Rack:** Bring a selection of Stoppers, small to medium Friends, extra slings, a few quickdraws, and two ropes, although a single rope works fine.

3. Foil (E3 6a) (5.10d) 2 pitches. First ascent by Pete Livesey in 1976. A stellar crack climb with sustained jamming and lots of protection up the steep face right of *Sabre Cut's* dihedral. **Pitch 1:** Climb Pitch 1 (5.7+) of *Sabre Cut* to its belay ledge. 100 feet. **Pitch 2:** Climb to the base of a crack splitting the face above. Jam the crack, which gets increasingly harder for some finger moves. More hard climbing leads to a rest at a pocket.

Continue up the crack with finger jams and laybacking to uncertain moves onto a ledge. Traverse left, and belay on blocks above *Sabre Cut*. **Descent:** Scramble left across ledges and then to the cliff summit. Descend a gully on the far right side. **Rack:** Stoppers, TCUs, and small to medium Friends.

4. Left Wall (E2 5c) (5.10c) 1 pitch. First ascent in 1956 and the first free ascent by Ado Garlick in 1970. Another one of the best Welsh routes. Steep, exposed, sustained, safe, and well protected, but also intimidating, exhilarating, and with a reputation as the most fallen-off route in the Pass. It climbs the striking forked cliff snaking up the Left Wall, the only obvious feature on the face. Begin by scrambling to a wide sloping ledge below *Cenotaph Corner*. **Pitch 1:** Climb up left to a shattered shelf below the obvious crack. Tricky moves lead into the crack and then sinking jams up the steep crack. The ground quickly falls away and gives a feeling of big air on a big lead. Continue to fingery moves to a good rest below a flake and the fork. Launch up left along the strenuous thin crack, using small edges until easy moves on big holds lead to the left arête. Finish up left at a spacious belay ledge. 140 feet. **Descent:** Stay roped and scramble right over the top of the corner to anchors with rappel slings. Make a double-rope rappel to the base of *Right Wall*. **Rack:** Bring a large selection of Stoppers and small to medium Friends, extra slings, a few quickdraws, and two ropes. You can place as much protection as you're willing to carry!

5. Resurrection (E4 6a) (5.11c/d) 1 pitch. First ascent by Rowland Edwards in 1975 with four points of aid, and first free ascent by Pete Livesey and Jill Lawrence in 1975. A stunning and brilliant piece of technical climbing up the right side of Left Wall. Begin at the base of *Cenotaph Corner*. **Pitch 1:** Climb up left to a shelf. Grab the left side of a rib to some hard moves that lead up left to *Left Wall*'s crack below the fork. Follow the sustained right-angling fingery crack up right, using small footholds on the face to a rest at a spike. Continue up right along the thin crack to a flat edge. Climb directly up easier rock to a belay ledge. 145 feet. **Descent:** Stay roped, and scramble right over the top of the corner to anchors with rappel slings. Make a double-rope rappel to the base of *Right Wall*. **Rack:** Bring a selection of RPs, Stoppers, TCUs, small to medium Friends, extra slings, a few quickdraws and free carabiners, and two ropes. Use double ropes on this pitch to equalize the protection.

6. Cenotaph Corner (E1 5c) (5.10a) 1 pitch. First ascent by Joe Brown in 1952. Simply the most famous rock climb in Britain. A must-do route up a perfect dihedral dividing two immaculate walls in the cliff center. Scramble to the base of the dihedral and belay. **Pitch 1:** Climb the corner for 25 feet to the first crux. Pull

through, and continue jamming, stemming, and laybacking up the unrelenting vertical crack and corner to a shallow niche 90 feet up. Leave the niche, and regain the crack above using extreme but well-protected moves (Stoppers). It seems harder if you're tired from the lower exertions. Good holds above finish up the dihedral to a belay on a ledge called The Valley. 120 feet. **Descent:** Make a double-rope from slings on a tree or other anchors. Be careful not to dislodge rocks, particularly if anyone is climbing or belaying below. **Rack:** Bring a good selection of Stoppers and small to medium Friends, extra slings, a few quickdraws, and two ropes. It's easy to lead on a single rope, but you need two for the rappel.

7. Lord of the Flies (E6 6a) (5.12d) 1 pitch. First ascent by Ron Fawcett in 1979. Another stunning line up the vertical wall right of *Cenotaph Corner*. Technical and sustained moves on small edges, and just enough protection—although you need to be imaginative to find it all! The route seeps after rain but gets sun from late morning to early afternoon. Begin 15 feet right of *Cenotaph Corner*. **Pitch 1:** Work up thin cracks until they end, then continue up good pockets to a wide edge. Traverse right along the edge, and climb to an indented pocket. Thin cruxy face moves up left lead to another pocket. Step right, and grab good holds to a narrow ledge. Climb the wall above to another wide edge; continue up a shallow corner with good gear and a few hard moves to the belay ledge. 130 feet. **Descent:** Make a double-rope rappel from slings on a tree or other anchors. **Rack:** Bring an assortment of RPs, Stoppers, small to medium Friends, extra slings, and two ropes. Best to double rope this climb to avoid rope drag.

8. Right Wall (E5 6a) (5.12a/b) 1 pitch. First ascent by Pete Livesey in 1974. Excellent, popular, and a bold necky lead.

Vertical with positive holds but wanders a bit to find the easiest line. It's the scene of many epics and long falls—don't underestimate its seriousness. Start at the right side of a grassy ledge below a short face with a corner above. **Pitch 1:** Climb the corner to a left-angling crack. Follow the crack, then move right and climb pockets to a fingery rail. Move up right to a good rest (find a nut placement on the right). Step onto a square foothold, and move up left to a large broken pocket (a stopper below the pocket and a #2.5 Friend above). Continue up left, using small pockets to a narrow shelf. Traverse right until you're 20 feet below the shallow Porthole. Edge up the vertical wall to the right until you can step into the hole—this is the crux. Above, grab great holds that head up right to a spike. Finish up a thin crack to the big belay ledge. 150 feet. **Descent:** Make a double-rope rappel from slings on a tree or from other anchors. **Rack:** Bring a generous selection of Stoppers, small to medium Friends, slings and free carabiners, and double ropes. The route wanders, so you'll get rope drag with a single rope.

9. Cemetery Gates (E1 5b) 2 pitches or 1 long pitch. A superb 1951 Joe Brown and Don Whillans route. Another Llanberis classic must-do 5-star route! Expect thrilling, exposed climbing with great position and good protection. To start, traverse right from the foot of *Cenotaph Corner* to a belay by a large flake below the blunt prow on the face's right side. **Pitch 1:** Climb the right side of the prow for a few feet, then work left to the base of a prominent crack. Bold tricky moves (5.10a) lead into the crack. Continue up steep but easier rock (one fingery 5.9 section) to a narrow shelf. Move up the harder crack above with finger jams to a narrow belay shelf. 110 feet. **Pitch 2:** Move right on the ledge, and climb a wide crack until you can step right around the prow (5.7). Finish steeply up the airy face on good jugs to the right side of the terrace above and belay. 60 feet. **Descent:** Make a double-rope rappel from slings or other anchors on the belay ledge. **Rack:** Bring a set of Stoppers, small to medium Friends, some slings, and two ropes. You can do the pitch in one long lead with a 200-foot cord. Use slings for rope drag.

10. Ivy Sepulchre (E1 5b) (5.9) 1 pitch. Another Dinas Cromlech classic. This interesting route climbs the obvious dihedral right of *Cemetery Gates.* Begin off a ledge directly below the dihedral. Reach the ledge by either scrambling up easy rock and bushes to the foot of the corner, or traverse right and up from the base of *Cemetery Gates.* You might want a rope for scrambling. **Pitch 1:** Climb and stem the steep corner to a good handhold on the left. Easier jamming leads to a niche below an overhang. Bridge up the strenuous dihedral past the overhang to small edges on the right wall. Crank to better holds on the left wall. Continue up the easier dihedral above to a tree belay just below the top, or continue to a belay on the right side of a large terrace. 130 feet. **Descent:** Make a double-rope rappel from a tree with a sling or other anchors at The Valley. **Rack:** Bring a set of Stoppers, small to medium Friends, slings, and two ropes.

11. Grond (E2 5b) (5.10b) 1 pitch. A 1958 Don Whillans jamming problem on the short headwall above *Ivy Sepulchre.* A fierce, thuggish crack that is not for everyone. Begin by climbing *Ivy Sepulchre* or *Cemetery Gates* to The Valley ledge. Scramble up right onto a flat ledge below a clean overhanging crack. Layback the crack for 20 feet, then begin brutal jamming or thrutching. Belay on the cliff top.

12. Flying Buttress (VD) (5.4) 6 pitches. First ascent by John Menlove Edwards solo in 1931. Recommended buttress and

ridge climb up the cliff's far right side with a bit of everything—slab moves, a hand crack, an off-width crack, traverses, and exposure—all at a easy grade. Belays, protection, and rock are solid, but parts are very polished. Some pitches can be combined, especially with slings to alleviate rope drag. The route is described with traditional short pitches. Begin by scrambling to the base of a worn ridge on the right side. **Pitch 1:** Climb directly up the ridge on large polished holds. 60 feet. **Pitch 2:** Continue up the ridge and over spiky gendarmes to a belay atop the ridge. 60 feet. These first two pitches can be combined. **Pitch 3:** Climb down and scramble to a belay on the left side of Castle Gully. 30 feet. **Pitch 4:** Up rock steps on the left gully wall to a step left around a corner. Cross a shallow corner, and make an easy traverse up left to an exposed belay stance at a large spike. 50 feet. **Pitch 5:** Climb the steep wall above the belay spike to a ramp that leads up right. Follow the ramp past a shelf to a belay stance below a chimney. 65 feet. **Pitch 6:** A few hard moves up the chimney (5.4) and then easier to the cliff-top belay. **Descent:** Walk right from the summit, and descend a gully down the south flank. The descent can be tricky if you go down the wrong gully or try to descend off the north side. **Rack:** A set of sStoppers, small to medium Friends, a few extra slings, and a single rope.

Dinas Mot

Dinas Mot, on the southwest side of Llanberis Pass opposite Dinas Cromlech, is readily seen from the parking area at Pont y Cromlech. The Nose is the obvious triangle-shaped slab in the middle of the cliff. All the described routes ascend The Nose. The Eastern Wing is the huge buttress crisscrossed by beetling overhangs and roofs left of The Nose. The Western Wing is the big buttress right of The Nose.

The Nose is Dinas Mot's most popular and friendly sector, with open slabs at an amenable angle on its lower section and steep cracks, dihedrals, and ribs on the upper headwall. All the routes are enjoyable outings with a combination of friction and edge climbing on the lower wall and jam cracks on the upper wall. Most route cruxes are on the upper wall. The rock quality is generally good, although loose bits are encountered. All routes are fairly well protected and have good belay stances.

Bring a generous traditional rack with a set of Stoppers, some TCUs, small to medium Friends, a few hexes, and free slings and carabiners. Most pitches are fairly short, so you should be fine with a single 165-foot (50-meter) rope. If you need British-style double-rope practice, then by all means climb with double 9-mm ropes.

Descent off the summit is by scrambling down either the left or right gully. The preferred descent is down Western Gully, the deep right-hand gully when facing the cliff. This dark cleft is easier than it looks. The Eastern Gully on the left is harder, with a few easy fifth-class moves at the bottom. Both are dangerous when wet, so use a rope and belay if necessary.

Finding the cliff: Dinas Mot is on the southwest side of Llanberis Pass, opposite Dinas Cromlech. The cliff is accessed via the A4086 highway between Llanberis and Pen-y-Pass. Dinas Mot is the slabby cliff directly west of Pont y Cromlech bridge. Park at the lay-by at the bridge, and follow a climber path to the cliff base. Hiking time is fifteen minutes. Parking is limited, so plan to arrive early, or park farther away and walk. Parking can be impossible on summer weekends. Routes are described from left to right. Belays are not shown.

1. The Cracks (HS) (5.6) 6 pitches. First free ascent by Colin Kirkus in 1930. This classic route ascends cracks and corners up the left side of The Nose. The route crux is a tricky mantle on the last pitch, but it can be avoided. Pitches are short, so some can be combined. Start left of the lowest part of the face. **Pitch 1:** Climb up and then right to a groove that leads to a belay stance. 40 feet. **Pitch 2:** Climb a slab up left to a crack. Follow the crack to a belay below a prominent roof. 60 feet. **Pitch 3:** Move right under the roof to a chimney, which leads to a good belay atop a big flake. 45 feet. **Pitch 4:** Fun climbing up double cracks in an open slab left of a dihedral to a belay ledge. 45 feet. **Pitch 5:** Climb a pillar, and make a tricky move right onto a ledge below a left-facing dihedral. Jam a steep crack up the dihedral's left wall to an airy belay. 60 feet. **Pitch 6:** Work up right, and make a strenuous mantle (5.6) onto a sloped ledge. Climb up left more easily, and move to the cliff top. 45 feet. **Descent:** Down-climb the Western Gully on the right side of The Nose.

2. The Direct Route (VS 5b) (5.8) 3 or 4 pitches. First ascent by Colin Kirkus and J. Dodd in 1930. Excellent route up shallow grooves in the slab's middle with clean rock, jamming and stemming, and balancey moves. It's also harder than it looks. The rock, despite being worn, is rough with lots of friction. This description combines Pitches 1 and 2 into a long lead. Begin at the lowest point of the face and left of a steeper face. **Pitch 1:** Climb up right on broken rock steps, and reach an alternate belay after 50 feet. Continue up right across a rib to the base of a tan corner system. Follow a narrow ramp up left until you can easily step right into the groove corner. Fun climbing up the groove with a harder bulge (5.7) leads to a belay stance. 140 feet. **Pitch 2:** The hand traverse pitch. Move up right on big holds to a right-angling finger rack. Hand traverse up the committing crack (5.7) until you can climb directly to a narrow ledge and a belay at large flakes. 50 feet. **Pitch 3:** A spectacular fun lead. Start off the left side of the narrow belay ledge. Hard moves off the ledge lead to wide stem-

ming up the smooth crux dihedral (5.8) to a 35-foot-high flake wedged in the dihedral. A few climbers lasso the top of the flake to aid through or use the traditional shoulder stand that Kirkus did on the first ascent! Layback and hand jam up the flake to a short corner, sometimes wet, that leads to the top. 55 feet. **Descent:** Down-climb the Western Gully on the right side of The Nose.

3. Superdirect (E1 5b) (5.9+) 3 pitches. Excellent and harder than its neighbors. The rock has a rough gritstonelike quality. Start at the toe of the face. **Pitch 1:** Clamber over a couple blocks and climb to a spike. Step down right, and make an obvious rising rightward traverse (5.7) until you can climb directly to a belay ledge below a small roof. 70 feet. **Pitch 2:** A long delicate pitch with many balance moves. Move past the overhang, and make a short traverse left to a crack system. Climb the crack (5.9) then right past a balanced flake. Step back left into the crack and follow straight up to *The Direct's* narrow belay ledge. 130 feet. **Pitch 3:** Short, thuggish lead. From the ledge's right side, climb a flake, and stem up a short corner to a triangular roof. Layback (5.9+) around the right side of the roof to big holds and the summit. 45 feet.

Descent: Downclimb the Western Gully on the right side of The Nose.

4. Diagonal (HVS 5a) (5.8+) 4 pitches. First ascent in 1938. A recommended classic but runout in spots, lots of delicate moves, and a hard mantle. Begin same as *Superdirect*. **Pitch 1:** Climb over two blocks to a short corner to a large flake. Make a long right-angling traverse (5.8) to a belay stance below a small roof, or climb the easier first pitch of *Superdirect* to the same stance. 80 feet. **Pitch 2:** Climb up right on good edges (5.8) to the right side of a roof. Work up a chimney on the right, and go left at its top to a roomy belay ledge. 40 feet. **Pitch 3:** Traverse straight right into a scoop. Climb the scoop, and pull up right to a hard mantle (5.8+) onto a shelf. Continue up right to an angling crack that leads up left to a ledge. Scramble over broken rock to a belay ledge below a dihedral. 100 feet. **Pitch 4:** Jam and stem a crack in the dihedral (5.7+) to a cliff-top belay. 40 feet.

Descent: Downclimb the Western Gully on the right side of The Nose.

5. Western Slabs (VS 4b) (5.8) 3 pitches. First ascent by J. M. Edwards and friends in 1931. A fine line up a series of shallow grooves on the far right side of The Nose. Start below the right side of the face and left of a stile and fence. **Pitch 1:** Climb over a block to a shelf, and continue up a shallow right-angling corner (5.7) to an arête. Step right, and climb to a small belay ledge. 50 feet. **Pitch 2:** Climb to an overlap, and edge past on the right to a spike (sling for pro). Climb up right under the next overlap to a corner (5.8), and follow it to a ledge. Head up another shallow corner to a belay ledge above Western Gully. 95 feet. **Pitch 3:** Go left from the belay, and climb an easy corner to a ledge with a flake. Continue right up a corner to hard exit moves up right (5.8) to a ledge. Cruise easier lower-angle rock to the top. 60 feet. **Descent:** Downclimb the Western Gully on the right side of The Nose.

Idwal Slabs and Walls

The popular and classic Idwal cliffs—The East Wall, Idwal Slabs, and Holly Tree Wall—sit at the southwest corner of the Llyn Idwal cirque west of Ogwen Valley. These crags offer traditional routes with a variety of grades. The main cliff is the broad north-facing Idwal Slabs, topped by steeper Holly Tree Wall, a broken cliff of slabs and faces. The steep East Wall, dropping sharply off the east side, is a spectacular face with superb routes. The cliffs offer great climbing amidst some of Britain's finest mountain scenery.

The Idwal area is generally relatively benign, despite the fearsome nature of some routes. The cirque's cliffs, including Idwal Slabs, East Face of Tryfan, and Milestone Buttress, were long a training ground for British climbers. The area is well suited for novice and moderate climbers with a large quota of reasonable, well-protected traditional routes. In 1936 the great Welsh climber John Menlove Edwards, in the book *Cwm Idwal Group,*

wrote about the Idwal Slabs: "It favours delicacy of technique, and makes excellent practice for beginners learning the balance and strategy that make the best additions to a climber's progress."

The rocky cirque is definitely a mountain area and has the rain to prove it. Rainfall in parts of Snowdonia is heavy and almost daily. Sunshine sometimes seems hard to find here, and the crags, especially those facing north or east, take a few days to dry. The Idwal Slabs, however, don't suffer that fate and usually dry quickly. If it's raining and you want to be British, then the slabs offer some good soakers. Popular outings are *Hope, The Regular Route,* and *Tennis Shoe,* depending on how much water gushes down the cracks. Watch for polished holds, and bring wool socks to slip over your rock shoes for added traction.

The rock is rough and coarse with plenty of friction. Footholds on the old slab routes are polished to a gleaming shine from the countless scrabbling of Tricouni nails from climbers in the 1920s

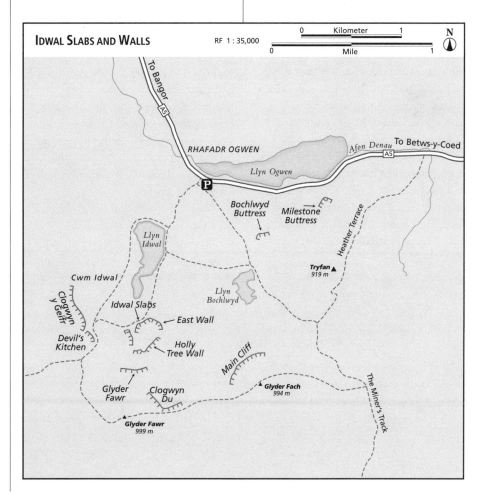

Descent

Continuation Wall

Glyder Fawr
Upper Cliff

Holly Tree Wall

West Wall

East Wall

Idwal Slabs

Trail ⟹

and 1930s. Shallow cracks seam the slab, allowing good protection. The East Wall is very climbable, with plenty of edges and holds, but difficult to protect. Some routes, like *Suicide Wall,* are serious and dangerous undertakings. You can put a lot of climbing mileage in at Idwal by combining routes like *Tennis Shoe* to *Lazarus* to a moderate finish up *The Arête*—more than 800 feet of fun 5.5 climbing. From there you can scramble to the lofty summit of Tryfan, a striking peak that is a Welsh high point.

Finding the cliffs: Llyn Idwal cirque lies west of Ogwen Valley, a wide glaciated valley that trends northeast toward the coast. The area is accessed from the A5 highway between Betws-y-Coed and Bangor. From either end, drive to Ogwen Cottage and park in there or in a lay-by along the road. This is difficult in summer because of hikers and tourists.

The cliff approach is straightforward from Ogwen Cottage. Hike about twenty minutes southwest on Cwm Idwal trail along the lake's south side to the obvious slabs at the far corner of the cirque. The

trail goes under Idwal Slabs. To reach The East Wall, follow a climber's path uphill through steep grass below the cliff.

The East Wall

The East Wall, a long vertical wall angling up the mountainside, forms the left boundary of Idwal Slabs. The vertical wall offers a selection of excellent classics, as well as serious harder routes that require steel nerves and good traditional climbing skills.

1. Heather Wall (VS 4c) (5.8) 2 pitches. 170 feet. First ascent in 1929 by F. E. Hicks, A. B. Hargreaves, and E. A. Stewardson. An excellent climb that is interesting but never hard. The route starts easy but finishes steep and exposed. Bring a thin sling or cord for a crucial thread on Pitch 2. Many climbers have problems finding the belay stance at the end of Pitch 2. It's best to belay below *Tennis Shoe's* last pitch, which gives a fun but polished finish. Start 200 feet up from the bottom of the buttress below a right-angling ramp. **Pitch 1:** Climb up right on a ramp, then up pockets to a shelf. Climb directly up a slab to its top, move left, and continue (5.7+) up a smooth face to a small belay shelf. 100 feet. **Pitch 2:** Traverse up left to a corner to the base of a bulge. Pull over the bulge (5.8), or go around on the left. Either way, step left into a groove and follow to a good belay stance. **Descent:** Lots of ways to go. The best option is to finish up *Tennis Shoe* and then scramble up left for a few hundred feet to a path that leads to the top of a gully above *Suicide Wall*. Downclimb a steep path left of *Suicide Wall* and then down the steep path paralleling The East Wall. Alternatively, scramble across the slab from the top belay point and downclimb *Ordinary Route*.

2. Ash Tree Wall (VS 4c) (5.8) 3 pitches. 175 feet. First ascent by F. E. Hicks and J. A. Smalley in 1929. A pleasant route with steep rock and exposure at an amenable grade. Start atop a square-shaped slab and below a pillar topped with a flat balanced boulder—Perched Block. **Pitch 1:** Climb good holds directly up a steep wall for 50 feet to a bulge. Pass this to the right (5.7+), and continue up lower-angle rock to a ledge. Belay on its left side from spikes. 100 feet. **Pitch 2:** Move left from the ledge, and climb straight up good edges past a couple small ledges to a belay stance below the pillar. 45 feet. **Pitch 3:** Go right onto the pillar, and climb airy rock to a hard move (5.8) to the Perched Block. Scramble up to the *Tennis Shoe* belay. **Descent:** Several options. Best to

finish up *Tennis Shoe* and then scramble up left for a few hundred feet to a path that leads to the top of a gully above *Suicide Wall*. Downclimb a steep path left of *Suicide Wall* and then down the steep path paralleling The East Wall.

3. East Wall Girdle (VS) 7 pitches. 500 feet. First ascent by John Menlove

Edwards and C. Palmer in 1931. One of the area's best routes and the wall's longest. This sustained girdle makes a rising traverse with interesting climbing and little vegetation. Begin at the bottom of the wall below a narrow slab (same start as *Tennis Shoe*). Climb up and left for 7 pitches with lots of 5.6 to 5.8 climbing. Consult the topo for the line.

4. Suicide Groove (E1 5b) (5.10a) 2 pitches. 110 feet. First ascent in 1948 by J. Lawton and D. Haworth. The first and easiest route on Suicide Wall, the uppermost face on The East Wall. Hike alongside the wall to the base of the obvious dihedral/corner on the right side of the face. **Pitch 1:** Climb a steep slab left of the groove (5.8) to a small belay stance below an overhang. 80 feet. **Pitch 2:** Move to the overhang and pull over with fingery moves (5.10a) to the corner above. Layback and stem up the corner on good holds to a belay ledge. **Descent:** Scramble up right and then back left for a few hundred feet to a path that leads to the top of a gully above *Suicide Wall*. Downclimb a steep path left of *Suicide Wall* and then down the steep path paralleling The East Wall.

5. Suicide Wall Route 2 (E2 5b) (5.10c) 1 pitch. 150 feet. First ascent by Pete Crew and Barry Ingle in 1963. Bold climbing with good edges but an underprotected crux on an intimidating face. Start by scrambling 150 feet from the base of *Suicide Groove* until you're below a scoop. **Pitch 1:** Climb to the crescent-shaped scoop, move right, and follow a rib to good edges. Pull edges and flakes to an old fixed piton. Step right to another rib, and move delicately using finger pockets (5.10c) to a shelf. Follow a corner system to a blunt arête to a belay on grassy ledges. **Descent:** Scramble up right and then back left for a few hundred feet to a path that leads to the top of a gully above *Suicide Wall.* Downclimb a steep path left of *Suicide Wall* and then down the steep path paralleling The East Wall.

6. Capital Punishment (E4 5c) (5.11c) 2 pitches. 160 feet. An excellent but serious climb with sustained moves, tricky protection, and great atmosphere. The second pitch can be divided. Begin same as #5. **Pitch 1:** Climb to the top of the crescent-shaped scoop and belay. 25 feet. **Pitch 2:** Continue up a steep slab to the base of a shallow corner. Work up the difficult corner to a jug. Continue up easier rock with good holds to a ledge (possible belay with poor anchors). Climb up left on a steep ramp from the left side of the ledge and join #7. Finish up left easily to a grassy ledge. **Descent:** Sometimes rappel slings are in place on the belay ledge to make a double-rope rappel to the ground. **Rack:** Bring a good rack of small gear including sets of RPs, Stoppers, and TCUs, along with some small to medium Friends, two ropes, and a helmet. Use double ropes to equalize protection and avoid rope drag.

7. Suicide Wall (E2 5c) (5.10c) 1 pitch. 100 feet. First ascent by Chris Preston in 1945. Bold, serious, and excellent. Be extremely careful—it's not a garden party. Start up left from #6 below the left side of a narrow grassy shelf. **Pitch 1:** Climb directly up small edges and flakes (5.10c) past a small spike to the left side of shelf. This polished and almost unprotected start

is the crux. The moves really aren't hard, and the crux is short, but you have the possibility of slipping off and hitting the ground. After reaching the ledge, breathe easier, although the protection is still inadequate here. Some climbers lasso a fixed piton 10 feet above the ledge with a long sling for protection on the next section or arrange small gear in various seams. From the right side of the shelf, make tricky moves up right to better holds. Climb

diagonally up right to hidden pockets that lead to a break. Climb up left on easier rock to a belay on a ledge. **Descent:** Sometimes rappel slings are in place on the ledge to make a double-rope rappel to the ground. **Rack:** Lots of small gear, including sets of RPs, Stoppers, and TCUs, along with small Friends, two ropes, and a helmet. Use double ropes to equalize protection and avoid rope drag.

Idwal Slabs

The Idwal Slabs, one of Wales's oldest climbing areas, is a sweeping slope creased by long left-facing corner systems and dissected by shallow cracks. The gently angled slab yields excellent, fun, easy climbs up a compact rock littered with edges and small pockets. Parts are glazed with a white quartz veneer. Some routes are polished from the old Tricouni nails used on early boots. Some of the first British routes climbed in "rubbers" or smooth-soled tennis shoes were here, including *Tennis Shoe* in 1919 by N. E. Odell. The routes are not overly endowed with protection, and belay stances are sometimes unobvious. It's common for newbies to steam past the stance and find themselves out of rope in an embarrassing and awkward place.

Bring a rack with a set of Stoppers, assorted Friends, extra slings, and a rope. All routes are safely climbed with a single rope. Don't leave your pack at the wall base because lots of foot traffic hoofs past it. Better to stash it in rocks along the base of The East Wall or carry it. Routes are described from left to right.

8. Tennis Shoe (S) (5.6) 6 pitches. 465 feet. Excellent classic route up the far left margin of the main slab. Some pitches can be linked together for expediency. Begin on the left side of the slab below a narrow slab. **Pitch 1:** Climb the narrow slab along its left edge until you can step right onto a belay ledge. 100 feet. **Pitch 2:** Edge up a scoop on the right and onto the main slab. Dance up the left edge to a spacious ledge. 50 feet. **Pitch 3:** Continue up the slab to a large flake and belay atop it. 60 feet. **Pitch 4:** Climb a gully/right-facing corner until you can step left onto a blunt rib. Head up the rib to a belay ledge. 110 feet. **Pitch 5:** Smear a fun slab to a spacious grassy ledge and belay. 100 feet. **Pitch 6:** Go to the ledge's left side below a pillar with the Perched Boulder. Climb the pillar face on slick, polished holds to a scoop (5.6). Friction up an upper slab to the balanced boulder. 60 feet. **Descent:** Finish up a Holly Tree Wall route, or scramble up and left to the top of *Suicide Wall* and carefully climb down a

steep trail to the base of The East Wall. Follow a climber path back to the base.

9. The Ordinary Route (Diff) (5.3) 4 pitches. 460 feet. This classic easy route is one of the oldest technical climbs in Britain with its first ascent in 1897. It follows an obvious crack system up the slab to the base of Holly Tree Wall. John Menlove Edwards described it in *Cwn Idwal Group* as "a good route for beginners with an ineptitude for steep places." The route is an easy downclimb, although not when other parties are climbing it. Begin

right of *Tennis Shoe* below the shiny crack. **Pitch 1:** Climb the easy but brightly polished crack to a good belay niche. Loop some spikes for extra pro on the pitch. 150 feet. **Pitch 2:** Work up a rounded nose for 25 feet right of the crack, and then move out left to the groove and follow its staircase to a scoop. Climb the scoop and then a rib above to a belay from a spike. 150 feet. **Pitch 3:** Climb a shiny crack up a steepening slab, make a short traverse right, and follow a crack directly to a good belay shelf. 85 feet.

Pitch 4: Easy climbing goes left and back right to a wide terrace and a belay below Holly Tree Wall. From here finish the adventure up a Holly Tree Wall route. **Descent:** Scramble up left to the top of *Suicide Wall.* Look for a block with slings that you can rappel off, or carefully downclimb a steep path to the base of The East Wall. Follow a climber path back to the base.

10. Hope (VD) (5.4) 4 pitches. 450 feet. First ascent in 1915. Another excellent and delightful excursion. It's the best of the *Charity, Hope,* and *Faith* triad. Start 75 feet right of #9 and right of the obvious Central Rib, a long rib bordered on its left by a left-facing corner system. **Pitch 1:** Edge directly up a quartz slab to a ledge. Climb the next slab, first up right and then back left to a thin crack to a quartz veneer. Continue to a long ledge and up a shallow corner to a belay ledge. 140 feet. **Pitch 2:** Best pitch. Work up polished twin cracks from the ledge's left end to big holds. Climb gingerly to a thin crack, and follow it to good edges and pockets to a shelf by a roof. Move past, and climb to a belay stance below a corner. 100 feet. **Pitch 3:** Edge up good holds on the slab left of the corner to a bulge. Pass on the left (5.4), and move up right. Climb up right through quartz to a belay stance. 150 feet. **Pitch 4:** Climb up left on easy rock to the large terrace below Holly Tree Wall. 65 feet. From here it's best to finish up by one of the Holly Tree Wall routes. **Descent:** Scramble up left to the top of *Suicide Wall.* Look for a block with slings for a rappel, or carefully downclimb a steep path to the base of The East Wall. Follow a climber path back to the base.

Holly Tree Wall

The Holly Tree Wall is the steep headwall above the wide terrace atop Idwal Slabs. Vertical crack systems, ribs, and slabs offer excellent routes that make good ending pitches to the easier slab lines. Access the wall by climbing any slab route or the lower routes on The East Wall. Routes are described from left to right.

11. Original Route (VS 5a) (5.8) 2 pitches. 130 feet. First ascent in 1918. Good line up the wall's left side. Begin from the left side of the terrace and right of #9's finish beside a boulder leaning against the face. **Pitch 1:** Climb 15 feet into a polished scoop and up to the base of a roof. Move right, and follow a ramp to a shelf below a chimney. Step left to another narrow ledge. Cross to its left side, and make a tricky move (5.8) up right to a mantle. Climb up right on exposed but easier rock to a belay stance above the chimney. You can avoid this semicircular section by climbing directly up the strenuous chimney/crack. 90 feet. **Pitch 2:** Several finishing options. Climb directly up the corner above the belay. Climb the wall left of the corner. Climb a series of short walls farther left, and then finish up right. **Descent:** Traverse left above the cliff to a downclimb onto a lower terrace. Continue left to the top of *Suicide Wall,* and descend a steep gully.

12. Lazarus (S) (5.5) 2 pitches. 140 feet. The wall's easiest way. Begin down right from the top of *Hope* and the terrace and at the base of Javelin Gully, an obvious gully that divides the wall. **Pitch 1:** Clamber up the gully over a couple short steps to a ledge belay. 50 feet. **Pitch 2:** Climb left around a block, then traverse up left to a corner. Pull past a short pol-ished section, and move up right (5.5) to a slabby corner. Follow the corner up right to a large belay ledge. **Descent:** Traverse left above the cliff to a down climb onto a lower terrace. Continue left to the top of *Suicide Wall,* and descend the steep gully.

13. Javelin Buttress (VS) (5.7) 1 pitch. 120 feet. First ascent by F. Graham and C. Jerram in 1925. Fine climbing on exposed rock up the buttress right of Javelin Gully. Begin by scrambling down past the base of the gully to the foot of the buttress. **Pitch 1:** Move right across a shelf to a corner system. Climb the groove corner for 40 feet, then step left onto a pock-marked slab. Edge up the slab for 15 feet, and climb up right through a scoop to a good natural thread (bring a sling). Traverse right a couple moves, and climb directly up a steeper face on good but widely spaced holds. The first is the route's crux mantle shelf (5.7). Above the angle lessens, and the climbing eases. End on a broad terrace below Continuation Wall. **Descent:** Traverse left along the terrace above the cliff to a downclimb onto a lower terrace. Continue left to the top of *Suicide Wall,* and descend a steep gully.

14. Javelin Blade (E1 5b) (5.9) 1 pitch. 120 feet. First ascent in 1930. This was one of the era's hardest climbs, with delicate movements and a paucity of protection. Start the same as *Javelin Buttress.* **Pitch 1:** Climb *Javelin Buttress* to the natural thread. Reverse back left onto the pocked slab, and edge up to the far left side of the buttress. Stem up a corner, and make a committing move (5.9) right onto a rib. Crank the rib to big holds, and finish on the terrace. **Descent:** Traverse left above the cliff to a downclimb onto a lower terrace. Continue left to the top of *Suicide Wall,* and descend a steep gully.

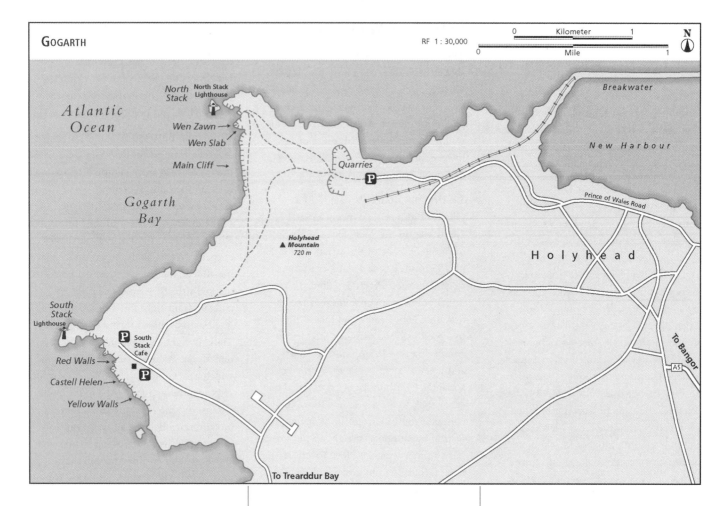

RF 1 : 30,000

N

Atlantic Ocean

Breakwater

North Stack

North Stack Lighthouse

New Harbour

Wen Zawn →

Wen Slab

Main Cliff →

Quarries

P

Prince of Wales Road

Gogarth Bay

Holyhead Mountain ▲ 720 m

H o l y h e a d

South Stack Lighthouse

P

South Stack Cafe

Red Walls →

Castell Helen →

P

Yellow Walls →

To Bangor

A5

To Trearddur Bay

Gogarth

The atmospheric sea cliffs at Craig Gogarth rim the northwestern tip of Wales, a fingered peninsula jutting into the Irish Sea. Here quartzite cliffs on Holyhead Mountain plunge abruptly into the foaming sea, forming an intimidating sea-cliff climbing area. The 3 miles of cliffs leap abruptly to heights of 350 feet above the surf.

Gogarth is a place to climb between the lonely sea and the sky, with only roiling water, a few manky RPs, and empty air below your sweaty hands. It's a frightening prospect to gaze from the cliff edge into the dizzy abyss, knowing that shortly you'll be rappelling down to the wave-tattered shore below. And matey, the only way to get back up is to climb.

The sheer cliffs are complex, intimidating, and committing. It's a place to go after you're friendly with locals who can steer you to the best routes and either give beta or sandbag you. This guide only details a single route, *Dream of White*

Horses, the most famous of Gogarth's 700-plus routes, simply because this is the first route to climb here.

Gogarth is a serious arena for adventure climbing by competent and skillful climbers. Come and do *Dream* and perhaps other moderate offerings like *Lighthouse Arête, Britomatis,* and *Red Wall.* Then you can suss out harder possibilities with an experienced eye. The local guidebook and area climbers are indispensable for a safe and enjoyable Gogarth experience.

The cliffs are reached by a quick hike from Holyhead, an hour's drive from Llanberis or Tremadog. A *caff* with endless pots of steaming tea is a short distance from Red Walls.

Be advised that sea-cliff climbing here is serious and dangerous. Tides and storms should not be taken lightly. Even on calm days, a rogue wave can smash into the cliff, soaking climbers at a belay stance 75 feet above sea level, or worse—tumbling you into foaming water. Use caution and check tide tables.

Finding the cliff: Drive to the island of Anglesey. Enter Holyhead on the A5, and follow it along the front, keeping right at the War Memorial. Continue past the harbor until you're forced to turn left onto Prince William Road and Beach Road (may be signed NORTH STACK). Keep straight ahead, with Holyhead Mountain visible in front and slightly left. Follow a dirt road alongside old railway lines that lead to an old quarry on the north side of Holyhead Mountain. Park at its end.

Follow a path uphill for 0.5 mile until it forks. Go left a short distance to another fork. Head right this time toward North Stack lighthouse. Wen Slab is directly below you now, south of the lighthouse. It's best to descend a grassy slope first to gain a vantage point on the promontory facing Wen Slab and Wen Zawn, to eyeball the route, and to ascertain the whereabouts of other climbers. Since *Dream* is a rising traverse, you won't be popular if other parties are on the harder direct routes. Before leaving the viewpoint, note the steep gully descending

right of the slab, terminating near an obvious spike at the slab's right-hand side about 100 feet up.

Choice 1: Decide at this point if you will climb Pitch 1 or not. Low tide is essential. Most parties omit Pitch 1 and start from the spike, making (some would argue) a more pleasurable route of an even standard.

Choice 2: If you are climbing Pitch 1, rappel from the spike to the base of the wall. Take extreme care here. Climbers have rappelled off with "too short" ropes

and fallen into the sea! Bring long ropes, and tie knots in the ends.

From grassy slopes above the cliff, traverse southward well above the cliff edge and rock outcrops until the main gully is seen. Avoid a steeper but less obvious decoy gully. Hide your rucksack in the numerous rocky outcrops. Descend the main gully with care (not as bad as it looks), and scramble downward until you can descend northward to the obvious pointed spike. Some people rappel this upper gully scramble following a line of

broken rock on the slab's right edge. A scramble down from the spike presents a grand view of Wen Slab. Rappel to the base of Pitch 1, or scramble behind the spike to a belay stance on the other side in a narrow gully. The first pitch climbs the left edge of an obvious groove from the sea up to the same stance.

1. A Dream of White Horses (HVS) (5.8) 3 pitches. This brilliant route on Wen Slab is one of Britain's best sea-cliff classics. Sustained, interesting, and exciting climbing throughout. No great difficulties are encountered, but make no mistake—this is a serious cliff and does not welcome complacency. A confident and bold approach is needed, as well as a calm mind. Dennis Jump says, "This is a rewarding climb that reminds you what climbing is really about. It jerks you back to reality. It makes you forget the wall back home or Sunday afternoons at the local crag. This is the real thing!"

Follow the directions above to find the start of the route. The first pitch begins from the zawn bed just above the sea. **Pitch 1:** An awe-inspiring place, and on stormy days it's obvious why Ed Ward-Drummond named the route. Climb the left side of a groove up the steep slab (5.7) to Wen Ledge. This is an alternative start-ing belay for Pitch 1 if the seas are rough below. Continue to a spike, then up right to a cramped belay stance in a corner. At first glance this pitch looks fairly tough, but it's delightful with good holds and friction. **Pitch 2:** The route follows an imposing line of flakes diagonally up left (5.7). Launch confidently up left from the stance. Not a lot of pro, so it feels serious. Bring thin webbing and rope slings to tie off short spikes. Look for hidden stopper placements or blunder past in ignorance. When the flake ends descend the other side, cross a broken corner into the aptly named Concrete Chimney, and belay at a stance from nuts directly above gaping Wen Zawn. Again, protection is sparse on the traverse and downclimb, but hang out and find gear to safeguard your second. 145 feet. **Pitch 3:** Atmospheric, exposed, exhilarating, and yes, a bit scary. Step left from the belay, and climb up left under a big roof. Descend down left to a rib. Reach around to a hidden hold. Continue left on exposed jugs (give a whoop of ecstasy!) to vivid orange rock. Make a difficult move (5.8) across to a square groove. Bridge the groove to a chunky peg, and exit left up easier slabs to the grass above. Belay from boulders back from the edge. 150 feet. **Rack:** An assortment of hexes and Stoppers, medium to large Friends, and plenty of quickdraws and slings (especially for the last pitch). Some thin pieces of webbing and cord are useful for slinging spikes. Brits double rope this route, so beware of rope drag with a single rope.

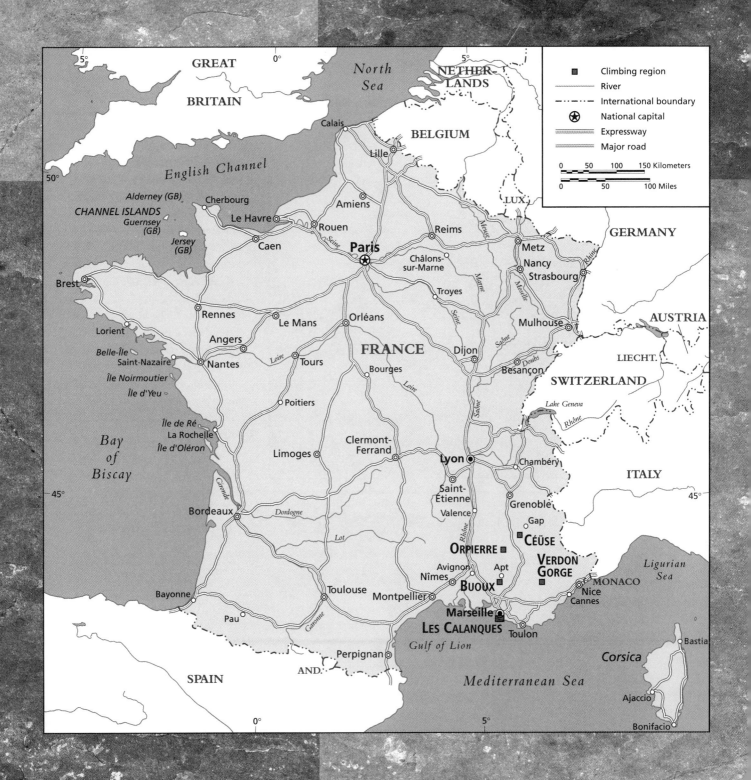
France

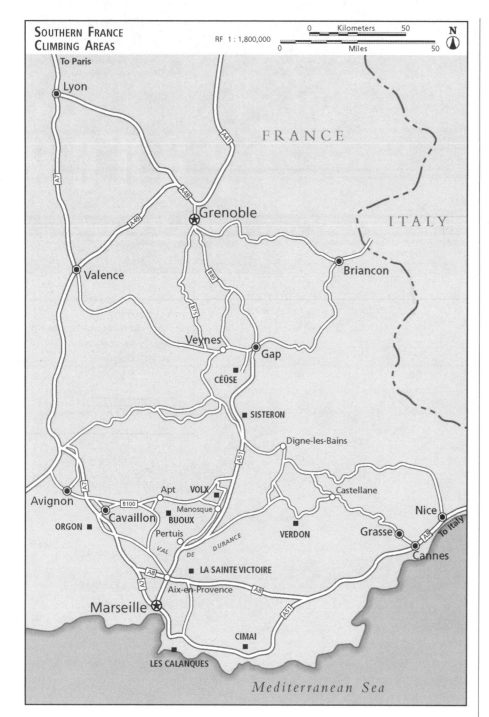

BUOUX

■ OVERVIEW

The Montagne de Lubéron, a hump-backed mountain range, straddles the middle of the Provence, stretching east from Cavaillon near Avignon to Manosque. The sinuous Durance River defines its southern boundary, separating it from stony hills bordering the Mediterranean Sea. The gentle range, topped by a rounded summit that rises to nearly 3,500 feet, is protected within the 247,000-square-acre Parc Naturel Régional du Lubéron or Lubéron Regional Natural Park. The sides of the range are green year-round with a dense woodland of cedar, pine, and oak; wildflowers, thyme, and lavender fill the air with aromatic scents.

The famed climbing area of Buoux, composed of the mile-long Falaise de l'Aiguebrun, is a sheer, imposing cliff that hides in a secluded, narrow canyon sliced into the northern flank of the Lubéron. The area, still considered one of Europe's premier sport-climbing areas, is an enchanting place of thick forests, a cool and refreshing creek, and the soaring textured cliffs that sharply rise 600 feet to the flat rim above. The bright gray and tan cliff is defined by huge pillars, immaculate faces, deep crack systems, steep corners, and streaked overhanging walls.

Buoux is a place to come and enjoy pure free climbing and its varied graceful movements. Climbing at Buoux, pronounced *boox* and named for a nearby village, is absorbing, interesting, and rarely repetitive. The limestone here is a fantastic medium for exploring the vertical world with an endless variety of intricate movements. It was on these steep walls, dubbed "The Laboratory" by *Vertical* magazine in the 1980s, that modern sport climbing evolved. Here climbers developed the movements, nuances, and vocabulary of today's hard climbing: drop-knees, back-steps, kneebar rests, dynamic throws to pockets, and gastons.

One word describes the climbing movements at Buoux: *athletic.* You need unabashed forearm and finger strength to

Ian Spencer-Green climbing the excellent *Rêve de Papillon* (8a) (5.13b).

succeed here on the hard lines. The stone, peppered with numerous characteristic *trou* or holes, dictates the aggressive yet delicate style and go-for-it attitude required for successful redpoint ascents. Steel fingers are necessary to pull on a variety of pockets. These range from shallow one-finger or mono-doigt dishes and scoops to full-hand mailbox jugs and large huecos. The two-finger pocket is considered the classic Buoux hold.

Some routes, especially those with holds that are not caked in chalk, are bouldery and difficult to on-sight because of the plethora of pockets. You reach up and grope around, trying to find the best pocket. You hook a sloping hole with two fingers and pull to the next move, only to find that 6 inches to the left hides a flat four-finger box. Flexibility is important here, with the ability to turn and keep the hip close to the face crucial for lifting weight off your fingers. High stepping is also helpful to stay in balance between pockets. It's key to wear shoes with

pointed toes for cramming in crucial pockets. Remember to tick the best toe pockets with chalk as you pass by, or else you'll end up hanging or falling.

The rock at Buoux lends itself to two distinct kinds of routes: vertical to overhanging faces with deep pockets and steep slabs laden with shallow divots and dishes. The hardest and best routes are generally the steepest ones. Usual difficulties on these are long reaches, successive dynos from tiny pockets, and strenuous moves off shallow pockets with no feet. Characteristic routes are the classic lines at Secteur TCF, *Rêve de Papillon,* and the routes at Bout du Monde sector, including *Chouca* and *La Rose et le Vampire*. The slab lines are tenuous and delicate, with upward movement from finger-stacks in the merest dents and high-stepping smears. The best of these routes ascend the smooth wall at Le Styx and the easier but polished lines at Mur Zappa.

This is a place generally reserved for the hard climber's enjoyment. There are many classic and excellent routes in the

middle grades, but the moderate climber will quickly exhaust the possibilities. This is not to say that lots of superb climbing is not found in the 5.9 and 5.10 grades, but these routes tend to be popular (so expect a queue on weekends or holidays) and subsequently can be very polished from myriad ascents. To really excel and enjoy Buoux, you need to be competent on at least 5.11 routes. This opens you to a wide variety of climbs. The strong 5.12 climber will find stacks of superb lines, including the area's finest pocket routes. It's best to come for a week or so to sample the classic routes and work on a couple projects.

Unlike the other major climbing areas in the south of France, Buoux's rock is composed not of limestone but of a calcareous sandstone deposited on a seafloor during the Miocene Epoch some twenty-five million years ago. The rough rock is composed of hard sand grains embedded in a soft calcareous cement that provides for more friction on polished rock surfaces than other area limestones.

The Falaise de l'Aiguebrun is not a long, clean sweep of stone, but rather broken by ledges, gullies, and terraces into thirty-five distinct climbing sectors. Not included is the beautiful West Face, seen from the access road as it descends from the village of Buoux into the valley, nor the roadside cliffs with old bolts and slings. Climbing on both of these cliffs was banned when the area got too popular in the mid-1980s. The main south-facing cliff, reached by various trails that begin at three designated parking areas, increases in height to the prominent Pilier des fourmis sector, the highest cliff section. Around the corner of the pillar is a huge amphitheater of excellent sectors. The easternmost sector open to climbing is Mur du Bout du Monde. Beyond this is another impressive cliff section above the auberge that is closed to climbing, although some routes do ascend that wall.

Through the 1980s and early 1990s, Buoux was considered the best crag in the world—the place where the best Euro-jocks came to play and to experiment. Here they honed the rock skills needed to open Céüse, today's "best crag in the world." On the other hand, it was also considered by some to be a mere outdoor gymnasium with a boring sameness to most of the routes. Buoux has fallen out of favor with myopic American climbers, who now come and forsake other French areas for Céüse, spending all their time at its single cliff. But if you dream of endless walls laced with two-finger pockets, short classic routes that have stood the test of time, perfect sweeps of overhanging limestone, and sunny Provencal days—then Buoux is a necessary destination on your European vacation.

Rack, Protection, and Descent

Almost all the routes are well protected by big beefy bolts, and few long runouts are found. The runouts that occur are found on steep routes where a fall drops you into empty space. Thick, glued-in eyebolts are normal on most routes because the underlying rock is often soft or porous while the surface is hard. Most anchors are quick-clip steel carabiners attached to stout chains, which allow you to clip in and lower without untying, threading, and retying the rope into your harness. The French make route finding easy too, with the names of many routes elegantly inscribed with paint and a fine-tipped brush on the rock at the route base.

A rack of fifteen quickdraws suffices for most routes, although if you're set on doing some of the longer ones, a set of wired nuts can come in handy for extra protection on long runouts. It's best to use a 200-foot (60-meter) rope; a 165-foot (50-meter) rope is too short to climb and lower on many routes. Accidents have occurred when the loose rope end slipped through a belay device. Be sure to tie a knot in the end to avoid becoming a statistic.

Descent off all routes is by lowering or rappelling from sturdy eyebolt anchors.

Climbing History

The first climbers here were undoubtedly early humans who inhabited the lush valley and surrounding mountains. They climbed into arching caves in the rocks and lived in the lofty aeries. Later, during the Wars of Religion, people lived on the cliffs in fortified dwellings perched on ledges such as that below La Plage. The remains of these buildings, mostly chiseled square holes for posts and beams, are found on the cliff.

Little technical climbing was done on these slumbering cliffs until the 1970s, when some mixed free and aid routes were established up cracks and corners.

The world's climbing attention shifted in the 1980s from the great American centers at Yosemite and Boulder to Europe, particularly France. The best European climbers of the 1970s had made rock pilgrimages to America and came back to their own continent sporting not only white painter pants and the skills to jam cracks, but the American free-climbing ethic that valued leading routes all free without resting or aiding on gear. The French quickly adopted the free climbing game and began freeing old aid lines and then establishing routes by a controversial new method: rappelling down and placing bolts. The absence of natural protection on the limestone cliffs at places like Buoux certainly contributed to this new ethic.

In the 1980s the French climbing magazine *Vertical* dubbed the Buoux cliffs "The Laboratory," because it was here that this new style of extreme free climbing—which included rappel-bolted routes, colorful Lycra outfits, desperate gymnastic movements, hang-dogging moves, and repeated falls—was experimented and improved upon. Climbers from across Europe as well as the United States came to Buoux simply to get better, to find new movements, and to climb the world's hardest routes. The Laboratory eventually led to today's sport-climbing ethos.

By late 1983 the local residents at the commune of Buoux were fed up with climbers invading their quiet Provencal corner, parking bumper to bumper on the access road, and camping in the valley. Their frustration led to the entire valley being closed to climbing. The following year a compromise with stringent restrictions reopened about half the cliffs.

Many of the harder routes were established and redpointed by Jibé Tribout and Antoine Le Ménestrel, along with British climber Ben Moon, who, in the early 1990s, snagged the first ascent of *Agincourt,* a longtime 8c (5.14b) project that he named for a famous battle between the French and English. Another significant ascent was Catherine Destivelle's 1988 ascent of *Chouca,* a 5.13c line of pockets that was at that time the hardest route ever climbed by a woman.

Getting Around

It's best to have a rental car to get around here, especially if you want to visit the superb outlying crags like Volx or Orgon. Many climbers, however, hitchhike to the crag daily or scam a ride from other climbers at the campgrounds. It's generally easier to find climbers at the Les Cedres campground in Apt, rather than at the more remote site at Bonnieux.

Driving is easy because traffic is usually light. Most of the back roads are

The classic village of Bonnieux is base camp for Buoux climbers.

narrow with blind corners. French drivers tend to speed on the winding highways, so if a Renault driven by a chain-smoking Frenchman is hugging your tail, pull over and let him pass—you're on vacation after all. A good road atlas or area map like the Michelin one is essential for finding your way to the cliffs and various points of interest. No matter how good your directions to a place are, plan on getting lost, especially in towns that have a bewildering maze of streets. Persevere, go slow, keep an eye out for signs pointing to the next village, and you'll be fine.

Seasons and Weather

Provence is hostage to the whims of the Mediterranean climate. The seasons are distinct and change abruptly. Climbing is possible all year at Buoux, but the operative word is "possible." Summer days, when many Americans visit, are often just too hot to climb comfortably. If you visit in summer, climb on the shaded walls at the front side in the early morning, and migrate to the shady east-facing sectors in the late afternoon and evening. Midafternoon is usually too hot to climb, making it a good time to rinse your feet in the cold stream below the cliff. Summer days can be humid, which makes every climb a steamy, sweaty affair—bring lots of chalk! The brutal heat of summer is directly tied to the vast and terrible Sahara spreading across northern Africa, a short hop across the sea from Provence.

The best months are April, May, and September through November. The days are usually pleasant and dry, although it can rain. Autumn showers end the storm of summer sunlight, whereas sustained rains fall in the spring months. Precipitation occurs on about seventy days annually. The crag dries quickly after rain, although some sectors are subject to water and dirt washing off the cliff top. Winter can be fine, but short days, cold nights, and occasional snowstorms conspire to make it a less than ideal time to visit.

The most distinctive weather feature of the Provence is the famed mistral, a cold, dry wind that begins far to the north and sweeps south down the broad Rhône Valley to the sea. It gusts when an inland high pressure funnels down the valley toward low pressure centered over the Mediterranean Sea. It's the one phenomenon that can impact your climbing holiday.

When it comes, the mistral blows for weeks on end, swirling around the cliffs, uprooting trees, rattling tiles off roofs, moaning through every nook and cranny in houses, and causing all kinds of domestic quarrels and a general malaise. The area between Avignon and Marseille, which includes the Lubéron, usually receives the worst of the mistral. It howls so hard here that locals say it will blow the ears and tail off a donkey. The area architecture reflects living with the mistral. Squat farmhouses lie low to the ground, their roofs weighted down with stones, and heavy shutters blind the windows. The good thing that comes with the mistral is the clarity of light after it scrubs the air clean. Every mountain detail and distant vista appears in stunning detail and color.

Camping, Accommodations, and Services

The two main base camps for a Buoux stay are the public campgrounds in Apt and Bonnieux. Camping Municipal Les Cedres, the Apt campsite, sits just north of the town center on Route de Rustrel and is a few minutes walk from the town center amenities. These include lots of cafes and restaurants, a large farmer's market on Wednesdays and Saturdays, banks and ATMs, a post office, and plenty of ambience. The campground is sometimes crowded and noisy, depending on the season, and the tent area is situated below a main road. The campground offers trailers for rent, a great option if the weather turns rainy. It also has a small cafe and sells essential supplies like fresh baguettes. The campground is open from mid-February through mid-November.

Bonnieux, a classic Provencal hill village, has a quiet campground tucked into a valley below the village. It is very busy here during holiday periods, but usually peaceful and secluded. The site is also cooler and higher than Apt. Be sure to get your shower first thing in the morning because the hot water runs out if it's at all busy.

Lots of hotels, *chambres d'hotes* (B&Bs), and *gîtes* are also found in the Apt and Bonnieux area. Ask at the main tourist office in Apt (Tel: 04 90 74 03 18) for suggestions and reservations. Some good places in Apt include Hôtel du Palais, Hôtel L'Aptois, and the Auberge du Lubéron. The Auberge de Jeunesse hostel offering bed and breakfast is south of Apt in the high village of Saignon. Several *gîtes* are in Bonnieux. You can also search out many marvelous inns scattered throughout the Lubéron. A recommended B&B is Les Peirelles near Ménerbes, the village made famous in Peter Mayle's *A Year in Provence*. For more places check with Fleurs de Soleil, an association of independent B&Bs in private homes, and Gîtes de France, with its comprehensive Web site.

Food and Drink

Besides climbing, exploring Provencal cuisine is reason enough to visit southern France. Eating well is important to the French, who know that properly prepared and presented fresh food is paramount to good living. It's possible to eat well in France without spending a fortune or visiting the best and most expensive restaurants. You can shop daily in the *supermarché,* shops, and town markets, picking up fresh fruits and vegetables, local cheeses and wines, and marvelous *boules* of French bread for your campground repast. Be sure to visit one of the local markets. They're great not only to people-watch but to build up your travel larder with the freshest local produce.

Provencal cooking is mainly country cooking and eating. Many dishes are prepared using the region's two main ingredients: *huile d'olive* or olive oil and *ail* or garlic. Olive oil from the tenacious olive tree is the most important element in Provencal cooking. Lots of other fresh vegetables regularly appear in regional dishes, including *tomates* (tomatoes), *aubergines* (eggplant), *courgettes* (zucchini), and *oignons* (onions). These are often combined into savory ratatouille, a hearty vegetable stew flavored with local herbs. It also makes an easy camp-stove meal. On one long road trip to Provence, all we subsisted on for three weeks were variations of ratatouille that depended on what was fresh and available. Also be on the lookout for the famed Provencal fish soup called bouillabaisse. It is usually made with several kinds of fish, as well as vegetables and a sprinkling of herbs. This wonderful *spécialité,* a symbol of the southern coast, is aromatic with the scent of saffron and intoxicating with its pungent flavor.

In Apt you have your choice of a couple good *supermarchés*—Le Clerc and Intermarche—on either end of town. Here you can explore all the cheeses, including superb Camembert and Brie at a fraction of the American price, various pâtés, delectable olives, and of course *vin* (wine). If you're unsure what wine to buy, look at what locals are purchasing by seeing which shelves are emptied of bottles. Most of them are inexpensive local table

wines. You can also visit the famous wine *caves* or caverns where the fruits of the Lubéron are cheaply pumped like gasoline into your own containers.

Many excellent restaurants are found through the Lubéron. In Apt's town plaza, an easy stroll from the campground, are several outdoor cafes with shaded tables. It's a good place to sip coffee, eat pizza, and watch the world pass on a warm evening. Some recommended area restaurants include Dame Tartine in Apt, Auberge du Presbytère in Saignon, Auberge de la Loube in Buoux, and Auberge des Seguins below the cliff.

Dame Tartine, its outdoor seating shaded by an ancient plane tree, offers tasty salads, imaginative quiches, and fresh fruit tarts. Auberge du Presbytère, an inn on Saignon's central square, serves superb regional dishes flavored with fresh herbs. The Auberge de la Loube in Buoux has a grand local reputation for delicious meals. My friend Howard Brooks calls his meal there the "best in my life—10 stars!" Auberge des Seguins, sitting in the valley below the cliff at Buoux, aims high with a passionate menu of wonderful Provencal food. Eating here after a day's climbing is unforgettable. The inn also offers rooms for overnight stays. These few suggestions merely hint at the gastronomic riches awaiting you—if your wallet and stomach can afford it. Otherwise, you can always head back to the campsite and stir up a pot of spaghetti and sauce with an appetizer of baguette and pâté.

Cultural Experiences and Rest Days

The Provence is that glorious region of southern France filled with sun, warmth, and color. It not only offers much of Europe's best climbing adventures, but it's also a place of ancient human history and stunning natural beauty. The Provence is soft and old with hazy mountains outlined by gentle contours, tan tile roofs etched against azure skies, and a formidable array of historical towns and villages dating before the Romans. Time slows to a crawl here. Locals spend summer days outside working in olive groves, sipping *pastis* at awning-covered tables in outdoor cafes, or playing the ancient ball game *pétanque* in the dappled shade of a plane tree.

No one except the native Provencan ever gets to really know the Provence as much as they remember it. For most it's a place of dreams and fantasies, a place of recollection and remembering, a place of food, drink, and sunlight. The dark green mountains and bright limestone cliffs burnished in evening sunlight; the aromatic perfume of lavender washing across afternoon fields; trickling creeks tucked away in leafy vales; medieval villages stitched onto fortified hilltops; sycamore-shaded benches surrounded by the shrill cacophony of a thousand cicadas; these are the visions you recall later when you're back home, away from that storm of sunlight and the ubiquitous mistral wind.

After cranking for a morning at Buoux, you will want to rest during the heat of the day before heading back to the cliffs. Before motoring off to other points, check out the historical places in this stunning mountain valley. The spectacular ruins of Fort de Buoux straddle the crest of the butte opposite the cliff. A trail heads up to the fort from a paved parking area opposite the cliff.

Area habitation dates back more than 100,000 years when both Neanderthals and Cro-Magnons existed in this rich landscape. Their prehistoric remains were found under the immense arching *baume* or cave along the access path to the fort. Past the *baume* are individual burial tombs excavated in bedrock, each chiseled out to the size of their occupant. This ninth-century necropolis was part of the village of Saint-Germain, which was destroyed in the wars between the Saracens and the Franks. Past the tombs pay a small fee at the guardian's house, and wend up chopped steps to the fort ruins atop cliffs. The sloping summit harbors the ruins of a thirteenth-century village and its Romanesque chapel, stone fortifications, arrow-slitted watchtowers, cisterns carved in rock, and deep trenches. The village was destroyed in the 1660s because it was a center for Protestantism. Walk to the edge of the north cliff for a stunning view of the

main climbing area across the valley before heading back down.

Some excellent hiking trails thread through the Vallon de l'Aiguebrun. One of the best heads up the valley from the Auberge des Seguin inn and restaurant to the tiny village of Chatebelle. You can purchase tasty and fresh *fromage de chèvre* (goat cheese) here before continuing on to the serene village of Sivergues. After resting and exploring the village, return to the valley via a loop trail that heads northwest and drops back to the valley floor near the village of Buoux.

Apt, a city with a population of 12,000, is one of Provence's main market towns. The old town, a maze of narrow medieval streets, centers on the eleventh-century Cathedral of Sainte Anne. The city was originally a Roman settlement called Apta Julia, an important colony along the Domitienne Way in the Calavon River valley. Local tribes destroyed the city in the fifth century, leaving its early remains buried beneath today's town. Apt flourished during medieval times and was a Catholic town during the Wars of Religion. A flood devastated it in the late sixteenth century, and then two plagues decimated the population. Now Apt is the business center for the Calavon valley. If you're staying at the campground or a nearby *gîte*, Apt is good to explore, especially since you'll see few Americans here. Lots of shops, supermarkets, bakeries, and cafes are found. Also visit the cathedral, which houses some relics of Sainte Anne. You can rent a bicycle and follow part of the Lubéron en Vélo cycling path, which runs 100 kilometers between Cavaillon and Forcalquier. The path passes alongside the campground. The main market day is Saturday, and the Fête de Sainte Anne is the last Sunday in July. For information on Apt stop by the Office de Tourisme.

After strolling around Apt, it's fun to head into the Provencal countryside and discover the beautiful villages. One of the closest is Bonnieux, a classic village perched atop a high ridge on the northern edge of the Lubéron massif. Its prominent twelfth-century *Eglise Haute* or high church lifts a pointed steeple above the village. Visit the church by hiking up

skinny streets, passing through arched tunnels under houses, and then up the final eighty-six steps to the church. Your reward is a stunning view west across vineyards and olive groves to Lacoste and a castle once inhabited by the Marquis de Sade. The church, surrounded by century-old cedars, is especially atmospheric at sunset when the wind whistles banefully through a metal cross. The village has shops selling pottery, artisan crafts, and art, as well as cafes and a restaurant that serves tasty pizza. Also of interest is the Musée de la Boulangarie (Bread Museum) in a seventeenth-century house. Bonnieux makes a good base camp to climb at Buoux and explore the Provence.

Lots of other interesting villages scatter across the area. Gordes to the north, although overrun with summer tourists, is one of the most beautiful. Nearby is the Village des Bories, which dates to the Bronze Age. The village contains about twenty *bories* or circular, dry-stone huts. These ancient huts are seen everywhere, including in fields around Buoux. Roussillon, north of Apt, is renowned for its red and orange ocher. The pretty village of Saignon, southeast of Buoux, is worth a ramble, with its ancient cathedral and castle ruins atop a limestone outcrop above the village.

On rest days head west 45 miles to the lovely walled city of Avignon. The city, built along the Rhône River, was the "French Vatican" and home to seven French-born popes between 1309 and 1377. It's best to park in one of the lots alongside the outer wall and walk into the city. Be sure to visit the lofty Palais des Popes, a fortified palace for the pontifical court, and the Cathédrale Notre Dame des Doms. Nearby is the Rocher des Doms, with numerous scenic overlooks. Several museums, lots of chic shops, and many outdoor cafes are available for your pleasure.

The Avignon area offers loads of other great cultural places to visit. To the west is the Pont du Gard, a famous Roman aqueduct. To the south is the picturesque town of Saint-Rémy-de-Provence, where Dutch artist Vincent Van Gogh was committed to St. Paul asylum in

1889–90. Many of his famous paintings are set in the surrounding countryside. Just south of Rémy are impressive Roman ruins at Glanum and Les Baux-de-Provence, a fortified village below an ancient castle perched atop a rock-rimmed butte. Nearby are Tarascon and Beaucaire, with their two classic castles facing each other across the Rhône. North of Avignon is the famed vineyard Chateauneuf-du-Pape, the winery of the popes, and still one of France's best wineries.

Trip Planning Information

General description: More than 450 excellent bolted routes are found on the south-facing, mile-long, 300-foot-high Falaise de l'Aiguebrun, one of Europe's premier sport-climbing cliffs.

Location: Provence region of southern France. The cliff and the village of Buoux are tucked into the Lubéron mountains 8 kilometers south of the town of Apt, east of Avignon.

Camping and accommodations: The two campgrounds frequented by climbers are in Apt and Bonnieux. Both are recommended. Camping Municipal Les Cedres in Apt is near the school on the north side of the river and just north of the town center. It offers good facilities, with showers and a small shop and cafe. It can be busy and is sometimes noisy from traffic, but most users are quiet and respectful. The site is popular with climbers since it's so close to the Apt center and within walking distance of supermarkets, banks, shops, and cafes. If you don't have a car, there are usually enough climbers here that you can hitch a ride. (Tel: 04 90 74 14 61).

Bonnieux is a mountain village southwest of Apt and west of Buoux. It's generally quiet, but can be crowded in summer. The campground has good facilities, but if it's busy, be sure to get your shower early; otherwise, the hot water runs out. The site can be windy and is usually cooler than Apt. There are fewer

shops in the village, but there are good restaurants and bars. (Tel: 04 90 75 86 14).

If you don't want to camp, parked trailers (caravans) can be hired at the Apt campground. They sleep two to four people and include a gas stove and electricity. Plenty of *gîtes* (guesthouses) are found in the Lubéron and Apt area. Prices are usually lower in the off-season than in summer. For more information and online booking, try www.gites-de-france.fr.

For those with unlimited budgets, plenty of excellent hotels are found in the region with five-star accommodations and restaurants. La Sparagoule, within walking distance of the cliffs, is a *gîte* in Buoux (Tel: 04 90 74 47 82).

Climbing season: Year-round. The best seasons are spring (April and May) and autumn (September to November). The cliff dries fast even after heavy rain, although some routes are wet with runoff from the plateau above. November is considered the perfect time to attempt the hard routes, with generally cool but dry

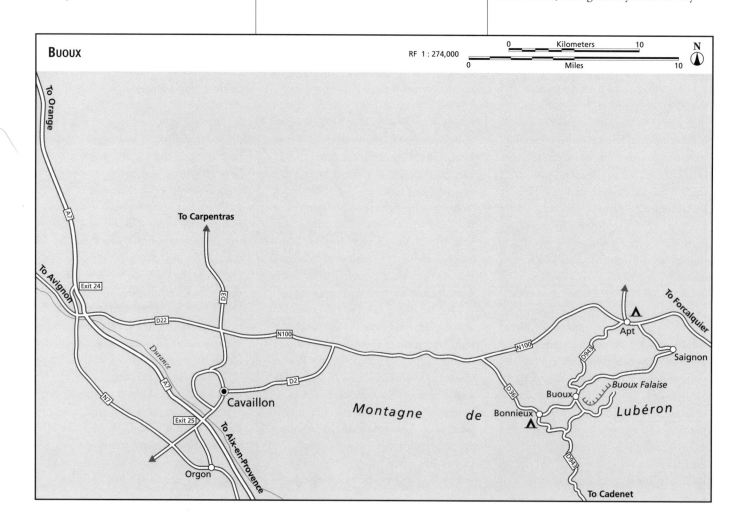

days. The summer is hot, although some days are cool enough for climbing. Plan on finding shade in the morning and evening.

Restrictions and access issues: The cliffs are on private land, so access is subject to an agreement between the FFME (Fédération Francaise de la Montagne et de l'Escalade) and the local landowners. Climbing is prohibited on the cliffs below the ancient fort, above the auberge at the road's end, and at the Confines. Park only in designated parking areas. Do not park on the road. The fort parking area is strictly for visitors to the fort, not for climbers. No camping is allowed in the area. No fires. Pick up all of your litter as well as any left by thoughtless climbers.

Guidebooks: *Buoux* by P. Duret, B. Fara, and S. Jaulin is a reliable topo guide to the area. It's on sale at local shops. *Buoux Kletterfuhrer* by M. Heinkel is a German-language guide.

Services and shops: All services are in Apt, with more limited and seasonal services in

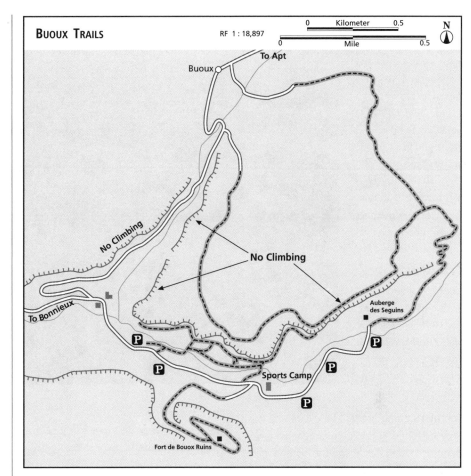

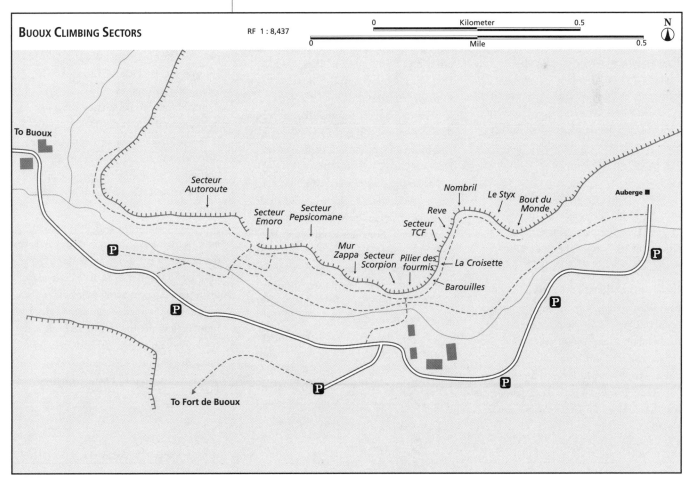

Bonnieux and Buoux. The nearest climbing shops are in Cavaillon, Avignon, and Aix-en-Provence. These include Intersport in Cavaillon, Sport et Montagne in Avignon, and Les Trois Mousquetons in Aix-en-Provence. A mobile boot resoler sometimes sets up shop in one of the Buoux parking lots on weekends.

Emergency services: In case of an accident, dial 18. Telephones are found in the village of Buoux and at the auberge just east of the cliffs at the road's end.

Nearby climbing areas: Many climbing areas are found in the mountains and valleys near Buoux. To the west is the pretty mountain chain called Les Alpilles. Numerous superb areas are found here, including Orgon and the nearby Falaise du Canal with many hard routes, technical face climbing at Mouriès, magnificent climbing and views at Saint-Rémy, and Fontvieille at the west end of the range.

North near Carpentras are excellent crags at Dentelles de Montmirail, Falaise d'Ubrieux, Rocher Saint Julien, and excellent steep climbing at St. Léger du Ventoux.

East of Apt are the Volx overhangs, a cave above the village of Volx in the Rhône Valley. Farther east is Verdon Gorge, one of Europe's best climbing areas.

Nearby attractions: Fort de Buoux; Apt; many classic villages, including Bonnieux, Saignon, Oppede-le-Vieux, Ménerbes (made famous in *A Year in Provence*), Lacoste, Gordes, and Roussillon; Pont Julien, a triple-arched Roman aqueduct; Village des Bories; Abbaye de Sénanque, a twelfth-century monastery; Avignon and all its attractions; Saint-Rémy-de-Provence; Les Baux-de-Provence; Tarascon Castle; and Glanum Roman ruins.

Finding the area: The closest international airport is at Marseille. The easiest way from here is to take the A51 north through Aix-en-Provence to exit 15. Head north on D556 to Pertuis, then west on D973 to Cadenet. Turn north onto D943 through Lourmarin to Apt.

From Avignon and the A7-Autoroute de Soleil from Lyon and Paris, take the Avignon Sud exit 24, and drive east on D22 and then N100 to Apt.

The Buoux crags are 10 kilometers south of Apt and 12 kilometers north of Lourmarin. Since Apt is your probable starting spot, directions to the cliffs are from downtown Apt. The roads are winding and narrow, and the signage is obscure. You might get lost, but not for long. A good local road map is helpful. Ask at the tourist office for one.

Follow the N100 to the east side of downtown Apt, and turn right at a large plaza and parking area where the local market is held. Follow the road south to a stop sign, and go right. Follow this street around the south side of the town center, and make a marked left turn onto the D113 road, which goes directly to Buoux. Drive uphill to the top of the plateau, cross the D232, and continue down to the village of Buoux. Wind through the village, and descend into the valley to an obvious left turn, which leads up the valley to the cliffs. Driving distance is 10 kilometers or 6 miles.

Park only in designated car parks. Do not park in the Fort de Buoux parking lot unless you are visiting it. Break-ins regularly occur at the parking areas, so leave nothing of value in your vehicle, open the glove box, and remove the lid over the trunk.

Trails lead to the cliff sectors from each of the parking areas. A path parallels the creek's north bank, and subsidiary paths head up to the cliff from this. From the main parking areas across from the school, walk down the road to the signed trailhead. Follow the trail down and across the creek, then up to the cliff base below the Pilier des fourmis. Hiking time to most sectors is from ten to twenty minutes.

Secteur Autoroute

The Secteur Autoroute is a fine cliff on the west side of the area. It is easily seen up high between the first and second parking areas. Many excellent routes ascend the vertical wall, with easier lines on the slabby right side.

Finding the cliff: The easiest approach is from the lowest parking area. Hike east alongside the creek past an old stone house. Continue to a huge log across the creek. Hike up the hillside on one of many climber paths before going up left through trees to the base of the wall. Hiking time is ten to fifteen minutes. Routes are described from left to right. Many routes not described here are left of #1.

1. Parties Carrees (7b+) (5.12c) This route goes up the middle of the cliff. Look for a hidden flake.

2. Unknown (7b+) (5.12c) Face climbing up the steep wall.

3. Docteur Jacques Hob (8a) (5.13b) 10 feet right of #2.

4. Voil de corbeau (7b+) (5.12c) Excellent and varied. 12 feet right of #3. Up a white streak to a break. Pockets to a large flake, then continues up a thin white streak to a roof. Pull over, and move up left to anchors.

5. Autoroute du soleil (7c) (5.12d) 20 feet right of #4. Stellar pocket route. Technical climbing with a high crux.

6. Valse aux adieux (7a+) (5.12a) 12 feet right of #5. Tricky slab moves. Begin directly below some bushes and trees. Climb into a scoop, then up left of trees over a bulge.

7. Belle de Cadix (7a+) (5.12a) 15 feet right of #6. Start below an arch. Climb over a bulge, then up right to a break to the upper headwall.

8. La mimi au champs (6b+) (5.10d) 15 feet right of #7. Start left of a detached flake/block. Climb the rib left of the flake. Clip out left, then up a corner to a bulge. Look for anchors at a horizontal break. 5 bolts to 2-bolt anchor.

Access the following routes via a short, steep, third-class ramp to an upper terrace.

9. Les gens d'ici (6c) (5.11b) Begin at the far left side of the terrace ledge. Climb a pocketed face for 25 feet to a horizontal break. Work up left then straight up to lowering chains below a long roof.

10. Le cœur en bandoulière (6c) (5.11b) Climb a short slab to a roof. Pull the roof and bulge, and finish up a slab to chain anchors.

11. L'amour à la plage (6a+) (5.10b) Start below the left side of a roof. Climb a short crack to the roof. Step left, and layback a left-facing corner to a final slab.

12. Noël au balcon (7a) (5.11d) Begin below the roof. Climb up and over the 4-foot roof. Continue up a black streak.

13. Nomades (5c) (5.9) Start at the far right side of the upper terrace. Climb past a small overlap on the right side of the wall. Make an obvious traverse left beneath some trees, and edge up a pocketed slab to the upper headwall.

Secteur Emoro

This short wall down right from Secteur Autoroute is deservedly popular with many moderate routes. Watch for polish on the easier lines.

Finding the cliff: Access is the same as for Secteur Autoroute. The easiest approach is from the lowest parking area. Hike east alongside the creek past an old stone house. Continue to a huge log across the creek. Hike up the hillside on one of many climber paths until you can make an obvious right turn on a cliff-base trail that quickly leads to Emoro.

14. Canaris de îles (5c) (5.9) The left-hand bolt route. Start off a ledge.

15. Unknown toprope

16. Chaton (5c) (5.9) Begin off the right side of the ledge. End at anchors.

17. L'émoro (6a) (5.10a) Very popular and so polished you can see reflections! Climb a steep face to a slab. Finish over blocky roofs.

18. L'oiseau bleu (6b) (5.10d) Start in trees. Steep face moves to a slab. End left of the upper roof. End at #17's anchors.

19. Sex pistol (6b+) (5.11a) Begin just left of a large flake-block at the base.

20. Meniskoté (6b) (5.10d) Route name is painted in big blue letters. Boulder 25

feet to the top of the flake. Edge up the slab to a roof above. End at #19's anchors.

21. Canabis (6a) (5.10a) Start off the flake in the trees. Climb a slab to tiered roofs. Anchors are above the roofs.

22. Les tontons macoutes (6c) (5.11b) The face just left of a left-facing dihedral. Finish at #21's anchors.

23. OK Carol (5c) (5.9) A bolted, left-facing dihedral.

24. Cyanolite (6c) (5.11b) Up the edge of a pillar right of a dihedral.

25. La No (6a) (5.10a) The obvious, bolted crack.

Secteur Mur Zappa

The Zappa Wall is a very good sector with lots of 5.10 routes. Most are popular and hence polished. This is not a spot to climb on a hot day. There is no topo to this cliff. Most of the route names are painted at the base.

Finding the cliff: Park at one of the upper parking lots. Follow the climber trail from the road, down and across the creek. Just past the creek, take the left fork, which goes up left through the thick forest. Follow this cliff-base trail about ten minutes to the base of the slabby gray wall. Routes are described from left to right.

26. Minouchette chérie (6a) (5.10a) Far left side of the sector.

27. Poupon la peste (6a) (5.10a) Same start as #26 then straight up.

28. PGF (6b) (5.10c)

29. Kadjet tropic (6a/b) (5.10b/c)

30. Ainsi parlait Zarathoustra *(Thus spake Zarathustra)* (6b) (5.10c) Traverse right up high, and finish up #32. The direct finish is 6b.

31. Couleur 3 (6b/c) (5.10c/d)

32. Bis (6b+) (5.10d)

33. Zappa maniac (6b/c) (5.10c/d) Finish up #32.

34. L'ombre d'in route (6b) (5.10c) Finish at anchors just left of a long roof and left-facing corner.

35. Bal des lazes (6a) (5.10a) Anchors under a prominent roof.

36. Schabada swing (6b/c) (5.10c/d) Anchors under a roof.

37. La quête de l'oiseau du temps (6b) (5.10c) Anchors just above the right side of the roof.

38. Paulo, si t'assures c'est pas dur! (6b) (5.10c) Up left at the top to #37's anchors.

39. Dardibule (6a/b) (5.10b/c) Start up #38 but go right to anchors just below trees.

40. Bas les masques (6b+) (5.10d) Directly up wall to anchors just right of #39's anchors.

41. Le bonté du forgeron (6b) (5.10c) End at #40's anchors.

42. Skud (6a+) (5.10b)

43. La marine (6a) (5.10a) Just left of a crack system.

44. Aptitude (6b) (5.10c) Face right of the crack. End at #43's anchors.

La Plage

Secteur Scorpion

The Scorpion Sector, left of the toe of the main buttress, yields a selection of good one-pitch moderate routes on its south-facing wall. All routes are bolted with lowering anchors. The names of many routes are painted at the base.

Finding the cliff: From the middle parking lot, follow the climber trail from the road, down and across the creek on a log bridge. Just past the creek, take the left fork, which goes up left through thick forest to the base of the wall.

Routes are described from left to right beginning at a large pillar/block with a couple routes left of a deep chimney.

45. Crank Frank (7b) (5.12b) Short stiff problem up the overhanging outside of the pillar.

46. Comme Papa (4b) (5.5) A kid's route! Easy pocket line up the right corner of the block.

47. La montée aux enfrers (6b+) (5.10d) Up left on a ramp, then over bulges to anchors below a big ledge.

48. Scorpion (6a) (5.10a) 2 pitches. Classic but polished and stiff for the grade. Usually only the first pitch is climbed.
Pitch 1: Polished crux down low. Pull huecos and edges right and then up left to a final corner and anchors on a ledge.
Pitch 2: Up right on white stone, then straight up to anchors below a small roof.

49. Deverdur (7a) (5.11d) Slab to bulges.

50. La nuit des morts de rire (8a) (5.13b) Thin face moves to a crack under a bulge.

51. Des verts pépères (6c) (5.11a/b) "The Green Peppers." Climb past a horizontal row of square holes once used for anchoring roof beams in an ancient fort. Above, work through a pumpy bulge.

52. Kamikazé (6c+) (5.11c) Begin up a thin crack then over the right side of a bulge.

53. Imitation granit (5c/6a) (5.9+/10a) Stem up a wide crack that doglegs right.

54. Bourreau d'enfants (6b) (5.10c) Climb the prow of a blunt buttress.

55. Le rut (6a) (5.10a) Follow a prominent crack system.

56. L'Anamour (7a) (5.11d) Climb onto a platform atop a slab, then up a technical face.

57. J'ai du vague à l'âme (6b/c) (5.10c/d) Edge up a slab with 2 bolts. Climb a steep prow left of a crack.

58. Gourgousse (7a/b) (5.12a/b) Excellent 3-pitch route to the top of the cliff. **Pitch 1:** A long lead. Climb the 2-bolt slab on #57 and then directly up the crack above to anchors, where it slabs off right of La Plage ledge (6a) (5.10a). **Pitch 2:** Superb face climbing up the steep wall just left of the pillar to a bolted belay stance (6b) (5.10c). **Pitch 3:** Wing up the steep, bulging wall above to anchors at the cliff top (7a/b) (5.12a/b). **Descent:** Rappel the face with double ropes, or walk along the cliff top to the Styx Wall and make a single rappel from chain anchors or a tree to the base of the wall.

59. Le roi de la jungle (*King of the Jungle*) (6b) (5.10c) Again start up the 2-bolt slab. Swing right above, and climb the face right of a crack.

Pilier des fourmis

The Pilier des fourmis is the central section and the tallest part of the Falaise de l'Aiguebrun. Some excellent routes ascend this magnificent wall, including *Gourgousse* (route #58 described above) and the mega-classic *Pilier des fourmis* up the central pillar. This classic route, first climbed with aid in 1968 and later free climbed by an unknown party, offers three pitches of increasing difficulty, lots of exposure on the upper headwall, and sustained and interesting climbing from bottom to summit. One of the good things is that you don't have to pull 7a (5.11d) to climb the route since you can French-free the 30-foot crux by pulling on a few strategically placed bolts, lowering the overall difficulty to 5.10d.

Finding the cliff: From the footbridge across the creek, hike directly up the right trail, which leads to the base of the pillar and the Secteur Barouilles. The route starts about 100 feet right of the pillar base below an obvious open corner. The route name is painted in red at the base.

60. Pilier des fourmis (7a or 6b+ A0) (5.11d or 5.10d A0) 3 pitches. **Pitch 1:** Climb the obvious corner (6a), and pass a small cave feature to a stance by a tree with bolted anchors (possible belay). Continue up left onto easier, lower-angle rock to a bolted belay on the left side of a spacious man-made terrace below a couple big flat roofs. This pitch is a full 165 feet. **Pitch 2:** Climb the wall immediately left and above the ledge/cave. Work up right over some small overlaps and then up right along an easier but exposed ramp to an airy bolted belay at a roof (6b) (5.10c). Keep along the right edge of the buttress on this pitch. Don't be misled by other bolts that go up left. **Pitch 3:** Move right from the belay, and work up to a narrow shelf on the prow of the buttress. Step left to a big edge, and then swing up the steep, gymnastic crux above to a scoop (7a) (5.11d) or aid it by grabbing slings (A0). Keep an eye out for hidden pockets at the crux. Continue right up a very exposed groove to easier rock and the summit. **Descent:** Rappel the face or walk along the cliff top to the top of Styx Wall. Make a single 100-foot rope rappel to the cliff base from chained anchors or a tree. Be careful not to knock any rock or debris off since people are usually at the base.

La Plage

Secteur Scorpion

Secteur Barouilles

60

Secteur Barouilles

This popular sector, lying right of the obvious main buttress that divides the wall, offers lots of good routes up pocketed faces and crack systems. This is a good sector when it's warm because the routes are in the shade from trees in the morning and in the shade all afternoon. Most route names are painted at the base, making route finding a snap.

Finding the cliff: Follow the trail from the road across the creek, but keep right at an obvious junction and go uphill a short distance to the base of the face. Routes are described from left to right.

61. Sourire Hawai (6b/c) (5.10d/11a) Up and left along a slab to an edge to anchors below some trees.

62. Unknown (6a) (5.10a) Up the corner and crack right of #61 to the same anchors.

63. Backstage (6b+) (5.10d) Steep face climbing to anchors by a bush.

64. Tora-Torapas (6b+) (5.10d) Up a blunt prow to thin face moves. Pass a roof and then up right to anchors on a stance.

65. Pilier des fourmis (6a) (5.10a) Also route #60 above. 3 pitches, or just do Pitch 1. Locate an obvious corner with the name painted in red at the base. Climb the corner to a bolted belay by a tree, or if you're doing the whole route, continue to a bolted belay in a cave above.

66. Vaugreray's Sisters (6c+) (5.11c) Start 5 feet right of the corner. Climb over pocketed overhangs.

67. Comme un loup blessé (6c+) (5.11c) A black and tan face above square post-holes chiseled in the rock.

68. Joe Klaxon (6a+) (5.10b) Begin up a right-angling corner system. When the corner straightens at bolt 3, work up left into another crack system.

69. Bonne nouvelle des étoiles (6a or 6c) (5.10a or 5.11a) Start by its name on the rock. Climb a steep slab, cross a corner, and go over a bulge on the right.

70. Barouilles (6a+) (5.10b) Climb a face up left into a dihedral. Keep left where the cracks divide.

71. Vice et verseau (6a) (5.10a) Move directly up a crack system and face, and join #69.

72. Tendance actuelle (6b) (5.10c) Face right of crack system.

73. Décadanse (5c) (5.9) 2 pitches. Fun climbing. Begin right of a corner system. Pitch 2 (#82) starts from anchors on a ledge.

74. Surfin' Rock (5b) (5.8) 2 pitches. **Pitch 1:** Climb a slab to a 3-bolt belay on a long narrow ledge. **Pitch 2:** (#81) Pull over a small roof to face climb to lowering anchors.

Secteur la Croisette

This sector offers a selection of good, popular routes above a long narrow ledge system. This area is good in the afternoon and evening on warm days since it is in full shade. More routes are on the wall above the finishing anchors for these routes. Some can be combined with the lower pitches into long leads. Most are in the 5.10 and 5.11 range.

Finding the cliff: Reach these next routes by continuing uphill on the cliff-base trail to a point where you can traverse left on a narrow ledge to belay anchors. These routes are described from right to left on the ledge.

75. Colonel six b (6b) (5.10c) No topo. Up the right side of a bulge and left of a broken crack to 2-bolt quick-clip anchor at a break.

76. Mega Top (7a+) (5.12a) Start just left of *Colonel six b*. Pockets over a steep bulge to a 2-bolt, quick-clip anchor at a break.

77. S'il te plaît, dessine-moi un mutant (6c) (5.11a/b) Scramble left on the ledge to belay anchors. Climb the left side of a big bulge to anchors.

78. Homo Grimpus Luberonus (6b+) (5.10d) Start off the ledge. Work over bulge left of *S'il te plaît* to anchors.

79. Prises Electriques (5b/c) (5.9) Over a bulge above the right side of the ledge, then face climbing to anchors.

80. Le Vieux qui lisat des romans d'amour (6a) (5.10a) Start from a belay bolt on the ledge left of *Prises Electriques,* and face climb to anchors.

81. Surfin' Rock (5b) (5.8) The second pitch of #74. Face climb from ledge anchors, up and right into scoop to anchors at break above.

82. Décadanse (5c) (5.9) The second pitch of #73. Face climb up left to anchors.

83. Soliel et nuit (5c) (5.9) The face just right of a big roof system.

Secteur TCF

The TCF sector is one of the crag's best cliffs, with superb pocket routes on excellent stone. All the routes are worth doing.

Finding the cliff: Cross the stream, and follow the right-hand trail up along the cliff base until you reach the sector, an obvious beautiful pocketed wall to your left. Begin all the routes from a wide flat ledge at the base of the face. Routes are described from left to right.

84. Fin de siecle (7a) (5.11d) Start from the far left side of the ledge below the wall. Route ascends a white streak.

85. Requiem (7c) (5.12d) Start up a white streak to a prominent hole, then tricky moves above to a ramp.

86. J'irai cracher sur vos tombes (7c+) (5.13a) Pull pockets up and right before veering left above bolt 4.

87. La cage aux orchidees (7b) (5.12b) Excellent. Climb pockets up a shallow groove, then up right.

88. Un zeste d'inceste (7b+) (5.12c) Thin, technical pockets up the steep wall. Begin with a bulge to twin pockets. Thin moves work up to better holds to a rest. Finish up a yellowish streak.

89. Dresden (7a) (5.11d) Superb climbing. Begin at the left side of the left-hand cave. Pockets over a bulge to a steep slab finish.

90. TCF (Turbo Cibi Facho) (7a) (5.11d) Popular and classic—one of the best routes at Buoux. Start at the right side of the small cave. Grab pockets up the gray wall.

91. Papa pas pou (6c) (5.11a/b) Start just left of the right-hand cave. Pockets over bulges.

92. Le zoo des robots (6c) (5.11a/b) Begin at the right side of the cave. Pull crux moves out the cave, then edge up the headwall above.

93. Alambic, sortie sud (6b) (5.10c) The easiest route here. A slab right of the cave to an interesting upper headwall.

Secteurs Reve and Nombril

Secteur Reve is a prominent bulging buttress with *Rêve de Papillon,* one of the area's best hard routes. Many other routes are found on the buttress and on the wall to the left. Consult the comprehensive guide for topos and grades.

Finding the cliff: From Secteur TCF, continue uphill to the base of the obvious pillar at Reve and Nombril's steep slab. Hiking time is about fifteen minutes from the parking area.

94. Rêve de Papillon *(Dream of the Butterfly)* (8a) (5.13b) Superb and excellent. One of Buoux's most popular 5.13s. Begin by scrambling up 3rd-class rock to a ledge below the route. Climb the left side of a corner and make "the Crawl," a difficult traverse left. Technical pocket pulling continues to a big hueco. Finish up a tricky, runout slab to anchors.

Secteur Nombril is the steep slab and hanging pillar right of *Rêve de Papillon's* buttress. Use a 200-foot (60-meter) rope for climbing and lowering off all the routes. Routes are described from left to right.

95. Tupinambis (6a) (5.10a) Follow bolts up the right wall of a huge right-facing dihedral.

96. La mouche à bière (6c+) (5.11c) Start from the angling corner below the left side of the wall. Climb the face right of the corner.

97. Le nombril de Vénus (6c) (5.11a/b) Excellent steep slab line. Start in the angling corner. Climb up and right, and then wander up the wall center to a dicey finish. The direct start is 6c+.

98. Bienvenue sur Aflolol (6b+) (5.10d) Steep slab climb left of the left-facing dihedral.

99. L'aspic (6a) (5.10a) Climb the face just left of the big dihedral.

100. Regards et sourires (7b+) (5.12c) Crimps and pockets up the left side of the hanging pillar.

101. Rose de sables (7a) (5.11d) Classic and highly recommended for its moves and position. Follow bolts up the narrow rib in the center of the pillar to the upper face. End with a roof problem.

102. Courage, fuyons (7a) (5.11d) Same start as *Rose de sables.* At the first bolt, diverge right onto the right-facing side of the pillar. Climb the steep, pumpy face to anchors atop the pillar.

Le Styx

Le Styx is the high, flat wall right of the *Rose de sables's* pillar. The wall overhangs on the left, is vertical in its midsection, and slabs off on its right side. Most of the routes are excellent and recommended. Use a 200-foot (60-meter) rope for climbing and lowering off all routes. Most of the route names are painted at the base.

Finding the cliff: Hike up to Secteur TCF. Continue uphill and then right to the base of the long, obvious slabby wall of Le Styx. Routes are described from left to right.

103. Mélodie Gaël (6b) (5.10c) Excellent. Begin right of a broken corner on the far left side of the wall.

104. Désidia (6b/c) (5.10d/11a)

105. Andéavor (6b) (5.10c)

106. Récréactivité (6b) (5.10c) Start at the right side of a low, narrow roof.

107. Buffet froid (*Cold Buffet*) (6b/c) (5.11a) Lynn Hill almost died on this route after free-falling from the anchors and landing in the trees at the base. She forgot to finish her tie-in knot before climbing the route, so when she lowered, the rope slipped through the harness.

108. Ultime violence (6c+) (5.11c)

109. Antidote (6c+) (5.11c) No topo.

110. Rhinoféroce (7a) (5.11d)

111. Vieux campeur (6c) (5.11a/b)

112. Ravi au lite (7c+) (5.13a) Shortest and hardest route on the wall. Thin moves up a white streak. Ends below a narrow roof.

113. Le hasard fait bien les choses (7b) (5.12b) Perfect pockets.

114. Plus de trois fois, c'est jouer avec (6c/7a) (5.11c/d)

115. Scaravangeur (7a) (5.11d)

116. Cupule radiale (7a+) (5.12a)

117. La dame aux camélias (6c) (5.11a/b) Begin right of a short, shallow, arching corner.

118. Handisport (7c) (5.11d) Bulge start.

119. Kilo de frites physique (6c+) (5.11c) Begin right of the steep wall.

120. Proxima nox (6c) (5.11a/b) On the slabby right side.

121. Voyage de l'incrédule (6b) (5.10c) An incredible slab-climbing voyage. Up the slab left of the gully with trees that mark the right side of the wall.

Bout du Monde

This sector, the farthest east part of the cliff open to climbing, offers a selection of excellent hard routes. Some have chipped and drilled pockets. The flat ledge below the wall is reputedly an early human habitation site. The views of the valley from here are quite spectacular—a good place to climb and hang out.

Finding the cliff: Hike up to Le Styx and continue east along the wall, passing by some fallen blocks, to the exposed ledge below the wall.

122. Tabou (8a+) (5.13c) Route climbs to anchors at a hole on the left side of a roof. The whole route from base to the top of the cliff is *Tabou zizi* (8b) (5.13d).

123. La Rose et le Vampire (8b) (5.13d) Excellent. One of the first 8bs in the world. Established by Antoine Le Ménestrel. Power pocket pulling up the overhanging wall to anchors under the roof.

124. La Voie (8b+) (5.14a) A long pitch. Crank over the cave roof, then work up the long overhanging wall above to anchors.

125. Chouca (8a+) (5.13c) Megaclassic desperate route and one of Europe's most famous routes. Up the right side of the white streak above the cave.

126. Le Minimum (8b+) (5.14a) Pockets and crimps up the wall above the right side of the cave.

127. Hiérogriffe (7b/c) (5.12c/d) Up the wall right of the cave.

CÉUSE

■ OVERVIEW

The Falaise de Céüse, perhaps the world's finest sport-climbing crag, is a long, immaculate limestone cliff that rims the southern edge of Montagne de Céüse in the Haute-Alpes region of southeastern France. This 2-mile-long cliff band, ranging from 200 to 500 feet high, simply offers some of the best pure rock climbing on the planet.

Climbing at Céüse is what rock climbing is all about. The cliff, reached by an hour-long uphill trudge, engages you with its sheer beauty, atmospheric views, and brilliant climbing. At 6,500 feet, the Céüse cliff yields stunning views of the surrounding landscape. Below its limestone aerie stretch forested slopes that plunge steeply to rolling, green farmland interrupted by pockets of trees and houses. The rugged skyscraping peaks of the Haute-Alpes punctuate the horizon

beyond. Céüse, lying at the interface between the Mediterranean and Haute-Alpes environments, lies at timberline in the alpine zone.

It's the impeccable stone that makes Céüse such a perfect climbing arena. The 140-million-year-old Jurassic limestone, burnished and streaked by a palette of steel gray, cobalt blue, and rich gold, is gritty and rough, but its holds, edges, and pockets are finger friendly and often smooth to the touch. The athletic movements on the cliff's overhanging walls are usually long reaches between perfect pockets and huecos interrupted by occasional kneebar rests. Between the steep walls rise vertical faces and tilted slabs that offer sustained, technical routes filled with crimps, mono-doigt pockets, and bouldery sequences.

Most climbers who hear the name Céüse think 5.13 and harder climbs. They think of Chris Sharma's route *Realization,* one of the world's hardest routes at the atmospheric 5.15a grade. Okay, it's true

that Céüse owns perhaps the best selection of 5.13 routes in the world, but it's just not true that the climbing begins at that lofty grade. The cliff offers more than 200 routes that range in difficulty from 5.8 to 5.15a, with the majority of climbs belonging in the popular 5.10a to 5.12a category.

Céüse, like most French crags, is divided into various sectors. The climbing varies dramatically between the fourteen different sectors. The popular Secteur de la Cascade offers long, arm-blasting, endurance routes up pockets and holes on steeply overhanging stone. Recommended routes here include the megaclassics *Ténéré, Mirage, Privilège du Serpent,* and *Super Mickey.* The Secteur Berlin yields edging masterpieces that require stamina and technique on vertical to slightly overhanging rock. The Secteur Demi Lune yields an array of delightful face climbs that utilize the maze of pockets that punctuate its vertical face. Farther right is La Grande Face, not described here, with gorgeous Verdon-quality rock and routes

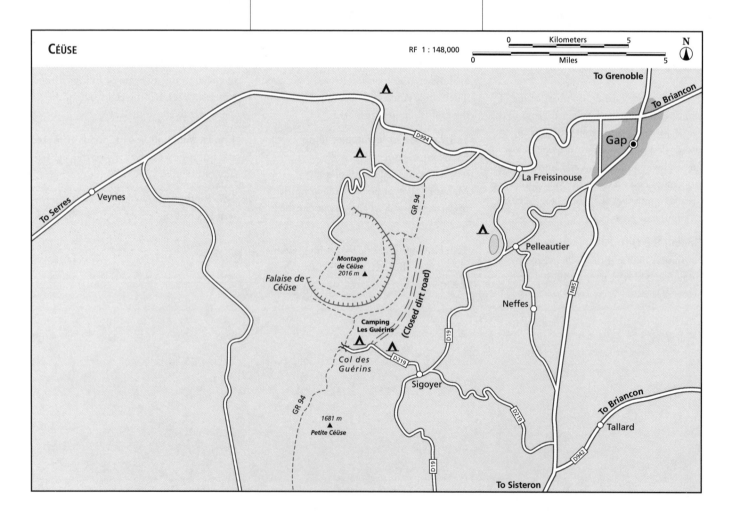

up to five pitches long. Two other excellent sectors not described in this guide are Golots à Gogo and Dalles du capeps on the far left side of the wall. Here you'll find some superlative moderate routes up amazing water channels and sustained slabs, as well as fewer crowds than at the more popular sectors.

Rack, Protection, and Descent

Céüse is a sport-climbing area with all the routes protected by bolts. Double-bolt lowering anchors, many equipped with quick-clip steel carabiners, are on all the routes. Bring a rack of twelve to twenty quickdraws, depending on whether you're going to leave draws hanging on any projects, and a 200-foot (60-meter) rope. Keep in mind that hanging quickdraws can be stolen, since some European climbers, particularly those from poorer eastern Europe, see any left gear as booty.

Céüse boasts a reputation for long runouts between bolts, especially on the older and the more difficult routes, turning a lot of redpoints into serious adventures in excitement and courage. Retrobolting, however, has taken the sting out of many serious climbs. Still, be prepared to take some major wingers on routes at your limit. All the big falls are into open air with no chance of hitting anything on the way down.

If you spend much time at the cliff, walking up on successive days, then you need to find a safe spot to stash your rope and draws so you don't have to lug them up and down the steep hill. The usual cache is under the Face de rat sector, which is also a popular bivouac spot.

Descent off all routes is by lowering from anchors on the one-pitch routes or rappelling from bolt anchors on the multi-pitch lines.

Climbing History

Serious climbing started at Céüse in the 1980s, although the first routes on the Falaise de Céüse were climbed in the mid-1970s. By the mid-1980s the area was a French hot spot and the private reserve

Anja Sparenberg on the vertical route *La magicienne trahie* (6a+) (5.10b).

of elite climbers, including Patrick Edlinger, who pioneered many of the area classics, and Jean-Christophe Lafaille. Back then the French climbing magazine *Vertical* called it the "Cliff of the Year 2000" for its astounding future potential and described the perfect limestone as a "pure marvel." The *Vertical* guide accompanying the article included Edlinger's comments on his routes, including "Sorry for the runout; the nervous should

abstain!" and "Above all, remain calm." With that the myth of Céüse began.

Through the 1990s Céüse lived up to the hype and became the crag of the future. When I first visited in 1994, we walked under the Secteur Biographie the day after Arnaud Petit had strung new Petzl logo quickdraws up a line of bolts on the overhanging project *Biographie*. The 8c+ (5.14c) route was free climbed by Petit in 1996, and the upper wall above

Biographie was bolted and became the *Biographie Extension* project. This futuristic problem, following a fat, blue streak, stretched another 65 feet above *Biographie's* anchors.

In 1997 Chris Sharma came and dispatched the first section in three days, then returned several more times over the ensuing years to work on the upper face. In 1997 alone Sharma spent almost a month working the route, falling from the high crux more than thirty times. Finally in July 2001 Sharma, who in *Climbing Magazine* called the route "the most beautiful and inspiring line I've ever seen," sent the route and dubbed it *Realization*. Sharma later said, "This route really confronted me with all my strengths and weaknesses. At a certain point I realized that the route was within me, that I had the strength and the control of my movements, and that I had to work on a much deeper level, on and within me."

Realization, one of the world's first routes graded 5.15a or 9b, is stacked with cruxes, beginning with the first 70 feet, which is rated 5.14c. Above, the route continues with sustained 5.13 climbing and no rests to a V10 boulder problem, then more sustained climbing to anchors. The route boasts more than sixty moves from ground to anchors. At press time it is unrepeated, but not for lack of suitors. The lower *Biographie* route was climbed by Americans Vadim Vinokur (fourth ascent) and Dave Graham (fifth ascent) in quick succession in July 2001. Near *Realization* is *No Futur,* another future project that will undoubtedly be one of the world's great endurance routes as it ascends more than 200 feet from base to cliff top.

Getting Around

It's best to have your own car to get around the Céüse area. With your personal wheels you can easily cruise into Gap for groceries, *biere,* and other essential supplies, or take in a disco at night. You can also check out nearby climbing areas and visitor attractions in easy day trips.

If you don't want or can't afford a car, then a small bus runs from Gap to Sigoyer. You can get a timetable at the Gap tourist office near the bus station.

The nearest international airport is at Marseille on the southern coast. You can also fly to Paris. From either place it's easy to catch a train. From Paris you'll want to go to Grenoble, and then take the Marseille train. From the train station catch the bus to Sigoyer. It is time-consuming to hitchhike. But once you're at the campsite, everything you need is within walking distance, or you can always bum a ride to town from other climbers. If you're spending much time here, then you're probably better off not having the car expense.

Seasons and Weather

Céüse is one of the best summer crags in southern France. While most Provence cliffs like Buoux and Verdon bake under the summer sun, Céüse, with its relatively lofty elevation of 6,500 feet, is cool, and shade is easy to find on hot days. It can, however, get hot here, with temperatures soaring into the 90s. Quick thunderstorms that rumble through in the afternoon are the only threat. So pack a raincoat on even the most benign days.

The usual climbing season is May through November. Spring and autumn are Céüse's prime climbing seasons with generally warm, dry days, although fog often develops in the lowlands and slowly rises to engulf the cliff. Although climbing does happen in winter, the crag is usually snowbound. The cliff seeps and is often wet from melting snow during spring.

Camping, Accommodations, and Services

Most climbers stay at the Les Guérins campground owned by Gerard, a farmer who also owns Bar de Guérins in the apartment building farther up the road. The rustic campsites are in a former field, now overgrown with grass and shaded by young trees. The campground has a toilet and shower block, some refrigerators to chill your food, a ping-pong table, a small bouldering wall, washing machine, and rental trailers with propane stoves, electric-

ity, and dishes for long-term visitors. Gerard also sells chalk, guidebooks, some groceries, and fresh bread in the morning. Prices are very reasonable.

You can hike to the cliff directly from the campground, which keeps your car safe from possible trailhead break-ins. The trail starts next to the barn and contours uphill to the west until it joins the regular trail from the parking lot. Lots of climbers from all over Europe as well as America stay here, so it's easy to meet climbers and find partners. You'll find more American climbers here than at any other southern France area. Another campground, Pre des Roses, is just down the road from Les Guérins.

If you don't haul camping gear over to France or just want a bit more luxury and warmth than the campground, a good alternative is La Grange aux Loups. This comfortable *gîte* is like a hostel, renting both dorm and private rooms. This is where Chris Sharma stayed while working on *Realization*. The hosts are excellent cooks and prepare exquisite evening meals. Other accommodations include Hôtel Muret in Sigoyer as well as other nearby *gîtes*.

The closest amenities are in Sigoyer, a couple kilometers down the road from the campground. Here you'll find an excellent bakery (*boulangerie*), a small grocery store, a cafe, and Hôtel Muret. For a major grocery outing, you need to go to Gap. One of the best stores is the Hyper U *supermarché,* with a big selection of fresh fruits and vegetables and cheeses, as well as everything else you need to make a week's worth of ratatouille. It also has a cafeteria for inexpensive meals or a coffee. It's usually open twelve hours a day, except for a few hours on Sundays. Lots of restaurants and cafes are also found in Gap, from gourmet haute cuisine to pizzerias and McDonald's.

Cultural Experiences and Rest Days

If you stay here for more than a few days, your arms and ego will have to take some rest days. The Gap area in the Haute-Alpes offers lots of outdoor activities as well as a smattering of cultural opportunities.

The Céüse massif is laced with trails for both hiking and mountain biking. Bikes can be rented at the campground as well as at Gap. A good hike ascends to the summit of Petit Céüse to the south. Walk up the road from the campground until you reach a road that goes left through the ski area and on to the summit. Bouldering is found along the trail. Another fun outing is climbing the *via ferrata* or iron ladders up the cliff right of the Demi Lune sector to the rolling grassy summit of Montagne de Céüse.

With a car you can explore all the narrow back roads below the *corniche*, as well as make day trips to Gap, Tallard, Sisteron, and Serres.

Gap, a scant 15 kilometers to the northwest, is a relatively large town with lots of shops and services. It's not a particularly old or quaint place, but it's fun to explore around and see what you discover. Lots of cafes with umbrella-shaded tables invite you to stop and sip a coffee or iced latte. Tallard to the south has a lovely castle overlooking the upper Durance valley.

Sisteron, a strategically located medieval town, lies along the Route Napoléon, the path taken by the emperor and a small following in March 1815. The fortified Citadel, built in the sixteenth century during the Wars of Religion, looms over the town at a rocky gap where the Durance and Buëch Rivers meet. Also be sure to stop in the Cathédrale Notre-Dame-des-Pommiers and view its seventeenth-century artworks and explore the skinny alleys of Old Sisteron. At Place de l'Horloge on Wednesdays and Saturdays is the local market, with stalls of fresh vegetables and fruits, lavender honey and oil, tasty nougat, regional cheeses, cages of pigeons and chickens, and occasional sheep. Across the river on the south and west flank of the Montagne de la Baume rises a dramatic uplift of gleaming limestone cliffs. Many excellent routes ascend the huge cliffs. A topo is available in town.

Serres, southwest of Céüse, is a lovely village perched on a rock-strewn hillside above the Buëch River. Ramble around

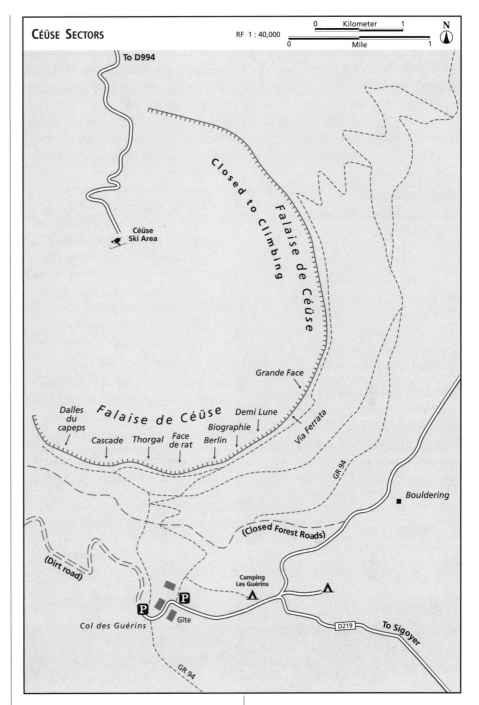

CÉÜSE SECTORS

RF 1 : 40,000

the village's narrow streets, some with arched passages, to peek at the fifteenth- and sixteenth-century houses.

Trip Planning Information

General description: Excellent climbing on the Falaise de Céüse, a 2-mile-long, south-facing, limestone escarpment that is one of the world's best climbing cliffs.

Location: Southeastern France in the Haute-Alpes region. The cliff is 10 miles

(16 kilometers) southwest of Gap and 20 miles (30 kilometers) north of Sisteron. It is 65 miles (105 kilometers) south of Grenoble and 120 miles (200 kilometers) north of Marseille.

Camping and accommodations: Most climbers stay at Les Guérins campground (Tel: 04 92 57 90 04 or 04 92 57 83 91) along the road to the crag parking. Prices are reasonable. The campground has showers, toilets, and running water. The campground Pre des Roses is down the road

(Tel: 04 92 57 81 66). Up the road is La Grange aux Loups, a comfortable *gîte* with either dorm or private rooms. The hosts, who speak some English, also provide excellent meals. If you're coming in summer, definitely make advance reservations (Tel: 04 92 57 95 30). Other accommodations include the Hôtel Muret (Tel: 04 92 57 83 02) in Sigoyer and Gîte Rural (Tel: 04 92 57 83 91).

Climbing season: April through November. Summer offers the best weather since the cliff is fairly high, but temperatures in the sun can reach 100 degrees (although that is a rarity). Much of the cliff is shaded on summer afternoons. May and June as well as September and October are prime climbing seasons. Some routes in May will be wet from melting snow above the cliff. The winter months are cold and snowy.

Restrictions and access issues: The cliff lies within La forêt domaniale de Céüse, a protected national forest of 1,900 hectares. The forest is rich in its variety of trees and vegetation because it's a meeting place of both the Mediterranean and alpine ecosys-

tems. The biggest danger is fire; building fires is strictly prohibited. Climbing is not allowed on the entire cliff, but only on the designated section between Secteur Golots à Gogo on the southwest and Secteur Natilik on the northeast, a cliff section about half its total length. Stay on the designated access paths to the cliffs to avoid creating new social trails, and pick up any trash along the cliff base.

A big problem here, like at many French crags, is toilet tissue and human excrement. There are no toilets near the crags, so most people use the shelter of the nearest boulder on the slopes below the cliffs as the outhouse. It stinks on summer days and the tissue flowers are unsightly and untidy. Don't contribute to the problem—use proper outdoor hygiene. Dig a cathole and bury crap, and tote your toilet paper out in a plastic baggie.

Guidebooks: The comprehensive area guide *Grimper dans les Hautes Alpes* covers Céüse and nearby areas. It's available in Sigoyer and the campground.

Services and shops: Basic provisions, including wine and bread, are available

from Gerard at the campground. The nearby village of Sigoyer has a few bars, a bakery, and a store. For large grocery stores, restaurants, theaters, discos, and everything else, go to Gap. Vertige (Tel: 04 92 51 91 78) is a climbing shop in Gap; Vertige Sport is in Orpierre.

Emergency services: Call 18 for rescue and 112 for emergency services. The nearest medical facilities are in Gap.

Nearby climbing areas: If you tire of Céüse and want a break, then lots of other crags are nearby. The area guide has topos to many of them. Northeast of the campground is a good bouldering area along the forest access road.

North of Céüse and highway D994 is La Roche-des-Arnauds, a good area with almost forty mostly moderate routes. Northwest of Pont-du-Fossé and above D994 are two crags, Les Dauphins and Corbières.

North of Céüse near highway D937 are several sport crags as well as some long mountain routes on the big faces. Near Saint-Etienne-en-Dévoluy is Falaises des Etroits with almost fifty sport routes. The

Southeast Pillar of 8,900-foot (2,709-meter) Pic de Bure is ascended by a classic twenty-three-pitch route (6a+ A0 or 6c). Farther north above the village Saint-Disdier are some big rock routes on Le Piéroux, Grande Roche, and Les Gillardes. Les Gillardes offers nine mostly bolt-protected routes up to fifteen pitches long on excellent rock. Topos for all the routes are in the Hautes-Alpes guide.

South of Céüse is the excellent Falaise de Ventavon, a long sport cliff above the villages Le Villard and Ventavon. To the southwest is the excellent midgrade area at Orpierre, and to the south are the great cliffs at Sisteron. The big overhanging cave at Volx is farther south above its namesake village.

Nearby attractions: Lots of places to see. Gap, a modern town, is good to walk around in and window-shop, drink coffee in an outdoor cafe, or visit a disco. To the south is Tallard, with a castle overlooking the Durance Valley. Farther south is the ancient town of Sisteron, with its cathedral and citadel. The mountain country around the area is well worth exploring by car. Get a good map, and drive lots of the back roads. You'll discover some interesting little villages and other points of interest.

Finding the cliffs: From Gap drive west on road D994 in the direction of Veynes and Valence. At La Freissinouse look for the sign for Sigoyer, and drive south 6 miles (10 kilometers) on the D19 to Sigoyer. Drive through the village, and on its south side, turn right (west) onto D219. Drive a couple kilometers to the 4,300-foot-high (1,312-meter) Col des Guérins. Park at a lot just north of the pass summit or on the right before a hut.

From Lyon take the highway southeast to Grenoble, then road N85 south to Gap. From Marseille and Aix-en-Provence, take highway A51 northeast to Sisteron, then road N85 north to Gap.

From the road two well-marked trails head north to the cliff base. One trail begins at a parking area on the right side of the col at the end of the paved road. It goes directly and steeply uphill to the cliff.

The preferred and easier trail follows a more gentle grade uphill from its beginning at the curve below the bar. Park at a lot on the north side of the road and southeast of a nursing home. The trail switchbacks uphill through pleasant woods to a forest road halfway up. Continue above this first road until you reach a horizontal path that runs parallel to the cliff about 500 feet below the cliff base. Go left on this trail to the Cascade sector. Look for a short path on the right that scrambles over boulders to the base of the sector. Or go right on the horizontal trail a short distance to a path that switchbacks up steep grassy slopes to the Berlin and Demi Lune sectors. The approach hike takes forty-five minutes to an hour.

If you stay at Les Guerins campground, you can reach the main trail by following a path that begins at the campsite barn. Contour west uphill to the regular access trail. Or walk up the road about a kilometer to the lower parking area by the nursing home. Doing either alleviates leaving your vehicle at the trailhead and worrying about a possible break-in.

Secteur de la Cascade

Cascade, on the southwest side of the cliff, is the first sector you get to after hiking up the trail. This beautiful overhanging wall is stacked with mind- and arm-blowing routes—some of the best in Europe! The sector is named for a waterfall that pours off the left side of the sector after rain or in the spring and early summer. The climbing is on steep, overhanging rock colored purple and gold. Lots of big holds abound. Cruxes are usually hard moves on small holds between jugs. Almost all the described routes are worth climbing. Routes are described from left to right.

1. Ténéré (7c+) (5.13a) Excellent and recommended. Good holds and long reaches.

2. Mirage (7c+) (5.13a) First ascent by J. C. Lafaille. Excellent continuous climbing on perfect rock. The runout, pumpy crux is at the very top of the route below the anchor. Plan on taking a 40-foot plunge unless you're strong and solid at the grade.

3. Vagabond d'occident (7c) (5.12d) Another 3-star route.

4. Blue blanc giorapare (7c+) (5.13a)

5. Blanches fesses (7c) (5.12d) Great climb. A jug haul with one crimp move.

6. Correspondance imaginaire (7c+) (5.13a) Recommended.

7. Corps étranger (7c) (5.12d)

8. Rosanna (8a) (5.13b) No topo. Look for bouldery sequences between steep climbing.

9. Question d'équilibre *(Question of balance)* (8b) No topo. Monos and tweaks.

10. Pieds nus sous les rodhodendrons (7c+) (5.13a) No topo.

11. Le privilège du serpent (7c+) (5.13a) Another contender for best route at the crag. Classic and impressive climbing. Big jugs with the crux at the top.

12. Super Mickey (7b) (5.12b) Super good and super popular with one of the best collections of buckets in Europe! A jug haul with the crux at the end. 100 feet. *Hyper Mickey* (7c) (5.12d) is a direct start to *Super Mickey*.

13. Kéket blues (7b) (5.12b)

14. Kéket direct (7c+) (5.13a)

15. L'atome de savoie (8a) (5.13b)

16. Ananda (7a) (5.11d) Classic and a good warm-up for the hard ones.

17. Médecine douce (6c+) (5.11c) Classic for its grade.

18. Women (7a+) (5.12a)

19. Fletcher Line (7b+) (5.12c) No topo.

20. Les Sales blagues à Nanarad (6c) (5.11a/b)

21. Des trous encore des trous direct (6b) (5.10c) Superb climbing on perfect rock. On the far right, uphill side of the sector.

22. Des trous encore des trous (5b) (5.8) No topo. Avoid the hard part of #21 by beginning just to the right. Climb up easier rock, then work up left above the crux of #21 to the same anchors.

Secteur Thorgal

Secteur Thorgal is the next cliff section uphill from Secteur Cascade. It begins right of a groove.

23. Baie des anges (7a+) (5.12a)

24. Clochette étalée (6c) (5.11a/b)

25. Pony Boy (6c) (5.11a/b) Excellent pocket pulling. Only the first pitch is usually climbed. The second pitch up the headwall above is 6c+.

26. Colombine panachée (6b+) Great climb up an impressive face. A dicey start, then technical face moves with a tricky finish to an ending jug.

27. Rumble gish (6b+) (5.10d) 3 pitches. Very good climbing. Most only do Pitch 1. Pitch 2 is 6c and Pitch 3 is 7a.

28. La femme piège (6b) (5.10c)

29. La ballade de la mer salée (6b+) (5.10d) No topo. Begin off a blocky ledge right of #28.

30. Alinoé (6b) (5.10c) No topo. Begin off a blocky ledge right of #29.

31. Le Maître des montagnes (6b+) (5.10d) No topo. Begin off a blocky ledge right of #30.

32. Pulp Friction (6b) (5.10c) 5 bolts to 2-bolt anchor.

33. Les daltons courent toujours (6b+) (5.10d) 6 bolts to 2-bolt anchor.

34. La touffe de ma dalton (6a+) (5.10b)
Fun climbing. Up right on a steep face, then back left to anchors. 6 bolts to 2-bolt anchor.

35. L'evasion des daltons (6b) (5.10c) A long pitch directly up the face to anchors below a headwall.

36. Le vol des daltons (6b+) (5.10d)

37. Les daltons se rachètent (6b) (5.10c) Anchors at the base of a bulge.

38. Les yeux de Tanatloc (5+) (5.9+) Good climb up a rib.

39. L'épée soleil (6a) (5.10a)

40. La forteresse invisible (6a) (5.10a) Fun pockets.

41. Gondalf le fou (6b) (5.10c)

42. Au-delà des ombres (5c) (5.9)

43. La chute de brek zarith (6c+) (5.11c)
6 bolts to 2-bolt anchor.

44. Entre terre et lumière (6b+) (5.10d)
5 bolts to 2-bolt anchor.

45. La cité du dieu perdu (6b) (5.10c)
Steep face to a slab finish. 5 bolts to 2-bolt anchor.

46. La magicienne trahie (6a+) (5.10b)
On the far right side of the face. 8 bolts to 2-bolt anchor.

Face de rat

The next sector uphill from Thorgal is Face de rat, a cliff characterized by a long overhanging section with few routes. The described routes are on the far left side of the sector, where the cliff-base trail begins to level off. The routes are moderate and very popular climbs up pocketed slabby rock. On the steep right side is the superb route *Face de rat* (8c+) (5.14b). The cliff usually gets sun from midmorning until late afternoon.

47. Le Meringoin (5c) (5.9) No topo. Left side of the sector.

48. L'heure du demi (5c) (5.9)

49. Le gros dard (5c) (5.9)

50. Pousse mousse (6a+) (5.10b)

51. FF MEUH (5c) (5.9)

Secteur Berlin

Excellent sustained routes up almost perfect, water-worn limestone ascend this sector on the right side of the cliff. Secteur Berlin is an ideal summer crag, getting lots of afternoon shade and breezes as well as sun for cool mornings. Many classic, must-do routes ascend this long cliff sector.

Routes are described from left to right.

52. L'errance d'une passion (7c) (5.12d) Far left side of the cliff.

53. Monnaie de singe (8a) (5.13b)

54. Blocage violent (7b+) (5.12c) Classic and continuous—one of the best 7b+ routes in France. One of the area's most famous routes put up by Patrick Edlinger in 1983. Directly up the wide streak. 85 feet.

55. Dolce vità (*Sweet life*) (8a+) (5.13c) Shorter line up the face right of a wide dark streak.

56. Petit Tom (8a) (5.13b)

57. La couleur du vent (*Color of the wind*) (8a) (5.13b) Excellent. Lots of continuous climbing with the crux up high. Follow blue water streaks up the left side of the sector.

58. Berlin (7c+) (5.13a) Another classic.

59. La chose (7c) (5.12d) Just right of *Berlin*.

60. Galaxy (7c) (5.12d) Starry climbing up a shallow corner system.

61. Makach Waloo (7c+) (5.13a) Beautiful rock and steeper than it looks. Start by flat boulders.

62. Queue de rat (7b+) (5.12c)

63. Rat man (8a+) (5.13c)

64. Bouse de douze (8a+) (5.13c)

65. Le concombre masqué (7c) (5.12d)

66. La petite illusion (7a+) (5.12a) One of the best 7a+s in France. Another Edlinger classic. Tricky start with a fat pinch and laybacks to sustained, delicate climbing up limestone perfection.

67. Cucubau setete (7b+) (5.12c)

68. Casse-noisette (7a+) (5.12a) Begin right of a water groove that runs the height of the cliff.

69. Le bleausard pressé (7a+) (5.12a)

70. Ricoco (7b) (5.12b) Up and left.

71. Zagreb (6c) (5.11b) Excellent, long, and sustained. It's easy to mess up the crux by slapping for the wrong hold.

72. Le moustik enragé (7a) (5.11d) Another long pitch.

73. Comme des phoques (6b) (5.10c) Great climbing.

74. Copu de blues pour Dom (6a+) (5.10b) Popular and good with plenty of pockets.

75. Super Mario (6b) (5.10c) Another popular and excellent moderate pocket route.

76. Le petit martien (7a) (5.11d)

77. Bleu comme l'enfer (6c+) (5.11c) Long lead up a light streak.

The next three routes are on a beautiful gray wall on the far right side of the sector. No topos for these routes, but they're easy to find. Walk right from #77 to the next wall panel. Routes are described from left to right.

78. Monzob sur mer (7b) (5.12b) No topo.

79. San John's pécos (7b+) (5.12c) No topo. A bouldery start to sustained climbing up an obvious blue streak.

80. Cent patates (7b+) (5.12c) No topo. Up the right wall of a big corner on the far right side of the Demi Lune.

Secteur Biographie

Secteur Biographie is the huge, overhanging midsection of the cliff. This sweep of stone, painted with wide vertical gray and blue stripes, is the home of *Biographie,* one of the world's hardest routes.

Finding the cliff: Find this sector by continuing to hike along the base of the cliff from Secteur Cascade until the area below the cliff widens. A direct access path is found by walking right or east along the horizontal path that the trail from the parking area intersects about three-fourths up the slope below the cliff. Look for an obvious path that leaves this main trail and heads up right across steep, grassy slopes. It ends at the base of this sector. Using this trail saves walking all the way to Secteur Cascade and then back along the cliff base.

81. Biographie (9a) (5.14c) No topo. First ascent by Arnaud Petit in 1996. Steep face climbing up a fat blue streak in the center of the wall to double-bolt anchors at 75 feet.

82. Realization (9b) (5.15a) No topo. First ascent by Chris Sharma in 2001. Dial in *Biographie,* then continue up the fatty streak past multiple cruxes to the high anchors.

83. Et on tuera tous les affreux ou le cadre *(And we'll kill all the bad ones)* (8c) (5.14b) No topo. This is marginally easier than the other hard ones here.

84. Project (5.14+) A project that goes up right and then works back left across some steep, impressive terrain.

85. Work but No More Love (8c+) (5.14c) First ascent by Dave Graham and Sylvain Millet. Begins at the same spot as

#84. Continue up right and then left over a bulge to anchors.

86. Les colonnettes *(The Columns)* (7c+) (5.13a) Classic, interesting, and recommended. An astounding and popular route up one of the cliff's best features—a series of vertical tufa columns. Look for pockets, strange laybacking, kneebars between columns, and a steep final headwall.

87. The Black Bean (8b+) (5.14a) An exposed continuation of *Les colonnettes* that ascends overlaps to anchors below a headwall.

88. Chronique de la haine ordinaire (8b) (5.13d) Pockets and edges up overhanging rock left of some tufa columns.

89. No Futur (5.14+) An unbelievable futuristic project. The long sustained pitch climbs to the top of the cliff.

90. Seredo Climbing Team (8a+) (5.13c) Steep climbing along a streak to anchors under the right side of a long roof.

91. Tout n'est pas si facile (7c+) (5.13a) Left of a streak to a white face to *Seredo*'s anchors.

92. Nitassinan (7a) (5.11d) Left of a left-facing corner.

93. Wounded Knee (7b+) (5.12c) Face to the left-facing corner to anchors under a big roof.

94. Sitting Bull (7b+) (5.12c) Companion route right of *Wounded Knee*. One of the best 7b+ routes in France.

95. Saint Georges picos (7a) (5.11d) Another best route for the grade. Lovely pocketed face on the right side of the sector.

Secteur Demi Lune

The Demi Lune sector on the right side of the wall is named for the huge half-moon bite chomped out of the top half of the cliff. It's easily visible from the campsite. The face runs east from a gully/crack system on its left margin to the right end of an immense roof that looms over the right side of the sector. The steep left side of the face offers a selection of startlingly hard face routes up slightly overhanging stone. The middle section yields some superb face-climbing gems up vertical, pocketed rock. The far right side boasts some overhanging routes, the best of which is *Carte blanche*. Routes are described from left to right.

96. La femme blanche (8a+) (5.13c) Brilliant line on the far left side of the face.

97. La femme noire (7c) (5.12d) Shares the start with #96, but continues straight up.

98. Le chirurgien de crepuscule (8b+) (5.14a) Excellent. Same shared start as previous route, but work out right and then up the steep face, passing the left side of a prominent roof.

99. Le poinconneur des lilas (8a+) (5.13c) Steep and technical. Finish over the right side of a roof.

100. Unknown

101. L'ami caouette (8a) (5.13b) 7 bolts to 2-bolt anchor.

102. Changement de look (7b+) (5.12c) One of Edlinger's famous routes and highly recommended. 9 bolts to 2-bolt anchor.

103. Joyeux boucher (7c+) (5.13a) Finishes through some roofs to a final headwall.

104. Jaune devant (7b+) 7 bolts to 2-bolt anchor.

105. Marron derrière (7b) (5.12b) 8 bolts to 2-bolt anchor.

106. Vieille canaille (7b) (5.12b)

107. Angel Dust (7a+) (5.12a)

108. Melody Nelson (7a+) (5.12a)

109. La Javanaise (7a) (5.11d) Just do it! One of the best of its grade at Céüse.

110. Koumac patome (7c) (5.12d)

111. Esparanza (7a+) (5.12a) Short, good, technical. 4 bolts to 2-bolt anchor.

112. El daü (7a) (5.11d) 8 bolts to 2-bolt anchor.

113. Les dessous chics (7a+) (5.12a) 6 bolts to 2-bolt anchor.

114. Harley Davidson (6b+) (5.10d) Excellent and engaging. The route was described in a French magazine as the best 6b+ in France, so it's deservedly popular and getting polished. Technical and sus-

tained pocket pulling up a vertical face. 6 bolts to 2-bolt anchor. 65 feet.

115. Marylou (6b) (5.10c) Another great pocket route.

116. Chant de cristal (6b+) (5.10d)

117. Papyrus (6b) (5.10c) Great climbing! The pitch above is *Minette a la plage* (7c) (5.12d).

118. Katina (6a+) (5.10b) Another great one and very popular. The recommended pitch above is *Beau f story* (7a) (5.11d).

119. Carte noire (6a) (5.10a) Popular and fun. The pitch on the overhanging wall above is *Encore* (8a+) (5.13c).

120. Sea Sex and Sun (6a) (5.10a) Recommended. All the ingredients for Provencal fun. End at anchors under the left side of the big roof. The route up the vast overhang above is *Radote joli pépère* (8b) (5.13d).

121. Les sucettes a l'anis (6a) (5.10a) Another popular moderate.

122. Face d'iguane (6a+) (5.10b)

123. Tête d'ampoule (6b) (5.10c)

124. Petit monstre (6a) (5.10a)

125. Couille de loup (6a+) (5.10b)

126. A. Patrick (6a) (5.10a)

127. Bonnie and Clyde (6c) (5.11a) Farthest right route on the lower face. A boulder problem start to a slab.

The following routes ascend the big overhanging face right of the slab. They're long, strenuous, and pumpy. No topos for these babies, but if you can climb them, you will find them no problem.

128. Lapinerie (7b) (5.12b)

129. Dures limites (8c) (5.14b)

130. Sueurs frodes (8a+) (5.13c)

131. Carte blanche (8a) (5.13b) Excellent, continuous, and spectacular. One move is way easier doing a rare Figure 4.

132. Sans peur et sanglier (8a) (5.13b) Same start as *Carte blanche* but climb up right on steep stone.

Other Sectors

There are more sectors with many routes. These are less populated than the popular areas described here. Consult the comprehensive guide for topos and grades.

On the far left side is Secteur Golots à Gogo with a great selection of routes from 5 to 6c. Features include water runnels and continuous slabs. It's shaded on summer mornings and in sun for the rest of the day. Some superb multipitch adventures await your fingers. Recommended routes are *Golots à Gogo* (6a, 6a, 4c), the sustained *Banzaille* (6c+), *Lili* (6a) with a tricky start, and *Joshua* (5b), a brilliant line up an excellent water runnel.

Dalles du capeps, the next sector east, offers more technical but moderate routes on a beautiful cliff section. Do these routes to sample some of the cliff's best moderates: *Régiment des Bananes* (6a) to anchors under a roof, *En baskets* (5c+) to its right, and the two-pitch *Un peu plus* (5c/6a).

Right of Secteur Demi Lune is Un pont sur l'infini sector, with many 5.11 and 5.12 routes on mostly vertical stone. Next is the *via ferrata,* a 150-foot-high series of iron ladders drilled into the rock, which allows easy access to the cliff top and the grassy plateau above—it's an exciting and exhilarating free solo!

Les maîtres du monde sector to the right is a radically overhanging cliff section with the must-do jug-haul route *Bibendum* (7b+). Grande Face farther right is the big wall here, with lots of airy routes up to five pitches long. Some lines are real stunners, including *Inespérance* (6a+, 6b+, 6c+, 7a), *Little Big Wall* (6b, 7b+, 7b+, 7b+, 4), *Captain Dada* (6c, 6c, 6c+, 6b+), or the mostly moderate *Plus tu ruses, plus tu t'uses* (6b, 5+, 5, 6c, or A0).

LES CALANQUES

■ OVERVIEW

The famed Mediterranean coast of southern France, the French Riviera, is notorious for pricey towns and developments replete with elegant villas, exclusive restaurants, movie star residents, the Cannes film festival, blocks of tourist hotels, and crowded beaches. It's a place that's hard on your pocketbook and harder on your sensibilities. It's where most of Europe seems to come for summer vacation, filled with caravans, tents, and tourists from the Netherlands, Belgium, and Germany. The coast is also Marseille, France's second largest city and a sprawling metropolis tacked onto a broad bay. But the Mediterranean coast is also Les Calanques, a wild coastal region of ragged mountains and one of France's best and largest climbing areas.

Les Calanques refers to a mountain massif that towers above the rocky coast between Marseille and Cassis. This rough, 12-mile stretch of coastline is lorded over by 1,916-foot-high Mount Puget and creased by a string of dramatic *calanques* or valleys drowned by the sea. The *calanques,* a French word translated as "rocky inlets," are Provencal fjords lined with limestone cliffs that tower above transparent turquoise water. These deep narrow inlets formed when the Mediterranean Sea was lower and creeks and rivers, swollen with glacial melt, chiseled deep canyons into the massif flanks. Later the sea rose and inundated the valleys, leaving today's seven main *calanques* and numerous coves.

Les Calanques is one of France's largest climbing areas with more than a thousand routes on numerous crags. The cliffs, composed of a rough, compact limestone, are made for climbing, with diverse features including cracks, slabs, caves, dihedrals, buttresses, arêtes, and pinnacles. Typical of limestone, most of the climbing is on open faces. The area is known not only for burly overhanging courses but also for a plethora of middle-grade routes. Lots of sport pitches are found on the small crags, along with multipitch lines

that ascend big walls. The lack of rainfall results in little vegetation crowding the cliffs, making for pleasant climbs rather than vertical bushwhacks, especially on easier routes. The area is famed for its traversing adventure routes on sea cliffs. The entire coast has been traversed using techniques including rappels, pendulums, and both aid and free climbing.

Les Calanques is a magical climbing arena and an enchantment of rock, sky, and sea. Climbing out there on the sun-polished cliffs is not soon forgotten. You long remember the vistas that unfold beyond a lofty belay aerie as much as the climbing movements—distant limestone ridges gleaming like alabaster castles; the air resinous with pine and wild rosemary; waves lapping against a stony beach below; the dancing sea reflecting the glitter spray of sunlight. It's an elemental place of basic earth elements that never fades against the wind-haunted sky, taut with streaming clouds and swept clean by the persistent mistral wind. It's a place that remains real. As Gaston Rébuffat, the great French alpinist, wrote in *Between Ground and Sky* about his Calanques adventures: "In the modern age, very little remains that is real. Night has been banished, so has the cold, the winds and the stars. They have all been neutralized, the rhythm of life itself is obscured."

Les Calanques Cliffs

Les Calanques is a complex area with more than twenty-five separate climbing locales scattered across the massif. The six main areas with concentrated climbing are, from west to east, the Marseilleveyre hills; the cliffs around Les Goudes, Sormiou, Morgiou, Luminy, and Gardiole; and En Vau. Marseilleveyre, in the hills south of Marseille, offers many sport cliffs with a wide range of grades.

Les Goudes has excellent big cliffs northeast of Calanque de Callelongue near the area's southwestern tip. The long wall of Rocher de St. Michel, with its overhanging cave Grotte de l'ermite or Hermit's Cave and jutting Rocher des Goudes, yields spectacular sport routes

along with multipitch moderates. Consult the comprehensive guide for directions to the area and cliff topos.

Calanque de Sormiou, a deep inlet separating the Puget and Marseille massifs, is easily accessible with lots of superb cliff, including L'Arche perdue and other cliffs at the tip of Bec de Sormiou and above the open sea on the west side of Crete de Sormiou, a long serrated ridge along the *calanque's* west side. At the Bec is the Momie or Mummy, a thin pillar leaning against the main wall with great three-pitch routes. On the opposite ridge side are more great crags with one- and two-pitch routes. Falaise de Tiragne, with more than fifty routes, is very popular.

Calanque Morgiou, running northwest from the sea, is a deep, narrow inlet lined with gleaming cliffs, stony slopes dotted with shrubs, and cobbled beaches. The area is reached via a narrow road that ends at the village of Morgiou and a safe parking area at the *calanque's* head. The village, sitting amid natural splendor, has a restaurant and bar for an after-climb repast. Above the village is the shady sport cliff of Les Cabanons, and farther southeast is the white cliff Falaise du Renard. La Triperie sector, west of the *calanque,* is a true sea cliff, with many routes reached by rappelling from the cliff top to hanging stances above the water. High above Morgiou looms the lofty 300-foot wall of Cret St. Michel, a big cliff with fun routes that bask all day in the sun.

Calanque de Sugiton, a shallow cove east of Morgiou, is a popular locale with numerous cliffs of all shapes and sizes. The site, also called Luminy since it is also accessed from the University of Luminy, offers a good variety of climbing and hundreds of routes. The area boasts three hard sectors: L'Oasis, La Grotte de L'Ours, and the magnificent La Paroi des Toits. L'Oasis is a hidden red wall stacked with superb lines. Grotte de L'Ours is a cave or *grotte* that overhangs forty degrees with lots of powerful routes up columns and pockets with *UFO,* the hardest one, checking in at 5.14b. The famed La Paroi des Toits yields a brilliant selection of hard routes on a long southwest-facing wall of roofs.

If you want moderate routes, Sugiton

is one of France's best places for long, middle-grade courses. The conspicuous pointed peak of La Grande Candelle or the Great Candle, coupled with the lower cliff Socle de la Candelle or the Candle Base, is the centerpiece of Les Calanques. La Grande Candelle offers more than twenty single-pitch sport routes on its south face along with many longer lines. Socle de la Candelle has many routes up to nine pitches long in the popular 5.9 and 5.10 range. You can cobble together routes up to 1,500 feet long on the lower cliff and upper wall to make superb all-day adventures in a beautiful setting. This guide describes *Le Temple* on the lower wall and the stunning *Arête de Marseille* up the west rib of Candelle's final blade.

La Gardiole, an area of rugged mountains and valleys on the east side of the Calanques, includes the excellent and popular Calanque d'En Vau. The area offers many adventure routes on what the French call *terrain d'aventure,* with few bolts, as well as sport climbs. Calanque du Devenson and Calenque de l'Oule, west of En Vau, have superb climbs, many of surprisingly moderate grades, up sheer cliffs that rear above the sea.

Calanque d'En Vau is not only the most popular *calanque,* but it's also the prettiest. The inlet, nicknamed "the pearl of the Calanques," is walled by lofty cliffs as well as a perfect beach. The wide Falaise de Droite or Right Cliff rises sharply from clear water. Many multipitch routes ascend the steep face, including *Eperon des Americains,* a classic first ascended by Americans John Harlin, Royal Robbins, and Gary Hemming in 1963. In the steep valley beyond the beach are more excellent crags, including Saphir, Petite Aiguille, the long vertical ribs of Sirène, Grande Aiguille, and the famous wall Le Pouce and its celebrated 1939 Gaston Rébuffat route *Pouce Integral* with a famous step over an exposed gap.

Rack, Protection, and Descent

Most of the described routes in this guide are equipped with bolt protection and bolt anchors. Protection is generally good, but some routes have runouts on easier pitches. Routes that are old or seldom climbed may have few bolts and fixed pitons, and those in place may be rusted. Use caution and either avoid these routes or back everything up. Many cliffs were retrobolted with stainless steel bolts. Most multipitch routes are set up in half-rope lengths, allowing you to climb and rappel the route with a single rope.

A standard Calanques rack includes twelve to fifteen quickdraws, a set of wired nuts, and a 200-foot (60-meter) rope. Carry a few small to medium cams on long routes. A 165-foot (50-meter) rope can also be used, but be careful on single-pitch sport climbs since some are longer than 85 feet.

Descent off sport routes is by lowering from bolt anchors, mostly quick-clip steel carabiners so you don't have to untie. The multipitch lines require rappels from fixed anchors. A single 200-foot (60-meter) rope is fine since most rappels are less than 100 feet long. Some routes also have walk-off descents.

Climbing History

Les Calanques boasts a long climbing history. The area, situated close to a major metropolitan area, developed parallel to other French centers, including Saussois south of Paris and le Salève near Chamonix. The first technical climbs were done here in the late nineteenth century. The local Le Club Alpine was founded in 1880 and the Société des Excursionnistes Marseillais in 1897, which by 1910 had more than 7,000 members, although most were hikers. The first ascents of Aiguille du Sorbet and some cliffs at Morgiou occurred at this time, although details are sketchy.

The Grande Candelle, the biggest and most aesthetic formation, was an obvious goal for early climbers. It's first technical route was up the back side in 1879. In 1913 Louis David made the first ascent of the Candelle's south face via the aid route *Corniches David.* In 1927 the great *Arête de Marseille* was climbed and is still considered one of the Calanques's great classics.

Over the next decades the area was used by climbers as a winter training ground to improve technique and rope work for the important summer sojourns to the Alps. Period climbers, putting up some stunning and difficult routes, included the great alpinist Gaston Rébuffat and Georges Livanos, one of the first confirmed limestone addicts. This pair climbed many of today's classic Calanques lines.

Sport climbing and the use of permanently drilled bolts came in the 1980s, and the area soon hummed with development. Many cliffs opened in the 1980s and 1990s, and local climbing exploded with hundreds of new routes.

Seasons and Weather

A typical Mediterranean climate, similar to southern California, brings warm winters and hot summers to Les Calanques. The best time to climb is from October through April. Like the Spanish coast, it's an ideal winter venue. This almost desert area is exceptionally sunny, receiving less rain than any other part of France. Rain falls on average a scant fifty days per year. Winter temperatures are usually ideal, with daily highs ranging between 50 and 65 degrees. The cooler months are best for cranking the harder routes. It occasionally gets cold in winter, but it's easy to find sun and warmth since most cliffs face south.

The main drawback to climbing at Les Calanques is the ubiquitous mistral wind, a violent and strong north wind that blows down the Rhône Valley whenever a low pressure system centers over the sea south of France. This irregular, cold airstream can last for weeks, wrecking havoc with people's moods, toppling trees, shattering windows, and ruining climbing vacations. The mistral huffs worst in the winter months, the ideal climbing season, making climbing all but impossible except on the most sheltered cliffs. If you're here during a mistral, be prepared to move to climbing sites east of Toulon, where it rarely visits.

Summer is usually too hot to climb at Les Calanques, especially on the sunny south faces. Heat and humidity conspire to drive visiting climbers north to the cooler Haute-Alpes or to Chamonix. If you come in summer, be sure it's June, when the weather is still pleasant. Pick your climbs carefully by traveling to shaded cliffs in the morning and evening. During the day's heat stash your gear on the rocky shoreline, and plunge into the warm water for an invigorating swim.

The area's hot, dry climate and its proximity to Marseille has led to rigorous prohibitions to protect the range from wildfire. Access to the entire Calanques region, including climbing and hiking, are forbidden from the beginning of July until the second Saturday in September because of extreme fire danger.

Food and Drink

Provence is great to visit if you love fine food. Eating well is taken for granted in France. It just happens. Walk through a village market in summer, and you quickly see why. Fresh fruits and vegetables, local cheeses, regional herbs and spices, crusty baguettes and flaky croissants, and vast selections of olives grace the colorful stalls and invite your palate. The French, although they patronize fast food joints like McDonald's, generally consider fast food as uncivilized, uncouth, and just plain bad. They use the word *gourmandise* for eating food simply because it tastes wonderful and is well presented. Inevitably, if you are sitting at the cliff base munching on a lunch of baguette and Brie, passing French climbers will always say *"Bon appetit."*

The south of France offers a *cuisine du soleil*—foods of the sun—that reflect the region's essence. Coastal Provence, including Marseille and the Calanques, offers superb seafood like shellfish, fresh fish, and *la bouillabaisse,* the famed Provencal fish stew. You can't visit here without sampling a tasty bowl of this famed *spécialité*. The dish originated as a humble one-pot meal for Marseille fishermen, who threw small bony fish that couldn't be sold into a pot on their boat. It was and still is served with slabs of dry baguette rubbed in garlic, fried in olive oil, and served with *rouille,* a spicy chili sauce. Now bouillabaisse is a gourmet dish, albeit an expensive one that is served in the finest restaurants. The best is made

with fresh fish—red *chapon,* spiny *galinette,* and *poissons de roches* or tiny rockfish— poached in a soup of tomatoes, olive oil, and spices. The *soupe* goes down easy with dry white wine from one of Cassis's fourteen vineyards—the only drink a Marseillais would think about sipping between spoonfuls of bouillabaisse.

Besides bouillabaisse, lots of fresh fish and seafood dishes are readily available. Look for *loup* or sea bass, particularly the delicious entrée *loup flambe au fenouil,* which is bass stuffed with fennel and flambéed in *pastis,* an anise liquor. Other tasty shellfish and fish are oysters, *telline* or clams, the ugly *chapon* or scorpion fish, and *lotte* or monkfish grilled over an open fire. Also sample *Fougasse aux anchois,* bread with anchovies.

The regional *fromages* or cheeses are, like elsewhere in France, spectacular. The assortment of cheeses in the *supermarché* and the *fromagerie* or cheese store is bewildering. Besides Camembert and Brie, try Provencal *banon,* a goat cheese wrapped in chestnut leaves, and superb Roquefort blue cheese. Roquefort, made from ewe's milk, is aged in underground chambers near Montpellier, west of Les Calanques, until ripe with characteristic blue veins and a strong taste.

The last thing about Provencal eating is olive oil, the basis for most regional dishes. The olive tree, introduced to here more than 2,000 years ago, flourishes in the dry climate. Olive oil is often coupled with garlic to make *pistou,* a paste of parmesan cheese, olive oil, garlic, and basil, and *aïoli,* a garlic and olive oil mayonnaise served with salt cod, vegetables, and baguette.

Cultural Experiences and Rest Days

On rest days you'll find no shortage of activities to do and places to see. Les Calanques offers a lot besides climbing. The hiking is superb, with trails exploring all the peaks and valleys in the range. A long-distance trail (Grande Randonnée 98-51) threads along the entire coast between Marseille and Cassis.

Another good excursion is taking an inexpensive boat trip out to the *calanques.*

Go to the Cassis harbor to buy tickets, or walk along the harbor to see which boats are loading. The trips go to three, five, or eight *calanques.* The best one is the eight-*calanques* trip, which visits the main ones and some smaller inlets. It's a great scenic trip to get acquainted with the area.

Swimming in the sea is another one of the Calanques's hedonistic pleasures. The water is generally warm, calm, and crystal clear. If you happen to be climbing a cliff overlooking the sea above Calanque de Sugiton, you'll look down wistfully at swimmers stroking between rocky islands. Later, after sending your project, jog down the slopes for a relaxing swim. The broad rock shelf below the cliff Les Pierres Tombées is a nude beach for immodest climbers.

Les Calanques is the site of one of Europe's great archeological finds—the underwater Cosquer Cave at Cape Morgiou. The cave, occupied 27,000 years ago when the sea was lower, was discovered by diver Henri Cosquer in 1985. After seeing cave paintings there in 1991, he notified archeologists. Now the cave, with an underwater entrance 125 feet below sea level, is an astounding art site, with more than 125 animal pictures of horses, ibex, bison, seals, and penguins and 55 stenciled handprints, many missing fingers, on the cave walls. Although you can't visit the cave, you can visit Musée d'Histoire de Marseille (Marseille History Museum) for a fascinating, virtual, three-dimensional cave experience.

The town of Cassis is one of those stunning places with both charm and beauty. It's understated charisma enchanted artists and writers, including French impressionist painters Matisse and Dufy. This fishing port, nestled below hills covered with olive and almond orchards as well as terraced vineyards that produce white wine, is a popular retreat for the Marseillais, as well as the well-heeled who want to avoid the tourist glitz of the Côte d'Azur to the east. Keep an eye out as you walk around for celebrities, such as resident actor Michael Caine.

Cassis dates back to Roman times, but was mostly rebuilt in the eighteenth century atop ruins. Walk about and

Cliffs rise above La Calanque de Sormiou.

explore. Look for old fountains and buildings and an open-air artist's market where you can buy paintings of Provence. The harbor is really the town's best feature, with fishing boats and yachts moored along the quay. Colorful restaurants and cafes line the harbor front. It's a pleasant afternoon diversion to sit at an umbrella-shaded table and waste a few hours sipping coffee or nursing a *biere* and watching the world pass by. East of the harbor is the popular beach Plage de la Grande mer and the tourist office, dispensing information and maps.

Marseille, France's second largest city after Paris, is a working city rather than a romantic one. It's not exactly beautiful nor filled with historic treasures, although it boasts some striking architecture. Instead, it's a simple city with a friendly populace that seldom looks down at you, the visitor, as is done in neighboring Aix-en-Provence or on the glitzy Côte d'Azur, which are more concerned with appear-

ances and money. The city is a cosmopolitan port that acquired a reputation as corrupt and run by the underworld. But Marseille is pretty safe, especially compared with American cities. Tobias Smollett's 1765 observations in the book *Travels Through France and Italy* still hold true: "I was much pleased with Marseille, which is indeed a noble city, large, populous, and flourishing. The streets . . . are open, airy, and spacious; the houses well built, and even magnificent."

You'll probably spend only a day or part of a day roaming about the city unless you're staying there. Highlights for your itinerary are the landmark cathedral Notre-Dame-de-la-Garde topped by a colossal gold Virgin; the Abbaye St-Victor, an ancient monastery with catacombs; Le Panier, the oldest part of the city with narrow streets and eclectic buildings; and Musée d'Histoire de Marseille, which includes displays about Greek and Roman settlements.

Trip Planning Information

General description: Les Calanques, one of France's best climbing areas, stretches along 15 miles of mountains and a rugged limestone seacoast.

Location: Southern France. The Mediterranean coast between Marseille and Cassis.

Camping and accommodations: Camping is a problem. No primitive camping is allowed because of litter, human waste, and fire danger. The best and closest campground is Les Cigales in Cassis. The 300-site campground is on Route de Marseille D559 about 1 kilometer from the port. Several campgrounds are in Marseille, including Bonneveine and Les Vagues. Another good campsite is at Gemenos. For rooms check out the La Gardiole Youth Hostel in Cassis. Numerous hotels are in Cassis and Marseille.

People will camp along the N559 between Cassis and Marseille, but it's very risky and not recommended. Stealing and robbery is a problem, and campers have been attacked—even in locked cars.

Climbing season: Year-round. Summers can be unbearably hot, especially on the south-facing cliffs, and no water is found. Les Calanques is France's driest region with only fifty days and 600 mm of rain annually. Spring and autumn are the best months, with warm, dry days. If it's hot, find shade, and when you're done climbing, take a refreshing dip in the sea. Winters are good, especially for harder routes, although the mistral, a strong north wind, often blows and makes climbing impossible except on protected cliffs.

Restrictions and access issues: Climbing and hiking is prohibited from July until the second Saturday of September, the hottest and driest months, because of extreme fire danger. Stoves, matches, and lighters are forbidden year-round. No camping or bivouacking is allowed, although it is done.

Robbery and car burglary is a business here because of the area's proximity to Marseille. In many areas your car and its belongings are not safe. Leave nothing in your car. Most Calanques parking areas are visited every day, and closed cars are broken into. Avoid problems by parking only in watched, protected car parks, or take public transportation to the cliffs. For En Vau, park in Cassis, or leave your car in the campground and walk (hour hike), or use a tourist boat to drop you off or pick you up at En Vau. It's safe to park at Morgiou and Sormiou since people live there.

Guidebooks: The comprehensive guidebook is *Escalade les Calanques* by Gilles Bernard, Daniel Gorgeon, Christophe Kern, and Bernard Privat. Proceeds of the book's sale go toward equipping routes. It's available in sport and climbing shops as well as *tabacs,* bookstores, and tourist shops.

Services and shops: All services, including restaurants, grocery stores, and accommodations, are in Marseille and Cassis. Nearby climbing shops are La Montagne, Alpina, and Decathlon Bonneveine in Marseille and Les Trois Mousquetons in Aix-en-Provence.

Emergency services: Call 18 in case of an accident. Les Marins Pompiers is the rescue group. Be sure you have the accident location, including *calanque,* cliff, and route name, as well as the type of accident. Telephones are in Callelongue, Sormiou, Morgiou, and Luminy. In case of accident you can also call at La Fontasse Youth Hostel and La Gardiole Forestry House.

Nearby climbing areas: Mte. Sainte-Baume above Gemenos offers an excellent selection of multipitch routes on several crags. Mte. Sainte Victoire east of Aix-en-Provence is another great climbing area, with hundreds of routes up to 2,000 feet long. Cimai is east of Cassis near Le Beausset.

Nearby attractions: Marseille, northwest of Les Calanques, has a stunning setting, almost perfect weather, and a lively selection of cultural and historical attractions. Visit the Vieux Port (the Old Port) and its open-air fish market; the Jardin des Vestiges with Greek and Roman ruins; Musée d'Histoire de Marseille; Musée Cantini, filled with twentieth-century art;

and Notre-Dame-de-la-Garde cathedral on the city's highest hill.

Cassis is a beautiful town nestled into a sunny cove. The town offers a bustling downtown, busy harbor lined with cafes, shaded square where residents play a bowling game called *pétanque,* and lovely beaches. Cassis is known for its excellent wines. One of the best vineyards is Clos Sainte-Madeline, with a mansion overlooking the sea and twenty-eight acres of vines.

Finding the area: Les Calanques is on the Mediterranean coast in southern France between Marseille and Cassis. The closest airport is Marseille-Provence International Airport. Fly here from Paris and major European cities, or fly to Nice farther east up the coast. Otherwise, it's a day's drive south from Paris on the autoroute.

It's best to stay in Cassis on the east side of Les Calanques. The town is easily accessed from the A52 autoroute east of Marseille and south of Aix-en-Provence. Calanque d'En Vau is easily reached from Cassis via a foot trail or by taking a boat from the harbor.

To reach Calanques Sugiton, Morgiou, and Sormoiu, drive into Marseille from Cassis on highway D559. As you descend into eastern Marseille from la Gineste Col, look left or south and see the Luminy campus. At the bottom of the hill, go left at a sign to Luminy to park for the Sugiton trailhead. To reach Morgiou and Sormiou, drive to the Mazargues Obelisk, a huge pillar in a roundabout. Go left, and follow signs from here through many small streets. You need to be alert for signs or you will get lost . . . then you will need to ask directions! Buy a good local map to stay on course.

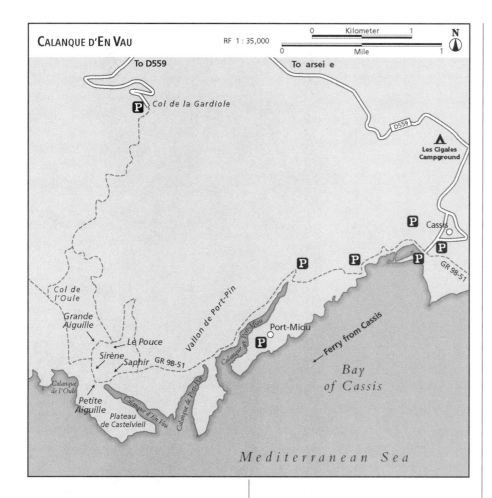

Map: CALANQUE D'EN VAU — RF 1 : 35,000

Calanque d'En Vau

Calanque d'En Vau, west of Cassis, is the most famous of the *calanques*. Gleaming limestone walls, some rising directly out of the water, line its deep channel filled with crystalline water. En Vau's stunning setting, sheer natural beauty, and relaxed atmosphere make it a popular destination for climbers, as well as hikers, bathers, boaters, and tourists. Its nickname is "the pearl of the Calanques." Despite its popularity, especially on weekends and holidays in summer, the *calanque* retains a peaceful serenity and secluded atmosphere. Shade is easily found on En Vau's cliffs, although the *calanque's* orientation makes it subject to the persistent mistral wind.

En Vau offers a huge assortment of sport and traditional routes that range from one to five pitches long on immaculate limestone. Most routes are protected with bolts, although a small rack of wired nuts and a selection of small to medium Friends should be carried on longer routes since bolts can be widely spaced.

The *calanque's* cliffs, unlike other nearby areas, are not difficult to figure out. When you stand on the beach facing the sea, the cliffs on the *calanque's* left side are called the Falaise de Gauche or Left Cliffs, and the ones on the right are called Falaise de Droite or Right Cliffs. All the described routes are on Falaise de Droite, ascending a couple pinnacles as well as some spectacular buttresses. The Falaise de Gauche offers many multipitch routes, including some excellent classics. Consult the comprehensive guide for topos to these routes.

Finding the area: Cassis offers the easiest access to En Vau. It is possible to hike to the *calanque* from the N559 highway between Cassis and Marseille, but it is safer to leave your car in Cassis and hike the coastal path to the area.

Leave your car and belongings at the campground in Cassis. Walk a kilometer down into the town center and the harbor. From the harbor walk west on several roads (part of trail #GR 98-51) paralleling the sea to Port-Miou. You can also drive, following signs, to Calanque de Port-Miou. Your car is safe here if nothing is in it. Leave the glove box open and the rear baggage cover off to deter thieves. From the Port-Miou car park, hike southwest on a wide path between an old quarry (the limestone base for the Statue of Liberty came from here) and the port. The trail climbs away from Port-Miou, crosses a ridge, and drops to the head of pretty Calanque de Port-Pin. Follow the trail uphill across rocky wooded slopes to the top of the plateau. Cross the plateau to the abrupt eastern edge of Calanque d'En Vau. A steep gully descent leads directly down to the beach from here, or hike along the rim for a half mile to an easier trail descent into the *calanque*. Hiking time from Cassis to the beach is forty-five minutes to an hour.

Alternatively, take a tourist boat from the Cassis harbor to En Vau. Numerous sightseeing boats travel along the coast, stopping at various *calanques*. They are used to drop off climbers along the way. Check at the booth in the town square next to the harbor for times and tickets to En Vau. Make sure your tickets, both one-way or round-trip, are specifically for En Vau. Also check the return time. If you go one-way, it's best to travel by boat to En Vau and then hike back to the campsite.

Petite Aiguille

This prominent, 90-foot-high, freestanding pinnacle looms in the middle of the canyon directly above the beach at the *calanque*'s head. Several fine, popular routes ascend the formation. A rack of ten quick-draws and a 200-foot (60-meter) rope is sufficient. Descent off all routes is by rappel or lowering from fixed anchors.

South Face

1. La Diagonale (4c) (5.6) First climbed in 1932 by Henri Barrin. Classic route.

2. Directe de Gauche (5c) (5.9) Directly tackles the center difficulties.

3. Directe de Droite (6a) (5.10a) Face moves trend up left.

4. Face à la Mer (4c) (5.6) Right side of face. 100 feet.

North and West Faces

5. La Face Nord-Ouest (4c) (5.6) First climbed in 1888. Up the left side of the face.

6. La B.B. (3c) (5.5) Climb to a ledge, then up a corner.

7. La Directe (4c) (5.6) The rib that separates the faces. 100 feet.

8. La Ratopenado (4c) (5.6) Good route up left side of the west face.

Secteur Saphir

This sector is an excellent ridge on the east side behind Petite Aiguille. The upper headwall offers three great moderates with beautiful views and fun climbing. Reach the start by scrambling up rocky slopes to the base of the obvious flat ridge. Descent is by scrambling down a gully on the left or north side of the formation.

9. La Saphir (4c) (5.6) 5 pitches. The top three pitches can be combined into two pitches. Begin at the ridge base. **Pitch 1:** Up the flat ridge (4c) to belay bolts. **Pitch 2:** An easy, laid-back ridge scramble (2b). **Pitch 3:** Up left (4b) on the headwall to a stance. **Pitch 4:** Work up the steep wall (4c) to a belay ledge. **Pitch 5:** Up the rib (3b) to the summit.

10. La Sortie des Artistes (5c) (5.9) 2 pitches. The middle finish to *La Saphir*. **Pitch 1:** Directly up (5a) to a stance by a bush. **Pitch 2:** Edge up the steep headwall (5c) to the top.

11. Directe de la Pierre Fine (5c+) (5.9+) 2 pitches. The right-hand finish to *La Saphir*. **Pitch 1:** Airy face climbing (5c+) to a stance. **Pitch 2:** The upper headwall (5c) to the top.

Secteur Sirène

Secteur Sirène is a magnificent flying buttress that juts from the *calanque* rim upcanyon from Secteur Saphir and Petite Aiguille. Several megaclassic face routes climb the narrow faces, including the beautiful route *Super Sirène,* established in 1941 by famed French climber Gaston Rébuffat and Paul Guerrin. Descent is best down the steep gully on the right (south) side of the pillar.

Finding the cliff: Scramble up the rocky hillside for 100 feet to the base of the face.

12. Sirène Liautard (4c) (5.6) 5 pitches. 325 feet. Good route up the left buttress. **Pitch 1:** Outside of pillar (4b). **Pitch 2:** Up pillar to ledge (4c). **Pitch 3:** Easier climbing up broken rock (3a). **Pitch 4:** Easily up right (2c). **Pitch 5:** Finish up the airy edge (4b).

13. Super Sirène (6a+) (5.10b) 4 pitches. 325 feet. Elegant, beautiful, and highly recommended. Polished in spots. **Pitch 1:** Sustained face climbing (6a+) to a semi-hanging belay from bolts. **Pitch 2:** More continuous face moves lead to a short crux (6a+) up left onto the rib. **Pitch 3:** Balance up the sharp arête (5a) to a good belay. **Pitch 4:** Edge up an exposed edge (4b) to the summit.

14. La Sans Nom (4b) (5.6) 3 pitches. 300 feet. A fun, easy outing up the right pillar. **Pitch 1:** Climb the narrow rib (4b). **Pitch 2:** Up the rib (3a) then right to a belay left of the tree. **Pitch 3:** Work up left and then up a face and crack to the summit (4b).

Grande Aiguille

The obvious Grande Aiguille, a 100-foot-high pinnacle, lies up the canyon from the beach. Several easily accessed routes ascend its south face.

Finding the cliff: Walk north from the beach up the canyon floor trail to the obvious aiguille on the right. Scramble to its base. Routes are described from left to right.

15. La Paillon (4a) (5.6) Climb the face and crack on the rounded left side of the south face to anchors below the finger summit.

16. Le G.H.M. (5b+) (5.8) Climb up and right of a cave feature, over the crux bulge, and up easier rock to anchors on the finger.

17. L'A.M.E. (4b) (5.6) Face climb to anchors in the notch.

18. Voie Abeille (3c) (5.5) First climbed in 1889. The normal route up the aiguille. Up the right margin of the face to anchors on the right shoulder.

Secteur Pouce

This sector is the tall, prominent face directly above and behind Grande Aiguille. Some excellent routes ascend the wall. One of the best is *Pouce Integral,* a 1939 Rébuffat route, up the huge buttress in the middle. This celebrated five-pitch line scales perfect rock to the top of a freestanding pillar. Here the climber makes a famous *pas* or step across the airy void to a finishing headwall. To the right are more excellent routes (not described here), including *La Paume* (6b+), a two-pitch bolted line directly up the next buttress, and *Les Petits Suisses* (6c), another two-pitch route up steep limestone.

Finding the cliff: Hike up the canyon from the beach to Grande Aiguille. Just past it find a climber's path that plods up steep, loose slopes to the pillar base.

19. Pouce Integral (6a) (5.10a) 5 pitches. Excellent climb up the prominent buttress. Begin at the toe of the buttress. **Pitch 1:** Work up a crack system (6a) and then up left to a belay ledge. **Pitch 2:** Face climb the right side of the buttress (6a) to a good belay ledge. **Pitch 3:** Up the right side of the white buttress (4c+) to another good belay. **Pitch 4:** Excellent exposed face climbing (5b) to the right side of the big nose. Climb the right side to the top of a freestanding pillar. **Pitch 5:** Step across the huge gap onto the main wall. Work up the headwall (5b) to the cliff top. **Descent:** Scramble down gullies left of the wall, or hike along the rim to find the trail back to Cassis. **Rack:** Bring a small rack of Stoppers, small to medium Friends, 10 quickdraws, and a 165-foot rope.

Calanque Morgiou

La Calanque Morgiou offers an excellent variety of climbing with a wide range of grades. The area gives traveling climbers a great sense of this mountainous seaside region and its semiwild character. Many cliffs scatter across the surrounding mountain flanks above the *calanque,* and more stunning crags and sea cliffs lie farther afield.

The village of Morgiou, straddling the head of the pretty inlet, is the center of the action. The narrow access road from Marseille twists over Col de Morgiou before dropping down a valley to the village. The picturesque harbor makes a good afternoon exploration, and a couple of restaurants and bars beckon you to sit on a terrace overlooking the port and sip a chilled Jupiler *biere* before dipping into a bowl of fresh *bouillabaise* soup. The village is a collection of about thirty stone and wood houses crowded against the road. Many of these *cabanons* or cabins are used only on weekends and holidays by vacationers.

In the off-season, the best time to climb, you'll find peace and quiet, with the place populated only by fishermen and their rusting trawlers. On busy weekends the village is teeming with swimmers, hikers, boaters, fishermen, and climbers. Parking is a serious problem then. This is a good place to park since the area is busy and your vehicle is safe from break-ins.

The main Morgiou crags are Les Cabanons, Cret-Saint-Michel, L'Abri Côtier, Falaise du Renard, Le Cap Morgiou, Le Cancéou, and Aiguille de Sugiton. These are all reached by trails that begin in the village. East of La Calanque Morgiou are excellent crags above La Calanque Sugiton in Luminy sector, including Paroi des toits, Pierres Tombées, Grotte de L'Ours, L'Oasis, Cathédrale, Socle de la Candelle, Concave, and La Grande Candelle. These cliffs are reached by hiking east along the coastal path from Morgiou or from the University of Luminy to the north.

The routes range from one-pitch sport climbs to full-day adventures. Most routes, especially the popular and classic lines, are laced with protection bolts and bolted belay and rappel anchors. Still, a small rack of

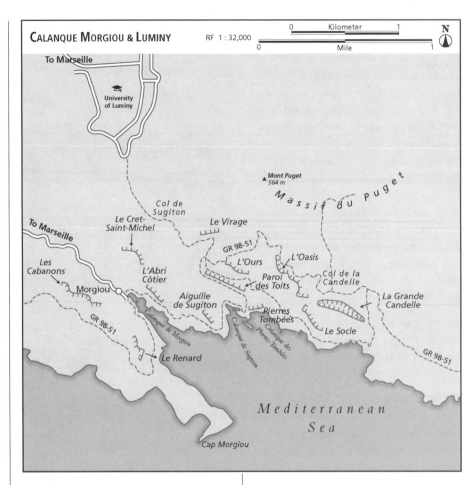

wires and cams should be carried because some climbs have runouts between bolts.

Finding the area: To reach Morgiou drive into the southeastern suburbs of Marseille. From Cassis drive west on highway D559 to Mazargues and a large roundabout with a tall obelisk (*Mazargues Obelisk*) in the middle. Go around the roundabout to its southwest side, and turn onto a narrow street that zigzags through Mazargues. Follow signs south toward les Baumettes and Morgiou. You might get lost since the streets are narrow with many turns. If you're lost, ask for directions. Eventually pass the climbing area Aiguille des Baumettes on your left. From there the road narrows and twists over Col de Morgiou. Continue down the winding road to the village, and park in a large area by the harbor. Road access is regulated in the summer because of fire danger and is often closed to all traffic.

Les Cabanons

Les Cabanons or the Cabins is a good, north-facing cliff west of the village of Morgiou. The shady cliff is a good choice on warm days. The crag has a good selection of routes ranging from 5.6 to 5.13c, with most climbs requiring technique and balance rather than strength and thuggery. Expect positive edges, slopers, some polish, and few pockets. Most routes are 5.11 and 5.12. Many routes are packed on the cliff, making it easy to get lost and not find a particular line. Bring a dozen quickdraws and a 200-foot (60-meter) rope. Some routes are long and need two ropes to abseil off.

Finding the cliff: Park at the Morgiou harbor lot. Look for a trail on the south side of the parking area. Follow it up and right to the cliff. Hiking time is ten minutes.

Routes are described from left to right. The names of most of the routes are painted on the base, so route finding isn't a problem. The first five routes are on a buttress on the left side by a small, freestanding pillar. Most routes are not on the topo.

1. Cotillon (5c) (5.9) Good fun. 6 bolts to 2-bolt anchor.

2. Chapeau Pointu (6a) (5.10a) Short crux on blunt prow. 7 bolts to 2-bolt anchor.

3. Serpentin (5c+) (5.9+) 7 bolts to 2-bolt anchor.

4. Confetti (5b) (5.8) 5 bolts to 2-bolt anchor.

5. Champagne (4c) (5.6) Broken corner. 5 bolts to 2-bolt anchor.

6. Le Grenouille et le Crapaud (6b) (5.10c) Excellent and highly recommended. Yellow wall left of a corner. A 130-foot pitch. 16 bolts to 2-bolt anchor.

7. Le Cimetiere des Arlequins (6b) (5.10c) 2 pitches. Begin right of #25. **Pitch 1:** Cross #25 at bolt 7, then up the wall above. Finish at #25's anchors. 130 feet. **Pitch 2:** Head up right (5c) to higher anchors.

8. Les Infants de la Magie (7a) (5.11d)

9. Delire Express (6c+) (5.11c)

10. Turluttutu (6b+) (5.10d) Excellent. Goes to *Les Infants*'s anchors.

11. Le Nouvel An (5c) (5.9) Goes to *Les Infants*'s anchors.

12. Contact Magazine (6b) (5.10c) Recommended.

13. Barbatruc (6c+) (5.11c)

14. Retour De Manivelle (7a+) (5.12a)

15. Barbibule (7a+) (5.12a) Thread up left through overhangs, crossing *Retour* and up to anchors. Second part above is 7b.

16. Juste Avant L'Oubli (7c) (5.12d)

17. Cendre de Lune (7b+) (5.12c)

18. Mort Jouit (6c+) (5.11c) Begin on the right side of the overhanging wall. Route traverses up and right to anchors.

19. Gagwell (7c+) (5.13a) Right side of cave. Directly up.

20. Passage a L'Acte (7a) (5.11d) 2 pitches. **Pitch 1:** Up to #37's anchors (6b). 4 bolts. **Pitch 2:** Up and left (7a) (5.11d). 5 bolts.

21. Scorpion (6c+) (5.11c) 2 pitches. **Pitch 1:** Follow a line of weakness up left to *Mort Jouit*'s anchors (5c+). **Pitch 2:** Straight up (6c+) (5.11c).

22. Fin de Partie (8a) (5.13b)

23. Bourre et Bam et Ratatoum (7c+) (5.13a)

24. Reves Truques (7c) (5.12d) The second part above the anchor is 7c+ (5.13a).

25. Prisonnier des Nuages (7c+) (5.13a)

26. Vertige (7a+) (5.12a) Recommended. Direct finish above anchors is 7b.

27. Ma Grande Mere est une Rockeuse (8a+) (5.13c)

28. Sous Haute Surveillance (7b+) (5.12c)

Le Cret-Saint-Michel

Le Cret-Saint-Michel, 300 feet high and 1,600 feet wide, is an excellent, southwest-facing cliff that overlooks Morgiou. Many superb multipitch routes lace this climbable wall, offering perfect limestone, good protection, spectacular views, and technical climbing.

All routes are bolted, but bring a small rack of nuts and cams just in case your pitch is runout. Otherwise bring a dozen quickdraws and a single 200-foot (60-meter) rope. Descent off most routes is by rappelling from fixed anchors or by scrambling off to the left (west) down gullies and rocky slopes.

Finding the cliff: The easiest approach is from the village of Morgiou. From Marseille drive over the narrow road through Col de Morgiou, and park at the harbor lot. From the parking walk back up the road and look for a footpath posted LUMINY between some houses. Follow the steep path up a stony drainage to the cliff base. Hiking time is twenty minutes. The described routes are on the buttress on the cliff's left side. Routes are described from left to right.

1. Le Marchand de Sable (6a) (5.10a) 4 pitches.

2. Le Grand Diedre Jaune (5b) (5.8) 5 pitches. Classic and excellent. **Pitch 1:** Up the right-facing corner system (5b) to a belay stance. 5 bolts. **Pitch 2:** Continue up the corner (5a), then right to a ledge

with bushes. 4 bolts. **Pitch 3:** Work up right along a weakness (4b) to a belay stance. 5 bolts. **Pitch 4:** Move right and climb the right-facing dihedral (4b) to a belay. 4 bolts. **Pitch 5:** Stellar climbing up the big right-facing dihedral (4c+). 6 bolts.

3. Hymne à la Vie (6b+) (5.10d) 4 pitches. Excellent climb. Begin just right of *Le Grand Diedre Jaune*. **Pitch 1:** Climb a long pitch up the white face (6b+) right of the right-facing corner system to the

second belay of *Le Grand Diedre Jaune*. **Pitch 2:** Continue up the face above (6a) to a belay ledge. **Pitch 3:** Climb the steep slab up and right (5c+) to a belay ledge below the big dihedral. **Pitch 4:** Work up the steep white rib on the outside of the dihedral (6b) to a belay ledge atop the cliff.

4. La Directe (5c+) (5.9+) 3 or 4 pitches. A classic adventure up corners and cracks right of the central pillar.

L'Abri Côtier

This southwest-facing sector, part of the larger cliff band on the north side of Calanque Morgiou, is a popular site with a good selection of moderate routes. The cliff receives morning shade.

Finding the cliff: Drive to the village of Morgiou, and park in the harbor lot. Walk east along the north (left) side of the harbor to a trail (GR 98-51) that switchbacks uphill to the cliff's base. Hike east on the trail, which goes to Calanque Sugiton, for about five minutes to the base of the obvious cliff band.

A few routes, not described here, are on the first face you reach. Continue along the cliff to the lower-angle, featured face. The routes are easy to find since most names are painted at the base. Routes are described left to right. Most routes are not on the topo.

1. Choupinette (3c) (5.5)

2. Nicolas (4a) (5.6)

3. Mes Pitchounets (4c) (5.6)

4. Passe Simple (5a) (5.7)

5. Intense Surprise Finale (5b+) (5.8)

6. Un Gout de Trop Peu (5b) (5.8)

7. Revenez-y!! (5c) (5.9)

8. Un Vrai Plaisir (5c) (5.9)

9. Danse Avec Les Clous (5c+) (5.9+)

10. Vestige d'un Jour (6a) (5.10a)

11. Pas Bloc! Pas Bloc! (6b) (5.10c)

12. Long Way (6b+) (5.10d) Halfway up *Pas Bloc!,* exit right and work up right on the steep wall. 100 feet.

13. Vas-y Frankie (6c) (5.11a)

14. Poupette (6c) (5.11a) Start at left side of hole. 115-foot pitch.

15. Voix de Fee (6a) (5.10a) Start at right side of the hole.

The last two routes are on the overhanging wall 100 feet to the right.

16. Golden Gate (7a) (5.11d)

17. Fee-Lyx (7a+) (5.12a)

Falaise du Renard

Falaise du Renard, or Fox Cliff, is a superb northwest-facing cliff on the right side of Calanque Morgiou facing L'Abri Côtier on the opposite side. Several classic multi-pitch routes ascend the cliff's white faces. The obvious feature is a huge, right-facing dihedral. Bring a small rack of Stoppers and small to medium Friends. Descent is by walk-off to the left or by rappel. Scramble left, and descend scree slopes from the first two routes. For the others, make two double-rope rappels (130 feet and 150 feet) down *Violences Passageres* or *Terminator*.

Finding the cliff: Drive to Morgiou, and park at the harbor. Walk west along the right side of the harbor, and locate a trail that begins in the rocks along the water's edge. Follow the trail (GR 98-51) past some cabins, and contour southeast above the water across a steep rocky slope. Farther along look for a path that contours up left across scree slopes and small cliff bands to the base of the face. Hiking time is twenty to thirty minutes. Routes are described from left to right.

1. L'Eperon (5b) 3 pitches. Left side of the obvious pillar. **Pitch 1:** (4c) **Pitch 2:** (4b) **Pitch 3:** (5b) **Descent:** Scramble to left and down scree slopes.

2. Le Noroit (6b) (5.10c) 2 pitches. Follows the corner up the right side of the obvious pillar. **Pitch 1:** (6b) **Pitch 2:** (5c) **Descent:** Scramble to left and down scree slopes.

3. Diedre du Renard (6a) (5.10a) 3 pitches. First climbed in 1942. The classic route up Renard's big dihedral. **Pitch 1:** (5b) Stemming and face climbing up the dihedral. **Pitch 2:** (5b+) Stemming and face climbing up the dihedral. **Pitch 3:** (6a) Climb the steep wall left of the corner before moving right and finishing up the right wall. **Descent:** Make two rappels (130 and 150 feet) with double ropes down *Violences Passageres* or *Terminator*.

4. Violences Passageres (6c) (5.11a) 2 pitches. Recommended. Direct line up the steep face right of the dihedral. **Pitch 1:** (6c) 150 feet. **Pitch 2:** (6c) 130 feet. **Descent:** Make two rappels (130 and 150 feet) with double ropes down the route.

5. Terminator (6a+) (5.10b) 2 pitches. Another fine face route. **Pitch 1:** (6a+) 150 feet. **Pitch 2:** (6a+) 130 feet.

Descent: Make two rappels (130 and 150 feet) with double ropes down the route.

On the face right of *Terminator* are three more routes: *En Deux Fois* (6b) (5.10c) 2 pitches; *Le Plan Droit* (5c) (5.9) 4 pitches; and *Directe du Plan Droit* (6b) (5.10c) 3 pitches. To descend make two rappels (130 feet and 150 feet) down *Violences Passageres* or *Terminator*.

Luminy Sector

Luminy, named for the University of Luminy on the north side of the massif, is a huge sector of cliffs among Calanque de Sugiton, a small *calanque* east of Morgiou. The cliffs include three excellent locales for hard climbing as well as a couple of excellent moderate areas. The hard routes are at L'Oasis, La Grotte de L'Ours, and La Paroi des Toits, whereas excellent mid-grade routes are at Socle de la Candelle and La Grande Candelle.

L'Oasis is a hidden crag tucked in the cliffs high above the *calanque*. The overhanging, 65-foot-high wall of yellow and red limestone is a tranquil spot. The crag offers fifteen routes from 6c to 8a+. Grotte de L'Ours is a quarter mile downhill from L'Oasis. This superb cave or *grotte* yields a selection of pumpy routes up a severely overhanging wall. Farther down the mountainside is the famous Paroi des Toits, a long overhanging wall lined with almost eighty routes from one to three pitches long. This imposing crag is a must for every hard climber. It's well known for

magnificent tufa climbs, including *Le Cimetiere des Elephants* (7c+) (5.13a) and *La Traversee du Desert* (7c+) (5.13a) in the central section. Most routes are long, sustained, and pumpy.

Farther east from Sugiton looms the Socle de la Candelle and La Grande Candelle. La Grande Candelle, the tallest rock formation, is the heart of the Calanques. From the west, "the Great Candle" appears as a pointed spire, whereas from the sea, its wide south-facing wall spreads across the escarpment. Below La Grande Candelle and a sloping terrace is Socle de la Candelle, "the Pedestal of the Candle," an immense rock bastion defined by an architecture of buttresses, faces, pillars, and gullies. Taken together, these two formations are a formidable wall more than 1,000 feet high. Numerous classic routes ascend the walls, making it one of the best and most scenic climbing areas in France. Everyone who visits Les Calanques needs to climb one of Socle's routes and finish up the superlative *Arête de Marseille* on La Grande Candelle's left skyline.

Grotte de L'Ours

This cave tucks into the base of a cliff band above Paroi des Toits. It offers many difficult roof routes that are technical and powerful. The cave, bolted by local climbers from the nearby university, is a good spot to crank hard routes. It gets morning shade and afternoon sun, making it good year-round.

Finding the cliff: The easiest way to access the crag is from University of Luminy on the south side of Marseille. Just as the D559 highway from Cassis enters the east side of Marseille in a valley, look for signs and a left turn to Luminy. Turn and drive up a valley to the university, and park in front of the campus. This is one of the safest places to park at the Calanques.

Hike south on a trail through pines and lavender to Col de Sugiton, where you can look south to the sea. Continue down the path a short distance to a junction. Go left and hike about ten minutes to a bend below Le Virage, a limestone wall. Reach L'Oasis via a faint path at the far side of the bend and cliff. For L'Ours

continue straight for another ten minutes to Grotte de L'Ours on the left. Hiking time from the university is about one hour.

Also reach the cliff from Morgiou by following the coastal path to Sugiton, then follow the trail up below Paroi des Toits to the junction below Col de Sugiton.

Routes are described from left to right. Not all the possible routes are listed here and shown on the topo, but the names are painted at the base. Left of the cave and the first described route are eight other routes that range from 6a to 7c.

1. La Javanise (7c) (5.12d) Excellent. On the left side of the roofs.

2. Parfum Sauvage (7c) (5.12d) or (8a) to the higher anchor. Recommended.

3. Les Massey Ferguson (8b+) (5.14a) Classic route on-sighted by Swiss climber Elie Chevieux; world's first 5.14 on-sight.

4. Virus (Project)

5. Un Instant dans le Vent (7b+) (5.12c) Harder than it looks! Features a tricky traverse right on stalactites.

6. Le Bilboquet (8b+) A second continuation pitch to #5. Up left to upper anchor.

7. Sacchi Shondelba (8b) Over the lower roofs, then up left to #6's anchors.

8. Electroman (Project) Awesome project for the strong. Head up right from *Sacchi* to anchors at the lip.

9. U.F.O. (8c) (5.14b) Classic hard climb but some "enhanced" holds. Out the bulging roofs in the center.

10. Rastata (8b) (5.13d) Pumpy and very physical.

11. Ysengrin (8a) (5.13b) Beautiful climbing.

12. Loopkin (8b) (5.13d) Not as steep but very technical.

13. Le Bilboqueur (8b+) (5.14a)

14. Rio de Janvier (8b) (5.13d) Great.

15. Pepito (8a+) (5.13c)

16. Solitude (Project)

17. Summer Time (6c+) (5.11c)

18. Ristourne (6c) (5.11a/b) Right edge of the cave.

19. Promesse de L'Aube (6a+) Right of the cave.

La Grande Candelle and Socle de la Candelle

La Grande Candelle is the most prominent peak in Les Calanques. This south-facing blade of limestone towers above the lower cliff Socle de la Candelle, the rocky shore, and the crystal sea. La Grande Candelle, with twenty-five routes on its flanks, is the Calanques's limestone masterpiece. Its varied face and crack routes are compared with the great alpine walls in the French Alps. The two megaclassic routes are the arêtes on either side of the great wall—*Arête de Marseille* on the west and *Arête de Cassis,* the longest route in the Calanques with lots of *terrain d'aventure,* on the east.

Socle de la Candelle is a long southwest-facing wall broken into several distinct sectors that are loaded with stellar multipitch routes on excellent stone. This easily accessed cliff yields some real gems, including *La Civa, Le Temple,* and *Gutemberg* on the left side.

Both cliffs face southwest and are generally protected from the persistent mistral wind in winter. They also receive morning shade, making them a good bet when temperatures heat up.

It's a full day adventure to climb at either or both cliffs. Plan accordingly by carrying plenty of water if it's hot. Despite the expanse of sea, you won't find any drinkable water out there. Also bring sturdy shoes if you climb La Grande Candelle since the descent is down steep gullies filled with gravel and loose rock.

Besides a dozen quickdraws, bring a small rack of Stoppers and small to medium Friends. A 165-foot (50-meter) rope is fine, although a longer 200-foot (60-meter) rope allows pitches to be strung together.

Socle de la Candelle

The Socle de la Candelle is the lower wall below the obvious Grande Candelle. The cliff is easy to access, making its routes very popular. The long cliff is divided into several sectors, which are, from left to right when facing it, Temple, Les Tours, Plaques Grises, Igloo, Vo2 Max, and Aiguille. Each sector is named for a classic route on that cliff section. The Secteur Temple, the only sector described in this guide, offers some of the best routes on this clean sweep of rock. Consult the comprehensive area guide for topos of the other sectors.

Finding the cliff: Follow directions to Calanque de Sugiton from the village of Morgiou. Past the *calanque,* drop down a trail, and follow the rocky coast around Calanque des Pierres-Tombées and its popular nudist beach below cliffs. At the far end of the cliff, scramble up and right on a rocky trail to the base of the wall. The three described routes focus on a huge left-facing dihedral and a pillar to its right. Hiking time is one to two hours from Morgiou.

Alternatively, approach from University of Luminy on the south side of Marseille. Just as the D559 highway from Cassis enters the east side of Marseille, look for signs and a left turn to Luminy. Turn and drive up a valley to the university, and park in front of the campus. Hike south on a trail through pines and lavender to Col de Sugiton, where you can look south to the sea. Continue to an obvious junction, and go left uphill to Le Virage, a white cliff. Walk under the cliff, and continue right along steep slopes past L'Ours to the Socle, a prominent cliff on your left. Scramble to the base of a big right-facing dihedral on the left side of the long wall to find the described routes. Hiking time is one to two hours.

1. La Civa (6a) (5.10a) 8 or 9 pitches. Combine pitches to do it in four or five pitches. Begin left of the big dihedral. The route climbs up and left on the vertical face, following a line of weakness for five pitches. **Pitch 1:** (5c+) **Pitch 2:** (5c+) **Pitch 3:** (5c) **Pitch 4:** (4c) **Pitch 5:** (5c) **Pitch 6:** Climb up right easily to a good ledge system below the final wall. **Pitch 7:** Climb the obvious crack system above, passing a big block on the right (5b+). Traverse left to a belay stance. **Pitch 8:** Continue up left along a crack system (5c) to a stance. **Pitch 9:** Finish up a short headwall (5b) to the top. These last pitches can be combined with a long rope.
Descent: Make three rappels—150 feet, 150 feet, and 115 feet—from three sets of anchors starting atop Pitch 6. Otherwise, scramble up slopes above and finish up La Grande Candelle, or descend steep gullies on the west side of the cliff. **Rack:** The route and belays are bolted, but bring a small rack of Stoppers and small to medium Friends. Bring two ropes to rappel from the top of pitch 6 or shoes for the walk-off descent.

2. Le Temple (5c) (5.9) 8 pitches. Combine pitches to do it in four or five pitches. Combine with *Arête de Marseille* on La Grande Candelle for a superb climb. Begin just left of the big left-facing dihedral below a wide crack. **Pitch 1:** Climb the wide crack using handholds inside (4c) to a bolted belay stance. **Pitch 2:** Face climbing using edges and layaways (5c) to a bolted belay stance. **Pitch 3:** Airy face moves lead up and right (5c) to an awkward finishing crack to a ledge with a large tree belay anchor. These first three pitches can be combined into a 165-foot-long pitch. **Pitch 4:** Make an airy traverse left to a flake crack (4b) to a spacious belay alcove. **Pitch 5:** Stem up two steps using loose flakes (5b) and a hanging block. Climb a rib up left to an exposed face with perfect rock to easy climbing that leads to a bolted belay ledge. **Pitch 6:** Climb the obvious crack system above, passing a big block on the right (5b+). Traverse left to a belay stance. **Pitch 7:** Continue up left along a crack system (5c)

to a stance. **Pitch 8:** Finish up a short headwall (5b) to the top. These last pitches can be combined with a long rope. A great finishing alternative is **Pitch 6:** Climb the obvious crack system, passing a big rounded block on the right (5b+). Continue straight up the splitter crack system with jams and laybacks (5c). At a roof exit right and voila—a belay ledge atop the wall. This is a 150-foot pitch.
Descent: Make three rappels—150 feet, 150 feet, and 115 feet—from three sets of anchors starting from atop Pitch 5. Otherwise, scramble up slopes above and finish up La Grande Candelle, or descend steep gullies on the cliff's west side. **Rack:** The route and belays are bolted, but bring a small rack of Stoppers and small to medium Friends. Also bring two ropes to rappel from the top of Pitch 5 or shoes for the walk-off descent.

3. Gutemberg (6a+) (5.10b) 4 pitches. A stellar face climb up the white rib right of *Le Temple*. Start on the outside of the buttress right of *Le Temple* and the big dihedral. **Pitch 1:** Face climb directly up the rib (5c) to a bolt belay. **Pitch 2:** Steep face climbing up left (6a) to a ledge belay at the big tree (shared with *Le Temple*). **Pitch 3:** Work up pebbles in the dihedral above (6a+) to easy climbing to a bolt belay. **Pitch 4:** Finish up a slightly overhanging crack system (6a+) to a bolt belay atop the buttress. **Descent:** Make three rappels from bolted anchors down the route—115 feet, 130 feet, and 150 feet. **Rack:** Bring a small rack of Stoppers and Friends, two ropes, and a helmet.

La Grande Candelle

La Grande Candelle is simply one of the Calanques's great walls. The south-facing formation offers a wide face flanked by the *Arête de Marseille* on the west and the *Arête de Cassis* on the east. The megaclassic *Arête de Marseille,* established in 1927, is one of the most popular routes in Les Calanques. This excellent route ascends a long, narrow arête with lots of exposure, just enough protection, and spectacular views across the mountains and sea. Set aside a full day to do the approach, the climb, the descent, and the long walk back to your car. The west-facing route is shaded in the morning. Because of its height and exposure, it is subject to the full force of the mistral wind. For topos and details to other routes, consult the area guidebook.

Bring a small rack of wires and cams to supplement bolts. A 200-foot (60-meter) rope is handy for stringing pitches together; otherwise, a 165-foot (50-meter) rope is adequate for climbing and rappelling.

Several Descents are possible. From the west end of the narrow summit ridge, scramble east along the crest to a shallow gully on the left (north) side. Scramble down and left to a set of beefy rappel bolts on a ledge. It may take work to find the bolts since they are not obvious. Make a single 80-foot rappel to the base of the north face.

If you parked at Luminy, take the high trail (GR 98-51) from the saddle called Col de la Candelle northwest to Col de Sugiton. Drop northwest down the valley on the trail to the university. If you are parked at Morgiou, hike to the Col de Sugiton, and descend a trail to the *calanque* head.

Or descend steep gullies on the west side of La Candelle. To reach these contour into a deep rock gully directly below the arête using a fixed cable. Descend a steep gully around the base of the arête and then down another steep gully called Couloir du Candelon between Socle on the east and Cathédrale on the west. Eventually reach a trail that descends sharply to the rocky shore and nudist beach. Take a swim if it's hot. Follow the trail west along the coastline to the head of Calanque de Sugiton, and continue west to Morgiou.

Finding the cliff: To climb Socle and then La Candelle, follow the directions to Calanque de Sugiton from the village of Morgiou. Past the *calanque* descend a trail, and follow it along the rocky coast around Calanque des Pierres-Tombées and its nudist beach below cliffs. At the far end of the cliff, scramble up and right on a rocky trail to the base of the Socle's wall. Hiking time is one to two hours from Morgiou.

To climb only La Candelle, it's easiest to approach from Luminy. Drive to the University of Luminy and park. Hike southeast on the marked trail to Col de Sugiton. Continue down the valley to an obvious junction. Go left on a trail to Le Virage, a white cliff. At the end of the cliff, go left on another path that leads up and across a long cliff (L'Ours) and under Cathédrale. Past this formation look for a steep, rocky gully, Couloir du Candelon, that divides Cathédrale from Socle. Scramble up the gully to a path partway up that exits right. Labor up gravel slopes to the base of a chimney on the south side of the prominent west ridge of La Candelle. Approach time is two hours.

4. Arête de Marseille (5c) (5.9) 4 to 5 pitches. Classic and recommended. Start below the obvious chimney. **Pitch 1:** Work up the slippery chimney (5c) to just below a notch. Climb up left on shelves to a bolt belay just below the top of a semi-freestanding pillar. **Pitch 2:** Do the famous step-across move between the pillar and ridge. Grab jugs and pull across. Climb the ridge (5a+) to a bolted belay ledge. Pitches 1 and 2 can be combined into a 165-foot lead. **Pitch 3:** Continue up the ridge (5a+) for 160 feet to a bolted belay on a ledge on the right. This can also be broken into three separate pitches. **Pitch 4:** Tricky face climbing (5b) up the flat arête leads to easier climbing on the ridge. Belay atop the ridge just below the summit. 150 feet. This can be done in two pitches. **Pitch 5:** Make a blind traverse on jugs around the exposed right side of a step, and scramble onto the summit. **Descent:** After reaching the west end of the narrow summit ridge, scramble east along the crest, and look for a shallow gully on the left (north) side. Scramble down and left, and find a set of beefy rappel bolts on a ledge. It takes some time to find the bolts since they are not obvious. Make a single 80-foot rappel to the base of the north face. Hike west along climber trails.

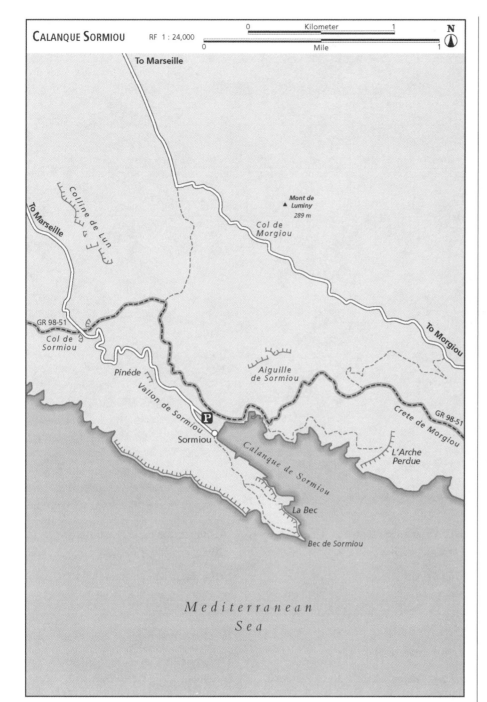

Kilometer

Mile

To Marseille

Colline de Lun

To Marseille

Mont de Luminy
▲ 289 m

Col de Morgiou

GR 98-51

Col de Sormiou

Pinéde

Aiguille de Sormiou

To Morgiou

Vallon de Sormiou

P

Sormiou

Calanque de Sormiou

Crete de Morgiou

GR 98-51

L'Arche Perdue

La Bec

Bec de Sormiou

Mediterranean Sea

Calanque Sormiou

La Calanque de Sormiou is a deep *calanque* separating the Marseille and Puget mountain massifs. The village and pretty harbor of Sormiou nestle at the end of the inlet. High mountains lined with soaring white cliffs rise above quiet water. This *calanque,* like the others, is frequented by hikers, picnickers, anglers, swimmers, and climbers. Lots of excellent cragging is found on the compact limestone cliffs surrounding the *calanque.* Popular climbing spots include several small crags atop Col de Sormiou; La Pinéde, a good moderate area just off the road; L'Arche Perdue, a superb cliff above the northwest shore; the excellent route *La Momie,* "the Mummy," at Le Bec; the well-equipped sector of Tiragne on the southwest side of Bec de Sormiou, facing the open sea with seventy routes; and the Luï d'Aï on the other side of the peninsula. The only described sector here is L'Arche Perdue.

L'Arche Perdue

L'Arche Perdue is an excellent sector on a northwest-facing cliff in a shallow valley on the east side of Calanque Sormiou. The sector, part of a long cliff, offers a good selection of routes from 3b to 6c+. It's relatively quiet and off the beaten track, giving solitude and fun climbing in a scenic setting above the *calanque.* All routes are well bolted and safe, making it a good spot to crank a lot of pitches. Most routes are about 60 feet long. It's shaded in the morning.

Finding the cliff: Drive to Sormiou from Marseille, pay the guardian at the hut, and park in the large lot. It's safe to park here since the lot is patrolled. Follow a trail that begins on the left side of the car park, and hike southeast above the rocky shore of the *calanque.* The trail eventually reaches a shallow ravine with a huge cliff walling its right side. Hike up the ravine along a stony trail to an obvious break in the lower cliff band. Scramble to the base of the vertical cliffs. Hiking time is thirty minutes. Routes are described from left to right. The first three routes are on a lower tier.

1. Les Aventuriers (3b) (5.4) No topo. No bolts. Toprope from anchors or solo.

2. Dernier Cri (4a) (5.5) No topo. No bolts. Toprope from anchors or solo.

3. Premisses (3b) (5.4) No topo. No bolts. Toprope from anchors or solo.

The main sector begins above the short lower tier of cliffs. Belay bolts are scattered along the cliff base. The first routes begin almost directly above the access scramble.

4. Typha (6c+) (5.11c) A long pitch. Up a white streak in the middle of a streaked wall.

5. Vanille (6c) (5.11a/b) Long 115-foot pitch. Name at the base. Starts up black streaks left of a corner.

6. La Virgule (5b) (5.8) Crack right of left-facing corner.

7. La Gri-Gri (4c) (5.6) A *gri-gri* is an African talisman and a belay device. Face right of corner to anchors in a diagonal crack.

8. Pitchounette (4c) (5.6)

9. Force Majeure (5b) (5.8) Good face climbing.

10. Mur Laque (6a) (5.10a) Big fun route up gray streaks.

11. Archimede in France (5c) (5.9)

12. Les Compagnons du Crepuscule (5c+) (5.9+) No topo.

13. Coup de Grisoo (5b+) (5.8+) Along a leaning crack system.

14. Didactique de la Masturbation (6a) (5.10a) Face left of corner.

15. La Balayette Enchante (4c) The obvious right-angling, left-facing corner system.

16. Chiva Tombe (6a) (5.10a) Slight bulge.

17. Tombe du Ciel (6a+) (5.10b) Excellent.

18. Moquette Chinee (5c+) (5.9+) Start out right on ledge.

19. Guigui le Homard (5c) (5.9)

20. Avec Vue Sure le Bec (5b+) (5.8) No topo.

21. Juste Avant la Plage (5b+) (5.8) No topo.

ORPIERRE

■ OVERVIEW

The south of France is stacked with great crags—Céüse, Gorges du Verdon, Buoux, Les Calanques, Mte. Sainte-Victoire, Presles, Claret, Cimai, and Orpierre stand out as some of the best. Orpierre, however, didn't always keep such illustrious company. Once it was empty of both climbers and routes, but in the late 1980s the town council and local climbers combined forces to create a new climbing area to revive the village's sagging fortunes. After visiting Orpierre you'll agree that they succeeded.

The climbing area's sand-colored limestone cliffs loom above Orpierre, an old medieval village of stone buildings crowding narrow streets in the Hautes-Alpes region of southeastern France. This mountainous region is a rough tapestry of rumpled peaks, lofty cliff-bound hills, slashing canyons, and broad valleys filled with wheat fields and farmhouses. The village of Orpierre, lying in the Buëch Basin, straddles the narrow gap below a winding gorge sliced by the Céans River through the mountain spine to the west. A restful beauty surrounds the village. If you sit in the dusty village plaza beneath shady sycamores or explore its ancient streets, it's easy to be transported back in time.

Orpierre, named for the adjoining village, is one of the most popular sport-climbing areas in southern France, with easy access to its cliffs, generally mild weather, lots of sunshine, and a rich range of easy and moderate routes. The area, unlike many French areas, offers lots of moderate lines, making it a paradise for the middle-grade climber. Some introductory routes are protected with bolts every 3 feet, allowing beginning leaders to safely explore their limits. The extreme climber also finds hard routes, including *Mission Impossible* (5.14b) (8c), Orpierre's hardest climb. The routes are mostly single-pitch affairs, although some multipitch lines are also found. The limestone cliffs range from 50 to 500 feet high.

The area is relaxed, and the emphasis for all climbers is fun. You see groups of friends that hail from all European nations: Germans that escaped from their cities; vanloads of Brits touring southern France's sun-rock areas; and Spanish, Italian, Belgian, Dutch, and Nordic climbers gathered at the base of routes and conversing in a plethora of tongues. Nearby a father tows a child up an easy route while the rest of the family has a picnic. Orpierre—it's an international climbing resort, with the number, quality, and safety of its routes as the main attractions.

The Orpierre climbing area is composed of eight different sectors, with most of them facing south, southwest, and southeast. The most popular cliffs surround a wide horseshoe-shaped valley north of the village. The popular Falaise du Château cliffs line the west side of the valley; the slabby wall of Belleric hems in the valley's northern end; and the high buttress and impressive cliffs of Quiquillon flank the upper east side of the valley. More cliffs stretch northeast from Quiquillon along the eastern mountain flank, including Quatre Heures, L'Adrech with several multipitch routes, and Les Blaches.

Quiquillon dominates the area with its huge walls and jutting southern prow, but it's the two smaller sectors, Falaise du Château and Belleric, that attract most climbers. At first glance both cliffs seem small and somewhat broken, without the immaculate limestone of the nearby famous venues of Verdon and Céüse. The rock, however, is surprisingly solid, with lots of edges, flakes, pockets, and jugs.

Other Area Crags

When you've had your fill of Orpierre or want to climb somewhere different, sample the other fine climbing areas scattered around the nearby mountains. Sigottier, about 15 miles to the north and above the village of the same name, is a climbing site composed of impressive limestone fins. The area yields some brilliant crack and face climbs in a wild and beautiful setting that is well off the beaten track. Some routes are steep, committing slab lines up perfect rock. Most of them ascend the main faces of Grande Dalle and Rocher d'Agnielle. A recommended route is two-pitch *Phebus* (5.10b), with a stunning second pitch transplanted from the Verdon. Note that climbing is forbidden on the cliffs above the village and for 500 feet (150 meters) on either side, above the road, and near the television antenna cables. Ask at Vertige Sport for a cliff topo.

Two other good nearby areas are Ventavon and Sisteron. Ventavon, east of Orpierre, is a long, south-facing limestone cliff with more than 100 great routes on excellent rock. The magnificent Montagne de la Baume looms above the Durance River and the medieval town of Sisteron. This huge cliff, tunneled through its base by a highway, yields many bolted routes up its wide, sunny south face. The easier lines follow crack systems, whereas the harder ones pick pockets and edges up blank faces.

Rack, Protection, and Descent

Bolts protect all of Orpierre's routes, making this a very safe climbing arena. The beginner routes are especially sewn up with protection, allowing novice leaders to push their on-sight levels.

A standard Orpierre rack is twelve to fifteen quickdraws and a 200-foot (60-meter) rope, although a 165-foot (50-meter) rope is adequate for most of the courses. It's a good idea, however, to check that you have enough rope to both climb and lower to the ground. Make sure your belayer is attentive and has a knot tied in the rope's end to avoid dropping you. If you climb any of the longer routes, then it's wise to carry a small rack of wires and a few cams to plug in between widely spaced bolts. A helmet is a good idea if you're climbing beneath other parties.

Descent off all routes is by lowering or rappelling from fixed bolt anchors.

Seasons and Weather

Orpierre offers year-round climbing, with the best months from March through mid-October. The spring months, March to May, are generally sunny and dry, although there can be cool periods with rain. Summers are busy with climbers, but it is often too hot in the sun. Unless the air is stifling hot, the Falaise du Château is perfect in the afternoon after the shade descends on it.

September through early October is an excellent time to visit Orpierre. Expect dry, sunny days and no crowds. In October the weather changes and becomes wet. October and November are the wettest months, with an average of 4 inches of rain and snow. Precipitation falls on average only eighty days each year. Winters are variable. It can be bright, sunny, and warm, but it can also be cloudy with rain or snow showers. The south-facing cliffs are warm on sunny winter days, even with snow on the ground. The good thing is that it's easy to bail from here if the weather changes and head south to sunnier climes like Les Calanques, which is only a couple hours away on the south coast.

Climbing History

Orpierre is not an old climbing area—it's one of France's newer developments. By 1980 the village was slowly shrinking, and few people lived there. So climbing activists and the local village council got together and came up with a plan to revive Orpierre's sagging fortunes by investing in "athletic tourism." The town, viewing the cliffs as an untapped resource, funded the climbers to establish routes and got the word out that climbers were welcome here—a refreshing attitude for Americans used to access problems. Pierre-Yves Bochaton, the patrone of Croq'Roc restaurant, opened and equipped many of the area's routes.

Getting Around

The village and cliffs at Orpierre are easily reached by car from the A51 autoroute to the east between Sisteron and Gap. The cliffs are 15 miles (25 kilometers) from Sisteron and 80 miles (130 kilometers) or an hour-and-a-half drive south of Grenoble.

Orpierre is also one of the few southern French crags easily accessible by train. Take the train between Paris and

Marseille and get off at the Laragne station, or take the train to Grenoble and then the bus on either the Grenoble-Marseille or Genève-Nice line. Disembark at Eyguians, and hitchhike the 6 kilometers to Orpierre.

Once you're in the village, it's easy to get around by foot. Most of the routes in the horseshoe-shaped valley north of the village can be reached in fewer than fifteen minutes from the campground, whereas the farther cliffs might take up to half an hour of hiking.

Camping, Accommodations, and Services

Most climbers stay in the spacious campground just south of the village. It has a small shop, a pool in summer, laundry facilities, and caravans for rent if the weather is bad. It can be extremely busy in summer with not only climbers, but also families on holiday. No wild camping is permitted in the area.

Alternatively, there are some hotels and many excellent *gîtes* or guesthouses in the immediate area. These are a great value if you're not carrying camping gear and just doing a quick crag tour of southern France. A good *gîte* in the center of the village is owned by the Vertige Sport climbing shop. Ask at the local tourist office for information and phone numbers for area *gîtes*. Also check the Appendix for some accommodation contacts.

Orpierre offers several shops, including Vertige Sport climbing shop, several restaurants and bars, a small market, and a good *boulangerie* or bakery for fresh baguettes and baked goodies. The nearest big supermarket is in Sisteron. A good restaurant is Croq'Roc, a vegetarian restaurant managed by the author of the local climbing guide.

Cultural Experiences and Rest Days

Orpierre is not only a great climbing destination, but it also offers lots of other outdoor sports for rest days. Nearby are several *via ferratas,* including the Motte du Caire Via Ferrata, which boasts a 200-

foot-long suspension bridge, the longest in Europe. Information, directions, and guiding for the *via ferratas* is available at Vertige Sport. Excellent mountain biking trails lace the area. Vertige Sport rents bikes. Some superb hiking trails also explore the surrounding mountains, including the GR 946 Grande Randonnée trail, which passes through the village. The trail climbs north to the range crest and the summit of 4,344-foot Le Suillet before descending to the village of Trescléoux. The south trail crosses the river and then ascends to Col de St. Ange, another climbing site. The Orpierre area is also well known for its paragliding opportunities.

A couple nearby towns are worth visiting. Sisteron, dating back to pre-Roman times, sits in a rocky gap at the confluence of the Durance and Buëch Rivers. An imposing thirteenth-century citadel protects the gap and town. It's an interesting town to explore, with a variety of shops and sites. Be sure to visit the peaceful twelfth-century Notre Dame des Pommiers cathedral and the Citadel. Serres, to the north, is a quaint village set on a hillside above the Buëch River. The village, filled with fifteenth- and sixteenth-century houses, is fun to explore and has some good restaurants.

Trip Planning Information

General description: One of southern France's best and most popular midgrade climbing areas with more than 250 bolted routes on several limestone cliffs perched above the ancient village of Orpierre.

Location: Orpierre lies in the Haute-Alpes region of southeastern France. It is 80 miles (130 kilometers) south of Grenoble and 102 miles (170 kilometers) north of Marseille. The area is 15 miles (25 kilometers) northwest of Sisteron.

Camping and accommodations: No primitive camping. Most climbers stay at Camping des Princes D'Orange (Tel: 04 92 66 22 53) on the south side of Orpierre. The site, which is very popular in summer, is open from April 1 to October 30. It's an easy walk to the cliffs from the campground. Cabins and trailers are also for rent if the weather is funky. Hotels and many gîtes are also found in the surrounding area. A couple gîtes are Les Drailles (Tel: 04 92 66 31 20) and Saint-Avons (Tel: 04 92 66 23 68). A hotel is Hotel le Céans (Tel: 04 92 66 24 22). Call the Office du Tourisme (Tel: 04 92 66 30 45) for a complete listing and more phone numbers.

Climbing season: Spring (April through mid-June) and autumn (September through mid-October) are ideal. Summer days can be extremely hot, although shady cliffs can be found in afternoon. Precipitation occurs on eighty days annually, with October and November the wettest months. The winter is usually dry and cool but often sunny.

Restrictions and access issues: None. Climbing is encouraged at Orpierre, and climber expenditures make up a good portion of the local economy. Keep to designated access paths to the cliffs so you avoid crossing private property, and pick up all your trash.

A big problem here is toilet tissue and human excrement. There are no toilets near the crags, so most people use the nearest big boulder on the slopes below the cliffs as their outhouse. It smells on summer days, and the tissue flowers are abominable. Don't contribute to the problem. Perhaps the town and area climbers will recognize the problem and put in a self-composting toilet on the flat area below Belleric.

Guidebooks: *Orpierre et Val de Meouge* with information in French, German, and English, is the complete guide to all of Orpierre's cliffs as well as nearby Châteauneuf de Chabre in Val de Méouge. It's available at Vertige Sport in Orpierre.

Services and shops: Vertige Sport is Orpierre's climbing shop, selling gear and guidebooks, renting bicycles, and offering area beta. Orpierre offers basic services, including a market and bakery. For a bigger supermarket, head to Sisteron or Gap.

Emergency services: Call 18 for rescue and 112 for emergency services. The nearest medical facilities are in Sisteron and Gap.

Nearby climbing areas: Besides the described sectors at Orpierre, there are several other excellent climbing sectors: the southeast face (Face Sud-Est) and Secteur du Ramier on Quiquillon, Falaise de Quatre Heures, Pilier Ouest de l'Ascle, Falaise de l'Adrech, and Falaises des Blaches. The sector Quatre Heures is stacked with lots of moderate routes and worth visiting.

Several nearby areas are described in the comprehensive local guide, available in the Orpierre climbing shop. Châteauneuf de Chabre in Val de Méouge just south of Orpierre on the D942 offers almost eighty midgrade routes. Ventavon, off the D942 east of Orpierre, is another good area.

Farther away near Gap is the great cliff of Céüse and La Roche-des-Arnauds. In the mountains above Gap are Ancelle, Pont-du-Fossé, and some high mountain rock climbs on Pic du Grillon, Les Gillardes, and at Gorges-du-Rif. Consult the local area guides for the beta on these and other areas.

Nearby attractions: Sisteron and its Citadel and Notre Dame Cathedral is

worth a day trip. The nearby towns and villages, including Serres and Gap, are fun to discover and explore. Drive around the countryside on the many minor roads and you'll discover some amazing places. For information and suggestions contact the Tourist Office/Office de Tourisme in Orpierre (Tel: 04 92 66 30 45).

Finding the cliffs: From Sisteron and the A51 autoroute, take exit 23 just north of Sisteron and drive northwest on highway N75 (Sisteron to Grenoble highway) toward Serres. After about 20 kilometers, turn left in Eyguians on highway D30, and follow it for 8 kilometers to Orpierre. Turn right just past the town square, and follow a narrow road to Parking du Belleric by the cemetery.

A trail goes uphill from here to Falaise du Château and continues north along the cliff base. Another trail heads north along the creek to Falaise du Belleric. At the mine tailings below Le Belleric, a trail contours east below Le Quiquillon to several other sectors.

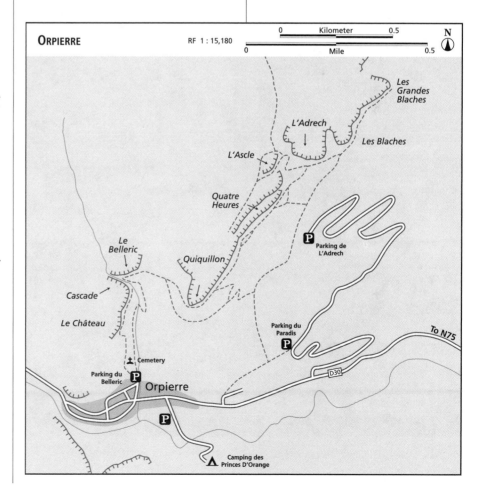

Falaise du Château

Le Château is the long, east-facing cliff escarpment on the left (west side) of the horseshoe-shaped valley north of Orpierre. Many fine routes ascend the long cliff, climbing everything from beginner slabs to the area's hardest routes out overhanging walls. The cliff is good on hot afternoons after it goes into the shade.

Secteur Les Racines du Ciel

This is the left-hand sector on the cliff. Access is fewer than ten minutes uphill from the parking area above the cemetery. A trail along the cliff base leads to the other sectors. Routes are listed left to right. The first three routes are on the first buttress. No topos.

1. Ciao Emile (5b) (5.8) Far left route up the first buttress.

2. L'éloge de la fuite (4c) (5.6) Fun middle route.

3. Paris-Texas (4b) (5.6) Right route on the buttress.

Routes #4 to #7 are popular easy lines up a slab.

4. Le serpent d'étoile (4c) (5.6)

5. Ini . . . (4b) (5.5)

6. Tiation . . . (4c) (5.6)

7. Traffic (4c) (5.6)

Routes #8 to #19 ascend the prominent buttress capped with a large roof on its right side.

8. Canardo (4c) (5.6)

9. Palmer (5a) (5.7)

10. Les clochards célestes (5b/c) (5.8+)

11. Le ficelou de Miss Waikiki (5c+) (5.9+)

12. Think Punk (5b) (5.8)

13. Cachou pour un lézard (5c) (5.9)

14. Les racines du ciel (6a) (5.10a)

15. Maudit manége (6b+) (5.10d) 2 pitches. **Pitch 1:** (5c+) (5.9) **Pitch 2:** (6b+) (5.10d) A short pumper over the big roof.

16. Sax, éponge et rodeo (5b/c) (5.8+)

17. Derniére prise avant le relais (5b/c) (5.8+)

18. Le ventre plein (5b) (5.8)

19. Les rescapés de la Côte d'Azur (5a) (5.7)

The following three routes are on the left face of a buttress right of a water pour-off.

20. Lent dehors (5a) (5.7)

21. Le fou d'Amérique (5a) (5.7)

22. Le fou direct (5c+) (5.9+)

Secteur Dévers

23. Les blessures de l'âme (7a) (5.11d)

24. Evitons d'emportuner l'étrangleur (7a) (5.11d)

25. Les copains d'abord (6c+) (5.11b/c)

26. Les vidanges du diable (pas de bloc) (7a/b) (5.11d/12a)

27. Mon ami Bart (6c+) (5.11b/c)

28. Pas de bras, pas de chocolat (7b) (5.12b)

29. Essayes Encore (7a+) (5.12a)

30. Tombe et tais-toi (7b) (5.12b)

31. 7 mai 1995, désillusion (7b) (5.12b)

32. Les kilos vont en enfer (7a) (5.11d)

33. La moulinette endimanchée (6a) (5.10a)

34. Poupoupidou ou le chant des étoiles
(6c) (5.11a) 2 pitches. **Pitch 1:** (6c)
(5.11a) **Pitch 2:** (6a+) (5.10b)

35. Ohm (7b) (5.12b)

36. Ca va couiner (7c) (5.12d)

37. Jesus inhyea (Unknown)

38. Mission Impossible (8c) (5.14b)
Orpierre's hardest route. Put up by J. B.
Tribout.

39. Pourquoi tant de haine? (7b+)
(5.12c)

40. Toutes les chances plus une (7b)
(5.12b)

41. L'ange gardien (7b+) (5.12c)

42. Les ailes du désir (6c+) (5.11b/c)

43. Pour un bébé robot (7b) (5.12b)

44. Le vol d'Icare (6b) (5.10c)

45. Costaud Lulu (6a) (5.10a)

46. Amélie Mélodie (6c) (5.11a)

47. Destruction (7c+) (5.13a)

48. Bookaro banzaï (8a) (5.13b)

49. Hurlement (8a+) (5.13c)

50. bis N'oubliez jamais (8a) (5.13b)

51. Heureusement il y a la bière (7c+) (5.13a)

52. Maman, je vais mourir (7c) (5.12d)

53. Même pas mal (7c) (5.12d)

54. Reste avec moi (7c) (5.12d)

55. Pourquoi t'est malheureux? (7c+)
(5.13a)

56. Dur, dur d'être un mutant (7c+)
(5.13a)

57. Jusque là, ca va (8a) (5.13b)

**58. La semaine prochaine, j'enléve le
haut** (8a) (5.13b) 2 pitches. **Pitch 1:** (6b)
(5.10c) **Pitch 2:** (8a) (5.13b)

59. L'exterminateur d'écailles (6a)
(5.10a)

60. Consommez-moi nature (6c) (5.11a)

61. N comme cornichon (7a+) (5.12a)

62. Duo d'amour pour vélo et trotinette
(7b) (5.12b)

63. Le guerrier pacifique (7b+) (5.12c)

Secteur Mur L'Anticlinal

This popular sector, laced with numerous one- and two-pitch moderate routes, is the prominent buttress on the far right side of Falaise du Château. It is reached via the cliff-base trail from the sectors to the left (south) or via the trail that follows the creek up the bottom of the valley. At the mine tailings walk west, and follow a short path to the cliff base.

64. Je t'aime moi non plus (7a) (5.11d)

65. Y'a plus de limites (6b+) (5.10d)

66. Le chant des baleines (5c) (5.9)

67. Sauve qui peut le vie (5c+) (5.9+)

68. Le cimetière des éléphants (6a) (5.10a) 2 pitches. **Pitch 1:** (4c+) (5.6) **Pitch 2:** (6a) (5.10a)

69. H2O (5a+) (5.7+)

70. Le piton inconnu (5c) (5.9) 2 pitches. **Pitch 1:** (5a+) (5.7+) **Pitch 2:** (5c) (5.9)

71. Poil dans la main (6a+) (5.10b) 2 pitches. **Pitch 1:** (5c) (5.9) **Pitch 2:** (6a+) (5.10b)

72. Raoul Petite (5b) (5.8) An alternate second pitch for #71.

The following short routes on the Anticlinal Secteur all end at anchors below a broken ledge on the anticline itself.

73. à 72 départs surplombants (Unknown) No topo.

74. Amnesty International (4a) (5.5)

75. Une lettre, une vie (4a) (5.5)

76. Les plumes qui grincent (4a) (5.5)

77. Conflit North Sud (5b/c) (5.8+) No topo.

78. La torture comme quotidien (6a) (5.10a) No topo.

79. Contre la peine de mort (6a) (5.10a) No topo.

Secteur Cascade

Around the corner to the right from Anticlinal is Secteur Cascade. This shady, north-facing cliff rises above the left entrance to a narrow canyon. The routes are very popular, particularly on warm days. Not all the routes are shown on the topo. Routes are described from left to right.

80. Spécial mammouth (6b) (5.10c) No topo.

81. Là où il y a une volonté, il y a un chemin (7a+) (5.12a) No topo.

82. Unknown. No topo.

83. Gaine ton corps (6b+) (5.10d)

84. C'est où qu'c'est dur (6c) (5.11a/b))

85. Chérie, fais-moi mal (6c+) (5.11c)

86. Tais-toi, tais toi (6b+) (5.10d)

87. What's Up (6a) (5.10a)

88. Yénenpéplou (6b) (5.10c)

89. L'homme débloque (6b) (5.10c)

90. 2000 bains, la baignoire de l'espace (5c) (5.9)

91. Etat d'urgence (5c) (5.9)

92. Rivière de pastis (6a+) (5.10b) No topo.

The next eight routes are on the next section of face with gray streaks.

93. Gourmandise (6a) (5.10a)

94. Envie (5c) (5.9) No topo.

95. Orgueil (5b/c) (5.8+)

96. Avarice (5b+) (5.8+)

97. Colère (5c) (5.9)

98. Paresse (6a) (5.10a)

99. Luxure (*Luxury*) (5c) (5.9)

100. Tout sur les pieds, rien dans la tête (5c) (5.9)

The last routes ascend the high, triangular-shaped face on the right.

101. Coupe-doights (5a) (5.7)

102. Maël first (4c) (5.6)

103. Calvaire one (4c or 5c) (5.6 or 5.9)

104. Babouin land (5c) (5.9)

105. Ceuf dur (5c+) (5.9+) No topo.

106. Eclectik Electrik (6a) (5.10a) No topo.

107. Capharnaüm (6a) (5.10a) No topo.

108. Chutes de pierres (5b) (5.8) No topo.

109. La Plage (*The Beach*) (3c) (5.4) No topo.

Falaise du Belleric

The excellent, south-facing Belleric Cliff sits at the head of the valley north of Orpierre. The 170-foot-high crag offers numerous moderate outings on its slabby wall. Use a 200-foot (60-meter) rope for most of the routes, or use intermediate belay stances on the longer pitches. Pay attention to your rope length to avoid toproping and lowering accidents by running out of rope. Two ropes are needed to rappel off some of the routes.

Finding the cliff: Park at the cemetery, and hike up the trail alongside the creek to the mine tailings. Scramble up to the base of the wall. Routes are listed from left to right.

1. Régime de bananes (6c) (5.11a) No topo.

2. Regards complices (6b+) (5.10d) No topo.

3. Echine (6a+) (5.10b)

4. Quatre kilos 170 plus tard, Mélodie (6b) (5.10c)

5. Le petit toit (6a) (5.10a) 2 pitches.
Pitch 1: (6a) (5.10a) **Pitch 2:** (5c) (5.9)

6. Un soir le téléphone (6a) (5.10a)

7. Jour de transes (6c) (5.11a) 2 pitches.
Pitch 1: (6a+) (5.10b) **Pitch 2:** (6c) (5.11a)

8. Amours toujours (6a+) (5.10b)

9. Le grand toit (6b+) (5.10d) 2 pitches.
Pitch 1: (6a) (5.10a) **Pitch 2:** (6b+) (5.10d) The direct on Pitch 2 is 7b.

10. Eh, super Jules, tu craques (6a) (5.10a)

11. La voie de son maître (5c) (5.9)

12. Le foc et l'enfant (5c) (5.9)

13. Les bijoux de Spaggiari (5b+) (5.8+)
2 pitches. **Pitch 1:** (5b+) (5.8+) **Pitch 2:**
(5b+) (5.8+)

14. Plus fort quie moi, tu meurs (6b)
(5.10c) 3 pitches. **Pitch 1:** (5b+) (5.8+)
Pitch 2: (5b+) (5.8+) **Pitch 3:** (6b)
(5.10c)

15. Rogntudju (6b) (5.10c) 3 pitches.
Pitch 1: (5a) (5.7) **Pitch 2:** (6a) (5.10a)
Pitch 3: (6b) (5.10c)

16. Rinocéphale (6b+) (5.10d) 2 pitches.
Pitch 1: (5c) (5.9) **Pitch 2:** (6b+) (5.10d)

17. Ironie du sport (6a) (5.10a) 2 pitches.
Pitch 1: (5b) (5.8) **Pitch 2:** (6a) (5.10a)

18. André-Aline shoot (5c+) (5.9+) 2
pitches. **Pitch 1:** (5b) (5.8) **Pitch 2:**
(5c+) (5.9+)

19. Violence en passion (6a) (5.10a)

20. Moins quarante a l'ombre (6b) (5.10c) 2 pitches. **Pitch 1:** (5b) (5.8) **Pitch 2:** (6b) (5.10c)

21. Tropique du Capricorne (5a/b) (5.7+)

22. Balai Brosse (5a) (5.7) 2 pitches. **Pitch 1:** (4c) (5.6) **Pitch 2:** (5a) (5.7)

23. Radio Lucien (4c) (5.6)

24. Les branchés (4b) (5.5)

25. Greenpeace (5b) (5.8) **Pitch 1:** (4a) (5.5) **Pitch 2:** (5b) (5.8)

The next four routes are on the lower-angled slab on the far right side of the cliff. No topos.

26. Les p'tits loups (3a) (5.4)

27. Mimi cracra (3a) (5.4)

28. Merlin l'enchanteur (3a) (5.4)

29. Mary Poppins (3a) (5.4)

Quiquillon

Quiquillon is the huge pointed peak split by a long pillar on the south that looms directly north of the village. Its big walls offer the longest routes in the area. An excellent route ascends the south pillar, and the big southeast face yields some other superb multipitch moderate gems.

Finding the cliff: Approach Quiquillon by hiking up to Le Belleric and following a trail that heads east around the head of the valley to the base of the south pillar. It takes about twenty minutes to walk it. Alternatively, you can drive out the road toward Eyguians. The first trail you come to on the left is a hiking trail to Le Quiquillon. Drive another 500 meters up the first road on your left that crosses Paradis estate to a car park. Follow a good trail up to the base of the southeast face. Allow twenty minutes to hike.

1. La Terreur du Chien Fou (7a or 6a A1) (5.11d or 5.10a A1) 6 pitches. An excellent long classic route up the big pillar. Begin left of the toe of the South Pillar beneath a smooth gray wall. The route ascends the immaculate face left of a huge, left-facing dihedral for six pitches. **Pitch 1:** 5c **Pitch 2:** 6a **Pitch 3:** 7a or 5b A1 **Pitch 4:** 4c **Pitch 5:** 6a **Pitch 6:** 5b **Descent:** Make three rappels from the summit down the southeast face and a big dihedral right of the route. **Rappel 1:** Rappel 130 feet (40 meters) to a big terrace with trees. **Rappel 2:** Rappel 130 feet (40 meters) to a stance. **Rappel 3:** Rappel 115 feet (35 meters) to the ground. **Rack:** Bring a small rack with a few Stoppers and small to medium Friends along with twelve quickdraws and two ropes.

Face Sud-Est

Face Sud-Est, Quiquillon's big southeast face, is laced with many one-pitch sport routes as well as a number of excellent multipitch routes. On the left side of the wall is four-pitch *Le dièdre sud* (5c) (5.9), followed by a dozen one- and two-pitch 5.10s. In the middle of the wall is Secteur du Ramier, with many excellent one- to

three-pitch routes, and some newer lines that climb to the cliff top, including six-pitch *Voie de la grotte* (5c) (5.9), seven-pitch *N'importe où nors du monde* (6a+) (5.10b), and eight-pitch *Brazil* (5c) (5.9). Another good sector farther right, Secteur du mur du Chamois, offers seven two-pitch routes.

Finding the cliff: The quickest approach is via a trail that climbs the hillside below the cliff. From the village, walk east to a short road on the left. Walk up it, and follow a trail up right until you join another trail. Go directly up the hillside to the base of

the cliff. Or you can drive east from the village, then follow the road on the left to Parking du Paradis. The trail begins on the west side of the lot and heads west to join the above-described trail. Hiking time is fifteen to twenty minutes. Alternatively, you can follow the cliff-base trail from Falaise le Belleric around Le Quiquillon to the base of the wall.

Many single-pitch sport routes are on the various sectors. Consult the comprehensive guide for details, names, and ratings. Routes are described from left to right.

1. Le dièdre sud (5c) (5.9) 4 pitches. A very good route up the big right-facing dihedral on the right side of the south pillar or on the far left side of the southeast face. **Pitch 1:** (5c) (5.9) **Pitch 2:** (5b) (5.8) **Pitch 3:** (5b) (5.8) **Pitch 4:** (5c) (5.9) **Descent:** Make two 135-foot (40-meter) rappels down the route. The second anchors are right of the route on *Mistral gagnant.*

2. Le mur bleu (6b) (5.10c) 3 pitches. The face right of the dihedral. **Pitch 1:** (6c) (5.11a/b) **Pitch 2:** (5b) (5.8) **Pitch 3:** (4c) (5.6) **Descent:** Two double-rope rappels to the ground.

3. Mistral gagnant (6a+) (5.10b) A long pitch. Follow a crack system past rappel anchors at 135 feet. Then angle up left to the second belay stance of #2.

Between #3 and #4 are eight one-pitch sport routes that are mostly 5.10.

4. Vivement la bonbe (7a) (5.11d) 2 pitches. **Pitch 1:** (7a) (5.11d) **Pitch 2:** (7a) (5.11d)

5. Heureusement il y a à la mer (7a) (5.11d) 2 pitches. Climb the wall right of #4 to the upper anchors just below the trees at the Jarin du Quiquillon. **Pitch 1:** (7a) (5.11d) **Pitch 2:** (7a) (5.11d)

The following is Secteur de Ramier with many routes. Between #5 and #6 are five two-pitch sport routes that are mostly 5.10.

6. Le Ramier (5c) (5.9) 6 pitches. A fun and long adventure up the central wall. Many parties just do the first three pitches and rappel off. **Pitch 1:** (4c) (5.6) **Pitch 2:** (5c) (5.9) **Pitch 3:** (5a) (5.7) **Pitch 4:** (3b) (5.4) **Pitch 5:** (5a) (5.7) **Pitch 6:** (5b) (5.8)

Right of #6 are twelve more sport routes, almost all single pitch. Most range between 5.5 and 5.9, making it a very fun, moderate venue.

7. Voie de la grotte (5c) (5.9) 6 pitches. A recommended, excellent, long moderate line to the top of the formation. **Pitch 1:** (5b) (5.8) **Pitch 2:** (5c) (5.9) **Pitch 3:** (5b) (5.8) **Pitch 4:** (5c) (5.9) **Pitch 5:** (5a) (5.7) **Pitch 6:** (5b) (5.8)

VERDON GORGE

■ OVERVIEW

The Gorges du Verdon in southeastern France is simply one of Europe's mythical climbing areas. The Verdon was, until Céüse was developed, the undisputed best climbing area on the continent and, along with Yosemite Valley, the world. The Verdon offers everything: superlative scenery, some of the planet's best rock, hundreds of five-star routes, and pure, unadulterated free climbing. It's a place to be inspired by both the splendor of this spectacular canyon and the beauty of the climbing. The gorge doesn't boast the hardest climbs in Europe, but it harbors some of the best routes on the most perfect limestone imaginable. Yes, this is all high praise—but the Verdon earns every word.

These days the Verdon Gorge is no longer the playground of the elite climbers, who prefer the radical overhanging walls at Céüse, Siurana, and other sport cliffs. Instead, these gorgeous gray walls attract climbers from around the world who come in search of the sheer aesthetic beauty of movement over vertical stone. It's at the Verdon that you can ascend surprisingly moderate routes up exposed faces overlooking the canyon void.

The Verdon experience is about free climbing in a safe and committing environment. Most routes are adequately protected with bolts, and the belays and rappel stations are fixed, so all you do is climb with the bare minimum: a rope and a rack of quickdraws. Verdon climbing is about moving across immaculate limestone, grabbing perfect pockets, laybacking off flutes and flakes, and finding an occasional hand jam. Since most routes tend to be either vertical or a bit slabby, footwork tends to be exacting. Sometimes the only foothold is a flared pocket that squeezes your shoe's toe box, a polished smear in a scoop, or a sharp, centîme-thin edge that catches only a daub of Stealth rubber.

The majority of Verdon routes ascend only the top half of the cliffs because the upper limestone is more pocketed, compact, and harder than the lower section.

The wealth of solution pockets or *gouttes d'eau* is unsurpassed. On some routes every hold you grab is perfect in some way. The routes ascend broad open faces, steep ribs, rounded buttresses, rising crack systems, long corners, and gently overhanging walls.

The Verdon procedure is disarmingly simple and different from anywhere else. Park near the rim, and walk a couple hundred feet. Locate your route's name painted on the polished rim rock. Anchor into a couple thick eyebolts, then step off the rim and rappel down the vertical face. Some rappels are free or require a pendulum to grab the next anchors at a hanging belay. Finally, you reach the last anchors, a couple bolts with rapid links or *maillons* in the middle of a seemingly blank face above a huge overhang. Your partner descends the cords, muscles in, and clips a daisy chain into the anchor. You pull the ropes, and you're suddenly in the moment and feeling very alive, with only empty air and the shining river far below and a great sweep of gray limestone above. Since you rappelled your route, you've already previewed it and know about the spectacular difficulties above. Now you climb—following small pockets over bulges, linking devious faces and technical slabs, finding invisible holds on blank faces, milking the occasional stance to rest your arms and cramped feet.

Most visiting climbers don't usually scale the great gorge walls, but frequent the many single-pitch sport routes found on smaller area crags. These attract more climbers because they're less committing and easier to access. The climbers who do come to the gorge itself usually only toprope routes from the rim, rather than rappel down and climb out. It is a big commitment to launch down a steep airy face to a hanging belay stance and then to brachiate back to the rim. But that is part of the Verdon's magic. Once you've done a couple long classic routes, you're addicted. And if you can't do the moves? Someone on the rim might toss you a rope, or maybe you can use a couple hooks to aid past the hard spot in the time-honored "French-free" method, where almost anything goes as long as you get to the top. As at any big

wall arena, it's fair to use some aid to finish your climb, particularly in the waning twilight or before an impending storm. You won't often see climbers following strict ethics here by lowering back to the belay and pulling their rope after a fall.

Verdon Gorge Cliffs

The Gorges du Verdon, dubbed the Grand Canyon of France, is a sheer rift that slices along a fault through an immense Jurassic-age limestone uplift, forming a rugged border between the mountains of the Haute-Alpes to the north and the wooded hills and valleys of picturesque Provence to the south. The 13-mile (21-kilometer) gorge reaches depths of 2,200 feet with cliffs as tall as 1,500 feet. The canyon was excavated by glacial melt in the swift Verdon River, which originates in the high mountains near the French-Italian boundary. The river plunges south, making a huge horseshoe-shaped bend through the gorge, and empties into wide Lac de Sainte Croix. Beyond the lake it descends a lower gorge before joining the Durance River. The gorge, like the rest of southern France, was inhabited by early humans. Hundreds of artifacts as old as 40,000 years were unearthed in the Grotte de la Baume Bonne in the lower gorge below the lake near the village of Quinson.

Most of the climbing at the Verdon is spread along a 9-mile stretch of discontinuous cliffs on the north side of the main gorge and below the 14-mile (26-kilometer) road Route des Crêtes, which makes an open loop from La Palud. The variety of routes is astounding, ranging from single-pitch lines to fourteen-pitch aid climbs that take a couple days. The canyon itself offers more than 1,600 routes, with even more on surrounding area crags. It's astonishing, though, that with all this developed climbing, there is even more rock that has never been climbed upon.

The gorge easily divides into several main climbing sectors. Just above the gorge and northeast of Point Sublime, the shallow canyon is lined with long cliff bands, mostly unclimbed. Below the twisting road is a small, steep cliff with the famed route

Les Spécialistes. The river section below is both accessible and private, offering superb swimming holes in summer.

The next sector is the overhanging 1,000-foot-high Falaise du Duc opposite Point Sublime and Couloir Samson. Beyond here the gorge narrows into a thin slit walled with towering faces. The Sentier Martel trail, beginning at Couloir Samson parking and ending at Chalet de la Maline, threads along the river's north shore in the canyon bottom and accesses the start of the routes *Ula* and *La Demande.* It passes through two long tunnels, originally created for workmen at a proposed dam here, before emerging into the gorge. Some serious routes ascend the big faces and buttresses in this area. The best are two aid routes—*Mescalito* and *La Paroi Rouge*—on the steep face just after the second tunnel. Above this cliff section is a hidden side canyon approached from the rim with the small but good Falaise de Valaute and its fine moderate sport pitches.

The next section is the famous Falaise de l'Escalès or Cliff of the Climbers, a huge southeast-facing cliff that is the gorge's main climbing sector. A few routes here start at the cliff base, but most are accessed from parking areas and fenced overlooks along the rim called *belvédères.* The first of these is Belvédère du Trescaïre at the first two hairpin turns. Belvédère de la Carelle, the next overlook, offers parking for the most popular climbing sectors, including the ones described in this guide. Last is Belvédère de la Dent d'Aire, which yields stunning views up the gorge toward Falaise de l'Escalès. The cliff is divided into various sectors named for their most famous route. These include Secteur Éperon Sublime below Belvédère du Trescaïre; Secteur la Demande, Secteur Pichenibule, Secteur Fenrir, and Secteur Chrysalis, all reached from Belvédère de la Carelle; and Secteur Mur Bleau and Secteur Frimes near Belvédère de la Dent d'Aire.

Beyond Belvédère de la Dent d'Aire, the road climbs to a high point and then drops west to a tunnel that bores through Secteur Miroir du Fou. This excellent cliff, 11 kilometers from La Palud, offers brilliant roadside cragging with a canyon view below. Nearby are Secteur Mur de Sale

Temps above the road and Secteur Envers du Miroir on the west side of the tunnel. The road continues descending west past more sectors, including Falaise de l'Eycharme, a hidden cliff laced with lots of hard routes, and a few long routes on cliffs below the road. The best of these is the excellent nine-pitch *Estamporanée* (5.10c), which is reached from Belvédère de Guègues. Falaise des Malines, the most notable cliff in the west gorge, begins at the CAF refuge Le Chalet de la Maline and runs northwest. This long, discontinuous cliff offers a few long moderate routes, including the classic *Arête du Belvédère* (5.8), an eleven-pitch outing up a blunt buttress. The last is Secteur l'Imbut below Belvédère Maugue.

Around the gorge scatter a number of smaller cliffs. Some are surprisingly more popular with visiting climbers than the big walls of the gorge since they require less commitment and are easy to access. These also offer a more social atmosphere. One of the busiest is Ayen or Le Col d'Ayen, a long low cliff with more than forty easy and moderate routes just west of La Palud. Another good one is Valaute in a remote setting on the north side of the gorge, just east of the first *belvédère.* Bauchet, an hour's drive from La Palud on the south side of the gorge, is an excellent alternative to the main cliffs. This perfect sport cliff, with almost one hundred routes from 5.8 to 5.14a, is composed of overhanging orange and blue limestone striped with tufa columns. The climbing here is much different than grabbing pockets on the sunny gorge walls.

Details, directions, and topos to all these cliffs are found in the comprehensive local French guidebooks *Grimper au Verdon* and *Aiguines: Verdon Rive Gauche.* The guides are available at Le Perroquet Vert climbing shop in La Palud.

Rack, Protection, and Descent

Solid bolt protection is found on almost all the Verdon routes, especially the popular classic lines, which are equipped with beefy bolts. Many routes were rebolted by Lei Lagramusas, the local climbing club, with proceeds from the sale of area guide-

books and badges. Some of the frightening routes with mandatory runouts were not rebolted because that would alter the scary character of the route, or the first ascensionist declined to offer permission.

On many longer routes, like *La Demande,* it's a good idea to carry a rack of wired nuts to protect the wide spaces between bolts. Some also require a set of Friends and perhaps a few tri-cams to wedge into pockets. Bring a rack of fifteen to eighteen quickdraws, a few free slings to tie off trees or thread holes, a good rappel device, a piece of cord for a rappel safety prussik knot, and a helmet. A helmet is important if you're climbing the popular routes because they are sometimes crowded. A clumsy party might be above you, or you might be dodging a wine bottle tossed off by a tourist.

You'll need two ropes at the Verdon. A 200-foot (60-meter) rope is best, although a shorter 165-foot (50-meter) cord works just fine since most of the pitches tend to be less than 85 feet long. If you're planning to rappel down to start any routes, then you will also need to bring the extra rope to make quick double-rope rappels. Many Verdon climbers use either an 8-mm or 9-mm rope. Some French climbers bring a 500-foot-long cord that is left fixed to the rim and allows them to make one long rappel to a hanging belay. It's also sensible to use a couple of 9-mm ropes for both leading and rappelling.

Last, a couple skyhooks are an important part of every experienced Verdon climber's kit. These are useful for aiding pockets between bolts if you get above your leading level or for a hanging rest on a long enduro pitch. Hooks are a matter of both practicality and expediency to get to the rim on sustained free pitches, especially with an approaching storm or in the evening light. The old-style "French-free" climbing, involving rests on fixed gear or aid with hooks, was often used here in the old days rather than today's *tout libre* climbing. Even old-style grades reflected this ethic, with some routes rated 5.9, whereas all free they are two grades harder.

The infamous Verdon descent is the first thing you do since most canyon routes are approached from the cliff rim.

It's both exhilarating and frightening the first time you approach the rim and peer off the edge into the stunning void below, knowing that momentarily you're going to clip in and slide down the ropes to your route's first hanging belay anchors on a smooth wall. After a couple days of rapping off the rim, though, you'll be saying, "No big deal." And it's not. Just remember to be safe, and build redundancy into your rappel system. It's a good idea to clip a prussik knot between your harness and rappel rope as a safety backup in case you lose control, especially on some rappels when you might have to pendulum sideways to the next anchors or swing under a roof and grab the anchors.

Remember that most problems at the Verdon occur during the descent, including getting your rappel rope stuck or becoming lost on the face. Descent route finding can be a major problem. Look for your next anchors, and don't rap blindly down the face with only a glimmer of hope of finding the next anchors. If you get into a difficult spot because of weather or an accident, remember that the only way out of the gorge is by rappelling to the base and hiking out, jumaring up a fixed line, or climbing out. If you don't know the cliff, then rappelling to the base is inadvisable, because many lower wall sections are either overhanging or have no anchors.

Always remember to always tie knots in your rope ends so you don't rappel off the loose ends. This is a major cause of fatal accidents at the Verdon. Some climbers lower the first man down if they're unsure of where the next rappel station is located. Likewise, if you're toproping routes from the rim, make sure the loose end is securely anchored into a bolt or tree so that your belayer doesn't lose the rope when he is lowering you. Fatal accidents occur annually at the Belvédère de la Carelle when the belayer loops the rope around the railing to lower the climber but neglects to secure the end, and it slips through their Gri-Gri. Be careful and double-check your system when rappelling or toproping to avoid becoming a European vacation statistic.

Climbing History

Climbing at the Verdon began late relative to other European areas. Most French climbers before 1970 considered themselves alpinists first and foremost, pitting ice axes and crampons against the great walls in the icy Alps. Rock climbing was simply training for the important alpine routes. The area was also ignored because most of the Provencal climbers, including Gaston Rébuffat, lived in the Marseille area and climbed at Les Calanques in the winter. And of course the Verdon Gorge is an intimidating place, and the blank walls appeared impossible to climbers armed only with pitons, hemp ropes, and mountain boots. The first climbers chose the easiest routes up obvious vertical crack and corner systems, usually free climbing up to 5.8 and 5.9 and then employing pitons for direct aid.

The Verdon's first major route was *Voie des Enrages* by Patrick Cordier and friends on the Falaise du Duc on the rarely visited south side of the gorge in August 1968. In October 1968 the most natural line on the Falaise de l'Escalès caught the eye of Joel Coqueugniot and Francois Guillot. The pair ascended this elegant 1,200-foot-long crack system from the cliff base to the rim, establishing *La Demande,* one of the Verdon's classic climbs. The route, often compared with Yosemite's *Steck-Salathe* route on Sentinel Rock, received its name after Guillot made *la demande* by proposing to his girlfriend after the first ascent.

Until the mid-1970s most Verdon routes followed crack systems because they were both secure and predictable. Some of these now-classic lines include *Ula, Luna Bong, Necronomicon,* and *L' Eperon Sublime.* A significant ascent came in 1974 when Parisian J. C. Droyer opened the new route *Triomphe d'Eros* using only nuts. Locals, however, didn't approve of his ascent and filled in his nut placements with cement and fixed a cable across a traverse.

The period from 1975 to 1990 was the golden age of Verdon climbing, with many classics opened on the majestic Falaise de l'Escalès. It also became one of Europe's biggest climbing scenes in the 1970s when all the rock stars came to hang

out. During this era the gorge, along with Buoux to the west, witnessed the evolution and development of modern sport climbing, including the concept of bolting on rappel from above. Single-pitch climbing and toproping also became accepted climbing methods since most of the routes are accessed from the cliff top. The finest face routes were established at this time, including *Papy On Sight* in 1983, *Je Suis une Légende* in 1984, *Pichenibule* in 1985, *Dingomanique* in 1987, and *Surveiller et Punir* in 1990. Most of the routes were put up by a small brotherhood of French climbers that included Jacques Perrier and brother teams Pernard and Daniel Gorgeon and Stephane and Jean-Marc Troussier. Jibé Tribout snared the first ascent of *Les Spécialistes,* one of the canyon's hardest routes, in 1987. Other important climbers were Lynn Hill and Patrick Edlinger.

After 1990 new route activity continued throughout the canyon, and aid was eliminated off most routes. The 1990s also saw the development of smaller crags in the surrounding area, including Ayen and Bauchet. New route activity has slowed considerably since the golden years, but a wealth of unclimbed rock on the south side of the gorge as well as on nearby mountains remains for future climbers willing to walk farther for new adventures.

Getting Around

The Gorges du Verdon lies two hours northeast of Marseille and three hours south of Grenoble. The closest international airport is in Nice, two hours to the southeast. The Verdon is somewhat remote and difficult to reach by French standards, especially for the budget climber. So like everywhere else in Europe, renting a car makes the most sense. You're more mobile, you can drive to other crags and sights, and if the weather turns rainy, you can escape to sunnier climes. Car rentals are easily obtained in the bigger cities; alternatively, you can fly to Paris and drive south, stopping at other climbing areas along the way. Make any car reservations from the United States since you'll get a much better rate than if you just show up at the rental kiosk or book in France.

The headquarters for your Verdon trip is the village of La Palud-sur-Verdon on the D952 between Castellene and Moustiers-Sainte-Marie. Moustiers is easily accessed from Manosque, Buoux, Sisteron, and the A-51 autoroute. Castellene is directly reached from Cannes and the A-8 autoroute. Most of the gorge climbing is concentrated along 9 miles of the 14-mile-long Route des Crêtes, a scenic loop road along the north rim of the gorge. All the roads in the Verdon area, particularly those on either side of the gorge, are narrow and winding. Use caution. Most curves are unmarked, and tour buses are regularly encountered.

The big problem here, as in the rest of southern France, is car burglary. Gangs of thieves regularly operate along the gorge roads during the busy season. They are particularly interested in fenceable items like cameras, climbing equipment, radios, and stereos, as well as money. The least risky places to park are the most crowded and busy parking areas, including Belvédères Carelle and Trescaïre, the Tunnel on the Route des Crêtes, Malines, and at Point Sublime near the restaurant. At these places you can leave your car locked with everything hidden and know that it will probably be intact when you return. No guarantees, though. Once I climbed over the railing at Carelle and heard a Belgian woman shrieking in the nearby lot. Thieves had just broken into her car in the full lot and snatched her purse and a video camera. To avoid problems leave your car as empty as possible, open the glove box, and remove the baggage lid over the trunk. French climbers usually leave their cars unlocked so it can be cased without the windows broken. If you're climbing at remote cliffs, it's best to park at a safer lot and walk a longer distance rather than risk a broken window or keyed lock.

La Palud and the Verdon Gorge are not well served by public transportation. If you come without a car, plan on walking and hitchhiking. There is one bus that runs on Monday, Wednesday, and Saturday in summer from Aix to Moustiers to La Palud to Castellene. The rest of the year it runs only on Saturdays. If you come from the north, take the train through Grenoble

Josh Morris leads *Starter* (6b+) (5.10d) at Secteur Belvédère de la Carelle.

to Digne-les-Bains, just east of Sisteron. You can catch a bus from here to Castellene in the morning, then hitch the last 15 miles to La Palud. Alternatively, you can take a bus from Cannes on the coast to Castellene. Once you arrive in La Palud, you're set, because there are always lots of climbers in the campground who you can bum rides off or hook up with as climbing partners. Groceries, restaurants, and shops are all found by walking from the campground into La Palud.

Seasons and Weather

Climbing is possible year-round at the Verdon Gorge. A broad statement, but it's true as long as you're willing to put up with some inclement weather. The Verdon myth is that the weather is often extreme—too hot in summer and too cold in winter. Unlike other Provencal climbing areas at lower elevations, the gorge's 3,000-foot elevation gives it an unpredictable mountain climate. The area lies at the juncture of a cool alpine climate to the north and the drier Provencal climate to the south and west.

It's rare that the Verdon summer is too hot for climbing, especially if you select shady routes and avoid direct sun during the hot midday hours. The L'Escalès cliffs generally face southeast, getting sun from morning until midafternoon. Many cliffs are shaded on summer afternoons, making them ideal for climbing. In July and August, the hottest months, most climbers go early in the morning, take a siesta or swim in the afternoon, and then climb again in the evening. The heat can be debilitating. If you do climb in the sun, be sure to slather on lots of sunscreen and carry plenty of water.

Thunderstorms are common on summer afternoons. Keep a wary eye out for them as they can start abruptly. Keep away from the exposed canyon rim and out of chimneys during lightning storms. Don't belay at the cliff edge during a lightning storm, and if you're caught below the rim, it's best to wait the storm out. Some of the grooves turn into waterfalls. Thunderstorms are frequent in May and late August.

Autumn is an ideal time to visit the Verdon, with no crowds and warm, pleasant days. The summer high pressure, bringing warm air up from Africa, usually lingers through September. October is traditionally rainy here. It's rare, however, to have more than a couple days of rain in a row. The rock dries quickly, particularly if it's windy.

Although climbing is possible through the winter, you need to pick your days—otherwise, you'll be frozen out. Obviously you want to climb sunny routes. Some winter days are absolutely stunning, with clear skies and warm temperatures. High-pressure systems sometimes park over southern France in January and February, bringing a succession of perfect days. It can also snow, and the temperature can plummet to zero degrees Fahrenheit. In that case you'll want to escape south to Les Calanques.

Spring weather tends to be unstable and unpredictable. March and April usually bring rain, cool temperatures, and even snow. May is one of the best months, with warm, dry days punctuated by cooler spells and rain.

The Verdon cliff orientation usually protects you from the persistent mistral winds, which come from the north and west here. Climbing on the main cliff is usually fine when the mistral blows, but belaying on the rim is an ordeal.

Camping, Accommodations, and Services

Almost every Verdon climber stays at the village of La Palud-sur-Verdon, rather than the busier tourist towns of Moustiers-Sainte-Marie and Castellene. The small village, the colorful French equivalent of Yosemite's Camp 4 or Hueco Tank's Petes, offers plentiful accommodations for a climbing holiday, including a couple of campgrounds, various *gîtes,* a nearby refuge, a hostel, and several hotels.

The two campgrounds, both popular with climbers, lie at opposite ends of the village. The municipal site on the east offers lots of grassy sites; some are shaded, but most are sunny. On the other side of the village is a more rustic and hence cheaper campsite. Be aware that this campground has experienced break-ins and theft. It's easy to walk into the village for groceries, bread, or a meal from both campsites. They're also the best places to hook up with climbing partners from all over Europe.

Several *gîtes* are found in the vicinity of La Palud. A favorite is L'Étable, with both dorms and private rooms, on the east side of the village. It also has a climbing wall for rainy days. Others include L'Arc-en-Ciel, Auberge de Jeunesses, and Auberge des Crêtes. Check online for others in the vicinity and to make reservations, which are a necessity in the busy summer season.

Some recommended hotels are Hôtel La Provence, Hôtel Le Panoramic just west of the village, and Hôtel des Gorges du Verdon atop a hill above La Palud. Perched on the rim of the gorge along the Route des Crêtes is Refuge de la Malines, a refuge run by the Club Alpin Francais. It has a spectacular scenic setting and is where the inner gorge trail begins.

Information on all the accommodations is available through the Office de Tourisme in La Palud. E-mail them at maisondesgorges@wanadoo.fr, or visit their Web site at www.lapaludsurverdon.com.

Food and Drink

The relatively unspoiled village of La Palud-sur-Verdon in a broad valley north of the canyon uplift is the main service center for both climbers and tourists. The village basically has everything you'll need.

You'll find a small *supermarché* with enough groceries at reasonable prices and an excellent *boulangerie* or bakery. It's easy to walk to the bakery first thing in the morning for fresh baguettes, as well as for a couple of their exquisite almond croissants. A limited number are made every morning, and when they're gone, you're out of luck. You can also pick up provisions at the weekly village market held on Wednesday mornings.

If you want to stock up on food before you arrive here, it's best to stop at one of the bigger supermarkets while driving to the gorge. A good one if you're coming from Buoux or Sisteron is the Mammoth store along the highway out of Manosque. There is also a larger supermarket in Castellene northeast of La Palud.

If you're not cooking or staying at a hotel or *gîte,* you can trek into the village to dine at a *creperie, pizzeria,* or restaurant. One of the most popular establishments is Lou Cafetier, a bar and restaurant. Pepino's Pizza Van in the village center is also worth a stop for a slice of French pizza.

Cultural Experiences and Rest Days

The Verdon region offers lots to do and see after you've spent a couple days cranking on the sun-swept walls. The first and best place you'll want to explore is the gorge itself. The Sentier Martel, the 8-mile footpath through the gorge, is a superb one-day hike. It's best to begin at the Chalet de la Maline and end at Point Sublime. You'll need to leave a car at the opposite end, though, and hitch to the

RF 1 : 125,000

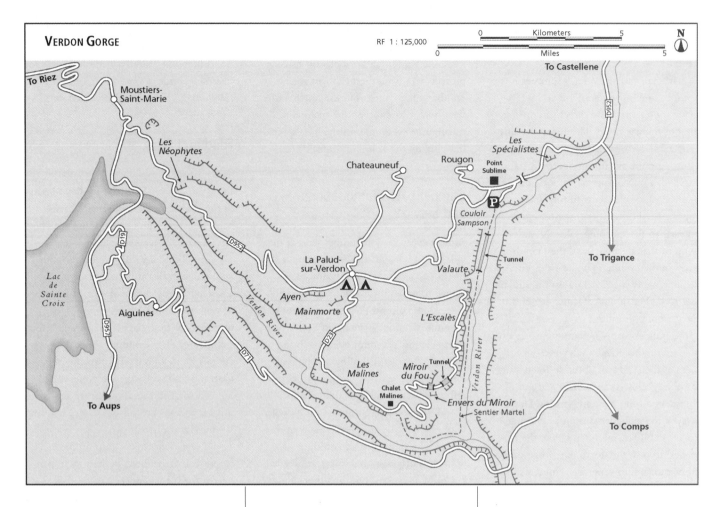

trailhead. The trail quickly descends from the refuge into the rugged canyon bottom, where it twists across steep slopes above the river. The climax for many is the long double tunnels at the east end. Bring a headlamp if you want light; otherwise, you can easily feel the way through the darkness as you slosh through ankle-deep water.

Another good rest-day activity during the warmer months is swimming in the river. You need to be careful, however, since the water flow is controlled by the EDF electricity board, which may open upstream dams and release large amounts of water. Some excellent swimming holes are off the Sentier Martel deep in the gorge depths. More accessible ones are along the stretch of river below the highway east of Point Sublime. You can park in a roadside pullout, scramble down bushy slopes to the river, and pick your spot. Another popular place is farther east, where the road reaches the river at a large cliff. Here you can slide down a steep smooth rock chute into a deep pool.

More water activities are found west of the gorge at Lac de Sainte Croix. This large lake, formed by an earthen dam above the lower gorge, is a fun summer playground for swimming and boating. The real challenge is the 45-foot leap from the highway bridge into deep water. You can rent a canoe and paddle far into the gorge, depending on lake levels. On hot summer days you'll sometimes pass other canoes paddled by bare-breasted Italian and French women. Europeans are very comfortable with nudity, especially in remote and secluded areas such as this, making nude swimming or sunbathing an accepted activity.

With a car you can make a daylong exploration of the road along the south rim or the Corniche Sublime of the Verdon Gorge. Start the drive by heading past the lake toward Moustiers. Make a left turn onto the D957 highway, and follow it across a large bridge over the lake at the gorge's gaping mouth. Take the first left turn onto D619, and follow it to the village of Aiguines. This lovely village,

perched high above the azure lake, is worth a walk around. It was once famous for woodworking, and the small *Musée des Tourneurs sur Bois* explains the ancient art of wood turning. In the village turn left onto the D71, and follow its twisting course high above the wild south flank of the gorge. Good climbing is found on a few cliffs along the way, including Bauchet, but most of these big walls are untouched. The road crosses Pont de l'Artuby, a lofty bridge over the Artuby River that is a popular spot for bungee jumping. Farther along is the *Balcons de la Mescla,* a magnificent viewpoint. From here the road climbs away from the gorge and runs through remote country to the River Jabron, which it follows north to the Pont de Soleils bridge. Go left here onto the D952 to head back to La Palud.

Moustiers–Sainte-Marie, although somewhat tourist ridden, is worth a visit because of its stunning natural setting among towering cliffs. The medieval village caters to the tourist flocks, so it's not a quaint Provencal village. The town is known for its beautiful faïence ceramics, a type of pastel glazed pottery. Buy some if you wish to cart it around with you, but you can buy it in the United States. The centerpiece of the village is the twelfth-century Notre Dame church, restored in 1928, and a curious star suspended on a chain across the Rioul Valley. It was first hung by Sir Blacas, a crusader who returned from captivity with a vow to hang the star. The current star was hung in 1957.

If you want to visit a real Provencal village, then continue west from Moustiers to the village of Riez. This ancient town, which began as a Roman village, is a great place to explore. The town economy relies on lavender and honey. Check out the *lavenderie* or lavender distillery, which creates essence for perfumes. The Maison de l'Abeille or House of the Bee is a research center with a shop that sells various local honeys. It's worth walking to the excavated cathedral ruins, a restored baptistry, and four standing Roman columns in a field. The village also has a small but interesting museum, Nature en Provence. Riez is a good place to find real Provencal food in its restaurants or to find an outdoor cafe where you can sit and sip coffee under the plane trees and listen to the cicadas.

Trip Planning Information

General description: The Verdon Gorge, one of Europe's best and most famous climbing areas, offers excellent sport and traditional climbing on beautiful limestone walls up to 1,500 feet high.

Location: Southeastern France. The Verdon is two hours from Marseille and Nice and three hours south of Grenoble.

Camping and accommodations: No primitive or illegal camping is allowed in the area or in the park. The village of La Palud, just north of the gorge and a fifteen-minute drive from the main sectors, has a couple of campgrounds, and there are several others in the immediate vicinity. Otherwise there are many *gîtes,* hotels, and rooms for rent. Ask at the tourist office in La Palud for suggestions.

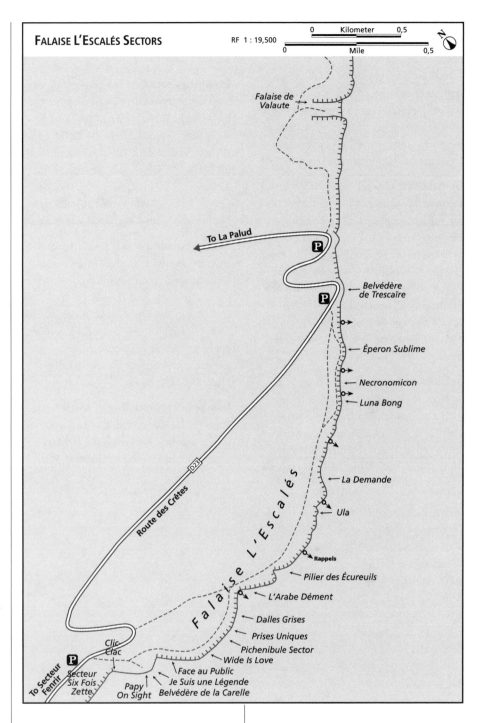

Climbing season: Spring and fall are the best seasons. Most climbers, especially Americans, visit in the hot summer months. It's best to climb in the early morning or evening in summer. Between November and March the weather can be unpredictable and cold. Hard frosts and snow regularly occur. The cliffs are generally sheltered from the mistral, the infamous wind of the Provence.

Restrictions and access issues: There are no restrictions on climbing at Verdon Gorge. The climbing area is in Le Verdon

Regional Nature Park. The park office is Mairie, BP 14, 04360 Moustier Ste-Marie (Tel: 04 92 74 63 95; fax: 04 92 74 63 94).

Use basic etiquette and good manners here. Avoid excessive noise. Do not throw rocks or anything else from the top of the cliffs as others may be below. Don't monopolize routes with topropes. Follow proper sanitary procedures by burying human waste well away from the cliff tops and trails. Pack all garbage out with you, including cigarette butts. Don't disturb nesting birds or vegetation. Respect local inhabitants by not walking on cultivated fields, not frightening stock animals, and not opening fences and gates.

Also be very wary of car thieves, especially on busy days or if your car is left at remote pullouts. Leave nothing of value in your car, and open the glove box. You can even leave the car open so the windows aren't broken by prospective thieves.

Guidebooks: *Grimper au Verdon* by Bernard Gorgeon and Daniel Taupin is a topo guide with sections in French, English, German, Italian, and Spanish. It's available in the climbing shop in La Palud. *Aiguines: Verdon Rive Gauche* by Phillipe Bugada covers the area on the south side of the gorge. The dated English guide *Rock Climbs in the Verdon* by Rick Newcombe offers basic information and description for some of the longer classics.

Services and shops: La Palud offers all services, including a bakery (get there early for the limited almond croissants), some bars and restaurants, grocery store, and a cash machine. Le Perroquet Vert (Tel: 04 92 77 33 39) is the local climbing shop on the village's main street. Chalk, guidebooks, and other climbing gear are available here.

Emergency services: For emergency services dial 18. Also telephone Pompiers, the fire brigade, at (04 92 31 27 06). You can also call the Gendarmerie (04 92 74 66 03) and Mairie de la Palud-sur-Verdon (04 92 77 38 02). Telephones are located at Auberge du Point Sublime, Auberge des Crêtes, La Palud-sur-Verdon, Chalet de la Maline, and Saint-Clair. Rescues are free.

Nearby climbing areas: Some smaller areas are around Castellene, Aiguines, and Moustiers. An excellent nearby area is Quinson's Cliffs near the village of Quinson in the lower gorge. It offers more than 130 routes from 5.4 to 5.13. A topo guide is available at Quinson's campground, at the Bar du Cours, and the Hotel Nôtre-Dame in Quinson.

Nearby attractions: Sentier Martel trail, Point Sublime, Rougon, Lac de Sainte Croix, Aiguines, Moustiers-Saint-Marie, Corniche Sublime drive, Quinson, Riez, Castellene, hiking, swimming, boating, sailboarding, bungee jumping.

Finding the cliffs: The gorge is difficult to reach by inexpensive means. The best way is to rent a car, especially since you need transportation to the cliffs from La Palud. The closest airport is in Nice, about two hours from Verdon Gorge, and alternatively at Marseille.

The quickest way to Verdon from Paris is to drive the Autoroute du Soleil A6 down through Lyon to the Avignon Sud exit. Head east on the N100 through Apt (past Buoux) to Manosque. Catch the D6 here, and drive through Valensole to Riez. Continue east on the D952 to Moustiers and then up the final winding road to La Palud. From the south and Nice, drive the N86 to Castellene, then follow the N952 to La Palud.

The Route des Crêtes, a 14-mile (23-kilometer) loop drive, makes a semicircle south of La Palud and allows access to all the major climbing sectors. This panoramic road is accessed on either the east or west side of La Palud.

Falaise L'Escalès

The Falaise l'Escalès or Cliff of Climbing is the Verdon's major wall. It runs 3 miles between Point Sublime and Jas d'Aire on the north side of the gorge. At its highest section the cliff rises 1,200 feet from base to summit.

Secteur Belvédère de Trescaïre

The Secteur Belvédère de Trescaïre, one of the first developed areas in the gorge, lies below the second hairpin curve on the loop road. This superb cliff section, although not as popular as it once was, offers a selection of exhilarating multipitch classics on the steep face above the Terrasse Mediane, a densely forested hanging terrace that divides the cliff. The terrace, the largest on the Falaise l'Escales, is best reached by making four rappels down *Luna Bong*.

Finding the cliff: Drive up the loop road, and park at the second switchback. Walk west along the cliff rim for about 500 feet to a gully. Downclimb 30 feet to a long narrow terrace above the steep cliff. Walk west along the terrace for another 300 feet to an obvious well-used set of rappel anchors (bolts and chains) at the top of *Luna Bong*.

Make three exciting rappels (double ropes) down the cliff to the Terrasse Mediane. Don't rappel with a single rope unless you want some hassles. Also use a prussik knot backup along with your rappel device for safety. The first rappel drops 30 feet to the cliff rim and then is a free rappel to the next anchors. A shorter rope will leave you hanging in space. Rappels are 165 feet, 165 feet, and 180 feet to the terrace. The last rappel can be split into two rappels.

Routes are described from left to right when facing the cliff.

1. Luna Bong (6c) (5.11a) 6 pitches. Allow three hours to climb. Many parties don't do the last long rappel and avoid the bottom two pitches. To find the start from the base of the rappels, walk west around the toe of a buttress. **Pitch 1:** A mediocre lead. Climb up right along a rib (5.8) to the last set of rappel anchors. **Pitch 2:** Jam

the crack above (5.9) to anchors. 85 feet. **Pitch 3:** Sustained jamming up the crack (5.10b) to a small belay stance. 80 feet. **Pitch 4:** More jamming up the crack with a detour right about halfway up the pitch (5.10b). 80 feet. **Pitch 5:** Continue up the crack (5.9+) to a belay by a tree. 75 feet. **Pitch 6:** The crux lead—your pitch! Climb to the big roof above, and move right. Pull up a short overhanging face (5.11a), and trend up left on easier climbing to cliff-top anchors. The crux moves can be aided. **Rack:** Carry a light rack with some Stoppers and Friends to supplement the bolts.

2. Necronomicon (6b) (5.10d) 3 pitches. A famous classic up a beautiful crack system right of *Luna Bong*'s upper pitches. To start make two rappels down *Luna Bong* to its third belay stance. **Pitch 1:** Face climb up right from the crack and belay stance to a crack. Follow the crack (5.10a) to a belay stance. **Pitch 2:** Work up the steep face and crack (5.10c/d) to a cramped belay stance. **Pitch 3:** Climb up right in corners to a tricky arête (5.10b). Continue up exposed rock (5.8–9) to cliff-top anchors.

3. L' Éperon Sublime (6b+) (5.10d/11a) 8 pitches or fewer. Super classic route up the right wall above the terrace with lots of exposure, varied climbing, and great rock.

The crux traverse can be easily aided and drops the overall grade to 5.10b/c. Some pitches can be combined. Begin by rappelling down *Luna Bong* to the terrace and walking east along the cliff base for 500 feet to the far right side of the terrace. The route, following an obvious crack through overhangs, starts right of a pillar base and below a big cave. **Pitch 1:** Climb a crack in a corner (5.9) then left across slabs (5.9) to a belay. **Pitch 2:** Face climb left into a vertical crack line and follow (5.9) to a belay. **Pitch 3:** Climb the crack up right (5.10a) to a stance. **Pitch 4:** Sustained jamming up the crack (5.10b/c) leads to a small belay stance. **Pitch 5:** Face climb (5.10a) directly above to another cramped stance at the start of an obvious left traverse. **Pitch 6:** Crux pitch. Make a wildly exposed traverse left (5.10d/11a) around the face of the pillar to a flake. Climb up left to a belay. Grabbing gear lowers the traverse grade. **Pitch 7:** A few hard face moves up right (5.12a or A0) lead to a crack. Climb past an overhang (5.10b) to a belay below a roof. **Pitch 8:** Edge across a slab (5.10a) below the roof, then climb through broken rock with trees to cliff-top anchors. **Rack:** Bring a small rack of stopers and Friends to supplement the bolts.

Secteur Demande

The Secteur Demande is a huge cliff sector that is split by *La Demande,* an elegant bottom-to-top crack system that is one of the gorge's all-time classic routes. To its west is *Ula,* another outstanding crack classic that also ascends the entire face. *La Demande,* one of the first routes climbed at the Verdon, is very popular and well traveled. It is, however, not to be taken lightly. This is a serious long route, especially if the weather is hot. *Ula* is equally demanding, with continuous crack climbing and lots of exposure.

Finding the cliff: Approach the start of *La Demande* and *Ula* by hiking down the gorge from Couloir Samson and through the tunnels. You need to leave a car at the nearest parking area on the Route des Crêtes loop road or plan on walking or hitchhiking. You cannot easily hike back to your car.

Drive to Couloir Samson, and park in the large lot. Follow the Sentier Martel trail into the canyon and up some steps to the tunnels. Walk through the long tunnels, sometimes sloshing through water, to the light. Continue along the trail above the north side of the river and past where the trail nears the cliff. Past a large cave is a huge bay of cliffs on your right. *La Demande* is the obvious left-angling crack system above. Scramble uphill on a rough path through brush and scree for about twenty minutes to the crack base. For the other big climb, *Ula,* continue up left along the cliff base to the route's start

right of a big cave. Hiking time from car to cliff is about an hour.

1. La Demande (6a) (5.10a) 11 pitches. 1,300 feet. First ascent by Joel Coqueugniot and Francois Guillot in 1968. Classic, excellent, and highly recommended—the *Steck-Salathe* of France. The first big route established on Falaise l'Escales. It's a very committing, exposed, strenuous, and sustained crack climb. Expect to be on the rock for five to eight hours or longer if a party is ahead. Try to go light, with only a small pack, since the upper part of the route climbs a tight chimney.

Approach the start by hiking down the gorge from Couloir Samson and through the tunnels (see above directions to the cliff base). Scramble up a rib for 35 feet to a belay ledge, and begin below an obvious left-leaning thin crack system. **Pitch 1:** Up the thin crack (5.10a). 100 feet. **Pitch 2:** Step left to gain the crack system, and follow it (5.9) to a belay. 150 feet. **Pitch 3:** Follow the angling crack system with continuous but good jams (5.10a). 130 feet. **Pitch 4:** Continue up the crack and then a corner/ramp (5.10a). 130 feet. **Pitch 5:** More jamming up the angling crack (sustained 5.9 and 5.10a) to a small stance. 100 feet. **Pitch 6:** Make an exposed step left, jam the steep bulging crack (5.10a) until it overhangs, and belay beneath a flaring chimney—the start of the upper pitches. 60 feet. **Pitch 7:** Pay attention to this pitch as it's possible to veer into difficult unprotected terrain. Don't climb the overhanging crack above. Climb up right to a shallow corner on the other side of the chimney. Continue up the corner crack (5.10a) past an overhang until you can traverse left to the main crack system. 115 feet. **Pitch 8:** Work up the steep crack and corner (5.9). 80 feet. **Pitch 9:** The route crux with continuous climbing, lots of exposure, and spaced protection. Follow the corner crack over a bulge (5.10a) and into the upper chimney. Sustained stemming leads up the widening chimney past a block to a belay stance. 150 feet. **Pitch 10:** Continue stemming up the airy chimney (5.9+) with tired legs past a tree to a stance. 150 feet. **Pitch 11:** Easier climbing up the chimney and then up slabs on the right (5.9) to the rim. 150 feet. **Rack:** Bring a rack with some medium to large Stoppers, an assortment of Friends, and 12 to 15 quickdraws. A 165-foot (50-meter) rope is fine, but a 200-foot (60-meter) rope will allow you to string some pitches together.

2. Ula (6b) (5.10c) 9 pitches. A superb companion route to *La Demande* with lots of varied crack climbing. Committing, sustained, and exposed. This description combines some pitches, speeding up the ascent time. It's possible to do it in fewer pitches with a long rope and lots of slings for rope drag. Begin by approaching *La Demande* but continue hiking west along the cliff base until you reach a corner topped by a roof right of a huge cave. This is directly below the long upper crack. **Pitch 1:** Steep face climbing (5.10a) leads to a belay by a pine tree. 85 feet. **Pitch 2:** Climb a crack to a huge roof. Traverse right (5.10a) under the roof, and work up a steep face past some trees and then left on a terrace to belay bolts. This pitch can be broken into a couple shorter leads. Use slings to avoid rope drag. **Pitch 3:** Start off the left side of the terrace and left of a cave. Pull up a short steep face (5.9) to Le Jardin des Écureuils, a tree-covered ledge. **Pitch 4:** Belay below the long crack. Work up the long crack, over some bulges (5.10a) to a belay stance on the left. **Pitch 5:** Continue up the crack and chimney (5.10a) to another stance on the left. **Pitch 6:** Jam the steep airy crack (5.10c) to a belay stance on the right by a small tree. **Pitch 7:** More jamming and stemming up the crack and chimney (5.10a) to a stance on the right. **Pitch 8:** Climb the strenuous crack and chimney (5.10b) to a small ledge. **Pitch 9:** Continue up the dihedral above and right of a big roof to a ledge (5.10b). Head over a bulge to a crack and over a final roof to the cliff top. **Rack:** Bring some medium to large Stoppers, a good selection of Friends to supplement the fixed protection, and 12 to 15 quickdraws. A 165-foot (50-meter) rope is fine, but a 200-foot (60-meter) rope makes for longer pitches.

Secteur Belvédère de la Carelle

This easily accessible and excellent sector lies directly below the guardrail at Belvédère de la Carelle, the third *belvédère* on the road. The area is popular with both climbers and tourists. Almost all the routes are single pitch and reached by rappelling from a fixed rope to belay stations with bolt anchors. These routes are commonly toproped. Be prepared when climbing here for lots of tourists to ask questions, take photographs of you, and possibly drop objects from the viewpoint. All routes are bolted.

If you toprope any of the routes, make sure the belayer is tied into the end of the rope and both the rope and belayer are securely anchored. Fatal accidents have occurred here after the belayer lowered the climber down and the unknotted and untied rope ran through the belay device. *Use extreme caution.*

Finding the cliff: Drive up the road to the Belvédère de la Carelle and park along the road. Walk 50 feet to the guardrail and the cliff top. Routes are described from left to right from the cliff top when facing out to the gorge, beginning from the left side of the guardrail.

1. Starter (6b+) (5.10d) Good warm-up route just left of the steep gully that divides the face from the slab to the left.

2. Je Suis une Légende (*I am a Legend*) (7a) (5.11d/12a) Continuous, strenuous, and famous.

3. Unknown (7b+) (5.12c) Steep bolted route left of *Je Suis.*

4. Papy On Sight (7c+) (5.13a) Classic hard climb. First ascent by England's Jerry Moffatt. Excellent and demanding face climb up slightly overhanging stone.

5. Scoumoune (7b) (5.12b) No topo. Recommended. Can be done in either 1 or 2 pitches. Rappel one rope length to a bolted hanging belay. **Pitch 1:** Sustained face moves (5.10a) to a hanging belay. **Pitch 2:** Climb left up a rib and then right (5.12b) into a corner.

6. La Baraka (6c+) (5.11c) No topo. Shares a start with *Scoumoune* but veers out left (5.11c) to belay anchors. Continue up the prow to the rim (5.10c).

7. Cercopitheque (6c+) (5.11c) No topo. 1 or 2 pitches to the guardrail.

8. Polpett (7a) (5.11d) No topo. Rappel or lower 150 feet from rim anchors to the start just left of a tree. Thin face climbing (5.11d) to easier rock (5.9).

9. Ticket Danger (6a) (5.10a) No topo. Excellent climbing. Top pitch of a 7-pitch route. Usually only the top pitch is climbed but the whole route is worthy. For the top pitch, rappel or lower 150 feet to anchors on a ledge. Face climb (5.10a) up the exposed wall, and end at the trees by the *belvédère.* To do the whole route, start by making six rappels to the base of the cliff. Pitch 1 climbs 150 feet to a terrace (5.11a). Go left, then climb five pitches of mostly 5.10 climbing to the stance below the final pitch.

10. Clic-Clac (5c) (5.9) No topo. Popular and easy to get to. Up to the right side of the *belvédère.*

The east side of the Secteur Carelle is the very popular slabby face just left (east) of the *belvédère* and readily seen from behind the guardrail. All the routes are good fun. Belay and rappel bolts are spaced along the cliff top. Be careful along the edge as the limestone is very polished and slippery. Use care when walking. The names of some routes are painted on the rim rock. Routes are described from right to left or from the gully right of *Starter* and the *belvédère*.

11. Mami Nova (5b+) (5.9) Excellent, fun, and you're in the flash of the tourist cameras on the *bélvédère* . . . and it's only a minute from the car. This is the first route from the gully. To start rappel 80 feet to a bolted belay by a tree. Climb up left on perfect rock to the cliff top.

12. Face au Public (5b) (5.8+) 2 pitches. An excellent introduction to multipitch Verdon climbing. Begin just left of *Mami Nova,* and make two rappels to a bolted stance by a small tree. Climb two pitches on beautiful stone.

13. Tarpet Farceur (5c) (5.9) 1 pitch. Rappel to a bolted stance. Edge up to a great finishing bulge.

14. Opéra Verticouenne (5b) (5.8+) 1 pitch. Rappel to a bolted stance. Face climb to a finishing crack.

15. À Mois les Vivants (5b/c) (5.9-) No topo. 2 pitches. These are the top leads of a longer route. Make two rappels down to an exposed bolted belay above a very steep wall. Pick pockets for two pitches up the steeper wall.

16. Tarsinge l'Homme Zan (5c) (5.9) 1 pitch. Rappel to the first stance on *À Mois les Vivants.* Climb up and right to a clifftop belay.

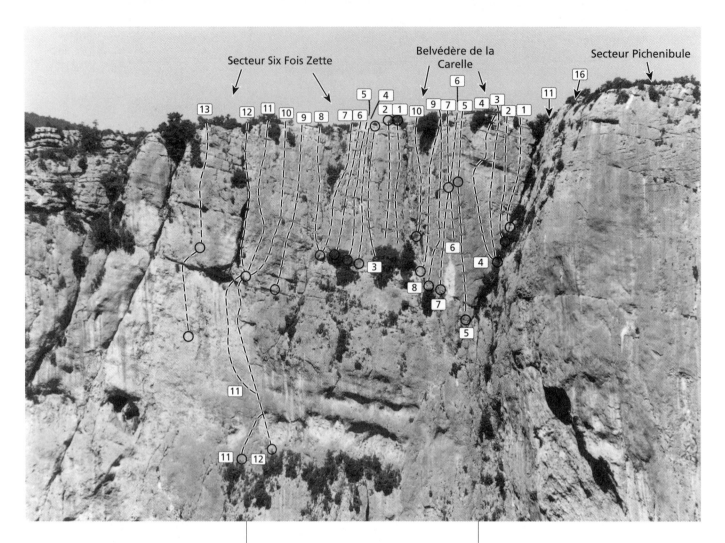

Secteur Six Fois Zette

This sector is just west from the Belvédère de la Carelle. It offers a selection of fun one-pitch routes that are usually toproped. This is an easy spot to come for a quick evening workout and crank a lot of moderate pitches on toprope. Of course you can always rappel down to anchors and lead back up. Most of the route names are painted on the rim rock next to the rappel anchors. Be careful along the cliff rim since it is very polished and slippery.

Finding the cliff: Park at the Belvédère de la Carelle lot, and walk west from the overlook. The first route is just right (when facing out) of the steep groove next to *Clic-Clac* and the railing's west end. Routes are described from left to right when facing the gorge from the cliff top.

1. Sérieux S'Abstenir (5b/c) (5.9) The top pitch of a 6-pitch route.

2. Delirium Très Mince (5.b/c) (5.9) The top pitch of a 5-pitch route. It begins from the same set of anchors as #1.

3. Fini au Pipi (5b) (5.8) A dihedral.

4. On Rase Bien les Poireaux (6c) (5.11a) Face next to dihedral.

5. Tire Flemme (5b) (5.8) Directly up the face of the buttress.

6. Rop'n Roll (5c) (5.9) Face climbing.

7. Escalebitte Dure (6a) (5.10a) Begin at base of dihedral, and climb up right.

8. Les Bidochon en Vacances (6c) (5.11a) Same starting belay as #7 but up the face left of a dihedral.

9. Karin's Line (6a) (5.10a)

10. Six Fois Zette (6a+) (5.10b) Up the middle of a face.

11. Love Me (6b) (5.10c) Up the left side of the face.

12. Kaboube (5b) (5.8) A right-facing dihedral.

13. Gaz Max au Verdon (6b+) (5.10d) Steep face climbing west of the dihedral.

More sectors are west of here. These include Troisième Ciel, Fenrir, Saut D'Homme, Armoire, Golem, Toboggan, Gousseault, Débilof, Sordidon, Mission, Surveiller et Punir, and Mort à Venise. Most have some great routes, and all are worth visiting.

The best routes at Secteur Fenrir are described below. Other recommended routes are *Saut d'Homme* (5.10a), a stunning dihedral climb; *Gravities Rainbow* (5.12d), a 150-foot pitch up a blank wall; *Pilier Gousseault* (5.12a or 5.11b A1), a 12-pitch expedition up a spectacular face; *Debilof Proffondicum* (5.11c), an excellent long sport pitch; *Chrysalis* (5.12a), *Séance Tenante* (5.13b), and *Liqueur de Coco* (5.13a), all spectacular sport pitches at Secteur Sordidon; *Frimes et Chatiments* (5.10d), a traversing route across Secteur Surveiller et Punir; and *Surveiller et Punir* (5.12a). This 4-pitch route simply climbs some of the best stone on the planet and is one of France's best routes. It has it all—perfect limestone, sustained and varied climbing movements, good protection, and lots of exposure. The last two pitches are the best. Consult the comprehensive French guide for topos and directions to all these routes.

Secteur Fenrir

This great cliff section, one of the Verdon's most famous sectors, has some excellent routes up a huge buttress. The following routes, the best at the sector, are located on the center of the buttress. They're easy to follow—just clip the bolts! Consult the comprehensive French guide for topos to the other eight routes.

Finding the cliff: Park at the Belvédère de la Carelle, and follow the rim trail west a few hundred feet to the sector, which is marked with a plaque and a large cairn. Route names are painted on the rim. To access the routes scramble down a gap to a large ledge with rappel anchors. All the routes require multiple rappels from good bolt anchors. Routes are described from left to right when facing out to the gorge. No topos.

1. L'Ange en Décomposition (7a) (5.11d) 3 pitches. An absolute stunner with some of the best free climbing at the Verdon. The cruxes are short, leaving most of the climbing pure fun up the immaculate face. To reach the start scramble down to a set of chains directly above the prow of the buttress. Make three rappels down the route to a belay station with bolt anchors. **Pitch 1:** Move up left, and climb a steep arête (5.11a/b) to a stance. **Pitch 2:** Steep exposed face climbing (5.11d) to an airy stance on the prow. **Pitch 3:** Climb up right, and finish up steep slabs to the ledge.

For a longer, harder route you can add the first three pitches of *Fenrir,* which makes this route even better. To start this linkup, rappel all the way to a tree-covered terrace below the sector. The easiest rappel line is to go east on the ledge to the top of *Rivière d'Argent.* Make four rappels with double ropes down the route—150 feet, 120 feet, 100 feet, and 185 feet. The last rap is very exciting as you descend freely past a huge cave. Scramble up left past a cave to the start of the route. **Pitch 1:** Climb up and right above the base cave (5.12a) to a belay at the big cave. **Pitch 2:** Traverse left, and climb the face left of the cave with one section 5.13a or 5.10a A0. Continue to belay bolts. **Pitch 3:** Face climb (5.9) to the start of *L'Ange,* and follow it to the top.

2. Alerte au Gaz (7a+) (5.12a) 3 pitches. A great route just left of *L'Ange.* The route starts at rappel anchors by a tree west of *L'Ange's* anchors. To start make three rappels down the route. **Pitch 1:** Face climbing (5.11c) up pockets and edges. **Pitch 2:** Sustained climbing with a high crux (5.12a) directly up the face. **Pitch 3:** Face moves (5.11b) to a higher crux (5.10d) after joining *Rêve de Fer* and then a steep slab to the tree and anchors.

3. Rêve de Fer (6b+) (5.10d) 4 pitches. A superb line at a manageable grade just left of #2. Begin from the same rappel station as #2. Rappel down left to a ledge with anchors. Make two more rappels from chain anchors to a small belay shelf perched on the face. **Pitch 1:** Face climb (5.10b) to a hanging belay. **Pitch 2:** Climb up, and move right to a scoop. Continue up a steep rib (5.10c) to a belay stance. **Pitch 3:** Work up a crack above for 15 feet, then climb up left on a steep face (5.10c) to a good ledge. **Pitch 4:** Climb up right, and follow a blunt arête (5.10d) that leads to belay/rappel chains by the tree.

Secteur Pichenibule

This excellent, south-facing sector, named for one of the Verdon's classic long routes, is a prominent flat face left (east) of the Belvédère de la Carelle. It's bounded on the right by a blunt prow and on the left by a steep rappel gully. Many routes are found on this wall. This guide describes the best classic routes here. Like most of the popular Verdon sectors, the rock is a grid of bolts. It takes some time to separate which routes are which, so you might be initially confused by all the possibilities. If you want to do the upper pitch or pitches, then look for the name of your prospective route painted on the rim rock.

Finding the cliff: Park at the Belvédère de la Carelle, and walk left along the cliff top above the slabby routes by *Mami Nova.* The routes begin at the end of the slab where the cliff bends left and drops vertically. Routes are described from right to left when facing the gorge. Most route names are painted next to anchors along the cliff rim.

1. Biscotte Margarine (6b+) 1 pitch to the rim. Super classic J. B. Tribout route. Rappel or lower 165 feet to an exposed hanging belay. Very good climbing leads back to the rim. The pitch below *Biscotte's* belay anchors is *Wall of Woodoo* (8a+).

2. Pichenibule (7b+) 8 or 12 pitches. The top seven or eight pitches are one of the Verdon's great multipitch routes. The bottom four pitches are below Jardin des Écureuils, the big vegetated terrace a third of the way up the cliff, and are seldom climbed. The route is basically a long left-rising traverse that ends with the crux climbing on the exposed gray wall right of *Biscotte Margarine*. Begin by making four rappels down the *Dalles Grises* rappel gully to the Jardin.

3. Wide Is Love (6a) (5.10a) 1 pitch to the rim. The wildest and best 5.10 route you will ever climb! Lots of exposure and perfect pocket pulling. Locate the faded name on the rim, and lower or rappel off nearby anchors for 150 feet to a hanging bolt belay. Open, airy pocket climbing to a crux overhang.

4. Ctuluh (6c+) (5.11c) 2 pitches. Another excellent climb. It goes right and up for two pitches above *Pichenibule's* Pitch 6 belay. Make two rappels with double ropes from the rim to a bolt belay. **Pitch 1:** Tricky climbing (5.11c) heads up right then back left to a welcome crack. Finish steeply up left to a hanging bolt belay (shared with a squeeze route *Le Genou de Claire* immediately left). **Pitch 2:** Airy pocket climbing leads up left (5.10a) to the rim.

5. Rideaux de Gwendal (6c+) (5.11c) 3 pitches. One of the Verdon's best climbs. The route begins at the base of the cliff, but the lower pitches aren't usually climbed. The top pitch (5.8) makes an exceptional moderate route itself. Begin by making three double-rope rappels down the line to a bolt belay on *Pichenibule*. **Pitch 1:** Face climb (5.11c) to a bolt belay. **Pitch 2:** Superb pockets and edges (5.10a) to a bolt belay. **Pitch 3:** A fun 150-foot face (5.8) pitch to the rim.

6. Bête À Sexe (5c) 1 pitch to the rim. Just east of *Gwendal's* top-out. Rappel or lower

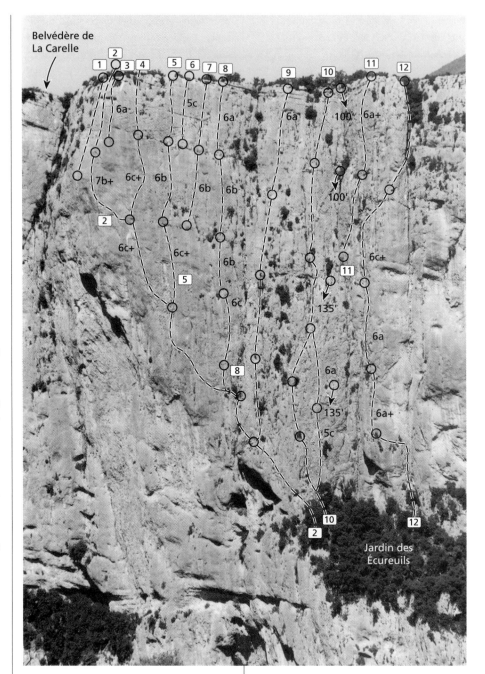

150 feet to a bolt belay. Face climb the gray wall to the rim. Bring 12 quickdraws.

7. Prises Uniques (6b) (5.10c) 2 pitches. A four-pitch route but the top two are best. To start locate the name on the rim, and make two rappels to bolt anchors. **Pitch 1:** Work up the steep wall and then right to a scoop. Climb back left to difficult moves (5.10c) below anchors. **Pitch 2:** Steep airy climbing (5.10c) on good holds back to the rim.

8. Trou Secs (6c) (5.11a) 5 pitches. A good line up the right side of the *Pichenibule* wall. Locate the route name painted on

the cliff rim, and rappel down the line using bolt anchors to a tree belay at the end of *Pichenibule's* Pitch 2. **Pitch 1:** From the tree and left of a big groove system, climb the left side of the groove (5.10a) and then right below a crack to anchors. **Pitch 2:** Move up the crack with good edges and then up left over a bulge (5.10c). Step left into another crack system and up to a belay stance. **Pitch 3:** Climb a shallow corner system (5.10c) to anchors at a stance. **Pitch 4:** Work up more grooves and corners to a tricky bulge (5.10c) to anchors. **Pitch 5:** Finish up left along a blunt prow (5.10a).

9. Afin Que Nul Ne Meure (6a) (5.10a) 5 pitches. Excellent, classic route with slabs and cruxy bulges on the buttress right of the *Pichenibule* wall. Access the route's start by making four double-rope rappels down the *Dalles Grises* gully just east of the route's top-out to the hanging forest Jardin des Écureuils. Scramble across the upper part of the Jardin to a tree belay. **Pitch 1:** Climb up left on the traversing first pitch of *Pichenibule* (5.9) to a belay. **Pitch 2:** Climb up and then left (5.8) to a ledge with anchors. **Pitch 3:** Work up right and over a bulge (5.9) to a belay ledge. **Pitch 4:** Edge up slabs to a crack (5.8). Above climb slabs up right to anchors near a tree. **Pitch 5:** Easy moves lead to a tricky bulge (5.9). Do more easy climbing to a final exposed bulge (5.10a) and the cliff top.

10. Les Dalles Grises (5c) (5.9) 6 pitches. A good moderate route up the wall left of the gully. Access the start by making four double-rope rappels down the *Dalles Grises* gully just east of the route's top-out to the Jardin des Écureuils. Watch for rockfall from other parties rappelling the gully. The route is bolt protected with bolted belays, so it's easy to follow. Start just left of the last rappel. The first three pitches climb faces and slabs up and then right to a rappel station. Alternatively, climb two pitches of 5.9 and 5.10a just right of the line on a steeper wall. Above the rap station continue up grooves, cracks, and slabs for three more pitches to the rim.

11. L'Arabe Dément (6a+) (5.10b) 2 pitches. Excellent, classic route up steep stone just right (when facing the cliff) of the *Dalles Grises* rappel gully. A stunning line up beautiful stone. Begin by making two rappels down the gully to the next anchors at some trees. **Pitch 1:** Start by traversing onto the face and then climbing a crack. Climb steep rock above (5.10a) to a thin crack to a belay stance near some trees. **Pitch 2:** Follow a shallow crack system up left and then move back right to tricky moves (5.10c) to an easier finish.

Many great routes are found on the wall between *L'Arabe Dément* and *Dinogmaniaque*. Recommended lines are five-pitch *À Tout Coeur* (6b+), *Passion d'Amour* (6a), and *L'Arabe Souriant* (6b+) and *L'Arabe en Decomposition* (6c).

12. Dingomaniaque (6c+) (5.11c) 5 pitches. A Verdon classic. Excellent and popular. The hard parts are easily aided. Reach the start by making four rappels down the *Dalles Grises* gully and then scrambling left (east) across the Jardin des Écureuils for about 150 feet to the base of a crack system right of a prominent nose. **Pitch 1:** Climb the crack system (5.8) for 75 feet and then traverse left above a big roof to a belay station. **Pitch 2:** Delicate face climbing leads up a blunt prow (5.10b) to a belay. **Pitch 3:** Continue up pockets and edges (5.10a) on the steep rib to a hanging belay. **Pitch 4:** Sustained face climbing (5.11c) up the steepening face to an obvious right-angling line of pockets. Grab these up right (5.9) to easier rock and a belay. 150 feet. **Pitch 5:** Continue up right along a crack system to an exposed wall. Finish up an airy, photogenic arête.

Secteurs Miroir du Fou and Miroir du Clou

The southeast-facing Secteur Miroir du Fou and south-facing Miroir du Clou, two excellent cliffs above a tunnel on the gorge loop drive, are among the most easily accessible crags at the Verdon. The rock is perfect, the climbs are technical and excellent, the approach is short, and the views across the gorge are stunning. Climb most of the routes using a variety of finger pockets. The cliffs are a good choice on summer afternoons since they get lots of shade. The popular routes are getting polished, so it's best to climb them out of the sun's heat. The crag and parking area also offer great views across the gorge, and it even feels somewhat secluded despite the road below.

Finding the cliffs: Drive up the loop Route des Crêtes from La Palud. Pass Falaise de l'Escalès, and ascend to a summit and start downhill. After 11 kilometers you reach an obvious tunnel boring through a cliff. Park on the left. All the Miroir du Fou routes begin below the left side of the cliff and left of the tunnel.

Miroir du Fou

The ultimate roadside crag! Descent off all routes is by double-rope rappel unless you just do half-pitches to the midheight anchors on *Miroir du Fou*. Routes are described from left to right.

1. Rond de Chaussettes (6c) (5.11a/b) No topo. Far left-hand route.

2. Voie Fawcett (7a+) (5.12a) No topo. A 1981 Ron Fawcett route up the left side of the face. Steep and fierce.

3. Une Ténébreuse Affaire (7a) (5.11d) Climb the first part of *Voie Fawcett,* then continue straight up steep rock. 10 bolts to 2-bolt anchor.

4. La Dülf du Fou (6a) (5.10a) Same start as *Miroir du Fou* but continue straight up above bolt 4 to a right-trending seam. 11 bolts to 2-bolt anchor.

5. Le Miroir du Fou *(Fool's Mirror)* (6c) (5.11a/b) 2 pitches. First ascent by Jacques Perrier in 1979. The cliff's megaclassic wanders across the face. **Pitch 1:** Excellent pocket climbing (6a) leads straight up. At bolt 4 begin a rising traverse up right (6c) to a 2-bolt anchor. 6 bolts. **Pitch 2:** Pull pockets up right, and then work back left to anchors on top. 7 bolts to 2-bolt anchor.

6. Pirouette Enchantée (6c) (5.11a/b) Sustained pocket climbing up the center of the face. Begin just right of *Miroir du Fou.* 13 bolts to 2-bolt anchor.

7. Grain de Folie (6c) (5.11a/b) No topo. Climb the right edge of the face just left of the scoop. Traverse right along the rounded lip of the scoop, and join *Miroir du Fou.* On the second pitch go above bolt 5 to a 2-bolt finish.

8. Brouette en Chantier (8b+) (5.14a) Short, steep, and technical. Over the left side of the bulge above the tunnel. 5 bolts to 2-bolt anchor.

Miroir du Clou

This small cliff parallels the road on the north and is a continuation of Miroir du Fou to the northeast. Access it by crossing the road from the parking and climbing a 30-foot-high ladder. Use a 200-foot (60-meter) rope for most of the climbs. Routes are described from left to right.

9. Unknown

10. Salut les Berlots (7a) (5.11d) A short line on the far left side of the sector.

11. Unknown (6b+) (5.10d) Left side of the main cliff.

12. Y'a Pas de Pet (6a+) (5.10b) Bouldery start to easier climbing.

13. La Dalle du Clou Que Rend Fou (5b) (5.8) Excellent moderate line up the center. 100 feet.

14. Le Fou de l'Extrême Droite (6b) (5.10c) A boulder problem start to fun climbing.

The West Sectors

Envers du Miroir is the next sector along the road. This south-facing cliff, offering twenty routes, forms the outside of the Miroir tunnel. To reach it park at the west side of the tunnel, and walk back to the trail down to the cliff. Most of the one- and two-pitch routes are 5.10 and 5.11.

If you need more adventure and want to get away from the tourists and climber crowds, then head west on the road past the Chalet de la Malines refuge. The trail through the gorge begins at the refuge and runs through the gorge to Couloir Samson.

East of the Chalet is Eycharme, one of the gorge's best small cliffs. This area, reached by a downhill hike, has a bunch of mostly hard routes up a beautiful cliff of orange limestone. The view across the canyon is stunning. Find the cliff by driving east up the D23 Route des Crêtes from the Chalet de la Malines for 1.5

kilometers. Park on the right, and descend south to the cliff.

West of the refuge is the Falaise des Malines, a big but somewhat broken cliff that runs northwest along the north side of the canyon. Some long moderate routes, traditional affairs with occasional bolt protection, ascend pillars and faces on the wall.

One of the best and most popular is *Arête du Belvédère* (5.7), a very pleasant eight- to ten-pitch route up the long prow of a buttress. To reach it drive west from the refuge for 0.9 kilometer to the *belvédère* pullout on the west side of the road. Scramble down some very steep gullies with iron spikes and trees for rappels. At the bottom of the descent, trend left to the base of the buttress. Climb cracks and faces up the buttress. The route is fairly straightforward to follow since it sees a lot of traffic.

The Petit Cliffs

Besides the big cliffs at L'Escalès, the Verdon Gorge offers lots of other smaller cliffs with many routes in the surrounding area. Some of these cliffs are more popular than the big walls since they are easy to access, generally short, and have a wide variety of routes in the popular easier grades.

One of the most popular is Le Col d'Ayen or simply Ayen. The long, south-facing cliff, ranging in height from 18 to 45 feet, lies south of the road between La Palud and Moustiers. Park 2.1 kilometers west of La Palud in a grove of pine trees on the south side of the road, and walk a couple minutes to the cliff top. The best way to reach the base is to walk east along the rim to a break that leads down. More than fifty routes ascend the short cliff, mostly between 5.4 and 5.10. Some routes are polished from lots of ascents. It's a good place to go if you want a break from the big walls and need some plain fun climbing.

Néophytes, another cliff off the road between La Palud and Moustiers, is a popular crag for hard climbers. The cliff, a minute's walk from the road, offers more than a dozen lines up its overhanging face that are 5.12 and 5.13. The cliff is 11.5 kilometers west of La Palud on the right side of the road.

Mainmorte is another cliff close to La Palud. This steep wall, with seventeen routes, sits 2 kilometers from La Palud on the road toward Chalet Malines. All the routes here are 5.12 and 5.13.

The lovely crag Valaute hides in a hanging valley above the main Verdon Gorge near the first *belvédère*. The cliff, from 30 to 100 feet high, has more than twenty-five easy and moderate, well-protected routes in a remote setting. Reach it by driving up the D23 Route des Crêtes to the first *belvédère* and park. Follow a good trail down left and parallel to the gorge. The trail follows the top of the gorge rim, bends left, and descends through pine woods to the cliff base.

Up the river canyon from Le Point Sublime is Spécialistes, a hidden cliff below the D952 highway. The route of choice here is *Les Spécialistes,* a classic 5.14a route up a severely overhanging face. This athletic route was first done by Jibé Tribout in 1987. To find it drive to Le Point Sublime, and continue on the D952 toward Castellene. Drive through the tunnel, and continue for another 0.75 kilometer to a small parking area on the right side of a left turn. Hike down a steep slope to the cliff top, and make a 60-foot rappel to the cliff base. Alternatively, scramble down slopes east of the cliff, and then contour over to the base. The river below the cliff harbors some excellent private swimming holes for hot summer days.

Okay, you've climbed at the Verdon for a week and gazed across the gorge at all that rock on the south side. Most of it is perfect and unclimbed. There is, however, an excellent sport crag over there—Bauchet. This beautiful blue, orange, and gray cliff, striped with tufa *colonettes* on its overhanging flank, offers more than eighty brilliant sport routes. Ask at the climbing shop in La Palud for precise directions and an up-to-date topo.

ROCHER DE FREŸR

■ OVERVIEW

"Belgium? There is climbing in Belgium?" That is the refrain sung by most American climbers who know little about European climbing except for the remarkable French Provencal limestone. Belgian limestone, however, is one of Europe's best-kept climbing secrets. Few Americans know about the sheer white faces that tower above the Meuse River and stud the rolling hills and hidden dales of south-western Belgium. This pastoral country-side hosts more than one hundred crags, some rivaling their French counterparts. The most famous and best of Belgium's climbing areas is the renowned collection of west-facing cliffs at Freŷr along the Meuse River.

Freŷr, with fourteen distinct crags, is a delightful climbing site as well as an eco-logical treasure with a diversity of lush forest and cliff ecosystems. Freŷr offers more than 600 routes and more than 1,000 pitches of bolted climbing on cliffs up to 400 feet high. The area, seldom vis-ited by Americans, is nonetheless a popular site with Belgian climbers as well as those from the Netherlands, Germany, and France, who flock here every summer weekend. The sheer number of bolted routes is mind-boggling. It's easy to spend a week here climbing routes and then linking pitch combinations to create even more climbs. Freŷr's solid and compact limestone, short approaches from the park-ing area, plentiful bolt protection, scenic setting, and wide assortment of routes ensures the area's continuing popularity with European climbers. And if all those reasons aren't enough, every route is fully bolted, allowing you to climb safely and easily push your leading standard.

The main Freŷr cliffs—Mérinos, Cinq Ânes, Tête de Lion, Le Pape, and Al'Legne—offer a variety of climbs from time-tested classics to cutting-edge sport lines up slabs, crack systems, vertical faces, bulges, roofs, and overhanging walls. The hard white limestone, varnished gray by rain and mist and streaked with black stains, is characterized by numerous hand-holds from fingertip crimps to full-hand buckets, steep sculptured faces, delicate friction slabs polished by thousands of passing feet, bulging roofs and overhangs, and incipient crack systems. The cliffs were weathered by eons of rain that smoothed and rounded the limestone into soft femi-nine shapes.

The biggest cliff is Al'Legne, a broad 400-foot-high wall that looms above a densely wooded hillside and the river. This impressive wall is Freŷr's most popular cliff with lots of classic lines and its hardest routes. More than twenty routes are graded 8a (5.13b) or harder, including *Razorblade* and *Le Clou*, both rated 8c (5.14b). The wall is also girdled by *La Trans-Freŷrienne*, a sixteen-pitch cliff tra-verse.

Le Pape and Tête de Lion are the next cliffs to the north. Both offer hard climbs up vertical walls above the gently flowing river. Cinq Ânes or Five Donkeys is a spectacular west-facing wall broken by vertical buttresses and cleaved by cracks and corners. The cliff acquired its unusual name after the 1937 first ascent of the classic *Cinq Ânes*. The gorgeous gray slabs of Mérinos, the northernmost major cliff, are often busy with climbers working up the brilliant moderate lines that dissect its two main faces.

Besides the main cliffs several fine smaller crags also offer superb climbing. These cliffs tend to be less busy than the main walls. North of Mérinos are three small cliffs—Les Fissures Georget, La Dalle Êcole, and La Carrière—with an assort-ment of easy climbs. South of Al'Legne are several cliffs, the best of which are Louis-Phillipe and La Jeunesse. Both cliffs, on the hillside below the camping meadow, yield fun climbing up their castellated flanks. More than sixty sport routes, mostly in the popular 5.9 to 5.11 range, lace Louis-Phillipe. La Jeunesse also offers more than sixty routes, mostly on its sheer south face. Information on these crags is in the comprehensive guide avail-able at Le Chamonix cafe or by asking any local climber.

If you tire of Freŷr, then check out some of the nearby climbing areas. Most are rarely visited by foreigners, with locals keeping them for themselves. Along the river between Dinant and Namur is a somewhat urban crag called Dave. The cliff, rising above a highway and railroad tracks, sports more than 150 routes from 5.6 to 5.13 up excellent limestone faces. Some are very steep or capped with over-hangs, making it a preferred alternative on rainy days. It also offers a good selection of easy routes.

Mozet in Samson Valley yields a peaceful experience on relatively unknown cliffs. Most routes are less than 80 feet long but ascend clean limestone with lots of bolt protection. Most of its routes lie in the ever-popular 5.10 and 5.11 range.

Marche-les-Dames by the village of the same name is a mile-long escarpment with twenty-three cliffs alongside the Meuse River north of Freŷr. The most popular sector is Beez, a group of nine crags with more than 200 routes. Expect long pumpy pitches up mostly vertical ter-rain and lots of beefy bolts. The area is known for stiff grading, so do some easier climbs before jumping on the hard ones.

Berdorf in the adjoining principality of Luxembourg is another area to visit on your European vacation. Here you'll find hidden sandstone walls and towers among peaceful wooded hills and valleys. Both the climbing and the atmosphere is magi-cal, with excellent bolt-protected climbing up steep faces and cracks as well as boul-ders. Berdorf's huecoed walls are similar to those at Kentucky's Red River Gorge. The village of Berdorf, a mere five-minute stroll from the nearest crag, offers good camping, a bakery, cafes and bars, and a grocery store.

To climb in Belgium you need a membership card from a legitimate climb-ing club or alpine association like the American Alpine Club, although a card from other groups like Sierra Club, Appalachian Mountain Club, and Colorado Mountain Club work fine. This system was implemented by the Belgian Alpine Club (BAC) to avoid overcrowding at the country's popular cliffs and to address access issues. You might be asked to produce a card by a BAC official at the cliffs, but if you don't have one, they most likely won't press the issue, especially if

Martha Morris belays Jean Bourgeois on *La Direttissima* (6a) (5.10a) on Al'Legne.

you're from North America. The system is applied more rigorously to climbers from nearby countries like the Netherlands, who inundate Belgium's crags every weekend, rather than climbers who travel halfway around the world to sample their cliffs. A friendly demeanor, however, goes a long way.

Rack, Protection, and Descent

Freÿr is a sport climber's paradise since virtually no traditional climbing exists, so leave your trad rack at home. Most routes are well protected with plentiful stainless steel bolts and beefy belay and rappel anchors. Bring a rack of fifteen to twenty quickdraws and at least a 200-foot (60-meter) rope. If you plan to do much toproping, then you need a 230-foot (70-meter) cord. Some routes may require double ropes to descend, but with creative rappelling acumen, a 200-foot rope is adequate. Many climbers bring a small rack of

wired nuts to supplement bolts on the older classic routes.

Toproping is the major cause of accidents at Freÿr. Make sure your toprope system is safe and secure before climbing to avoid problems. Use carabiners with locking gates to thread your rope through, and make sure both ends of the rope reach the ground if you're rigging from above. Also tie a knot in the rope's end to avoid having a loose bight snake through your belay device as you lower your partner to the ground.

Climbing History

Belgium, despite being ignored by the climbing masses, is storied with a rich climbing history and heritage. In the 1920s climbing began at the classic areas, including Freÿr, Dave, and Marche-les-Dames. Belgian climbing was popularized during this era by Albert I and Leopold II, the third and fourth kings of Belgium.

Both were passionate climbers, and their various exploits were well publicized. Albert I cut his teeth on hard routes in the Alps and Dolomites before exploring his native crags and making early first ascents at Freÿr in the 1930s. Unfortunately, the popular king tragically died after a soloing fall at Marche-les-Dames in 1934.

Climbing almost ceased during the war years, with climbers more intent on fighting for their country than pursuing vertical pleasures. Climbing returned in the 1950s, however, with a dedicated cadre of climbers pushing standards into today's 5.10 range and establishing some of Europe's hardest routes. A dominant climber that emerged from this era was Claudio Barbier from Brussels. In 1963 Barbier began free climbing routes without grabbing pitons or slings for upward progress. He eliminated aid from many Belgian routes and painted the unnecessary pitons and bolts yellow.

By the early 1980s Belgian climbers pushed Freÿr's standards and developed today's sport-climbing ethos. French climbers, including Jean Claude Droyer and Laurent Jacob, also discovered the Belgian cliffs and made many trips before shifting their attention to the limestone cliffs in southern France. Some of the world's hardest climbs in the 1980s were in Belgium. These included Arnauld t'Kint's first ascent of *13 Boulevard du Vol* (5.13b) at Freÿr in 1983.

Through the late 1980s and 1990s, Belgian climbers kept pace with the rest of the climbing world by bolting and establishing hard routes on steep walls. Jean Paul Finné, a well-traveled Belgian climber, made the third ascent of *Just Do It* at Smith Rock and cranked hard routes at Rifle and other American crags. Freÿr remains atop Europe's cutting-edge sport routes with Nicolas Favresse's two 8c or 5.14b routes: *Le Clou,* realized in 2002, and *Razorblade* in 2003. *Razorblade,* up Al Legne's South Face, is a 100-foot-long endurance pitch that finishes with an overhang.

During the 1990s the Belgian Alpine Club spearheaded the replacement of old bolts and updated fixed equipment on most of Freÿr's routes, a practice that continues today.

Getting Around

Renting your own automobile is the best plan when you visit Freÿr. Your own car affords more freedom and convenience than if you were stuck here without wheels, particularly when the weather turns rainy.

The cliffs are about an hour's drive and 60 miles south of Brussels International Airport. Flights to Brussels from North America are more expensive than flights into the major European air hubs at Paris or Frankfurt. Car hire costs are also cheaper in France and Germany than in Belgium. If you fly to Paris, Amsterdam, or Frankfurt, you can easily combine a trip to the Frankenjura or Fountainbleau with a few days at Freÿr. Both Paris and Frankfurt are a four- to five-hour drive away, depending on traffic and weather conditions.

Your American license is fine for renting a car and driving if you're staying less than ninety days in Belgium. Speed limits are 50 km per hour (31 mph) in the city, 90 km per hour (56 mph) outside the city, and 120 km per hour (75 mph) on four-lane highways. Speeding fines are imposed by cameras, and rental cars are not immune. There are no tolls on Belgian highways. Seat belts must be worn by all passengers at all times, and children younger than twelve are prohibited from sitting in the front seat. Maximum blood alcohol level is 0.5g/L or about a single glass of wine. Penalties are stiff for drinking and driving, so don't do it.

If you decide not to rent a car, then you can take advantage of Belgium's extensive and relatively inexpensive train and bus systems. You won't have a problem hitching a ride from Dinant to the crags and Le Chamonix cafe. All the cliffs and the camping area are within easy walking distance of the cafe.

Seasons and Weather

The best climbing weather at Freÿr is between April and late October. Spring can be wet and cool, with periods of rain and clouds. Summer days can be excellent but are also hot and humid. Daily summer high temperatures jump into the 90s, although shade is easily found on most cliffs. The polished routes will seem way harder for their grades on hot days. September and October, with mostly warm dry days and cool nights, are perhaps the best months to visit Freÿr. The beauty of the changing foliage is an added bonus. November through March is usually too cold and wet for climbing. A better bet in winter is to head south to France or Spain like the Belgian climbers.

Camping, Accommodations, and Services

The best place to stay at Freÿr is across the road from Le Chamonix cafe in either the free camping site or at Duchesne Refuge. The free campsite, accommodating about fifty tents, spreads across a lovely meadow

surrounded by tall trees along the rim of the river valley about 600 feet south of the main parking area. The site, owned by the Belgian Alpine Club (BAC), is for tent camping only. Park at the main lot, and carry all your gear to the site. The only stipulation is that you cannot leave a tent set up nor any gear at the site from 8:00 A.M. until 5:00 P.M., necessitating a ritual packing every morning.

The Duchesne Refuge, immediately west of the main parking area, is a spacious hut that sleeps twenty-four. It offers flush toilets, a hot shower (one euro for five minutes), drinking water, and food preparation areas. It is busy on weekends but often deserted during weekdays. The refuge, like the campground, is owned and operated by the Belgian Alpine Club.

If you want more privacy or luxury, your best bet is to drive to Dinant and find a hotel. You'll find quaint family-run hotels or chain hotels like Ibis on the south side of town. Out in the countryside are numerous *gîtes* or rural rooms in farmhouses and villages. Ask at the Dinant visitor center on the west side of the river, opposite the cathedral, for information on accommodations, or check online.

Food and Drink

The place where climbers hang, especially on rainy days, is at Le Chamonix cafe on the east side of the highway opposite the cliff parking lot. They serve reasonably priced meals, including breakfast, and have a pleasant outdoor dining area with covered tables. Many climbers stop for an invigorating beer after the day's climbing and compare notes on their ascents. This is a good place to ask locals for beta and recommendations on other cliffs. You just might get a tour of secret crags reserved for Belgian climbers. Also be sure to order a refreshing glass of *Caracole* ("Snail") beer, a local microbeer brewed in a nearby village.

Since the Middle Ages Belgium has been renowned for its superb assortment of specialty beers, which most beer connoisseurs consider the finest in the world. Beer writer Michael Jackson notes on his beerhunter.com Web site, "No other country . . . has among its native styles of

The Freÿr cliffs tower above the Meuse River.

beer such diversity, individuality, idiosyncrasy, and color. Nor does any other country present beers so beautifully." High praise, but well earned by the nation's brewers. As you travel around Belgium, you'll find an immense variety of regional beers in different towns and villages.

The monastic and abbey beers are the most famous. Only a dozen or so abbey breweries remain in Europe, and of those, six are Trappist breweries in Belgium. The Trappist monks, knowing that divine *biere* is a way of being close to the Almighty, brew rich dark ales with time-honored recipes that date to the Middle Ages at six monasteries: Achel, Chimay, Orval, Rochefort, Westmalle, and Westvleteren. The abbey beers are fine ales similar to the Trappist ones but are not brewed in monasteries but rather by commercial brewers. A good gastronomic outing to sample monk beer is to drive northwest of Dinant to the Abbey de Maredsous, where you can sample their beer and handmade cheese.

The surrounding towns and villages offer no shortage of good eating. You'll find lots of restaurants in Dinant and in Givet to the south across the French border. Dinant is well known for a unique hard cookie made from flour and honey and baked in various shapes. If you're camping at Freÿr, drive a couple kilometers south to the village of Falmignoul and its excellent bakery for morning baguettes, croissants, and pastries.

Last, Belgian chocolate. Those dark sweet bars are revered by chocoholics as the best in the world. You can easily find great chocolate to sample from shops if you wander around Dinant's side streets.

Cultural Experiences and Rest Days

Belgium, like Freÿr's climbing, is one of Europe's best-kept secrets—a marvelous gem that packs the best of Europe within its nutshell borders. This Maryland-size

kingdom is divided into two distinct cultural regions and personalities. In the north is Flanders or Flemish Belgium, a flat land seamed with canals and three of Europe's great art cities: Antwerp, Bruges, and Ghent. Wallonia or French Belgium, straddling the southern half of the country, offers the historic cities of Namur, Leige, and Tournai, as well as the picturesque hills of the Ardennes, castles and châteaus, and the Freÿr cliffs. Brussels, roughly in Belgium's center, is the nation's busy capital and headquarters to the North Atlantic Treaty Organization (NATO) and the European Union.

The two parts of Belgium are almost polar, with Flanders being all business and work oriented and Wallonia being laid-back, quiet, and very French. The dichotomy is linguistically based. The Dutch-speaking Flemish have long been competent merchants and seamen. The Walloons speak French and enjoy good food, beer and wine, and the pleasures of life.

Freÿr lies in Wallonia, only a few

miles north of the French border. After a few days of cragging or if it rains, explore the surrounding countryside. The obvious first place to visit is Château Freÿr on the opposite side of the Meuse from the cliffs. This beautiful Renaissance mansion offers an elegant touch to the Ardennes hills. It also has 300-year-old orange trees, 6 kilometers of mazes, and several classical gardens. It's open daily for tours most of the year.

Dinant, north of Freÿr, is the area's main city, with a population of 13,000. It hems onto a narrow strip of land between the Meuse and towering cliffs capped with a fortress. The city's name, dating back a couple thousand years to Celtic times, means *Deo-nant* or "divine valley" in the ancient tongue. The town was an industrial center, particularly for brassworks, but now is primarily a tourist attraction. Dinant gave its name to the craft of dinanderie, the art of working in copper.

The main points of interest are the Notre Dame Church and Citadel of Dinant. The striking church, topped with a 225-foot-high Gothic steeple, is quiet, dark, and intimate inside, especially after you step in from the busy street. The Citadel is a fortress built in 1820 by the Dutch and later occupied by German invaders in World Wars I and II. Reach it by clambering up a 420-step rock stairway or taking a cable car from the town center. It offers a museum, shelter cave, restaurant, and spectacular view of Dinant and the Meuse. Dinant is also famous as the 1814 birthplace of Adolphe Sax, a famed instrument maker and inventor of the saxophone. A giant saxophone monument commemorates his invention on the city's north side.

Also explore the surrounding countryside and poke around the ancient villages. One of the best is Bouvignes, which has kept its maze of medieval alleys and streets. Or drive north to the Flemish cities and visit the country's grand art museums, where the paintings of great Flemish artists, including Van Gogh, Bosch, and Rembrandt, are exhibited.

Trip Planning Information

General description: Rocher de Freÿr offers superb climbing on several large limestone faces and buttresses towering above the River Meuse.

Location: Southern Belgium in the province of Namur. The cliffs are a few miles south of Dinant and north of the French border. Dinant is 58 miles south of Brussels.

Camping and accommodations: A free campsite run by the Belgian Alpine Club lies southwest of the parking lot. A short trail leads to the area. It has shaded grassy areas for about fifty tents. You cannot leave a tent up during the day and must vacate the campsite until evening. Nearby is the CAB Refuge Duchesne with bunks, running water, a toilet, and a 1-euro shower with hot water. Across the road from the parking are some hotels. Otherwise, drive to Dinant for a hotel. Check at the Dinant visitor center on the west side of the bridge and river for suggestions, addresses, and directions.

Climbing season: The climbing season is April to October. It often rains but the cliffs dry quickly. Summer temperatures can be hot and humid, with highs in the low 90s. Shady climbs are easily found. September and October are often dry and pleasant. From November until the end of March, it is usually too cold and wet for climbing. For weather information dial 0900 27003.

Restrictions and access issues: The Freÿr cliffs are private property and are managed by the Belgian Alpine Club. To climb or hike here, you must be a member of the club or another accredited organization. Bring a membership card of an official alpine club like the American Alpine Club. This system was implemented to prevent overcrowding at the country's crags. In practice you probably will not be asked for a card, nor will you as a visiting climber be booted from the cliffs. Camping is only permitted at the bivouac tent site atop the cliffs. You can only stay here at night and may not leave a tent or belongings at the site. Follow the well-

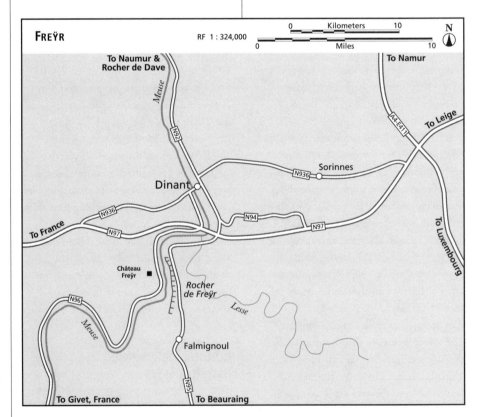

trodden, marked trails to the cliffs. Don't litter or leave cigarette butts.

Guidebooks: *Freÿr* by Marc Bott and Pierre Masschelein is the complete guide to the cliffs. The French-language guide is available at the Le Chamonix cafe. The only English-language guidebook is *Selected Rock Climbs in Belgium and Luxembourg* by Chris Craggs.

Services and shops: Alpi Rando, a small climbing shop, is along the N95 highway between Dinant and the cliff-top parking area. Le Chamonix cafe, across the street from the parking, is the popular place to eat and drink and to meet other climbers. It also sells the area climbing guide. All services and shops are in Dinant. Water is available at the CAB refuge and at Le Chamonix cafe.

Emergency services: Call 112 for emergency services and 100 for the Gendarmerie. Also call the *gardien de rochers* or guardian of the cliffs at 082 22 73 57. A pay telephone (you need a phone card unless it's an emergency) is at the car park. Other telephones are at Le Chamonix and other nearby businesses.

Nearby climbing areas: Many cliffs are found in the vicinity. Rocher de Dave near Namur is a good roadside cliff with many easier routes. Mozet in the Samson Valley offers a quiet collection of crags and towers in a birch forest. Marche-les-Dames, by the town of the same name, is a mile-long stretch of twenty-three crags along the River Meuse north of Freÿr. The best sector here is Beez, with nine cliffs and more than 200 routes, including many moderates. Lastly, Berdorf in Luxembourg, a two-hour drive south, yields excellent sandstone climbs up to 5.13c. The nearby village of Berdorf has campgrounds, bakery, grocery store, and other amenities.

Nearby attractions: Château Freÿr, Dinant, the Citadel, Notre Dame in Dinant, Saxophone Monument in Dinant, Ardennes Hills, village of Bouvignes.

Finding the area: Freÿr is in the province of Namur in southern Belgium close to the French border. It's about an hour drive south from Brussels International Airport and four to five hours drive north from Paris.

The easiest way to reach the cliffs is from the Motorway E411 between Brussels (Bruxelles) and Luxembourg to the east. If you're coming from Paris or France, you will probably be on the E42, which intersects the E411 north of Namur.

From either the north or the south E411, take exit (*sortie*) 20 and drive west on the N97 highway. Just before you reach the big bridge over the River Meuse, look for a right turn onto the smaller N94 highway. Follow this down to Anseremme immediately south of Dinant. Turn south or left onto N95 highway, and follow this a few miles until it climbs steeply up a long hill to the parking areas for the Freÿr cliffs. (Main parking lot GPS: N50° 13.213' E4° 53.695'. Elevation 665 feet).

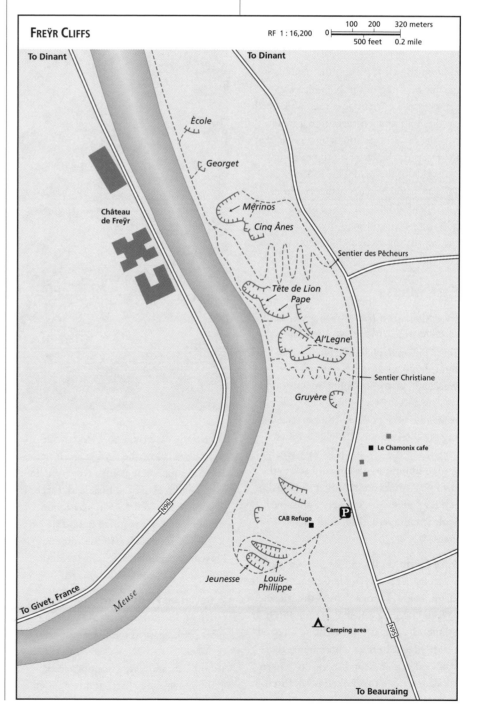

Le Mérinos

Le Mérinos is the west-facing cliff directly opposite Château Freÿr. The formation is composed of three main sectors: Face Nord, or North Face, with some short extreme routes; Face Meuse with moderate classics up big dihedrals and ribs; and Face Sud, or South Face, with superb slab lines. The cliff offers many routes and pitches, which can be linked for further adventures. Mérinos is extremely popular, especially on weekends. Some cliff sections are loose, especially the La Casserole ledge system across the upper South Face; avoid climbing under other parties whenever possible, and wear a helmet.

Finding the cliff: Park in the roadside lots on the west side of the N95 highway across from Le Chamonix cafe. Walk north on the N95 to a left turn onto a trail just past the Friterie restaurant and a road that intersects the highway on the opposite (east) side of the road. This is *Sentier des Pêcheurs* or fisherman's path. (Trailhead GPS: N50° 13.491' E4° 53.712'. Elevation 596 feet.) Descend steps then the path all the way to the river, and go right to the cliff base.

Face Meuse

Face Meuse is the river-facing west wall of Le Mérinos. Many excellent routes cover this wall, including popular easy and moderate lines. It is crowded on nice weekends. Watch for falling rocks or other objects, and wear a helmet. The easier routes are very polished in places, requiring good technique. The cliff is easy to access, and the descent is an easy scramble off the summit to a footpath back to the road. The routes are mostly well bolted, but it's a good idea to carry a small rack with wired nuts and small to medium cams.

1. Le Mérinos (4b) (5.6) 4 pitches. 360 feet. First ascent by X. de Grunne in 1930. Begin below a broad slab on the left side of a right-facing dihedral system. **Pitch 1:** Climb easy cracks up the slab to a bolted belay ledge. **Pitch 2:** Continue up the slab's left side (5.5) and then easy broken rock up a ridge to a bolted belay. **Pitch 3:**

Follow the easy ridge to a ledge with belay bolts below the final ridge. It's possible to scramble left along a ledge system from here to avoid the final lead. **Pitch 4:** This pitch is called *La Savonnette*. Fun climbing up very polished holds (5.6 or 5.7) leads to easy rock to the summit. **Descent:** Scramble across the summit ridge to a trail back to the road.

2. Deviation Poids Lourds (6a+) (5.10b) 1 pitch. An interesting, athletic, and long sport pitch. Start in the forest just right of *Le Mérinos's* slab below a steep face. Climb a short slab, and pass a diagonal crack. Continue up steep rock, and cross a left-angling ramp on *Les Crêpes*. Pull up the face above, and continue to bolt anchors on a ledge. 115 feet. **Descent:** Rappel with two ropes, or continue up other routes to the summit.

3. Les Crêpes (5c) (5.9) 3 or 4 pitches. 400 feet. A recommended classic opened in 1940. Pitches 2 and 3 can be combined. Start right of #2 below a left-angling crack system. **Pitch 1:** Climb a smooth slab to a high bolt, then traverse delicately up left and pass an overhang (5.9). Continue up left and then back right to a belay ledge. **Pitch 2:** Traverse right across a bushy gully, and climb a gray slab (5.5) to a belay stance. **Pitch 3:** Work up a crack system (5.6) to Vire de la Casserole, a ledge system on the South Face, and belay below a blunt prow. **Pitch 4:** Climb a short pillar to the right (5.7), then work up easier rock to the summit. **Descent:** Scramble across the summit ridge to a trail back to the road.

4. Mickey Mousse (6a+) (5.10b) No topo. A bolted sport route up steep terrain just right of *Les Crêpes's* first pitch.

5. Disney Land (6a) (5.10a) No topo. The rightmost sport route. Climb a slab to a couple of small roofs. End at the same bolt anchors as #4.

Face Sud

6. Le Lézard *(The Lizard.)* (6c) (5.11a) 3 pitches. Recommended classic up the left side of the Face Sud. Start from a niche below an overhang on the left side of the South Face. **Pitch 1:** Clear the overhang (5.10a), then climb more easily up left to a slight downward traverse. Continue up to a good bolted belay ledge. **Pitch 2:** Climb up right across a slightly polished slab (5.6) to good belay ledge. **Pitch 3:** Climb a slab to a steep face, and make a tricky dynamic move to a bucket (5.11a), cross *La Jaunisse,* and finish up a slab on *Vire de la Casserole.* **Descent:** Do a pitch on the upper wall or traverse left along the *Casserole* ledge and walk off.

7. Les Hermétiques to Super Vol-Au Vent (6a) (5.10a) 4 pitches. Two pitches on *Les Hermétiques* to two pitches on *Super Vol-Au Vent.* Start on the far right side of a terrace. **Pitch 1:** Climb out left and then upward for about 35 feet. Traverse hori-
zontally right on slippery holds to a short but hard crack (5.9+) that leads to ramp. Move up right to a good bolted belay ledge with bushes. **Pitch 2:** Make a 50-foot traverse up right along a crack system to the base of a steep wall. Edge up the wall (5.10a) to the ledge system of Vire de la Casserole. **Pitch 3:** Climb up left above an overhang to a technical slab to a belay stance. **Pitch 4:** Climb directly up a slab to the summit, or move right partway up and climb past a small roof.

8. La Gamma (6a+) (5.10b) 2 pitches. An excellent alternative to the last two pitches of #7. **Pitch 1:** Climb up and left across the steep wall (5.10b) to a small belay stance. **Pitch 2:** Work directly up the thin slab to the summit.

Cinq Ânes

Cinq Ânes or Five Donkeys is one of Freÿr's most beautiful cliffs. The steep west-facing wall offers some stunning multipitch routes up steep dihedrals and open faces. The cliff was unnamed until the route *Les Cinq Ânes* was opened in 1937.

Finding the cliff: Access is the same as Le Mérinos. Park in the roadside lots on the west side of the N95 highway across from the Le Chamonix. Walk north about 1,500 feet on the N95 to a left turn onto a trail just past Friterie restaurant and a road that intersects the highway on the opposite (east) side of the road. This is *Sentier des Pêcheurs* or fisherman's path. (Trailhead GPS: N50° 13.491' E4° 53.712'. Elevation 596 feet.) Descend steps, and follow the path until you are four switchbacks above the river. Exit onto a climber's path here,

and walk right (north) to the base of the cliff.

Routes are described from left to right.

1. La Can-Can (6a+) (5.10b) 1 pitch. This superb route ascends the far north margin of the cliff for 165 feet. It can be broken into two pitches with a belay to the left halfway up. Bring 20 quickdraws to do it in one pitch. Descend by rappelling the route with two ropes or walking off.

2. Les Cinq Ânes (4c) (5.7) 2 pitches plus one of three finishing pitches. "The 5 Asses" did the first ascent of this excellent and exposed route in 1935. The varied climb directly ascends an obvious cracked central pillar to the cliff summit. Begin at the broken base of the pillar. **Pitch 1:** Climb steps up the pillar to a chimney on the left (5.6) to a belay on a terrace. **Pitch 2:** Grab buckets up right on a steep face, then step right and climb up the airy edge

of the pillar (5.7) to a good belay stance. **Pitch 3:** Do one of the following three routes to finish *Les Cinq Ânes*.

3. La Traversée Bourgeois (4a) (5.6) First ascent by Jean Bourgeois in 1958. An elegant escape left across a break in the upper white headwall to a belay on the left shoulder.

4. La Fissure des Cinq Ânes (6a+) (5.10b) A spectacular and exposed finish up the original aid line. Climb above the belay and then angle up right along a thin crack that splits the compact upper slab right of the pillar edge.

5. Le Tour de Cochon (5c) (5.9) Also the last pitch of route #7. Climb out right and then up right-angling cracks to the summit.

6. La Therese (6a) (5.10a) 1 pitch. This is a direct sport pitch up the prow of the pillar to anchors halfway up *Les Cinq Ânes's*

Pitch 2. Start right of the pillar base. **Pitch 1:** Climb a white dihedral up left to a thin fingery crux (5.10a). Continue up a corner and then the exposed white pillar to the bolted belay stance. Rappel from here with double ropes, or continue up *Les Cinq Ânes.*

7. Le Tour de Cochon (6c) 3 pitches. A classic tour up terrain right of the main pillar. **Pitch 1:** A succession of pleasant cracks lead to a large obvious V. Go right up the lower ramp to a slippery crux (5.8). Climb up left along the upper ramp to a belay stance. **Pitch 2:** Climb up left along cracks (5.9) to the second belay ledge of *Les Cinq Ânes.* **Pitch 3:** Work up right along a crack system (5.9) that splits the great gray slab right of the pillar.

8. Pino-Prati (5b) (5.8) to **Le Scarabee** (6a) (5.10a) 2 pitches. This route attacks the big dihedral right of the pillar. Begin on the right side of a broken pinnacle below the dihedral. **Pitch 1:** Climb the right side of the pinnacle and then up the white left-facing dihedral (5.8+), passing a slippery overhang, to a good niche belay. 120 feet. *Pino Prati's* Pitch 2 exits right here on easy steps (5.4) to the top center of the cliff. **Pitch 2:** Jam, bridge, and layback up the airy dihedral (5.10a) to the cliff summit.

9. Les Taches Rouges (*The Red Spots*) (6a) (5.10a) 1 pitch. A great sport pitch up the white face between two main pillars. From the start of *Pino Prati,* walk right to the base of the second dihedral. Climb the dihedral and then cracks and corners up the technical white face to a bolted belay. **Descent:** Make a two-rope rappel to the ground.

10. Le Culot Qui Manque (6a+) (5.10b) 1 pitch. Another good long pitch up the central face. Jam and stem up the long technical left-facing dihedral just left of the right-hand pillar. **Descent:** Rappel the route with two ropes.

11. Le Parapluie (*The Umbrella*) (6a+) (5.10b) A brilliant face route up the white face on the right pillar. Start just right of *Le Culot.* Climb an apron and then a compact wall with a crack system to a

stance. Continue up the stunning white pillar above, and join the upper part of *La Sanglante.* Finish up *La Sanglante's* crack, and pass the superb final roof on the left to a belay and rappel stance. **Descent:** Two rappels (240 feet) with double ropes to the ground.

12. La Sanglante (6b) (5.10c) 2 pitches. An excellent climb directly up the right pillar. It can be done in two pitches as well as one long lead. Climb up the right side of an obvious dihedral and past a roof to a stance (possible belay here). Launch up an athletic crack system on the steep white face. Skirt the exposed upper roofs on the left, and end on a belay stance just below the cliff top. **Descent:** Make a two-rope rappel to the ground.

13. L'envie Folle (*Insane Desire*) (6b+) (5.10d) 2 pitches. Another great route up the right side of the wall. **Pitch 1:** Climb a bulge and gray wall (5.10c) to a good belay ledge. **Pitch 2:** Edge up the steep white face left of the leaning corner (5.10d) to a final pumpy roof. Belay atop the pillar. **Descent:** Two rappels down the route. **Rack:** Bring 16 quickdraws.

14. La Faucille (*The Sickle*) (7b) (5.12b) 2 pitches. The line follows the prominent sickle-shaped corner system. Do Pitch 1 of *L'envie Folle* to avoid the 5.12 finger crack. **Pitch 1:** Climb a technical finger crack (5.12b), and then work up left to a good belay below the sickle. **Pitch 2:** Stem and layback up the superb corner system (5.10d) to a cliff-top belay. **Rack:** Bring 15 quickdraws.

15. Le Pilier Cromwell (7a) (5.11d/12a) 1 pitch. Excellent route up the steep right wall. Do it in one long pitch with a 230-foot (70-meter) rope, or break it into two leads. The route was inspired by Alister Crowley, the nineteenth-century British climbing warlock. To start climb the left side of a small pinnacle, then launch up left. Grab pockets and edges up left on the vertical face until you're just right of the sickle corner. Pull up the steep and pumpy face right of the corner to a cliff-top belay. **Rack:** Bring at least 15 quickdraws.

Tête de Lion

Tête de Lion or Lion's Head, a small massif resembling a lion's head, juts into the green waters of the Meuse. The formation is characterized by streaked limestone, roofs, and steep walls. It's divided into three sectors: North Face, Meuse Face, and South Face. Most routes are steep and fingery, although a few easier classics are found. All the described routes are on Meuse Face.

Finding the cliff: There are two ways to access the cliff base. The first is the same as for Le Mérinos. Park in the roadside lots on the N95 highway across from Le Chamonix. Walk north about 1,500 feet on the N95 to a left turn onto a trail just past Friterie restaurant and a road that intersects the highway on the opposite (east) side of the road. This is Sentier des Pêcheurs, or fisherman's path. Descend steps, and follow the trail to the river. Turn left or south on the riverside trail, and walk to base of the first cliff.

The second access is the same as for Al'Legne. Park in the roadside lots on the west side of the N95 highway across from Le Chamonix. Walk north on the west shoulder of the N95 for about 900 feet and past the last restaurant on the opposite side of the highway. Look for the Sentier Christiane trailhead signpost (Trailhead GPS: N50° 13.365' E4° 53.734'. Elevation 734 feet) on the left marked G.R. 126 FALMIGNOUL G.R. 125 HASTIERE. Step left onto the trail, and descend to the base of Al'Legne. The fun begins here. Follow the cliff-base trail right or north below the cliffs. Eventually it reaches a dead end at the river below Tête de Lion's Meuse Face. An underwater concrete path, however, continues along the cliff base to the north side of the formation. The path is usually under between 6 inches and 2 feet of water.

Routes are described from left to right when facing the cliff from the river. Descent from the summit is by scrambling off the back of the summit and descending slopes on the north side to the cliff base and trails back to the highway and rim. You can also rappel from your route. Plenty of belay and rappel anchors are found on the face.

Meuse Face

The steep, striped wall facing the Meuse River.

1. La Tête de Lion (5c) (5.9) 3 pitches. A classic up the left side of the face. Start from boulders beside the river at the base of a long blunt ridge. **Pitch 1:** Easily climb the ridge (5.5) to a belay under the roofs. **Pitch 2:** Climb to the roofs, and move left and climb the bulging wall just left of the ridge (5.9) to a belay stance on a shoulder. **Pitch 3:** Scramble up easy rock to the summit.

2. La Sirene *(The Siren)* (6c+) (5.11c) 2 pitches. A serious hard line up the center of the face. Begin beside the Meuse where the trail goes into the water. **Pitch 1:** Climb a wall and a steep slab left of a shallow left-leaning chimney/corner to an overhang (5.10d). Continue past a hole and the steep face to a vertical hole and belay. **Pitch 2:** Climb a short wall up right to a leaning ramp to a stance. Climb up left along a crack system to anchors. **Descent:** Rappel the route.

3. Lachez les Fauves (7c) (5.12d) 1 pitch. Excellent with a range of moves. Begin up *La Sirene,* and climb it to the first hole. Work up left on the steep gray wall above the river to a crack below a bulge. Crank over the muscular overhang, and end at *La Sirene's* upper anchors. **Descent:** Rappel the route.

4. Cocaine Fingers (7a+) (5.12a) 1 pitch. An absolutely superb and sustained pitch. Climb *La Sirene* to its first set of anchors at the small cave. Launch out left across a white slab and then over the striped overhang to *La Sirene's* upper anchors. **Descent:** Rappel the route.

Route hidden →

5. La R? (6b) (5.10c) 2 pitches. Great climbing up the dark gray face on the right side of the wall. **Pitch 1:** Climb a short crack, then move up left on the steep gray face (5.10b) to a belay stance. **Pitch 2:** Go up left from the belay, and pass a thin roof. Continue up the steep face on small holds to the rock summit.

Le Pape

Le Pape or The Pope is the huge cliff looming over the Meuse immediately south of Tête de Lion. This big cliff is secluded and usually less busy than its neighbors. Some fine routes ascend the steep face, which is divided into three parts: Face Ouest or West Face, Face Sud or South Face, and Secteur Jurassic.

Finding the cliff: The cliff access is the same as for Al'Legne, the cliff to the south. Park in the roadside lots on the N95 highway across from Le Chamonix. Walk north on the west shoulder of the N95 for about 900 feet and past the last restaurant on the opposite side of the highway. Look for the Sentier Christiane trailhead signpost (Trailhead GPS: N50° 13.365' E4° 53.734'. Elevation 734 feet) on the left marked G.R. 126 FALMIGNOUL G.R. 125 HASTIERE. Step left onto the trail, and descend to the base of Al'Legne. Follow the cliff-base trail right or north below the west face of Al'Légne to the base of the wall.

Routes are described from left to right when facing the cliff from the river.

1. Le "Z" (6c) (5.11a/b) 2 pitches plus *Les Tourtereaux's* last pitch. A beautiful route up Secteur Davaille on the left side of the West Face. The route initially follows a long left-arching corner system. Start right of the arch by a corner. **Pitch 1:** Climb the crack and corner system to a shelf, then traverse up left to the base of the arching corner. Follow the arch up left (5.11a/b) to a small belay ledge under a small roof. **Pitch 2:** Pull past the roof at the end of the arch, and work up right on a dark vegetated slab (5.10b) to an open corner to a belay ledge shared with *Les Tourtereaux*. **Pitch 3:** Climb *Les Tourtereaux's* last pitch up left of the black overhang (5.10a) to the summit.

2. Les Tourtereaux (6a) (5.10a) 4 pitches. Superb, sustained, with varied styles of climbing. Begin same as #1. **Pitch 1:** Climb the corner crack to a shelf, and traverse 20 feet up left to the base of the left-arching corner (5.10a). Continue up left to a small belay ledge below the arching roof. **Pitch 2:** Climb up right through

a break in the roof, and climb a steep airy face (5.10a) to a good belay ledge with rappel anchors. **Pitch 3:** Climb a ramp up left and then crack systems up the steep muscular wall (5.10a) to a good belay ledge under a black roof. **Pitch 4:** Climb up left around the black overhang (5.10a) and onto the cliff summit.

3. Samarkande (6c) (5.11a/b) 1 pitch. Excellent and recommended. This pitch parallels #2's first and second pitches and ends at its second belay ledge. Begin just left of *Les Tourtereaux's* opening corner. Climb a short crack, then face climb past

the right side of an overhang. Continue up pockets and edges and over a bulge to finish on thin crispy holds. Belay on a good ledge. **Descent:** Rappel from here or do #4.

4. Les Murs ont des Oreilles (6c) (5.11a/b) Delightful and exposed face climbing. A second pitch to #3. Begin by climbing either #3 or #2 to the belay ledge. Face climb directly up the beautiful white pillar to a bolted belay stance below the big black overhang. **Descent:** Make two rappels to the ground, or climb *Les Tourtereaux's* Pitch 4.

5. La Herman Bull (6c) (5.11a/b) 2 pitches plus the last pitch of *Le Pape*. Good exposed climbing up the heart of The Pope. Begin right of *Les Tourtereaux* below a crack system. **Pitch 1:** Climb the crack system and then a smooth face. Traverse up right for 25 feet, then climb a system of thin slanting cracks (5.10c) to a belay stance below a black corner. **Pitch 2:** Climb up and pass the impressive roof above on the right (5.11a or 5.10a with one point of aid) to a bolted belay/rappel station. Descend in two rappels from here, or continue up right on easier rock to a large terrace and finish up *Le Pape's* last pitch to the summit.

To the right of *La Herman Bull* are five sport routes: *Les Mots Bleus* (6a+) (5.10b), *La Tire-Ligne* (6b) (5.10c), the long and excellent *Hazawee à Laeken* (6c) (5.11a), *Bourrin Malin* (6b+) (5.10d), and *Ventru Velu* (6c+) (5.11c).

6. La Francaise (6b+) (5.10d) 2 pitches and *Le Pape's* finishing pitch. A classic expedition up the steep central wall. The beginning is a little confusing, but the upper section is straightforward. **Pitch 1:** Climb dark vegetated rock (5.10b) to a belay stance below the white face. **Pitch 2:** Move up right and climb the big left-facing dihedral, then surmount a couple roofs (5.10d). Finish up easier but exposed rock to a belay on a ledge. **Pitch 3:** Climb the steep last pitch (5.10b) of *Le Pape*.

7. Le Pape (6a+) (5.10b) 3 pitches. Another great Freÿr classic. Start at a smooth wall right of a cavity. **Pitch 1:** Climb the wall to a shelf and then over a slight bulge. Continue up vertical cracks (5.9+) and then right to a niche belay. **Pitch 2:** Thrutch up the famous chimney above (5.9), and end on a good ledge. **Pitch 3:** Follow cracks up left (5.10b) and then back right to the summit.

Al'Legne

Al'Legne is Freÿr's most impressive cliff as well as the biggest and most important crag in Belgium. The 400-foot-high cliff divides into two walls: the narrow West Face fronting the Meuse and the broad, sunny South Face above the forest. Many routes and pitches ascend the cliff, allowing you to climb almost anywhere by linking various pitches together. This guide describes most of the best classic routes as well as some newer moderate sport lines. The right side of the South Face offers hard single-pitch sport routes. Check the comprehensive area guide for complete details to all the cliff's routes.

Finding the cliff: Park in the roadside lots on the west side of the N95 highway across from Le Chamonix cafe. Walk north on the west shoulder of the N95 past the last restaurant on the opposite side of the highway. Look for the trailhead signpost on the left marked G.R. 126 FALMIGNOUL G.R. 125 HASTIERE. (Trailhead GPS: N50° 13.365' E4° 53.734'. Elevation 734 feet.) Step left onto the trail, and descend to the base of the wall.

Face Ouest

The West Face of Al' Legne is the tall narrow wall facing the river at the west side of the formation. Some excellent multipitch routes ascend this face. Wear a helmet, particularly on busy days or weekends, since the routes above see a lot of traffic.

Finding the cliff: Follow the access trail all the way down slopes south of the main face to the river. Walk north or right a short distance along the cliff-base, river-side trail to the base of the big west-facing cliff.

1. L'Arête Jongen (5c) (5.9) 1 pitch. This is a long, popular sport lead and also Pitch one of a three-pitch route combined with *La Sérénade*. Face climb an elegant pillar of pocketed limestone to a bolted belay stance below line of roofs. Rappel from here, or continue up route #2.

2. La Sérénade (6a) (5.10a) 2 pitches and 1 lower pitch. Climb route #1, and belay from bolt anchors below the roofs. **Pitch 1:** Pull through the overhangs above the belay (5.10a) into a shallow corner system.

Grab easier rock up right along an exposed prow to a belay niche below a roof (belay shared with *L'Al Légne* so it's sometimes crowded). **Pitch 2:** Climb steep, fun rock (5.10a) above the belay. After the angle eases look for a bolted belay in a notch on the ridge. Scramble to the summit via a low-angle ridge.

3. Le Spigolo (5a) 1 pitch start to *L'Al Légne*. Start from the riverbank at the cliff's lowest point. **Pitch 1:** Climb a wall into the base of an immense chimney and couloir. Work up right, and follow the edge of an aesthetic pillar to a bolted belay stance. Finish up *L'Al Légne*'s last two pitches to the summit ridge.

4. Le Parrain de Juliette (6a) (5.10a) 2 pitches. Excellent recommended route that travels two long pitches from the riverbank to the summit. Begin just right of *Le Spigolo*'s start. **Pitch 1:** Work up a dark left-facing dihedral with some delicate stems (5.10a), and cross over *Le Spigolo*. Climb a beautiful streaked face right of a gully system, and belay at the same stance as *Le Spigolo*. **Pitch 2:** Climb a series of superbly sculpted faces (5.10a) up right of the face's prow to a bolted belay in a notch on the summit ridge. Continue to the summit on easy rock. **Rack:** Bring at least 18 quickdraws for these long pitches.

Face Sud

The South Face is the biggest and grandest piece of rock at Freÿr. The south-facing wall offers many routes up friendly slabs, vertical pocketed walls, and striped overhanging faces. If it's possible to climb the rock, then a route ascends that section. Almost 150 pitches ascend the wall. It is easy to link up different pitches to form lots of routes of varying grades. This guide details some of the classic multipitch routes along with some newer sport leads accessed from those routes. Consult the comprehensive area guide for information on other routes.

5. L'Al Légne (4a A0) (5.6 A0) 5 pitches. Very popular classic. The first route on the face, established in 1933. This grand traversing line follows the path of least resistance up the left side of the wall with a final finish up the west ridge. To find the start descend the access path almost to the river, but look right for a path that scrambles up through woods and talus to the top of a wide terrace below a groove/dihedral system. **Pitch 1:** Climb the chimney/groove for about 40 feet, then head up left along a slanting crack system (5.4) to a bolted belay ledge. **Pitch 2:** Descend down left along a series of ledges to a face equipped with a fixed pendulum cord—*La Banane*. Pendulum left or free climb the move (5.7). Climb past a left-facing corner, and continue left on horizontal ledges to a bolted belay below a prow. **Pitch 3:** Climb left and up easy vegetated rock (5.4) to a bolted belay in a niche below an overhanging rib. **Pitch 4:** Excellent pitch. Go up left from the niche and onto the north face just left of the rib. Climb the steep wall (5.6) to the ridge and a belay at a notch. **Pitch 5:** Scramble up the easy ridge (5.0) to the summit.

6. L'Hypothénuse (4a A0) (5.6 A0) 5 pitches. Excellent, classic, and extremely popular. Some sections are polished. Start by scrambling up the base of the groove/dihedral system and the start of *L'Al Légne*. **Pitch 1:** Same as *L'Al Légne*. Climb the chimney, then up left to a belay ledge. **Pitch 2:** Climb easily up left to a smooth slab equipped with a pendulum

Pendulum

cable. Grab it and pendulum left, or free climb the slippery 5.10a moves left and then climb easily up left to a bolted belay ledge. **Pitch 3:** Traverse left on grassy shelves to a groove. Climb the groove, then traverse left across a broad slab (5.6) to a bolted belay at a niche below a steep rib. **Pitch 4:** Climb up left from the niche onto the north face. Face climb (5.6) to the ridge above and a belay in an exposed notch. Alternatively, if it's busy, you can climb directly up the rib (Pitch 2 of *La Sérénade*) above the niche (5.10a) to the notch. **Pitch 5:** Scramble up the easy ridge to the summit.

7. L'Amour (6a) (5.10a) to **Le Chainon Manquant** (5c) (5.9) to **La Lecomte** (5c+) (5.9+) 5 pitches. This combination of three routes makes a brilliant and sustained climb from base to summit. Begin the two pitches of *L'Amour* downhill from the pedestal and below a left-facing dihedral system. **Pitch 1:** Climb the dihedral to a small roof (5.9). Pull past it on the left, and belay above from bolts. **Pitch 2:** Continue up the thin dihedral (5.10a) and then up easier shelves to a bolted belay ledge. **Pitch 3:** *Le Chainon Manquant's* pitch. Edge and smear up left along a crack in a slab (5.9) below the *L'Hypothénuse* pendulum. Belay at the stance for *L'Hypothénuse*. **Pitch 4:** Last two pitches are *La Lecomte*. Climb a slick slab below double roofs. Thread your way through the roofs on hidden holds (5.9+), and finish up a steep exposed slab to a belay in a left-facing dihedral. **Pitch 5:** Work up the dihedral (5.9+) to a belay on the ridge above.

8. Pull Marine (6a+) (5.10b) 1 long pitch. A brilliant technical and exposed line up a steep slab. Climb *L'Hypothénuse* to the belay just past the pendulum. Edge and smear up the wall to a bolted belay on the summit ridge. **Rack:** Bring at least 18 quickdraws.

9. Les Pétoles (6a+) (5.10b) 1 pitch. Another great lead. Begin by climbing the first pitch of *L'Al Légne*. From the belay ledge, work up left, then directly up the steep gray face, edging over a thin roof, to a bolted belay stance on the face. Rappel from here, or continue to the summit via *Le Zig-Zag* or *La Direttissima*.

10. Full Monty (6a) (5.10a) A bolted pitch just right of *Les Pétoles*. Start from the same belay as *Pétoles,* and climb up and left for 65 feet to join *Pétoles* under a small roof. Climb up right to the belay stance. Finish up *Le Zig-Zag*.

11. Marchand de Cailloux (5c) (5.9) Another fine long face climb on the face just left of *La Direttissima's* dihedral. Face climb up slabs and walls to a final small roof. Belay above at the same stance as *Les Pétoles*. Finish up *Le Zig-Zag*.

12. Le Zig-Zag (5c) (5.9) 1 pitch. First ascent in 1942 by De Warty and A. Régneir. An excellent zigzag route up the beautiful *Dalle des 3 Saurets,* the high slab left of the big *Direttissima* dihedral. Start by climbing *La Direttissima* to its second belay in a niche. **Pitch 1:** Traverse left to a fine shelf (belay stance for *Les Pétoles*). From its left end climb the steep slab past a hole, then make a rising traverse to the left. Climb broken rock on the left edge of the slab and a small face to the summit ridge and bolted belay.

13. La Direttissima (6a) (5.10a) 3 pitches. Another great line directly up the big left-facing dihedral that divides the wall. Start off the pedestal at the base of the dihedral system. **Pitch 1:** Work up the chimney/

groove in the dihedral (same as *L'Al Légne*), but stay right and continue up the bushy groove (5.5) to a good belay terrace. 115 feet. **Pitch 2:** Short lead. Climb a bright wall (5.8) and then an enjoyable corner to a niche belay. **Pitch 3:** A great pitch with airy climbing. Climb up left in the dihedral below a series of roofs. Continue face climbing up the dihedral until it's blocked by a roof. Exit right, and pull up steep exposed rock (5.10a) to a final overhang. Belay on the summit ridge.

14. L'Infant (6b) (5.10c) 2 pitches. A wild route up the outside of the *Direttissima*

pillar. Free climbed by Frenchman Jean Claude Droyer in 1978. To begin climb *Direttissima* to the niche belay below the final dihedral. **Pitch 1:** Work up through the steep white overhangs (5.10a) to a semihanging belay by a flake. **Pitch 2:** Move up right, and follow the beautiful exposed arête (5.10c) to a cliff-top belay.

15. L'Echec du Siècle (6c) (5.11a/b) 3 pitches. The local guidebook calls this "the classic of classics." It's a hard, sustained, and technical line up a couple dihedrals and faces right of *Direttissima*. Begin uphill from *Direttissima*. **Pitch 1:** Scramble right up an easy ramp, then face climb a wall and short corner (5.6) to a bolted belay stance on a ledge. **Pitch 2:** Climb a left-facing corner to a shelf and the route *La Traversée des 6 Jours.* Traverse left about 20 feet, and swing up a steep face (5.10c) to the left side of a long bulging roof. Pass on the left, and belay at a small stance above the roof. **Pitch 3:** Climb the steep technical left-facing dihedral above (5.11a/b), and exit right to the summit.

16. Le Pilastre (6c) (5.11a/b) 4 pitches. Yet another great classic climb up dihedrals and the obvious feature Le Pilastre. Begin uphill from *Direttissima* at the same place as *L'Echec du Siècle.* **Pitch 1:** Climb a long easy ramp up right to a ledge belay at the base of the monolithic pillar. **Pitch 2:** Jam cracks up the left side of Le Pilastre (5.10a), and belay atop it. **Pitch 3:** Crank up left on the steep white wall (5.10c) to a belay shelf below a dihedral. **Pitch 4:** Climb the gorgeous and airy dihedral (5.11a) until a roof bars the way. Exit right, and climb up right to the summit.

17. La Variante Duchesne au Pilastre (6a) (5.10a) 2 pitches or 1 long pitch. Good classic start to *Pilastre.* To start scramble right onto a pile of blocks. **Pitch 1:** Climb a thin corner system for about 50 feet, then work up left along thin cracks (5.9) to a belay under the left side of Le Pilastre, the hanging pillar. **Pitch 2:** Traverse back right, and climb vertical cracks up the right side of the pillar (5.10a) to a belay atop the monolith. You can avoid the belay by keeping right and connecting the two pitches. **Descent:** Make two rappels from the anchors back to the base, or continue up *Pilastre* to the summit.

18. La Grippe Intestinale (*The Intestinal Flu*) (6b+) (5.10d) 1 long pitch. Begin up *La Variante Duchesne.* Just after beginning the left-angling traverse, climb directly up the gray wall to a small roof. Edge up the perfect gray wall above, then up right through a white area to a belay stance below the arching bulge. **Descent:** Make two rappels to the ground with a 200-foot (60-meter) rope.

19. La Cerise (*The Cherry*) (7a) (5.11d) 3 pitches. An audacious route up the intimidating wall. Begin up right of *La Variante Duchesne* at a broken corner. **Pitch 1:** Climb past the corner system and up a steep slab to a 25-foot horizontal traverse left past a block (5.12a or 5.10b with one point of aid) to a belay stance. **Pitch 2:** Athletic climbing up the white face (5.10c) to a leftward-rising traverse to the left side of the bulging wall. Climb past the stance for *La Grippe Intestinale,* and pull up the steep face to a belay stance above it. **Pitch 3:** Work up left across exposed rock to an arching crack (5.11d). Continue up left where the angle and difficulty eases.

Many difficult and excellent routes ascend the steep striped wall on the right side of the South Face. Recommended routes include *Manathan Transfer* (5.12b), the long endurance route *Big Bang* (5.13b) with 22 bolts, *Tartine de Clous* (5.12b), *Le Clou* (5.14b), the classic *Scharzennegger* (5.13b), *Ninja* (5.13a), and *Bayou Minou* (5.13b). The complete topo is in the comprehensive area guide.

COSTA BLANCA

■ OVERVIEW

The Costa Blanca, a gleaming landscape of sharp mountains, limestone cliffs, and sea along Spain's eastern Mediterranean coast, is blessed with two hearts. The obvious heart is that of sun-warmed winter tourists, high-rise hotels, throbbing discothèques, and sandy beaches. This is the Spain loved by the northern European snowbirds—the British, Germans, Dutch, and Scandinavians—who own houses and villas here and fly down for weeks in midwinter to escape the grim clouds and snow. The other heart beats inside the real Spain—that ancient inland empire of dusty whitewashed villages, twisting single-lane backroads, donkeys towing plows across fertile terraces, and fragrant orchards filled with oranges, almonds, and olives.

Spain, after Switzerland, is Europe's most mountainous country. The broad shovel-shaped Iberian Peninsula is filled with crumpled mountain ranges. Through the 1990s climbers from across Europe began developing Spain's immense climbing potential by opening new areas and crags. Many of these areas are found along the long Mediterranean coast, including the Costa del Sol and El Chorro near Malaga, and the Costa Blanca and Costa Daurada between Murcia and Barcelona. Besides offering excellent climbing, the coastal areas are relatively cheap and uncrowded during the ideal winter climbing season, with weather that is usually perfect.

The Costa Blanca, encompassing the developed coastal strip as well as the coastal mountain ranges, stretches north from Murcia to the famed city Valencia. Costa Blanca, translated "White Coast," is named for its characteristic white beaches and limestone cliffs. The wealth of limestone, including long cliff scarps, isolated faces and walls, and towering stone peaks, offers a staggering variety of climbing adventures that make the Costa Blanca perhaps Europe's best winter climbing venue. This is a place where you can come

for two weeks and crank at a different area every day on routes that range from bolted 25-foot-high roadside climbs to full-day traditional routes up mountain faces.

The climbing is generally on good to excellent limestone, riddled with pockets and edges and ranging from immaculate gray slabs to overhanging tufa-lined faces. The rock is often rough and sharp, except on the popular routes, whose holds are rapidly being polished to a gleaming shine by the passage of countless hands and feet. Most routes tend to be single-pitch bolted sport lines on cliff bands, along with multipitch sport and trad routes that ascend the bigger walls. The bolts tend to be plentiful and good, although some areas—none included in this guide—are still protected by older, somewhat rusty bolts. Most routes are well protected, allowing you to safely push your climbing limits. Anchors are usually two bolts with either chains or quick-clip steel carabiners for quick, safe lowering. Route-finding difficulties are minimal since your only problem is finding the right line of bolts up your prospective climb.

Costa Blanca Cliffs

Lots of cliffs, both developed and undeveloped, scatter across La Marina, the rugged, arid mountain ranges of the Costa Blanca. The Spanish climbing magazine *Desnivel's* annual crag guide lists more than forty separate climbing areas in the southern part of the Valencia province. This guidebook describes two of the Costa Blanca's best classic areas—the Valle de Sella and the Peñon d'Ifach. After climbing a few days at these excellent areas, you can branch out and explore some of the more remote and lesser known areas for further adventures.

The Sella climbing area straddles the Valle de Sella, a lovely hidden mountain valley a few miles inland from the highrise hotels of Benidorm. Most of the climbing at Sella, the largest and most important area at the Costa Blanca, are sport routes up both sides of a limestone ridge that divides the valley. Nearby is The Wild Side, a superb wall laced with hard

routes. Unfortunately, it is now closed unless you have permission from the landowner. Above Sella is the long escarpment of Pared De Rosalia, with more excellent routes up to four pitches long. The Puig Divino, a towering pyramid-shaped peak, lords over the lower cliffs. It yields some stunning long routes, including those up the Pared de la Taula, a 400-foot-high shield of perfect limestone.

The Peñon d'Ifach, a monumental 1,000-foot-high block of limestone, dominates the city of Calpé on the coast north of Benidorm. This huge landmark offers many classic long routes up its steep flanks. Expect great climbing, plentiful protection, and lots of airy moves high above the dark sea.

Many other cliffs and cragging areas also invite exploration. In the north part of the Costa Blanca are lots of good crags, including Gandia, one of the older areas, with many hard routes on mostly vertical stone. Farther inland is Salem, named for a village, with more fun climbing in an amphitheater. This classic Costa Blanca crag is rarely crowded. Pego's two sectors offer lots of moderate climbs. A bit farther north is El Aventador, one of Spain's first sport crags. More than seventy-five face-climbing routes ascend this long south-facing wall in an open valley. It sports many 5.9 and 5.10 routes, allowing for a productive afternoon of climbing.

The Calpé region has other cliffs besides the imposing Peñon. Sierra de Toix is both a roadside crag and a sea cliff with lots of easily accessible climbs over a wide range of grades. It's usually dry and sunny but sometimes windy. It's a popular venue but suffers from surrounding housing development. Nearby is Mascarat Gorge, an impressive canyon that the N332 twists through just south of Calpé. Although not as popular as it once was, the gorge does offer some excellent long routes. Recommended climbs are *Via Sulfada* (5.10c), *Cleoplaca* (5.12c), and the fine classic *Via U.P.S.A.* (5.8), a seven-pitch line up the outside pillar above the highway tunnels. Dalle d'Ola, a compact minor cliff above the N332 also called Altea, is a fun outing with a bunch of sunny one-pitch moderates.

The rocky buttresses of 4,613-foot Puig Campana, the prominent notched peak towering above Finestrat and Sella, was one of the first developed climbing venues at the Costa Blanca in the 1960s. These long mountain routes, although not as popular as the sport areas, are nonetheless worthy additions to any area tick list. Most of the routes are long, moderate, traditional affairs up the peak's 2,000-foot-high south face. Recommended routes include *Via Rompededos* (5.11a) with its marvelous crux first pitch, the excellent and continuous *Diedros Magicos* (5.10b), *Via Diedros Gallego* (5.10a) up corners in the face's middle, and the easy twelve-pitch classic *Espero Sur Central* (5.6). The climbing and wilderness atmosphere more than make up for the long approach hike from Finestrat and the descent.

The mountains west of Alicante offer lots of brilliant small crags with hundreds of sport routes. The best of these are Salinas, El Marín, Cabreras or Sax, Peña Rubia, Reconco, Alcoy, and the excellent cliff Foradá. Foradá, a superb crag with more than one hundred routes, offers an assortment of 5.10 routes as well as harder ones at the famous Sector Superheroes. Alcoy, a featured cliff above the town of Alcoy, has fine overhanging pocket routes but is a long drive from the coast and has an urban setting. Reconco yields enjoyable slabby one- and two-pitch gems up its big southeast cliff. Peña Rubia is a shady and popular crag near the Boreal factory—a good place for a quick stop to try out your new shoes. Cabreras is composed of several cliffs scattered along a ridge north of Sax. The best sectors, Peñas del Rey and Sector Cumbre, have fine routes in the 5.10 range. El Marín, an obvious 200-foot-high dome perched above the village of Onil, is an excellent crag for fun sport routes up to 5.9. Salinas, also called Alto de Don Pedro, is a ridgeline cliff with a wide variety of routes by the town of Salinas. The busy area has a lovely setting and perfect rock. Its eighty routes are closed from February to April for nesting birds.

If you want to spend a couple days away from the madding climbing crowds, then journey either north or south from

Kristian Merwin grabbing tufa on The Wild Side.

Benidorm to find some fantastic climbing cliffs. Leiva, south near Murcia, is a huge limestone wall comparable with France's Verdon Gorge. The cliff, one of Spain's best climbing sites, is a long day trip from Benidorm, so consider spending a couple days there to acquaint yourself with its vertical charms. The area, with more than 150 routes, is divided into several sectors. Routes up to five pitches long grace the Main Face, and sectors Pared de las Cuevas and La Pecera are stacked with worthy single-pitch sport climbs.

North of Benidorm are more great climbing areas, including Chulilla and Montanejos. Chulilla is simply extraordinary, with beautiful climbing and an exquisite setting. The whitewashed village of Chulilla stair-steps up hillsides below an ancient Moorish castle in a sharp canyon lined with limestone walls. The canyon offers more than 350 routes of all grades. Camping is prohibited here, but you can stay in quaint hotels and *pensiones* and eat in classic Spanish restaurants. Visiting and climbing at Chulilla is a true off-the-beaten-track cultural experience. Buy the comprehensive guidebook *Chulilla Guia de escaladas* at the village.

Montanejos, a series of cliffs tucked in a mountain canyon along highway CV-20, is considered one of Spain's most important climbing areas, with more than 1,200 routes from 6b to 8c. Allow a few days of climbing to crank a lot of great routes. You'll find the area guide at the nearby Refugio de Escaladores.

Details, directions, topos, route names, and grades are found in the comprehensive area guidebooks. The best ones in English are published by Rockfax and Cicerone Press. Spanish topo guides to many areas are found in local climbing shops. Most cliffs are well frequented through the winter, so if you show up at any crag, you will find climbers who will allow you to peruse their guides. Like elsewhere in Spain most of the route names are painted at the route base, making route finding easy.

Rack, Protection, and Descent

Spain and the Costa Blanca is a sport climber's paradise. Almost every cliff and every route is protected by solid bolts and lower-off and rappel anchors equipped with chains or quick-clip steel carabiners. Bring a basic sport rack with twelve to fifteen quickdraws and a 200-foot (60-meter) rope. If you bring a shorter cord, then pay attention to your route of choice to make sure your rope is long enough to climb and lower back to the base. As always, tie a secure knot in the end to make sure the rope doesn't slip through your belay device. It's probably worthwhile to bring a set of wired Stoppers or Rocks in case you want to plug a nut into a runout between bolts.

If you plan on ascending any of the long routes on the Peñon de Ifach or Puig Campana, then bring a larger traditional rack with sets of Friends or Camalots along with a set of wired nuts.

Descent off sport routes is by lowering from bolt anchors, whereas the bigger cliffs require rappels from bolt anchors. The descent off the summit of the Peñon

requires an easy hike down the tourist trail to Calpé. Bring sneakers or sandals for the walk-off. Use caution since the descent path is brightly polished from the scrabble of myriad tourist shoes. It's a good idea to bring a headlamp for the descent on any of the long routes on the short days in December and January.

Climbing History

Technical climbing began on the Costa Blanca back in the 1950s with a couple routes on the imposing monolith Peñon de Ifach. *Via Pany* on the North Face was put up by Panyella and Salas in 1955, and the popular easy classic *Via Valencianos* was established by A. Marti, M. Gomez, A. Botella, and A. Tebar in 1958. The 1960s saw first ascents of the classic routes up the South Face of the Puig Campana. Starting in the late 1970s, the Peñon became the focal point of Costa Blanca climbing, with more than twenty new routes opened on the formation between 1976 and 1982.

During the 1980s the region was discovered by foreign climbers, mostly from Germany and Great Britain, who came down for climbing and adventure during the mild Spanish winter. They, along with a strong contingent of local climbers, were the impetus to develop many of the older crags, including Gandia, Sierra de Toix, and the easily accessible walls of Mascarat Gorge. The first English-language guide, by British climber Chris Craggs, came out in 1990 and detailed 200 routes on nine crags.

It was during the late 1980s that climbing exploded here. The seemingly limitless limestone potential was quickly exploited as all the best routes were installed on today's best cliffs, like Sella and Fornadá. Through the 1990s local climbers developed more cliffs, keeping them secret from the visiting hordes until they had plucked the crème of the routes. This trend continues through the early 2000s, with more and more "secret" crags being opened every year.

Getting Around

A rental car is a necessity to reach all the widely spaced climbing areas. Car rentals are reasonable in Spain and usually cheaper than in France, Great Britain, or Italy. You can fly into Madrid in the morning, rent a car, and be on the Costa Blanca by midafternoon, or you can change planes in London, Paris, or Madrid and fly into Alicante on the southern Costa Blanca and be edging up a sun-swept face by afternoon on your jet-lagged legs.

Be sure to make reservations before you leave the United States to ensure the best possible price. If you wait until you arrive, the cost will be exorbitant. All the usual car hire companies are found, like Hertz, Avis, National, Alamo, and Europcar, Europe's largest rental agency, as well as smaller companies, including Javea Cars. These offer some great rates but are harder to book in advance. Some like Victoria Rent-a-Car and Premier Car Hire can be booked through English offices. Take your current driving license as well as an international driving license to hire the car.

Driving in Spain is a lot like driving in America with well-signed roads, lots of stoplights rather than roundabouts, and big highways that quickly shuttle you across the country. Some of these motorways, like the A-7 through the Costa Blanca, are toll (*peaje*) roads. It's much faster to jump on the toll highway rather than to slowly meander through lots of towns and villages on the jammed coast road—unless you're just out Sunday driving. The tolls can be paid by credit card. Spanish law requires you carry all legal car and travel documents as well as an extra pair of eyeglasses in the car. Also don't drink and drive. The alcoholic limit in Spain is only 50 milligrams or 0.05% blood alcohol limit. Nonresidents can be fined for traffic violations on the spot and are expected to pay immediately.

Like everywhere else in southern Europe, car crime is a big problem here. Local thieves regularly cruise the various parking areas, especially the more remote ones, and break and plunder any vehicle with items of value inside. As elsewhere, leave absolutely nothing of value in your car, leave the glove box open and empty, and remove the parcel shelf in the back of hatchbacks so the thugs can see that nothing is hidden except a week's worth of dirty underwear.

Public transport, including buses and taxis, is available and generally fine for travel between villages, but avoid it unless you want to spend your Spanish vacation camping at Sella and walking to the village for food and *cervezas*.

Seasons and Weather

The best time to climb at Costa Blanca is during the American winter, although you can expect generally great weather between October and May. The winter months from December through February are ideal. The area, lying at the same latitude as southern Colorado, boasts a climate more akin to southern California. Winter weather is usually pleasant, reliable, and fairly settled, although periods of rain or showers can settle in for a few days. It cools at night, so bring a sweater and a raincoat as layers. On most days expect colorful sunrises and sunny days, with terraces on the surrounding mountains covered with green grass, flowers, and trees laden with ripe oranges. The resorts are quiet in winter, and prices are correspondingly low. The average daily temperature—the average of highs and lows—in January is 54 degrees.

October is mild and warm, but it's the wettest month on the coast. Still, the rain rarely sets in for more than a day or two. It's usually spread out sporadically, so the day varies depending on where you're climbing. But it can also bring strong winds, heavy rain, and even hail. November and December are calmer, and lots of bargains are found since the winter snowbirds haven't flown south yet.

The summer months from June through September are too hot for comfort, with daily high temperatures in the 90s and even hotter. It's also high season, when everyone across northern Europe seems to head here for beach fun in the sun. Prices are also very high.

Camping, Accommodations, and Services

The Costa Blanca is a busy tourist area, particularly in winter and then again in late summer when Europeans flock to the Spanish beaches, so there is no shortage of accommodations here to fit both your purse and taste. You can lease an apartment, stay in a country villa, hang at the climber's *refugio,* rent a room in a guesthouse or motel, or camp.

Lots of visiting climbers, particularly those from Britain and other northern European countries, buy a holiday package from a travel agent. If you can track down an English agent on the web, this is one of the cheapest ways to go. With a flexible schedule, you can buy packages with round-trip airfare from London, a week's lodging in a Benidorm high-rise hotel, and a meal a day for as cheap as $150. The last-minute deals, often just before or after Christmas, are the best value. The downside is that you don't know where you will be staying, but you can bet it will be a large hotel, which may not be so bad if all you'll be using the room for is sleeping.

Most climbers end up in either Benidorm or Calpé since both have lots of hotels and other accommodations, as well as many restaurants, bars, and beaches. Of course it will be too cold in midwinter for beach lounging. The best way to find a hotel if you don't arrive with a package is to visit the tourist information office in each town. They can give you a list of hotels and prices within your range and will even call ahead to make reservations. If you drive around, you will also find big hotel and apartment blocks with signs in English that read ROOMS FOR RENT. All the desk folks in the big hotels speak English, making it easy to shop and compare.

If you want, however, to experience the real Spain, then it's best to move inland and find lodging in one of the mountain villages. The whitewashed village of Finestrat, perched atop a hillock below the magnificent Puig Campana, is a great choice. Several small hotels are here, along with The Orange House, a guesthouse and bunkhouse just outside the village. The house, owned and operated by British climbers, has double rooms, a bunkhouse, communal kitchen, a swimming pool, and bar. The owners can also orient you to climbing areas, help you find a climbing partner, or set you up for mountain biking or canyoneering. Sella, west of Finestrat, is another good village for climbers. This lovely village, just south of the famous crag, has a good bed-and-breakfast inn called Villa Pico, as well as other accommodations. Lots of other small villages in the surrounding mountains offer rooms for rent.

The option for the rich and famous is to lease an apartment or, better yet, a villa for a week or two. This is actually a good alternative if you're traveling with a large group so the exorbitant fee is sliced into manageable bites, which can be as little as $100 apiece for a week's lodging. A villa is a better deal than an apartment. Most apartments are part of tasteless building blocks in the larger towns like Benidorm. Their noisiness and lack of charm, however, is offset by the convenience of shops and restaurants. Most villas are in the country and often come with amazing views of the rugged coast, the sea, and the sunrise. They also have amenities like a swimming pool, jacuzzi, barbecue grill, and television set.

If you're counting your euros and want cheap, then consider staying at the friendly Casa Refugio below the cliff at Sella. Be warned that it is rustic and very noisy on weekends when it fills with Spanish climbers. Still, you'll have a great time, improve your Spanish, and probably make some new friends.

Camping, although the preferred cheap option at many climbing areas, is not the best way to go at the Costa Blanca. The campgrounds in towns like Calpé cater more to the caravan crowd, who muscle their way down here from Belgium, the Netherlands, and Germany. Hence the tent sites tend to be stuck on the side of the area as an afterthought, and the ground is rock hard from rolling cars. Bring a hammer for pounding in your tent stakes and double foam pads for ground comfort. The traditional place to camp is near the Casa Refugio at Sella, but at press time they had lost their government camping license. A newer campsite, with

The Peñon de Ifach towers above Calpé's beach.

toilets and hot showers, is on the west side of Sella. Another recommended campsite is at Olta near Calpé.

Food and Drink

Since the Costa Blanca is a vacation playground, you'll find no shortage of restaurants and cafes. Most Spanish *restaurantes* offer good value, with plentiful food at reasonable prices. The best value is the *Menú del Dia* or Menu of the Day, a fixed-price daily special. Restaurants are mandated by law to provide a *Menú del Dia,* which usually includes an appetizer, choice of entrees, bread, dessert, and perhaps a small carafe of wine or bottle of *cerveza.* The menu is often posted outside. If you want to splurge, then order a la carte rather than *el menú.* Your meal will be better but more expensive. The menu usually offers *ensaladas* or salads, *entremeses* or hor d'oeuvres, as well as main courses with meat, fish, seafood, eggs, and vegetables.

You'll find lots of dining options in Calpé and Benidorm since these are tourist centers. Ethnic restaurants abound, serving Chinese, Indian, and Arabic meals. You'll also find places owned by northern European expatriates who cater to their visiting countrymen. These include authentic English pubs pouring Guinness from the tap, German *ratskellers* serving *wurst* and steins of *bier,* and Dutch bakeries filled with sweet treats. Cafes are good for *desayuno* or breakfast, with strong *café* and a toasted roll or *tostada.* For authentic Spanish food it's best to head into the mountains and stop at a village restaurant. These are usually basic eateries, often a dining room attached to a bar, with a simple menu. A few good Calpé restaurants include El Santo, a busy place with a superb *estampa ensalada;* The Regata, with haute cuisine and great bouillabaisse soup; as well as any of the seafood restaurants at the harbor below the Peñon de Ifach.

Be sure to try *paella* on the Costa Blanca. This Spanish specialty began on the Valencia coast north of here. It's a dish of saffron-flavored rice topped with a variety of seasonal vegetables and seafood tidbits or chunks of meat or chicken slow cooked in a wide, shallow pan, preferably over an open wood fire, which allows the rice to simmer in juices. Some bars here serve it as a *tapa,* whereas others make it only for two or more diners. Try to avoid it as a fast food; otherwise, you'll wonder why people rave about *paella.*

A good alternative to restaurant eating is to head into the towns and feast at a *tasca* or bar that specializes in *tapas. Tapas,* translated literally as "lid," are bar snacks that are a unique cuisine. They originated in southern Spain when bartenders placed a lid of sliced bread atop a drink to ban the ubiquitous flies. Over time they began putting a slice of sausage or a stuffed olive atop the bread. Now *tapa* bars serve a huge selection of usually salty snacks (to encourage more drinking) with lots of regional specialties and variations.

The *tascas* display an array of *tapas* on the bar counter, a detailed listing on a blackboard, or even a menu in the fancier places. Ask what's available because not every item is displayed. On the Costa Blanca the *tascas* offer lots of *muy delicioso* seafood *tapas,* including bite-size pieces of fried fish, oysters, clams, fish balls, octopus, prawns or *gambas,* marinated anchovies or *boquerones,* along with cheeses, spicy *chorizo* sausage, *jamon,* and olives. It's fun to try lots of different *tapas,* or even to go *tapa*-crawling from *tasca* to *tasca* to sample a variety. Be careful to order exactly what you want—a *ración* or large serving, a *media ración* or half-serving, or single *tapas*—otherwise, the bill might shock. Also remember that *tapas* will be cheaper if you sit at the bar rather than a table.

Cultural Experiences and Rest Days

The Costa Blanca is part of Comunidad Valenciana, a state with three provinces—Castellón, Valenica, and Alicante—stretching along a narrow strip of Spain's east coast. It's famed for Valencia, its beautiful and exciting capital city, and Valencia oranges, its namesake citrus crop. The Costa Blanca, an important cog in Spain's thriving tourist industry, is one of Europe's most visited areas. Fortunately visitation is low during the cooler months, when climbing conditions are ideal. The area has gotten a bad rap; it is not all concrete high-rise hotels, ghastly urban sprawl, and pasty package-vacationing fugitives who have escaped from the gloomy northern countries for a week of winter sun.

After a few climbing days you'll want to leave the coast and drive inland to visit the real Spain. It's easy to go to Benidorm, the only city in Spain that is never accused of being charming, and dance at the nightclubs along the beach or barhop around town, but after a night or two you'll want to get away from the madness. Lots of narrow roads thread through the mountains, passing quaint villages, soaring cathedrals, ancient Moorish terraces, stone farmhouses, and great scenery.

First, though, check out Benidorm with its skyscrapers, one of Europe's best beaches, and its three big attractions: sex, sun, and sin. Travel guides pan Benidorm, dubbing it "Tacky City" and "Manhattan on the Med," yet despite these nasty monikers, it continues to prosper and pack tourists into its urban jungle. To be fair, the city is trying to attract a better clientele than the beer-guzzling louts that crowded in during the 1980s. Now it's a somewhat genteel and tame haven for northern European senior citizens and expatriates. Levante, Benidorm's hippest beach, is good for sunbathing, sand sculptures, walking at sunrise, and great views north to the Peñón. Walk down the beach to a promontory and Balcón del Mediterráneo park, with its giant spouting water fountain. A couple miles offshore is triangular Isla de Benidorm, an island you can visit by boat.

West of Benidorm is Terra Mitica, Spain's answer to Disneyland. If you have a rest day to kill, take in this pricey, history-based theme park where you explore all the ancient civilizations of the Mediterranean. Here you can voyage past the pyramids on the Nile River, watch gladiators battle in a replica of Rome's Coliseum, and enjoy traditional Spanish folk dances.

North of Benidorm are Altea and Calpé, both enjoyable towns to visit. Altea, 6 miles north of Benidorm, is a picturesque whitewashed town that stair-steps up a prominence to a cathedral. Home to hundreds of artists, Altea is reputedly the most painted town in *España*. It's a good place to prowl around, peeking in galleries and antiques shops, grazing at restaurants, walking its stony beach, and shopping an excellent outdoor market. Pick up a map and information at the beachfront tourist office.

Calpé is a smaller, more intimate version of Benidorm. Despite the high-rise apartment blocks and hotels, it feels more Spanish, especially the old part of town with its steep, narrow streets. It's a great place to dine at sumptuous restaurants or to find a *tapa* bar with a great view across the beach to the Peñón. Stop at one of the two tourist offices at Plaza del Mosquit in town or on Avenida de los Ejércitos Españoles en route to the Peñón for maps and suggestions.

It's easy to drive into the La Marina mountain range and explore the many peaks, valleys, and hospitable villages. The back roads are simply spectacular, twisting across high ridges and winding along pastoral valleys lined with olive tree–studded terraces and small villages. Exploring out here is not to be missed—this is the real Spain. Driving around the mountains you discover lots of unknown villages and places like the bullring at Bocairent, carved from rock in 1813, and the nearby man-made caves Les Covetes dels Moros or the Moors' Caves. Be sure to stop at a restaurant for real country cooking or at a *tasca* for *tapas.* A rudimentary knowledge of Spanish is helpful outside the larger towns.

Castell de Guadalest, one of the best villages, lies over the rocky Sierra de Aitana from Sella. Despite drawing tourists and buses on day trips, it is still relatively unspoiled. The old Muslim part of the village is accessible only on foot and by passing through a rock tunnel below a castle. After peeking at the castle, stop at the fascinating Museo de Miniaturas, with its micropainting of da Vinci's *Last Supper* on a rice grain and Goya's *The Naked Maja* detailed on a fly's wing.

Alcoy, surrounded by good climbing crags, is an interesting stop. It's industrial but has a good atmosphere. Places of interest are the Iglesia de Santa Maria church and the Convento de San Agustín. Other interesting villages include Callosa de Ensarria, Jijona, Ibi, Biar, and Villena with an archeology museum and Castillo Atalaya.

Trip Planning Information

General description: Excellent bolted sport climbing and longer traditional routes on numerous limestone cliffs and walls in the La Marina mountains along the Mediterranean coast.

Location: The Costa Blanca. On Spain's east coast between Alicante and Valencia.

Camping and accommodations: The best camping, if it's open, is at Sella Refugio near the crags. Other campgrounds that cater more to trailer campers are found in nearby cities like Calpé and Benidorm. In the off-season definitely spend only a few more euros to stay in relative comfort at a hotel or guesthouse in nearby villages like Finestrat or in self-catering apartments, villas, or hotels in the surrounding area and cities. Check the Appendix for suggestions, or ask at the local tourist offices.

Climbing season: Year-round. October through April is the best time. The winter months are excellent with generally perfect climbing temperatures in the sun. Rain showers are usually spotty and short-lived. October can be wet. The summer months are too hot for climbing, although shady cliffs can be found if you happen to be there.

Restrictions and access issues: None except on the Peñon de Ifach, which has a climbing ban on its northwest face in the spring and early summer because of nesting birds. Check at the park visitor center for details.

Guidebooks: A couple of English guidebooks are available. The best is *Costa Blanca, Mallorca, El Chorro* by Alan James and Mark Glaister. It covers most of the area crags with topos and descriptions. *Costa Blanca Rock* by Chris Craggs covers most of the area climbing. Either one is indispensable if you're planning on spending more than a week here and plan to venture to other cliffs. They are, however, difficult to find in Spain and in the United States.

Some good Spanish guides are available. They can be purchased at local sport shops like Sport Zero 95 in Calpé or online at *Desnivel*. *Sella Escalada* by Ignacio Sanchez is a topo guide to Sella and surrounding cliffs, including the Puig Divino. *Guia de Escalada del Peñon de Ifach* by Roy de Valera is a guide to the Peñon, Sierra Toix, and Mascarat Gorge. *Escaladas en le Medio y Alto Vinalopo* details the crags along the Vinalopo River, including Sax and Foradá. *Guia de Escalada del Puig Campana* by Carlos Tudela is a good guide to the big rock. A foldout topo guide to the Peñon is available for free at the Calpé tourist offices.

Services and shops: All services are found near the crags, including supermarkets, restaurants, bars, and anything else you desire. The nearest climbing shops are Zero 95 in Calpé and K2 Esports in Alicante. Check the Appendix for addresses and phone numbers.

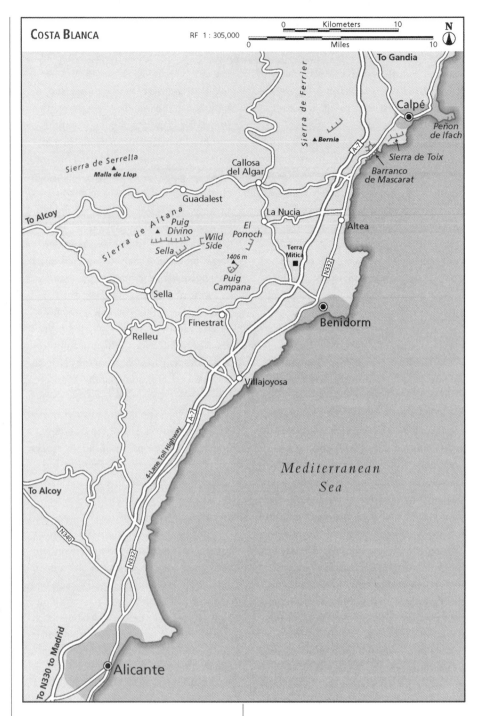

Emergency services: In case of emergency dial 532 or the official European emergency number, 112. Complete medical services and hospitals are at Benidorm, Calpé, and Alicante.

Nearby climbing areas: Lots of crags and cliffs are in the Costa Blanca region. These include Alto de Don Pedro (Salinas), Agujas Rojas, Barranc del Sinc (Alcoy), Barranc de les Coves (Pego), Barranquet de Ferry (Alcoy), Cabezo de Oro (Buset), Cabreras (Sax), Foradá, El Marín, Onil, Pared Negra, Peña Rubia (Villena), Penya Roc, Ponoig, Racò del Corv, Reconco, Redován, Gandia, Salem, and Peña Roja. To the north are some great areas, including Jérica, the world-class area Montanejos, La Pedrera, Penyagolosa, Torrebadún (Peñíscola), and Chulilla, another great area. You can find information and topos to most of these places by asking at climbing shops, going to the nearest village where you can usually buy a topo guide, or checking online at the *Desnivel* magazine Web site.

Nearby attractions: Lots of urban attractions at Benidorm, Calpé, and Alicante. Terra Mitica, a history theme park, is just west of Benidorm. Altea, Villajoyosa, Callosa de Ensarria, Guadalest, Alcoy, and Villena are all worth visiting. Check out "Cultural Experiences and Rest Days" in the overview above for more details.

Finding the area: Costa Blanca is on the east coast of Spain between Valencia and Alicante. It's easiest to fly into Alicante from Madrid, Paris, or London. There are lots of package vacations with airfare from London to Alicante all winter. Otherwise, fly to Madrid from the United States, and fly or drive to the coast. Driving time from Madrid via the four-lane N330 Autovia Alicante-Madrid highway is about four hours.

All the climbing areas are easily accessed from the A7 Autovia north of Alicante. Check the area maps and cliff descriptions for detailed directions.

Peñon de Ifach

The Peñon de Ifach, the symbol of the Costa Blanca, is a massive limestone fortress that juts into the Mediterranean Sea. It towers more than 1,000 feet above the Calpé harbor and the high-rise hotels that line its pale beaches along a narrow strip of land that joins the headland to the mainland. This amazing formation, an ancient landmark visible from miles away, attracts climbers that swarm up its vertical flanks during the winter months while the rest of Europe huddles around woodstoves. The Peñon is not only an interesting geologic oddity but also boasts a unique variety of endangered plants and flowers. These interesting plant communities, as well as the formation's singular geology, are protected in a natural conservation park that encompasses most of the Peñon.

The limestone is variable in quality, with occasional loose and broken sections and some very polished and slippery holds on the popular lines. Loose rock is commonly encountered on the lower pitches. Definitely wear a helmet. Rockfall is common, particularly off the busy routes. The routes are long, exposed, multipitch affairs set spectacularly above the sea and finish atop the airy satisfying summit. The climbing is fun and interesting, the views are stunning, and protection ranges from good to excellent. The modern routes like *Costa Blanca* are completely bolted, allowing for safe and friendly upward journeys. The older classic routes like *Via Valencianos* are equipped with older gear and require a rack in addition to quickdraws. Plan on at least four hours to climb most routes. Some might take longer, particularly if you're stuck behind a slow party. Bivouacs on the long classics like *Diedro UBSA* are not uncommon on short winter days. Start early, or come prepared for a chilly January night.

The Peñon de Ifach is divided into two climbing sectors. The white North Face, looming above the Calpé harbor and Playa de Levante, offers a selection of brilliant moderate routes that are mostly

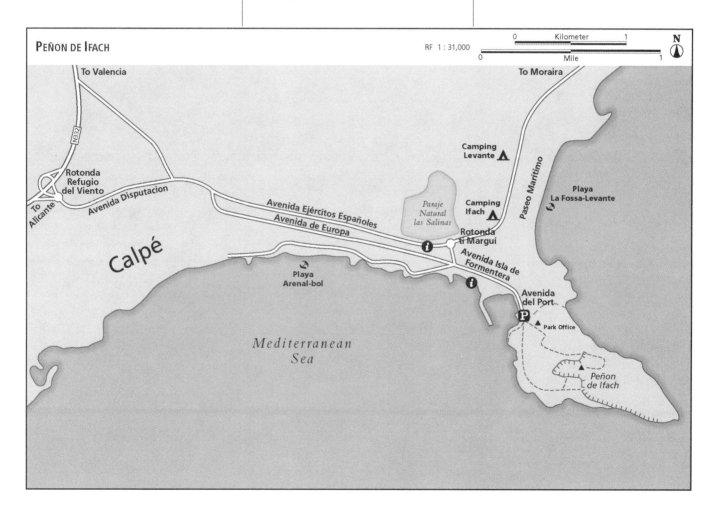

shaded. The face is closed for nesting birds from May to September, and the left side above the summit trail is also closed because of possible rockfall onto hikers. The South Face, a broad 1,000-foot-high cliff, is a complex sweep of sunburnt stone broken into steep slabs, smooth immaculate faces, steep cracks and corners, huge shallow caves, and imposing buttresses. This wall receives full winter sun, although it can be disconcertingly windy on the higher pitches or shrouded in gray morning mist. Sunscreen and water are the usual necessities.

Bring a good-size rack for most routes that includes sets of Stoppers and Friends, fifteen to twenty quickdraws, some extra slings, and a 200-foot (60-meter) rope. You can also climb with a 165-foot (50-meter) rope but will need two if you need to rappel from the face. It's a good idea to wear a helmet, especially on the busy routes. Bring a small pack with water, some food, a jacket or sweater, and shoes for the walk-off. Also be very careful walking down the slippery

limestone on the descent path. It's polished to a bright sheen from myriad scrabbling shoes on this popular tourist hike. A jacket is a good idea in winter since the upper sections of the routes can be windy and are in the shadows by the time you reach the summit on short days.

Finding the cliff: The Peñon rises above the Calpé harbor. It's easily reached from the car park at the harbor. Drive into Calpé on the north-south highway N332, which is easily accessed from the toll highway at exit 64 for Altea. Turn east onto Avenida Disputacion, which turns into Avenida Ejércitos Españoles, the obvious road that descends past the town center and past the tourist office to an obvious junction at a roundabout called Rotonda Tí Marguí. Go right here to another roundabout, and go right onto Avenida Isla de Formentera to Avenida del Port and the harbor. Park in a long parking area below the west side of the obvious Peñon. Walk along a brick esplanade alongside the sea for about a quarter mile to the south side of the cliff. Behind the

public restrooms, look for a rough trail that scrambles uphill over loose talus to the base of the cliff. Hiking time from car to cliff is ten to fifteen minutes.

South Face

The complex South Face of the Peñon is an immense wall broken into a varied rock architecture of slabs, pillars, dihedrals, overhangs, and caves. Many routes, mostly bolt protected, lace the wall and offer excellent multipitch, daylong adventures on great climbing terrain amid spectacular scenery.

Most routes are straightforward and require only basic route-finding skills. Come prepared, however, to climb quickly to avoid being benighted on the shorter days in December and January. The popular easy classics usually require an early start to avoid being tangled behind large and garrulous parties of Spanish or British climbers. Allow at least four hours to climb the routes. The newer lines are bolt protected with beefy belay bolts, which allow for a quick, easy escape off the line if the weather turns or night falls. The face

Valenciano's slab

Diedro UBSA

is often hot and bakes in the sun. Bring plenty of water and sunscreen.

1. Via Valencianos (5+) (5.9) 8 pitches. An easy classic expedition up the big dihedral and slab on the left side of the face. It's usually busy, so get there early and try to avoid climbing behind a big party. Expect mostly easy climbing except for a slippery bit on Pitch 3. The route is easily rappelled if the weather moves in or it's late. Scramble up rocky slopes below the face to the foot of the huge left-facing dihedral on the left side of the wall. Look for the route name painted on rock at its start. The pitches can be combined for speed with a long rope. It's easy to follow the route—look for the shiny polish. **Pitch 1:** Climb up right and then leftward to a steep slab. Edge past a fixed piton (5.4) to easier rock and a 3-bolt belay on a spacious ledge. 100 feet. **Pitch 2:** Traverse up left on bushy, easy rock to a rib and crack (5.4) to a ledge system. Follow the ledge back right to a bolted belay above the Pitch 1 stance. 115 feet. **Pitch 3:** Climb easy rock up right to a terrace (possible belay here) below the big dihedral. From the right side of the ledge, work up the very polished, well-protected (2 bolts) crux crack on the right wall (5.9) by stemming (easy to frig this section) to a jug. Continue on easier rock to a ledge on the left below the broad slab. 110 feet. **Pitch 4:** Move up left across the lower slab (5.6) to a bolt and bush belay stance. 65 feet. **Pitch 5:** Excellent long pitch but can be divided into two shorter leads. Climb directly up the center of the great slab (5.6) to an airy belay stance with stunning views atop the ridgeline. 150 feet. **Pitch 6:** Walk along the exposed ridge to the mountain bulk. Climb leftward along a shelf to a crack up a slab. Grab good holds (5.6) over a bulge, and belay from a spike of rock. 100 feet. **Pitch 7:** Climb up and right on easy rock, following the obvious line, to a 2-bolt belay stance in an exposed notch above *Diedro UBSA*. **Pitch 8:** Climb a long pitch up an easy groove to a belay stance. 100 feet. Scramble from here to the summit.
Descent: Hike down the summit trail to the car park at the harbor (thirty to forty-

five minutes). Bring shoes for comfort.
Rack: Bring a set of Stoppers or other wired nuts along with a small selection of small to medium Friends to supplement fixed protection. A 200-foot (60-meter) rope is best, but a 165-foot (50-meter) rope is fine. Wear a helmet to protect yourself.

2. Polvos Magicos (6a) (5.10a) 8 pitches. A great route that climbs the big dihedral right of *Via Valencianos*. It's easy to escape left onto *Valencianos*. Begin at the same

place as *Valencianos*. **Pitch 1:** Same as *Via Valencianos*. Climb up right and then leftward to a steep slab. Edge past a fixed piton (5.4) to easier rock and a 3-bolt belay on a spacious ledge below a corner. 100 feet. **Pitch 2:** Climb directly up the steep, sustained, and polished corner (5.10a) past many bolts and fixed pitons to a crux at the top. Belay above from bolts. 85 feet. **Pitch 3:** Pitch 3 of *Valencianos*. From the right side of the ledge, work up the polished, well-protected (2 bolts) crack on the right wall (5.9) by stemming to a jug. Continue on easier rock to a bolted belay ledge on the left below the broad slab. 100 feet. **Pitch 4:** Climb easy rock into the big dihedral above. Continue up the dihedral (5.8) to a niche belay. 75 feet. **Pitch 5:** Interesting laybacks, stems, and face moves (5.9) up the dihedral to a bolted belay on the exposed ridge atop the slab. 85 feet. **Pitch 6:** Work up a groove in the ridge, climb left over some airy bulges, then up easier rock to a belay stance. 65 feet. **Pitch 7:** Climb up right on easy rock along the obvious line to a 2-bolt belay stance in an exposed notch above *Diedro UBSA*. **Pitch 8:** Climb a long pitch up an easy groove to a belay stance. 100 feet. Scramble from here to the summit. **Descent:** Hike down the summit trail to the car park at the harbor (thirty to forty-five minutes). Bring shoes for comfort. **Rack:** Bring a set of wired nuts along with a small selection of small to medium Friends to supplement fixed protection. A 200-foot (60-meter) rope is best, but a 165-foot (50-meter) rope is fine. Wear a helmet.

3. Costa Blanca (6c+) (5.11b) 7 pitches. One of the Peñon's great climbs—excellent, highly recommended, short cruxes, a stunning finish, and mostly bolted. It ascends the obvious pillar between *Diedro UBSA* and the *Valencianos's* slab. Follow the route by following the bolt line. Begin left of the pillar at the start of *Via Valencianos*. **Pitch 1:** Scramble up right on easy, broken rock to a bolted belay stance below the steeper pillar. 65 feet. **Pitch 2:** Edge up a thin slab, then flakes and edges (5.10c) to a bolted belay stance on the right. 115 feet. **Pitch 3:** Work up a slab to a corner. Climb up right over small bulges (5.10c) to a good bolted belay stance. 145 feet. **Pitch 4:** Climb a gray slab to left up a pocketed wall (5.10a) to a final loose crack system. Finish at a spacious bolted belay to the top of the pillar. 105 feet. **Pitch 5:** Step across the chimney gully behind the pillar. Swing up the wall over bulges with good holds except for one thin section (5.10d). Belay from bolts on a long ledge at the bottom of the *Diedro UBSA* rappel. 85 feet. **Pitch 6:** Climb tufa to a face with good holds (5.10c) to a bolted belay stance on the left side of the

large upper cave. 95 feet. **Pitch 7:** Pull up jugs on the cave's left edge until you can make some wildly exposed moves on good holds up left (5.11b) on the steep face. Easier climbing above leads to a final steep face. Finish up a fine and airy crack to a bolted belay stance. An easy 65-foot pitch leads to the summit ridge. Scramble to the peak's summit. **Descent:** Hike down the summit trail to the car park at the harbor (thirty to forty-five minutes). Bring shoes for comfort. **Rack:** Bring 15 to 18 quickdraws and perhaps a few wired nuts to supplement the plentiful bolts.

Wear a helmet, particularly if a party is on its popular neighbor *Diedro UBSA*.

4. Diedro UBSA (5+) (5.9+) 10 pitches. An excellent and highly recommended route up the big wall. Lots of interesting climbing up a long corner system that culminates in a rappel from a cave to an exposed ledge. Some route finding is involved near the top, but most of the climb is straightforward. It has good belay stances with big bolts. Reach the start by scrambling up the climber's path until you're below a scrubby apron and the obvious corner system. **Pitch 1:** Several ways to tackle the first section but it's easiest on the left. Easily climb to a ledge with bolt anchors below the corner. 50 feet. **Pitch 2:** Move up right across a slightly polished slab, and climb the steep corner groove (5.7) to a good bolted belay stance where the corner becomes a chimney. 100 feet. **Pitch 3:** Grab slick holds up the bolt-protected right wall of the chimney (5.9+ route crux). Above stem up the groove to a bolted belay ledge. 100 feet. **Pitch 4:** Continue up the corner system (5.8) by stemming off polished holds to a good belay stance with bolts. 85 feet. **Pitch 5:** Edge right across a slab, then back up left into the corner (5.7), which is now a deep chimney. Climb this quickly to a scenic bolt belay behind the top of a pillar. 100 feet. **Pitch 6:** Easy climbing leads to a jammed block atop the chimney. Make a tricky move around it (5.8). Superb climbing heads up right on a clean face to a bolted belay stance. Look for threads for extra pro. 85 feet. **Pitch 7:** Climb underprotected shattered rock to the upper left edge of the big shallow cave and an obvious ball of rappel slings on your left. Belay here. 85 feet. **Pitch 8:** Rappel or lower 65 feet from the fixed slings and a bolt to the right side of a long narrow ledge. Scramble across the ledge to a good bolted belay station. After rappelling you need to swing left to a jug and the ledge. Use a safety prussik knot to allow you to use both hands to safely gain the belay ledge after rappelling. **Pitch 9:** Traverse left on pockets across the exposed ledge system into a big obvious dihedral (5.6), and climb good holds to an obvious bolted belay stance above a bush. 100 feet. **Pitch 10:** Bridge up the dihedral (5.7) to a notch in the summit ridge with a 2-bolt belay anchor. 100 feet. Climb to the summit from here by scrambling up a corner and then easy rock and grass to the top. **Descent:** Hike down the summit trail to the car park at the harbor (thirty to forty-five minutes). Bring shoes for comfort. **Rack:** Bring 12 to 15 quickdraws, a set of wired nuts, small to medium cams, a rappel device, and some extra slings. A 200-foot (60-meter) rope is best. A helmet is a good idea.

5. El Navigante (7a) (5.11c) 9 pitches. Another stunning adventure with steep, sustained, and spectacular climbing up the face right of *Diedro UBSA*. If you pull on bolts on a couple pitches, the grade drops to 5.10b/c. The route is easy to follow since it has lots of bolts. Begin at the same spot as *Diedro UBSA*. **Pitches 1 and 2:** Climb the first two pitches of *Diedro UBSA* to the belay below the initial chimney. **Pitch 3:** Climb the crux 5.9+ section of *Diedro UBSA* up the right wall of the chimney above the belay. Continue up the easier corner to a ramp on the right. Climb the awkward ramp to a small belay stance with 3 bolts below steep rock. 85 feet. **Pitch 4:** Work up good holds on disconcerting strange rock that is surprisingly solid, then up right to a corner (5.10c). Higher, move left to a bolted belay stance. 100 feet. **Pitch 5:** Follow the bolts to some hard moves onto flowstone (5.10c). Continue on big holds to a crack system and then a loose corner. Belay from bolts on a ledge above the corner. 115 feet. **Pitch 6:** Move up left to an arête. Tricky laybacking (5.11a) leads up the arête to a niche. Climb up right to a bolted belay ledge. 75 feet. **Pitch 7:** Climb a corner and then a steep crack (5.10a) up left on the exposed wall to a bolted belay stance. 85 feet. **Pitch 8:** A stunning and exciting pitch! Pull edges up the overhanging face above (5.11c), or clip and grab up a short A0 bolt ladder to the left. Above, work up right on steep rock and follow a crack to a leftward hand traverse. Pull out of a niche and then up a corner and slab to easier rock and a bolted belay on the summit ridge. 90 feet. **Pitch 9:** Scramble to the summit from here. **Descent:** Hike down the summit trail to the car park at the harbor (thirty to forty-five minutes). Bring shoes for comfort. **Rack:** The route is mostly bolted, so bring 15 to 18 quickdraws, some extra slings, and a set of wired nuts and a few small and medium Friends for the first *Diedro UBSA* pitches.

The imposing face right of *El Navigante* offers other excellent long routes, including the superb *Puto Paseo Ecologico, Via Manual, Linea Magica, Via Gomez-Cano,* and *Via Angalada-Gallego.* The right-hand face, which culminates in a pointed summit, also yields great climbs like *Directa Manfred, Directa Rusa, Super Directa, Revelacion,* and the neoclassic *Nueva Dimensions. Nuevo Dimensions* (5.12c) is a fantastic and atmospheric 10-pitch journey up the huge, steep face, with the final pitches some of the best on the Costa Blanca. The third pitch is a full 165 feet long and protected with 20 bolts! The upper leads over a huge bulge are exposed, strenuous, and unforgettable. Details and topos for these routes are found in the area guidebooks.

North Face

The white, triangular-shaped North Face of the Peñon rises directly above the Calpé harbor and the park visitor center. The countenance of the face is startlingly different than the huge South Face, being smooth, split by diagonal crack systems, and mostly shady. The routes on the face's left side above the summit trail and its tunnel are closed. The entire wall is closed from May through September for nesting birds.

Finding the cliff: Park at the Calpé harbor lot, and hike up a road to the visitor center on the northwest flank of the Peñon. Continue up the summit trail, which switchbacks uphill before bending left toward a tunnel that it goes through. When you're below the face, look for a faint climber's trail that scrambles up right to the base of the wall. Hiking time is thirty minutes. Routes are described from left to right.

6. Via Roxy (6b) (5.10c) 7 pitches. Some scrubby lower pitches but stunning leads up the upper face. A great, sustained, moderate route with good protection and thrilling exposed climbing. Start left of a big obvious chimney. **Pitch 1:** Climb up left from the chimney base to a crack. Stem up the crack to a shelf (5.8), and work left to a belay ledge. 100 feet. **Pitch 2:** Stem or thrutch up a wide crack (5.9) above the belay to a good ledge. 65 feet. **Pitch 3:** Face climb for 25 feet (5.8), then work up right to a left-angling ramp. Downclimb the ramp to a good belay from bolts. 100 feet. **Pitch 4:** Climb up and right to a corner. Work up the corner, and stem another corner (5.9+) to a bolted belay ledge. 100 feet. **Pitch 5:** Crux climbing. Make an exposed and fun traverse left (5.9) across the steep face to a stance. Face climb up right to a tricky mantle (5.10c) and then to a steep, difficult crack (5.10a/b) to a small belay stance. 100 feet. **Pitch 6:** Hard moves off the belay lead to superb jamming and stemming up the crack and corner above (5.10a/b) to a belay stance on the left. 85 feet. **Pitch 7:** Continue up the crack system (5.10a) to a double-bolt belay ledge. 85 feet. Do an easy pitch to the summit from here. **Descent:** Hike down the summit trail to the car park at the harbor (thirty to forty-five minutes). Bring shoes for comfort. **Rack:** Bring sets of wired nuts and cams, including a few big pieces, 15 quickdraws, a 200-foot (60-meter) rope, and helmets.

7. Via Pany (4) (5.7) 7 pitches. An excellent easy tour of the North Face with some interesting climbing, good position and exposure, and plentiful protection. It's a bit vegetated down low but cleaner up high. Start at the base of a prominent chimney. **Pitch 1:** Climb the chimney using polished holds (5.6 and protected by threads) to a chockstone. Pass on the right to a good belay ledge. 85 feet. **Pitch 2:** Scramble up easy 5th-class rock and bushes to a bolt belay atop a buttress. Divide this into two shorter pitches with a shorter rope. 180 feet. **Pitch 3:** Move up a rock rib and climb a corner (5.5). Move left to a bolted belay stance in a niche

below a block. 130 feet. **Pitch 4:** Good aesthetic climbing on this lead. Work up a corner (5.7) to a bolt, step right, and climb another corner to a bolted belay on a good ledge. **Pitch 5:** Do a short airy traverse left, and climb a ramp to cracks (5.6). End at a bolted belay atop a buttress. 95 feet. **Pitch 6:** Edge up right across a slab (5.7) to an obvious crack system. Good climbing up the crack leads to a belay stance. 100 feet. **Pitch 7:** Follow the crack (5.7) until it becomes bushy. Look

left to a bolt, and climb past it into another crack system that is easily followed to a high belay stance. 100 feet. Scramble up easy rock to the summit from here. **Descent:** Hike down the summit trail to the car park at the harbor (thirty to forty-five minutes). Bring shoes for comfort. **Rack:** Bring a rack of wired nuts and cams, 15 quickdraws, some extra slings, a 200-foot (60-meter) rope, and helmets.

Sella

Sella, a climbing area 10 miles directly west of Benidorm and the coast, is the largest and most important sport area on the Costa Blanca. So much climbing is found on the Valle de Sella cliffs that you can easily spend a winter week just exploring this single area. The most popular cliffs are along the flanks of a long ridge that splits the secluded valley north of the picturesque village of Sella. Climbing is found on both sides of the ridge, with most of the routes ascending the southeast-facing wall, the tallest and most popular sector. The northwest-facing sector offers mostly harder, shorter, and more overhanging routes up its tufa-lined cliff. These routes are usually dry during wet spells and shady during hot periods.

All kinds of sport routes of all grades are found at Sella, from easy beginner leads to sustained technical lines. The main cliff routes tend to be slabby to vertical, with fingery sections on crimps and small pockets. The easier routes ascend clean faces with lots of good edges and jugs. One of the fine characteristics of Sella's limestone is the variety of finger pockets, called *gouttes d'eaux* or "drops of water" in French, that pock the cliffs. Most routes are friendly and well bolted, making Sella a good place to push your limits. The variety of cliffs allow for climbing in either sun or shade, depending on the temperature and sunshine. The area dries quickly after rain, which rarely happens in this desert part of Spain.

The main cliff is roughly divided into seven sectors. The Cabeza de Rino, a short, steep cliff facing the refugio, is on the northwest side of the ridge. The other sectors on the east side of the ridge are Culo de Rino, El Cajón de los Cuartos, Techo del Rino, Sector Marión, Sector Competición, Ojo de Odra, and Sector Final on the far right. All offer some excellent routes. All the sectors are within a two- to ten-minute walk from the parking areas.

The Wild Side in Hidden Valley, lying farther up the road from Sella, is a wonderful cliff covered with steep, hard routes that pull pockets, smear on slopers, and grab overhanging tufa columns. Most of the routes, almost all recommended and excellent, require a combination of power and endurance for successful redpoints. Unfortunately, access is now curtailed. The base of the crag as well as the access trail is on private property, and the current owner, at press time, is restricting climbers because of excessive noise, lots of litter, and climbers crapping in the woods. Ask the owner—Mr. Sjaak (Jack) Blejilevens at the house above the parking area—for permission to climb. If he isn't home do not climb, but come back another day when he can grant permission. Park at the small lot by the gate, and walk to the house. He will give you permission based on his interview with you.

Other excellent cliffs are found around Sella. The biggest is the immense and dramatic mountain Puig Divino, which looms 3,500 feet west of the Sella crags. The south face of the pointed mountain is divided into several big walls. A selection of long traditional routes

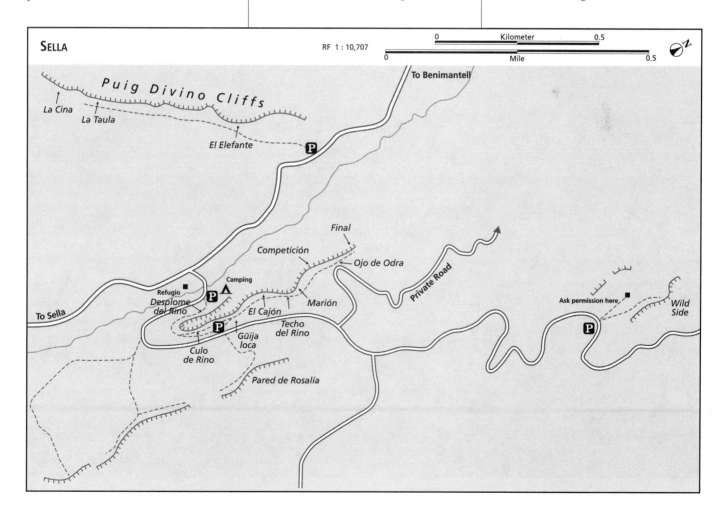

ascend the easier sections, and some well-bolted multipitch sport courses offer superb and exposed climbing up the other clean vertical faces. One of the best sport routes is four-pitch *La Taula* (5.12c) up the left side of a broad shield. Its neighbors *Fisura de Edwards, Excitación,* and *Edwards-Lloret-Pérez* are also three-star adventures. El Elefante, the Elephant, is a spectacular 200-foot-high face on the lower right side of the Puig Divino's south wall. This immaculate limestone bastion yields the area's hardest routes, including several technical 5.12 and 5.13 climbs. The slightly overhanging sector is both quiet and easily accessible. The comprehensive book *Costa Blanca, Mallorca, El Chorro* and the Spanish guide *Sella Escalada* offer both beta and topos.

Finding the cliffs: Sella is easy to reach from the A7 toll highway (*autopista*). Take either the Villajoyosa exit or the Benidorm exit for Terra Mitica. From the Villajoyosa exit drive west on a winding road for 17 kilometers to Sella. From the Benidorm exit follow signs and highway CV770 for 6 kilometers to Finestrat. Continue along a winding road for 7 kilometers, then go right to Sella. Just before the village, turn right, and drive past the cemetery. Drive 4.2 kilometers until the pavement ends at a Y fork. Go right. The refuge is the house on the right. Camping is on the left side of the road. Plenty of parking is available. To park at the cliff base, continue for another kilometer to two large parking areas. A network of trails spreads out from here to the various sectors. The longest walking approach is ten minutes. The shortest is a minute. Continue up the road to the Wild Side parking.

If you don't have a car, there is regular bus service from the Alicante bus station to Villajoyosa. A train also leaves every hour from Alicante. From Villajoyosa take a taxi or the school bus, which leaves town at 3:00 P.M. and 6:15 P.M. Monday through Friday. It goes from Sella to Villajoyosa at 7:00 A.M. and 4:00 P.M. It's a 4-kilometer walk to the area from Sella, although it's easy to get a lift hitchhiking—if any cars pass you.

Sector Desplome del Rino

This short, overhanging, west-facing wall is opposite the refuge on the west side of the Cabeza del Rino. It's easily approached from the campground and refuge parking lot. The cliff is in the shade most of the day, making it a good destination for warm days. Expect short, pumpy routes with big jugs.

1. L'eura (6a+) (5.10b) Begin off a pedestal on the left side of the cave. 4 bolts to 2-bolt anchor. 40 feet.

2. Chapo el 2° y me bajo (6a) (5.10a) Start on the pedestal. 6 bolts to 2-bolt anchor. 40 feet.

3. Menestrel Pescanova (7b+) (5.12c) 5 bolts to 2-bolt anchor. 40 feet.

4. Sindrome del Betún (7a+) (5.12a) Up left after bolt 1. 3 bolts to 2-bolt anchor. 45 feet.

5. Próximo Bautizo (7a+) (5.12a) Start up #4, then up right at bolt 1. Finish up #7. 4 bolts to 2-bolt anchor. 40 feet.

6. Comtitapel (7a) (5.11d) 5 bolts to 2-bolt anchor. 40 feet.

7. Hombres de poca fe (8a) (5.13a) 5 bolts to 2-bolt anchor. 40 feet.

8. Diagonal (7a) (5.11d) Start on #4, then up right to high anchors. 5 bolts to 2-bolt anchor. 50 feet.

9. Multigrado (7c) (5.12d) An excellent pump up the middle of the wall. 5 bolts to 2-bolt anchor. 40 feet.

10. Región Pagana (7c) (5.12d) 5 bolts to 2-bolt anchor. 40 feet.

11. Julio Cesar (7a) (5.11d) 3 bolts to 2-bolt anchor. 40 feet.

12. Chulerías (6b+) (5.10d) On the far right side of the cave. 4 bolts to 2-bolt anchor. 35 feet.

Cuerno de Rino or Horn of the Rhino is to the right of the cave. Seven routes ascend this buttress. From left to right they are *Pequeñecos* (3), *La Tina de Turner* (5+), *Tais tos tolais* (6b), *Frustración agricola* (5+), *Quisiera ser un octavo* (5+), *Verglas que sí* (5+), and *Registro Sanitario* (6b). Approach the wall via a path below it. Most route names are painted below the route.

Sector Culo de Rino

This is the leftmost sector on the east side of the Sella ridge. Approach from the parking by hiking left (south) on a climber trail to the cliff base.

Left Side

13. Timatiriticón (5+) (5.9+) No topo. On the left side of a small buttress. 3 bolts to 2-bolt anchor. 55 feet.

14. Pies de minio (5+) (5.9+) No topo. Middle of the buttress. 4 bolts to 2-bolt anchor. 55 feet.

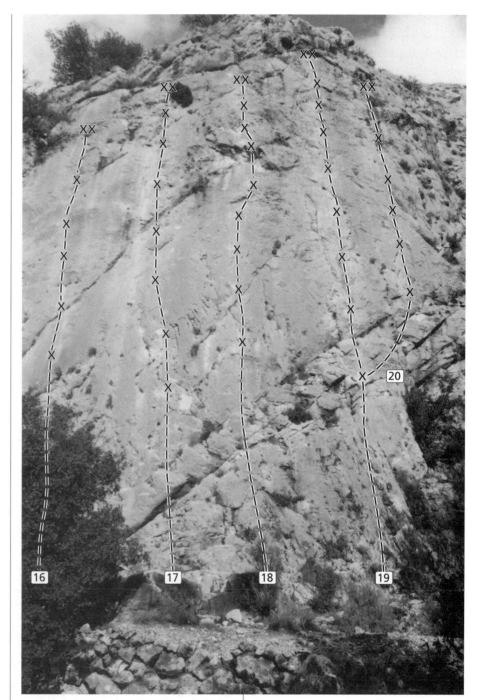

15. Chusmaniática (6a) (5.10a) No topo. Right side of the buttress. 4 bolts to 2-bolt anchor (same anchor as #14). 55 feet.

16. Otigofrénica (7c) (5.12d) A smooth pocketed face. Technical and bouldery. 5 bolts to 2-bolt anchor. 65 feet.

17. Denominación de origen (6a) (5.10a) 7 bolts to 2-bolt anchor. 85 feet.

18. Camilo el rey de los Kumbayas (6a+) (5.10b) Superb climbing up a steep slab. 8 bolts to 2-bolt anchor. 90 feet.

19. Valor y coraje (6a+) (5.10b) Gets harder higher. A rope-stretching pitch; tie a knot in the free end. 8 bolts to 2-bolt anchor. 100 feet.

20. Martillazos de maricona (6b) (5.10c) 6 bolts to 2-bolt anchor. 100 feet.

Right Side

21. Los refugiados (5) (5.9) 7 bolts to 2-bolt anchor. 60 feet.

22. A diestro y siniestro (5+) (5.9+) 8 bolts to 2-bolt anchor. 70 feet.

23. A golpe y porrazo (5+) (5.9+) 7 bolts to 2-bolt anchor. 80 feet.

24. Vía del Indio (5+) (5.9+) 7 bolts to 2-bolt anchor. 80 feet.

25. Divinas Chapuzas (6a) (5.10a) Polished in spots but a good route with a fine flake finish. 7 bolts to 2-bolt anchor. First hanger is missing. 80 feet.

Sector Güija loca

This popular sector yields a stunning selection of sustained and technical lines up steep limestone.

26. Tú dirás (6a+) (5.10b) Crux is a long reach on small but good edges. 8 bolts to 2-bolt anchor. 80 feet.

27. Vino d'Oporto (6b+) (5.10d) Watch out for the slopers at the crux. 8 bolts to 2-bolt anchor. 80 feet.

28. Güija loca (6c) (5.11a/b) 9 bolts to 2-bolt anchor. 80 feet.

29. Kina Borregada (7b) (5.12b) Continuous and technical. First bolted for a climbing competition. 9 bolts to 2-bolt anchor. 80 feet.

30. No frenes mis instintos (7a) (5.11d) This was originally led with gear and called *Edward's Wall*. 6 bolts to 2-bolt anchor. 80 feet.

31. Suspiros de dolor (7a) (5.11d) 10 bolts to 2-bolt anchor. 80 feet.

32. La Cosa (6c+) (5.11c) Recommended. Groove to a headwall. 7 bolts to 2-bolt anchor. 80 feet.

33. A golpe de pecho (7a) (5.11d) 6 bolts to 2-bolt anchor. 80 feet.

34. Con las manos en la cosa (6c) (5.11a/b) Fine route. Tufa groove to a short crux. 6 bolts to 2-bolt anchor. 80 feet.

35. Días de lluvia *(Days of Rain)* (6a+) (5.10b) Far right side of sector. 7 bolts to 2-bolt anchor. First hanger is missing. 65 feet.

El Cajón de los Cuartos

This sector, Sella's most popular area, offers some fun easy routes that are perfect for beginners. It can be crowded on weekends.

36. Dime, dime (3+) (5.5) Fun, easy, and classic. A great first lead. 6 bolts to a 2-bolt anchor by a tree. 40 feet.

37. Con mallas y a lo loco (3+) (5.5) 6 bolts to 2-bolt anchor. 45 feet.

38. Pequeñecos II (4) (5.6) 5 bolts to 2-bolt anchor. 65 feet.

39. Pequeñecos III (4+) (5.6) 7 bolts to 2-bolt anchor. A second pitch climbs to a higher set of anchors at the cliff top. 70 feet.

40. Porko niente lire (7a) (5.11d) Up a smooth headwall right of the corner. 6 bolts to 2-bolt anchor. 75 feet.

41. Cuidado con mi sombrero (6b) (5.10c) 8 bolts to 2-bolt anchor. 70 feet.

42. Fulanita y sus menganos (6b) (5.10c) No topo. 4 bolts to 2-bolt anchor. 55 feet.

43. Zig-zag atómico (6a) (5.10a) Popular. Ends under blocky roofs. 4 bolts to 2-bolt anchor. 55 feet.

Sector Techo del Rino

This sector is a sunny buttress with a deep groove and a huge roof on its left side. The cliff, Sella's steepest wall, offers perfect limestone laced with many popular and excellent routes. Approach time is a couple of minutes from the parking area.

44. Two Nights of Love (5+) (5.9+) 2 pitches. **Pitch 1** has 4 bolts to a 2-bolt anchor at the base of a deep chimney. **Pitch 2** (4+) works up the face left of the chimney.

45. Blanco nato (6b) (5.10c) Start in a crack (same as #44), then up right. 7 bolts to 2-bolt anchor.

46. Martín Galas (6c+) (5.11c) Nice technical climb up two kinds of stone. First part is small crimps on sharp rock. 7 bolts to 2-bolt anchor.

47. Pesos pluma (6b) (5.10c) Climb either #45 or #46, and belay at the anchor. This line goes up left across a steep, exposed slab below the big roof. 6 bolts to 2-bolt anchor.

48. La Explanada (8b+) (5.14a) Hardest route on the crag, put up by Ivan Hernández. Originally done using a bolted-on hold but later repeated without it. Climb either #45 or #46, and belay at the anchors. Edge up the slab past another possible belay, and crank over the roof to anchors above the lip. A fixed line aids the hard part. It can also be climbed in a single pitch with a long rope.

49. Via Pecuraria (6b) (5.10c) Climb #45 or #46 to the belay. Climb out under the airy right side of the roof to anchors.

50. Vaya tipo el de Oti (6c) (5.11a/b) 5 bolts to 2-bolt anchor on a narrow ledge.

51. Unknown (6a+) (5.10b) Popular. An obvious crack left of a bush. 6 bolts to 2-bolt anchor (same as #50).

52. Cardo Borriquero (6c+) (5.11c) Excellent line up the left side of the main headwall. Best done as a single 100-foot pitch from the ground by first climbing either #50 or #51. Continue up the blunt arête to anchors. 7 bolts to 2-bolt anchor

plus either 5 or 6 bolts on starting pitch. Use a 200-foot rope. 100 feet.

53. Acróbata procino (7a) (5.11d) Start left of a short pillar. 8 bolts to 2-bolt anchor. 77 feet.

54. Ssorbe verga (7b+) (5.12c) Dynamic moves. Begin by climbing center of broken pillar. 10 bolts to 2-bolt anchor. 97 feet.

55. Kashba (6c+) (5.11c) One of Sella's best routes. Begin right of pillar, and pull

up slightly overhanging tufas on the steepest part of the sector. 10 bolts to 2-bolt anchor. 97 feet.

56. No me bajes tan (7a) (5.11d) 7 bolts to 2-bolt anchor. 90 feet.

57. El torronet (5+) (5.9) Excellent route up the wall just right of the main cliff with a high crux. The right holds are there when you need them. 8 bolts to 2-bolt anchor. 100 feet.

Sector Marión

Lots of moderate and popular classics, from one to three pitches long, ascend this sector. The high cliff rises directly northwest of the parking area. The first three routes ascend a smooth slab on the far left side of the sector. It's not unusual to see as many as ten parties on the wall on a nice Saturday.

58. Colp de cot (6a+) (5.10b) 4 bolts to 2-bolt anchor. 50 feet.

59. Hola Patricio (6a+) (5.10b) High first bolt. 4 bolts to 2-bolt anchor. 50 feet.

60. Puntea (6a) (5.10a) 9 bolts to 2-bolt anchor. 65 feet.

61. Culo Ipanema (6b) (5.10c) No topo. 10 bolts to 2-bolt anchor on a ledge. Use the intermediate anchor on #62 for lowering with a 200-foot rope, or else rappel with double ropes. 125 feet.

62. Rosalind Sutton (6b) (5.10c) No topo. The right-hand companion to #61. End at the same 2-bolt anchor. Use the intermediate anchor for lowering with a 200-foot rope, or rappel with double ropes. 125 feet.

63. Bolt Tax (6a) (5.10a) Good intro to 5.10a. Continuous pocket climbing at the top. 5 bolts to 2-bolt anchor. 75 feet.

64. Deja Vu (5) Crux is below the anchors. 6 bolts to 2-bolt anchor. 85 feet.

65. Cartujal (5+) Excellent with nice moves on a long pitch. Move right then back left halfway up to bypass a blank part. 7 bolts to 2-bolt anchor. 100 feet.

66. Cul de Sac (5, 4+) 2 pitches. Both pitches are 65 feet long. Pitch 1 is good climbing on flakes and edges along a left-leaning groove. **Descent:** Rappel the route.

67. Prusik (5+, 6a+) 2 pitches. **Pitch 1:** 65 feet. **Pitch 2:** Long sustained lead with a tricky move on a flake. 100 feet. Watch for a loose flake out left high on Pitch 2. **Descent:** Rappel the route with a 200-foot rope.

68. Anglopithecus Britainensis (6a+) (5.10b) A short crux that is out of character with the rest of the route. 95 feet.

69. Mister Pi (6a) (5.10a) Start left of a left-facing corner. 10 bolts to 2-bolt anchor. 95 feet.

70. Marión (4+, 5, 5+) 3 pitches. Classic, popular, and recommended. Look for the name at the base. **Pitch 1:** 7 bolts to 2-bolt anchor. 65 feet. **Pitch 2:** 5 bolts to 2-bolt anchor. 85 feet. **Pitch 3:** Runout with easy climbing. 3 bolts to 2-bolt anchor. 65 feet. **Descent:** Rappel the route.

Sector Competición

This popular and superb area, named because a competition was once held here, is on the right side of the cliff. A left-angling ramp splits the sector. The routes on the lower wall are all great moderates. The routes right of the ramp are generally vertical face climbing on crisp edges and finger pockets. A 200-foot (60-meter) rope is necessary for many of the routes.

71. El gran coscorrón (6a+) (5.10b) Recommended route. Crimpy in places. Crux halfway up. 10 bolts to 2-bolt anchor. 65 feet.

72. Nido de Piratas (6b) (5.10c) Recommended. Good, unpolished rock. Reachy in places. Crux at the top. 11 bolts to 2-bolt anchor. 65 feet.

73. Y tú Quién eres? (6a) (5.10a) 10 bolts to 2-bolt anchor. 65 feet.

74. Desbloquea (5) 9 bolts to 2-bolt anchor. 65 feet.

75. Perleta (5+) 8 bolts to 2-bolt anchor. 65 feet.

76. Wasp Factory (6a, 6c+) 2 pitches.

77. Ratito de gloria (6a, 6c+) 2 pitches. **Pitch 1:** 7 bolts to 2-bolt anchor. **Pitch 2:** Climb to anchors below a long roof.

78. Martxa d'aci (6a) (5.10a) 8 bolts to 2-bolt anchor. 85 feet.

79. Relleno de crema (6a+) (5.10b) 8 bolts to 2-bolt anchor. 75 feet.

80. Dingo boingo (6c) (5.11a/b) No topo. 9 bolts to 2-bolt anchor. 90 feet.

81. Pedro, estás inspirado (7c) (5.12d) Excellent. 11 bolts to 2-bolt anchor. 125 feet.

82. Unknown (7c) (5.12d) 10 bolts to 2-bolt anchor. 90 feet.

83. Unknown (7c) (5.12d) 9 bolts to 2-bolt anchor. 90 feet.

84. Sopa de marsopa (6b+) (5.10d) Recommended but stiff for the grade. Hard for the short. Sustained above bolt 5. 10 bolts to 2-bolt anchor. 100 feet.

85. Adio los domingos (6c+) (5.11c) Continuous, fingery, and excellent. 10 bolts to 2-bolt anchor. 100 feet.

86. Tecnócratas (6c) (5.11a/b) 11 bolts to 2-bolt anchor. 85 feet.

87. El vuelo de la maquina (6b) (5.10c) 10 bolts to 2-bolt anchor. 100 feet.

88. Unknown (6b) (5.10c) On the far right side of the sector. 7 bolts to 2-bolt anchor. 80 feet.

89. Unknown (6a+) (5.10b) 7 bolts to 2-bolt anchor. 80 feet.

90. Almorranas salvajes (4+) (5.6) No topo. A popular outing. Around the corner from #89. 8 bolts to 2-bolt anchor. 80 feet.

91. Alí Babá (4) (5.6) No topo. Another well-traveled easy one on slabby rock. 6 bolts to 2-bolt anchor. 80 feet.

Sector Ojo de Odra

The sector beside the eyehole. Look through the hole for a great view of Puig Divino. Five additional routes are found between routes 91 and 92. These northeast-facing lines are (left to right) *Kamikaze* (7a+) (5.12a); *Seventh Samurai* (6b+) (5.10d); *Fisura con finura* (6a) (5.10a), great route; *Roberto Alcázar y Merlin* (6a+) (5.10b), crimpy start to jugs; and *Espíritu de Satur* (6b+) (5.10d). *Kamikaze* is highly recommended. Reach the sector by hiking along the cliff base.

92. Ojo de Odra (6b+) (5.10d) Polished but sweet. Up the wall left of the eye *(ojo)*. 4 bolts to 2-bolt anchor. 55 feet.

93. Los coreanos (6c) (5.11a/b) Good route. Climbs an arching break right of the eye. 4 bolts and 1 fixed thread to 2-bolt anchor (same anchor as #92). 55 feet.

94. Els nuciers (7a) (5.11d) Right of a groove. 5 bolts to 2-bolt anchor. 50 feet.

95. Mel de romer (6a+) (5.10b) No topo. Recommended. Pumpy with lots of hidden holds. The ending is exciting, with a long reach for the last handhold.

96. Skid Mark (6b+) (5.10d) Recommended. A hard first clip. 6 bolts to 2-bolt anchor. 60 feet.

97. Los remeros (6c) (5.11a/b) 5 bolts to 2-bolt anchor. 40 feet.

98. Baladas para un sordo (6b) (5.10c) 6 bolts to 2-bolt anchor. 55 feet.

Sector al Final

This is the rightmost section of developed cliff. It, along with the road that switchbacks below the cliff base and the continuing cliff to the right, is on private land. Do not drive up the road or park on it. Park only in the two parking lots below the main cliff. A trail follows the cliff base up right to the sector. Hiking time is ten minutes.

99. La vergûenza (3+) (5.4) This and its twin are Sella's easiest routes. 60 feet.

100. La vergûenza (3+) (5.5) Left of gully crack. Anchors right of tree. 65 feet.

101. Speedy González (5+) (5.9) First route right of groove. 6 bolts to 2-bolt anchor. 60 feet.

102. El Pixoncet (6a) (5.10a) 60 feet.

103. Con mallas y a lo loco (5+) 60 feet.

104. Aquí no nos dejan apaarcar (6a) (5.10a) Hard to bolt 1 and a tricky move onto the upper headwall. 8 bolts to 2-bolt anchor. 60 feet.

105. Aquí tampoco (6b+) (5.10d) A long route with a pumpy finish over the big roof. 12 bolts to 2-bolt anchor. 65 feet.

106. Wagageegee (6a+) (5.10b) Classic climb up the big right corner. Be careful above bolt 1—it's polished and has bad fall potential. 8 bolts to 2-bolt anchor. 60 feet.

107. Desperate Dan (6c) (5.11a/b) 50 feet.

108. Kilroy was 'ere (6c+) (5.11c) 50 feet.

109. El agûi (6c+) (5.11c) 55 feet.

110. Grillos navajeros (6c) (5.11a/b) 55 feet.

111. Mandolin Wind (7a+) (5.12a) 55 feet.

112. Anno Dracula (6c) (5.11a/b) 50 feet.

113. IQ 18/30 (6b) (5.10c) No topo. 60 feet.

The Wild Side

The Wild Side is a superb crag in the next valley northeast of Sella. Many excellent hard routes ascend the steep wall on the right side of the valley. Unfortunately, it changed owners in 2002, and the new owner severely limits access. Check the above Sella information to learn how to climb at this great cliff. Do not just show up and expect to climb. You will need to cultivate a relationship with the owner to be able to continue to climb here. It may or may not be open. Use utmost discretion and courtesy. I considered removing this cliff from the Sella section altogether, but on the chance that it stays open, it stays in the book—it's that good!

Finding the cliff: Check the Sella directions to find the cliff. Park only in the designated area. Routes are described from right to left.

1. Si te dicen que caí (7a) (5.11d) No topo. Up a left-facing corner on the right side of the cliff. 85 feet.

2. Todos los caminos conducan al romo (7b) (5.12b) 85 feet.

3. Llanuras bélicas (7b) (5.12b) 85 feet.

4. Celia (7c+) (5.13a) Excellent. Works up and right. 9 bolts to 2-bolt anchor. 85 feet.

5. La forqueta del diablo o Romocop (8a) (5.13b) Recommended. Begin a few feet left of #4. 10 bolts to 2-bolt anchor. 85 feet.

6. La hora de Millau (7c) (5.12d) Superb climbing. Begin below tufa. 10 bolts to 2-bolt anchor. 85 feet.

7. El pito del serano (7c) (5.12d) Another worthwhile crank. 7 bolts to 2-bolt anchor. 95 feet.

8. El gremio (7b+) (5.12c) 9 bolts to 2-bolt anchor. 90 feet.

9. Dimension diamante (8a) (5.13b) Recommended. Start right of a tree on the face. 9 bolts to 2-bolt anchor. 90 feet.

10. Sweet Lady (8a) (5.13b) Very sweet indeed. Right of a short arête. 7 bolts to 2-bolt anchor. 85 feet.

11. Septiembre (8b+) (5.14a) Over roof to tricky headwall. 8 bolts to 2-bolt anchor. 70 feet.

12. La criatura (8b) (5.13d) Thin and technical. 7 bolts to 2-bolt anchor. 65 feet.

13. Nido amoroso (7b+) (5.12c) Superb route. Finishing right is 7b+, whereas finishing left is 7c. 7 bolts to 2-bolt anchor. 65 feet.

14. Discípulo traidos (8b) (5.13d) 9 bolts to 2-bolt anchor. 75 feet.

15. El último mono (8a+, 8b+) (5.13c, 5.14a) An endurance masterpiece. It's 8a+ to the first anchors and 8b+ to the upper anchors. 13 bolts to 2-bolt anchor. 100 feet.

16. Océano (7b, 8b) The first section (7b) (5.12b) to the lower anchors is a good warm-up. Above, work over a roof. 10 bolts to 2-bolt anchor. 96 feet.

17. Project Will it go? 90 feet.

18. Ergometría (8a) (5.13b) Light 8a! One of Sella's best hard routes. Boulder problem start. Look for a kneebar rest up high. 9 bolts to 2-bolt anchor. 85 feet.

19. Project Another sick-looking project. 80 feet.

20. Dosis (8b+/c) (5.14a/b) Technical line up tufa flutes, finger pockets, and edges. 8 bolts to 2-bolt anchor. 80 feet.

21. Cuestión de estilo (7b) (5.12b) Redpointing this great line is a question of style. Follow the right-angling crack system. 6 bolts to 2-bolt anchor. 75 feet.

22. Keep the Faith (7c) (5.12d) Begin below a bushy crack. Climb up right, and finish up #21. 5 bolts to 2-bolt anchor. 66 feet.

23. Propiedad privada (7a+) (5.12a) A short tufa route with the crux clipping the anchors off a monopocket. 4 bolts to 2-bolt anchor. 45 feet.

24. Ya somos olímpicos (7b+, 7b) (5.12c, 5.12b) Another excellent route—highly recommended. Most only climb up the tufa curtains to the first set of anchors. 10 bolts to first 2-bolt anchor. 85 feet to first anchors.

25. Watermark (8a, 8a+) (5.13b, 5.13c) 11 bolts to first 2-bolt anchor. 125 feet to top anchors.

26. Black Is Black (7b) (5.12b) Left route on the cliff. Up and then right to finish up *Watermark*. 11 bolts to 2-bolt anchor. 80 feet.

EL CHORRO

■ OVERVIEW

El Chorro, one of the most important climbing areas in southern Spain's glorious Andalucía province, centers on Garganta del Chorro, a deep gorge carved by the Rio Guadalhorce as it plunges from interior Andalucía south to the Mediterranean Sea. The abrupt 4-kilometer-long gorge, narrowing at its southern entrance to a scant 30 feet wide, slices through a 1,000-foot-high upheaval of rock that is both heroic and violent. Towering cliffs and fins composed of impeccable Jurassic-age limestone line the gorge and rear up the steep mountain flanks above the river, offering excellent climbing adventures on a wide assortment of routes that include some classic multipitch adventures, some of Europe's best limestone slab climbing, and lots of single-pitch sport climbs.

El Chorro itself is a small village with a handful of shops, houses, three grocers, a few restaurants, and a couple hotels built up the hillside above the dammed river below the awesome gorge. The village, however, is overwhelmed by the surrounding spectacular scenery as well as the abundant decaying engineering works built in the last century in an attempt to harness the power of the river. The most amazing of these industrial landmarks is the famed El Camino del Rey, a concrete catwalk pinned to the vertical walls of the gorge 300 feet above the river. The now-abandoned walkway was built in the 1920s to allow workers to enter the gorge to build railway tunnels and a hydroelectric plant. After Spanish King Alfonso XIII officially opened the project in 1921 and edged along the airy catwalk, the walkway was dubbed "The King's Way." Later the project failed, and the walkway began slowly falling into disrepair, leaving gaping holes.

Although the decaying walkway is officially closed, climbers still use it to reach some spectacular climbing sectors both above and below it. The starting and ending sections of walkway were removed a few years ago to keep tourists from killing themselves by stumbling off or falling through one of the many holes left by falling rocks. If you insist on airing your pants out on the walkway, ask at the village climbing store or Finca la Campana for up-to-date access information. None of the cliffs in the Lower Gorge accessed by El Camino del Rey are described in this guide. For complete beta pick up a copy of the area guidebook.

The cliffs at El Chorro, named for the village at the southern base of the cliffs, range in difficulty from 5.5 to 5.13 and in length from 30 feet to eleven pitches. El Chorro particularly shines in the middle-grade routes, making it a popular destination for European sport climbers. That's not to say that there aren't lots of excellent hard routes, because they're here too, including Spanish classics like *Lourdes* (8a) and the five-pitch *Poema Roca* (7c+), complete with hanging wooden belay seats. Frequent and substantial bolts protect most of the routes, allowing leaders to push themselves without risking life and limb.

The limestone here is just about perfect for climbing, with plentiful edges, pockets, and occasional cracks to jam a hand or cam into. Almost all the routes are bolted, although it eases the mind to carry a small rack of wires to plug between bolts on the more runout routes. The crags are generally easy to access, thanks to the walkway, the railway tunnels on the line between Málaga and Seville, and a variety of roads and good trails. This is a rare European climbing area where a car is not a necessity; you can fly to Málaga and take the train to El Chorro.

El Chorro went through a period in the 1990s when it was one of *the* places to climb in Europe. Since then it's fallen from that lofty perch and slipped into a quieter period, which is good since it's not so busy. There are also lots more routes to climb at a variety of grades.

The El Chorro Sectors

El Chorro is divided into four main sectors: Las Frontales, Lower Gorge, Central Gorge, and Upper Gorge. Some excellent outlying sectors are also found, including Las Encantadas, Valle de Abdalajis, Desplomlandia, Túron, Campillos Gorge, and El Torcal.

Las Frontales is the huge cliff escarpment that towers above the village of El Chorro. This immense fin of limestone, reaching heights of 1,000 feet, begins just above the reservoir below the village and stretches east below the rounded 3,907-foot (1,191-meter) summit of Sierra de Huma for more than a mile before ending. This long cliff is divided into three sections. Frontales Bajas, the lower wall above the village, hosts the sector Albercones and the Amptrax area. Farther east is Frontales Medias, the middle section dominated by Poema de Roca, a huge cave nestled below its tallest wall, and Placas del Olimpo on its right side. Frontales Altas, the high, somewhat broken section on the east, is bounded on its left by the long cliff Escalera Arabe and on its right by El Pilar, a semidetached pillar.

This guide describes a few of the routes at the Amptrax area, as well as most of the routes at the excellent Escalera Arabe. The routes at Albercones, although popular and close to the village, are generally not the best the area offers. The Poema de Roca, centered on a couple large caves, is a well-developed sector with many of El Chorro's most difficult routes. Consult the comprehensive area guidebook for details and topos to these excellent lines.

The ridge in front of Las Frontales is studded with three excellent crags—Las Encantadas, Bedees, and El Corral—which unfortunately are closed to climbing because of access issues. On the west side of the river, opposite El Chorro and Las Frontales, is a small roadside crag named Sector Caliza. A selection of short, bolted, easily accessible routes ascend this scrappy cliff.

The gorge itself divides into three main sectors, predictably named the Lower Gorge, the Middle Gorge, and the Upper Gorge. The gorge, running north to south, is often shaded, cool, and very windy. The Lower Gorge offers a selection of exposed routes that begin off the catwalk perched 300 feet above the river. Most of these routes are fairly serious and difficult, and see little traffic because of the commitment required to reach them. One of the best is eleven-pitch *Zeppelin,* El Chorro's longest route, which ascends the full height of the gorge cliffs from river to rim. This excellent line offers two pitches of 5.11c with the rest somewhat easier.

The Central Gorge offers some of El Chorro's best climbing venues, including the slabs at popular Los Cotos, the excellent vertical wall of El Polverin, and the spectacular overhanging wall at El Makinodromo. The Central Gorge receives more sun and less wind than the other gorge sectors. It is accessed by walking through three railroad tunnels, beginning on the south side of the gorge cliffs. This guide describes a selection of the best and most popular routes at Los Cotos and the climbs up El Polverin. The impressive El Makinodromo and its two adjoining lower sectors El Invento and Los Bloques are part of a long ridge that marches up the hill on the east side of the canyon. The 100-foot (30-meter) endurance route *Lourdes* (8a), described as a "gothic nightmare," is El Makinodromo's most famous route. The prized and polished route threads through an overhanging maze of tufas and stalactites. The sector's many superb hard routes are not included in this guide. Consult the *Costa Blanca, Mallorca, El Chorro* guide for cliff details and beta.

The narrow Upper Gorge yields an excellent assortment of atmospheric routes, but they are now closed to climbing because several rare endemic plants, including *Ruphicapnus Africana,* grow on the cliffs.

Other Climbing Areas

Valle de Abdalajis, lying a scant 10 kilometers east of El Chorro on the east side of the mountain massif, is the best outlying cliff for moderate routes. The topos and descriptions in this book are the first published information in English for this delightful little area.

Farther afield is the magnificent karst limestone landscape at El Torcal, a small national park south of Antequera and east of El Chorro. This 4,000-foot-high mountaintop has been eroded into a maze of outcrops, sinks, ravines, alleys, temples, and

towers with whimsical names like La Muela ("the molar"), La Copa ("the wine glass"), and El Lagarto ("the lizard"). It's a beautiful spot, windswept and overgrown with ivy, hawthorn, many rare flowers, and more than thirty species of orchids. It also gets a lot of precipitation. An old adage in Andalucía says: If there is a cloud in Andalucía, then it is at El Torcal. While Torcal has excellent hiking trails, climbing opportunities are limited by the park administration. Ask at El Chorro for up-to-date climbing information and topos.

North of El Chorro and the gorge is Desplomlandia. Several excellent cliffs here overlook a large lake from the flank of the high mountainside to the southeast. These include Sector Buena Sombre just off the road; Sector Como la Vida Misma; the excellent hard routes at Triangulo, the base of which doubles as a smelly sheep pen; and El Pozo de la Mona. If all these climbs aren't enough, check out the two walls in Campillos Gorge carved by the Rio de la Venta. Túron, a half-hour's drive from El Chorro, is a newer unspoiled area with more than eighty routes from 5 to 8a. Archidona, northeast of Antequera, is a major area with many overhanging routes, including *Orujo,* which checks in at 9a. And lastly, Loja, a nice north-facing crag with 150 routes, is near the town with the same name.

The El Chorro climbing area lies within Paraje Natural Desfiladero de los Gaitanes or the Gorge of Los Gaitanes Natural Park, one of thirty-one parklands in Andalucía that protect natural areas and wildlife habitat. The park includes the river gorge, the lofty Sierra de Huma, and surrounding ridges and canyons. The area, covered with scrubby forests of pine and evergreen oak, is also important habitat for increasingly rare fauna and flora. Wildlife includes vultures, eagles, hawks, and owls, along with Spanish ibex, which are often seen clambering on the cliffs above Escalera Arabe. Because of the landscape's unique status as a natural park, regulations are enforced by authorities. These include camping only in designated areas; not damaging trees or shrubs; no fires; no hang gliding; and some rock climbing restrictions, which include not

climbing in the Upper Gorge. A permit system for climbing has been in place since the mid-1990s, but it doesn't seem to be enforced anymore. This could, however, change in the future. Permits are available at the Station Bar in El Chorro and from the park warden.

Rack, Protection, and Descent

There is little objective danger on most of the well-traveled sport routes. Keep watch for the occasional loose flake on some climbs. Longer routes might have loose rock, so a helmet is a good idea, particularly if you're climbing below another party.

All the routes described in this guide are sport routes, so a rack of fifteen quickdraws and a 200-foot (60-meter) rope is all you need. A handful of wired nuts is also useful, taking the sting out of runouts between bolts on some lines. You can get by with a 165-foot (50-meter) rope on many of the climbs, but carefully eye the route to make sure you don't need a longer cord. A few routes require a 230-foot (70-meter) rope.

Descent off all routes is by lowering or rappelling from fixed anchors. Most of the long routes are set up as shorter sport pitches, so a single rope is all you need to get off.

Climbing History

Serious technical climbing at El Chorro, like at most Spanish climbing areas, began in the 1980s as area climbers began exploring the nation's limestone wealth. The easily accessible cliffs in the spectacular gorge were among the first to be climbed. The higher cliffs of Las Frontales were explored later, and even still, new routes are being established on the bigger walls.

Seasons and Weather

Climbing is possible year-round at El Chorro. The best seasons are from March through May and from September through November. Rainy and unsettled periods can occur in early spring and late autumn. The weather can be very good in winter, although it is sometimes cold and windy. Shaded cliffs are usually too cold for comfort in midwinter, but many cliffs receive lots of sun. Reconsider traveling here in summer since it is usually hot or very hot. You can, however, find shaded cliffs, and mornings are usually cool. El Torcal is best in summer.

Getting Around

El Chorro is one of the few European climbing areas that doesn't require a car. Many visiting climbers ride the train here and then walk to the cliffs above the village. This limits you to the cliffs around the village and shopping in the small El Chorro shops but saves a bundle of cash. A car is essential to visit the outlying crags, to drive to Alora for better shopping, and to cruise the area's spectacular back roads on rest days.

El Chorro lies about 40 miles inland from Málaga and the Costa del Sol, a popular winter destination for northern Europeans. Lots of bargain flights and charters regularly fly to Málaga's international airport, particularly in the off-season cooler months when the climbing is best. Málaga is served by Easy Jet, a budget British airline. Work with a travel agent to find the best deals, which might entail flying to London, changing terminals or even airports, and then flying on to Spain. You can also book flights from London by surfing the Internet or reading the travel section of London newspapers.

It's easy to fly into the airport, ride the underground Metro to Málaga Renfe, the city's central train station, and then take the train to El Chorro. Although the timetable is changeable, right now only one daily train stops at the tiny El Chorro Station, so you need to carefully check the schedule in the main station before buying tickets and getting on the train. Trains stop at Alora, a larger village about 6 miles south of El Chorro, every hour. One bus a day runs from Alora to El Chorro around noon; otherwise, you can hitchhike or take a taxi for those last miles. If you're staying at Finca la Campana, the owners can

A climber on *Birdy* (7b+) (5.12c) at Escalera Arabe.

arrange picking you up for a fee with advance warning.

Alternatively, you can fly to either Málaga or Madrid, rent a car, and drive. El Chorro is an hour northwest of Málaga and about seven hours south of Madrid via a fast divided highway and some final winding roads. Remember that it's cheaper to book your car from the United States rather than in Spain. Lots of car rental companies operate here, including Hertz, Avis, National, Alamo, and

Europcar. You can also find local hire companies. Be sure to bring your current driving license as well as an international driving license to rent the car.

Driving is easy here with divided highways, winding country roads, plenty of good signs, and generally polite drivers. You're required by law to have all legal car and travel documents and extra eyeglasses with you in the car. Don't drink and drive. The penalties are severe. The alcohol limit for drivers is only 50 milligrams or

0.05% blood alcohol limit. Likewise, you can be fined on the spot for traffic violations and are expected to pay immediately. Car crime is a problem like elsewhere in southern Europe. Don't leave anything of value in your car, especially at remote parking areas. Cars are safe in towns and villages.

Camping, Accommodations, and Services

The Costa del Sol is a big tourist destination with lots of high-rise hotels and beaches jammed with sunbathers. The good news, however, is that the sweltering summer is high season and the worst time to climb at El Chorro. In the off-season lots of accommodations are found along the coast, many at bargain prices, but it's just too far to drive from the coast to El Chorro every day to climb. You want to stay locally nearer the cliffs.

Most climbers stay near the village of El Chorro, which offers lots of accommodations that cater to the climbing clientele. Possibilities include a *refugio,* cottages, apartments, hotels, a bunkhouse with apartments, and a campground.

Camping El Chorro is just north of the village beside the river. It's clean and basic with hot water, showers, telephone, and a bar. It's easy to walk to the gorge climbing areas from the campsite. The downside is that the site is shady, so it can be cool if the weather is bad.

Finca la Campana, a mile east of El Chorro, makes an excellent base camp for climbers. It offers a bunkhouse, double rooms, apartments, and cottages, along with kitchen amenities, hot showers, and a pool for hot days. The *finca,* owned by Swiss climbers John and Christine, also has a small shop that sells basic groceries, *cervezas,* and climbing gear. They rent mountain bikes and offer guided climbing, mountain biking, and caving trips.

Another good place is La Almona Chica, with two cottages sleeping up to five and two smaller ones for two people. It's owned by a couple ex-pat Brits and is part of a working farm with olives, lemons, clementines, and almonds. The cottages, rented by the week, are self-

catering and fully equipped. El Chorro and many of the cliffs are within walking distance.

In El Chorro is a rough Spanish *refugio,* which is rustic and often noisy, and La Gargantua Hotel opposite the Station Bar and railroad station. The hotel offers reasonably priced rooms and apartments, a pool, and restaurant. Another place is La Pension de Isabel next to the station. Alternatively, you can find inexpensive rooms in Alora.

A couple small shops in El Chorro offer basic necessities including bread, fresh eggs, vegetables, some canned goods, and drinks. If you have a car, it's easy to drive to Alora and shop in the large, well-stocked supermarket there. A small climbing shop in El Chorro sells shoes, gear, ropes, chalk, and other guides. The owner is knowledgeable about the area and can give you beta on routes, cliffs, accommodations, and directions.

Food and Drink

The regional cuisine of Andalucía is usually dismissed by northern Spaniards as uncomplicated and light with its simple casual dishes. That, however, is the charm of the Andalucían diet, which is filled with a variety of vegetables, fruits, and fresh fish. The kitchen here is distinctly Mediterranean with a strong Moorish flavor from northern Africa.

Andalucía is famed as the true home of the celebrated *tapa,* a delectable appetizer accompanied by wine or beer. The humble *tapa,* Spanish for "lid," began as a thin crisp of baguette placed over a glass of wine served to travelers waiting for their carriage horses to be changed. The barkeep would rush outside to greet the travelers and offer them the wine with its bread lid to keep dust and flies out. Added inducements like a bite of ham or cheese were placed atop the *tapa* to encourage customers to linger and perhaps buy more wine or a meal.

Now as then, basic *tapas* like bread, cheese, or a plate of olives are often served free with drinks in traditional bars. If you drive about the region on rest days, be sure to stop in some of the towns and cities, like

Antequera, Málaga, and Sevilla, to sample a variety of *tapas.* Typical ones include *pavias,* strips of salted cod dipped in batter and fried; *pringa,* a pork and vegetable stew; and *espinacas con garbanzos,* made from spinach and chickpeas. Most bars serve an assortment of cold and hot *tapas.*

Sherry, a usually sweet wine, gazpacho soup, and olives are Andalucía's other major contributions to cuisine. The most popular sherry is *fino* or dry and served with *tapas.* Gazpacho is a cold soup with an enhanced flamenco flavor of minced garlic, onions, and peppers. Olives and olive oil are mainstays in the regional diet and economy. Endless rows of dull green olive trees carpet all the available hillsides in parts of Andalucía, creating a huge monoagriculture that exports millions of gallons of olive oil.

In El Chorro you will find good food, but since many foreign visitors stay there, it pales in comparison to the special meals you find by venturing into the countryside. In the scattered whitewashed villages and towns, you can discover authentic country food in quiet restaurants where you are a guest of the *casa.* Dinner entrees include rabbit; venison; fresh fish, including squid and swordfish; shellfish, like prawns and mussels; fruits; vegetables; and cheeses, all washed down with local table wine or a cold *cerveza,* like San Miguel, which is brewed in Málaga. Also look for helpings of the famous rice dish *paella* as well as thin slices of excellent *jamon serrano.* None of the restaurants will have English translations, so bring your dictionary or be surprised.

Cultural Experiences and Rest Days

El Chorro is a great place for climbing, but it's also in the center of one of Spain's most historic and diverse regions. Andalucía offers not only climbing, but is the native home of both bullfighting and flamenco, and the birthplace of the guitar. Great cities like Granada, Sevilla, Cordoba, and Málaga are filled with cultural monuments and museums and lie within a few hours drive of El Chorro. These make ideal rest-day excursions.

Málaga, the birthplace of artist Pablo Picasso, is usually bypassed by tourists but it offers some great sights. The Alcazaba, a Moorish palace, overlooks the city and houses an Archeological Museum, and the adjoining Castillo Gibralfaro is a castle ruin on the hill above. The beautiful Málaga Cathedral is worth visiting for its wood carvings and side chapels. The best place, though, is the Picasso Museum, a few blocks from the master's birthplace, with a stunning masterpiece collection. The city is known for its lavish Easter processions, some of the best in Spain.

Near El Chorro are the famous Andalucían *pueblos blancos* or white villages, ancient Moorish-style villages that spill across steep hillsides in the surrounding mountains. Castle ruins usually lord over the narrow streets and the local cathedral.

A few kilometers south of El Chorro is Alora, with skinny streets lined with white buildings, an old Muslim castle, a good *supermercado,* and plenty of Spanish ambience. On a mountaintop above El Chorro looms Bobastro, the ninth-century ruined hilltop fortress of Omar ibn Hafsun.

Antequera, to the northeast, is a modest-size market center with a Muslim castle, lavish Baroque-style church, bullfighting museum and Plaza de Toros ring, and interesting megalithic dolmens. The dolmens, some of Europe's best-preserved ancient burial chambers, date back more than 4,000 years. The town also has twenty-six churches, many worth visiting, including the sixteenth-century Iglesia del Carmen. Antequera is a good place to ramble around, stopping at its many shops and restaurants.

Places around Antequera include the magnificent upland plateau and diverse natural history of El Torcal; Garganta de Teba, a sharp gorge cut by the Rio la Venta; the walled Moorish town of Teba; the intriguing and lovely town of Archidona; and Laguna de Fuente de Piedra, a flamingo breeding ground, to the west.

If you have a couple extra days, then definitely drive the Ruta de Pueblos Blancos, a scenic drive that passes through

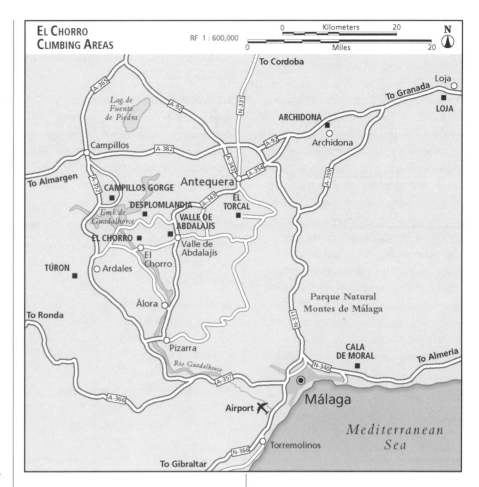

a series of stunningly beautiful hill villages, including Arcos de la Frontera, Zahara, Grazalema, and Ronda, sitting astride the deep El Tajo Gorge. Nearby is Cueva de la Pileta, with a stunning gallery of prehistoric cave art.

Of course, if that's too much culture and sightseeing for you, then head for the beaches of the infamous Costa del Sol. This string of banal resorts from Málaga to Gibraltar are crowded with sun-worshipping northern Europeans and are a prime example of Europe's worst tourist development.

Trip Planning Information

General description: An excellent limestone sport-climbing area centered on a deep gorge and high ridges in the Gorge of Los Gaitanes Natural Park near the village of El Chorro.

Location: Andalucía in southern Spain. El Chorro is 40 miles north of Málaga and the Mediterranean coast.

Camping and accommodations: A good campground is along the river between El Chorro and the gorge. It is reasonably priced and offers amenities including hot showers. It's possible to walk to most of the crags from here. No primitive camping is allowed in the area.

Look for some excellent, reasonably priced accommodations in the El Chorro area. Lots of climbers stay at Finca la Campana, which has a bunkhouse, private rooms, and apartments for rent. La Almona Chica offers four large cottages that rent by the week only. Other choices are Gargantua Hotel across from the Station Bar and train station, and a noisy but cheap *refugio* on the road coming into El Chorro.

Climbing season: Spring and autumn are the best seasons. The temperatures are pleasant and mild, although it can rain in spring. Winter is often good, with warm sunny days, but it can also be chilly in the shade with periods of rain. Summers are very hot. If you insist on coming then, you can find shaded cliffs in the morning.

The gorge can be very windy any time of the year.

Restrictions and access issues: All the climbing at El Chorro is in Paraje Natural Desfiladero de los Gaitanes or Gorge of Los Gaitanes Natural Park. They have required a permit to climb in the past, but it hasn't been enforced for a few years. If you need one, they are available at the Station Bar and from the park warden. You need your passport to obtain the permit. Climbing is allowed everywhere except in the Upper Gorge. No climbing is currently allowed at Las Encantadas because of access issues with the landowner. No primitive camping is allowed in the park, especially in the meadows at the Middle Gorge. Other rules include no damage to plants and trees, no fires, no hunting, motor vehicles only on roads and tracks open to the public, and no hang gliding.

Guidebooks: A couple good English-language guidebooks are *Andalusian Rock Climbs* by Chris Craggs and *Costa Blanca,*

Mallorca, and El Chorro by Alan James. A good Spanish guide is *El Chorro—Escalade en Málaga* by Javier Romero Rubiols. It's available in El Chorro.

Services and shops: A small climbing shop in El Chorro offers all essential climbing gear, including shoes, clothes, and chalk. El Chorro has three small groceries with limited supplies. Complete services, including large supermarkets and many stores, are in Alora, 10 kilometers south of El Chorro.

Emergency services: Call 112 for emergency services. Nearest medical facility is a clinic in Alora.

Nearby climbing areas: North of the gorge is Desplomlandia, with several excellent cliffs overlooking the reservoir. Campillos Gorge, also called Rio de la Venta Gorge, offers excellent routes on limestone from slabs to caves. Túron near Ardales is another worthy nearby area. El Torcal has unique climbing on pinnacles

atop a high limestone mountain. Archidona to the northeast of Antequera is a massive cave laced with many steep and sustained routes, including *Orujo,* Spain's first 9a and only 150 feet long! Loja offers some excellent crags near the town of Loja off the N-342 highway west of Granada. On the coast near Málaga are Mijas with eighty-five routes and La Cala del Moral.

Nearby attractions: Near El Chorro is the hilltop fortress ruins of Bombastro, the Garganta del Chorro, and its famed Camino del Rey walkway.

Also check out El Torcal Natural Park, the towns of Antequera and Ronda, cave paintings at Cueva de la Pileta, flamingos at Laguna de Fuente de Piedra, and excellent hiking at Parque Natural Sierra de las Nieves southeast of Ronda.

Just south of El Chorro is the old town Alora, with shops and markets as well as a Muslim castle. Farther south is Málaga, a cosmopolitan port city with wide avenues, some good museums and monuments, and good walking adventures for a rest day. Check out the Muslim Alcazaba palace and Gibralfaro castle overlooking the city; the city's main cathedral; and the Picasso birthplace and the new Museo Picasso, which displays the work of the famed Málaga-born artist.

Farther away is the famed Alhambra palace at Granada; the diverse architecture, museums, and excitement of the great city Sevilla; the British colony Gibraltar near the southern tip of Spain; and Córdoba's old quarter, the Mezquita.

Finding the area: The easiest way to El Chorro is to fly to Málaga, the region's principal airport. Fly to Madrid and catch a flight from there, or alternatively, fly to London and get a cheap Easy Jet (a cheap British airline) flight from London's Luton Airport to Málaga. From Málaga you can either rent a car and drive, or catch a train from the city's main station to El Chorro.

If you drive, leave the airport and turn left onto the N-340 highway, following signs toward Málaga. After the highway turns into the ring road that bypasses Málaga, look for signs toward Cártama and the A-357 highway. Follow the four-lane

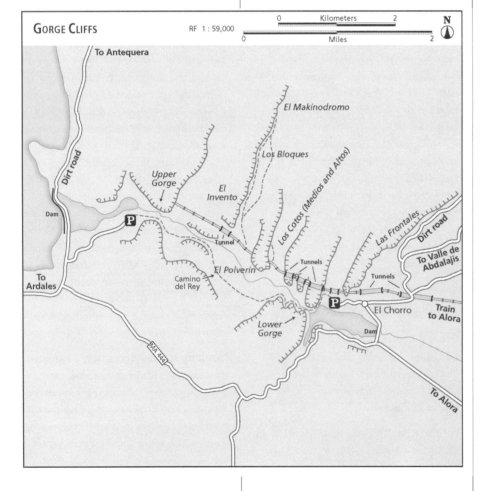

GORGE CLIFFS   RF 1 : 59,000

and then two-lane A-357 highway past Cártama and northwest up the west side of the Rio Guadalhorce valley to a marked right turn onto the A-343 toward Alora and Pizarra. Look for a quick left turn, and head north, following signs for Alora. Drive through the town, and follow signs for El Chorro (follow highway MA-404). Continue 10 kilometers up the winding road to a right turn. Cross a dam, and enter the village of El Chorro. This 50-kilometer drive takes just more than an hour, depending on traffic.

Alternatively, you can continue up the A-357 past the turn to Pizarra to a marked El Chorro turn, just past the village of Ardales. Follow this winding road (MA-444) for 11 miles to the dam, and make a left turn to El Chorro.

If you don't rent a car, you can catch the train to El Chorro from Málaga's main train station, Málaga Renfe. First, take the underground train from the airport to the station. Many trains leave from here to Alora, and one a day continues to El Chorro. Check the timetable, or ask when the train leaves. Trains run about once an hour to Alora. If you miss the connection to El Chorro, you can hire a taxi for that last 10 kilometers.

Cotos Medios

Most El Chorro visits begin with a trip to Cotos Medios, the middle section of Los Cotos, in the open Middle or Central Gorge. This excellent, south-facing sheet of slabby limestone lies right of railroad tunnel #6, which punches through the rock ridge. Expect some superb cranking here on edges and pockets with beefy protection bolts and quick-clip anchors on many of the routes.

More than eighty routes are found on the cliff's three sectors, with the best selection of moderates found on Cotos Medios or Middle Cotos. Expect a bit of polish on some of these routes since they get a lot of traffic. The slabs continue up right as Cotos Altos. A selection of harder edging and pocket climbs on the left side of this sector are described also. Cotos Medios is a good cool-weather cliff, getting lots of sun and being protected from the winds that sweep down the gorge.

It's exciting to access the crag since you walk through either three or four railway tunnels, depending on where you park. The trains run through the gorge at a good speed, so keep alert and stay on the wider side of the tunnel when walking through. The wind often blows strongly through the tunnels, and you don't always hear the trains sneaking up behind you.

Finding the cliff: Drive past the campground along the lake, and park at the end of the road below a railroad bridge. Hike up an old, narrow road that swings north from the parking above the lake to a railroad bridge between two tunnels. Do not drive this road! There is no good place to turn around. Or walk up the road a short distance from the parking area, then follow a trail up to the right side of a narrow draw to the railroad tracks and walk north through a long tunnel to the bridge. Continue for a half-mile (1 kilometer) through three more tunnels into the Middle Gorge. Los Cotos Medios is the sector right of the next tunnel in the middle of the gorge. (Base of cliff: GPS N36° 55.286' W04° 46.442'.)

Routes are described left to right from the railway tunnel.

1. Fisuroterapia (5) (5.9) Good continuous climb. The obvious left-hand crack to the right of and below the tunnel. Climb a thin crack past 2 bolts, then straight up to bolt 3. Continue up the crack above to another bolt. Finish on a ledge with a 2-bolt anchor. 4 bolts to 2-bolt anchor. **Rack:** Large Stoppers are useful and a 200-foot (60-meter) rope.

2. Fisura de los Santos (5) (5.9+) Very good route. Start the same as route #1. Climb up left from the first 2 bolts, and make an obvious step right into the middle crack system. Work up the crack (some hand jams) and over a small roof. Above, step left to a bolt, and climb up left to #1's 2-bolt anchor. **Rack:** Bring some Stoppers or small Friends for the start and a 200-foot (60-meter) rope.

3. Fisura de Hombre (5) (5.9+) Brilliant climbing! Same starting point as #1. Climb past 2 bolts, then work up right on the steep slab to excellent climbing up a vertical crack system. Finish up right of some bushes at anchors. 10 bolts to 2-bolt anchor. Use a 200-foot (60-meter) rope.

4. Bitchitos on the Wailers (4+) (5.8) Uphill to the right from *Fisura de Hombre*. Begin below the left side of a slab. Climb over a bulge, then edge to anchors below a tree. 4 bolts to 2-bolt anchor.

5. El Monstruro de las Galletas (5+) (5.9) Fun climbing. Start right of *Bitchitos*. Up and right on the slab. 8 bolts to 2-bolt anchor.

6. Mordiscos de Amor (5) (5.9) The slab just left of the broken corner system. Begin up #5, then up right above bolt 3. 8 bolts to 2-bolt anchor.

The next routes are on the triangular-shaped slab. All routes are recommended and popular, although some are getting polished.

7. Cat (6a+) (5.10b) Short route on the left side of the slab. Bouldery start. 4 bolts to 2-bolt anchor.

8. Alucinosis (4+) (5.8) Popular and fun, but polished. Bolt 2 is blue. Face to thin crack to headwall finish. 5 bolts to 2-bolt anchor.

9. Unknown (5) (5.9) An excellent, recommended route. Begin at the belay bolt, and work up left along a seam and then straight up to the same anchors as *Alucinosis.* 7 bolts to 2-bolt anchor.

10. Number One (4) (5.8+) A great route but the polished crux at the top has increased the difficulty. Begin at the edge of the stone pavement at a belay bolt. Follow a flake system up right then back left to a slippery crux. 8 bolts to 2-bolt anchor.

11. Bruja Intrepida (5) (5.9) A direct start to *Number One.* Begin right of #10. Edge up 20 feet to bolt 1 and then up left past two more bolts to join *Number One.* 6 bolts to 2-bolt anchor.

12. Numero Dos (5) (5.9 R) Excellent but a little runout at the top. Heady moves lead to the high first bolt, then work up right to the left-angling crack system. Traverse easily up left here, or preferably climb 30 feet directly up the unprotected headwall above on good edges (5.8) to anchors. 4 bolts to 2-bolt anchor.

13. Galleta (4) (5.8) Classic. *Galleta* means "cookie." Begin right of *Numero Dos* at the base of a long, left-angling crack system. Fun climbing heads up left along the crack to a bolt. Continue up the crack to a ridge, and scramble up right to anchors on a stance. **Rack:** Nuts and small cams.

14. Super Galleta (5+) (5.9) Super excellent "cookie" route. Begin at the same spot as *Galleta.* Edge and smear up an incipient crack system directly up the middle of the face. A bit polished in spots. 9 bolts to 2-bolt anchor.

15. Gaby (6b+) (5.10d) An excellent link between #16 and #14. Climb up and left along a leaning corner. At bolt 2, step left, edge to the last bolt on *Super Galleta,* and scramble to anchors. 9 bolts to 2-bolt anchor.

16. Los Mandriles No Comen Galletas (6a+) (5.10b) Another great route. Climb along the left-leaning corner. 7 bolts to 2-bolt anchor.

17. Mandriles (7a) (5.11d) On the far right side of the triangular face. Climb over an overlap to a steep slab. Lower from the top bolt. 4 bolts to 1-bolt anchor.

Cotos Altos

The next sector to the right is Cotos Altos. Only the first routes are described. Many other very fine routes are on this steep slab farther up the slope. Most of the routes are more difficult than the Cotos Medios lines, tending to be thin and technical face climbs. Strong fingers are a must.

18. Emportrador Empodrado (4+) (5.8) 2 pitches up the left side of Cotos Altos, the next face right of Cotos Medios. **Pitch 1:** Start at the left side of the face. Fun climbing leads to a ledge. 5 bolts to 3-bolt anchor. **Pitch 2:** Work up the slab above to a stance. 4 bolts to 2-bolt anchor. **Descent:** Rappel the route.

19. Cebolla Oscilante (5+) (5.9) Easier than it looks. Edge up the smooth slab to a tricky finish. 6 bolts to 3-bolt anchor.

20. Genesis (6a+) (5.10b) An incipient crack system. 2 bolts to 2-bolt anchor on ledge.

21. Mongroni Fear (6a+) (5.10b) Recommended. The right-hand incipient crack. 2 bolts to 2-bolt anchor.

22. Arbola (6a+) (5.10b) Thin left-leaning cracks. 5 bolts to 2-bolt anchor.

23. Bruner and the Bruns (6a+) (5.10b) Delicate face climbing past an obvious hole. 6 bolts to 2-bolt anchor with cable.

24. Ley de la Selva (6b+) (5.10d) The name is painted on the rock. Thin face climbing. 5 bolts to 2-bolt anchor with slings, or keep climbing to a higher lower-off.

25. Embolia Cerebral (5+) (5.9) Usually climbed only to the first anchors. Bolts are far apart. 3 bolts to 2-bolt anchor.

26. The Policeman Stole My Walkman (6b) (5.10c) Climb #25 to the anchor, and make tricky moves up right to anchors. 6 bolts to 2-bolt anchor.

27. Güirilandia (7a) (5.11d) Thin, technical, and excellent. The faded name is at the base. 6 bolts to 2-bolt anchor on a narrow ledge.

28. Café Bonk (7a+) (5.12a) More technical face climbing. Over a small roof to thin moves. 4 bolts to 2-bolt anchor.

29. Penetración Analgésica (6c) (5.11a/b) Over a small roof to a thin right-facing corner. 4 bolts to 2-bolt anchor.

El Polverin

El Polverin is simply one of the best crags at El Chorro. If 5.11 face climbing on perfect, vertical limestone is your cup of tea, then El Polverin is your place. The northwest-facing cliff yields numerous one- and two-pitch routes up its 200-foot-high face. All the routes are recommended. Sharp rock is found on some of the routes. The cliff has also been rebolted, making the routes safer for both climbing and lowering off. The wind can whip down the gorge in the afternoon, and El Polverin often gets its full brunt. The cliff gets shade in the morning and sun in the afternoon.

Descent is by lowering or rappelling off bolt anchors. Alternatively, you can walk left off the top, clipping into a couple fixed cables where it's exposed.

Finding the cliff: Walk along the railroad tracks, and continue past Cotos Medios through railroad tunnel 6. Just past this long tunnel, go left immediately onto a path that contours out to a wide ledge that overlooks the cliff. This platform is a good spot to check out the routes. Scramble across slabs and ledges to the base of the wall. Routes are described from left to right.

1. Alerta Roja (Red Alert) (6c) (5.11c) A good long pitch up the far left margin of the face. Start below the leftmost line of bolts. It's easiest to stem up the gully and face to bolt 1. Continue up the left edge of the face to an anchor left of a hanging tree. 11 bolts to 2-bolt anchor.

2. Sueño de Venus (Dream of Venus) (6a+) (5.10b) 2 pitches or 1 long pitch. An excellent and recommended route. Start just right of #1. **Pitch 1:** Fun climbing (5+) to a belay. 3 bolts to 2-bolt anchor. **Pitch 2:** Climb up and left on edges and great pockets to high anchors. 7 bolts to 2-bolt anchor.

3. Pilier Dorado (6c) (5.11c) 3-star classic. A long pitch that finishes through a triangular roof up high to anchors left of a tree. 15 bolts to 2-bolt anchor.

4. Generación Espontanea (6c) (5.11c) Start up *Pilier Dorado* but head up right at bolt 4. Continue to anchors left of a huge hueco. 12 bolts to 2-bolt anchor.

5. Revuelta en el Frenopático (6c+) (5.11d) 2 pitches or 1 long pitch. Climb up the center of the wall past a set of lowering anchors or alternate belay anchors if you're doing it in two pitches. End at chain anchors right of a cave. 13 bolts to 2-bolt anchor.

6. Habitos de un Perturbado Irremediable (6c) (5.11c) One of the best routes on the wall—don't miss it! Climb a brilliant long pitch up the center of the wall to anchors. Look for a sit-down rest in a cave partway up. 12 bolts to 2-bolt anchor.

7. La Pregiera Tonta (6c) (5.11c) Another great route. Long and sustained. 10 bolts to 2-bolt anchor left of a narrow hole.

8. Games Moya (6a+) (5.10b) A good warm-up. This shorter route ends at the obvious horizontal break. 5 bolts to 2-bolt anchor with slings.

Descend the steep loose slope below the face for the next routes. Don't knock rocks off since people may be below.

9. Obsesion Perma Nente (6c) (5.11c) 2 pitches. Work out right to the first bolt. Edge up a thin face (6b+) to a 2-bolt chain anchor. Belay here, or continue up the steep face to cliff-top anchors. 15 bolts to 2-bolt anchor.

10. Anaña Mecánica (6b+) (5.10d) Start off a ledge with 2-bolt anchor. Crimp up and right to anchors on a leaning ramp. 6 bolts to 3-bolt anchor.

11. Paco Eugene (6a) (5.10a) 3 pitches. A good, long route that is the easiest on the wall. The first two pitches, which require gear, begin down the slope. This description makes it a sport climb, although some wires and small cams add extra security between bolts. Begin at the same 2-bolt anchor as #10. **Pitch 1:** Climb up right along a crack system (5) to a belay ledge. 5 bolts to 2-bolt anchor. **Pitch 2:** Pull a face (5) to a zigzag crack to a cramped belay niche with 2 bolts. **Pitch 3:** Good crack lead. Work up left along a crack, then up cracks and corners to the cliff top. 5 bolts to 2-bolt anchor.

12. Nirvana (6b+) (5.10d) No topo. 2 pitches. Good climbing up the right side of the face. **Pitch 1:** Climb the first pitch of *Paco Eugene* described above. 5 bolts to 2-bolt anchor on a ledge. **Pitch 2:** Straight up the face above to a 2-bolt anchor on the cliff top.

13. Urbi et Orbe (7a) (5.11d) A one-pitch bolt route up a steep rib right of #11's first pitch.

14. Los Crocodrilos (7a+) (5.12a) No topo. Another one-pitch bolt route up the face right of #13.

On the cliff band up left of El Polverin are a couple short routes. No topos.

15. Pedro el Grande (6a+) (5.10b) Obvious route above the descent path off the top of El Polverin.

16. El Gordo Ya No Come Guarro (5+) (5.9) Left of #15. Mostly easy climbing with a short stiff crux.

Amptrax

The Amptrax sector is on Las Frontales, the huge south-facing cliff escarpment above the village of El Chorro. The lower wall by the railroad is Albercones, and although many routes are here, they are not described in this guide since they are generally of lesser quality than the described sectors. Consult the comprehensive guide for topos for these routes. At Amptrax, however, several excellent routes, including the seven-pitch *Amptrax,* ascend the center of the wall.

Finding the cliff: Drive through El Chorro from the Station Bar, heading north toward the cliff on a narrow road. Park at the road's end, and walk up a trail over the tunnel and up the hillside alongside the cliff to the base of the routes. Look for the lines of bolts up the cliff.

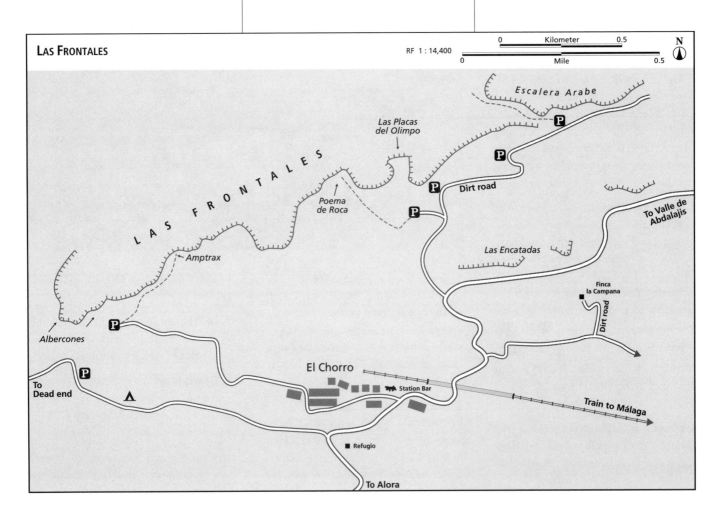

LAS FRONTALES

RF 1 : 14,400

1. Pa Lante Amigos (6c) (5.11a) 2 pitches. A worthy exploration. **Pitch 1:** Bolted face climbing (6a) to a 2-bolt belay. 65 feet. **Pitch 2:** More difficult face moves (6c) to a 2-bolt belay. 100 feet. **Descent:** Rappel the route.

2. Son Quartos (6b+) (5.10d) 2 pitches. Right of #1 and similar in quality and character. **Pitch 1:** Easy climbing (4) to a 2-bolt anchor. 55 feet. **Pitch 2:** Face climbing up and left (6b+) to #1's anchors. 115 feet. **Descent:** Rappel the route with two ropes.

3. Amptrax (5+) (5.10a) 4 or 7 pitches. Excellent, recommended, and popular. A bolted, moderate route up this big cliff sector. Most parties only do the first four pitches since they are bolted. The upper three pitches require gear and a walk-off. Start by scrambling up easy rock above the cliff-base trail to a ramp. Continue up the ramp until you need to rope up below the steepening wall. **Pitch 1:** Climb the easy ramp (3) to a 2-bolt belay. Need a bit of gear for this pitch. **Pitch 2:** Climb up left, and make an exposed move to the top of a big flake. Then face climb (5+) to a 2-bolt belay. 55 feet. **Pitch 3:** Swing up steep rock on good holds (5) to a 2-bolt belay. 50 feet. **Pitch 4:** Climb directly up (5) to a 2-bolt belay beneath a roof. 65 feet. Rappel from here or continue to the cliff top. **Pitch 5:** Work up 30 feet, then make a long rising rightward traverse (5) to a belay. 65 feet. **Pitch 6:** Continue up right (4+) to another belay stance. 85 feet. **Pitch 7:** Climb easier rock (4+) to the top. 100 feet. **Descent:** Rappel from the top of Pitch 4 or scramble from the cliff top down the back side following the easiest possible way. The rappels back down the route can be problematic if other parties are climbing and belaying at the anchors. Best to be polite and smile. Or look for a big chain anchor near the end of Pitch 5, and rappel back to the ground using double ropes from separate sets of anchors. **Rack:** 200-foot (60-meter) rope and 15 quickdraws for the first four pitches. Bring a selection of wired Stoppers and small to medium Friends for the upper pitches. Some nuts are useful on the first pitch if you're uncomfortable.

Escalera Arabe

Escalera Arabe, called the Arab Steps after a series of stone stairways below the cliff, is an excellent sector of buttresses and faces on the upper east wall of Las Frontales. The cliff section rises from right to left above a broken section of wall. The south-facing area offers many bolted routes with a wide variety of grades, making it a popular sector. The routes are on faces and slabs between broken cliff sections.

Finding the cliff: The sector can be accessed from either El Chorro or by driving to the base. These directions are for driving. Drive east from El Chorro toward Valle de Abdalajis. Drive up this steep, narrow, paved road to a square water tank on the left about a kilometer from the village. Turn left here, and follow a narrow dirt track for 2 kilometers across the valley and up along the base of Las Frontales. When you reach an S turn below the cliff face, park on the left at the top turn near power lines across the road. Follow a trail that contours west along the cliff base for five minutes to the sector. If you hike up from El Chorro, a trail heads up the valley below the cliff. Allow forty-five minutes to an hour to hike up. Routes are described from right to left.

The first three routes are on a slab on the right side of the cliff band and left of a deep gully below a big face. No topos.

1. La Gaita (4+) (5.7) Good climbing and sustained for the grade. Up the right side of the slab. 8 bolts to 2-bolt anchor.

2. Kiwi (5) (5.8-) Fun route up the center of the slab with pockets and edges. 8 bolts to 2-bolt anchor.

3. Unknown (4+) (5.7) Not as good. On the left side of the slab. Bring some gear. 2 bolts to 2-bolt anchor.

Walk 325 feet to the next steep slab behind six big pine trees.

4. Marlen Suzuky (6c) (5.11a) 2 pitches. Popular and good. **Pitch 1:** Face climbing up narrow slabs (6a+). 7 bolts to 2-bolt anchor at a stance. **Pitch 2:** Steeper face climbing. 7 bolts to 2-bolt anchor on a ledge. **Descent:** Rappel the route.

5. Highway to Africa (6b) (5.10c) 2 pitches. **Pitch 1:** Good face climbing (5+). 8 bolts to 2-bolt anchor. **Pitch 2:** Long pitch (6b) up right to bolt anchors on a ledge. **Descent:** Rappel the route.

The next two routes are 120 feet to the left of #5.

6. Mas que un Carretta (6a) (5.10a) Good and popular. 5 bolts to 2-bolt anchor.

7. Dos Tetas Tiran (6b) (5.10c) Excellent. A long pitch up a yellow wall. 9 bolts to 2-bolt anchor.

Walk left a few feet to the next routes on a broken slab left of a big dihedral.

8. El Artista (4) (5.6) No topo. Left of the big, left-facing, left-leaning dihedral. 4 bolts to 2-bolt anchor.

9. Los Timbales (4) (5.6) Fun climbing up a broken slab. 6 bolts to 2-bolt anchor.

10. O Sole Mio (4) (5.6) Another fun juggy slab line. 5 bolts to 2-bolt anchor under a tree.

11. La Chillona (6a) (5.10a) 3 pitches. Popular multipitch affair up the right side of a gully system. **Pitch 1:** Pleasant climbing (4) up left to a big ledge. 8 bolts to 2-bolt anchor. **Pitch 2:** A dicey slab (6a) right of the gully. 7 bolts to 2-bolt anchor on a ledge. **Pitch 3:** Steep face climbing (6a) to a short left-facing corner to a belay stance. 7 bolts to 2-bolt anchor. **Descent:** Rappel the route.

Walk west down and around the edge of a buttress to a long wall with a gently ascending terrace in front of it. The first routes are on a flat face on the right.

12. Double Edged (6b) (5.10c) Fine sustained route. Begin just left of a 20-foot-high pillar. Thin face climbing up the vertical wall. Keep right of the bolts to keep the grade at 6b. 8 bolts to 2-bolt anchor.

13. For Fite (6b) (5.10c) A 3-star adventure. Climb to a small ledge, then monkey up the superb face above to high anchors. 120 feet. 13 bolts to 2-bolt anchor. Use a 230-foot (70-meter) rope or double ropes to get off.

Walk west up the terrace 125 feet to a good-looking face with two routes. Start off a ledge below the face. Look for the route names painted on the rock. No topos.

14. Yo y Mi Resaca (5) (5.9) Great climbing up the right-hand line. 8 bolts to 2-bolt anchor.

15. Antonio y Sergio (6a) (5.10a) More superb movements up the left route. 7 bolts to #14's 2-bolt anchor.

Continue west up the ascending terrace until it narrows above a stone wall. The next three routes are on slab above the trail.

16. La Raya a la Izquierda (5) (5.9) Right side of the slab. 5 bolts to 2-bolt anchor.

17. Soló Afeiter (6a) (5.10a) Steep face to a slab. 5 bolts to 2-bolt anchor.

18. Unknown (4+) (5.7) No topo. 50 feet left of #17. Climb a rib. 6 bolts to 2-bolt anchor.

Walk west on the trail to an excellent cliff sector that overhangs some of the Arab Steps. All the routes are excellent and popular.

19. Rock the Kasbah (7b) (5.12b) Up the right side of the face. 6 bolts to 2-bolt anchor.

20. Coming on Strong (7a) (5.11d) Steep face climbing to a slab finish. 6 bolts to 2-bolt anchor.

21. Calvo Potrun (7c) (5.12d) Steep moves up the center of the face. Polished on the bulge. 6 bolts to 2-bolt anchor.

22. Birdy (7b+) (5.12c) Really good. Same start as #21 but up left to a low anchor, or continue past another bolt on easier climbing to a higher anchor. 9 bolts to 2-bolt anchor.

23. Sheik Tu Dinero (6c+) (5.11c) Easier than the others here and well traveled. Swing up the left side of the face, then run it out on easy rock. 5 bolts to 2-bolt anchor.

A prominent buttress rises above the trail left of route #23.

24. Arabesque (7a) (5.11d) Superb and recommended. Thin face climbing up the outside of the pillar. Poke around for a hidden pocket at the crux. 9 bolts to 2-bolt anchor.

25. Diedre Torpedol (6c) (5.11a/b) Another great climb! Up a shallow corner to an arête finish. 6 bolts to 2-bolt anchor.

26. Lococolo (7a+) (5.12a) Face climbing up a steep rib right of a crack and corner system. 9 bolts to 2-bolt anchor.

27. El Arabe Perdido (6c+) (5.11c) Left of a big flake. Good face moves on perfect rock. 6 bolts to 2-bolt anchor.

The next routes are on a high vertical face between buttresses.

28. Escalopendra Guajani (6a+) (5.10b) 2 pitches. First pitch is good. **Pitch 1:** Steep thin face climbing over a bulge. 8 bolts to 2-bolt anchor. Alternatively, go left at bolt 4 to another set of anchors—7 bolts to 2-bolt anchor. **Pitch 2:** Traverse up right and then up the face above, left of a left-facing corner. 7 bolts to 2-bolt anchor.

29. El Amor Sandunguero (6c) (5.11a/b) 2 pitches. *Muy bueno.* **Pitch 1:** Face climbing (6c) with some good pockets. 6 bolts to 2-bolt anchor. **Pitch 2:** Great exposed face movements. 8 bolts to 2-bolt anchor.

30. Engendro Caneki (6c) (5.11a/b) 2 pitches. Another worthy climb. **Pitch 1:** Face climbing (6b+) right of a big dihedral to a belay in a hole. 4 bolts to 2-bolt anchor. **Pitch 2:** Up the face right of a groove dihedral (6c). 7 bolts to 2-bolt anchor.

The last routes are on a bulging buttress

with big holes at the top of the steps and above a narrow col.

31. Filou (6a) (5.10a) Recommended. Left of the deep groove on the right side of the buttress. 5 bolts to 2-bolt anchor at the horizontal break.

32. Lucky No Come Pan (6a) (5.10a) *Bueno ruta.* Face climb to a belay under a big roof and on the edge of a wide hueco. 8 bolts to 2-bolt anchor.

33. El Beso de la Flaca (5+) (5.9) Up the left side of the buttress. 7 bolts to 2-bolt anchor.

The last route and easiest one at this sector is up the east ridge of a freestanding pillar directly south of #31 to #33. No topo.

34. El Pilarito (3) (5.5) Fun climbing up the low-angle east ridge of the pillar. Bring some gear.

Las Placas del Valle de Abdalajis

This excellent sector, the bottom part of a huge broken cliff above the village of Valle de Abdalajis, offers an excellent assortment of mostly midgrade routes in a pretty and bucolic setting. The routes are either unnamed or no one knows the names anymore. No matter, the climbing and position is great. The south-facing cliff is 11 kilometers east of El Chorro on the front of the same abrupt mountain escarpment.

Finding the cliff: From El Chorro drive east from the village on a narrow road for 11 kilometers to the village of Valle de Abdalajis. Just before reaching the village, if you look left, you will see the cliff sector above an orchard. Drive into the village on a narrow street, watching for oncoming traffic. Partway through the village, look for a very sharp left turn just past an inobvious sign on the left that reads EL CHORRO. Make this turn onto a narrow road that leads west out from the village. It quickly becomes a one-lane, rutted, rocky uphill track. Follow the rough road for 1 kilometer to a small, obvious parking area in an almond grove near a small sign that says ZONA DE ESCALADE or "Zone of Climbing." Hike up a short steep trail through the orchard to the cliff base. Routes are described from left to right. Two routes are located around the corner to the left of #1.

1. Unknown (6c) (5.11a/b) Left side of a steep smooth slab. Runout at the top with possible groundfall unless you can fit a medium cam in a pocket. 5 bolts to 2-bolt anchor.

2. Unknown (6a) (5.10a) Excellent. Follow a left-angling crack system that starts on the right side of a slab to a tricky crux up high. 8 bolts to 2-bolt anchor right of a tree.

3. Unknown (4+) (5.7) An excellent deep-water groove/chimney just right of the

smooth slab. 8 bolts to 2-bolt anchor on a ledge.

4. Unknown (4+) (5.8) Good climb up groove and crack system. Climb broken rock to an A-frame, then up left along a left-angling crack to anchors at a stance.

5. Unknown (6a) (5.10a) Same start as #4, but above the A-frame, head left up the angling crack, then back along an arching crack to anchors on a high ledge. 13 bolts

to 2-bolt anchor. 115-foot pitch. Descend with two ropes or lower with a 230-foot (70-meter) rope.

6. Unknown (6a) (5.10a) Great long pitch. Clamber over broken rock at the base then up to an A-frame. Climb cracks and face right and up to a tree. Anchors are on a ledge to the left. 12 bolts to 2-bolt anchor. 115-foot pitch. Descend with two ropes or lower with a 230-foot (70-meter) rope.

7. Unknown (5) (5.8) A short access pitch to a ledge. 4 bolts to 2-bolt anchor.

8. Unknown (5+) (5.9+) The easiest of the long routes. Climb #7 and belay. Start off the ledge, and climb straight up the face to a zigzag crack to anchors on a stance below a bush. 11 bolts to 2-bolt anchor.

9. Unknown (5) (5.8) The right-hand access pitch to the belay ledge. 5 bolts to 2-bolt anchor on ledge.

10. Unknown (6b) (5.10c) Begin from the belay ledge. Traverse up right from the ledge. Climb a rib to a face to a large hole. Excellent face climbing up left then back right along a crack leads to the finishing headwall. 10 bolts to 2-bolt anchor.

11. Unknown (5) (5.8) Short face and crack climb (45 feet) to a tree. 5 bolts to 2-bolt anchor under left side of the tree.

12. Unknown (6c) (5.11a/b) A technical testpiece with thin, continuous face movements. 50 feet. 7 bolts to 2-bolt anchor.

13. Unknown (5+) (5.9) *Bueno escalade.* Cool moves up the right side of a deepwater groove to anchors below a bushy crack out right of the groove top. 8 bolts to 2-bolt anchor.

14. Unknown (5+) (5.9) Good face climbing to #13's anchors. 8 bolts to 2-bolt anchor.

15. Unknown (6a+) (5.10b) A long pitch. Climb #14 to its third bolt. Step right, and climb flakes, pockets, and horizontal cracks to anchors at the cliff top. 15 bolts to 2-bolt anchor. Descend with two ropes, or do two rappels from #13's anchors.

16. Unknown (6a) (5.10a) Edge along a left-angling crack transecting a smooth gray wall. 7 bolts to 2-bolt anchor below a tree.

17. Unknown (5) (5.8) Climb to bolt 1 below a triangular roof. Follow the left-leaning crack past three more bolts—some grass blocks the crack—to anchors behind a tree. 4 bolts to 2-bolt anchor. Bring a selection of cams and wired nuts.

18. Unknown (5) (5.8) 3 pitches. A long route up a crack system. Fun but vegetated in spots. **Pitch 1:** Climb 45 feet up easy rock (4+) to a ledge with a 2-bolt anchor. **Pitch 2:** Up grassy cracks to bolt 1, then up the grassy crack to a 2-bolt anchor under a small roof. **Pitch 3:** Continue up cracks past two bolts to a 2-bolt anchor under a small roof to the left. **Descent:** Rappel the route.

19. Unknown (4) (5.6) An easy, well-protected beginner lead. 6 bolts to 2-bolt anchor.

The next routes are on an excellent, 45-foot-high slabby wall below a long ledge system on the right side of the sector. All the routes are well protected and very fun.

20. Unknown (4) (5.6) Face between cracks. 5 bolts to 2-bolt anchor.

21. Unknown (4+) (5.7) Face to a shallow left-facing corner. 5 bolts to 2-bolt anchor.

22. Unknown (5) (5.8) Fun climb. 6 bolts to 2-bolt anchor.

23. Unknown (4) (5.6) An obvious left-leaning crack to #22's anchors. 6 bolts to 2-bolt anchor.

24. Unknown (5+) (5.9) Up the center of the face between two left-leaning cracks. Crux is a tricky bulge. 6 bolts to 2-bolt anchor.

25. Unknown (4+) (5.7) Left-angling crack to #24's anchors. 7 bolts to 2-bolt anchor.

26. Unknown (5) (5.8) More joy. Face right of the crack. 7 bolts to 2-bolt anchor.

The last two routes are on the steep wall above the ledge. Access by climbing one of the lower routes to belay anchors. See topos on the previous page.

27. Unknown (6b+) (5.10d) Long pitch. Climb directly above the 2-bolt ledge belay past 2 bolts to a grassy stance.

Continue past long pockets to a thin, hard crux move. Finish up broken cracks to anchors. 8 bolts to 2-bolt anchor.

28. Unknown (6a+) (5.10b) An absolutely brilliant bit of climbing. Another long pitch. Begin on the big ledge at a 2-bolt belay anchor. Scramble up easy rock, then weave your way up through bulges to right-angling cracks to anchors. 8 bolts to 2-bolt anchor.

Italy

SWITZERLAND · LIECHT. · 8° · 12° · **AUSTRIA** · 16° · **HUNGARY**

DOLOMITES

Bolzano · **ARCO** · Trento · Belluno · **SLOVENIA**

Como · *Lago di Garda* · Padua · Trieste · **CROATIA**

FRANCE · Bergamo · **Milan** · Verona · Venice

Turin · *Po* · Ferrara · **BOSNIA AND HERZEGOVINA**

Parma · Ravenna

Genoa · La Spezia · **Bologna** · Rimini · **YUG.**

44° · Pisa · Florence · **SAN MARINO** · Ancona · 44°

MONACO · Livorno · Perugia · *Adriatic Sea* · **YUG.**

Bastia · *Elba* · **ITALY**

Corsica (Fr.) · Terni · Pescara

VATICAN CITY · **Rome**

Foggia · Bari

Sassari · **Naples** · Salerno · Brindisi

40° · Taranto · Otranto · 40°

Sardinia · *Tyrrhenian Sea*

Cagliari · Cosenza

Catanzaro

Palermo · Messina · Reggio

Mediterranean Sea

Catania · *Sicily*

Siracusa

Legend

■ Climbing region
— River
–·–·– International boundary
✪ National capital
═══ Expressway
═══ Major road

0 50 100 150 Kilometers
0 50 100 Miles

12° · 16°

ARCO

■ OVERVIEW

Arco is one of those European places that is at once seductive, intriguing, and simply breathtaking. Arco has it all—a picturesque medieval town, a fertile valley lush with olive groves and palm trees, towering mountains, and superb rock climbing and outdoor adventures. The town sits on the west side of the flat, narrow Valle dei Laghi, a north-south trending valley drained by the Sarca River and flanked by immense limestone mountains and ridges.

Arco is a place where you get used to ancient history, to narrow streets almost unchanged from medieval days, to historical houses and grand castles, to places where you can time travel in a few footsteps back to the Renaissance. It's a place to sojourn into the arts, antiquities, timeless history, and delicious food of northern Italy. It's also a superb place to explore the spectacular natural beauty of the dominating mountain landscape, by hiking its footpaths, clambering up *via ferratas,* biking old Roman roads, and scaling the multitude of limestone faces that scatter across every mountainside.

Arco is justifiably famous for the excellent climbing on its many cliffs. The comprehensive area guidebook details fifty-eight separate climbing areas with 1,921 routes. And that's not counting all the new crags or the secret ones. But it's no secret that there is limestone here, and lots of it. Crags stud the mountainsides and hide in the woods. Limestone mountains, polished and sculpted by ancient glaciers, loom thousands of feet above the fertile valley floor.

The limestone-rich valley and mountains yield amazingly varied climbing experiences, ranging from single-pitch sport routes to twenty-five-pitch routes on the mountain faces up the valley. The visiting climber finds every type of climbing movement: blocky walls with big holds and easy routes; delicate gray slabs that require deft foot smears and palms pressed on dimples; vertical face climbs where progress is measured in crimps and sidepulls; and overhanging walls laced with sequential and powerful moves up an array of pockets, from shallow one-finger cavities to full-hand mailbox jugs. The Arco cliffs are as near as a five-minute stroll from the popular coffee bar Caffè Trentino in the town center and as far as a 15-mile drive up the valley to the southern edge of the Dolomites.

Arco is a climber's paradise and not only because of the abundance of limestone. Climbers are welcomed, and their visits translate into big bucks for the local economy. European climbers, especially Germans and Austrians, congregate here and visit the crags as often as the local Italians. Americans, both climbers and tourists, are seldom seen, so a visiting Yank is a novelty. The locals are generally friendly toward climbers, partly because climbing has been an important part of the area sports scene since 1980. The town views itself as a climber's paradise, a reputation that is secured by not only the area's many routes, but also by the annual elite climbing competition held on a permanent wall along the river and numerous climbing shops. One of the campgrounds even owns a bouldering gym for rainy days, and many bars, restaurants, hotels, and shops offer *prezzi speciali*—special prices for climbers.

The town of Arco itself is compact and walkable, with narrow cobblestone streets lined with old stone buildings and homes capped with red tile roofs. The town center is composed of skinny, shop-lined streets or *vias* populated by pedestrians and bicycles. A spacious plaza or *piazza* sits in the middle of the old town behind the cathedral. Caffè Trentino on the east side of the piazza is a popular climber's hangout on dreary off-season days, and a pizza-slice-to-go restaurant and a *gelateria* or ice cream shop on the west side offers dinner and dessert. The *gelati* or ice cream is highly recommended on a hot afternoon or after sending your 7c project. Nearby are shady gardens, parks with benches, and the town visitor center, which offers maps and information. Away from the old center are tree-lined streets graced with stately houses and mansions built by aristocratic visitors who came for Arco's salubrious winter climate and ambience. Arco offers a wide assortment of restaurants and bars with a variety of food and prices. A couple of supermarkets are just south of the park on the main street through town.

Arco is one of Europe's best and most popular climbing areas, one of those crème de la crème venues. It's a rock arena that offers a huge range of climbing adventures for everyone from beginners to tough guys. Most American climbers who regularly visit Arco, including Chris Sharma and Boone Speed, love its diversity of climbing and the sheer number of routes, as well as all the marvelous cultural experiences available. Speed, a longtime Utah climber and boulderer, says, "I love Arco. There are lots of cliffs, and the village is so beautiful. I like to walk into town every evening, eat some great Italian food, and then walk back. It's the best!" So come to Arco and climb for a few days on the stellar limestone crags, walk into town to sip coffee and eat pasta, and explore its hidden wonders and historical places—you'll be a believer too.

Rack, Protection, and Descent

All you need to climb at Arco is a basic rack with twelve to fifteen quickdraws, a 200-foot (60-meter) rope, and a small rack with wired Stoppers and small to medium Friends. A 230-foot (70-meter) rope is useful on some crags, including Massone, since the pitches can be very long. If you don't have one, scope out your chosen route to make sure the rope will reach the ground when doubled. It's a misnomer to designate cliffs here as either sport or trad, since some sport routes require a rack of wired nuts to protect runouts between bolts, and many so-called traditional routes are also protected with occasional bolts or "spits" for protection and belays. If you climb any of the long routes, it's always a good idea to carry a small rack of gear and wear a helmet. Many routes are busy, especially on weekends, and loose rock falls off. Protect your head.

Descent off all sport routes is by lowering or rappelling from fixed bolt anchors. The longer routes require a walk-off descent or a descent down a *via ferrata.*

Climbing History

Arco has a long climbing tradition that began when alpinists used the area's cliffs as a training ground for mountain routes in the Alps and neighboring Dolomites. The blank faces, however, limited ascents to crack and corner systems. In the early 1980s the area's climbing fundamentally changed with the use of rappel-placed bolts. This new protection allowed Italian craggers to explore, bolt, and climb Arco's diverse cliffs. This new breed of sport climber was led by Roberto Bassi, Manolo, and the famed Heinz Mariacher. These three in particular began climbing the steeper, overhanging faces and finding new gymnastic lines up seemingly blank walls. Many classic 5.12 routes were established during this time as German and Austrian climbers came and established easier moderate lines.

Arco's wide variety and huge number of cliffs allowed climbing to proliferate. The town of Arco took it all it stride, seeing the opportunity to make a few lire off visiting climbers and spreading the word that this was one of Europe's great free-climbing centers. Since 1986 Arco has hosted a prestigious international climbing competition with a lucrative prize purse that has attracted the world's best climbers, including such American notables as Lynn Hill, Robyn Erbesfield, Katie Brown, and Chris Sharma. Since climbing competitions were in their infancy during the Arco invitational's inception, the organizers created competition routes by drilling and chipping on a crag now called Sport Roccia 86 at the eastern base of Mont Colodri's towering east face. Trees were also clear-cut below the cliff to allow better views for spectators. Since those first tentative comps, the summer competition has been held on the Rockmaster Wall, a huge outdoor wall along the river. It's open for climbing every day from April to November.

Seasons and Weather

Arco is generally viewed as a year-round climbing area, but summer, when most Americans visit the area, is usually just too hot for comfort. That's not to say that

A climber cranks on the cliff at Nago.

summer can't be fine since cool days regularly occur and shady cliffs are always found. If you come in summer, however, be prepared for heat and humidity with high temperatures in the 90s. If the temperatures are unbearable, remember that the cool Dolomites are only an hour's drive to the north. Since Arco is at a relatively low elevation, it enjoys a mild and pleasant climate. Autumn and spring, like elsewhere in southern Europe, is the ideal time to visit, with daily highs in the 60s and 70s. Winter can be fine, but it is also when cold winds sweep south off the Alps. Additionally, inversions of mist and fog can make winter climbing pretty miserable.

Camping, Accommodations, and Services

Arco, being a popular tourist center, is wealthy in its accommodations. Most climbers stay in the two campgrounds along the River Sarca just north of town.

The cliff Cima Colodri Est above Arco.

To reach them turn north at the river bridge on the north side of Arco, and head up the west side of the river below the towering walls of Mont Colodri.

The first site is Arco Campground, a large area will lots of facilities and campers, especially in summer, when it seems that all of Germany and Austria stays here. Their Web site calls it a "touristic-sport centre" with a tennis court, Olympic-size pool, table tennis, bouldering room, beach volleyball court, climbing school, playground equipment for the bored climber, and bicycle hire. It has a small supermarket, snack bar and cafe, complete laundry facilities, and showers and toilets. They also rent bungalows and apartments, which are a good choice if you didn't come prepared to camp.

The campground is extremely busy in summer, with wall-to-wall tents and cars. Lots of climbers are here, so you can hook up with a partner if needed. You can also use the pool as part of your warm-up or on hot afternoons when you can submerse yourself and study the vertical cliffs above.

Up the road is Camping Zoo. This site is more primitive than its neighbor but makes up for it with more peace and quiet. It too is popular with visiting climbers. It was named for a motley collection of local wildlife and barnyard animals that once inhabited cages here.

If these sites are too busy for you, especially in summer, than head north up the highway from Arco for fifteen minutes to the old village of Pietramurata. Camping Daino offers a stunning view of surrounding limestone peaks and faces that tower above the valley. It's uncrowded and quiet, with grassy tent sites shaded by spreading trees. The nearby Hotel Daino offers discounted rooms for climbers.

Many hotels are found in the Arco area, ranging in price from moderate to ritzy. Ask at the Arco tourist office for suggestions and directions to various hotels. They also make reservations for you. Some recommended places are Hotel Garni Toresela in Nago-Torbole, Alla Grotta near the lake, and Guesthouse with eight apartments.

All services are found in Arco, including several supermarkets, lots of shops, and several excellent pizzerias and cafes. The most popular climber hangout is Caffè Trentino on the east side of the square behind the cathedral. Many afternoon hours are whittled away here in the warm sunlight slanting across the piazza.

Lots of climbing shops with relatively inexpensive prices await you in the Arco area. You find particularly good deals on Italian-made equipment such as La Sportiva shoes, which cost about half the U.S. price. Local shops include Vertical Sport, Red Point Mountain Equipment, Vertical La Sportiva (an outlet shop), and Vertical Sport Outlet in Pietramurata.

Cultural Experiences and Rest Days

The Valle dei Laghi, a north-south trending valley drained by the Sarca River and flanked by immense limestone mountains, was one of the first settled valleys in the northern Italian province of Trentino. The bucolic region, protected from the chill central European winds and winters by the lofty mountains, boasts a mild Mediterranean climate, a long growing season, and many plants typical of more southern latitudes, including citrus trees, holm oaks, cypresses, and olive trees. South of Arco stretches Lago di Garda, the largest and most visited lake in Italy. The 30-mile-long lake, reaching a maximum depth of 1,113 feet, sits between the Alps and the broad Po Valley. It froze only once in recorded history—during a record cold spell in 1709. The lakeshore is heavily developed with villages, towns, resorts, and holiday cottages.

The most popular resort is Riva del Garda at the head of the lake southwest of Arco. It's a classic Italian village with cobblestone streets, whitewashed houses, and spacious piazzas. It also offers plentiful hotels, restaurants, and activities for the well-heeled tourist. But after visiting Riva on a rest day, you will undoubtedly agree that Arco is calmer, prettier, and more relaxed.

Besides visiting Riva on rest days, drive down to Lago di Garda for sun and surf. Torbole at the northeast side of the lake is renowned as one of Italy's best sailboarding areas. You can rent boards to catch afternoon breezes. Nearby you'll find topless beaches and great swimming. Mountain biking is popular, with lots of trails and bike rentals in Arco. The visitor center hands out maps of biking itineraries in the mountains. If you haven't climbed enough, pack up shoes, harness, and slings, and scale a *via ferrata*. These climbing routes ascend steep faces, gullies, and ridges equipped with safety cables, ladders, and iron pegs. Guides in German and Italian are available in book shops. One of the best for hot days is a 1-kilometer adventure up a narrow, wet slot canyon to Castello di Drena. Another great rest day activity is driving into the mountains on the narrow, twisting roads and exploring quaint villages, lakes, and valleys, and finding spectacular viewpoints.

The Arco area is rich in prehistory and history. The valley is littered with ancient habitation sites, as well as early Roman roads and villages. Later, three of Trentino's five fortified towns—Arco, Riva del Garda, and Tenno—were settled. Arco was established and owned by the powerful Arco family. This ancient, fortified town nestles against the soaring flanks of Colodri Sud, a limestone bastion capped by Castello di Arco or Arco Castle. This exquisite castle, surveying the narrow Valle dei Laghi north of Lago di Garda, overlooks what was once the route south for invading armies marching to the Po plain. The striking castle, initially built by the Arco family in the twelfth century, protected the fertile valley. The family occupied it until the sixteenth century, when they moved down from their mountain aerie and settled in luxurious manor houses in the village below. Left to the owls and lizards, the castle slowly decayed, with a final blow dealt by the French, who sacked it in 1703 during the War of the Spanish Succession. The castle is now preserved and is explored on daily tours.

North of Arco is Castel Toblino. This famous castle sits on a peninsula that juts into Lago Toblino in the north part of Valle de Laghi below the Bassilandia and La Gola climbing sectors. The romantic castle is built on what was a prehistoric and then Roman village. An inscribed stone dating from the third century in the castle portico explains that a temple dedicated to the adoration of The Fates was erected here. In the thirteenth century the strategically located castle was built, guarding the northern approach to the valley.

Trip Planning Information

General description: Excellent climbing on numerous limestone cliffs and walls in the mountains surrounding the town of Arco.

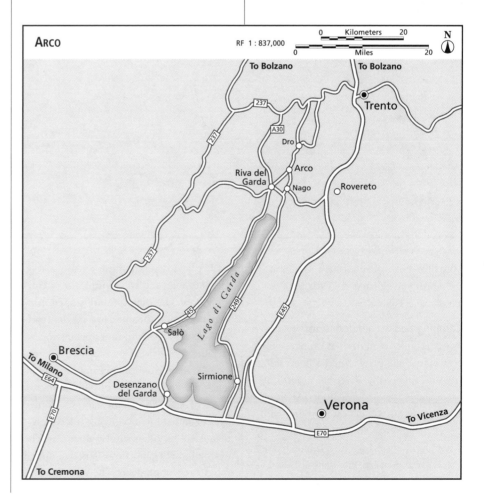

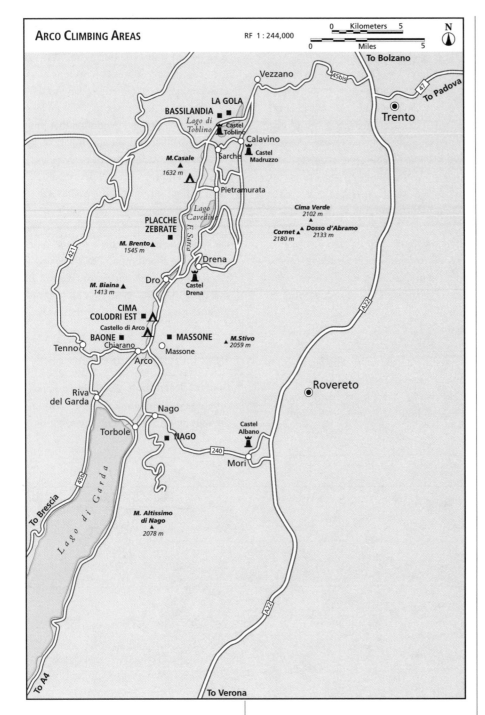

ARCO CLIMBING AREAS

RF 1 : 244,000

fifteen-minute drive north of Arco, making a car necessary to reach climbing areas.

Climbing season: Year-round. Arco, despite its northerly position by the Alps, is surprisingly temperate. The mild climate allows citrus and palm trees to flourish. The best months to climb, as in all Mediterranean areas, is from October through May. Spring and fall months are warm and usually dry, with daytime temperatures in the 60s and 70s. The winter months are often good, although periods of rain and stormy weather occur. These off-season months are less crowded than the busy summer, when most of Europe goes on vacation, filling Arco with German and Austrian tourists. Summer, when most Americans visit, tends to be hot, with stifling heat and humidity for weeks at a time. Look for shaded crags or cliffs at a higher elevation such as Nago in summer.

Restrictions and access issues: None. Remember that many cliffs are on private property, so conduct yourself accordingly. Parking is a problem at many cliffs. If lots are full, then you park farther away and walk. The only crag in this guide that will have this problem is Massone. Also remember that car break-ins are a problem here like anywhere in Europe. Leave as little as possible in your car.

Guidebooks: *Arco Falesie* by Diego Depretto and Margareth Eisendle is the thick, comprehensive local guidebook. It's available at Arco climbing shops and in newspaper/magazine shops (cash only).

Services and shops: All services are in Arco, including fabulous restaurants, grocery stores, and upscale shops. Caffè Trentino on the plaza behind the cathedral is a popular place to hang and chat. Climbing shops in Arco include Red Point Mountain Equipment, Gobbisport Mountain Equipment, and Vertical World Sport.

Emergency services: For an ambulance (*Ambulanza*) dial 118. For highway rescue (*Soccorso Stradale*) dial 116. For police (*Carabinieri* or *Polizia*) dial 112 or 113.

Location: North-central Italy. Arco is at the north end of Lago di Garda between Verona and Trento.

Camping and accommodations: Two campgrounds are in Arco. Both have similar facilities and prices, and both are along the west side of the River Sarca north of town and below Mont Colodri. Arco Campground is a huge campground with many amenities, including toilets, showers, a bouldering wall, bike hire, minimarket, snack bar and tavern, safe deposit boxes, freezers with keys, laundry room with washers and dryers, bungalows and apartments to rent, and an Olympic-size swimming pool. The campground is open from March through October. Just up the road is Camping Zoo with more primitive facilities.

Another good campground is Camping Daino in the village of Pietramurata north of Arco. This scenic campsite, lorded over by limestone mountains, is less busy than Arco but offers similar amenities. The nearby Hotel Daino also offers discounted room rates for climbers. The village is a

Nearby climbing areas: Many climbing areas near Arco are not described in the comprehensive guidebook. Ask at the climbing shops for the guide to the long mountain routes on the big faces up the valley.

Ceredo, on Monti Lessini north of Verona, is an excellent area with almost 200 routes from slabs to overhangs. A guidebook can be bought in the pizzeria Gavinel in Ceredo. Erto to the northeast was one of Italy's original hard crags. The area is east of Longarone. To the north near Vicenza is the excellent classic crag Lumignano. Lots of excellent and sustained routes are found on this huge limestone wall.

Lastly, the Dolomites boast literally thousands of routes, from sport climbs to long alpine routes. After climbing at Arco be sure to head up to the *Dolomiti* for a few days of cranking and sightseeing.

Nearby attractions: Lots to see and do around Arco. At Riva del Garda check out the Museo Civico, a city museum with archeological and art displays. North of town is spectacular Cascata Varone, a 300-foot waterfall fed by Lago di Tenno.

To the southeast is Verona, one of Italy's most beautiful cities and the setting for Shakespeare's *Romeo and Juliet*. The surprisingly compact old town offers excellent attractions and museums, including a Roman arena; Piazza delle Erbe, a plaza in the city's heart; Casa di Giulietta, the supposed location of Juliet's balcony; the exquisite Piazza dei Signori, one of Verona's best Renaissance buildings; Castelvecchio, a castle that is now a museum; and the Romanesque church Basilica di San Zeno Maggiore. The city also offers excellent restaurants and lots of entertainment.

Venice, perhaps Italy's most famous and certainly most beautiful city, sits on the coast southeast from Arco. The city is built on 117 small islands with 150 canals and 409 bridges. There is much to see here. Start with a boat trip down the Grand Canal to check out the incredible buildings alongside it. Walk around to see the rest, including Piazza San Marco, the

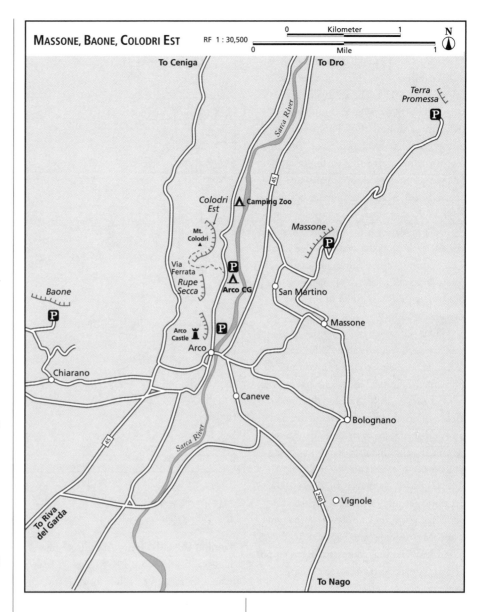

great cathedral Basilica di San Marco, Palazzo Ducale, and the wonderful art museum Gallerie dell'Accademia. It's best to drive to the outskirts of Venice, park, and ride the train into the city center or to take the bus from Arco to Rovereto and then the train to Venice. Plan on staying for at least one night.

Finding the area: Arco is in northern Italy just north of Lago di Garda. To reach Arco from the north, from Germany, Austria, and the Dolomites, drive south on the A22 Autostrata to Trento. Exit and drive west on highway 237 for 19 kilometers to Sarche. Turn south at the roundabout in Sarche, and drive south 22 kilo-meters on highway 45 *bis* to Arco. From the south drive north on the A22 Autostrata, and take the South Rovereto exit. Turn west onto highway 240, and drive through Mori and Nago to Arco.

If you don't have a car, take the train from either the north or south to Rovereto. Catch a bus to Arco outside the train station.

The closest international airport is at Milan, about 140 miles to the west. To drive to Arco from Milan, follow the A4 Autostrata past Bergamo and Brescia. Just west of Verona go north on the A22, and follow it to the South Rovereto exit. Follow the above directions to Arco.

Massone

Massone, a long east-facing cliff northeast of Arco, offers more than 150 sport routes from 5.7 to 5.13+. The easily accessed crag is deservedly popular and one of Italy's most famous cliffs. The routes are mostly excellent, with a diversity of climbing movements up compact limestone. Cliff features include roofs, slabs, tufa columns, edges, and occasional pockets. A definite downside to Massone's accessibility and popularity is the weekend crowding and polish on the well-traveled lines. The majority of the climbs are between 5.11a (7a) and 5.13a (7c+), making Massone an ideal destination for on-sighting routes.

The cliff is generally divided into three sectors. Massone Basso, the left-hand sector, yields many routes from 5a to 7a on slabby to vertical limestone broken by corners and roofs. La Valletta, the middle sector, offers superb and sustained test-pieces that require both strength and stamina to clip the anchors. Routes on this mostly overhanging section range from 7a to 8a. Il Pueblo, the third sector on the right side of the crag, boasts the cliff's hardest routes up steep overhanging stone. Most routes here begin at 7c.

Most Massone routes are between 65 and 100 feet long. On the left sector, however, some climbs are shorter (35 to 50 feet), whereas some on the right are as long as 130 feet.

If you plan on climbing any of Massone's longer routes, you need to bring a 200-foot (60-meter) cord, or better yet a 230-foot (70-meter) rope; otherwise, expect some scary descents. A rack of

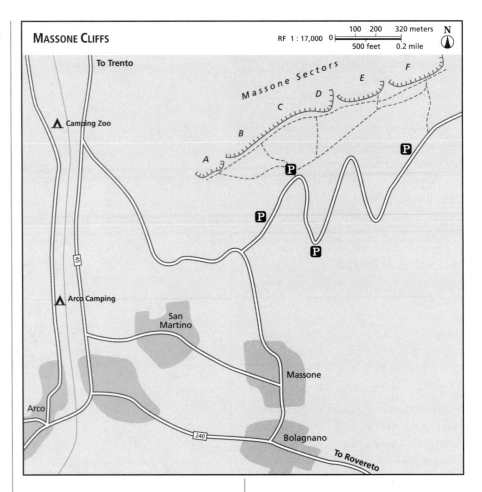

twelve to sixteen quickdraws suffices for the rest of your gear.

Finding the cliff: From Arco drive on highway SS 45 toward Rovereto. In less than a kilometer, turn left (north), and follow signs for the village of Massone. Enter the village, drive through a narrow gateway, and bear left at the fountain (you can fill water bottles here). Follow the narrow road up through olive groves, and park at the obvious pullout directly below the cliff. If this lot is full, park down the road toward Massone in the olive grove. All this

land is private property. Be respectful of the owner's property rights and the olive trees. Approach time from car to crag is thirty seconds.

An alternative driving route is to go north on the highway toward Trento. In about a kilometer make a very sharp, unmarked right turn in front of a store, and follow a narrow road up through olive groves to the cliff.

Massone is close enough to Arco that you can easily walk to the crag from the campground in fifteen to twenty minutes.

Sector A

The first section, Sector A, is two slabby faces on the far left side of the cliff. The routes are fun and popular.

1. Piccola Luna (4a) (5.5) 50 feet.

2. Formica Lodovica (5a) (5.7) 50 feet.

3. Giacca gialla (5b) (5.8) 50 feet.

4. Banane fisch (5a/b) (5.7+) 55 feet.

5. Lara Croft (5c) (5.9) 60 feet.

6. Gelateria Tarifa (6a+) (5.10b) 35 feet.

7. Easy Rider (6c) (5.11a/b) 35 feet.

8. Alce volante (6a) (5.10a) 40 feet.

9. Boiacca (5c) (5.9) 40 feet.

10. Giuditta (6a) (5.10a) Right-hand route on the first face. 60 feet.

11. Pesce d'aprile (6a) (5.10a) Just right of a groove that divides the two faces. 65 feet.

12. Skoda (6b) (5.10c) 65 feet.

13. Gocce d'ansia (6b) (5.10c) 65 feet.

14. Pegasus (6a+) (5.10b) Face to slab to anchors above a final small roof. 65 feet.

15. Zac (5a) (5.7) Ends at anchors under a roof. 60 feet.

16. Tac (5a) (5.7) Ends at anchors under a roof. 60 feet.

Sector B

17. Unknown (6a+) (5.10b) 65 feet.

18. Fra fra (6b) (5.10c) 65 feet.

19. Fur eine Hand (6a+) (5.10b) 60 feet.

20. Dottor Plantier (6a) (5.10a) 50 feet.

21. Zlù (6a) (5.10a) 65 feet.

22. Nino (6a) (5.10a) 65 feet.

23. Tangram (6a+) (5.10b) 72 feet.

24. La bamba (7a+) (5.12a) 35 feet.

25. The Mirror (6c) (5.10d) 65 feet.

26. Spectrum (6b+) (5.11a/b) 65 feet.

27. Red Point (7a+) (5.12a) 65 feet.

28. Mirta del Pineto (7a+) (5.12a) 65 feet.

29. Marsabit (7c) (5.12d) 50 feet.

30. Stressami (7c) (5.12d) 50 feet.

31. Desiree (7b) (5.12b) 50 feet.

32. Loacher (7b+) (5.12c) 50 feet.

33. Not Normal (7a) (5.11d) 50 feet.

34. Vite minori (6c) (5.11a/b) 85 feet.

35. Let Me Life (7b) (5.12b) 75 feet.

36. Il ladro (8a) (5.13b) 75 feet.

37. C'è qualcuno (7b/c) (5.12b/c) 85 feet.

38. Deasy (6c) (5.11a/b) 85 feet.

39. Tis sa arc (6b+) (5.10d) 85 feet.

40. Cannonau (7a) (5.11d) 85 feet.

41. Crisi (7a) (5.11d) 85 feet.

42. Via le man (7a) (5.11d) 85 feet.

43. Marlene (7a+) (5.12a) The name is at the base. 85 feet.

44. Greta (7a) (5.11d) Name painted at the base. 85 feet.

45. Sulla pancia (7c+) (5.13a) 85 feet.

46. Mantide Atea (6c+) (5.11c) 85 feet.

47. Variante diretta (7b+) (5.12c) 85 feet.

48. I buoni cattivi (7c) (5.12d) 85 feet.

49. Sangit (7a+) (5.12a) 85 feet.

50. Panico sopra l'orlo (7c) (5.12d) 85 feet.

51. Profumo di invisibile (8a) (5.13b) 85 feet.

52. Soviet Supremo (7b) (5.12b) 85 feet.

53. Beverly Hills (7b+) (5.12c) 85 feet.

54. Kabul (6b) (5.10c) 85 feet.

55. I Like Gorba (6c) (5.11a/b) 90 feet.

56. Killer Event (7b+) (5.12c) 65 feet.

57. Action Direct (6c+) (5.11c) 85 feet.

58. Incantesimo (8a) (5.13b) 65 feet.

59. Ricky Bike (8a) (5.13b) 65 feet.

60. Musetto e Big Gim (6b) (5.10c) 75 feet.

61. Super Golia (6c+) (5.11c) 85 feet.

62. Heliotrop (7b) (5.12b) 85 feet.

63. Berny (7c+) (5.13a) 85 feet.

64. Ictus (6c+) (5.11c) 85 feet.

65. Destinzione Arena (7c+) (5.13a) 85 feet.

66. Sabato turistico (6c) (5.11a/b) 80 feet.

67. Prime impressioni (6a) (5.10a) "First impression." 82 feet.

68. Tullio e l'amore (6a/b) (5.10a/b) 75 feet.

Sector C

Sector C is a vertical wall that begins right of a prominent roof system. Most of the routes are good and popular.

69. Hurgada (6b) (5.10c) 60 feet.

70. Over Booking (6a) (5.10a) 60 feet.

71. Raper (5c) (5.9) 60 feet.

72. Settima luna (6c+) (5.11c) 53 feet.

73. Ektoplasma (6b) (5.10c) 60 feet.

74. Odio la polvere (6b) (5.10c) 60 feet.

75. L'unicorno (5c/6a) (5.9/10a) 50 feet.

76. Stattento (5c/6a) (5.9/10a) 50 feet.

77. Impetrite's (5b) (5.8) 50 feet.

78. Marina's (5a) (5.7) On the far right side of the sector. 50 feet.

Sector D

Sector D is the uppermost cliff section described here. The sector is steep, with bulges and roofs. Expect technical and powerful climbing. The area is accessed by hiking north on the trail along the terraces at the cliff base.

79. Rettoscopie (6b+) (5.10d) 73 feet.

80. Il culto (6b) (5.10c) 65 feet.

81. Fata Morgana (7a+) (5.12a) 65 feet.

82. Il ritorno di Aly (6b+) (5.10d) 65 feet.

83. Ulla (6c) (5.11a/b) 65 feet.

84. Un bacio di Karin (7a+) (5.12a) 65 feet.

85. Halloween (7a) (5.11d) 65 feet.

86. Otto promille (6c+) (5.11c) 65 feet.

87. Unknown (6c+) (5.11c)

88. Briciola (6c) (5.11a/b) 60 feet.

Cima Colodri Est

Cima Colodri is one of the best and most accessible traditional crags at Arco. This towering, east-facing limestone mountain, dominating Arco's northern skyline, is divided into two peaks—Colodri Est on the right and Rupe Secca on the left, when viewed from the campgrounds. The impressive wall of Colodri Est towers a thousand feet above the broad river valley. An easy five-minute stroll along a climber trail from the campgrounds leads to the base of the routes. The routes are ideal for sunny autumn mornings or shady summer afternoons.

Cima Colodri offers an excellent selection of multipitch routes that are climbed in a traditional style. Occasional bolts as well as fixed pitons, however, supplement whatever gear you place to protect pitches. Most belays are bolted. Most of the routes are worth climbing, but this guide describes the best classic lines. A couple recommended routes on Rupe Secca, the big face looming over the road

south of Colodri Est, are *Tyskyewic* (6b+) and *Mescalito* (7a). Between the two faces is Sport Roccia 86, a bolted face with drilled and chiseled holds that was used in a 1986 climbing competition.

Bring sets of wired nuts and cams, along with extra slings and ten quick-draws. A 200-foot (60-meter) rope is adequate for all routes, especially if you want to run pitches together.

Descent off the peak is by walking down to the south. Scramble down the ridge toward the southern summit with the castle. Past a white cliff look for the *via ferrata* or iron railing and cable route that descends slabs on the broken face between the two major faces.

Finding the cliff: From either campground just north of Arco, the cliff is apparent. If you're camping there, rack up and trek across the road to your chosen line. Otherwise, locate a small car park near Arco Campground. Walk from here to the cliff base. Approach time is about five minutes.

Routes are described from left to right.

1. Somadossi (6a+) (5.10b) 9 pitches. Excellent route up the left side of the wall. Pitch grades: 5b, 5a, 5b, 6a, 6a, 5a, 5c, 5c, 5c.

2. Renata Rossi (6a+) (5.10b) 9 pitches. Excellent and varied climbing with lots of exposure and good movements. Pitch grades: 4a, 5a, 5b, 5c, 6a, 5c, 5b, 5c, 5b.

3. Barbara (6b) (5.10c) 10 pitches. Excellent climbing but polished in places because of its popularity. The line ascends the obvious right-facing dihedrals right of the obvious pillar on the high right side of the wall. Pitch grades: 3a, 5a, 5b, 5c, 4a, 6a, 5b, 5b, 5c, 6a.

4. Zanzara (7a+) (5.12a) 11 pitches. Up the prominent steep faces on the right side of the wall. Expect technical, exposed, and sustained climbing on many of the pitches. The route is mostly bolted. Bring a small rack to supplement bolts. Pitch grades: 4a, 6b, 7a+, 6c, 7a, 6a, 6a, 6b, 6b, 6b+, 6a.

Baone

Baone, stretching across the mountain slopes northwest of Arco, is a long, easy-angled slab with a selection of extremely popular, easy and moderate routes up to 650 feet long. The climbing area is divided into two sectors. The left sector offers easier routes than the right sector. The slab is often used by local climbing schools for beginner lessons. Weekends can be very busy. The south-facing slab can be roasting hot in the sun.

A simple rack of ten quickdraws and a 200-foot (60-meter) rope is all that is needed for a morning's fun. Descent off the routes is by rappel from bolted belay/rappel stations.

Finding the cliff: Baone, while easy to see from town, is trickier to find. The driving approach requires navigating some narrow village streets in Chiarano, the next village west of Arco, and a narrower one-lane road that climbs to the parking area below the cliff. Begin by driving west from the

park and plaza in Arco, following signs toward the hospital. Pass the hospital, and jog right into the village of Chiarano. Drive into the village, and pass through an archway over the road. Go left just after the arch onto a narrow road that climbs out of the village and onto a slope terraced with olive trees. Take a sharp right turn, the only possible turn, at the crest of the road, and continue up the one-lane road to a parking area below the cliff. Follow a trail to the slabs for a couple minutes.

Routes are described from right to left.

1. Unknown (4b) (5.6) The farthest right route on the slab. Smear to a 2-bolt anchor under the obvious overlap.

2. Unknown (4c) (5.6) Straight up to a 2-bolt anchor under the overlap.

3. Unknown (4b) (5.5) Friction to a 2-bolt anchor under the overlap.

4. Mucillero (4b) (5.5) 3 pitches. Pitch grades: 4a, 4a, 4b.

5. Ondulina (5a) (5.7) 3 pitches. Pitch grades: 4a, 5a, 4a.

6. Cade la coda (4b) (5.5) 3 pitches. Pitch grades: 3a, 4b, 4b.

7. Figoviz (5a) (5.7) 3 pitches. Pitch grades: 4b, 5a, 4a.

8. Strati sensuali (5c) (5.9) 3 pitches. Good climbing through the lower overlaps left of the main slab. Pitch grades: 5c, 4a, 3b.

9. Unknown (5c+) (5.9) Directly up through the overlaps on the left side of the big slab to a 2-bolt anchor.

10. Solarium (5b) (5.8) 2 pitches. **Pitch 1:** Up left along an angling crack and then past some overlaps on the left (5b) to a 2-bolt anchor. **Pitch 2:** Easy friction (3+) to anchors.

11. Unknown (5c) (5.9-) Over the overlaps to #10's anchors.

Walk left along a cliff-base trail to the left-hand slab. All these routes are easy, low-angle affairs.

12. Unknown (3) (5.5) 4 pitches. Pitch grades: 3, 3, 2, 2.

13. Unknown (3) (5.5) 4 pitches. Pitch grades: 3, 3, 2, 2.

14. Via D.B. (3) (5.5) 4 pitches. Pitch grades: 2, 3, 2, 2.

15. Via C.G. (3) (5.5) 3 pitches. Pitch grades: 2, 3a, 3a.

Nago

Nago is an excellent collection of southwest-facing cliffs perched on a steep mountainside southeast of Arco. The area, with stunning views across the valley, yields a brilliant selection of moderate routes, as well as many superb harder lines. The cliffs are often hot in the sun, but because they are at a high elevation, they are usually cooler than the lower crags around Arco, making it an ideal summer area.

Finding the cliffs: From Arco drive southeast on highway 240d toward Mori. The highway leaves the valley and climbs steeply to the village of Nago. As soon as you reach Nago, go right at a big round-about and then immediately left into the village. Follow signs toward Monti Baldo. Go straight into the village on the narrow street, and make a sharp right at an arch-way. Follow the very narrow road south through the village, and leave Nago after 0.4 kilometer. Just past the village the road splits. Keep right on a narrow road, and continue southeast past a farmhouse. The road passes through olive groves, then climbs steeply up the mountainside. After driving 2.6 kilometers from the turnoff to Nago, park at a large parking area on the left or at a small area on a switchback turn.

A couple of climber trails access the cliffs. Start from the small car park on the

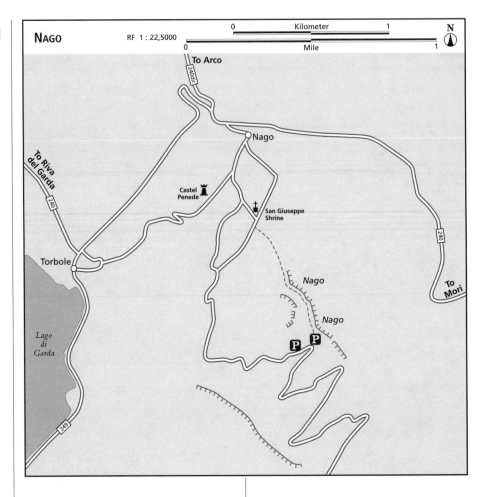

switchback. Walk straight north, and after 50 feet you reach a good trail. Go left, and hike downhill about ten minutes. Keep an eye on the cliffs to your right to find the various trails that branch off to the right to the base of the cliffs. The farthest described cliff and the first one in this guide is a fifteen-minute hike down the trail. A trail follows the base of the cliff uphill to the farthest east sectors. To directly access these sectors, which lie directly north of the car park, a path runs north from the trail junction to the cliff base. Hiking time is about five minutes.

The first routes are on a couple faces divided by ledges and bordered by leaning crack systems.

1. Bali (6a) (5.10a) A short white face to anchors below the trees. 33 feet.

2. Bisigoti (6a) (5.10a) Right of Bali. 33 feet.

3. Unni (4c) (5.6) Up left along an angling crack system. 30 feet.

4. Zuppa Zuppa (6a) (5.10a) 2 pitches.
Pitch 1: Easy face to a ledge (3). 40 feet.
Pitch 2: Up the left side of the face (6a). 50 feet.

5. Parampampoli (6b) (5.10c) 2 pitches.
Pitch 1: Easy face to ledge (3). 40 feet.
Pitch 2: Face (6b) to anchors below the top. 50 feet.

6. Alcor (5b) (5.8) Left-angling crack system. 40 feet.

7. Winkinbongo (5b) (5.8) Next angling crack system to anchors up right at the top. 40 feet.

8. Asdù (5c) (5.9) Up the obvious leaning crack to anchors. 35 feet.

9. Enzo Molinari (5c) (5.9) The narrow face left of a crack. 35 feet.

The next face is a slightly overhanging wall of perfect limestone laced with a selection of excellent routes.

10. Il Capriccio (7c) (5.12d) No topo. Far left side of the face. Route follows along a steep crack. 65 feet.

11. Super Mario (7b+) (5.12c) Thin and sustained. 80 feet.

12. Gobazio (6a+) (5.10b) Easier than it looks! 85 feet.

13. La mandria (6a) (5.10a) Classic and recommended. Directly up the center of the face. 85 feet.

14. Mario Polenta (6a) (5.10a) Excellent and popular. 85 feet.

15. Lillila (6a+) (5.10b) Killer climbing up the right edge of the face. 85 feet.

Walk uphill from *Lillila* along the cliff base, passing a broken face, to the base of a pale wall with a stunning arête up its middle.

16. La placca (6a+) (5.10b) 2 pitches. **Pitch 1:** Climb moderate rock (5c) to a ledge with a 2-bolt belay. 65 feet. **Pitch 2:** Edge up the steep white wall to cliff-top anchors. 65 feet.

17. Cato-Zulù (6b+) (5.10d) Up white arête.

18. Lo sconosciuto (6b+) (5.10d) Face right of arête.

The next wall is just right and uphill from the *Cato-Zulù* arête. The routes begin up and left from the base of the face.

19. Peach-Pitt (6c) (5.11b) Left side of the face. 65 feet.

20. Torpedo (7a+) (5.12a) Steep and technical. 65 feet.

21. Mammalucco (7a) (5.11d) Good moves up the white rock left of a gray streak. 85 feet.

22. Genesi (7a) (5.11d) Sustained and technical. 85 feet.

23. Unknown (6b+) (5.10d/11a) Over a roof, then up the gray face left of an arête. 85 feet.

A cleft separates two walls. The first route climbs a short wall at the base. The others are on the steep wall above.

24. Astuzio (6b+) (5.10d/11a) Short route up the base of the face. 40 feet.

25. Esuli lontani (7a) (5.11d) Sustained climbing on the left side of the face. 85 feet.

26. La nonna va (6c+) (5.11c) Just right of #25 up the steep face. 85 feet.

27. Tasmania (7a) (5.11d) Thin and continuous. 85 feet.

28. Crisalide (6b+) (5.10d/11a) Over bulges and vertical faces. 85 feet.

29. Coda di Porco (6b) (5.10b) Up the outside face of the buttress. 85 feet.

30. Facile (4c) (5.6) Fun climbing. On the right side of the buttress. Angle up right to anchors. 85 feet.

The next sector is an excellent cliff with lots of routes up its streaked face. Most of the routes are recommended and offer good climbing. A trail leads up to the face from the main descent path and from the right side.

31. Asdo da Melch (7c) (5.12d) Far left margin of the face. 85 feet.

32. Grisù (7a+) (5.12a) 85 feet.

33. Lucacappiotti (7b+) (5.12c) Up left along a crack system, then straight up the steep face. 125 feet.

34. Dago (7b+) (5.12c) Same start as #33, but work straight up. 125 feet.

35. Eh Mersh (7b) (5.12b) Long and sustained. 125 feet.

36. Culo dritto (7b) (5.12b) White face. 75 feet.

37. Uligani Dangereux (7a+) (5.12a) 85 feet.

38. Passeggeri del Vento (7b+) (5.12c) Continuous, airy climbing. 130 feet.

39. Lunatica (7b) (5.12b) Short and popular. 60 feet.

40. Boulevard (7c) (5.12d) Up left along a break, then directly up the brown streak. 130 feet.

41. Per Sempre Mary (7b+) (5.12c) Same start as *Boulevard* but break off right early and then up the brown streaks. 130 feet.

42. I soliti Ignoti (7a) (5.11d) Short route up a brown streak. 65 feet.

43. Sbargek (6b+) (5.10d) Along a crack system. 65 feet.

44. Lupo Alberto (7a+) (5.12a) 2 pitches or 1 long pitch. **Pitch 1:** Steep face to anchors. 65 feet. **Pitch 2:** Up the bulging wall above. 65 feet.

45. Titanic (7b+) (5.12c) Long, continuous climbing up the right side. 115 feet.

46. Iceberg (7a+) (5.12a) Keep moving so you don't crash. 115 feet.

47. Gandalf (6c) (5.11a/b) White face to a roof, then a gray slab. 85 feet.

48. Esodo (6b) (5.10c) 85 feet.

49. Cohelet (6b+) (5.10d) On the right side of the face. 85 feet.

The next routes are on a slabby wall just right of the above routes.

50. Troppo buoni (5b) (5.8) Popular and fun. Up face right of the roofs. 50 feet.

51. Unknown (5b) (5.8) Just right of #50.

The next cliff to the right of #51 is an excellent face with a good selection of moderate climbs. No topos to these routes, but they're easy to find. Routes are described from left to right.

52. Nevermore (6c+) (5.11c) 65 feet.

53. Spleen (6b) (5.10c) 65 feet.

54. Equinox (6a) (5.10a) 65 feet.

55. Gerico (6a) (5.10a) 50 feet.

56. Night'fly (5c) (5.9) 65 feet.

57. Super Tramp (5c) (5.9) 60 feet.

58. Good Bye Stranger (6a) (5.10a) 50 feet.

59. Cif (5b) (5.8) 50 feet.

60. Ragioner Filini (5c) (5.9) 50 feet.

61. Mega Direttore (5c) (5.9) 50 feet.

Uphill to the right and directly opposite or north from the parking area are more cliffs with some excellent routes. Check the comprehensive area guide for topos, names, and grades to these routes.

Placche Zebrate

The great east-facing slab Le Placche Zebrate towers as high as 1,600 feet above the wide Sarca River Valley near Pietramurata between Arco and Sarche. Despite the slab's size and height, however, it is dwarfed by the immense limestone faces on the mountains above. The cliff is easily seen and identified from the highway between Dro and Pietramurata.

The cliff is very popular, with a large selection of excellent bolted, multipitch routes that edge and smear up the bright slab. Most routes are friendly, but don't be lulled into complacency, because some lines sport long runouts between bolts. The slab varies in height between 600 and 1,600 feet, with the shorter lines on the left side of the wall.

For most routes bring a small rack of wired nuts and small to medium cams, along with fifteen quickdraws and a 200-foot (60-meter) rope.

Descent off the cliff top is by walking south along a climber's path that descends scree slopes on the south side of the slab. Descent time from the summit to the cliff base is fifteen to twenty minutes.

Finding the cliff: Drive north from Arco and pass through Dro. Continue north a few more kilometers, and look for the slab on your left below another big mountain wall. After passing Bar Placche Zebrate on your right, look for a large parking lot on the left with a kiosk and map. Park here, and follow a trail directly west for fifteen minutes to the slab base. A trail also runs along the cliff base, accessing all the routes.

1. Via Trento (5a) (5.7) 6 pitches. On the cliff's left side and just left of a broken angling ramp system. Pitch grades: 4b, 4b, 5a, 5a, 4c, 2. 650 feet.

2. Via Olocausto (7a) (5.11c) 7 pitches. Great route up the right side of the next slab shield. Pitch grades: 5c, 6c, 6b, 6b, 6b, 7a, 4c. 725 feet.

3. Via Gabri-Camilla (6b or 6a A0) (5.10c or 5.10a A0) 9 pitches. Brilliant climbing up the middle of the big striped slab. Pitch grades: 5b, 5a, 4c, 6a, 6a, 6a+ (A0), 6b (A0), 3b, 3b. 1,200 feet.

4. Via Claudia (5b) (5.8) 16 pitches. Excellent long route up the right side of the slabs with mostly easy climbing. Pitch grades: 5a, 3c, 3c, 4a, 3c, 4a, 3c, 4c, 4a, 5b, 5a, 4c, 4b, 3c, 3c, 4a. 1,600 feet.

Bassilandia

Bassilandia is a superb area above Lago di Toblino and Castel Toblino (Toblina Castle) just northeast of the village of Sarche, north of Arco. This easily accessible, east-facing cliff offers a great assortment of difficult, one-pitch sport routes on perfect limestone in a stunning setting. The area, developed in 2002 and 2003, is not described at press time in any other guidebook. Right of Bassilandia is another small area called Toblino, with fourteen routes from 6b to 7c.

Finding the cliff: Drive north from Arco on highway 240d for about 20 kilometers to the village of Sarche. Pass through Sarche, and angle right toward Vezzano and Trento. The highway passes under the cliff on the hillside above the road and lake. Park at the north end of the lake at a large scenic pulloff on the right. Cross the highway, walk up the road through a grape vineyard, and pass a house on the right. Continue up the road to a power pole just before a waterfall. Go left here, and scramble up a slab and then up a steep trail to the right side of the cliff. Hiking time is fifteen minutes. A climber trail runs southwest along the base of the cliff.

Routes are described from right to left. Some route names are painted on the rock at the base.

1. Crotalo Wall (7a) (5.11d)

2. Novecento (7a) (5.11d)

3. Brillantina (7a) (5.11d)

4. Gong Ho (7b) (5.12b)

5. Tim (7a+) (5.12a)

6. Giamaica (7a/b) (5.12a/b)

7. Trutta Bianca Blue (7b+) (5.12c)

8. Mad Wadl (7c+) (5.13a)

9. Il Mare Calmo (7a) (5.11d)

10. Cucciolo D'uomo (7a) (5.11d)

11. Guideo Sul Muschio (8a) (5.13b)

12. Messico e Nuvole (7a) (5.11d)

13. Diedrin Volll (7b+) (5.12c)

14. Quo Vadis (7b) (5.12b)

15. Qui Resting (7c+) (5.13a)

16. Il Signor (7c) (5.12d)

17. Goganga (7c/7c+) (5.12d/13a)

18. Bod Pa (7c) (5.12d)

19. PKK (Project)

20. Da Zanca a Zanca (7c) (5.12d)

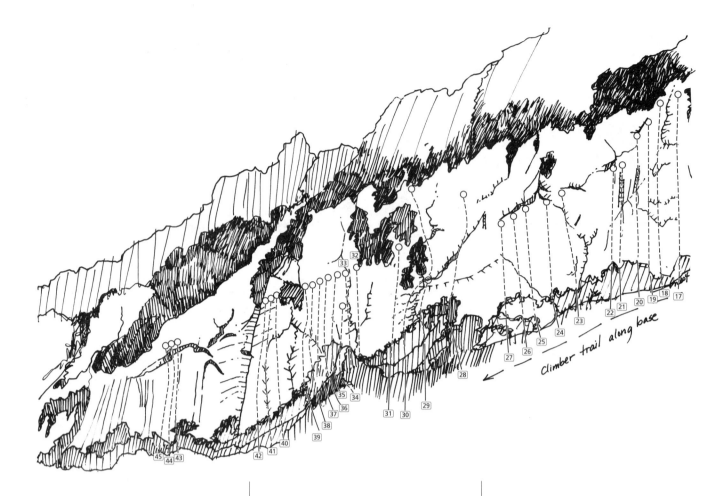

21. Will Coyote (6c+) (5.11c)

22. Extraterrestre (7a) (5.11d)

23. L'Andalopiteco (8a+) (5.13c)

24. E Chiove (7c+) (5.13a)

25. Mohammed Califfa (7c+/8a) (5.13a/b)

26. Tsumani (7c+) (5.13a)

27. Cerutti Gino (8a) (5.13b)

28. Frisco (7c) (5.12d)

29. Nix is Nicht (6b+ or 8a)

30. Il Patto (6c+) (5.11c)

31. Su e Giu (7a/b) (5.12a/b)

32. Sapori di Lagolo (6c+) (5.11c)

33. Adalpina (6c+) (5.11c)

34. 6 Marzo (6a) (5.10a)

35. X Pile (7b) (5.12b)

36. Unknown (7a+) (5.12a)

37. Unknown (7b) (5.12b)

38. Unknown (7a+) (5.12a)

39. Unknown (Project)

40. Unknown (6b+) (5.10d)

41. Unknown (7a+) (5.12a)

42. Unknown (7b) (5.12b)

43. L'Abuelito (7c) (5.12d)

44. El Flaco (7c) (5.12d)

45. El Gordo (7c+) (5.13a)

La Gola

La Gola climbing area, a collection of superb limestone crags, hides in a tranquil, hidden canyon just north of Bassilandia and west of Castel Toblino and Lago di Toblino. Thick woods and melodious bird-songs fill the deep canyon, floored with a creek that tumbles over rounded cobbles and boulders. This quiet area is nonetheless one of the best sport-climbing sectors in the Arco area, offering more than one hundred routes from 4 to 8b. The majority of lines are between 6a (5.10a) and 7b (5.12b), making it a good alternative when the other cliffs are too crowded or too hot. Both shade and solitude are easily found at La Gola. Some cliffs are closed to climbing because they are in a protected biological zone for rare plants.

The area's limestone is perfect, with plentiful edges, flakes, pockets, and even tufa formations. All the cliffs border the closed road that follows the narrow canyon floor, allowing easy access.

La Gola is divided into seven sectors. One of the best is Settore A, the farthest west cliff and just right of the road. A good selection of routes lace the crag, including a couple bolted layback cracks and some superb face routes. Settore B, a perfect cliff that rises directly above the road, yields more great routes. Not to be missed is *Hollenganda* (7a), a long line up tufa columns. The cliff continues up right on the hillside with more good climbs. Settore D, hiding in the woods right of the road, offers a collection of ten routes from 5c (5.9) to 7b+ (5.12c). This is a cool, shady crag. Lastly, the tough guy will want to check out the severely overhanging routes up Settore E, a huge, obvious cave on the right side of the road. Many of the lines pinch and layback up exciting tufa columns. On the left side of the cave, try *Ray Man* (8a+) (5.13c) and *Destino Fatale* (8a) (5.13b). In the back of the cave are the classic *Danza Macabra* (7a+) (5.12a) and *Hei Joe* (7a+) (5.12a).

None of La Gola's routes are described in this guide. Check out the comprehensive area guide for topos and identification. Or just visit the canyon and pick what looks good and feasible. You won't go wrong!

Finding the cliffs: Follow the same directions as for Bassilandia. Drive north from Arco on highway 240d for about 20 kilometers to Sarche. Pass through Sarche, and angle right toward Vezzano and Trento. Park at the north end of the lake at a large scenic pulloff on the right. Cross the highway, walk up the road through a grape vineyard, and pass a house on the right. Continue past a waterfall on the left in a grotto, and walk west up the road along the floor of the canyon. Most of the cliffs are on the right, with the first one being an obvious cave.

DOLOMITES

■ OVERVIEW

The Dolomites, part of the eastern Italian Alps, is a complex and extraordinarily beautiful mountain range and simply one of Europe's most famous and best climbing arenas. The sky-scraping range, lying between the Austrian Alps and the Venetian Plain, is composed of many groups of peaks divided by deep glaciated valleys. The jagged landscape is characterized by craggy peaks, snow-covered mountains, sheer spires, and immense rock walls. Scattered throughout the region are numerous cliffs that were originally used as training sites. Now the crags, laced with sport and traditional routes, offer diverse climbs of all grades in gorgeous alpine settings.

Twisting mountain roads link the Dolomite massifs, traversing high passes, descending wildflower-strewn meadows, passing under lofty peaks, and dropping into valleys. Picturesque villages nestle among the mountains, with wooden chalets dominated by soaring church steeples. Some are resort towns, like Cortina d'Ampezzo, that cater to the winter skier and summer tourist.

The Dolomites, or *Dolomiti* in Italian, are named for Deodat de Dolomieu. In 1789 this French geologist discovered an unusual carbonate rock that was called dolomite, a name applied to both the rock and the mountains where he discovered it. The rock appears loose and rotten at first glance, but the climber discovers its rough surface is surprisingly solid and compact with an abundance of holds. Many faces and buttresses that appear holdless, smooth, and unclimbable are ascended at moderate grades.

Dolomite climbing is unforgettable. The sport routes ascend steep cliffs surrounded by fir and spruce forests or tower above meadows studded with wildflowers. These routes are ascended with a full vocabulary of movements—gastons, laybacks, crimps, open-hand grips, gymnastic sequences, dynos, backsteps, hand jams, and fingerlocks. The rock terrain includes

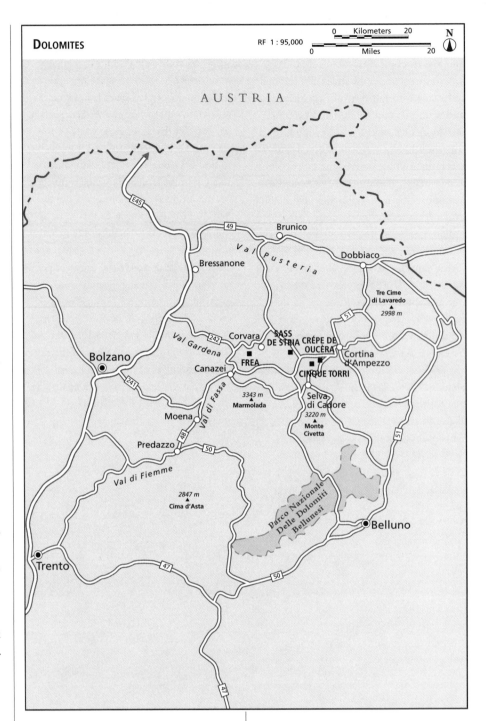

juggy slabs, vertical faces, overhanging prows, and leaning walls.

The sport cliffs described in this guide make a good introduction to the Dolomites. These crags are easy to find and access, offer a plethora of routes, and are usually dry. They're the best way to acquaint yourself with Dolomite climbing adventures. After climbing these "training" routes for a few days, you want to venture onto the higher peaks and climb the long routes. Suggestions for the best massifs and

recommended routes are included here. But you need to pick up a local guidebook (German or Italian) for topos and directions.

The best climbing strategy is to alternate crag days with mountain days. Rest days can be spent hiking and scrambling up a *via ferrata*. The Dolomites' famous *via ferratas* or "iron ways" are climbing routes that ascend mountains using iron ladders, cables, and even metal bridges. It's exhilarating to scale a *via ferrata*. You're unencumbered by gear and can move quickly across exposed, technical terrain that is unattainable without fifth-class climbing. Instead, you slip on mountain boots, a harness, a helmet, a couple self-locking carabiners with daisy chains, and go climbing. Some climbers carry a short rope as well as crampons and an ice axe. The easier *via ferratas* are generally short with low-grade climbing, whereas the demanding ones require competent mountaineering and rock skills. Like any mountain experience, a host of objective dangers are found on *via ferratas,* including rockfall, missing ladders and cables, damaged protection, snow and ice, bad weather, and lightning. Numerous German and Italian guides are found in local climbing shops.

The Dolomites should be on every American climber's European tick list. This magical place offers grand adventures moving over stone. The area's sheer immensity astounds first-time visitors, with thousands of climbing routes awaiting their hands and feet. Beyond the climbing, though, this is a place to let the spirit of the mountains sink into your soul. That's what you'll remember back home.

As Hermann Buhl, the great Austrian climber, wrote in his book *The Lonely Challenge:* "The Dolomites . . . soar above the green and pleasant valleys beyond counting, their spires, towers, and needles crowning sheer ridges and walls. Exciting, wildly romantic, their yellow faces soar perpendicular from the green meadows or gray tongues of rubble at their feet."

Dolomite Cliffs and Peaks

The Dolomites are complex. When you come here, you need a plan. Remember that you won't see everything, and you definitely won't climb every route on your list. Instead, immerse yourself in a few massifs by climbing the smaller cliffs and then doing a few long routes. But also remember to hike across the spectacular meadows, stay overnight in *rifugios,* and linger atop the airy summits. And always remind yourself: I'll be back.

The Cinque Torri or Five Towers is a group of blocky pinnacles and towers perched high atop a mountain ridge overlooking Cortina. This beautiful group is a climber's playground with more than 200 routes of all difficulties, from hard sport climbs to traditional classics. It's also popular and usually a visiting climber's first introduction to the Dolomites. Many excellent routes ascend Torre Grande, the biggest formation.

In the forest below Cinque Torri are the limestone cliffs of Crépe de Oucèra Bassi and Alti. Many excellent sport routes, including lots of popular moderates, climb the crags. Near Cortina are Sasso di Colfiere with a short vertical face, and Campo e Volpèra, an easily accessed area with more than fifty routes. North of Cortina is Són Póuses, a single face with twenty-two routes and gorgeous panoramas. South of Cortina by the village San Vito di Cadore are San Bodo and La Zoppa, two small areas that are good in cold weather.

Falesia Sass de Stria is below the summit of Passo di Valparola and west of Cinque Torri. This high cliff, on the east flank of Sass de Stria, is a popular face with a selection of fun moderates. North of the pass toward Armentarola is the big cliff and smaller crags of Sass Dlacia. The west-facing wall is warm, sunny, and quick to dry. Superb bolted routes up to five pitches long ascend the vertical wall. Nearby is an overhanging block dissected by perfect single-pitch routes from 5.9 to 5.13b.

The marvelous sport cliff of Frea lies on the north side of the Sella Group or Gruppo di Sella below Passo Gardena. Assorted rock adventures ascend this excellent wall, making it a destination for any visiting climber.

Farther west is Cansla, another brilliant cliff with nineteen perfect multipitch routes up Traumpfeiler, its northwest-facing wall, that range from 5.10b to 5.13b. Expect sustained, technical climbing up immaculate slabs and vertical faces covered with pockets, edges, slopers, and sidepulls. *Traumpfeiler* (5.11d or 7a), the wall's first route, is highly recommended. Nearby is the Wasserfall sector, with easier warm-up

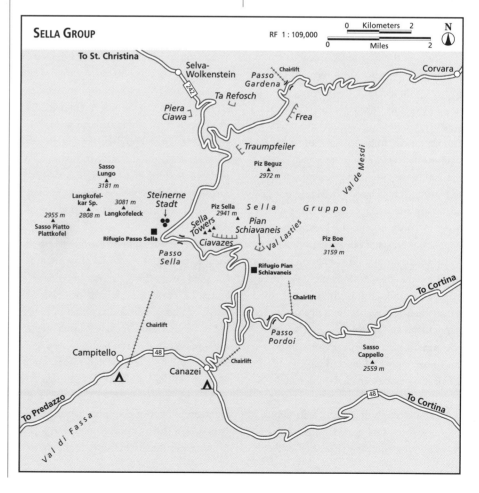

routes, and Woodstockplatten sector, with a good selection of 5.10 and 5.11 routes.

The valleys north of Cansla and Frea harbor several small cliffs, including Ta Refosch, Sas dala Piera Ciauda, and the busy beginner area Busc dl Preve. West of Cansla is Steinerne Stadt, an area of scattered boulders with bolted routes below Passo Sella and the massif Sasso Lungo.

The big wall Ciavazes on the south side of Passo Sella offers excellent classic routes. These include *Micheluzzi* (5.9), a wandering fourteen-pitcher put up in 1935; eight-pitch *Schubert* (5.8); *Kleine Micheluzzi* (5.6), with ten pitches up ramps and corners; ten-pitch *Rampenfuhre* (5.6) on the right side; and the elegant and exposed twelve-pitch *Abram* (5.7 A0 or 5.10d) up the far right. Pian Schiavaneis, a controversial crag with manufactured routes, hides in a beautiful alpine cirque on the west side of the Sella Group.

More cliffs are in Val di Fassa and its side valleys. The oldest and best known are in lovely Val di Sèn Nicolò east of the village Meida. This spectacular *klettergarten* features bolted crags that range from boulders to 700-foot walls. Find beta, topos, and directions to the Val di Fassa areas in the local guidebook.

Besides the cragging areas, the Dolomites offer thousands of multipitch routes up the peaks. The following are a few suggestions to start. Remember that weather, temperature, season, and snow conditions can impact your route choice. The north-facing routes are usually shady but can be wet, requiring several warm days to dry out. The south-facing routes are sunny and dry. It's best to come with a short to-climb list and then revise the list depending on what's in condition.

Ask the local guides what might be good for the season. Many climbers come and hire a guide, at least for a couple days, to get their feet wet on one of the longer easy classics and to get acquainted with the area. Not a bad idea if you want to maximize your Dolomite time. Lots of English-speaking certified guides are found in the area.

The Gruppo di Sella or Sella Group in the western Dolomites is one of the most popular climbing areas. Approaches from the roads are generally short, the climbing is varied and beautiful, and the massif's mountains, faces, and cirques are stunning. An astounding number of routes lace the numerous walls, leaving the visiting climber agape with the selection.

Some of the best, most popular, and easiest accessed routes ascend the Sella Towers or Sellaturms, a group of spiked towers and mountains towering east of Sella Pass. Many superb and recommended routes ascend these towers. A great adventure is traversing the First, Second, and Third Towers via the *Stegar Route* (5.7) on the First Sella Tower (Erster Sellaturm in German), the *Kostner Route* (5.4) on the Second Sella Tower (Zweiter Sellaturm), and *Jahn Route* (5.5) on the Third Sella Tower (Dritter Sellaturm). The seven-pitch *Stegar* is an elegant ridge and face climb up the west side of the First Tower. After summitting, scramble down the descent, and climb the superlative four-pitch *Kostner* up the sunny south face of the Second Tower, finishing up an airy dihedral. Scramble down again to a notch below the huge southwest face of the Third Tower. Finish the long day by climbing seven excellent pitches up *Jahn,* a 1918 route, on the exposed wall to the tower summit. Then there's the exhilarating descent—a complex downclimb of the *Normal Route (Normalweg)* on exposed but easy rock (if you're on route), followed by five rappels. This alpine traverse yields eighteen technical pitches, along with lots of scrambling, and a couple thousand feet of downclimbing and rappels. Go ahead and sleep in the next day—you've earned the rest! These routes are also good single-day climbs.

On the west side of Passo Sella is Sasso Lungo, another massif of peaks and glaciated cirques, and the adjoining Sasso Piatto. These obvious mountains tower north of Campitello and Canazei in upper Val di Fassa. More excellent classics ascend these peaks. One of the best traverses is the Punta delle Cinque Dita, a small uplift of sharp pointed peaks in Sasso Lungo. The entire traverse makes a long day, with eighteen pitches of climbing (never harder than 5.6), a half a dozen rappels, and lots of down climbing. The route highlight is swinging up an exposed knife-edged ridge on The Thumb, a sparsely protected pitch with big holds.

Northeast of Cortina is the spectacular Tre Cime di Lavaredo, the most famous Dolomite peaks. The Tre Cima or Three Peaks (Drei Zinnen in German) are renowned for their stunning and epic routes up the vertical north faces, a place for airy free climbing in an alpine setting. First scope out the routes up these massive limestone peaks. A fantastic climb for a strong party is Emilio Comici's *Spigolo Giallo* (The Yellow Edge), a 1,200-foot-long, south-facing, vertical nine-pitch line that is mostly 5.8 and 5.9 up a magnificent arête on Cima Piccola. Other famous climbs include the 1933 fifteen-pitch *Comici Route* (5.10c) directly up the intimidating North Face of the Cima Grande, Comici's *Gelbe Kante* (5.10a) on Cima Piccola, and the *Hans Dülfer Route* (5.8) up the West Face of Cima Grande. Climb it, and you'll be humbled knowing it was first done in 1913. Two other good ones are *Dibona* (5.7), an eighteen-pitch extravaganza on Cima Grande, and *Mosca Chimneys* (5.4) on the South Face.

This Dolomite subrange, protected in Parco Naturale delle Dolomiti di Sesto, offers beautiful mountain scenery. On rest days you can scramble below the faces, sunbathe on boulders, and break out binoculars to watch climbers grappling above. A great hike circumnavigates the towers, with an overnight stay in the excellent Rifugio Locatelli hut near Tre Cima. The trails and routes are very busy in August. Get to the base at the crack of dawn to have a crack at being first on the rock. Three high huts—Auronzo, Lavaredo, or Locatelli—serve as good base camps for the cliffs.

This is a basic primer to the Dolomites. So many cliffs. So little time. Come and climb these, then discover other hidden peaks to add to your life tick list. Suggestions include the Tofana de Rozes Group, the huge walls on Marmolada, the excellent Civetta Group, the marvelous Vajolet Towers, the Catinaccio Group, and of course the wild and scenic Brenta Dolomites west of Bolzano. When you climb here, you'll always find new faces and peaks that speak to you. Let that be your inspiration.

Rack, Protection, and Descent

Most of the described routes are bolted sport climbs, so all you need is a rack of ten to fifteen quickdraws and a 200-foot (60-meter) rope. The multipitch routes at Cinque Torri, especially the older classics, are not sewn up with bolts, although some used by the local guides are well bolted. For these routes bring a basic rack with sets of Stoppers and TCUs, a selection of mostly small and medium Friends or Camalots, a fistful of runners, and twelve quickdraws.

You can usually climb and rappel with a single 200-foot (60-meter) rope, although many climbers prefer bringing a couple 8.8-mm or 9-mm cords and climbing with British double-rope technique. The advantage is that you lessen rope drag on wandering pitches and quicken rappel descents. If you plan on scaling the longer mountain routes, then double ropes are your best bet.

Bring and use a helmet. Many areas, particularly Cinque Torri, are busy with climbers. Those above you are not always careful, and rocks are regularly dislodged by carelessness or by their rope. This is an alpine area, with snow, ice, and frost wedging liberating boulders and cobbles throughout the year. It's also important to wear a helmet when belaying at the cliff base. Other useful gear on long routes are a headlamp, a lightweight fleece, a wool hat, and proper rainwear.

Remember that all the YDS American grades are translations of French and UIAA grades commonly used in the Dolomites. Consider the European grade as the more accurate rating.

Descent off most routes is by lowering or rappelling from bolt anchors. The rappels are never longer than 100 feet, so a 200-foot (60-meter) rope is adequate. Tie a knot in the end on long rappels. The most complicated descent is off Torre Grande. Carefully read the descent information, then study the formation so you can find the rappels, downclimbs, and traverses on the descent. It's not difficult

Ivo Gamper on *Linea Mortale* (8b/c) (5.13b/c) at Pian Schiavaneis.

to follow the descent since the rock is polished. If you have difficulty, ask a local climber, or follow another party down.

Seasons and Weather

The Dolomite climbing season runs from May through October, with the best and driest weather in July and August. Summer is, as the Italians say, absolutely *magnifico,* with sunny mornings, afternoon thunder-storms, and calm weather systems. The season shoulders, May and October, can be unstable, with the possibility of snow and rain.

The lower-elevation crags tend to be in shape and drier sooner than the higher ones, although the south-facing cliffs at Cinque Torri are climbable all year. These crags offer more dependable weather than the mountain routes, making them ideal if you're stormed off the big climbs. The disadvantage to August is that it's crammed with not only Italians but other Europeans who swarm over the cliffs, queue up for *via ferratas,* and throng the hiking trails during their monthlong holiday.

Even on the most benign summer days, toss a rain parka into your pack in case an afternoon thunderstorm parks over your crag. Quick-drying clothes are also a good bet, rather than heavy, slow-drying cotton garments. If you're climbing the mountain routes, pack warm clothes, because the alpine weather is fickle and cold. Snow or sleet can fall anywhere and anytime in the higher elevations through the summer.

Climbing History

The Dolomites, one of Europe's oldest areas, played a major role in rock climbing. Here climbing techniques and equipment evolved to meet the vertical challenges. Pitons, *etriers* or aid stirrups, and specialized footwear were developed to safeguard early climbers on the peaks. Whole books are written about the Dolomites climbing history, so the following is a brief summary of the highlights and characters that developed the range.

The first climbers here were undoubtedly the early people who inhabited the fertile valleys. Evidence that they roamed high into the mountains was confirmed after the 1991 discovery of Ötzi, the mummified ice man discovered in the Similaun glacier in northern Italy, just meters from the Austrian border. The man died on the glacier some 5,000 years ago and was buried by snow and ice before melting snow exhumed his remains, which are now displayed at a Bolzano museum.

Modern climbing began in the Dolomites in 1856 when two British friends, Josiah Gilbert and George Churchill, explored the region as part of a "Grand Tour." They climbed several peaks over the next few years and published the classic book *The Dolomite Mountains* detailing their exploits. John Ball, another English climber, inaugurated the Dolomites into a golden era of alpinism in 1857 with his remarkable ascent of Pelmo. Over the next forty years, numerous climbers ascended most of the major

peaks. Austrian Paul Grohmann with area guides scaled many summits, including Marmolada in 1865 and Tofâna di Mezzo in 1863.

The Cinque Torri, described in an Italian tourist brochure as "a small kingdom of sharp spires," attracted lots of attention. The North Face of Torre Grande was climbed in 1880 by C. G. Wall and Cortina guide G. Ghedina, and the South Face was reached by L. Trepton and guide Sepp Innerkofler in 1892. Torre Inglese was climbed in 1901, and the Romana, del Barancio, and Lusy towers were climbed by area guides between 1911 and 1914.

The great peak of Monte Civetta was initially climbed by unknown parties before the turn of the twentieth century and was nicknamed "L'Università dell'Alpinismo" or the University of Alpinism. Its big northwest wall was first opened in 1895 by Englishmen John Pillimore and Arthur Raynor, accompanied by guides Antonio Dimain and G. Siorpaès on the route *Via Degli Inglesi.* In 1925 Emil Solleder and Gusta Lettembauer pushed a classic line up the center of the face. The route, the first known Grade VI climb in the Dolomites, was *a goccia cadente* (a falling drop) route since it was a *directissima.*

Later pioneers established classic passages up the Dolomite walls, including Emilio Comici and Ricardo Cassin. These skilled and brave climbers opened the doors to harder gymnastic climbing by exploring the realm of the possible. You will be impressed by their ability and nerve when you come and climb these old established routes.

Except for Cinque Torri, route development at the lower-elevation cliffs began in the 1970s as climbers wanted more practice to improve technique and proficiency. The Scioattoli climbing group in Cortina was important in finding, equipping, and climbing many crags. They generally opened new routes on sunny cliffs with solid rock and a wide variety of grades. Likewise, the proximity of Val di Fassa to the La Sportiva shoe factory farther down the valley led to climbers, including the great Hans Mariacher and

Luisa Jovane, exploring new crags in Val Di Sèn Nicolò and farther afield in Erto. New route activity still continues throughout the region, with new crags opened every year.

Getting Around

Your own car is essential for a fulfilling Dolomite experience. The range is vast and complex, with difficult, time-consuming travel across deep valleys, high passes, and higher mountains. The climbing areas are scattered throughout the region, making it necessary to use your own wheels to find the sites. Public transportation exists, but if you rely on buses to get around, then much precious time will be spent figuring out bus schedules, waiting for the bus, and walking long distances to the crag. Hitchhiking is perhaps easier, but you're at the mercy of drivers in small cars. It's easier and more time efficient to set up a base camp in one of the surrounding towns and then motor out every day to different areas.

Some climbers fly into Munich, Innsbruck, or Milan and buy a train pass that allows them to ride the rails to the larger Dolomite towns like Bolzano, Trento, Cortina d'Ampezzo, or Belluno. Reserve a car ahead of time at the train stations, pick it up when you arrive, and hit the road to the mountains. If you're only traveling in Italy, it's cheaper not to purchase a Eurail or Inter-Rail pass since Italian fares are relatively inexpensive.

It's imperative that you acquire a detailed Dolomite road map, otherwise it's easy to get lost or sidetracked in the maze of roads. Maps with sufficient detail are almost impossible to find in the United States but easy to locate in Italy. Check the local tourist office first for a free area map. The main offices in Trento and Bolzano stock reams of practical information, updated accommodation lists, and maps. Otherwise, look in area bookstores or climbing shops.

The roads and highways are generally paved and in good condition, although they have no shoulders and boast as many curves as a swimsuit model. Highways are extremely busy during the summer, so focus your complete attention on driving to avoid accidents. You share the road with other drivers, including Italian speed demons in red Ferraris who treat the winding roads as personal Le Mans courses, middle-aged couples out Sunday driving, creeping tourists unsure of their direction, huge tour buses that hog most of the road, bicyclists out for a 100-kilometer spin over a few passes, and, of course, the ubiquitous German motorcycle riders decked out in black leather suits. Groups of motorcycles roar along the highways, traveling en masse between pubs and cafes. It's usually best to slow and wave them past. The funny thing is that later, at the top of a pass, you see those same riders, without helmets, sipping a latte, smoking a cigarette, and looking exactly like the accountants, teachers, and software designers that they are in real life in Munich.

Driving in the Dolomites and the rest of Italy is not ordered and polite as in Britain. Drivers are aggressive, fast, forceful, and always take the right-of-way. As a visitor, yield to avoid problems. Petrol is expensive and widely available. Parking is never an issue since most villages have free parking. Car crime is not a big problem, but you still need to be vigilant, especially when leaving your vehicle in remote areas. Gangs of thieves canvas the area in summer and break into cars. Do like the locals and leave nothing of value, open the glove box, and remove the luggage hatch. It's safer to leave valuables locked in your tent back at a secure campsite or ask your campground host if they have a safebox to stash them.

Lastly, distances are not what they seem on the map. It's very time intensive to drive around this rugged area where a trip of a dozen kilometers might include 200 turns and switchbacks, 2,000 feet of elevation gain and loss, and passage through three small villages. It's best to take your time, enjoy the view, and drive safely.

Camping, Accommodations, and Services

The popular Dolomites offer a wealth of accommodation choices that include a multitude of campgrounds, refuges, hotels, and guesthouses. It's best to pick a village near the climbing areas and set up base camp there. Most long routes and visits to other crags are easily done in day trips with a car. To climb on the other side of the range, it's easier to move to another village closer to those cliffs. Stay at Canazei or another village in Val di Fassa or Val Gardena if you plan on climbing in Sella Gruppo or other parts of the western Dolomites. If climbing at Tre Cime di Lavaredo or mountains in the east, then it's better to base around the famous resort of Cortina d'Ampezzo. It's time-consuming to bunk in Cortina and drive to Sella for a day's climbing, particularly if the roads are busy. And forget about staying in the bigger towns like Trento or Bolzano expecting to drive to the mountains every day, because that drive gets old real fast.

The best places to stay are in the extensive and well-organized network of mountain huts or *rifugi* spread across the Dolomites. There are few climbing sites that do not have a nearby hut. The *rifugi*, typically open from July through September, range in style from a basic but comfortable hostel with dorm rooms to lavish digs with double rooms. As a rule the refuges closer to a chairlift, cable car, or road are more expensive and more crowded with tourists than those at higher elevations reached by hiking. These remote locations are used only by serious hikers, mountaineers, and rock climbers. The pricey *rifugi* offer tasty but costly meals. If you're planning on spending much time and want to save cash, then bring a stove and cook some meals.

It's important to book a bed ahead of time, especially in August, or you might show up at the *rifugio* and be out of luck. In that case you might have to hike a couple hours to the next one with openings. Phone numbers for a few refuges near Cinque Torri are in the Appendix; otherwise, ask for telephone numbers at the local tourist offices, or visit the Club Alpino Italiano (CAI) Web site at www.cai.it/rifugi for more information. Expect to pay between $20 and $40 per person each night.

If you're climbing at Cinque Torri, then the two nearby refuges—Rifugio Cinque Torri and Rifugio Scoiattoli—are recommended. A short walk away is the Colazione hut, an excellent refuge with modern, wood-paneled rooms, showers, and wonderful food and views.

Lots of accommodations are found at fashionable Cortina d'Ampezzo, Italy's answer to Aspen or Vail. This resort town is well equipped with hotels, including some surprisingly reasonable ones in low season. Ask at the tourist office for recommendations, or try Cavallino, Hotel Montana, or Pensione Fiames just north of town. The International Camping Olympia is a good campground.

Valzoldana, 20 kilometers south of Cortina, is quieter and cheaper than its illustrious neighbor. It's also close to the spectacular Civetta Group. You'll find lots of places to stay here, including good hotels and the Rifugio Casera di Bosconero.

Canazei and surrounding villages in the beautiful Val di Fassa are a good base for exploring the excellent Sella Group, the spiked peaks of Sasso Lungo, Val di Sèn Nicolò, and Marmolada, the highest peak in the Dolomites. Lots of hotels are found in the valley, a popular ski resort. Again, ask at the tourist office in Canazei for recommendations. Campgrounds are in Canazei and Campitello, a couple kilometers to the west. The Campitello site is quieter and has spacious tent sites by a river.

Many *rifugi* scatter around Gruppo di Sella, including the roadside Rifugio Monti Pallidi near the Pian Schiavaneis cliff, Rifugio Passo Sella just west of the pass summit, and the beautifully situated Rifugio Demetz-Hütte below the Sasso Lungo peaks, as well as several remote refuges tucked into the Sella backcountry. If you're climbing at Frea or the north part of Gruppo di Sella, a good hut with an enchanting view is Rifugio Passo Gardena atop the pass.

The third base camp area is beautiful Val Gardena in the northwest part of the Dolomites. This is a popular ski area in winter, so lots of hotels and *garni* or B&Bs are found, although many are not open in summer. Stop in any village and ask about local accommodations and camping.

No camping outside of established campgrounds is allowed in the Dolomites.

A climber pulls up strenuous *Fulminetor* (8+) (5.13c) on the Massi boulders below Cima Grande.

Like elsewhere in Europe there are no public campgrounds on public lands, only private ones. Most are fairly expensive, although camping is cheaper than staying in hotels or even refuges. Climbers do bivouac in the mountains, sometimes at the base of their next day's climb. This is technically illegal but a generally accepted and necessary practice.

Food and Drink

The Dolomite populace are reluctant Italians since most are Germanic descent, with almost 70 percent speaking German rather than Italian. The area was once South Tirolo or *Südtirol,* an Austrian province, until ceded to Italy after World War I. The food here, a mingling of Teutonic and Latin cultures, is very different from what Americans consider typical Italian fare and flavors. Even within the Dolomites' two provinces of Alto Adige and Trentino, significant gastronomic variations are found in the two cuisines.

The Alto Adige offers an Austro-Tyrolean cooking that is heavy on *wursts,* potatoes, cabbage, hearty rye bread, and dumpling soups. In short, food that is easy to cook from local ingredients in a relatively harsh environment with long winters and a short growing season. Main food elements include pork, rye, wheat, and dairy. The province of Trentino immediately south offers a mixed cuisine of Italo-Venetian cooking with an emphasis on polenta and pasta accented by alpine foods like butter, cheese, mushrooms, and game.

The famed specialty of Alto Adige is smoked meat, particularly *speck,* a boneless smoked pork. Speck is a basic part of the Dolomite diet and is only now being produced commercially. The best speck, of course, is homemade and comes from the rich variety and tradition of family secrets, recipes, and preparations. Pigs are slaugh-tered in February, and the best and leanest pork is diced into small chunks and placed in saltpeter along with spices and herbs that include garlic, juniper, pepper, and laurel, along with secret family herbs. It's then hung in a smokehouse and gently smoked for a few hours a day for five or six months. It's served in thin slices for breakfast, as an antipasto, or a snack.

The Dolomites are well known for excellent cheeses, including goat's milk *Ziegenkäse,* mild *Pusteria,* and sharp *Graukäse.* All of which make a fine mountain lunch with a thick wedge of dark rye bread. A delicious gourmet cheese, if you can find it, is *formaggio grigio,* made from unpasteurized milk in Val Pusteria. The area is also Italy's leading apple producer. These are particularly tasty in thick *strudel* as well as in apple fritters called *Apfel-küchel.*

Traditional dishes include *knödeln* or *canederli,* hefty bread dumplings laced with bits of liver or speck; *spätzli,* a small dumpling topped with melted gorgonzola cheese; wholesome soups with barley and tripe; peppery *Rindsgulasch* or goulash; *Sauerbraten,* a pot roast made with wine, vinegar, and onions; *testina di vitello* or lamb intestines; and wild game dishes like venison, brook trout, and *polenta e coniglio* or rabbit with polenta. My favorite local dish is ravioli stuffed with mashed pear and gorgonzola.

Southern Trentino serves food with a definite Italian flair, although the northern cooking influences are still strong. Trentino offers excellent fish, mushrooms, cabbage, and potatoes, and its famed wines including merlot and pinot grigio. A basic food is polenta, an Italian cornmeal usually enriched with other grains. Trento, the provincial capital between the Dolomites and Arco, has a famed market that sells more than 250 different mushroom varieties. This is the place to order superb *Risotto ai funghi,* a risotto pasta with strong and tasty *brisa* mushrooms. Trentino's desserts are also wonderful. Look for *Fregolotta* cake in the bakeries for a crunchy almond treat.

Lots of restaurants are found in the Dolomites. Unfortunately, finding quality dining is a hit-or-miss situation, with many establishments catering to tourism and skiing. The smaller villages away from the resort business offer better value for your money. Besides traditional foods, which can admittedly be coarse and heavy, you'll be able to eat great pizza and pasta dishes. Most refuges serve up hearty meals with lots of food at a good price. Those close to chairlifts and ski areas are pricey, especially for a mug of beer or glass of wine.

If you're camping or want food for lunch and nibbling, then you'll find groceries, bakeries, and shops. The larger towns offer better selections and prices. Shop where the locals shop, and you won't go wrong. Remember that most grocery stores shutter the doors on Saturday afternoon and don't reopen until Monday morning. On other days they close by 5:00 or 6:00 P.M., so be prepared by purchasing food in the morning if you'll be out climbing all afternoon.

Cultural Experiences and Rest Days

The Trentino-Alto Adige region stretches along the rugged border of Austria and northern Italy. This stunning landscape offers lots besides climbing for the intrepid visitor. The area, relying on a tourist economy, is renowned for its superb and varied hiking adventures, which are among the best in the Alps. The trails range from relaxing half-day strolls across undulating meadows to strenuous hikes up peaks and ridges.

The Dolomite trails are well marked and easy to follow. Painted bands on trees and rocks along the route mark the trail, whereas others are designated with colored triangles. The local tourist offices have maps with the popular trails and *rifugi*. Lots of great trails surround the climbing areas. Some of the best are in the Sella Group, Sasso Lungo, the lovely mountains bordering Val de Sèn Nicolò, the Cortina area, the Alpe di Suisi, and the western Brenta Dolomites. The four Alta Vie or High Trails, taking about two weeks each to hike, are of particular interest to many walkers who ramble the linked trails and stay in huts along the way.

Other outdoor activities are mountain biking, road biking, and parasailing. The local tourist offices can point you toward biking trails and bike rentals. The area is famous for road biking, with many challenging rides over the high passes. You won't come in winter to rock climb, but the skiing is awesome, with plenty of slopes of all levels.

The Dolomites are not one of Italy's great cultural areas. Most villages tend to cater to the tourist and ski industry so they're fairly nondescript, with blocks of hotels and condos rather than cute chalets. Spend some time, though, driving around the region and gawking at the mountain massifs. The views from every pass are spectacular and different. Also visit the La Sportiva factory and outlet store in Ziano di Fiemme in Val di Fiemme. The hard-to-find factory is in an industrial complex on the south side of the village. Ask for directions.

Besides the German and Italian ethnic groups, the Ladino culture is a third group that hides in the Dolomite valleys. This small population speaks Ladin, an ancient language originating from Latin. The minority lives in valleys below the Sella massif, including Val di Fassa, Val Gardena, Val Badia, and Val Pusteria. It's worth visiting the Ladin Cultural Institute and adjoining Museum Ladino di Fassa in Val di Fassa to understand this unique and ancient living culture.

For other cultural experiences it's best to go downhill to either of the provincial capitals Trento or Bolzano.

Trento is an ancient city with beautiful cathedrals and buildings. Visit the cathedral and Palazzo Pretorio at Piazza del Duomo plaza; the Museo Diocesano with its religious artifacts; the Museo Tridentino di Scienze Naturali science museum; and the impressive Museo di Arte Moderna e Contemporanea, a modern art museum. The Trento area is also filled with enchanting castles overlooking peaks and valleys.

Bolzano is well worth the drive over the mountains. This Austrian-feeling city is a pleasant city with a historic center and peaceful ambience. It's good to park outside the city center and ramble around. Gothic architecture abounds, including the cathedral. The most fascinating display is at the South Tirol Museum of Archeology where Ötzi, the famed "ice man" is displayed. This forty-five-year-old hunter disappeared from his village some 5,300 years ago, after trekking into the Alps near the Italian-Austrian border. He died on a glacier in leather clothes, wrapped in his woven reed, fur-lined cape, with a pouch containing an axe, flint knives, tools, and a fire-starter kit. Snow covered him, and he was mummified. Forensic analysis indicates he was wounded in the back by an arrow, possibly in a fight, before dying. Now he is displayed in a climate-controlled chamber. In the museum's gift shop you can purchase an assortment of Ötzi souvenirs, including baseball caps, T-shirts, and postcards. Nearby shops sell Ötzi ice cream and iced tea, as well as Ötziwein beer with his image on the label.

Trip Planning Information

General description: A selection of the best lower-elevation crags in the Dolomites, including the famous Cinque Torri towers.

Location: Northern Italy. The Dolomites are a sky-scraping mountain range composed of many smaller massifs in Trentino and Alto Adige provinces.

Camping and accommodations: It's best to base out of a specific area and then explore the nearby mountains. Almost every town or village offers a campground. If you don't camp, the Dolomites have many *rifugi* or mountain huts scattered over the massifs. A good one is below Cinque Torri. Since this is a tourist area, lots of hotels, *garni* or bed and breakfast inns, and other accommodations are found. Ask at any of the local tourist offices for recommendations, addresses, and phone numbers.

Climbing season: June through September is best. The weather is often unpredictable in this mountainous region. Expect a mixture of sunny days interspersed with cool, rainy days. Summer temperatures range from 50 to 80 degrees, with cool mornings. In September it can snow in the higher elevations. Be prepared for sudden changes in the weather. Rain drops the temperature as much as twenty degrees. Bring rain gear every day, regardless of the morning weather.

Restrictions and access issues: No restrictions at any of the described crags. Like everywhere else, adopt a sensitive, environment-friendly consciousness to keep these special climbing areas clean and unaltered by your passage. These rules should be followed: Pick up all trash; dispose of human waste properly (best to pack out your toilet tissue in a plastic ziplock baggie rather than burying it under a rock); follow existing trails wherever possible, but especially across fragile alpine tundra; park in pullouts, not along the grassy road shoulder; refrain from smoking or lighting fires; and don't disturb nesting birds, cut vegetation or trees, or

remove any bolts or hangers. Some areas are sometimes closed for nesting raptors, including eagles and owls.

Guidebooks: Several books are available. *Arrampicata Sportiva a Cortina d'Ampezzo* by Roberto Casanova is a good guide to crags around Cortina. It also has sections in English. *Klettern in Groden Dolomiten* by Mauro Bernardi is a good German guide to many long routes as well as sport areas in the central Dolomites.

Services and shops: Climbing stores are scattered across the region in all the main towns, including Bolzano, Trento, Cortina, and Canazei. The La Sportiva factory store, offering some good shoe deals, is in Val di Fiemme near Cavalese. All services and supplies are easily available throughout this popular mountain area.

Emergency services: Dial 112 for all emergency services.

Nearby climbing areas: Besides the described areas, there are many sport and trad crags throughout the Dolomites, as well as thousands of technical mountain routes. Some of the other bolted crags are Busc dl Preve, with twelve easy and moderate routes; Sas dala Piera Ciauda, with routes from 6c to 7a; Ta Refosch, with routes 6c to 7a; the excellent wall of Cansla near Frea, with many great multipitch routes from 6c to 8a+ (best are on Traumpfeiler wall); and many small blocks and bolted boulders at Steinerne Stadt on the north side of Passo Sella. A small roadside crag is just east of Canazei and Penia on the road to Marmolada. The well-bolted cliff is on the left just past the river Avisio.

Near Cortina are Sass Dlacia, a good sport area with a big wall and an overhanging buttress; Bèco d'Ajàl, with many overhanging pillars; Sasso di Colfiere, a small block of steep limestone; sunny San Bodo; Crèpe de Oucèra Alti, the higher companion to the described cliff below; Campo e Volpèra, a good area near Cortina with many 5.10s; and Són Póuses, a fine crag in the beautiful Natural Park of the Ampezzo Dolomites.

Val di Sèn Nicolo near the village of Meida in the Val di Fassa has excellent sport cliffs with lots of routes established in the 1980s. The valley's vertical face Maerins (picnic area on the right side) has several excellent sectors with lots of bolts.

Another small crag is in Val de Sèn Pelegrin near Ronchi. The south-facing limestone face offers more than twenty sport routes.

Farther afield is the excellent summer crag of Erto near Longarone. Hans Mariacher in *Climbing Magazine* calls it some of "the best overhang climbing in Italy." Expect steep pumpy routes, including Luca Zardini's *The Big Mother,* weighing in at 5.14c. Nearby is the No-Big Sector, with easier slab routes.

Lumignano is an important area, with beautiful limestone and many technical routes on its huge cliff. It's a few kilometers south of Vicenza.

Italian guidebooks are available to all these areas but are very difficult to find anywhere but in the Dolomites or the immediate vicinity of the cliffs. Good crag hunting!

Nearby attractions: There are lots of attractions near Trento and Bolzano, including museums, castles, and interesting architecture. Check the above "Cultural Experiences and Rest Days" section for suggestions and more information. It's also good to drive around the Dolomites to get a full view of the mountain massifs and spectacular scenery.

Finding the area: The closest international airports are in Milan and Innsbruck, Austria. It's easiest to approach the Dolomites from the big north-south A22 *autostrada*. Both Bolzano and Trento, the two major cities in the area, are along the highway. Several highways head into the mountains from the A22. The S48 highway runs up to Val di Fassa, and the S242 goes up Val Gardena. Cortina d'Ampezzo, on the east side of the range, can be accessed from the south and Belluno via the S51 highway. Purchase a comprehensive road map to find your way around this complex region.

Cinque Torri

The Cinque Torri or Five Towers is a superb and popular group of five spires perched high on a mountain ridge west of Cortina d'Ampezzo. This is one of the best places to sport climb in the Dolomites, although be in your best form to keep up with the stylish Italian climbers. Besides offering great climbing, the Cinque Torri is also good to visit if you have nonclimbers in your bunch since the area hiking is spectacularly beautiful. A convenient refuge on the slope below the towers is an excellent place to stay overnight or to eat a meal.

The towers, at 7,500 feet, straddle a grassy ridge above timberline on the eastern slopes of Mount Nuvolau. The area, despite its high elevation, offers relatively good weather in comparison to the surrounding mountains. Climbing is possible on most days since you can usually find sunny faces out of the wind.

The towers are composed of principal dolomite, a variety of pale limestone with thin horizontal strata that often fractures along vertical planes, perpendicular to the strata. This characteristic gives the towers their unique blocky appearance. The blocky east-facing cliffs tend to be colored yellow, be vertical to overhanging, and have horizontal edges and holds. These faces are out of the rain and dry quickly after storms. The north- and west-facing cliffs receive more precipitation, so they're gray with black streaks. These faces are usually solid, with lots of pockets and holes from water erosion, and dry more slowly than the other faces.

The area is complex at first glance, but if you eyeball the towers and take a quick hike around, the layout is easier to understand. Torre Grande, the biggest tower, sits on the ridge crest on the south side of the towers. It's divided into three distinct peaks—Cima Sud, Cima Nord, and Cima Ovest—separated by deep notches.

The second tower, northeast of Grande, is also divided into three peaks—Torre Romana, Torre del Barancio, and Torre Lusy.

The third-highest tower, Torre Latina, sits northwest of Grande and is divided into two fractured blocks.

The fourth tower lies north and downhill from Grande. It is split into two towers—Torre Quarta Alta and Torre Quarta Bassa. Torre di Mezzo or Middle Tower is a small pinnacle on the south side of Torre Quarta Alta.

The fifth tower, Torre Inglese, lies northwest of Quarta Alta and is the northernmost and lowest tower. It's further divided into two pinnacles.

On the northeast side of the massif is a jumble of smaller, mostly insignificant formations except for Torre Trephor. This large rock has an excellent west face for climbers.

The last formations are Massi, a group of three immense boulders below the west face of Torre Grande, and Sasso Cubico, a large round boulder below the Cima Nord face of Torre Grande. Both boulder groups have short, hard sport routes on steep faces.

The Cinque Torri offers almost 200 routes from one to eight pitches long.

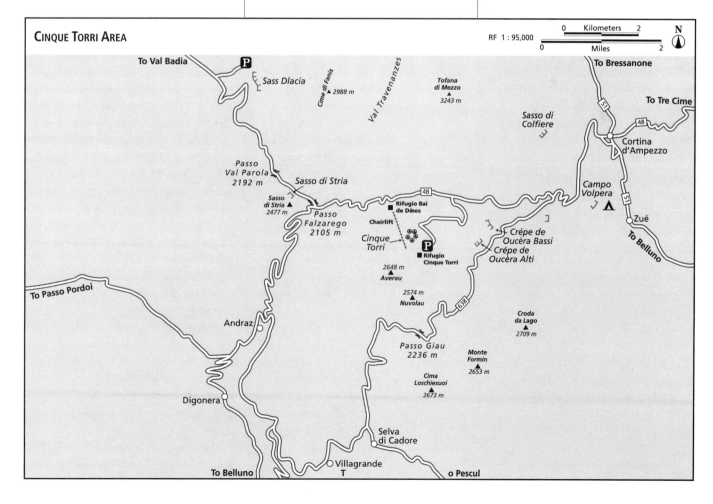

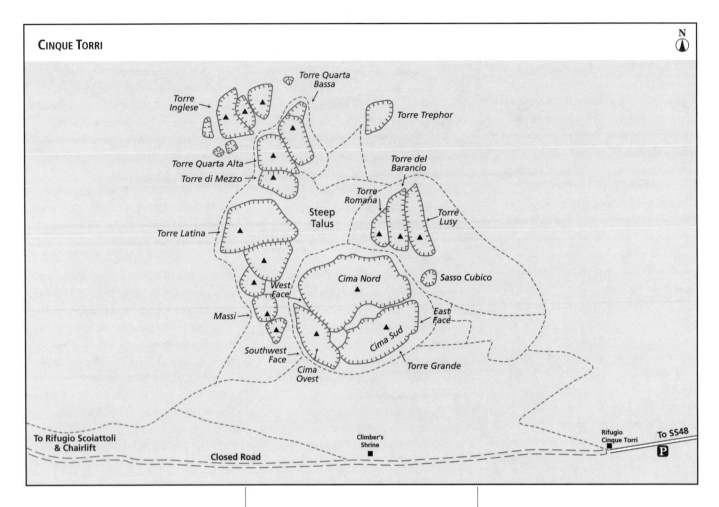

Many excellent moderate classic lines ascend the towers, making this a fun area to visit. Most routes, especially the modern lines, are well equipped with bolts, or *spits* in Italian. Not all the classics are equipped with bolts, although most have secure bolted belays.

If you plan on climbing more than single-pitch sport lines, bring a standard alpine rack with sets of Stoppers, TCUs, Friends, and hexes. Hexcentric nuts work perfectly in many Dolomite placements. Also bring a couple of ropes to ease rappelling, although you can do all rappels with a 200-foot rope. Double ropes are good to carry if you plan on doing the longer Dolomite routes since these lines can wander. Double-rope technique helps you avoid rope drag.

Descent off most of the towers is by rappelling from bolt anchors. The anchors are usually visible on the small towers. Torre Grande is tricky to descend. The descent route involves some downclimbing, route-finding difficulties, and rappels. If you're there when it's busy, local

climbers can help you on the descent, or you can follow them down. Use extreme caution on the descent since lots of loose rock is encountered, and it would be deadly to knock any onto parties below.

Likewise, be very aware and cautious at the base of the faces since rocks fall off from gravity, weathering, and careless climbers. Bring and wear a helmet when belaying at the cliff base and when climbing. Also watch out for dangerous lightning strikes on all of the towers during electrical storms. Be aware of impending bad weather, and do your best to either retreat from your route or begin the descent from the summit to avoid becoming a lightning target.

One of the best parts of climbing at Cinque Torri is the close proximity of two mountain huts—Rifugio Cinque Torri below the rocks and Rifugio Scoiattoli at the top of the chairlift to the west. Both offer food and shelter in the summer and autumn. Get there early or make reservations because they are often full.

Finding the cliffs: Cinque Torri lies west of Cortina d'Ampezzo in the eastern Dolomites. The access road can be reached from several directions—from Cortina to the east, Passo di Falzarego to the west, and Passo Giau to the southwest. From either Cortina or Passo di Falzarego, drive on highway SS48 to a road on the south at kilometer 112.200 post. Drive up this steep, winding, paved, single-lane road for a couple miles until you can park along the road shoulder or in several small lots before the Rifugio Cinque Torri hut below the towers.

This road is usually snow-free by early May and stays open until the end of October. It is extremely busy, especially on weekends, holidays, and during the August vacation period. Watch for oncoming traffic on the narrow road, and look for places to pull over to pass. Parking is very difficult to impossible at times. Traffic and parking restrictions are in force during August.

In August or on busy weekends it's best and easiest to park a couple kilometers west of the road turnoff at kilometer 110 on highway SS48. Turn and drive up to Rifugio Bai de Dònes and park. Take the chairlift up the mountain slope to Rifugio Scoiattoli just west of Cinque Torri. The chairlift is open from July through early September and during the winter, when it is the only way to reach the cliffs.

Torre Grande—Cima Sud

Torre Grande, the largest formation in Cinque Torri, is the most popular tower, with many classic multipitch routes as well as lots of shorter sport lines. The tower, split by chimney and crack systems, divides into three separate peaks—Cima Nord (North), Cima Sud (South), and Cima Ovest (West). Routes are described on each peak and their respective faces. Some route names are painted at the route base.

Cima Sud is the large, flat-summited, south peak of Torre Grande. Routes ascend both its southwest and east faces. The peak is divided from Cima Ovest by a large, broken chimney and gully system on the southwest, and from Cima Nord by a wide chimney that cleaves the east face.

The descent off the peak requires route finding and downclimbing. Watch for loose rock! It's easy to knock it off onto climbing parties below you. It's possible to downclimb the entire formation, but most choose to rappel down the gully on the north side. From the summit begin by scrambling down easy rock to the southwest to a ledge with lots of belay anchors. Facing toward the wall follow the ledge left. Eventually you reach a ramp, which you descend. Continue down right and through a tunnel to the base of a steep gully on the north side of Torre Grande. This last section can be avoided by rappelling from anchors.

For sport routes bring a rack of quickdraws and a 200-foot (60-meter) rope. For longer, classic routes, bring a set of Stoppers and a selection of small to medium Friends, some quickdraws, and a 200-foot (60-meter) rope. A helmet is necessary on the crowded classics.

Routes are described from left to right, beginning at the blocks and chimneys on the southwest face that separate it from Cima Ovest.

Southwest Face

1. Thomas (6a) (5.10a) Sport route up the left side of a semifreestanding pillar right of a deep chimney on the southwest face of Cima Sud. 60 feet.

2. Agrodolce (6b) (5.10c) Up the left margin of the vertical face right of a gully. Usually only the first pitch is climbed.

3. Equipe 84 (6a+) (5.10b) 2 pitches. **Pitch 1:** Climb up and right across the face (6a+) to a belay under the roof. 75 feet. **Pitch 2:** Pull over a break through the roof (6b) to anchors on the vertical rock above. 50 feet.

4. Ramba Balù (7b+) (5.12c) Thin face climbing to anchors under the roof. 85 feet.

5. Ci Vuole un Fisico Best . . . (6b+) (5.10d) Direct up the vertical face to anchors under the big roof system. 80 feet.

6. Fandango (6c) (5.11a/b) Recommended. Good face movements up the white wall to #3's anchors. 80 feet.

7. Tommy Tom (6c) (5.11a/b) Superb climbing. Over the left side of a narrow roof, then up the white face to a roof finish. 80 feet.

8. Calippo (8a+) (5.13c) Steep stone over the lower roof, then out right of a hanging nose to anchors above. 80 feet.

9. Franceschi (6b) (5.10c) 5 pitches to the summit. Classic route. **Pitch 1:** Face climb up right along a diagonal crack system across a narrow roof (6b) to the base of a crack in a right-facing dihedral. Belay above at a stance. 82 feet. **Pitch 2:** Fun climbing up the dihedral (5+) to a belay ledge on the left. 90 feet. **Pitch 3:** Continue up the easier crack above (4+) to a large ledge. 140 feet. **Pitch 4:** Traverse right on the ledge system to a belay. **Pitch 5:** Climb easy rock (4) to the summit. 55 feet.

10. Footuk (7b) (5.12b) Edge up the pale, bolted face, over a roof, then steep rock to #9's first set of anchors at the base of the big dihedral. 80 feet.

11. Via Col Vento (6c+) (5.11c) 2 pitches. **Pitch 1:** Start up a shallow right-facing corner, then exit left and over a narrow roof (6b+). Crimp up right to belay anchors on a stance. 82 feet. **Pitch 2:** Climb the white face above the belay, then work up right (6c+) to high anchors. 90 feet.

12. Directissima Scoiattoli (6c+) (5.11c) 6 pitches. A classic *directissima* up the face and south pillar of Cima Sud. **Pitch 1:** Begin at the same place as #11. Up the corner to a narrow roof, then a long right traverse under the roof until it ends (6c+). Work above to a belay stance. 75 feet. **Pitch 2:** Edge directly up the wall (6a+) to a bolted belay. 105 feet. **Pitch 3:** Easier rock up right (4) leads to a belay ledge below a large dihedral. 65 feet. **Pitch 4:** Work up right (6a+) across the exposed face to the right edge. Airy climbing to a belay stance. 115 feet. **Pitch 5:** Edge directly up the prow of the buttress (6a) to a ledge belay. 65 feet. **Pitch 6:** Run up easy rock (4) to the summit. 65 feet.

13. Spit Express (7a+) (5.12a) 2 pitches. Start just right of #12. **Pitch 1:** Pull up the steep face past the narrow roof (6c+) to a bolted belay stance above (shared with #11). 65 feet. **Pitch 2:** Endurance climbing (7a+) up the white wall above to anchors. 100 feet. **Descent:** Rappel the route.

14. Pazzia Rock (7c+) (5.13a) Powerful climbing through bulging roofs. 65 feet.

15. Sulle ali di Dedalo (7a+) (5.12a) 3 pitches. **Pitch 1:** Muscle through bulges (6c+) to anchors. 60 feet. **Pitch 2:** Thin face climbing (7a+) up the steep wall. 66 feet. **Pitch 3:** Continue up the face (6c) to anchors. 45 feet. **Descent:** Rappel the route.

16. Nordica (6b) (5.10c) No topo. Sport pitch on the lower right side of the wall. 55 feet.

17. W lo Spot (7a) (5.11d) No topo. 3 pitches. Begin near the toe of the buttress just right of #16. **Pitch 1:** Thread

through bulges and roofs (7a) to anchors. 55 feet. **Pitch 2:** Up and left across the face (7a) to bolt anchors. 55 feet. **Pitch 3:** Easier climbing up the face (6b). 60 feet. **Descent:** Rappel the route.

18. Myriam (5) (5.8) 6 or 7 pitches. Megaclassic route up the prow and face. The route was first climbed by American Miriam O'Brien in 1927. Begin below an obvious crack system below the peak's south pillar. **Pitch 1:** Climb the crack to a face, then left into a large dihedral (5) to a belay. 125 feet. **Pitch 2:** Continue up the dihedral (4) to a belay. 65 feet. **Pitch 3:** Traverse out left across shelves (4th class) to a stance. 85 feet. **Pitch 4:** Follow cracks up left and under a big flat roof (4+). Traverse up left to a belay below a crack system. 120 feet. **Pitch 5:** Climb the crack system (5) to a belay stance. 65 feet. **Pitch 6:** Continue up the cracks (4) to a big ledge. 50 feet. **Pitch 7:** Climb moderate rock (4) to the summit. The last 2 pitches can be combined into a long lead.

East Face

The East Face of Torre Grande's Cima Sud is the wall right of the south pillar. Several excellent long routes ascend the wall, as well as a couple single-pitch sport routes. Routes are described left to right from *Myriam* to the deep chimney that splits the face and separates Cima Sud and Cima Nord.

19. Unknown (6c+) (5.11c) No topo. A long sport pitch up the wall right of *Myriam*. 80 feet.

20. Unknown (6a+) (5.10b) No topo. Sport route right of #19. 72 feet.

21. Direct Dimai (6a+) (5.10b) 8 pitches. Excellent classic adventure up the exposed left side of the face. Begin by climbing the first 2 pitches of *Myriam*. **Pitch 3:** Continue up the groove (4) to a large ledge. **Pitch 4:** Traverse left along a shelf and then up right (6a) to belay anchors. 80 feet. **Pitch 5:** A short lead up left (4) to anchors. 65 feet. **Pitch 6:** Face climbing

(5+) to anchors. 100 feet. **Pitch 7:** Crux face climbing to a horizontal break, jog left, and then back up right (6a+) to anchors. 65 feet. **Pitch 8:** Easy climbing up grooves and cracks above (3) to the summit. 150 feet.

Access the next three routes by scrambling up an easy blocky chimney below the deep splitter chimney. Scramble up left above onto a terrace below the steep face.

22. Via Delle Raponzole (6a+) (5.10b) 4 pitches. **Pitch 1:** Face climb up left and then back right on the white wall (6a+) to anchors. 80 feet. **Pitch 2:** Continue up the white wall (6a) to exposed anchors. 75 feet. **Pitch 3:** Up to a break, left a few moves, then up right on streaked rock (6-) to a belay stance. 80 feet. **Pitch 4:** Easy climbing up right to the summit. 100 feet.

23. Fessure Dimai (6a) (5.10a) 4 pitches. Interesting route up the obvious crack. **Pitch 1:** Follow a crack up left (5), then up the wide crack to belay anchors. 100 feet. **Pitch 2:** Chimney up the crack (5+) to anchors near the top. 85 feet. **Pitch 3:** Continue up the crack, which pinches down, and work up left above (6a) to a belay ledge. 100 feet. **Pitch 4:** Easier rock leads up right to the summit. 100 feet.

24. Nuova Germana (7a+) (5.12a) No topo. 2 pitches. Good route up the face left of the huge chimney. **Pitch 1:** Begin up #23, but partway up the first crack, head up right on the steep white face (7a+) to anchors. 105 feet. **Pitch 2:** Climb edges up the streaked face (6b) to anchors. 65 feet. **Descent:** Rappel the route.

Torre Grande—Cima Nord

Cima Nord is the North Peak of Torre Grande. The peak, smaller than Cima Sud, is characterized by its abrupt east face seen from the *rifugio* and the steep, loose north face. Routes are described from left to right, beginning below the big chimney that divides Cima Nord from Cima Sud. Many parties climb just the lower pitches on the east face routes and descend by rappelling from bolt anchors.

From the summit descend northwest through a passage past many bolt anchors. Continue down over boulders wedged in a

big crevice between Cima Nord and Cima Sud. At the middle terrace scramble to the other side of the crevice using a fixed rope across a smooth face. From the terrace descend into the steep gully on the north side of the formation. Descend the gully, or locate rappel anchors on the left to reach the base of the north face. Be very careful not to dislodge loose rocks on the descent since climbers and hikers are below.

Finding the cliff: Follow the access trail up rock and grass slopes below the east face to the base of the wall. Hiking time from the *rifugio* to the face is ten minutes.

25. Idefix (7a) (5.11d) 4 pitches. Excellent. Up the steep white face right of the huge chimney. Pitch grades: 4, 6b+, 6a+, 7a. **Descent:** Rappel the route.

26. Finlandia (6b) (5.10c) 5 pitches. Recommended. Brilliant climbing that wanders up the middle of the white wall. Pitch grades: 2, 6a, 6b, 6b, 6a.

27. Columbus (7b) (5.12b) 4 pitches. Great route! Do the first couple pitches at least. Pitch grades: 6b, 6c, 7b, 6a+.

28. Farouk (7a+) (5.12a) 3 pitches. Another superb climb. Pitch grades: 6a+, 7a+, 7a. **Descent:** Rappel the route.

Sasso Cubico

Sasso Cubico is a huge boulder that sits below the east face of Cima Nord. Several short, excellent sport routes ascend the boulder's overhanging east face. The routes are easy to find. Routes are described from left to right when facing the boulder. No topos.

29. Swing (6a) (5.10a) 50 feet.

30. Unknown (6a+) (5.10b) 50 feet.

31. La Danza di Pier (6a) (5.10a) 45 feet.

32. Telefono Azzurro (8a) (5.13b) Excellent little route. 45 feet.

33. Cliffhanger (8a) (5.13b) Right-hand route on the overhanging face. 45 feet.

Torre Grande—Cima Ovest

Cima Ovest, the West Peak of Torre Grande, is the formation's pointed west summit. The West Face yields many excellent sport routes. A huge left-facing dihedral cleaves the face, dividing a slabby right wall and a vertical left wall. The right wall offers long, easy routes as well as an assortment of single-pitch lines. The first pitches of the left wall routes are climbed often, whereas the upper pitches see less action.

Finding the cliff: Hike up the trail toward the east face of Grande Torre until you can traverse left across the slope to the base of the south face. Hike west up the slope to the base of the west face.

Southwest Face

The southwest face is the face left of the big chimney/gully that divides Cima Ovest from Cima Sud. Many fun, moderate sport routes ascend the bottom of the face, along with an easier classic to the top of the peak.

Descent from the sport routes is by lowering off. To descend from the flat peak summit, scramble down about 10 feet on the north side to rappel anchors. Rappel 65 feet to a ledge. Move left, while facing the wall, to another set of anchors. Make a second 65-foot rappel to the upper part of a north-facing gully. Scramble down to another set of anchors, and make a third 65-foot rappel to the base of the north face, or scramble down a narrow tunnel protected with pitons and continue down the gully. Be extremely careful not to dislodge loose rocks on the ledges or in the gully.

Routes are described from right to left. Route #1 is right of #34 on the right side of a deep chimney.

34. Rosamunda (5) (5.9) Up the steep wall on the left side of a deep chimney. 75 feet.

35. Unknown (6b) (5.10c) Right side of the face to anchors. 65 feet.

36. Unknown (6a) (5.10a) Good climbing. 65 feet.

37. Zebra Zabra (5) (5.8) Over a low roof then vertical rock to anchors. 65 feet.

38. Fra Fra (5) (5.8) Left-hand sport route. 65 feet.

39. Via Delle Guide (4–) (5.6) 4 pitches. Classic and recommended route opened in 1930. Lots of perfect holds on surprisingly solid rock. Start below the left side of the wall, just right of a pillar. **Pitch 1:** Climb up right, and pass through an overhang (4–). Belay at a stance above from a cemented piton. 115 feet. **Pitch 2:** Work up right (3) to a belay. 80 feet. **Pitch 3:** Climb left of a big roof, then up left along a break (4–) to a high ledge. 80 feet. **Pitch 4:** Climb directly up easier rock (3) to the summit. 150 feet. **Descent:** See above description.

West Face

The West Face is a vertical wall left of a big, left-facing dihedral. Some excellent sport routes climb the face. Many parties only do the first pitches of the routes. For descent from the top of the peak, see the above descent directions.

Routes are described from right to left.

40. Via Olga (5+) (5.9+) 3 pitches. Classic and excellent. Up the face just left of the dihedral. Pitch grades: 5, 5+, 3.

41. Sir Biss (6a) (5.10a) 3 pitches. Face left of the dihedral. Pitch grades: 6a, 5+, 6a.

42. Chiaro di Luna (6a+) (5.10b) Single pitch to obvious horizontal break. 90 feet.

43. Onorevole Cicciolina (6b+) (5.10d) 3 pitches. Recommended. Excellent route up the middle of the face. Pitch grades: 6a, 6a, 6b+. Usually only Pitch 1 is climbed.

44. Fulmini e Saette (6a+) (5.10b) Single pitch to the horizontal crack. 85 feet.

45. Armida (6) (5.10) 4 pitches. Classic excursion up the left edge of the face. Pitch grades: 4, 4+, 6, 3.

46. Mimosa (5+) (5.9) Good climbing up the far left margin of the face. 75 feet.

The following three sport routes are on the north face of Cima Ovest, around left of an arête and the west face. No topos. Routes are described from right to left.

47. Pompa Pompa (6c) (5.11a/b) Excellent. 75 feet.

48. Alta Marea (6b+) (5.10d) 65 feet.

49. Sinonia da Hilti (6b) (5.10c) 65 feet.

Massi

Massi is a collection of three immense boulders lying below the northwest corner of Torre Grande's Cima Ovest. The rocks have popular toprope routes as well as a few short, bouldery lines.

Finding the boulders: Follow directions to Cima Ovest's West Face. The boulders are on the slope below the face. Routes are on the west face of the boulders and in the slices between them.

Routes are described from left to right starting on the west side of the boulders.

50. Nirvana (7b) (5.12b) Short pumpy line up a steep wall to anchors on the slab above. 40 feet.

51. Blob (5+) (5.9+) Slab on the left side of the southern boulder. 35 feet.

52. Strip Strip (5) (5.8) Follow the crack system up left. 35 feet.

53. Tetto Marcello (6b) (5.10b) Over a small roof to a slab. 40 feet.

54. Bibì e Bibò (5+) (5.9) Popular and fun. Up the right slab. 50 feet.

55. Fulminetor (8a+) (5.13c) Short, overhanging pumpfest up the steep side of the slice. 22 feet.

56. Match 3 (6c+) (5.11b/c) No topo. East face of middle boulder. 25 feet.

57. Strapiombino Poliruga (7c) (5.12d) No topo. Excellent. Up the overhanging north wall of the slice between the north and middle boulders. 35 feet.

58. Sequenza da Oscar (8a) (5.13b/c) No topo. East face of the north boulder. 40 feet.

Torre del Barancio
and Torre Lusy

These two small towers sit at the northeast corner of Torre Grande. Both have steep south faces and long slabby north faces. All the described routes are on the south faces.

Finding the towers: Hike to the northeast corner of the East Face of Torre Grande from the *rifugio*. The obvious towers are on the right.

Routes are described from left to right.

Torre del Barancio

This is the west tower with two summits. Five sport routes are on the south face. The north face offers a five-pitch route up its slabby wall called *Via Ignazio Dibona* (4+) (5.7). This classic route ascends the narrow face for three long pitches and then traverses right for two short pitches to rappel anchors above the tower's west face.

59. Via del Camino (3) (5.5) 2 pitches. Begin below an obvious chimney that splits the south face of the tower. **Pitch 1:** Up the chimney to a belay. **Pitch 2:** Continue up the chimney and then the face on the left to a traverse leftward to rappel anchors about 10 feet below the west summit. **Descent:** Make one double-rope rappel or two 80-foot rappels to the base.

60. Attenti al Lupo (6a+) (5.10b) Left side of the face right of the chimney. 75 feet.

61. Via Crupp (6a+) (5.10b) Begin down the slope to the right. 80 feet.

62. Alba Chiara (6b) (5.10c) Good climbing on the right side of the face. 80 feet.

63. Zandalee (7a) (5.11d) Up the right edge of the face. 80 feet.

Torre Lusy

Torre Lusy is the east companion tower to Torre del Barancio. Again, only the south

face routes are described. A great outing is *Via Lusy Pompanin* (4-) (5.7), the tower's narrow north face. This mostly easy six-pitch route ascends the left side of the face for three pitches and then works up right and back left to a ledge. Finish up the east face of the summit block. Scramble down the east side to the base of the face to start.

64. Fantasia (6c+) (5.11c) No topo. A 1-pitch route up the steep west-facing wall

down and right of the south face of Torre del Barancio. 65 feet.

65. Per Elisa (6b+) (5.10d) 2 pitches. Recommended. **Pitch 1:** Climb the face right of *Fantasia* to anchors. 65 feet. **Pitch 2:** Work over a roof, and edge up the slightly overhanging face above to anchors just below the summit.

Torre Trephor

This small tower sits alone at the bottom of the steep, bouldery slope below the north face of Torre Grande. The described routes are on the southwest flank of the spire.

Finding the tower: Hike to the east face of Torre Grande from the rifugio. Descend down the steep boulder field to the base of the tower. Hiking time from the *rifugio* is fifteen to twenty minutes.

     Routes are described from left to right.

66. Pelle di Leone (6c) (5.11a/b) Sport climb up the left side of the face. 80 feet.

67. Trapanetor (6c+) (5.11c) 75 feet.

68. Rispitta il Prossimo Tuo (6b+) (5.10d) 2 pitches.

69. Fulvia Che Dorme (6b+) (5.10d) 2 pitches. **Pitch 1:** 65 feet.

70. Unknown (6b) (5.10c) Up the right side of the face, passing left of a big roof. 77 feet.

71. Vertigo (6c) (5.11a/b) No topo. On the west side of the tower. 80 feet.

Crépe de Oucèra Bassi

Crépe de Oucèra Bassi, reaching heights of 100 feet, is a popular sport crag near Cortina. This long, northeast-facing wall, at an altitude of 5,300 feet, tucks into the evergreen forest between Val del Falzarego and Val Costeana. The cliff's compact Cassian dolomite rock is sprinkled with weathered holes and pockets formed by seeping water, and with edges and flakes. The vertical cliff, with only a few overhanging sections, requires a variety of climbing styles and techniques. The crag, coupled with Crépe de Oucèra Alti on the slopes above, is one of the most important sport areas in the Dolomites.

Almost ninety single-pitch, bolted routes, ranging from 5.6 to 5.12d, ascend the cliff. Most routes, however, are 5.10 and 5.11, making Crépe de Oucèra Bassi an excellent venue for moderate climbers. The easier routes offer closely spaced bolts for novices. The bolting is excellent, and the bolts themselves are relatively new and reliable. The cliff dries rapidly after rain, although the base is sometimes muddy, so bring a small towel or piece of carpet to keep your shoes dry. Bring twelve quickdraws and a 200-foot (60-meter) rope.

The cliff is divided into three sectors. Settore Sinistro, the first one reached on the path from the parking, is sometimes wet but offers a selection of steep pumpy routes. Its right side has a few easier and popular lines. Settore Centrale, the middle sector, includes the cliff's longest and most difficult routes. Settore Destro, up a slight hill from the middle, is shorter but is composed of solid, pocketed rock.

The cliff was almost single-handedly developed by local climber Diego Ghedina "Tomasc." He located the area, built trails, cleaned the cliff, and installed most of the routes.

Finding the cliff: The easiest access is from Cortina to the northwest. From Cortina drive west on highway SS48 toward Passo Falzarego. Turn left at the Pocol junction onto highway SS638 toward Passo Giau. Drive 2.8 kilometers up the road. Past the first hairpin turns, look for an area on the left (south) side of the road and park. The roadside marker post here reads IX 2. If you are coming down from Passo Giau, drive about 6 kilometers, and look for the marker post and the parking area on the right.

Follow a footpath on the road's opposite side from the parking, and hike across a hillside through a forest for about ten minutes to the cliff base.

Routes are described from left to right. Many route names are painted at the base.

Settore Sinistro

This is the first cliff section reached from the parking area.

1. Zachetac (6b) (5.10c) 40 feet.

2. Sei a Milleei (6b) (5.10c) 60 feet.

3. Unknown (6c) (5.11a/b) 65 feet.

4. Unknown (6c) (5.11a/b) 72 feet.

5. Non c'è tanga che tenga (6c) (5.11a/b) 80 feet.

6. Cielo Duro (6b+) (5.10d) 88 feet.

7. Nessuno che rompe (6b) (5.10c) 88 feet.

8. Tettona (6c) (5.11a/b) 88 feet.

9. Regno di Ragno (6b+) (5.10d) 88 feet.

10. Cosce Che Capitano (6b) (5.10c) 82 feet.

11. Primo Pelo (6a+) (5.10b) 74 feet.

12. Souplesse (6b+) (5.10d) 65 feet.

13. Yabba Dabba Doo (6c+) (5.11c) 88 feet.

14. Busillis (6a+) (5.10b) 72 feet.

15. Curve Perigolosi (6b+) (5.10d) "Dangerous Curve." 75 feet.

16. Stress da Sass (6c) (5.11a/b) 88 feet.

17. Unknown (7a) (5.11d) 85 feet.

18. Visita Parenti (5+) (5.9) 86 feet.

19. Zanzare a Zonzo (5+) (5.9) 84 feet.

20. Fun Tomas (5) (5.8) 84 feet.

21. Piche Peche (4) (5.6) 86 feet.

22. Escluso Autoveicoli (4+) (5.7) 89 feet.

23. Troppa Trippa (6c+) (5.11c) 60 feet.

24. Topless (6b+) (5.10d) 69 feet.

25. Stai Zitto Che Non Sei Altro (6a+) 75 feet.

26. Palle al Balzo (6b) (5.10c) 79 feet.

27. Callipigia (6b) (5.10c) 82 feet.

28. Ochiti Pochiti (5+) (5.8) 79 feet.

29. Gommapiuma (4+) (5.7) 80 feet.

30. Promenade (5) (5.8) 80 feet.

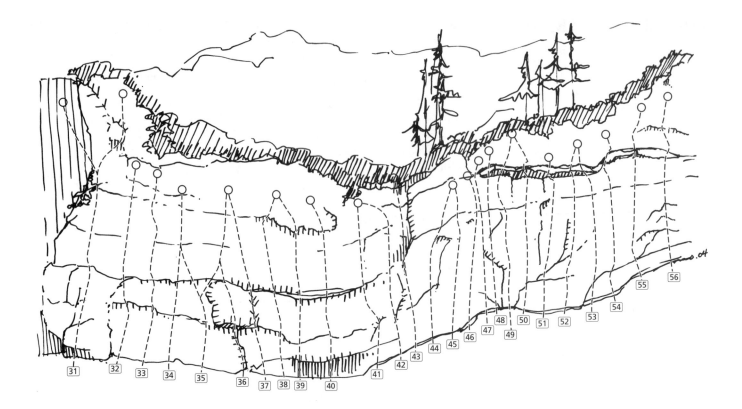

Settore Centrale

The sector right of a broken crack system.

31. Tipa al Top (5+) (5.9) 80 feet.

32. 33 Marzo (6c) (5.11a/b) 78 feet.

33. Effetti Collaterali (6b+) (5.10d) 80 feet.

34. Hoo Issa (7c) (5.12d) 80 feet.

35. Variante Hoo Issa (7a) (5.11d) An easier start to the right.

36. Sex Appeal (7a) (5.11d) Begin up a shallow left-facing corner. 80 feet.

37. Tutto Pepe (6c+) (5.11c) End at *Sex Appeal*'s anchor. 80 feet.

38. Sorci Verdi (6b) (5.10c) 82 feet.

39. Uso del Buso (6c+) (5.11c) 82 feet.

40. Miss Popa (6a) (5.10a) Excellent. 82 feet.

41. Sembra Facile Ma Non (6b+) (5.10d) 82 feet.

42. Ostrega Che Mona (6b+) (5.10d) 72 feet.

43. Finta di Niente (6a) (5.10a) 80 feet.

44. Kappa 0 (6c) (5.11a/b) 65 feet.

45. Overdose (6c) (5.11a/b) 65 feet.

46. Patatrac (6b+) (5.10d) 65 feet.

47. Unknown (6b) (5.10c) 82 feet.

48. Messa per Parte (5+) (5.9) 72 feet.

49. Follie (6c+) (5.11c) 72 feet.

50. Uscita Dai Gangheri (6c) (5.11a/b) 72 feet.

51. Brodo di Giuggiole (6b+) (5.10d) 72 feet.

52. Ghereghereghez (6b) (5.10c) 72 feet.

53. Augh (6b) (5.10c) 72 feet.

54. Attività Sassuale (6c) (5.11a/b) 75 feet.

55. Elogio Della Pazzia (6c+) (5.11c) 85 feet.

56. Buco Nell'azona (7a) (5.11d) 85 feet.

The cliff continues to the north with Settore Destro to the right and slightly uphill. Another twenty-five sport routes lace this cliff section. Consult the comprehensive guide *Arrampicata Sportiva a Cortina d'Ampezzo* for a cliff topo.

Falesia Sass de Stria

Sasso de Stria, a small 8,110-foot (2,472-meter) peak in the Fanis group, towers above 6,906-foot (2,105-meter) Passo Falzarego west of Cortina d'Ampezzo. The east side of the peak facing the pass is tiered with cliffs, with the base of the face a steep slabby wall creased with diagonal cracks called Falesia Sass de Stria. Local mountain guides bolted most of the routes in 1996, creating one of the Dolomites' easiest crags.

The popular east-facing wall receives morning sun and afternoon shade. The climbing season is generally short, from June through September, because of the crag's high elevation. A large snowdrift along the base of the wall doesn't melt back completely until July. The rock is slabby and compact, with lots of edges and flakes. All the described routes are bolted

with abseil chains. Some routes have a second pitch. A basic rack of ten quickdraws and a 165-foot (50-meter) rope is all that's needed for a morning's fun. Descent off all the routes is by rappel or lowering off.

Finding the cliff: The crag and Passo Falzarego are easily reached from Cortina, Livinallongo, Caprile, and anywhere else via winding mountain roads. Drive to Passo Falzarego, and turn north onto the road to Passo Val Parola. Drive 0.7 kilometer up the road, and park on either side of a huge roadside boulder. The cliff is obvious from the car park. A climber's path leads downhill for five minutes through a boulder field to the base of the obvious cliff.

Routes are described from left to right. The names of many routes are painted at the cliff base.

1. S.N. (4a) (5.5)

2. Friends (4a) (5.5)

3. Nuts (4a) (5.5)

4. Ossodi Banana (5a) (5.7)

5. Black Rain (5a) (5.7) 2 pitches.

6. Totem (5b) (5.8)

7. Blowing in the Wind (5c) (5.9)

8. Bozano (4b) (5.6)

9. Wily Coyote (5a) (5.7)

10. Bip Bip (5b) (5.8+) Short and tricky. Keep right at the top; otherwise, it's 5.10a. 5 bolts to 2-bolt anchor.

11. Nurajev (5a) (5.7) 7 bolts to 2-bolt anchor.

12. Incas (4b) (5.6)

13. Bilanciamento (4a) (5.5)

14. Super Trombetta (6a) (5.10a)

15. Mano Morta (4b) (5.6)

16. Welcome in Padania (4a) (5.5)

17. Gatto Vecio (5a) (5.7)

18. Semi de Papavero (5b) (5.8)
Excellent.

19. Non Stringere (5b) (5.8) Great route!

20. Pamir (5b) (5.8) Another super climb.

21. Sfigoi (6a) (5.10a)

22. Sacripante (5b) (5.8)

23. Progressione Fondamentale (5b)
(5.8)

24. Son Cotto (6a) (5.10a) 2 pitches.

25. Rioby (6a) (5.10a)

26. Citrullina (5b) (5.8)

27. Nuvolari (4a) (5.5)

Rodelheilspitze

Murfrëitspitze

Val Culea

Himmelsleiter

Rechter Pfeiler

Felsnelke & Herbstzeitlose

Bittersuss & Fingerkraut

To parking

Frea

Frea, lying below jagged peaks and an alpine cirque in the northwest section of Sella Gruppo, is an impressive cliff laced with brilliant one- and two-pitch sport routes. The easily accessed cliff looms above the road just below Passo Gardena. A grassy ledge system divides the wall into upper and lower halves. The cliff divides naturally into five distinct sectors. The upper cliffs, characterized by steep pocketed rock and exposure, yield excellent routes.

The lower cliff, divided from the upper by a narrow ledge system traversed by a *via ferrata*, is split into three distinct sectors: Settore Sonnentau, Settore Felsnelke and Herbstzeitlose, and Settore Bittersüss and Fingerkraut. The upper cliff offers two excellent walls: Settore

Himmelsleiter on the left and Settore Rechter Pfeiler on the right.

The Frea cliffs are seen above highway SS243 as it switchbacks west from the summit of Passo Gardena. The highway passes directly below the cliffs, allowing quick access to this beautiful climbing area.

The north side of the Sella Group also offers classic long routes up the big mountain faces. Many local climbers view these smaller sport crags as simply training for the long routes. While climbing at Frea, check out the possibilities for these multipitch affairs, and do one. Recommended routes are ten-pitch *Vinatzer* (5.7) up the North Face of Rodelheilspitze and eleven-pitch *Nordwand* (5.7) on Murfrëitspitze.

Finding the cliff: (See Dolomites map.) Frea is easily reached from Val Gardena, Fal di Fassa, and the villages of Corvara, Canazei, and St. Christina. From Corvara to the east, drive up the road over Passo Gardena. From the col summit the cliff is obvious to the south. Continue down the road, and park in a small pullout on the right (north) side of the road. From Passo Sella and Val Gardena, turn east onto the road toward Passo Gardena. Drive 4 kilometers on the road to the parking area on the left (north) side of the road.

Hike steeply uphill on a climber's path for seven minutes to the cliff base. A *via ferrata* ascends the obvious cleft in the bottom of the cliff, allowing access to the upper walls. The *via ferrata* also traverses under the upper walls, allowing safe access to both these excellent sectors.

Settore Bittersüss and Fingerkraut

This sector, with a left and right section, flanks a deep gully on the lower right side of the cliff. Almost all of the routes are single bolt-protected pitches with bolt lowering anchors. Most are thin, technical face problems, except for the right side lines, which are easy, slabby affairs. The names of some routes are painted at the base. Routes are described from left to right.

1. Weisswurz (7a) (5.11d) Leftmost route in sector. 40 feet.

2. Kratzdistel (6c) (5.11a/b) 40 feet.

3. Bittersüss (6b) (5.10d) 40 feet.

4. Federnelke (6b+) (5.11a) 40 feet.

5. Wundklee (6b+) (5.10d) 40 feet.

6. Iris (5a) (5.7) Blunt prow. 40 feet.

A *via ferrata*, allowing access to the upper walls, ascends the left side of the deep gully/cleft between the sectors.

7. Fingerkraut (7a+) (5.12a) Just right of gully. 65 feet.

8. Mauerpfeffer (7a+) (5.12a) 65 feet.

9. Vergissmeinnicht (7a) (5.11d) 65 feet.

10. Barbarakraut (6b+) (5.10d) 65 feet.

The next routes are on the slabby wall divided by a headwall and overhang. No topos for these, but they're easy to find. The routes are described from left to right.

11. Peru (6a) (5.10a) Shares anchors. 65 feet.

12. Unknown (6a+) (5.10b) 65 feet.

13. Unknown (6a+) (5.10b) 65 feet.

14. Unknown (6a) (5.10a) 50 feet.

15. Unknown (5a) (5.7) 50 feet.

16. Alpenmohn (5a) (5.7) 50 feet.

17. Unknown (4b) (5.6) 50 feet.

18. Unknown (4c) (5.6) Slab (4b) to anchors. 50 feet. A second pitch (4c) goes up the right side of the slab above to the *via ferrata* below the upper wall.

19. Unknown (4a) (5.5) Far right margin of slab. 50 feet. A second pitch (6b) climbs the steep wall above to the *via ferrata* below the upper wall.

Settore Rechter Pfeiler

Settore Rechter Pfeiler, the upper right wall, yields a great selection of long pitches with interesting and sustained climbing. The one- and two-pitch routes up this popular section are surprisingly moderate. All the routes are bolted for safety with lowering or rappel anchors. Be very careful on the ledge below the climb. The cliff below drops off steeply, and it's easy to knock loose rocks onto parties climbing below. Use a 200-foot (60-meter) rope on the routes, and be sure to tie a knot in the end before lowering.

Finding the cliff: From the parking area on the highway, hike up the climber's path to the base of a gully between Settore

Bittersüss and Settore Fingerkraut on the lower wall. Climb the *via ferrata* up the left side of the gully, and follow the cables up right to the base of the face. The cables continue both right and left along the base, providing both safety and belay anchors. Routes are described from right to left.

20. Löwenzahn (7b) (5.12b) No topo. Thin face climbing up the wall right of an arête. 95 feet.

21. Unknown (6c) (5.11a) Just right of the arête. 95 feet.

22. Kante (6b+) (5.10d) Excellent. Directly up the arête. 95 feet.

23. Unknown (6b) (5.10c) 2 pitches. Recommended. **Pitch 1:** Edges and pockets up the 9-bolt face left of the arête. 95 feet. **Pitch 2:** Up the face left of a crack (5b) to cliff-top anchors.

24. Unknown (6b) (5.10c) Anchors at break. 90 feet.

25. Unknown (6b) (5.10c) Goes to same anchors as #24. 90 feet.

26. Knöterich (5c) (5.9) 2 pitches. Fun climbing. **Pitch 1:** Climb the face right of a crack system (5c) to ledge anchors. 90 feet. **Pitch 2:** Up the face right of the crack (5a).

27. Unknown (5c) (5.9) 2 pitches. **Pitch 1:** Slab left of a crack system (5c) to a belay stance below the steeper wall. **Pitch 2:** Up the headwall to a bolt belay.

28. Unknown (6a) (5.10a) 2 pitches. **Pitch 1:** Slab to anchors under bolt headwall. **Pitch 2:** Headwall to bolt anchors.

29. Peru (6a) (5.10a) 2 pitches. Good climbing. **Pitch 1:** Edge up a slab to a pocketed headwall (6a) to anchors at a stance. **Pitch 2:** Pull up a steep wall (6a) above the belay to a white slab.

30. Unknown (5c) (5.9) A direct line just left of *Peru* to shared anchors. 65 feet.

31. Trollblume (5b) (5.8) 2 pitches. On left side of the face. **Pitch 1:** Climb the slabby wall to a shallow left-facing corner (5b). Belay above at a bolted stance. **Pitch 2:** Face climb left of a corner (5a), then up fluted rock to anchors on a ledge.

32. Unknown (4c) (5.6) Face to slab to anchors. 65 feet.

33. Unknown (6a+) (5.10b) 2 pitches. **Pitch 1:** Face to slab (5c) to anchors. 65 feet. **Pitch 2:** Work left up steep rock (6a+) to anchors.

34. Sterndolde (6b) (5.10c) 2 pitches. On the far left side of the face. **Pitch 1:** Climb a face and slab (6b) to a stance with anchors. **Pitch 2:** Swing up the steep edge just right of a deep chimney (6b).

Settore Herbstzeitlose

Settore Herbstzeitlose, a buttress on the bottom left side of the wall, offers a fine assortment of one-pitch sport routes. All routes are bolted with lowering anchors.

Finding the sector: Hike up the steep path from the parking area until a trail leads left along the cliff base to the sector.

Routes are described from right to left.

35. Unknown (5c) (5.9) Climb the rib right of a gully. 50 feet.

36. Unknown (5b) (5.8) Stem up the gully. 60 feet.

37. Unknown (5c) (5.9) Route just left of the gully. 60 feet.

38. Knabenbraut (6a) (5.10a) 60 feet.

39. Alpenrose (6b) (5.10c) 65 feet.

40. Arnika (6b) (5.10c) Fun climb. 65 feet.

41. Anemone (6b+) (5.10d) Good face climbing. 65 feet.

42. Herbstzeitlose (6b) (5.10c) Up the left margin of the face. 65 feet.

43. Mondviole (7b) (5.12b) Steep face just left of prow. 50 feet.

44. Schattenblume (6a) (5.10a) No topo. Direct up the center of the narrow face. 60 feet.

45. Wintergrün (6a) (5.10a) No topo. Left side of the narrow face. 60 feet.

Settore Felsnelke

This sector is just left of Settore Herbstzeitlose on the left side of the wall. Some routes are two pitches long, but only the first ones are described since they are usually climbed. Most of the lines are popular with varied climbing and grades.

46. Unknown 17 (5c) (5.9) Left of the left-facing dihedral. 65 feet.

47. Unknown (6a) (5.10a) A few tricky sections. 65 feet. Continue up for two more pitches—6b+, 6c+—to the *via ferrata* on the ledge above.

48. Unknown (5a) (5.7+) Popular face route. 65 feet.

49. Blauer Eisenhut (6a) (5.10a) Popular and excellent. Up the rib right of a corner system. 55 feet. Continue up the cliff for four more pitches: 6b+, 6b, 6b+, 4a.

50. Unknown (7a+) (5.12a) First route left of the broken corner system. 65 feet.

51. Blauer Enzian (6c) (5.11a/b) Good pitch with interesting face movements. 65 feet. Continue above for two pitches: 6a, 6c.

52. Waldvöglein (6b) (5.10c)

53. Türkenbund (6c+) (5.11c)

54. Unknown (6b+) (5.10d) A bulge start to more bulges. 65 feet.

55. Unknown (6b) (5.10c) Left finishing variant to above route.

56. Sonnentau (6a+) (5.10b) Starts just right of the big roof. Continues above the first anchors for three more pitches: 6b, 6b, 6c.

57. Eisenkraut (6c) (5.11a/b) No topo. Over the right side of a big roof on the sector's left side. Continue for three more pitches: 7a, 6b, 7b.

Settore Himmelsleiter

Settore Himmelsleiter, an excellent sector above Settore Herbstzeitlose, is a high, open wall with superb views and perfect climbing. It takes a bit of clambering up the *via ferrata* to reach the sector, but the routes are worth the extra effort. Be careful not to knock rocks down since climbers are often climbing below.

Finding the sector: Scramble up the *via ferrata* to the ledge system halfway up the wall. Follow cables left along a series of ledges with grass and rock to the base of the wall.

Routes are described from right to left.

58. Rapunzel (7b+) (5.12c) Right side of the face. Finish left of a crack system. 98 feet.

59. Belladonna (7a+) (5.12a) Up a gray wall. 98 feet.

60. Rittersporn (7a+) (5.12a) Follow a white streak to a bulge. 98 feet.

61. Himmselsleiter (7a) (5.11d) 4 pitches. Left side of the white streak to a belay ledge. Climb three more pitches—4c, 5a, 4c—to the cliff top. **Descent:** Rappel the route.

62. Blaustern (7b) (5.12b) 4 pitches. Pitch 1 goes up the white streak right of a vertical crack system (7b). Continue for three more pitches—4c, 6a+, 4c—to the cliff top. **Descent:** Rappel the route.

63. Spatzenzunge (7b) (5.12b) Face just left of crack and corner. 95 feet.

64. Kletterrose (7a) (5.11d) Pockets and edges up gray face. 95 feet.

65. Bergdistel (6c) (5.11a/b) Directly up the middle of the left face. 95 feet.

66. Felsnelke (6b+) (5.10d) 3 pitches. On the left edge of the face. **Pitch 1:** (6b) (5.10c) **Pitch 2:** (6b+) (5.10d) **Pitch 3:** (4a) (5.5)

To the immediate left of *Bergdistel* are the upper pitches of *Blauer Eisenhut* and *Felsnelke,* both of which go to the cliff top. You can climb these pitches from the ledge, avoiding the lower pitches.

Settore
Gabriel

Settore Centrale

Pian Schiavaneis

The Sella Gruppo or Sella Group, one of the most beautiful Dolomite massifs, is a stunning complex of peaks, walls, buttresses, towers, cirques, and valleys. Val Lasties, a cirque and valley lined with immense cliffs, splits the southern part of the group. In the lower valley at timberline nestles Pian Schiavaneis cliff, a tiny crag compared with its surrounding neighbors.

The cliff, however, is hardly insignificant. Instead, this white, overhanging, southwest-facing wall is the training arena for the area's fittest and strongest climbers. Not only is it a pumpy playground and an outdoor climbing gymnasium, but Pian Schiavaneis is also one of Italy's most controversial sport cliffs. Every route on the Central Sector has been chipped, glued, drilled, and sculpted into modern testpieces that require both power and endurance. This chipping neoethic hardly dims the crag's popularity, but many Italian climbers refuse to climb here or even

acknowledge its existence because manufacturing routes is so far removed from traditional ethics and the venerable sense of rock preservation.

In my past guidebooks I refrained from knowingly including manufactured and chipped routes and crags since I believe that creating routes destroys climbing as well as the rock itself. We need to bring ourselves up to the level of the rock. The rock dictates whether we are able to climb its steep flanks. By drilling and chipping anyone can climb anything. That said, the reality is that cliffs like Pian Schiavaneis are out there. Go and climb its routes and decide for yourself. If you do not climb at the level required, at least walk back and have a look at the cliff. This sculpted cliff certainly raises important questions, such as "Is this the end of climbing as we know it?"

Pian Schiavaneis offers a large selection of difficult bolted sport climbs. Most have continuations above the first anchors, making longer, harder routes. These are designated with "Plus" after the route

name. A selection of easier routes, ranging from 5b to 6c, are found at Settore Placca, left of the central section. The far right section also has some easier lines. The cliff is a good alternative for stormy days since it stays dry in all but the wettest conditions. Also check out the marmots that thrive along the base. More than twenty live here and are well adjusted to climbers. They'll even take snacks from your hands. But be advised they will also forage through your pack or any unattended food.

Finding the cliff: The cliff is between Val di Fassa and the village of Canazei and Passo Sella. From Canazei drive up the winding road past the turn to Passo Pordoi, and keep toward Passo Sella. Park at the Pian Schiavaneis and Monti Pallidi refuges on the right (east) side of the road. From Val Gardena drive over Passo Sella, and continue down to the refuges on the left side of the road. From the refuges walk up a path along the right side of the road to a large boulder and a gate on the right. Follow an old road along the river until you can cross. Continue up a path to the base of the obvious white cliff left of a big waterfall. Hiking time is ten minutes.

Settore Centrale

Settore Centrale is the cliff's main central sector. Steep, pumpy routes ascend the overhanging white face. The dominant features of the sector are a right-angling break and an obvious nose that marks its left side. If you bring food, put it in a hole in the middle of the cliff to keep it safe from marauding marmots.

Left of this sector is a slabby wall with about a dozen routes on it that range from 5b to 8a.

Routes are described from left to right. Names are painted at the base. No topos.

1. Pian Schiavaneis (6b) (5.10c)

2. La Tettona (8a) (5.13b)

3. La Tettona Plus (8a+) (5.13c)
Continuation of *La Tettona*.

4. Linea Mortale (8b/c) (5.13b/c)

5. Non Mollare (8b+) (5.14a)

6. Super Polentin (8b) (5.13d)

7. Polentin Plus (8a+) (5.13c) Upper continuation.

8. Supergrimpe (8a) (5.13b)

9. Ce Chi Dice No (8a+) (5.13c)

10. Samba (7b) (5.12b)

11. Samba Plus (7c) (5.12d)

12. Clape e Tira (7b+) (5.12c)

13. Clape e Tira Plus (7c+) (5.13a)

14. Clape e Tira Plus Plus (8a) (5.13b)

15. Pascal (7a+) (5.12a)

16. Pascal Plus (7b+) (5.12c)

17. Lambada (6b) (5.10c)

18. Lambada Plus (7b) (5.12b)

19. Lambada Plus Plus (7b/c) (5.12c/d)

20. Dirty Dancing (7b+) (5.12c)

21. Dirty Dancing Plus (7c) (5.12d)

22. Pregio e Privilegio (7b) (5.12b)

23. Pregio e Privilegio Plus (7c) (5.12d)

24. Benvenuto Etienne (7a+) (5.12a)

25. Benvenuto Etienne Plus (7b+) (5.12c)

26. Capuvers (8a) (5.13b)

27. René's Line (7b/c) (5.12c/d)

28. Bebé a Bordo (7c) (5.12d)

29. Benedick (7b) (5.12b)

30. Puffo Scalatore (7b) (5.12b)

31. Pensavo Peggio (6c) (5.11a/b)

32. Pensavo Peggio Plus (7a+) (5.12a)

Settore Gabriel

Settore Gabriel is the shorter right-hand section of the cliff. Scramble up steps on the hillside to these fine routes. A small, detached cliff to the right also has a couple short routes on good stone. Route names are painted at the base. "Plus" routes are continuations of the lower pitch, making a longer route. Routes are described from left to right. No topos.

33. Donna dal Cuore Nero (7a) (5.11d)

34. Sebastiena (6b) (5.10c)

35. Sabastiena Plus (6c+) (5.11c)

36. Voglia de Volare (6a) (5.10a)

37. Voglia de Volare Plus (7a+) (5.12a)

38. Maldestra (7c) (5.12d)

39. Petra la Dura (7b) (5.12b)

40. Calanques (7a) (5.11d)

41. L'Amico é (Project)

42. Sei Forte Papà (6c) (5.11a/b)

43. Friends (6b) (5.10c)

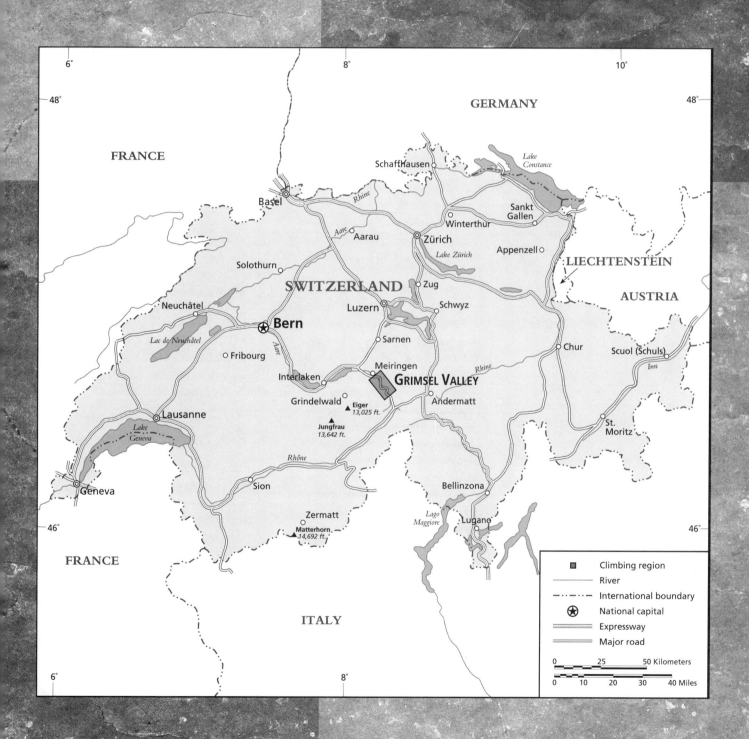

Switzerland

GERMANY

FRANCE

Schaffhausen

Lake
Constance

Basel

Rhine

Sankt
Gallen

Aare

Aarau

Winterthur

Zürich

Solothurn

SWITZERLAND

Lake Zürich

Appenzell

LIECHTENSTEIN

AUSTRIA

Neuchâtel

Zug

Luzern

Schwyz

Chur

Scuol (Schuls)

⊛ Bern

Inn

Lac de Neuchâtel

Aare

○ Fribourg

Sarnen

Meiringen

Rhine

GRIMSEL VALLEY

Interlaken

Andermatt

Lausanne

Grindelwald

▲ Eiger
13,025 ft.

St.
Moritz

*Lake
Geneva*

▲ Jungfrau
13,642 ft.

Rhône

Geneva

Sion

Bellinzona

FRANCE

Zermatt

*Lago
Maggiore*

Lugano

▲ Matterhorn
14,692 ft.

ITALY

▪	Climbing region
	River
— ·· —	International boundary
⊛	National capital
	Expressway
	Major road

0   25   50 Kilometers

0   10   20   30   40 Miles

GRIMSEL VALLEY

■ OVERVIEW

The Aare River tumbles out of the glacial debris of the Swiss Alps below the rounded col of Grimsel Pass. The milky river, impounded and tamed behind a couple dams, dashes north down a deep U-shaped valley walled with shattered granite cliffs and long sloping slabs. The Grimsel Valley has a bold, sharp newness, emerging newborn after the retreat of an immense valley glacier that melted away a scant 10,000 years ago.

The valley's perfect granite is an ancient bedrock with a compact matrix that peels off in great exfoliated sheets, leaving overlaps and long roofs. Climbing here requires a combination of techniques: laybacking on thin flakes, crimping fingertip edges, smearing sticky-rubbered toes on shallow depressions, palming rounded dimples, and finding the occasional hand jam or fingerlock. The many friction routes, particularly the harder ones, require delicate smearing, a cool head for long runouts between bolts, and grace under pressure. The brute strength needed for limestone climbs won't get you up these holdless routes. The climbing is similar in nature, quality, and length to Yosemite's Tuolumne Meadows.

The Grimsel Valley slabs, with some of Europe's best friction climbing, are extremely popular. On summer weekends the slabs are jammed with parties from all over central Europe who come to sample the long routes up these high-altitude cliffs. Here you'll find elegant lines with intricate moves, delicate footwork, intimidating runouts, well-protected cruxes, and breathtaking scenery. Most of the routes are long, multipitch affairs up glacier-polished slabs.

Eight major climbing sectors are found in Grimsel Valley. Each offers its own unique climbing experience and adventures. The most popular sectors—Gelmerfluh, Gerstenegg, and Azalée Beach—lie in the central valley below the Räterichsbodensee dam. The huge orange slab of Gelmerfluh, on the east side of the valley, yields *Moby Dick* (5.9+), one of Grimsel's finest short crack routes. Across the valley is Gerstenegg, a big slabby wall with a handful of corner and slab routes. Up left is Foxie Slab, a big dome with a couple long classics, including its namesake, *Foxie* (5.7). This excellent line smears up a slab apron on the right side. To the left of Foxie and above the tram station is Azalée Beach, a popular small cliff with many brilliant one- and two-pitch routes. These easy and moderate climbs are great introductions for beginners or climbers getting acquainted with the area's granite.

Farther upvalley is the huge shield of Räterichsbodensee Dome above the west side of the lake. Many excellent, long routes lace this hunk of granite. The upper cliffs tower above the rocky north shore of Grimsel Lake just north of the Grimsel Pass summit. Dome de la Márée is an immaculate slab that rises directly out of the milky lake waters next to the dam. From the dam viewpoint the cliff is imposing and blank looking. A closer inspection reveals a gentle angle and some superb smearing lines beginning just above the water line.

The trail west along the north shore leads to Dome de la Cascade, the excellent 1,500-foot-high Eldorado Dome, and the even bigger Bärenwand farther west. Eldorado, not described in this guide, yields some stunning crack climbs, some of Switzerland's longest granite routes, up its smooth flanks. The two best routes, similar to climbs on Yosemite's Fairview Dome, are *Motörhead* (5.10b) and *Septumania* (5.10a). The megaclassic *Motörhead* motors up fourteen pitches of perfect cracks, corners, and slabs. *Septumania*, another megaclassic, wanders for sixteen pitches up friction slabs and crack systems on the left side of the wall. Another fifteen routes ascend this big dome.

The lower section of the valley below Gelmerfluh and a long highway tunnel also offer some excellent cliffs and climbs. The Handegg Slabs, composed of immense sweeping slabs flanked by buttresses, looms above a power station. On its right side is *Quarzriss* or *Quartz Crack* (5.10a), a marvelous four-pitch crack and slab route to the base of a huge roof. Farther right is the obvious buttress ascended by *Fair Hands Line* (5.10c), one of the first classic long routes established at Grimsel. Bügeleisen, a smaller triangular-shaped wall, lies across the valley from Handegg. Mittaglfue, the last major cliff, is a 1,000-foot wall farther north on the east side of the valley and just south of the small village of Guttannen. This blocky wall, split into faces and pillars, offers steeper face routes than the slabs up the valley. Most of the routes, some excellent 5.10s, are on the left slabby wall of a huge dihedral that diagonals up the face.

The high peaks and cirques in the Alps above Grimsel Valley also yield some stunning rock climbs and mountaineering routes. Gelmerhörner, a high peak east of Handegg, offers long rock climbs up ridges and faces. A beautiful cirque west of Räterichsbodensee dam and Azalée Beach, reached by a two-hour hike, is an excellent midsummer alternative to the valley slabs. Some great climbs ascend the various alpine slabs here, ranging from one-pitch sport lines to eight-pitch courses. The Bächlital-Hütte, a mountain hut below the Heidiland and Bächlital (Beach) sectors, is available for overnight stays.

Details, directions, and topos for all the cliffs not described in this book are available in Jürg von Känel's comprehensive area guidebook *Plaisir West*.

Rack, Protection, and Descent

Bolts protect almost all the routes in the Grimsel Valley. Some bolts on the older lines are small and sometimes rusted. Use these with caution, and always back them up at belays. All the newer routes are protected by stainless steel bolts, with double bolts for anchors.

For friction climbs carry a small rack with a set of wired nuts, some small to medium-size cams, twelve quickdraws, a few extra slings, a couple free carabiners, and a 165-foot (50-meter) rope. On the longer crack routes, bring a set of wired nuts and a couple sets of cams, depending

Climbers smear up the excellent friction slabs at Azalée Beach.

on the route. It's best to eyeball the line and determine if you'll need any big cams for off-width cracks. A 200-foot (60-meter) cord is useful on many routes, making it easier to run pitches together. Also, many climbers use two ropes to alleviate rope drag on long pitches and for ease in rappelling off.

Descent off many routes is by rappel from fixed bolt anchors. Since most of the pitches are set up as sport pitches or a half-rope length, it's easy to climb and rappel with a single rope. A 200-foot rope gives you more flexibility to locate the next anchors without reaching the rope's ends. Double-rope rappels are faster, but you have to carry two cords. Some routes require a walk-off descent via ledges, gullies, and grass slopes. Bring a pair of shoes or sandals to save your feet unless you're climbing in approach shoes.

Seasons and Weather

The Grimsel Valley lies squarely in the Swiss Alps in an alpine and subalpine environment. Many of the routes are above timberline and are subject to severe storms. The climbing season begins sometime in June, depending on how much snow has melted away, and ends in early October, when the snow begins to fly. The best months are July, August, and September, with generally warm, dry weather. Expect to find snowdrifts along the base of many walls early in the season. In June the cliffs usually seep from snowmelt in the higher cirques. It can rain, sometimes for several successive days, even in the best months. Be prepared by bringing good rain gear and being ready to climb as soon as the rain stops. The granite dries quickly, especially if the sun comes out. Again, the rock will weep for days after heavy rain, so check if your prospective route is wet before heading up

it. October can be wet and cold, so have alternative plans to climb in the lower elevations if storms settle in for a few days.

Climbing History

Climbing began in earnest in the Grimsel Valley in the 1970s. Before that alpinists had ventured onto the high peaks towering above the valley, cramponing up couloirs and scaling alpine ribs and buttresses. In 1978 Swiss climbers Jürg von Känel and Martin Stettler established *Fair Hands Line* (5.10c), a stunning crack and slab line up a prominent buttress. After this landmark ascent the route rush was on, and new lines wove their way up almost all of the major slabs and cliffs in the valley. Many of these original routes, however, are seldom climbed now since they were established on the lead and bolted sparsely with hand drills. Today's climbers owe particular thanks to Claude and Yves

Remy, a pair of brothers who established the majority of the valley's routes and continue to seek out new Grimsel slab climbs.

Getting Around

This area of Switzerland is traversed by scenic two-lane highways, which twist and turn over high mountain passes and speed down deep glaciated valleys. A car is a necessity for getting around and out to the cliffs. The Grimsel Pass road is narrow, steep in places, and busy in the summer months. Keep an eye peeled for speeding motorcycles on sharp curves.

Park only in designated pullouts along the road as described in each cliff section below. Don't pull off and park on the shoulder. All the cliffs are easily seen from the road and parking areas. The access trails are generally obvious. The only difficult one is approaching the Handegg Slabs and *Fair Hands Line* in the lower valley.

Camping, Accommodations, and Services

The best place to stay is Innertkirchen below the north end of Grimsel Valley. This lovely village offers four campgrounds, so take your pick. The Camping Grund on the south side of town is good and close to the village, so you can walk around in the evening. At some of the campgrounds you can rent caravans for the night. Innertkirchen also has a hotel, along with restaurants and pubs. A couple of small shops sell groceries and fresh bread.

The larger town of Meiringen, just a few kilometers to the west, offers a larger selection of hotels and inns, many restaurants, lots of shops, and a grocery store. Climbing gear and guides are also available in outdoor shops. Ask at the local tourist office for details and directions for accommodations.

No wild camping is allowed in Grimsel Valley. It is possible to camp, but only if you have permission from the landowner. Climbers often bivouac in the mountains, away from the highway. A

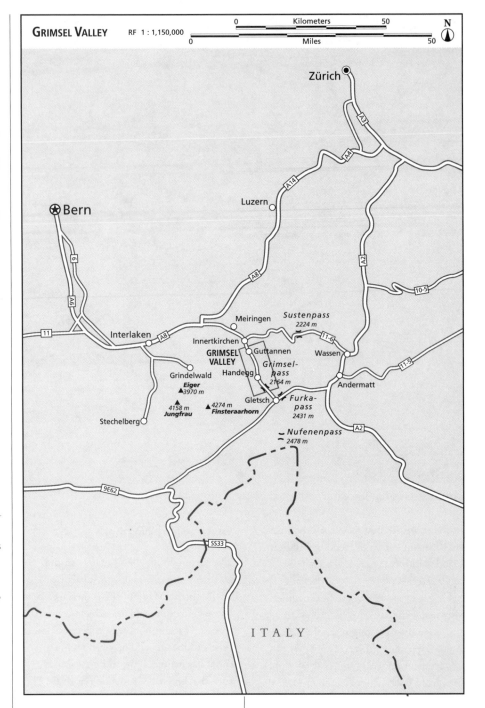

good alternative to staying in Innertkirchen is at the Grimsel Hospiz hotel above the Grimsel Lake dam, Hotel Handeck below Handegg Slabs, or at one of the lofty hotels atop Grimsel Pass.

Cultural Experiences and Rest Days

Central Switzerland's alpine area offers many activities and sights for climbing rest days. It's famous, of course, for outdoor sports, including mountain biking and excellent hiking on the many area trails. The mountains and valleys surrounding Grimsel Valley are among Europe's most famous sightseeing areas, with lots of spectacular alpine scenery, as well as interesting towns and historic places.

Meiringen, just west of Innertkirchen, is an old town between the Grimsel, Brunig, and Susten passes. The major town in the Haslital district, it's famous for meringue, a dessert invented here. The dessert was created a couple hundred years ago when Napoleon passed through and a local chef beat leftover egg whites into creamy mounds. They were baked and served with sweet cream to the general's gastronomic delight. Try a delicious meringue at most local bakeries. Also visit the old parish church with its eleventh-century crypt.

The region includes more than 185 miles of marked hiking trails as well as scenic destinations, including Rosenlaui Glacier and Reichenbach Falls. Sherlock Holmes fans need to visit the Reichenbachfall. This gushing waterfall south of Meiringen so impressed Sir Arthur Conan Doyle, the creator of Sherlock Holmes, that he used the place for the detective's final struggle with his archenemy Professor Moriarty. The evil professor pushed Holmes off the cliff-bound trail into the turbulent falls. He, of course, survived the spill and lived to solve more cases, to the relief of Holmes fans. The Rosenlaui Gorge carved by glacial melt is another nearby natural wonder above the falls. Between Meiringen and Innertkirchen is the impressive Aare Gorge, an abrupt 700-foot-deep, mile-long cleft excavated by the rushing Aare River below Grimsel Valley. Some marvelous scenic drives explore this section of the Alps. A good loop drive twists east from Innertkirchen over Sustenpass to Andermatt, west over Furkapass to Gletsch, and back north over Grimselpass and back down to Innertkirchen.

Last, make sure you head over to the resort town of Interlaken. After strolling around its busy streets, drive up to Grindelwald for a view of the famous Eiger Nordwand and the snowy 13,642-foot Jungfrau. The tourist office in Interlaken provides lots of information on hiking, cable car rides, and lots of other fun activities.

Trip Planning Information

General description: Excellent slab climbing on many granite domes in a glaciated alpine valley.

Location: Central Switzerland in the eastern Berner Oberland south of Zürich and northeast of Genéve (Geneva). The climb-

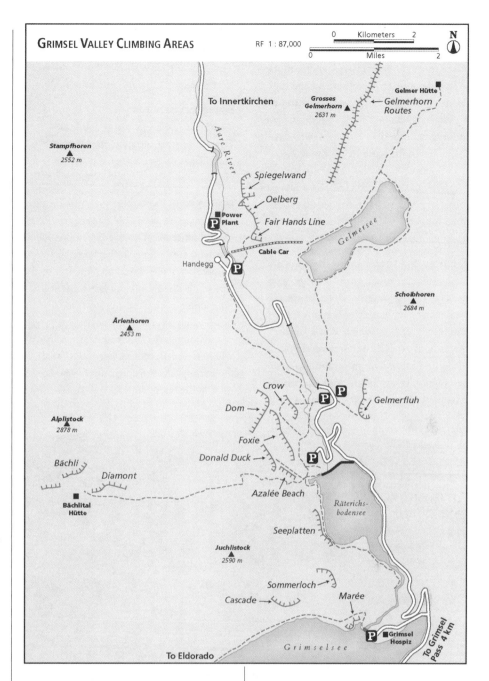

ing is in Grimsel Valley along the Grimsel Pass road between Innertkirchen and Grimsel Pass.

Camping and accommodations:
Innertkirchen offers four campgrounds with reasonable rates, good mountain views, and plentiful sites. Camping Grund on the south side of the village is my preferred site. Another is Camping Aareschlucht. Several hotels are found in Innertkirchen, as well as in Grimsel Valley. The Grimsel hotels include Hotel Handeck at Handegg, Hotel Urweid in Guttannen, and the scenic Hotel Grimsel Hospiz. A recommended hotel in Meiringen is Hotel Meiringen.

Climbing season: June through September. The valley cliffs are sometimes wet in June because of melting snow in the alpine cirques. The cliffs are also wet and seeping after heavy rains, but the popular slabs usually dry quickly. September brings fine weather, and sometimes you can climb well into October, depending on the cliff's aspect.

Restrictions and access issues: No access issues. Park only in designated parking areas, not on the road's shoulder. Follow climber paths whenever possible to avoid damaging the grasses and flowers. No wild camping unless you have the landowner's permission.

Guidebooks: The valley is covered in *Plaisir West* by Jürg von Känel. This book covers many moderate areas and mountain routes in the Bernese Oberland and the Haute Savoise in France. Other books in the series, including *Schweiz-Extrem,* cover the extreme routes in Switzerland. Useful maps are Landeskarte der Schweiz No. 255 Sustenpass 1:50,000 and No. 5004 Berner Oberland 1:50,000. The Sustenpass map is very useful; the Berner Oberland map is necessary if you want to climb mountain routes.

Services and shops: Innertkirchen has a couple small markets that sell bread, fruit, vegetables, and other food. There are also restaurants and bars. Meiringen, a few miles west of Innertkirchen, is a larger town with grocery stores; more shops, including a climbing store; and lots of restaurants. If it's raining, visit Kletterhalle Haslital, a climbing gym in Meiringen.

Farther west is Interlaken, a large town with loads of restaurants, hotels, and shops. The climbing shop Vertical Sport offers a large selection of gear and clothes.

Emergency services: Dial 112 for all emergencies. Phones are available at Grimsel Hospiz, atop Grimsel Pass, and in the villages of Guttannen and Innertkirchen.

Nearby climbing areas: Several limestone sport crags are above Meiringen, just west of Innertkirchen. The five developed sectors here are Tschorrenflue, Rotsteini, Hundsflue, Staldenflue, and Beretli. The alps south of Meiringen offer some stunning alpine rock climbs up to fifteen pitches long on the Engelhörner.

Mountain granite routes are everywhere in the Bernese Oberland. One of the prize peaks is Salbitschijen (9,800 feet or 2,984 meters), with lots of superb bolted routes and the traditional routes up

ridges. Excellent limestone climbing is found at Tellistock and Wendenstock.

Nearby attractions: Area attractions include Aare Gorge, Rosenlaui Glacier, Rosenlaui Gorge, Reichenbach Falls, Sustenpass, Interlaken, Grindelwald, Eiger, and the Jungfrau. Farther southwest is Zermatt and the Matterhorn. Ask at the tourist office in Interlaken or Meiringen for information and maps.

Finding the area: The nearest international airports with regular flights from the United States are Zürich to the north and Geneva to the west. You can also fly to Milan, Italy, and drive north to the area. The Grimsel Valley cliffs are along the road between Innertkirchen and Grimselpass. All distances to the described cliffs begin in Innertkirchen at the north end of the valley.

Spiegelwand   Oelberg   Fair Hands Line

Parking

Handegg Slabs

The Handegg Slabs is a huge, west-facing sector that towers above Handegg on the east flank of Grimsel Valley. The sector is divided into three sections: Spiegelwand on the left, the stunning slabs of Oelberg in the middle, and the obvious buttress of Fair Hands Line on the right. The best routes ascend the huge central slabs of Oelberg and the elegant long rib of *Fair Hands Line*.

Oelberg

Oelberg is the huge sweep of granite slab above Handegg. Several long routes ascend the slab. This guide details the best and most popular route, which is divided into two separate routes since many parties rappel after climbing *Engeliweg* to the base of the steep headwall that divides the slab. Other good routes are *Boulder Highway* (6c) (5.11b) and *Katzenpfad* (4c) (5.7), an easier nine-pitch route up the left side of the slab.

1. Engeliweg (5b) (5.8) 5 pitches. The first few pitches up the central slab, first ascended by Christel Feederle and Hans Howald in 1979, make a good afternoon outing. Start right of a dark water-streaked wall capped by a large roof. **Pitch 1:** Up a slab right of the roof (5b) to bolt anchors. **Pitch 2:** Continue up left across a clean slab (5a) to bolt anchors on a ledge. **Pitch 3:** Move left on the ledge, and work up a crack and slab (4b) to bolt anchors. **Pitch 4:** Good friction climbing (5a) to bolt anchors. **Pitch 5:** Up left and over an overlap, then straight up to a ledge (5b) with bolt anchors. **Descent:** Rappel the route. **Rack:** Bring two 165-foot (50-meter) ropes and a dozen quickdraws.

2. Siebenschläfer (6b+) (5.11a) 15 total pitches: five pitches on *Engeliweg* plus ten pitches. Climb *Engeliweg* for five pitches. **Pitch 6:** Thin slab climbing up left (6b)

to a bolt anchor. **Pitch 7:** Continue up left, surmounting a big overlap (6a), to a bolted belay under the steep headwall. **Pitch 8:** Tricky face and crack moves up the headwall (6b+) to a bolted belay on the slab above. **Pitch 9:** Move out right, up a bit, then up right (6a) to bolt anchors. **Pitch 10:** Up left around some

flakes, then back right (6b+) to bolt anchors. **Pitches 11–15:** Continue straight up the slab—5c, 5c, 6b, 6a, 5c—to the final set of bolt anchors. **Descent:** Rappel the route. **Rack:** Bring two 165-foot (50-meter) ropes and a dozen quick-draws.

3. Handeggverschneidung (5c+) (5.9+) 5 pitches. A great route up the big right-facing dihedral left of a slab on the lower right side of Oelberg. Start below the obvious dihedral. **Pitch 1:** Low angle climbing up the dihedral (4c) to a bolted belay. **Pitch 2:** Up the steepening dihedral (5a) to bolt anchors. **Pitch 3:** Good climbing up the dihedral (5c) to bolt anchors. **Pitch 4:** Over a blocky roof system (4a) to bolt anchors. **Pitch 5:** Thin edging up the dihedral (5c+), then up right below the immense roof to bolt anchors. **Descent:** Rappel the route. **Rack:** Bring two 165-foot (50-meter) ropes and 12 quickdraws.

4. Quarzriss (5c+) (5.9+) 4 pitches. "Quartz Crack," right of route #3, is an excellent line up a shallow crack system on the streaked slab capped by a large roof on the lower right side of Oelberg. **Pitch 1:** Climb up left and then straight up a slab (5a) to a bolted anchor. **Pitch 2:** Follow the crack system (5a+) to a bolted belay shelf on the right. **Pitch 3:** Superb climbing up the crack (5c+) to a bolted belay. **Pitch 4:** Finish up the crack (5c), then move left to bolt anchors under the big roof. **Descent:** Rappel the route. **Rack:** Bring two 165-foot (50-meter) ropes, a set of Stoppers, and 10 quickdraws.

Fair Hands Line Sektor

The Fair Hands Line Sektor is the prominent buttress right of the Handegg Slabs. Several routes ascend the buttress; the best is *Fair Hands Line,* established in 1978 by Martin Stettler and Jörg von Känel. Just right is another great route called *Mummery* (6b+) put up by Yves and Claude Remy in 1994.

Finding the cliff: Park at the parking lot on the left (east) for the Hotel Handeck just past a tunnel and 0.8 kilometer up the road from the parking for Handegg. Cross the river on a bridge, and hike up left on a well-defined trail for about fifteen minutes to the base of the buttress.

5. Fair Hands Line (6a) (5.10a) 10 pitches. This long excellent climb ascends a prominent buttress to the right or south of the Handegg Slabs. The first eight pitches ascend a mixture of corners, cracks, and slabs. **Pitch 1:** Crack (5b) up left-facing corner. **Pitch 2:** Face left of corner (6a-) to a good ledge. **Pitch 3:** Move left and climb a right-facing corner, then left and up a face left of a corner and roof to a belay (5c+). **Pitch 4:** A left-facing corner to a face (5b). **Pitch 5:** Face climb up left to the top of a right-facing corner. More face climbing leads to a belay (5a+). **Pitch 6:** Face climb out right and then directly up to a belay (5a+). **Pitch 7:** Easier climbing (4b) up the slabby wall to a belay. **Pitch 8:** Face climb up right and then up left along a crack system to a belay above (5a+). **Pitch 9:** Move up right, then up a left-facing corner. Above, work back left on the smooth slab (6a) to a belay ledge. **Pitch 10:** Easier slab climbing (5a) leads up to the trees above and a belay. Continue climbing up through the trees and easy slabs until you can traverse off right to the top of the cable line.

Descent Tram

Descent: Quick, easy, and painless. Ride the cable car back to the base. It's also possible to rappel from fixed belay anchors down the route if the weather craps out.
Rack: Bring medium to large Stoppers, a few small and medium Friends, a dozen quickdraws, and a 165-foot (50-meter) rope. A 200-foot (60-meter) rope lets you easily string pitches together to speed up your ascent.

Gelmerfluh

Gelmerfluh is a gorgeous, west-facing, orange and gray-colored slab hanging on the east side of the wide valley just past the long highway tunnel partway up Grimsel Valley. The central slab section offers a half-dozen hard routes with somewhat scanty protection. The best of these is *Wildheuer* (6a) (5.10a) with four pitches of steep smearing before rappelling back down. This section of the wall can be wet and seeping in June and after rain. Ask around for beta on this and the other routes. The cliff's best lines ascend the blunt buttresses on the right side of the cliff, with the classic *Moby Dick* being the best route. This aesthetic line laybacks up a couple left-facing dihedrals. *Via Birra* is a fine crack and corner climb to the right.

Finding the cliff: Drive south from Innertkirchen for 17 kilometers. Just past the long, uphill tunnel are two parking lots. Drive past the first one on the right, and park in the smaller lot on the left. The obvious cliff is above the road to the east. Hike up a climber's trail that meanders up a steep grassy slope to the base of the left side of the slab. Walk right along the base to the routes, which are on the right side of the cliff. Approach time is fifteen minutes.

6. Moby Dick (5c+) (5.9+) 2 pitches. A Grimsel classic, must-do route. Begin at a belay bolt below the obvious left-leaning dihedral on the right side of the slab. **Pitch 1:** Exciting fingertip laybacking (5.9+) leads up the dihedral past 3 bolts. Exit right with tricky face moves, and climb to a 2-bolt belay at the base of the upper dihedral. **Pitch 2:** Layback up the excellent left-facing dihedral to a 2-bolt belay stance. You can climb three more pitches above here, but the rock and climbing isn't as good as the first two leads. **Descent:** Rappel the route with two ropes. **Rack:** Bring two ropes, #3 to #9 Stoppers, and #1 to #2.5 Friends. Some small cams are also useful.

7. Via Birra (5a) (5.7) 3 pitches. A fine crack route up the outside buttress. Begin

75 feet right of *Moby Dick* at a belay bolt. **Pitch 1:** Climb double cracks up a left-facing corner on the left side of a giant flake to a ring bolt belay stance. **Pitch 2:** Continue up and right in corners and cracks past a bolt and a couple fixed pitons to a bolted belay. **Pitch 3:** Step right, and jam a long corner crack to a bolted belay. **Descent:** Rappel the route with double ropes. **Rack:** Bring two ropes, a set of Stoppers, and Friends to #3.

8. Little Big Man (5c+) (5.9+) 3 to 4 pitches. A good route on the far right side of the wall. Begin just right of *Via Birra* below a right-angling crack and corner system. The first pitch edges up left past a bolt, then works up the corner system to a belay. Continue up corners and flakes for two to three more pitches. **Descent:** Make three rappels down the route, with the last rappel from anchors on the slab to the right of the corner. **Rack:** Bring a set of Stoppers and Friends to #3.

Dom

Donald Duck
Sector

Foxie Slab

Azalée Beach

Parking

Crow Slab →

Gerstenegg Cliffs

The Gerstenegg area lies on the west side of the valley opposite Gelmerfluh and is composed of several large, distinct slabs that form five different sectors. These are, from right to left, Crow, Dom, Foxie, Donald Duck, and Azalée Beach. Crow, Foxie, and Azalée Beach are all named for routes on their respective slabs. The sectors are justifiably popular, with many long, excellent moderate routes.

Crow Slab

Crow Slab is an east-facing, 900-foot-high (270-meter) slab directly west of the parking area just south of the tunnel. This beautiful dome, creased by vertical crack systems and dissected by two large roofs, yields a superb assortment of long, moder-ate routes up its granite flanks. Besides the classic routes described here, another worthy line is *Crow* (6a) (5.10a). This moder-ate route has a short crux up a couple of steep, 15-foot steps. The route parallels *Fliegender Teppich* on the right.

All the described routes, like most in the valley, are set up as half-rope-length pitches, so you can climb and rappel with a single 200-foot (60-meter) rope. If you bring enough quickdraws, you can easily run pitches together and shorten your climbing time. All the routes are bolt pro-tected, although runouts do occur. Carry a small selection of gear for each climb that includes Stoppers from #3 to #9 and Friends from #1 to #2.5.

Descent off all the routes is by either rappelling the route from bolted stations or walking off to the south. If you choose to rappel, it's a good idea to have a 200-foot (60-meter) rope or two ropes. The walk-off descent takes about fifteen minutes.

Finding the cliff: The slab is approached from either the east or from the south. For the east approach drive up the road from Innertkirchen, and park at the large lot on the right at 17 kilometers, just past the long tunnel. Follow a path downhill, cross the creek on a stone bridge, and scramble up to the base. For the other approach drive 18 kilometers up the highway, and make a right turn onto a narrow road below the large dam. Follow this paved road to a parking area at the cable car station. Cross slopes to the west on a path to a good trail that leads down and north to the base of the cliff. Hiking time from car to cliff is fifteen minutes.

Routes are described from left to right.

9. Krümel (5a) (5.7-) 9 pitches. Very good and very fun with some interesting pitches. The route is bolt protected with bolt belay anchors. Begin on a ledge at the toe of the far left side of the cliff. Climb up right on a tongue of rock for two pitches. Pitch 1 is 4c with one point of aid or 5b (5.8). Pitch 2 is 4b. Halfway up Pitch 3 angle up left to a belay below the left sweep of slab. Climb three easy pitches up the smooth slab: 4b, 4c, 3b. Pitch 7 works up left and ascends a rib (5a) to a belay ledge on the left. Pitch 8 continues (5a) to just below the cliff top. Rappel from here, or continue up left (3b) to the top or right and up to the top of *Fliegender Teppich* and rappel down it. **Descent:** Rappel the route or walk off to the south.

10. Fliegender Teppich (5a) (5.7) 10 pitches. Classic climbing. Established by Roger Meier and Jürg von Känel in 2000. Begin at the same place as *Krümel* at the bottom left side of the slab. Climb Pitches 1 and 2, same as *Krümel,* but continue up right to a ledge belay at the end of Pitch 3. Pitch 4 features spectacular smearing (5a) up right above the big arching roof. Pitch 5 works up and left across the great slab (4c) to a belay. Pitch 6 edges up the headwall (5a), then up right. Pitch 7 climbs easily (4a) to a steep step. Pitch 8 pulls up the step (5a) then up left. Pitches 9 and 10 follow cracks and corners (4b) to a belay at the cliff top. **Descent:** Walk off to the south or rappel the route with double ropes.

11. Gämsipfad (5a) (5.7) 8 pitches. This good route up slabs and cracks offers mostly easy climbing with only one tricky section. Start below a right-angling dihedral on the right side of the slab. **Pitch 1:** Climb the dihedral (4a) to the right side of a roof system. **Pitch 2:** Edge up a nice slab (3b) to a belay. **Pitch 3:** Bypass the right side of the next roof system (3c) to a belay above. **Pitch 4:** Up cracks (4c). **Pitch 5:** Up left along cracks (4c). **Pitch 6:** Up a crack (4a) to a belay below a buttress. **Pitch 7:** Jam a steeper crack (5a) to a ledge. **Pitch 8:** Up and left on easier

climbing (4a) to the cliff top. **Descent:** Rappel the route from the top of Pitch 8, or walk off to the south.

12. Bazi und Bizi (5a) (5.7) 8 to 12 pitches. Up the far right side of the slab. Pitches can be easily combined together, and the upper pitches can be avoided. Begin just right of *Gämsipfad.* **Pitch 1:** Up a short slab (4a). **Pitches 2 and 3:** Up and right in cracks (4a and 4c). These can also be broken into three pitches. **Pitch 4:** Up right from the gully and past the right side of a roof (5a). **Pitches 5 and 6:** Along the right edge of a slab (4b

and 3c) to a belay right of a long thin roof. **Pitch 7:** Up left across a slab (5a). **Pitch 8:** Slab and face climbing to a ledge (5a). **Pitch 9:** Three options here: 1. Traverse up left from here on easy climbing to the cliff top; 2. Move right on the ledge, and climb a crack to a belay below trees (5a). Rappel from here back to the big ledge; 3. Excellent crack and face climbing (4c) to the high point of the cliff. **Descent:** Scramble up through trees to the walk-off, rappel back to the ledge and finish up left (4a), or rappel the route.

Foxie Slab

This immense, east-facing slab offers three excellent and popular routes up narrow slab aprons on its right side. The routes are almost 1,000 feet long. The beautiful central slab is deceptively low angle and offers mostly easy friction climbing.

The routes are well protected by bolts, so you only need a rack of twelve quickdraws. Beginning leaders should bring a few wires and cams. All the belays are bolted.

Walk off south from the cliff top, and descend grassy slopes above the slab to Azalée Beach. Continue down the trail to the car park.

Finding the cliff: The slab is approached via a trail from the south. Drive up the highway from Innertkirchen for 18 kilometers, and make a right turn at a switchback below the dam onto a narrow road. Follow this paved road west and uphill to a large parking area at the cable car station. Cross slopes to the west on a path to a good trail that leads north to the base of the cliff. The routes are on the far right side of the slab. Approach time is fifteen minutes.

Routes are described from right to left.

13. Dousche inklusive (4b) (5.5) 7 pitches. Fun easy route to run up on the far right side of the slab. Begin on the right side of the wall, just left of a grassy area. Follow the line of bolts up the white slabs. Pitch grades: 3c, 3c, 4b, 3b, 4a, 3b, 3b. **Descent:** Walk-off to the south.

14. Foxie (5a) (5.7 A0) 8 pitches. *Foxie,* established by Claude and Yves Rémy in 1981, is one of Grimsel's best classics, with excellent climbing, good protection, and an airy finish. Some pitches can be combined into longer leads to save time. Start left of a low roof. **Pitch 1:** Pass the left edge of a roof, and trend up right (4b) on a slab. **Pitch 2:** Up right on the smooth slab (5a). **Pitch 3:** Friction up left, then up the big left-facing dihedral (5a). **Pitch**

← Walk off

4: Easy climbing up the dihedral (3c). **Pitch 5:** Climb slabs and cracks above the dihedral (4c). **Pitch 6:** Work over a roof and then up a prow (4c). **Pitch 7:** Up the left edge of the slab (3c) to a belay at the left side of the big roof. **Pitch 8:** Two ways to go. Climb the right wall of the roof (4c with two points of aid or 5c), or edge up the slab left of the roof (4c). Either way, belay on the slab above.

Descent: Scramble to the cliff top, and hike off south.

15. Alpiner Abstieg (5a) (5.7) 8 pitches. Another fun outing on the slab's right side. Begin at the same place as *Foxie.* Climb eight pitches with bolt protection and bolt anchors up the left side of a long, narrow slab apron. Pitch grades: 5a, 4c, 4b, 4b, 4b, 3b, 3c, 3b. **Descent:** Scramble to the cliff top, and hike off south.

Azalée Beach Dome

Azalée Beach, the smallest cliff in the Gerstenegg area, is an east-facing, easily accessible slab that offers an excellent selection of climbs from one to three pitches long. Most routes are well protected and offer a variety of climbing that includes friction, edges, short cracks, flakes, corners, and occasional roofs. The Beach, a good introduction to Grimsel climbing, is usually busy and popular, especially on weekends.

The only necessary gear is a dozen quickdraws and a rope, preferably a 200-foot (60-meter) rope. Descent off all routes is by rappel from fixed anchors or by walking off to the left or south from the cliff top.

Finding the cliff: The Beach has a short approach from the cable car station parking area. Drive south up the highway from Innertkirchen for 18 kilometers, and make a right turn at a switchback below the dam onto a narrow road. Follow this paved road west and uphill to a large parking area at the cable car station. Hike south from the parking area toward the dam, and pick up a trail that switchbacks up the grassy slope to a small saddle near the dam and beside an aqueduct. Follow a trail north alongside the aqueduct to the cliff base. Hiking time is fifteen minutes from the parking to the cliff.

Routes are described from left to right.

16. Alphorn (5c+) (5.9+) 1 pitch. An edging problem up the far left side of the slab. 85 feet.

17. Moritz (3b) (5.5) 1 pitch. Fun and easy. 85 feet.

18. Kristall (4c) (5.6) 2 pitches. **Pitch 1:** Up and left (3c) to belay bolts. 85 feet. **Pitch 2:** Fun climbing left and then back right (4c) to anchors under the dark headwall. **Descent:** Rappel the route.

19. Finisch (6a) (5.10a) A top finishing pitch for *Kristall*. Edge up and right on the steep headwall to bolt anchors.

20. Felix (4a) (5.6) 1 pitch. Start off a boulder. Fun edging and smearing up and slightly left to anchors. 85 feet.

21. Zizigutti (5c) (5.9) 3 pitches. **Pitch 1:** Easy climbing (3b) to anchors under the big overlap roof. 85 feet. **Pitch 2:** Over the right side of the roof, then thin edging up left (5c) to bolt anchors. **Pitch 3:** Climb the leaning blunt arête (5c) up left to bolt anchors.

22. Nils Holgersohn (5a) (5.7) 4 pitches. A good tour up the big, left-slanting corner in the center of the face. **Pitch 1:** Flakes and smears (3c) to anchors right of the roof. **Pitch 2:** Up the big corner (4b). **Pitch 3:** Stemming and edging (5a) up the corner. **Pitch 4:** The groove and face (4a) to bolt anchors at the cliff top. **Descent:** Rappel the route or walk off left.

23. Traverse Stupid (5c) (5.9) 4 pitches. Superb climbing. Friction up the face right of the corner system. **Pitch 1:** Flakes and edges (5a) to anchors. **Pitch 2:** Up left and over the overlap (5b). **Pitch 3:** Around the right side of a roof and then up left (5c). **Pitch 4:** Up and then traverse left (5c). **Descent:** Rappel the route or walk off left.

24. Härdöpfel (5c) (5.9) 4 pitches. Another good one up the central slab. Pitch grades: 5a, 5b, 5c, 5b. **Descent:** Rappel the route.

25. Unknown (5c) (5.9) 3 pitches. Recommended. **Pitch 1:** Friction to anchors up left of an overlap. **Pitch 2:** Over the overlap above. **Pitch 3:** Edge to anchors just below the top. **Descent:** Rappel the route.

26. Grimsel Life (5c+) (5.9+) 3 pitches. Fun route. **Pitch 1:** Edge (5a) to anchors. **Pitch 2:** Friction up and left (5b) to belay anchors under an overlap. **Pitch 3:** Around the overlap and straight up (5c+) to anchors. **Descent:** Rappel the route.

27. Azalée Beach (5c+) (5.9+) 4 pitches. Classic climb. Smear up four excellent pitches—5b, 5c+, 5b+, 4b—to anchors just below the top. **Descent:** Rappel the route or walk off left.

28. Sellsorger (6a+) (5.10b) 2 pitches. **Pitch 1:** A sort of runout slab to a short headwall. Go right (6a+) or left (5c) to anchors below an overlap. **Pitch 2:** Straight up (5c) to anchors. **Descent:** Rappel the route.

29. Chüngel (5c) (5.9) 3 pitches. Thin edging and friction up the right side. Bolts are spaced, so keep your wits about you. Pitch grades: 5c, 5c, 5b. **Descent:** Rappel the route.

30. Wadenchrampf (6a-) (5.10a) 3 pitches. The smooth white slab on the far right side. Again, watch the runouts. Pitch grades: 6a-, 5c, 5c. **Descent:** Rappel the route.

The other Gerstenegg sectors also offer good climbs. Donald Duck, the slab right of Azalée Beach, has four good routes:

Donald Duck (5a) (5.9) 4 pitches; *Roadrunner* (4c) (5.6) 7 pitches; *Dagoberts Goldspeicher* (5a) (5.9) 6 pitches; and *Speedy Gonzalez* (4c) (5.6) 6 pitches. This streaked slab is often wet, particularly early in the season when snow is melting in the cirque above. All routes are bolted with fixed anchors.

Above Azalée Beach and Donald Duck is Bächlital. This excellent area above the Bächlital-Hütte is a high alpine cirque below Alplistock (9,450 feet or 2,878 meters) and the Bächligletscher or Bachli Glacier west of Grimsel Valley. It's reached by hiking west from Räterichs-bodensee, the dam that plugs the valley above the Gerstenegg slabs, for two hours uphill on a trail that begins at the dam parking area. The area offers great sport-climbing cliffs with single-pitch routes, as well as some bigger crags with routes up to eight pitches long. Consult the guide-book *Plaisir West* for topos and directions.

Seeplatten

A large dam blocks the Aare River above Gerstenegg, forming a long reservoir called Räterichsbodensee at an elevation of 5,797 feet (1,767 meters). The highway twists along the eastern shore of the lake, and a long parade of immense slabs marches along the western shore. The main slab sector here, called Seeplatten, is divided into three sectors framed by rock gullies. The right-hand section is a 1,300-foot-high (400-meter) slab with a half-dozen long routes that wend their way up cracks, corners, and open slabs. The middle section, reaching a height of 720 feet (220 meters), yields some brilliant moderate routes. These climbs are more sustained than the Gerstenegg routes. The described routes and topos are on this cliff section. Consult the comprehensive guidebook for topos to the long routes on the right slab. To the left is another large slab called Sommerloch. Several good routes ascend its streaked flanks. All the routes are divided into half-rope lengths, making them easy to climb and descend with a long cord. You can also run pitches together for quicker ascents.

Like the other Grimsel slabs, all the routes are bolted, although runouts are found. Carry a small selection of nuts and cams for the occasional placement between bolts. Also bring two 165-foot (50-meter) ropes or a 200-foot (60-meter) rope. Descent off all the routes is by rappel.

Finding the cliff: Drive up the highway from Innertkirchen for 18 kilometers, and turn right below the dam. Follow the narrow road up to the parking area at the cable car station. This is the same parking lot to access the Gerstenegg slabs. From here hike south on a trail that switchbacks up to the far right (west) side of the dam. Follow a good trail along the western lakeshore to the base of the slabs. Or continue driving up the highway another kilometer, and park in a lot on the east end of the dam. Walk across the dam, then follow the level lakeside trail to the slabs. Approach hiking time is twenty to thirty minutes.

Routes are described from right to left. To the right of route #31 are two other good routes—*Chly Häx* (5c+)

(5.9+) and *Paradiesvogel* (5c+) (5.9+). Both are 5 pitches long and easy to follow. Locate the lines of bolts just right of *Bluttä Buch* and crank.

31. Bluttä Buch (5c+) (5.9+) 5 pitches.
Pitch 1: Up left on a slab right of corners (4b). **Pitch 2:** Up left and over obvious overlap (5c) to belay bolts. **Pitch 3:** Wander up and right on slab (5c) to belay bolts. **Pitch 4:** Over right side of thin roof (5c) to bolted belay. **Pitch 5:** Thin face climbing (5c+) to a bolted belay. **Descent:** Rappel the route.

32. Maa mit Bart (6a) (5.10a) 5 pitches.
Pitch 1: Slab above trail (5b) to belay bolts below a roof. **Pitch 2:** Pull over the roof, and climb a slab and crack (5b) to a bolted belay ledge. **Pitch 3:** Face climbing on a steeper slab (5c+) to a bolted belay. **Pitch 4:** Climb up right, then yard over a roof (5c) to a bolted belay stance. **Pitch 5:** Thin, tricky face climbing up and left (6a) to a ledge with belay bolts. **Descent:** Rappel the route.

33. Schnäggäsiider (5a) (5.7) 5 pitches. Begin on the trail cut into the cliff base.

Pitch 1: A smooth slab to a corner, then climb over a notch roof (5a) to a bolted belay stance. **Pitch 2:** Step left, and climb (4b) directly up to a bolt belay. **Pitch 3:** Edge up the left side of a slab (4c) to a bolt belay. **Pitch 4:** Face moves up the slab (5a) to a belay left of a big roof. **Pitch 5:** Easier climbing up broken rock to belay bolts right of some bushes. **Descent:** Rappel the route.

34. Grims (5a) (5.7) 5 pitches. Good clean friction route. **Pitch 1:** Friction up a compact slab (4b) to a bolted belay. **Pitch 2:** Jam a crack, then face climb (4a) to a ledge with belay bolts. **Pitch 3:** Climb a short corner up right, pull an overlap, and friction (4a) to a stance with belay bolts. **Pitch 4:** Smear left and up (4a) to belay bolts on a pedestal. **Pitch 5:** Face climb (5a) to belay bolts. **Descent:** Rappel the route. The rappel from the top of Pitch 2 to the base is 168 feet.

Dome de le Marée

Dome de le Marée is a beautiful golden-colored dome that drops directly into murky Lake Grimsel next to the dam below Hotel Grimsel Hospiz in the upper valley. This superb 500-foot-high dome offers a great introduction to the heady climbs found farther west above the north shore of Lake Grimsel. The main face offers several multipitch routes, and the shorter west face yields three good, one-pitch lines, including a perfect hand crack. The crag is a stunning place to climb, with spectacular views up the lake toward the higher Alps towering to the west.

Rack: The slab routes require a small rack with a set of Stoppers, ten quickdraws, and a 165-foot (50-meter) rope. A 200-foot (60-meter) rope is preferred, especially for the rappel to the base on the east side of the dome. Descent off the dome routes is by walking off to the east and descending grassy gullies, terraces, and slabs to the access trail. The routes on the west face require rappelling with two ropes or lowering from bolt anchors.

Finding the cliff: Drive up the valley for 22.3 kilometers to the obvious right turn marked HOTEL GRIMSEL HOSPIZ on the east side of Grimselsee, the large lake. Turn right, and drive up the cobblestone road to the hotel and park. Walk west across the lot to a viewpoint overlooking the lake. Marée is the dome rising out of the water next to the dam.

Descend a staircase near the viewpoint for three floors and exit onto a trail that heads west to a stone viewpoint and then back right above the lake to the top of the dam. Walk across the dam, and follow a trail cut into the cliff face above. The airy trail heads up right and then traverses back left across the cliff face to a tunnel. Just before the tunnel are some bolt anchors for rappelling. Abseil from here to access the right-side slab routes. Otherwise, walk through the long dark

tunnel to the west side of the crag. Look for more anchors on a slab next to a grass gully or anchors at the cliff base. Rappel from here down the gully to access the slab routes on the left side of the wall. Hiking time from the car park to the west side of the tunnel is fifteen to twenty minutes.

Routes are described from left to right.

35. Pile-Poils (5c) (5.9) No topo. 1 pitch. A 3-star, perfect hand crack left of the west tunnel entrance on the west face of the dome. Jam the steep, sustained hand crack (no bolts) to a bolt anchor. 150 feet. **Rack:** Bring #3 to #9 Stoppers, a couple sets of Friends #1 to #3, 10 quickdraws, and two ropes. **Descent:** Rappel the route.

Between *Pile-Poils* and the tunnel entrance are a couple 5.11 bolted slab routes.

36. Rösti Blues (5c) (5.9) No topo. 1 pitch. Start down and right from the tunnel. Climb a crack and steep slab to bolt anchors. **Rack:** #3 to #9 Stoppers, some small cams and TCUs, 10 quickdraws, and two ropes. **Descent:** Rappel the route.

37. H2O (6a+) (5.10b) No topo. 1 pitch. Edge up the black streak right of #36 to bolt anchors. **Rack:** #3 to #9 Stoppers, some small cams and TCUs, 10 quickdraws, and two ropes. **Descent:** Rappel the route.

To reach *Euréka* descend the grassy gully below #37 by down climbing or rappelling from anchors on the wall down right from the start of #37 or from a big iron bar on a slab to the west. Left of *Euréka* is *Mistral* (7a) (5.12a), a bolted friction route up the smooth slab.

38. Euréka (6b) (5.10c) 5 pitches. An excellent route up the dome's left side. Begin at the high-water mark on the left side of the slab. **Pitch 1:** Friction up right along a shallow crease (6a) to a hollow, then climb straight up to a bolted belay ledge. If the water is high, you will slide into it if you fall! **Pitch 2:** Work delicately up left (6b) to a bolted belay below a thin right-facing corner. **Pitch 3:** Brilliant smearing up the corner (6a) leads to a bolted belay. **Pitch 4:** Move up right on

the slab to a break. Continue up a crack system (5b) to a bolted belay on a ledge. **Pitch 5:** Climb a short headwall (5a) to the cliff top and a building. **Rack:** Bring a set of Stoppers, 10 quickdraws, and a single rope. **Descent:** Hike east down grassy gullies, terraces, and rock slabs to the access trail.

39. Les pieds et les mains (6b) (5.10c) 5 pitches. Great climb! Begin by rappelling from anchors on the access trail just before the east tunnel entrance. Rappel down the gully 150 feet to another anchor. Make a

50-foot rappel down to the base of the cliff. If the water level is low, traverse onto a white shelf to belay. Otherwise, belay by the gully, and traverse out to a bolt at the route's start. **Pitch 1:** From the far left side of the white shelf, climb up and left (5c) to bolt anchors (same first anchors as *Euréka*). **Pitch 2:** Smear up right on the beautiful slab (5c) to bolt anchors at a ledge. **Pitch 3:** Climb a short headwall (6b), and then work up left onto the upper slab and bolt anchors at a break. **Pitch 4:** Easier climbing (4a) leads up right to belay bolts at a break. **Pitch 5:** Edge up a steep wall (5c) to a ledge. Belay here, or walk left and climb another short wall (5c) to the cliff top. **Rack:** Bring a set of Stoppers, 10 quickdraws, and a single rope. **Descent:** Hike east down grassy gullies, terraces, and rock slabs to the access trail.

40. Les O.S. (6c) (5.11a) 5 pitches. A good line up the right margin of the cliff. Use the same approach as #39 to the white ledge below the slab. If the water level is high, you will have to use some creative traversing to get to the route's start. **Pitch 1:** Tricky face climbing up the steep slab (6a) leads to a short traverse to a belay ledge with bolts. **Pitch 2:** Step right, work up a short corner system, then do some hard face climbing (6b) to a bolted belay. **Pitch 3:** A short pitch. Face climb (4b) to a ledge with bolts and bushes. **Pitch 4:** Climb up left (4a) to a bolted belay ledge. **Pitch 5:** Edge up the steeper headwall right of the "window" (5c) to a ledge. Belay here, or continue up another steep step (6c) to the top. This last hard step can be avoided by going left on the ledge and climbing a 5c wall. **Rack:** Bring a set of Stoppers, 10 quickdraws, and a single rope. **Descent:** Hike east down grassy gullies, terraces, and rock slabs to the access trail.

Dome de la Cascade, Eldorado Dome, and Bärenwand

Some of the Grimsel Valley's best climbs are on immense hidden slabs—Dome de la Cascade, Eldorado Dome, Bärenwand—that tower above the north shore of Grimsel Lake west of the dam and highway. After climbing the classics described in this guide, you will want to hike up the valley and do some of the long classic friction and crack routes on these remote domes. Besides superlative climbing you'll find lots of solitude and isolation and a setting that is simply stunning. To the west loom some of the highest and most dramatic 13,000-foot-high (4,000 meter) peaks of the Bernese Alps, including the Wetterhorn and the pointed Finsteraarhorn, as well as the Oberaar Glacier.

Dome de la Cascade is the large broken dome near a rushing waterfall west of Dome de le Marée. The best routes here are *Razamanaz* (6a) (5.10a), up a long crack and corner, and *Manitoba* (6a A0) (5.10a A0 or 5.10d), up the central slab. Reach the dome by walking west from the tunnel through Dome de le Marée and then uphill over grass slopes and low-angle slabs to the cliff.

Eldorado Dome is the biggest and perhaps the best dome at Grimsel. It's a huge, 1,600-foot-high (500-meter) face of perfect granite split by long cracks and corners. *Septumania* (6a+) (5.10a/b) and *Motörhead* (6a+) (5.10a/b), two of Switzerland's megaclassic routes, ascend the left side of the face.

Septumania, a beautiful climb on the lower-angle left side of the wall, ascends friction slabs and occasional cracks and corners up the general line of least resistance. The bolt-protected, 16-pitch route keeps your attention all the way up. Pitch ratings are 5c+, 5c, 5a, 5a, 5b, 6a, 5c, 6a-, 5c, 6a+, 5a, 4a, 5c, 5b, 5c, 4a.

The elegant *Motörhead,* just right of *Septumania* and right of a grassy ledge and bushes, is a much different route. The first half of the 14-pitch line jams cracks and corners before the angle eases and it becomes a face climb. Pitch ratings are 4a, 5c, 6a, 4b, 5a, 5c, 6a, 6a+, 4b, 5b, 5c, 6a, 5c, 4a.

The pitches on both routes are a half-rope length so you can run pitches together to shorten belaying and leading times. The routes are also bolt protected, although a rack of gear is needed, including sets of Stoppers and Friends to #3, along with a dozen quickdraws. All belay anchors are 2 bolts. Descent is by walking off to the east and descending grassy gullies.

Find the dome by following the directions to Dome de le Marée. After the tunnel continue walking west along the trail above the north shore of the lake for another hour to the base of the cliff. Many other excellent routes ascend Eldorado, including the bold *Marche ou Crève* (6c) paralleling *Septumania, Vénon* (6b A0 or 7a+) on the pillar right of *Motörhead, Hirnriss* (6c), the classic *Métal hurlant* (6b), *Schweiz plaisir* (6a+), *Yeti* (6c), the friction classic *Forces Motrices* (6a A0), and *Gletscherweib* (6a A0) on the right side of the dome.

The last dome is Bärenwand, a huge 1,800-foot-high (550-meter) dome hidden around the slope west of Eldorado Dome. Few routes ascend the dome, but the best and most traveled is *Himmelsleiter* (6b) (5.10c). This 12-pitch outing follows an obvious line up cracks and corners on the central left side of the wall. Fixed protection is limited, so bring a generous rack that includes sets of Stoppers, TCUs, and Friends (a few extra mediums are good), 15 quickdraws, and two ropes. Descent off the top is by rappelling the route. Find the dome by hiking another half hour past Eldorado Dome to the cliff base.

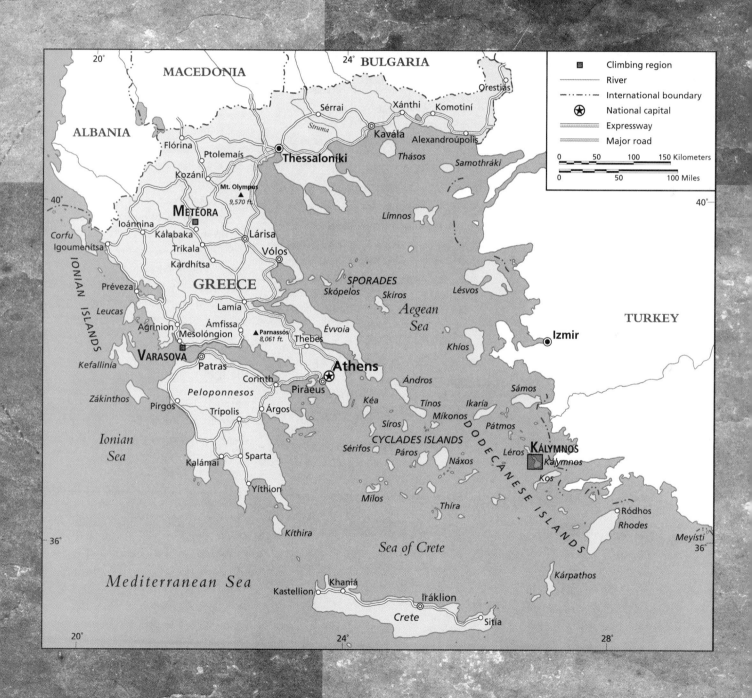

Greece

Map Legend

- Climbing region
- River
- International boundary
- National capital
- Expressway
- Major road

0 50 100 150 Kilometers
0 50 100 Miles

BULGARIA

MACEDONIA

ALBANIA

Orestiás

Sérrai
Xánthi
Komotiní
Kavála
Alexandroúpolis

Flórina
Ptolemaís
Struma
Thessaloníki
Thásos
Samothráki

Kozáni

Mt. Olympus
9,570 ft.

METÉORA

Ioánnina
Kálabaka
Lárisa
Límnos

Corfu
Igoumenítsa
Tríkala
Vólos

Kardhítsa

GREECE

SPORADES
Skópelos
Skiros
Lésvos

Préveza
Lamía
Aegean
Sea

Leucas
Ámfissa
Évvoia

Agrínion
Mesolóngion
Parnassós
8,061 ft.
Thebes

Khíos

TURKEY

Izmir

VARASOVA

Kefallinía
Patras
Corinth
Athens
Piraeus

Ándros

Sámos

Zákinthos
Pirgos
Peloponnesos
Árgos

Kéa
Tínos
Ikaría
Pátmos

KÁLYMNOS

Ionian
Sea

Trípolis
Síros
Mikonos
Kalymnos

Sérifos
CYCLADES ISLANDS
Léros
Kos

Kalámai
Sparta
Páros
Náxos

Yíthion
Mílos
Thíra

Ródhos
Rhodes

Kíthira
Sea of Crete
Kárpathos
Meyísti

Mediterranean Sea

Kastellion
Khaniá
Iráklion
Sitía

Crete

IONIAN ISLANDS

DODECANESE ISLANDS

KÁLYMNOS

■ OVERVIEW

Kálymnos (pronounced *cal-im-nos*) rises starkly out of the obsidian-colored waters of the East Aegean Sea a scant 20 miles west of Turkey and Asia Minor. The island, open to the sea and the sky, is a rocky land circumscribed with bays that slice into its barren, scalloped edges. It has precipitous limestone cliffs and a few trees scattered across its dry hillsides. The famed Greek poet Ovid described ancient Kálymnos in his *Poems of Exile* as "shaded with trees and rich in honey." Today, however, all the ancestral forests have long since been mowed down, and the hills are clad in grass and shrubbery.

The island is an unprepossessing, quiet place that generally attracts few of the tourist groups that flock to the nearby holiday isles of Kos and Rhodes. The visitors who do come to Kálymnos make an effort to get there; the island has no airport. But those who do visit find deserted stony beaches, lonely bays, and miles of superb limestone cliffs that loom above the coastline. The island's limestone, found mostly along the west coast, is a perfect arena for athletic climbing challenges. The climbing is never monotonous, with a plethora of varied movements, from delicate pulls up steep slabs and vertical walls to pumpy endurance routes up overhanging walls and caves.

More than forty-two equipped crags scatter along the west coast of Kálymnos, with more than 500 bolt-protected pitches. This guide describes most of the best and most popular crags, including Grande Grotta—called one of the world's top-ten sport crags—Poets, Odyssey, Kastéli, and Arhi. Other good sectors are Monastery and Austrians south of Kantouni; Spartacus, Panorama, and Afternoon on the long stretch of cliff above Massouri; Ocean Dream and North Cape, with some of the island's longest routes; and the Seaside Kitchen, Palace, Baby House, and Kreissaal above Emborios and the end of the west coast road. The offshore island Telendos also offers a few good routes and lots of potential.

Kálymnos is a barren, mountainous, 67-square-mile island with a rugged 60-mile-long coastline. Much of the island is composed of limestone cliffs and crags, with few fertile valleys and almost no trees. The land is, however, abundant in aromatic shrubs and plants, including thyme, sage, and oregano, which suffuse the island air with a rich fragrance.

Kálymnos is one of the Dodecanese or Twelve Islands scattered along the west coast of Turkey. The islands, including Rhodes, Kos, Kálymnos, Leros, and Patmos, have long been of strategic importance to Greece and coveted by Turkey. They were under the Turkish yoke until the Greeks were liberated in 1912. The islands were promised to Greece at the end of World War I but instead were ceded to Italy as a reward for war service. It wasn't until 1948 that they were finally returned to Greece.

Most of the rocky and rugged island is uninhabitable and untrammeled except by goats. Agriculture, mostly small family farms that grow fruits and vegetables, is restricted to a couple of pastoral valleys on the island's south side, where most of the towns and villages are located. Kálymnos is famed for its rich honey flavored by thyme and oregano. The island is inhabited by 15,500 permanent residents, most of whom live in Pothia, the modest island capital. Pothia, built around the natural horseshoe-shaped harbor on the southeast side of Kálymnos, offers all the necessary conveniences for the climber-traveler, with banks, a post office, hospital, restaurants, and a diversity of shops. The town is the center of the island's commerce and activity. It's a good place to stroll down the narrow streets, dodging maniac motor scooters, finding icon shops, or having an afternoon coffee at a cafe overlooking the harbor.

Kálymnos is nicknamed "the island of the sponge fishermen" for its most famous business. Until twenty years ago the island was the largest center for sponge production in the Aegean Sea. For the past five centuries, the Kalymnians were famed as deepwater free divers with incredible stamina, mental control, and the ability to hold their breath underwater for five min-

utes. The divers roamed the sea in small boats, diving to harvest sponges that were sold around the world. A combination of factors, however, caused the sponge business to falter, including a rare disease in 1986 that decimated the sponges and the easy manufacture of artificial sponges. With the demise of the sponge industry, Kálymnos looked to surrounding islands and began to develop itself as a resort destination.

Rack, Protection, and Descent

Kálymnos is strictly for sport climbers. All the routes are bolted, mostly with stainless steel bolts and clip-gate carabiners on the anchors for quick lower-offs. Most of the bolts are safe and solid, but beware of old, rusty bolts that are weakened by constant exposure to the salty sea air. A leader fall onto a derelict bolt can result in it shearing off and the climber being injured. Also, never lower from a single anchor here.

Bring a rack of twelve to fifteen quickdraws and either a 200-foot (60-meter) or 165-foot (50-meter) rope. The longer cord is preferable for a week's climbing, but you can get by with the shorter rope. Descent off all routes is by lowering off or rappelling from bolt anchors.

Climbing History

Most travelers to Greece's sunlit islands are generally concerned only with the warm, turquoise water, tranquil sandy beaches, and picturesque whitewashed villages stair stepping up steep hillsides above rocky bays. The idea that rock climbing occurred on these lovely isles was a distant thought until the island of Kálymnos was discovered by Italian climber Andrea di Bari on his honeymoon in 1997. He noted the amazing variety and quality of the island's limestone and returned that autumn to establish fifteen routes at Arhi and Odyssey. The islanders, having never seen climbers before, thought they were in trouble and needed rescue, so they called the police. And so began rock climbing on Kálymnos, which now dubs itself "the island of the climbers."

Since 1997 most of the island's 500-plus routes have been opened and equipped by Italian, German, and Greek climbers. Activists besides di Bari include Italian Manolo; Swiss Marcel Schmed, Kaspar Ochsner, Michel Piola, and the Remy brothers, Yves and Claude; Germans and Austrians Karsten Oelze, Martin Chepers, and Klaus Hildenbrand; British climber Neil Gresham; and Greek climbers Aris Theodoropoulos and Tomas Mihailides.

It was through the efforts of Aris Theodoropoulos, a respected Athens climber and guide, that climbing took off on Kálymnos. In 2000 he organized a climbing course for locals, as well as Kálymnos 2000, an international rock climbing meeting that officially opened the island to climbing and made its presence known to the world climbing community. He now works with the island government to ensure that all the routes are safe and properly bolted. In the past the island recreation department has provided the necessary hardware, including a drill, stainless steel bolts, and hangers for qualified climbers to establish new routes. This is good public relations, but they don't always have bolts. If you want to open new routes, it's best to bring your own bolts and hangers and try to borrow the drill from the government. Kálymnos is indeed a climber-friendly place!

Getting Around

It's not easy to get to Kálymnos, one of the most far-flung Greek isles. The quickest way is to fly to a major European city like London, Paris, or Athens and catch an Olympic Airlines flight to Kos, since there is no airport on Kálymnos. A ferry, taking forty-five minutes, runs three times daily from Kos to Kálymnos. You'll have to check ferry schedules for times, which are usually early morning, midafternoon, and evening. You can also fly to Rhodes (Rotos) and ferry to Kos and then Kálymnos. Cheap charter flights are available from London to Rhodes. If all that flying is beyond your budget or you want to combine a trip to Kálymnos with climbing at Metéora, then catch an inex-

Catherine Herve leads *Gefaerliche brandung* (6a) (5.10a/b) at Kasteli.

pensive ferry from Piraeus in Athens for a twelve-hour ride to Pothia (183 nautical miles). If you can afford it, book a cabin rather than a deck passage since it's more comfortable and private. The best ferry leaves in midafternoon and arrives in the wee hours in the morning. You need to book a hotel room ahead of time so when you arrive, a taxi can whisk you to your room.

It's relatively easy getting around Kálymnos since it is traversed by only a

few roads. It takes less than an hour on a busy day to drive from Vathi on the east coast to the end of the road at Emborios. You can catch a taxi from the harbor in Pothia to your accommodations on the west side of the island and from there walk to some cliffs like Poets and Odyssey.

You need transportation to get to the other cliffs. Most climbers rent scooters to get to the crags. They are cheap and easily rented in Pothia. Be advised, though, that some of the island scooter riders are kamikaze maniacs. Be very careful when riding and walking through Pothia. People are regularly killed in scooter accidents. Alternatively, you can rent a car, mountain bike, or take a local bus, which connects Pothia with the beach towns on the west coast. Most grocers and shops are closed on the west side of the island during the off-season, so if you don't have a car, you need to ring a taxi to head into Pothia for supplies and groceries. Some excellent year-round restaurants are within walking distance of the Massouri hotels.

Seasons and Weather

Kálymnos offers a generally warm, dry climate with sunny days. You can climb on the island year-round, finding shade in summer from the day's heat and sun in winter on cool afternoons. The best seasons are spring and autumn. Spring runs from March through May and autumn from September until November. Expect sunny days and mild nights. It can occasionally storm, usually with light rain. It can also be windy since most of the cliffs face toward the sea.

Summers are usually just too hot, although the majority of the cliffs face west and southwest and are in morning shade. Summer, especially July and August, is also the big tourist season, with more crowds and higher prices. Off-season, the rest of the year, is calmer, with few tourists and better deals on accommodations and meals.

Winter does offer many climbable days, but it can also be very cool and windy. The flip side is that you won't have to share the crags.

Camping, Accommodations, and Services

Primitive camping is prohibited on Kálymnos, but suitable and affordable accommodations are abundant, especially in the off-season when the climbing is best. Two kinds of hotels are found: full-service hotels and self-service studio apartments. The villages of Myrties, Massouri, and Arginonta, offering plenty of rooms,

Martha Morris leading a classic route at Kasteli.

are only minutes from the cliffs. Farther from the cliffs but closer to Pothia and the main shopping and dining area are the villages of Panormos and Kantouni.

Prices vary depending on the season and how many people are in your party, but they are generally inexpensive, with a studio costing between $20 and $30 a night, and a double room in a hotel between $30 and $50. The prices are regulated, but if you shop around, you can probably negotiate a better deal than the first one you're offered, especially if you're staying for a week or more. Check the Appendix for some suggestions and phone numbers. Also, all the hotel pools on the island are open to the public, allowing a relaxing afternoon swim after a hard day's cragging. If you're staying for a week or more, it's best to rent a studio since they are equipped with a kitchen, pots, pans, and dishes.

Several small shops on the west side of the island sell groceries and drinks, but their hours are variable. If you want to stock up on food, then go to Pothia and visit one of the larger grocery stores. One is on the right just as you enter town. Down in the town center are other groceries, bakeries, and butchers.

Food and Drink

Visiting other countries means experiencing the local culture, customs, holidays, and food. While you're on Kálymnos you will want to stroll around the old town of Pothia. Many interesting shops and restaurants await exploration. After a morning's cranking it's pleasant to relax along the harbor and sip coffee.

Definitely eat at one of the seafood restaurants. The waiter will walk you to the kitchen to select fresh fish from the cooler. Try some of the local dishes, including grilled octopus, octopus marinated in ouzo, and octopus balls. Other unique dishes are *Mermizeli* (a salad with *krithines kilocuries*), *Karkani, Ouzo Mezedes,* and at Easter the *Mououri,* a goat roasted in an earthen olla. One of the best seafood restaurants is Martha's Taverna on the waterfront. For dessert try *galaktoboureko,* a sweet and gooey Kálymnos specialty.

Some fine restaurants are also found in Massouri and Myrties close to the usual climber accommodations. These include Noufaro, with a brilliant wine list and its excellent entrée Lamb Noufaro; Aegean Restaurant and Kokkidinis, with great grill dishes in Massouri; and Smuggler and Selene's in Myrties.

Cultural Experiences and Rest Days

Easter on Kálymnos is famous throughout Greece. Ask any mainland Greek about Kálymnos and he will invariably say, "Dynamite!" Easter here is literally a blast. It begins earlier in the year when groups of men begin to collect explosives, some from wrecked ships, and make crude bombs. In the weeks before the big day, test explosions occasionally rock the har-

bor, jolting the cafe coffee drinkers. On Easter opposing groups climb to the hilltops on either side of the town and begin tossing their explosive devices. Needless to say, Pothia really rocks. It's also extremely dangerous, with death and disfiguration regularly occurring among the combatants.

Besides climbing lots of other activities as well as points of interest will amuse you. In Pothia visit the Archeological Museum with its collection of Neolithic and Bronze Age artifacts and the Nautical and Folklore Museum on the waterfront. The ruins of the Castle of the Knights of Rhodes and the Monastery of Christos of Jerusalem from the sixth century are both near the village of Chorio. The monastery Moni Agiou Savra sits atop a hill south of Pothia. Admittance requires long sleeves and either long pants or skirts. For more adventure you can sailboard between Kálymnos and Telendos, cycle out to Emborio, or hike across the hills on old footpaths. Over at Vahti on the east side of the island is a fabulous, low-water bouldering traverse that stretches more than 1,500 feet. Bring extra shoes or sandals for the return swim.

If you need more than a day's rest from the arm-bending rigors of the tufa walls, then take a couple days and ferry over to some of the nearby islands. The third-largest Dodecanese island Kos, popular with the European beach-lounging set, is usually overrun with tourists. The island is famed as the birthplace of Hippocrates, the father of medicine, in 460 B.C. If you visit, go to the archeological sites, including the Shrine of Aphrodite, Temple of Hercules, the eighteenth-century Turkish mosque, the imposing fourteenth-century Castle of the Knights, and the Hippocrates Plane Tree, under which, according to local lore, the master himself taught his pupils.

Leros, Patmos, and Lipsi, along with some smaller remote islands, glimmer in the sea to the north. All are hilly isles with indented rocky shorelines. Patmos is perhaps the most visited, with many pilgrims coming to pay homage at the cave where St. John the Divine received his divine guidance and penned the book of

Revelations after he was banished here in A.D. 95. The site, inside the Monastery of the Apocalypse, includes the rock he used for a pillow and the three ceiling cracks through which the voice of God spoke. Lipsi, Arki, and Agathonisi are small secluded islands. If you head out to these remote rocky islands, you are guaranteed peace and quiet.

Another good day trip is to take the ferry to Kos and then another ferry over to the resort town of Bodrum in Turkey, where you can browse the bizarre bazaars, trod palm-lined streets, and take in the silent mausoleum or ear-throbbing discos. Ephesus, perhaps the best preserved of all of Turkey's ancient cities, is another amazing Turkish place, with its well-preserved Greek and Roman ruins, the Temple of Artemis (one of the seven wonders of the ancient world), and the Temple of Hadrian. This ancient Ionian city flourished during the Greek Empire and later became an early seat of Christianity. St. Paul wrote the Epistle to the Ephesians here, and legend avers that the Virgin Mary lived out her last days in Ephesus.

Trip Planning Information

General description: Many excellent limestone cliffs that offer a wide selection of bolted sport routes on the island of Kálymnos.

Location: Kálymnos in the Dodecanese Islands in the eastern Aegean Sea. The easiest way to Kálymnos is to fly from any major European city to the isle of Kos, and hop a forty-five-minute ferry ride from there to Pothia, the capital city of Kálymnos. You can also take a long ferry ride from Athens to Kálymnos. The ferry drops you in Pothia at 3:00 A.M.

Camping and accommodations: Unregulated and primitive camping is prohibited on the island. There are, however, many reasonably priced rooms available in both full-service hotels and self-service studio apartments, so you can leave your tent at home. Hotels often include breakfast in their price. Studio amenities vary, but often include private cooking facilities as well as private bathrooms. It's not necessary to reserve ahead of time except in the summer high season, although when you arrive on the ferry at 3:00 A.M., it's good to have a reserved room waiting. The villages closest to the climbing are Myrties, Massouri, and Arginonta. Panormos and Kantouni are farther away, but closer to Pothia, the largest town on the island. Check the contact info in the Appendix, or sign onto the Kalymnos Web site www.kalymnos-isl.gr for more information.

Climbing season: Year-round. The best months are March through May and September through November. The winter months are usually good also, although it can be cool, windy, and sometimes rainy. The summer months, which is island high season, are usually too hot for comfortable climbing, although shade can be found in the morning on the west-facing cliffs.

Restrictions and access issues: No new routes at the main Grande Grotta from *Aegialis* to *Panoroma*. All the cliffs are privately owned, but the landowners welcome climbers. Don't abuse the privilege. No primitive camping or bivouacking.

Guidebooks: *Kalymnos Rock Climbing Guide* by Aris Theodoropoulos, a complete bilingual guide to the cliffs and routes. It is available on the island and on the Internet at www.kalymnos-isl.gr. Also check the Greek Web site www.oreivatein.com.

Services and shops: The Climber's Nest, near Lambrinos Studios, sells climbing gear, including chalk, quickdraws, ropes, clothes, and cams. Bring all your own gear if possible. Everything else is found on the island in Pothia, the largest town.

Emergency services: Call the police at 29301. The hospital number is 23025.

Nearby climbing areas: A bouldering area is found at Kardamena on Kos. Climbing areas are found on the island of Rhodes to the south.

Nearby attractions: The Archeological Museum and the Sponge Factory is in Pothia, the island capital. The nunnery Ag Savas is worth visiting. Other Kalymnos points of interest are the citadel of Péra Kástro, the Cave of Seven Virgins, sunset over the isle of Telendos, the fortified castle ruins of Kasteli, Kolonóstilo or Cyclops Cave with its huge stalactites, and Daskalió Cave. Lots of great hiking is found on the island. The other Dodecanese Islands are also worth visiting, including Rhodes, Symi, Kos, and Patmos. A good day trip is to Bodrum, Turkey, by taking the ferry to Kos and then to Bodrum. For Internet information check out www.kalymnos-isl.gr.

Finding the area: Fly, sail, ferry, or swim to Pothia. You can reach the island by air via the airport on Kos to the south. From the Kos airport take a bus to Mastichari and then a ferry (forty-five minutes) to Pothia. The ferry runs three times daily between the islands. The airport on Kálymnos is not finished at press time.

From Athens and Piraeus the ferry journey takes between ten and twelve hours. Ships depart daily in the afternoon between 2:00 and 4:00 P.M. on Dane and GA Ferries. The ferry docks at Pothia in the wee hours of the morning. On the return trip the ferry leaves Kálymnos in the evening and arrives in Piraeus the following morning. Tickets can be bought at the ferry offices near the docks or from travel agents in Athens.

After arriving in Pothia head west from town along the road toward Kantouni and Massouri. The cliffs are along this road. A taxi can take you to accommodations on the west side of the island. Consult each cliff's description for specifics on finding and accessing the various sectors.

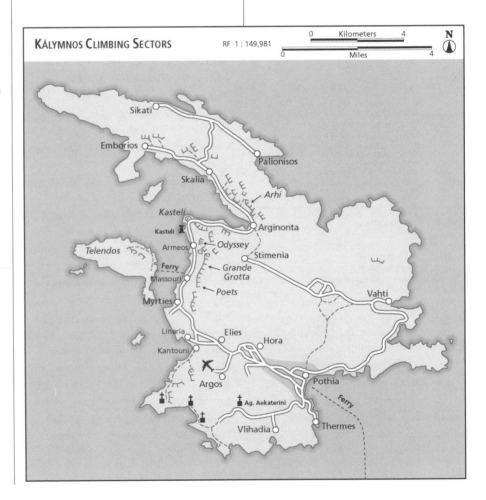

KÁLYMNOS CLIMBING SECTORS   RF 1 : 149,981

Poets

This superb, west-facing, gray wall is on the cliff band above the town of Massouri. It offers several excellent routes from 5.9 to 5.11. All the routes are bolted with lowering anchors and are worth climbing. It's in the shade all morning, making it a good warm-weather crag. Sunsets over Telendos and the Aegean Sea are also phenomenal from the cliff. The routes on the main wall are named for famous Greek poets. The route names are painted at the base of all the routes.

Finding the cliff: In Massouri park on the street just past the Hotel Continental and below Studios Lambrinos. Look for a sign on the side of a building on the street that marks the start of the trail. Walk east up the steep street to a large boulder left of the studios. Follow the blue-marked trail uphill for twenty minutes to the sector. Routes are listed right to left. The first four routes (no topos) are on an obvious gray slab right of the main wall.

1. Kalispera (6b+) (5.10d) 60 feet.

2. Kalimera (6b+) (5.10d) 60 feet.

3. Metaxas (6a) (5.10a) 65 feet.

4. Oyzo (5c/6a) (5.9+) 85 feet.

Walk to the left around a rib to the main wall.

5. Ione (7a+) (5.12a) 9 bolts to 2-bolt anchor.

6. Ibria (6b+) (5.10d) 80 feet. Sustained and technical climbing. 10 bolts to 2-bolt anchor.

7. Anacreonte (5c) (5.9) 65 feet. Sustained climbing. 8 bolts to 2-bolt anchor.

8. Alocamne (6c) (5.11a/b) 90 feet. 10 bolts to 2-bolt anchor.

9. Licimnio (6c) (5.11a/b) 82 feet. 10 bolts to 2-bolt anchor.

10. Alceo (6b) (5.10c) 80 feet. Slab climbing leads to sustained thin moves on sharp holds. 9 bolts to 2-bolt anchor.

11. Pindaros (5c) (5.9) 40 feet. Devious moves. The clips are difficult. 4 bolts to 2-bolt anchor at a large hole.

12. Saffo (6a) (5.10a) 72 feet. Relatively easy climbing to a steep crux at the top. 8 bolts to 2-bolt anchor.

13. Omero (6c) (5.11a/b) 8 bolts to 2-bolt anchor.

On the wall left of Poets are a couple more routes. No topos.

14. Mustass (6a) (5.10a) 60 feet. Excellent. Edge up a slab, and then climb flowstone to anchors.

15. Quando tramonta il sol (6b) (5.10c) 60 feet. A stiff start to interesting moves on a range of holds from crimps to jugs.

Grande Grotta

The Grande Grotta, the great cave at the end of the wall left of Poets, offers a selection of spectacular routes up stalactites and tufa columns. The cave yields the steepest sport routes on Kálymnos, including *Priapos,* the excellent *DNA,* and the exceptional tufa line *Aegialis,* one of the best routes here. Boulder climber Chris Archer calls it one of the two best sport pitches he's every climbed. These routes are big-hold, endurance lines, but are difficult to on-sight. Lots of hidden jugs and unobvious rests are found, with many kneebars (some hard to find unless you're used to this type of climbing) and some bridging between columns. It's unlikely that more routes will be established in the cave since the locals are concerned about damage to the tufas. They are also considering closing the cave in spring, when the tufas are seeping and more fragile and susceptible to damage by climbers.

Left of the cave is the Afternoon sector, with thirteen fine pitches from 5.7 to 5.11a. Most routes are slabs and vertical face climbs. One of the best is *By By Doc* (5.10d/11a).

Right of the Grande Grotta is the Panorama sector, with numerous three-star outings from 5.10b to 5.12b, most in the 5.10+ to 5.11+ range. Among the best are *Trella* (5.11b), *Rastopopoulis* (5.12b), *Aegean Sea* (5.11d), *Cigarillo* (5.11b/c), *Pansellinos* (5.10d), *Carpe Diem* (5.10b), *Chosi Family* (5.11b), and *By By Felix* (5.11c). Consult the comprehensive island guide for beta for both sectors.

Finding the cliff: After driving through Massouri, park at the Hotel Filoxenia (where you can go for a swim and sip a cold Mythos after a hard day of cragging). Follow red marks up a steep uphill path past a large olive tree to the cave. Allow about twenty minutes to hike up.

Routes are described from left to right. Most of the route names are painted at the base of the routes. Not all the routes are included here.

16. Massalia (6a+) (5.10b) 4 pitches. A long, exposed route along and above the lip of the entire cave. **Pitch 1:** 6a+. **Pitch 2:** 5c. **Pitch 3:** 5c. **Pitch 4:** 5c.

17. Aegialis (7c) (5.12d) Highly recommended endurance route. Follow a line of bolts up the left edge of the cave to anchors. Look for kneebars for good shakeouts. The no-hands rests end after the first 30 feet. 100 feet.

Immediately right is *Sawi Nul Syndicate* (5.13a).

18. Aphrodite (7a/b) (5.11d/12a) A short but powerful and tricky route with large holds right of #17. Crux is a few powerful moves up to and off an undercling between bolts 3 and 4. Easier if you're tall. 35 feet.

19. DNA (7b) (5.12b) Classic jug-haul, but watch the pump factor. No move is harder than 5.10! Excellent overhanging moves on jugs with two tricky rests, including a no-hands rest halfway up. Skip the second to last (13th) bolt. 14 bolts to 2-bolt anchor. 65 feet.

Ocean Dream

Odyssey

Trail

20. Ivi (7b+) (5.12a) Another good long endurofest. It's a little harder than *DNA* but of equal quality. If you value your life, then lower from the *DNA* anchors rather than the single bolt with a fixed biner that many lower off.

21. Priapos (8a+) (5.13c) 2 pitches up the back of the cave. **Pitch 1:** 5.12d to lowering anchors at 115 feet. **Pitch 2:** 8a+. 25 bolts to 2-bolt anchor. 180 feet.

22. Fun de Chichunne (8a) (5.13b) A stiff outing on the right side of the cave. It's a bit scruffy—needs more traffic. The top half is loose and dirty. 28 bolts to 2-bolt anchor. 130 feet.

More good routes with tufa and stalactites are right of #22 on the back wall. The best are *Trella* (6c+) (5.11c); *Monahiki Elia* (6a+) (5.10b); *Rastapopoulos* (7b+) (5.12c); *Aegean Sea* (7a+) (5.12a), excellent and sustained; *Cigarillo* (6c+) (5.11c), with a big tufa; and *Panselinos* (6b) (5.10c), a tufa climb.

Spartacus

The Spartacus sector above Afternoon is another great wall with a dozen three-star outings from 5.10c to 5.13b. The best routes are *Spartacus* (5.12b/c), good holds to a powerful crux; *Daniboy* (5.13b), a fabulous power endurance route; *Kebapals* (5.11b/c), great long route left of *Daniboy;* *Jellyfish* (5.11d/12a), technical and pumpy sections; *Gladiator* (5.12a), brilliant and continuous; *Hari-Kiri* (5.10b), fabulous climb; *Les amazons* (5.11a), amazing route up a prominent tufa; *Nebuchadonmosor* (5.11a), excellent long moderate (use 70-meter rope); and *13 Travels of Hercules* (5.11a), sporty but worth the effort.

Odyssey

Odyssey, one of the most popular sectors, is a long northwest-facing cliff with some of the best climbing on Kálymnos. The cliff is shaded for most of the day, receiving sun only from early to midafternoon. Sector Merci Marc stays shaded until late afternoon and is sheltered from the south wind. The cliff is long enough that even if other parties are climbing, it usually doesn't feel crowded. Not surprisingly, most of the route names derive from Homer's epic poem, *The Odyssey*. Route names are painted at the base of most routes, which makes locating them easy. All the routes are bolted with clip-gate anchors for easy lower-offs. The crux of many routes is clipping the anchor, which makes some grades based on whether you clip or grab the anchors!

Finding the cliff: Drive past the village of Massouri, and park on the left just past Big Blue, a restaurant. A white pillar marks the start of the trail. Hike left up a road to a level road. Go right (south), and follow the road until it ends. Continue to a group of boulders. The blue-marked trail heads uphill here along a draw before traversing left along the right side of Odyssey. Hiking time is twenty minutes. Routes are described from right to left.

23. Nessuno (5c) (5.9) Up a slabby tongue to a corner on the far right side of the cliff. 6 bolts to 2-bolt anchor.

24. Laertes (6a) (5.10a) Shares *Nessuno's* start but veers left, climbs past a tufa, and finishes up steep rock to shared anchors. 6 bolts to 2-bolt anchor.

25. Femio (6a+) (5.10a/b) Steep gray rock. 6 bolts to 2-bolt anchor.

26. Circe (6b) (5.10c) Highly recommended. Pockets and edges on gray limestone. 6 bolts to 2-bolt anchor.

27. Atena (6b+) (5.10d) Excellent! Begin this classic on the right side of a recess. Crank slightly polished but good holds. 6 bolts to 2-bolt anchor.

28. Omiros (7b+) (5.12a/b) Steep and thin. Fantastic climbing until the final desperate two-finger pocket anchor clip. 8 bolts to 2-bolt anchor.

29. Dionysos (7a) (5.11b/c) Named for the god of wine. Left side of the recess. Climb to a shelf with a hands-free rest, then up and right to an anchor crux. 9 bolts to 2-bolt anchor.

30. Alcinoo (7b) (5.12b) Height dependent. Begin just right of a deep recess. Great climbing to a big lunge up and right. 8 bolts to 2-bolt anchor.

31. Calipso (6c+) (5.11b/c) Superb climbing. Start up the right wall of the recess to a juggy, overhanging headwall. 8 bolts to 2-bolt anchor.

32. Ulisse coperto di sale (7a+) (5.12a) Begin just left of the recess. 8 bolts to 2-bolt anchor.

33. Ciao Vecio (6c+) (5.11c) Recommended. Interesting moves on widely spaced holds up vertical rock. 10 bolts to 2-bolt anchor.

34. Itaca (6c+) (5.11c/d) Stiff for the grade. Fun climbing up a slab to desperate overhanging finish and cruxes. Beware of old rusty bolts. 8 bolts to 2-bolt anchor.

35. Lotofagos (6c) (5.11a/b) Sustained. Can be done as 2 pitches. Finish up an obvious corner. 9 bolts to 2-bolt anchor.

36. Eryriklea (5b) (5.8) Short route up a gray slab to anchors below the steep. 5 bolts to 2-bolt anchor. 50 feet.

37. Poly Retsina No Good (6a+) (5.10b) Traverse left to anchors where the wall slabs off. 7 bolts to 2-bolt anchor.

38. Mermizeli (6b) (5.10c) Short and steep. Crux is a move left at the overhang. 6 bolts to 2-bolt anchor.

39. Mikrotera Kalamarakia (6b+) (5.10d) Short and tricky. Left side of a short wall. 6 bolts to 2-bolt anchor.

40. Haryvdi (6a) (5.10a) Good climb. A steep start to the right edge of a prow. Go left at bolt 2 and then up to bolt 3 to avoid looseness. 11 bolts to 2-bolt anchor.

41. Lestrygon (6c) (5.11b/c) Recommended with terrific position. Balance climbing that follows the left edge of a prow. 11 bolts to 2-bolt anchor.

42. Penelope (6a) (5.10a) Recommended. Right side of a gray slab. Thin crux over the bulge at bolt 4. 7 bolts to 2-bolt anchor.

43. Telemaco (5b) (5.8) Fun cranking. Best of its grade on the cliff. 7 bolts to 2-bolt anchor.

44. Argo (4c) (5.6) Fun, easy slab. 6 bolts to 2-bolt anchor.

45. Eumeo (4c) (5.6) Big holds up a slab to anchors in a hole. 4 bolts to 2-bolt anchor.

46. Imia (6b+) (5.10d) Highly recommended. Climb a gray slab past a scoop, then up an interesting headwall. 11 bolts to 2-bolt anchor.

47. The Beast (7b+) (5.12c) Angle up left to high anchors. 8 bolts to 2-bolt anchor.

48. Why Not? (7a) (5.11d) A 40-foot route with good moves up tufa columns and a flake. 4 bolts to 2-bolt anchor.

49. Alfredo Alfredo (7b+) (5.12c) Great route! Technical moves but some old bolts and a bit of polish. Bolts are poorly positioned and rusty—use caution. 6 bolts to 2-bolt anchor.

50. Polifemo (7c) (5.12c) Another must-do line. Pumpy start leads to thin, technical climbing. Bolts are rusty and need replacing. Beware of the rusty bolts at the crux moves onto the tufa. 8 bolts to 2-bolt anchor.

51. Gaia (8b) (5.13d) One of the island's hardest routes. Sustained and unrelenting bouldery moves up an overhanging wall in the deep recess. 9 bolts to 2-bolt anchor.

To the left is *Fouska* (7a+) (5.11c), another difficult but fun overhanging line with an anchor crux.

52. Nausicaa Nausica (6a) (5.10a) Fun climbing up a long, slabby tongue. 9 bolts to 2-bolt anchor.

53. Odisseo (6a+) (5.10b) Steep face climbing up vertical rock. Cruxy moves through the midheight bulge. 8 bolts to 2-bolt anchor.

54. Fourtouna (7b/7b+) (5.12b/c) 9 bolts to 2-bolt anchor.

55. Sirene (7b+) (5.12c) Begin just right of a cave. 14 bolts to 2-bolt anchor.

56. Amphora (7b) (5.12a) Excellent. Pumpy technical climbing to a powerful finish.

57. Marci Marc (7c) (5.12d) Excellent— one of the island's best hard routes. Long and sustained with the crux at the top. 12 bolts to 2-bolt anchor.

58. Lucky Luka (7a+ to fixed carabiner) (5.12a) 8 bolts to a fixed carabiner at the top of the cave. An 8b/c project on the upper wall. Drilled pockets.

59. Dafni (Daphne) (7b) (5.12b) Fabulous long technical pitch with a tricky high crux.

Just left of #59 is *Patroclos* (7b) (5.12b), a 115-foot pitch with 10 bolts and anchors.

60. Meltemi (7a) (5.11d) Begin below a rib right of a recess. Go right, and avoid the original 7b crux. 11 bolts to 2-bolt anchor.

61. Orion (8a) (5.13b) Light for the grade. Crux is a boulder problem. 7 bolts to 2-bolt anchor.

62. Andromeda (7c+) (5.13a) Similar in difficulty and movement to *Orion*. 6 bolts to 2-bolt anchor.

Between #62 and #63 are three routes: *Babu pensaci tu* (7b+), 75 feet; *Satyros* (6c+) (5.11c), excellent climbing with long reaches; and *Il gigante e la bambina* (6c+) (5.11c), 72 feet.

63. Island Highway (7a, 6b+) (5.11d, 5.10d) 2 pitches. Not very good. Lousy placement of the anchors, making the rope abrade on an edge when you clean. **Pitch 1:** 6c. 9 bolts to 2-bolt anchor. 72 feet. **Pitch 2:** 6b. 65 feet.

64. Lucky Strike (7b+) (5.12a) Brilliant route. Superb climbing up a tufa curtain to the crux at the top. 10 bolts to 2-bolt anchor.

65. Island in the Sun (7a+) (5.11c/d) Excellent continuous climbing. Avoid the one-move extension. Can be done in 2 pitches. 11 bolts to 2-bolt anchor above a roof.

66. Feta (6c+) (5.11c) Recommended. Great climbing to the last move, then a hard crux move to the chains. The grade is 6c+ if you don't grab the chains! 9 bolts to 2-bolt anchor.

67. Elies (7a+) (5.12a) Just left of *Feta*. 10 bolts to 2-bolt anchor.

68. Arugliopulos (7c+) (5.13a) 7 bolts to 2-bolt anchor.

69. Mythos (6c) (5.11a/b) Good rock, good climbing, long pitch. A gray wall on the left side of the cliff. 13 bolts to 2-bolt anchor.

70. Clyde (6b+) (5.10d) Loose at the overhang. 8 bolts to 2-bolt anchor.

71. Bonnie (5c) (5.9) Leftmost route on the crag. Use the first bolt on *Clyde,* or run it out to bolt 1. Some route finding en route to the anchors. 7 bolts to 2-bolt anchor.

Kasteli

Kasteli, a northeast-facing wall and a west-facing wall, sits on the flank of a promontory topped with the ruins of an ancient Byzantine castle above the sea. Most of the routes are good, although some are sharp because of their close proximity to the water. The cliff is shaded much of the day, with the west face receiving sun only by midafternoon. After climbing, hike south across the ruins, and visit a small white chapel perched above the sea on the south side of the promontory.

Finding the cliff: Drive north from Massouri. The road makes an obvious sharp bend east of Kasteli. Park here on the west side of the road. Follow a rough path around the right slope of the hill to the crags. Routes are described left to right.

72. Tsarouhis (6a) (5.10a) Fun climbing with good crimps. 6 bolts to 2-bolt anchor.

73. Gyzis (5b) (5.8) Follows a shallow corner system. 5 bolts to 2-bolt anchor.

74. Gikas (4c) (5.6) Just one hard move and lots of jugs. 5 bolts to 2-bolt anchor.

75. Pillar of the Sea (6a+) (5.10b) Excellent, classic, and photogenic. One of the isle's best 5.10s. Edge up a blunt arête to a roof, move left, and finish up a headwall. 7 bolts to 2-bolt anchor.

The following routes are on the west side of the promontory and face the sea. They're a little sharp but are mostly fine climbs with a great view.

76. Mikros Prigipas (6a) (5.10a) Over a roof to a slab to a headwall. 10 bolts to 2-bolt anchor.

77. Ruheloser pirat (6a+) (5.10b) An overhanging start. 7 bolts to 2-bolt anchor.

78. Gafaerliche brandung (6a) (5.10a/b) Sustained edging. 6 bolts to 2-bolt anchor.

79. Piccolo diavolo (6a) (5.10a) Very good. Continuous with lots of 5.9 moves on sharp holds. 6 bolts to 2-bolt anchor.

80. Hocla (5c) (5.9) Superb and fun. Name is below the first bolt. 7 bolts to 2-bolt anchor.

81. Gruselino (5c+) (5.9) A chunky start to a fun finish. 5 bolts to 2-bolt anchor.

82. Gónegili kiz (Sunshine Girl) (5c) (5.8+) Fun climbing on interesting holds. 7 bolts to 2-bolt anchor.

83. Scarabeus (5b) (5.7+) Good finish. 6 bolts to 2-bolt anchor.

84. Damokles (6a) (5.10a) No topo. Easy to bolt 3, then move up left to a steeper finish.

85. Aaolaa (4c) (5.5) Right-hand route up a broken rib. 6 bolts to 2-bolt anchor.

Arhi

Arhi, "beginning" in Greek, is the sector at the base of a huge cliff on the north side of a long cove. The sector, one of the first developed on the island, is deservedly popular, with many excellent moderate routes and a short approach. The cliff is divided into five main sectors, with four of them described here. Helvetia (Switzerland), the fifth area, is a large cave on the upper right side of the wall. The cliff's main feature is the huge central cave, which is mostly featureless and offers few routes. Most of the routes ascend the gray slabs on either side of the cave.

The Arhi routes are characterized by crisp edges and occasional pockets. Some follow tufa columns. All are well bolted, although some of the clips are hard to make. Most of the routes are worth doing. Almost all of the route names are painted along the base, making route finding a snap.

Finding the cliff: Drive north from Massouri along the coast road. Just past the village of Arginonta, look for a parking area on the right side of the road. A white post marks the start of the trail. Follow a blue-marked trail for eight minutes to the cliff base. Routes are described right to left. Hike up right along the base to the first routes on a gray slab.

86. Alba (5c) (5.9) No topo. On the far right side of the cliff.

87. Aristos (5b) (5.8) 6 bolts to 2-bolt anchor.

88. Pinipon (4c) (5.6) 6 bolts to 2-bolt anchor.

89. Caronte (4c) (5.6) Free and easy slab climbing. 6 bolts to 2-bolt anchor.

90. Arhaggelos (5a) (5.7) Right of a scoop. 4 bolts to 2-bolt anchor.

91. Cerbero (5a) (5.7) Left of the scoop. 5 bolts to 2-bolt anchor.

92. Arianna (5a) (5.7) 7 bolts to 2-bolt anchor.

93. Optassia (5a) (5.7) Fun climbing with sharp holds. 7 bolts to 2-bolt anchor.

94. Carlo non Farlo (5a) (5.7) Right of a scooped wall section. 7 bolts to 2-bolt anchor.

The next routes ascend a stellar gray wall on the right side of the deep, yellow cave. Most of these routes are excellent.

95. Minotauro (5c) (5.9) A short line left of the scooped wall. Good holds. Good climbing. 5 bolts to 2-bolt anchor.

96. Perseo (6a+) (5.10b) Easy climbing to a thin, fingery finish. 7 bolts to 2-bolt anchor.

A route called *Kalymnian Cheese* continues up the wall above the anchors for a couple more pitches. Do not climb it, especially if other climbers are on the base routes, as it is loose, rotten, and dirty.

97. Medusa (6a) (5.10a) Great route. Steep finish. 7 bolts to 2-bolt anchor.

98. Dedalo (6a+) (5.10b) Very thin crux up high and a hard clip. 7 bolts to 2-bolt anchor.

99. Orione (6a) (5.10a) Excellent with perfect crimps up a clean slab. 7 bolts to 2-bolt anchor.

100. Triana (6b+) (5.10d)

101. Icaro (6c+) (5.11c) A broken slab to a brown streak. 8 bolts to 2-bolt anchor.

102. Nereidi (6a+) (5.10b) Start on *Icaro,* and go up left at bolt 3. 8 bolts to 2-bolt anchor.

103. Mofeta (7a) (5.11d) 88 feet.

104. Poseidon (6b+) (5.10d) Stemming along a tufa column and a technical slab finish. 10 bolts to 2-bolt anchor.

105. Thetis (6b) (5.10c/d) Highly recommended. One of the coolest routes here. Stem up the left side of a pronounced hanging tufa column to anchors atop it. Lots of stemming. 5 bolts to 2-bolt anchor.

106. Il Pittore (6b+) (5.10d) Pockets and tufa. Hard start to tufa jugs. 6 bolts to 2-bolt anchor.

107. Polydeykes (7b) (5.12a) Cool route. A stiff pull leads to a pumpy entry into a corner formed by tufa. Wild stemming up the corner, and finish under a roof. 8 bolts to 2-bolt anchor.

108. Kastor (6c+) (5.11c) Continuously good climbing up this classic line. More pockets and weird tufa formations. 6 bolts to 2-bolt anchor.

109. Eros (7c) (5.12d) No topo. Left-hand route on right side of the cave. 60 feet.

The next routes are on a slabby gray wall left of the main cave. All the routes are recommended and fun.

110. Ziwi (5c) (5.9) Up the yellowish rock left of the cave. 9 bolts to 2-bolt anchor.

111. Ercole (5c) (5.9) Anchors are in the yellow stone. 9 bolts to 2-bolt anchor.

112. Centauro (5c) (5.9) Recommended. 8 bolts to 2-bolt anchor.

113. Pegaso (5a) (5.7+) Fun. 7 bolts to 2-bolt anchor.

114. Teseo (5a) (5.7+) 6 bolts to 2-bolt anchor.

115. Argonauti (5b) (5.8) 6 bolts to 2-bolt anchor.

116. Scacco (5c) (5.8+) Perfect route! 5 bolts to 2-bolt anchor.

117. Pares (5c+) (5.9+) Another superb line with an interesting tufa handle. 9 bolts to 2-bolt anchor.

118. Deimos (6b) (5.10c) Right of some flowstone. 7 bolts to 2-bolt anchor.

119. Phobos (6c+) (5.11c) Steeper rock on the left side of the sector. 7 bolts to 2-bolt anchor.

The next section is a buttress up left from the previous routes. Scramble to a ledge below to start the routes.

120. Adonis (6b) (5.10c) Goes to a high set of anchors. 12 bolts to 2-bolt anchor.

121. Dell Mabul (6a) (5.10a) 7 bolts to 2-bolt anchor.

122. Apoplus (6a) (5.10a) 8 bolts to 2-bolt anchor.

The last routes are on an excellent gray slab a couple hundred feet to the left of route 122. No topos for these easy-to-find routes. All three are recommended.

123. Ewa (6a) (5.10a)

124. Dodo (6a+) (5.10b)

125. Thia Fotisi (5c) (5.9)

Vahti

If you're traveling around the island on a rest day and want a memorable adventure, then head east to the small port of Vahti at the head of a deep inlet. On the wall of the inlet is *Socratic Swimming Lessons,* a 1,500-foot-long traverse above the sea.

Drive east from Pothia to Vahti at the head of a long sea arm. A couple of good restaurants are in the village. At the harbor facing the sea, walk out a concrete road on the south (right) side of the bay. The traverse starts where the road ends. Traverse left on easy rock (some 5.9 and 5.10a moves) for about 1,000 feet. Eventually the traverse turns a corner and reaches the crux—a short overhanging 5.12 section with small holds. You'll probably fall off, but no problem. Your feet are only a few inches above the clear water. The difficulty eases here. Continue traversing around a lovely cove to a prominent point. Either climb out (watch for sea urchins), or swim back to the start. Bring extra shoes and an extra chalk bag because you'll probably take the plunge.

METÉORA

■ OVERVIEW

Lofty ridges and rounded snowcapped peaks in central Greece's province of Thessaly surround Metéora, one of Europe's most magical and intriguing places and one of its most amazing climbing sites. Metéora, pronounced *meh-teh-o-rah,* is a simply stunning place and a refuge from the noise and bustle of the modern world. Here, on the northern edge of the broad agricultural valley of the Pinios River, lies a maze of immense pinnacles, pillars, fins, castles, towers, and buttresses tucked into the southern flank of the Andikhasia Mountains. This natural rock architecture, formed by a coarse conglomerate, offers a spectacular assortment of classic rock climbs up the soaring faces and ridges on more than fifty formations and eighty peaks scattered over four major groups in Metéora.

Metéora yields a mixture of both traditional routes and sport climbs, although most are bolted face climbs. The older classic lines, established by German climbers, tend to be minimally bolted with large ringbolts, so protection is widely spaced. This keeps your attention from wandering too far from the holds at hand, even on easy climbing. The bolts on these routes are often hard to spot from below, making route finding a somewhat tricky proposition on some lines. The large, beefy bolts are also used at both belay and rappel stations. These are usually single bolts, but they're safe because of their size and placement.

The more modern sport climbs, mostly established by Greek climbers, are bolted with a responsible eye toward leader safety. Many of these new routes are exceedingly popular, whereas nearby older classics are climbed less often because of their risk. Most new Metéora leaders, until they get used to the conglomerate and the necky, runout climbing, drop a grade or two for their leads on the classics. Traditional routes, protected by cams and nuts, commonly follow chimneys and wide cracks. Jam cracks and chimneys are usually found on at least one or two

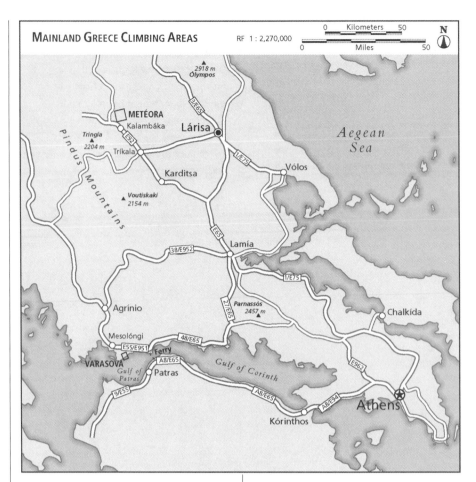

pitches on the longer routes. Register books are found on the summits of most formations to record the date of your adventures. They're interesting records to read in the afternoon sunshine while eating your lunch atop a spire.

The highest wall at Metéora is the 1,000-foot-high Wall of the Great Saints looming above the town of Kalambáka. The most important pillars and formations for climbing are found in the central area, including Kastraki Tower (*Kastrákiturm*), Devil's Tower (*Teufelsturm*), Ypsilotéra Rock (*Ypsilotérafels*), Doupiani Rock (*Doupianifels*), The Holy Ghost (*Heiliger Geist* or *Aghion Pnéwma* in Greek), Alyssos, Modi, Sourloti, and Pixari. Most of the towers were unnamed until the Germans began climbing here in the 1970s. They tried to find the old names for the rocks, but found that most were unnamed.

The Metéora conglomerate is a strange surface for climbing. Its concrete-hard matrix cements an irregular assortment of pebbles, cobbles, and boulders into the cliffs. The rock, despite its appearance as a vertical streambed, is surprisingly

solid, with lots of positive pebble edges, rounded potato-shaped jugs, scooped incuts, and shallow dishes where cobbles have fallen out. The climbing, if you haven't pinched cobbles before, seems odd, but you quickly learn to trust the holds. Metéora locals, however, warn that the larger cobbles liberate themselves more often than the more solid smaller knobs. All the routes offer the same kind of climbing, with the only variations being the size of the cobbles and the angle of the rock. This conglomerate was deposited along an arm of a sea on the west side of an ancestral mountain range during the late Tertiary Period some twenty-five million years ago.

Rack, Protection, and Descent

How much gear you carry on a Metéora route depends on whether it is an older classic or a newer line. The older routes tend to be somewhat underprotected by today's sew-'em-up sport-climbing standards. The conglomerate tends to be difficult to protect without drilled bolts. Cracks are generally few and far between.

Carry a rack of ten to fifteen quickdraws as well as six to ten free carabiners; an assortment of nylon runners, slings, and cords of various thicknesses for tying off and threading cobbles; a selection of Stoppers or other wired nuts, which work when wedged between cobbles; some chocks, including large Hexentrics, which also work well in funky placements; and an assortment of cams, depending on how much crack climbing is on your chosen route. Large Camalots are useful on many of the longer crack routes. Also bring a couple long slings for aiding off bolts. Bring two 165-foot (50-meter) ropes for climbing and descending. Double-rope technique is sometimes useful on intricate pitches. A longer 200-foot (60-meter) rope is useful for running short pitches together to save time. Use extra slings to avoid rope drag. A helmet is your last essential piece of equipment. Rockfall occurs regularly, especially on seldom-climbed routes. A helmet also protects your head in the event of a long fall.

Descent off most Metéora routes is by rappel. Sturdy fixed anchors are found on all the towers. Many older rappels are from thick, single eyebolts. Remember to tie knots in your free rope ends to avoid rappelling off them. Also try to find the next set of anchors before committing to a rappel. A couple of prusik cords make a good backup safety system on long rappels.

Climbing History

No records exist of Metéora's early climbers, but evidence found by Heinz Lothar Stutte and Dietrich Hasse, the German authors of the area guidebook, as well as other climbers, indicates that many formations were ascended long ago. An early account by the nun Theotekni says that before the establishment of the monastic hermitages, local climbers, shepherds, and hunters in the nearby town of Stagon knew the ascent routes and took monks to the summits. The early climbers, besides free climbing up conglomerate walls on routes as difficult as 5.8, suspended multistory ladders from corbels chiseled into the rock. The corbels can still be seen every 15 to 20 feet on the original climbing routes up Ypsilotérafels, Monifels, and Alyssos. They also built platforms on wooden braces hammered between rocks.

One of the area's great unsolved climbing mysteries is how a metal cross now kept at the Varlaam monastery was erected atop the Holy Ghost. It was supposedly planted there in 1348, more than 600 years ago, on a tall pillar that today requires fifth-class climbing, ropes, and bolts to both ascend and descend. The cross was removed from the summit by helicopter in 1975.

Modern Metéora climbing began at the relatively recent date of 1975. Before that German soldiers ascended some formations during World War II, but few other ascents were made until German climbers Bodo Zophel and U. Weinreich discovered the area's potential in 1970 and reached several summits that year.

By the mid-1970s Heinz Lothar Stutte and Dietrich Hasse, along with other Germans, including Sepp Eichinger, came to Metéora and spent the next couple of decades opening new routes and bagging the first ascents of many formations. These included the classic *Ostkante* on Doupiani Rock, Glocke, Teufelsturm, Ypsilotérafels, and Geierwand in 1976; *Archimedes* on Pixari in 1977; and *Traumpfeiler* (*Pillar of Dreams*) on Heiliger Geist (Holy Ghost) and *Hypotenuse* on Sourloti in 1981.

By the 1990s many Greek climbers were establishing new routes. While respecting the German climbers' strict ethics and boldness, the Greeks opened their own routes with more bolts and better protection. Some of the hardest routes were climbed by local climbers Christos Batalogiannis and Vangelis Batsios. A couple of their best lines are the *directissima Action Directe* on Heiliger Geist and *Orchidea* on Alphasporn in 1995, and the severely overhanging sport pitch *Crazy Dancing* on Doupianifels in 1997. Other active Greek climbers include Aris Theodoropoulos, Steanos Nikologiannis, and Aris Mitronatsios. During the 1980s and 1990s, the German climbers Stutte and Hasse continued to open more new routes throughout the Metéora region.

Getting Around

The best way to get from Athens (Athínai) to Metéora is by car. Lots of car rental agencies are found in Athens, including at the airport and around Syntagma Square (*Plateia Syntagmatos*) in downtown Athens. Most of the car hire companies in Athens will drive you to the city outskirts so you don't have to deal with the horrendous traffic and difficult route finding in the maze of streets and highways. Driving is a breeze once you're out of Athens on the main highway heading north.

You need to exercise extreme caution, be alert, and use all your defensive driving skills here. After driving around Greece you won't be surprised to learn that it leads Europe in road fatalities. Passing on the narrow roads is the leading cause of accidents here. Remember on two-lane highways that slower traffic usually drives on the far right in the breakdown lane or on the shoulder. It's best to yield to the speed demons—you're on vacation, after all.

The Greek highway system is generally good, with clear signs and bypasses around most towns and villages, which saves lots of time and navigation nightmares. Remember that Greece, like other European countries, uses different road signage than America. Look for signs pointing toward the towns in the direction you want to go rather than specific highway or route numbers. Make sure to check the map ahead of time, and write down place names in both Greek and Roman letters; otherwise, you will be unable to read the signs if they're in Greek.

If you don't want to hire a car, then you can easily reach Metéora by train. From the airport take a taxi to Larisis Train Station in downtown Athens. Taxis are relatively cheap and fast. Trains regularly run to Kalambáka, a ten- to twelve-hour journey. Before you get in line to buy a ticket, go to an information point, and ask the clerk there to write down the train you need. Then get in line to purchase tickets. It's best to ride the more expensive intercity express trains, which are more modern and comfortable than the cheaper station-to-station service, which crawls across the countryside and takes twice as long. You will switch trains partway along the journey. Be sure to write the town's name in Greek so you don't miss the stop. When you disembark in Kalambáka, catch a taxi or walk a couple miles to Kastraki. From there it's easy to hike to most cliffs.

Seasons and Weather

Metéora lies at a latitude of thirty-nine degrees, roughly the same latitude north as Denver, Colorado. The area, however, experiences a vastly different climate than Denver. Lying close to the Mediterranean Sea, Metéora sits in a region of generally temperate weather with mild winters and hot summers. Winter conditions are variable, with occasional cold and wet periods and only rare snowfalls. Summers, when most Americans visit, are usually very hot, with climbing only happening in the morning before 10:00 A.M. You can also climb in the evening on shaded faces.

Spring and autumn are the best seasons to visit Metéora. Spring, beginning in March, is mild and warm with infrequent rain. Greek climbers traditionally visit Metéora on Easter weekend. Come then, and you're assured of finding plentiful climbing partners and making lots of new friends. September and October are also reliable, with warm, dry days and few tourists or climbers.

Camping, Accommodations, and Services

Metéora, justifiably popular with both foreign and Greek visitors, offers lots of accommodations in both Kalambáka and Kastraki. Most climbers stay in Kastraki because it's closer to the rocks and quieter than Kalambáka. Some good campgrounds are found in Kastraki, including the preferred site, Camping Vrachos, on the left side of the road just after you enter the

village. The campsite is climber friendly and offers discounts for long-term stays. It has clean toilets, hot showers, a swimming pool in the warmer months, a covered area for cooking and socializing, and a small *taverna*. The other campgrounds are Cave Camping on the other side of Kastraki (good since it's closer to the cliffs), Metéora Garden, and Boufidis Camping.

Lots of rooms are found in Kastraki for the traveler who forgot camping gear. Rooms are found in both guesthouses and hotels. Check in the Appendix for suggestions and phone numbers. A popular option for budget-minded climbers are *domatia* or *dhomatia,* the Greek equivalent of a bed-and-breakfast inn—without the breakfast. These family-run rooms are generally modest but clean. Around the bus and train stations in Kalambáka you can usually find a *tout,* often a family member, greeting passengers and offering rooms for rent. You'll want to eyeball the room and its location, and get a firm price before agreeing to anything.

Kalambáka, the bigger town on the south side of the rocks, offers lots of hotel rooms as well as complete services, including grocery stores, restaurants, coffee shops, and many shops vending tourist trinkets. If you stay here, remember that you'll need transportation to travel to the main cliffs. Kastraki has more limited services, especially in the less busy seasons.

Food and Drink

Metéora is in rural Greece and as such offers standard Greek country fare, which translates to a lot of meat dishes. This is a difficult place to be a vegetarian. Meals tend to be simple, plentiful, and relatively inexpensive. *Tavernas,* usually a traditional place with a rough ambience, tend to be the best places for good, hearty Greek food. The menu is often posted on a window or door, and it's always in Greek. But you can usually translate the main dishes with a bit of practice and a dictionary. It's also acceptable to venture into the kitchen to see what's cooking and to point out which dish you want. This ensures that you'll make new friends who will remem-

ber you next time you visit the *taverna,* and you'll know what you're eating. Not everything on the menu is available every night, as some dishes are seasonal.

Begin your *taverna* repast with some *mezedes* or appetizers. These include *tzatziki,* a refreshing mixture of yogurt, cucumber, and garlic scooped up with pita bread; *taramasalata,* a fish roe dip; *dolmades,* stuffed grape leaves; *keftedes* or meatballs; *saganaki,* a fried cheese; and flavorful black olives. You can always order a mess of *mezedes* for your main meal. Be sure to eat a Greek salad, called *horiatiki salata,* with onions, tomatoes, olives, peppers, and feta cheese made from sheep or goat's milk, all doused in olive oil and squeezed lemons. The main dish here is often *souvlaki,* skewers of grilled meat like lamb or beef, dished up with fries. *Moussaka,* layers of eggplant, zucchini, and meat covered with a cheese sauce, is another common dish.

Greek coffee (*ellinikos kafes*) is the national drink. The thick sludge of coffee, served in a small cup with the grounds, usually comes three ways—*sketo,* without sugar; *metrio,* medium sweet; and *glyko,* the very sweet variation. Coffee is served with a small cleansing glass of water and often a bite of chocolate. If you haven't acquired a taste for Greek coffee, you can order Nescafé, an American-style instant coffee. Nescafé is made into a delicious iced *frappé* in summer. For your morning coffee it's fun to drive over to Kalambáka and fuel up at one of the places at the plaza. I visited the same coffee shop for two weeks, and after the first couple mornings, the proprietor started preparing my favorite coffee as soon as I walked in the door—now, that's customer service.

The most common Greek beers (*byra*) are Amstel and Heineken from northern Europe, both brewed in-country, as well as Mythos. Also sample the popular aperitif *ouzo,* a clear anise-flavored drink served with a separate glass of water for dilution. It's often served in a special *ouzeri* bar, often with a small plate of *mezedes.* The other local drink is *retsina,* a pine-resinated wine that is usually served chilled. It's definitely an acquired taste; the first impression is that it tastes like a combination of wine and paint thinner.

Rock formations loom over the town of Kastraki.

Cultural Experiences and Rest Days

Metéora climbing has been under threat of closure for a few years. The national archeological service, with the support of the Greek Orthodox church, has been pushing to ban climbing in the area. The thousands of climbers from Greece and the rest of Europe who visit the area every year, however, are well aware of Metéora's significance to the cultural heritage of Greece. Climbers have always approached the area with respect for its religious and historical importance as well as its sensitive ecology. A ban on climbing rock formations topped by active monasteries has been in place since 1976, and climbers abide by those restrictions. Climbers along with most residents of the nearby towns do not support any sort of further climbing restrictions, partly because of the importance of climbers to the area's economy.

Having said that, Metéora and its rock-bound monasteries are truly one of Europe's most special historical and natural places, as well as one of the world's most spectacular sacred sites. The word Metéora means literally "hovering in the air," a term applied by pilgrims who thought that the monasteries appeared to hover above the rock pillars. Although hermits and ascetics lived in the region long before the Christian era, it was the arrival of Christianity in the eighth century that turned the rocks into monastic retreats.

The formations, seemingly inaccessible without modern climbing gear, were first climbed by early shepherds and religious hermits seeking solace and solitude from the world's sorrows, as well as for safety from the Turks and lawless bandits. As the number of monks increased, the Theotokos of Doupiani was established as a religious community in the eleventh century, and the first monasteries were built. By the fourteenth century the Turkish Byzantine Empire was waning in influence, and the monasteries on the Athos peninsula to the northeast were harassed by pirates and brigands. Three monks—Athanasius, Gregory, and Moses—left Athos and came to the "rock forest" at Metéora, retreating atop the pillar Stylos. Endowments from wealthy Orthodox believers allowed them to build the Church of the Transfiguration in 1356, which emerged as the dominant Grand Metéora (Moni Megalo Meteoro) community.

Over the next few centuries, twenty-four monasteries were built, including Moni Varlaam, which took almost 200 years to complete. The monasteries kept alive Hellenic culture, traditions, and religion during the Turkish occupation, serving not only as religious centers but also places of learning and artistry. For security and seclusion, the monasteries were difficult to enter. Main access was by nets and baskets hoisted up by ropes and pullies or retractable wooden ladders up to 130 feet high. In the 1400s Metéora plunged into disorder for a couple centuries, until a revival of monasticism during the reign of

Suileman the Magnificent. In the eighteenth century the area was a refuge from the harsh administration and heavy taxation of the Ottoman overlords. Later, in the nineteenth century, the remote rocks served as a hideaway for rebels fighting the Turks during the war for Greek independence. During World War II Germans occupied the area, looting and destroying some of the monasteries and Kalambáka.

Today only six monasteries are occupied by a handful of nuns and black-bearded, long-robed monks. Most now prefer living in peaceful refuges like the famed sanctuary at Athos. Now the monasteries are living museums, rather than strictly religious retreats—especially when the loop road crawls with tour buses disgorging visitors who come to marvel at this mystical place of peace and solitude. Still, it's discouraging to see the mobile shops in the parking lots hawking souvenirs and trinkets next to the sacred gates.

It's best to visit the monasteries in the off-season, which happens to be the best climbing season. Although they're crowded in summer, it's highly recommended that you visit a few of the monasteries on rest days. They are usually open in the morning, closed for lunch, and then reopened in afternoon. A small entrance fee is charged. You also need to dress appropriately to visit them. This means men cannot wear shorts, and arms must be covered. Women must wear skirts below the knees, and their arms also must be covered. Improperly attired visitors can pick from a big stack of full skirts piled on the floor beside the ticket booth. If you sit and watch the tourists, you will inevitably spot a man heading back to his car after refusing to don a skirt for his once-in-a-lifetime visit to Metéora!

Trip Planning Information

General description: A magical and unusual climbing area with more than 600 established, multipitch climbing routes on pinnacles, towers, and pillars composed of excellent conglomerate rock.

Location: Thessaly in central Greece. 220 miles (355 kilometers) northwest of Athens.

Camping and accommodations:
Campgrounds, guesthouses, and hotels are found in both Kalambáka and Kastraki. Most climbers stay in Kastraki since it's closer to the cliffs. The recommended climber campsite is Camping Vrachos, on the road into Kastraki from Kalambáka. A discount is offered for long-term stays. The other site is Cave Camping near Doupiani Rock. Several campgrounds are found in Kalambáka, including Theopetra Camping, Camping Philoxenia, Rizos International, and Camping Kalambáka.

Hotels in Kastraki include Hotel Kastraki, Pension Patavalis, Papastathis Rooms, Tsikeli Rooms, Dupiani House, Hotel Spanias, Hotel Sydney, and Hotel France. Many hotels are also found in Kalambáka, including the chain hotel Divani, a favorite with tour groups; Hotel Metéora; and Koka Roka Rooms at the start of the Agia Triada Moni trail.

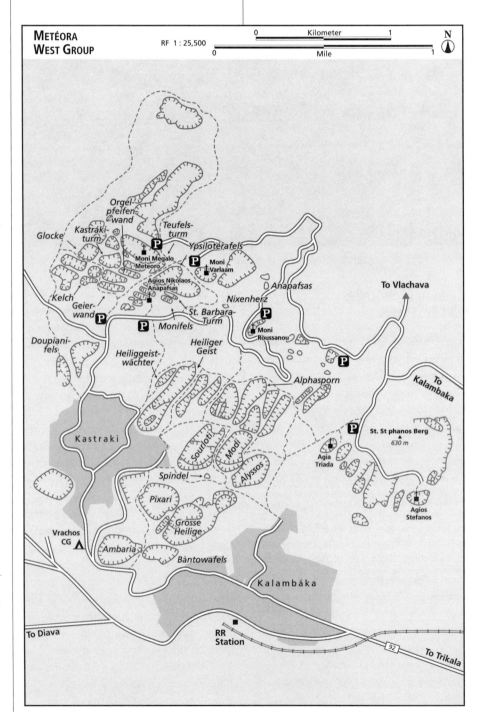

Climbing season: Year-round. The best seasons are April to June and late September to early November. Easter is the traditional time for Greek climbers to visit. Autumn is generally warm and dry. Summer, when most Americans visit, is uncomfortably hot, although shady morning routes are easily found. Most of the big routes can be climbed between 5:00 A.M. and 10:00 A.M., before the heat is unbearable. Hot afternoons are best spent at the campground swimming pool. Winter conditions vary greatly. It can be cold, wet, and even snowy, but good days also regularly occur.

Restrictions and access issues: Climbing is prohibited on all rocks and summits with inhabited monasteries. This rule was negotiated by climbers with the church in 1976. Local ethics dictate that all first ascents must be done ground up with all bolts drilled on the lead. Otherwise, visiting climbers should follow standard protocol by picking up trash, using chalk sparingly, not camping or bivouacking among the rocks, and following existing trails whenever possible.

Guidebooks: *Meteora Klettern und Wandern* by Heinz Lothar Stutte and Dietrich Hasse is a comprehensive topo guide to all the classic routes and those established before 1986. *Meteora Klettern* is Stutte and Hasse's updated guide to the newer routes. Both books have sections in English as well as German, Italian, French, and Greek.

Services and shops: All services are found in Kalambáka and Kastraki. Kastraki is smaller but closer to the monasteries and the climbing. It has many traditional Greek *tavernas* that serve traditional Greek food, including *souvlaki, gyros,* and Greek salads with lots of feta cheese. Some favorites include Paradiso Café, Gardenia, and Philoxenia Restaurant. Kalambáka offers more shops, *tavernas,* restaurants, and hotels. It's good to go into town for a morning coffee by the town plaza. Motorbikes and scooters can be rented in Kalambáka. Sideris Konstantinos in Kalambáka sells a selection of climbing

gear. Remember that both towns have a thriving tourist industry, so prices during tourist season will be high.

Emergency services: Dial 100 in Greece for all emergency services. Medical facilities are in Kalambáka and Trikala.

Nearby climbing areas: Some excellent limestone sport climbing is found near Metéora. This includes Theópetra, Mouzaki, Pyli, and Elati. More information is available at: www.geocities.com/pascuale.geo (Mouzaki); www.geocities.com/rizomaboulder (Rizoma bouldering); and www.oreivatein.com/climb/rock/e_rock.htm (Metéora, Theópetra, Mouzaki, Pyli, and Elati).

Nearby attractions: Visit the six Metéora monasteries open to the public. These World Heritage Sites are historic and beautiful. They are Moni Agios Nikolaos Anapafsas, with its beautiful frescoes painted by monk Theophanes Strelizas from Crete; Moni Megalo Meteoro (Grand Meteora), the largest and most famous monastery; nearby Moni Varlaam; Moni Roussanou, perched atop a lofty rock; the spectacular Moni Agia Triada (Holy Trinity), featured in the James Bond movie *For Your Eyes Only;* and the nunnery Moni Agios Stefanos, overlooking Kalambáka. Opening and closing times vary depending on the season. Most are open in the morning, closed over lunch, and then open in the afternoon. Most are closed a day or two every week. A visitation fee is charged. A strict dress code is enforced, with women required to wear skirts below their knees (sometimes provided when entering a monastery) and men in long pants and covered arms.

The town of Kalambáka nestles at the foot of the cliffs. The ancient city was called Eginio in ancient times, and later Stagon. During Turkish occupation it was renamed Kalambáka, possibly derived from the Turkish *kale mpak* meaning "prestigious castle," and referring to the Metéora rocks. The town of 15,000 residents was destroyed by the Nazis in World War II and is mostly modern buildings.

Other points of interest include the deep gorge at Pyli, the Pindos Mountains, and the nearby city of Trikala, with its sixteenth-century Turkish mosque Koursoun Tzami.

Finding the area: Metéora is in central Greece northwest of Athens. The best way to get there is by driving from Athens. The three- to four-hour drive is on good, easy-to-follow highways. Many car rental agencies in Athens will drive you and your rental car to the outskirts of the city to avoid the traffic jams and route-finding nightmares. Most Greek towns and villages are ringed by highway bypasses so you can avoid getting lost and driving through their congested centers. Athens is hell to drive in, but the rest of Greece is relatively easy—however, be very cautious. Greece has the highest road fatality rate in Europe, with passing the greatest cause of accidents. Greeks often drive on the highway shoulders to allow faster vehicles to pass.

To get to Metéora from Athens (Athinai), head north from the city on the big highway 1/E75. Drive 215 kilometers to Lamía, and exit onto highway E65, following signs for Karditsa and Trikala. Drive 96 kilometers to Karditsa and another 26 to Trikala. Bypass the city on the highway, and continue another 26 kilometers to Kalambáka. Drive through the town and continue, following signs, a couple kilometers northwest to Kastraki. The road continues through the village and then threads among the rock formations and monasteries.

If you don't have a rental car, take the train from the Larisis Train Station in Athens to Kalambáka. Trains depart throughout the day. The journey takes ten to twelve hours. Ask at the information center at the train station before buying tickets, and write down the names and numbers of the trains. Write down the names in Greek also. You change trains in Paleofrsalos. It's best to buy a ticket on the express train since it's faster and less crowded than cheaper ones.

Kastrakiturm

Glocke

Doupianifels

Echofels

Kelch

Geierwand

Parking

Doupianifels (Doupiani Rock)

Doupiani Rock, lying on the northwest side of Kastraki, is Metéora's most popular climbing site, with numerous excellent multipitch routes and easy access.

Almost all the routes can be rappelled. The following descriptions are of the two main rappel routes.

South Face rappel: The original descent route is two rappels from the notch just south of the summit down the southeast side of the formation. Scramble down to the notch, and look for anchors. Make a 135-foot rappel with double ropes.

Traverse left (facing the rock), and follow a ramp to a stance above a small cave feature. Make a 35-foot rappel, and walk down low-angle rock to the road.

North Face rappel: A few meters above the notch, look for a ringbolt on flat rock. Make a short rappel north and then two 100-foot rappels to the ground.

Southwest Face

1. Regenpfeiler (V) (5.7) No topo. 5 pitches. 460 feet. This route, a good introduction to Metéora, is on the south side of the rock. To reach the start take the road that leads to the monasteries, and just past the Hotel Kastraki, turn left onto a

narrow road. Park at the first bend, and follow the streambed on the right to the base of the rock. The route ascends the obvious ridge above you. **Pitch 1:** Face climb (V+) to a bolt belay. 3 bolts. 112 feet. **Pitch 2:** Continue up the lower-angle ridge above (III) to a bolt belay. 115 feet. **Pitch 3:** Easy climbing to a bolt belay below the upper ridge. 65 feet. **Pitch 4:** Steeper face climbing (V+) leads onto the summit slab (IV) and a bolt belay. 4 bolts. 115 feet. **Pitch 5:** Edge up the slab above (IV) past 1 bolt to the summit anchor. 50 feet. To reach the summit register, scramble right along the ridge to a col, then climb curved steps to the top.

Southeast Face

The popular Southeast Face of Doupiani Rock looms directly above the town of Kastraki.

2. En Psychro (VIII-) (5.11c) 4 pitches. Up the middle of the face. **Pitch 1:** Face climb (VIII-) to a belay stance near the top of a large right-angling dihedral. 6 bolts. 100 feet. **Pitch 2:** Climb the dihedral to its top, and climb steeply (VII-) to a pothole. Traverse left across the pothole and below another pothole to a belay at its left side. 5 bolts. 100 feet. **Pitch 3:** Climb a steep slab (VII-) to a belay left of a groove and chimney. 9 bolts. 135 feet. **Pitch 4:** Face climb the rib (VI) left of the chimney to a ledge belay just below the summit. 4 bolts. 100 feet.

3. Black Out (VII+) (5.11a/b) This pitch is a stiff direct start to *Südoustwand*. You can rappel from its anchors, or continue up *Südoustwand's* upper pitches to the summit. Climb directly up (VI-) to a rightward traverse (VI+). Edge up the steep slab above (VII+) to a belay anchor at the top of the large right-angling dihedral. 6 bolts. 135 feet.

4. Efialtis (VII+) (5.11a/b) 5 pitches. Start directly below the left side of a thin roof. **Pitch 1:** Straightforward face moves (VII+) up the pebbled wall lead to a belay on a sloping stance. 6 bolts. 85 feet. **Pitch 2:** Climb up and pass the left side of the thin roof. Continue up (VI) to an airy stance just left of the huge hole and ledge. 6 bolts. 150 feet. **Pitch 3:** Work up steep, thin rock (VIII-) to a stance up right. 6 bolts. 85 feet. **Pitch 4:** Climb a crack system (VIII) in a corner above the belay to a small stance. 8 bolts. 85 feet. **Pitch 5:** Climb up right on lower-angled rock (VI+) to a belay just below the summit. 6 bolts. 85 feet.

5. Duett (VIII) (5.11d) 5 pitches. **Pitch 1:** Climb a slab and water groove (VI) to a belay at a horizontal break. 6 bolts. 100 feet. **Pitch 2:** Climb a slab to a thin roof. Pull over (VII-), and continue to a belay at the left side of a long hole. 5 bolts. 85 feet. **Pitch 3:** Step left from the hole, and face climb (VIII-) up past the huge hole. Work up right to a bolted belay stance. 9 bolts.

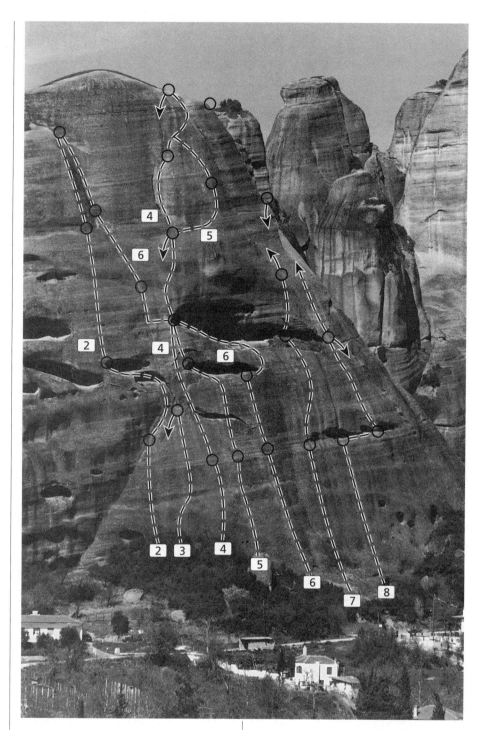

150 feet. **Pitch 4:** Traverse right, then climb directly up the steep wall (VIII) to a small stance. 5 bolts. 85 feet. **Pitch 5:** Climb up left and then back right (VII+) to a slab belay just below the summit. 8 bolts. 100 feet.

6. Südoustwand (VII- or VI A0) (5.10c or 5.10a A0) 6 pitches. A recommended 3-star classic. **Pitch 1:** Face climb to a groove (VI-) to a belay stance. 5 bolts. 85 feet. **Pitch 2:** Continue straight up (VI) to a belay in a long pothole. 9 bolts. 100

feet. **Pitch 3:** Traverse right to the right side of the pothole, and climb easy rock to the large cave. Move left, and belay at a bolted stance on the left side of the cave. **Pitch 4:** Traverse left (VI-) into a groove and climb steep, thin rock (VII- or VI-AO) to a belay. 6 bolts. 50 feet. **Pitch 5:** Move up left along the groove (V) to a belay. 3 bolts. 65 feet. **Pitch 6:** Chimney up the groove/corner (V+) to a belay ledge on the shoulder left of the summit. 3 bolts. 115 feet.

7. Crazy Dancing (IX+) (5.13a) 5 pitches. One of Metéora's hardest routes. Established by Vangelis Batsios and Christos Batalogiannis in 1997. If you want to climb just the hard bit, ascend *Ostkante,* and traverse up left after the first pitch to the cave. **Pitch 1:** Face climb (VI) to a belay stance left of some potholes. 6 bolts. 115 feet. **Pitch 2:** Work up right (VI+) to a belay at the right side of the cave. 4 bolts. 85 feet. **Pitch 3:** Begin in the back of the cave. Follow a crack system out the cave, and pull onto the steep wall above (IX+). Continue pebble pinching to a belay stance. 9 bolts. 45 feet. **Pitch 4:** Climb the wall just left of a crack system (VI) to a belay near the top of the crack and corner. 6 bolts. 150 feet. **Pitch 5:** Step right from the belay, and move up steep rock (VIII-) to a belay on the shoulder just below the summit. 6 bolts. 100 feet.

8. Hammer und Sichel (VII+) (5.11a/b) 5 pitches. Begin in a line directly below the largest pothole. **Pitch 1:** Face climb up right and then up a groove (VII) to a belay in the large pothole. 9 bolts. 100 feet. **Pitch 2:** An easy traverse right to a belay between potholes. 35 feet. **Pitch 3:** Climb the bulge above (VII+/VIII-), or do a shoulder stand (V+) and move up steep slabby rock to a belay stance just right of the big cave. 6 bolts. 85 feet. **Pitch 4:** Face moves lead to a groove to a belay by a pillar. 3 bolts. 150 feet. **Pitch 5:** Climb the last pitch of *Ostkante* up the rib to the summit. 5 bolts. 115 feet.

9. Dickes Ende (VI+) (5.10b) 5 pitches. 475 feet. A classic face line. **Pitch 1:** Climb up and left past several small potholes (V+) to a belay stance. 3 bolts. 150 feet. **Pitch 2:** Move up left to a shallow groove (V+) to a traverse left on a carved monk ledge. Belay from bolts just right of the cave. 3 bolts. 85 feet. **Pitch 3:** Climb up and follow a deep groove (V) to a stance. 1 bolt. 115 feet. **Pitch 4:** Continue up the groove/left-facing corner (V+) to a belay. 65 feet. **Pitch 5:** The crux lead. Follow the corner until it ends. Make thin moves up the steep face above (VII- or VI A0), and move right to a bolted belay. 3 bolts. 65 feet. **Rack:** Bring a set of Stoppers and some small to medium cams.

10. Ohne Vorbehalt (VI-) (5.9) 4 pitches. Just left of the prominent ridge. **Pitch 1:** Face climb up cobbles (IV+) to a belay right of a series of potholes. 3 bolts. 115 feet. **Pitch 2:** Continue up left on relatively easy rock (V-) to a belay below a small roof. 4 bolts. 135 feet. **Pitch 3:** Climb up left into a groove. Partway up, exit left, and climb the face (V+) left of the rib to a stance. 3 bolts. 115 feet. **Pitch 4:** Edge up a steep face (VI-) to a belay on the rounded shoulder just below the summit. 3 bolts. 115 feet.

11. Ostkante (VI) (5.10a) 4 pitches. 400 feet. A super classic line up the obvious

east ridge. Opened by Dietrich Hasse and Heinz Lothar Stutte in 1976. Begin below the ridge. **Pitch 1:** Climb the easy ridge (III) to a belay stance. 3 bolts. 135 feet. **Pitch 2:** Continue up the ridge to a stance right of a narrow roof. 2 bolts. 85 feet. **Pitch 3:** Traverse straight left (III) to a groove and up (V+), or angle up left (V) past a bolt to the groove. Continue up the shallow groove to a belay by a pillar. 2 bolts. 85 feet. **Pitch 4:** Climb directly up the rib (VI) above to the summit. 5 bolts. 115 feet.

Northwest Face

Doupiani's northwest face lies on the shaded side of the rock northwest of Kastraki. Almost all the routes are recommended. The newer lines are better protected than the older classics. Descent is by rappelling back down the routes or by the standard rappel descent down the south side of the rock.

Finding the cliff: Park in one of the pullouts on the left just past Doupiani Rock. Walk up the narrow paved road that heads west below the north side of the rock. Follow a climber's trail to the base of the face. Approach time is about five minutes.

12. Nightmare (VI-) (5.9) 3 pitches. **Pitch 1:** Edge up a steep slab (VI-) to a belay at a hole. 5 bolts. 150 feet. **Pitch 2:** Move around the right side of the hole, and climb easy rock to a grass patch. Belay above. 1 bolt. 100 feet. **Pitch 3:** Climb a rib and then up right on an easy slab to a belay just below the rounded summit. 2 bolts.

13. Schritte am Abend (V+) (5.8) 2 pitches. **Pitch 1:** Stem up the obvious groove (V+) on the left side of the face. 6 bolts. 135 feet. **Pitch 2:** Follow an easy trough up right to the shoulder right of the summit.

14. Orektika (V-) (5.6) 2 pitches. **Pitch 1:** Grab cobbles up the face (V-) to a belay stance on lower-angle rock. 5 bolts. 135 feet. **Pitch 2:** Climb the easy slab above the belay to a trough. Follow up right.

15. Boulatapfeiler (VI–) (5.9) 2 pitches. 230 feet. Begin right of a deep chimney groove. **Pitch 1:** Work up the steep wall (V+) to a belay. 5 bolts. 115 feet. **Pitch 2:** Climb steepening rock between two grooves (VI–) to the top. 3 bolts. 115 feet.

16. Ostria (V+) (5.8) 2 pitches. Fun and well protected. Start just left of a Y groove. **Pitch 1:** Steep slab climbing (V+) to a belay on the left fork of the Y. 8 bolts. 100 feet. **Pitch 2:** Edge up the wall just right of the groove. 6 bolts. 100 feet.

17. Isidora (VI–) (5.9) 2 pitches. Begin just right of the Y groove. **Pitch 1:** Pull cobbles (IV) to a belay on a slab. 6 bolts. 100 feet. **Pitch 2:** Climb the headwall above (V+). 6 bolts. 100 feet.

18. Zwischenhoch (V+) (5.8) 2 pitches. **Pitch 1:** Fun climbing (IV) leads to *Isidora's* belay. 3 bolts. 100 feet. **Pitch 2:** Edge up the steepish wall (V+) to a belay just below the top. 2 bolts. 100 feet.

19. Tausendmal berührt (V+) (5.8) 2 pitches. **Pitch 1:** Climb a right-angling groove corner (V+) to a groove. Belay on the slab above. 5 bolts. 115 feet. **Pitch 2:** Work up the steep wall (V+) left of a right-angling groove to the top. 1 bolt. 85 feet.

20. Viper (VII–) (5.10c) 2 pitches. **Pitch 1:** Climb a groove up a right-angling corner and then up the vertical wall above (VII–) to an anchor on a sloping stance. 6 bolts. 115 feet. **Pitch 2:** Continue up steep rock (VI+) left of a crack system to the top. 6 bolts. 100 feet.

21. Schwein gehabt (V+) (5.8) 2 pitches. **Pitch 1:** Follow a groove (V+) to a belay. 5 bolts. 150 feet. **Pitch 2:** Continue up the easier groove above the belay. 65 feet.

22. Reflektor (VI+) (5.10b) 2 pitches. Start just right of *Schwein gehabt* and just left of a right-angling corner. **Pitch 1:** Climb steep rock (VI+) to a belay. 4 bolts.

135 feet. **Pitch 2:** Surmount a bulge, and then work up rock (VI–) right of a crack system. 2 bolts. 100 feet.

23. Nordlicht (V+) (5.8) 2 pitches. Classic. **Pitch 1:** Climb a slab up the right side of a right-angling corner to a short headwall (V+). 5 bolts. 135 feet. **Pitch 2:** Move up right, and climb a water groove to a steeper wall. Work up right past a couple large holes to the summit. 5 bolts. 115 feet.

24. Apocalypse (VIII–) (5.11b/c) 3 pitches. **Pitch 1:** Climb the first lead of *Nordlicht*. **Pitch 2:** Move up right to the base of a groove. Continue up right across a slab past a bolt to a belay. 100 feet. **Pitch 3:** Climb a steep crack and wall (VIII–) to the top. 7 bolts. 85 feet.

Glocke

Glocke, meaning "bell," is a 400-foot-high, bell-shaped tower on the northwest side of the west group of towers immediately north of Doupiani Rock. The rock is difficult to see from the road.

Finding the tower: Park just past Doupiani Rock, and hike northwest into the maze of towers. Pass under Geerwand, and continue through a narrow canyon past Kelch and Echosfels on the left. Eventually you reach the west side of the group of towers. Go right, and follow a trail along the west base of Bischofsmütze to the west face of Glocke. The route ascends the southwest side of the tower. Approach time is fifteen to twenty minutes.

25. Glockenspiel *(Carillon of the Bell)* (VI) (5.10a) 6 pitches. Excellent and classic. Runout in places, but all the cruxes are protected. Start below the southwest edge of the tower. **Pitch 1:** Climb 30 feet on cobbles to the first bolt, and head up right (V+) to a belay stance. 3 bolts. 100 feet. **Pitch 2:** Work up the steep face above (V) to a belay up right. **Pitch 3:** Climb the steeper wall above until it's possible to move left. Edge through the crux (VI), and then traverse up right to a belay below slabbier rock. 3 bolts. 85 feet. **Pitch 4:** Cruise the easier slab above to a belay below the rounded summit cap. 1 bolt. 65 feet. **Pitch 5:** Traverse right below the summit cap (IV-) to a belay. 65 feet. **Pitch 6:** Follow a groove (IV) up left onto the rounded summit. 35 feet. **Descent:** Two rappels. Rappel 65 feet from the summit to an anchor at the base of a slab on the northeast side. Then rappel 65 feet to a notch. Scramble from here into a gully, and descend it alongside the east face to the base of the rock.

26. Allemannischer Schelledanz (VII+) (5.11a/b) 4 pitches. A happy climb for late afternoon or as a morning warm-up. The route begins left of *Glockenspiel* and just

right of a large boulder. It's in the morning shade and afternoon sun. **Pitch 1:** Moderate, almost vertical face climbing. Climb past 3 bolts (VI), then traverse right and climb past 6 more bolts (VI) to a ringbolt belay. 115 feet. 9 bolts. **Pitch 2:** Face climb (VI-) straight up to a bulge. Surmount (VII- or A0) to a ringbolt belay.

10 bolts. 100 feet. **Pitch 3:** More face climbing (VI- and VI) to a break below the summit cap. Traverse left to a bolt belay. 7 bolts. 115 feet. **Pitch 4:** Pull over a small overhang (VII+), and climb an easy groove to the summit. 3 bolts. 50 feet. **Descent:** See above description for #25.

Kelch

Kelch, meaning "Holy Grail" because the rock looks like a grail communion cup, is a prominent two-summited tower on the south edge of the west group of towers. It's easily identified from the road. *Eiertanz,* ascending the east ridge of the north summit to an airy step across, is the classic route up the tower.

Finding the tower: Park in one of the pullouts just past Doupiani Rock, and hike northwest toward the tower on a narrow path that leads to the base of the obvious route. Approach time is ten minutes.

27. Eiertanz (VI- A1) (5.9 A1) 5 pitches. Superb and popular climb. Begin below the slabby east ridge. **Pitch 1:** Climb up left over a short steep section (V) and then up the cobbled slab above to a belay stance. 3 bolts. 85 feet. **Pitch 2:** Continue up the steepening, wide ridge (crux VI-) to a belay directly below a crack system. 8 bolts. 85 feet. **Pitch 3:** Work up the steep wall above (V), and climb the crack to a belay at its top. Protect the crack with nuts #4 to #9 and Friends #2 to #3. 1 bolt. 135 feet. **Pitch 4:** Do a short scrambling pitch (III) around a knob to a belay atop a higher summit. Watch for loose rock. 65 feet. **Pitch 5:** Classic pitch with lots of exposure! Down climb into the deep gap, and step across to a bolt. Aid (A1) or free climb (VII/VII+) up the vertical face to the airy summit. The step across and free climbing is easier for tall climbers. Use just a few slings instead of carrying aiders. **Descent:** Normal descent is three rappels down the west side. Rappel 65 feet from the summit to a stance. Then rappel 50 feet from a tree to a ledge with a tree. Finally, rappel 100 feet to the ground. Another rappel route is on the opposite side. Make two airy rappels (135 feet and 150 feet) to the ground. **Rack:** A set of Stoppers and some small to medium Friends.

Kastrakiturm
(Kastraki Tower)

Kastrakiturm is a huge tower that sits in the middle of the west group. *Talweg,* the described route, follows an obvious crack system up the right side of the south face. This excellent traditional route, one of Metéora's best crack climbs, was first ascended by Dietrich Hasse and Heinz Lothar Stutte in 1983.

Finding the tower: Park in one of the pullouts on the left just past Doupiani Rock. Follow a path that heads north along a ravine. Past Geierwand, look for another path that works up a short steep hillside to the base of the prominent crack system.

28. Talweg (VII) (5.10d) 6 pitches. Recommended. A strenuous and serious trad climb with retreat almost impossible. Begin by scrambling up an easy groove on a slab for a couple hundred feet to a belay (anchor is a #3 Camalot) in a cave below the crack system. **Pitch 1:** Chimney and stem up the corner crack to a bulge crux (VII-). Belay above in a niche. 1 bolt. 85 feet. **Pitch 2:** Chimney up the wide crack (IV) to a niche belay. 1 bolt. 65 feet. **Pitch 3:** Steep moves (VI+) lead to a back and foot chimney. Move left to a belay stance. 85 feet. **Pitch 4:** Step right, and work up the right-hand crack (V+) until it's possible to traverse back left into the left crack. Alternatively, you can climb directly up the left crack (VII) above the belay. Work up the steep off-width crack (VII) to a belay below a roof. 3 bolts. 100 feet. **Pitch 5:** Climb the exposed summit dihedral (VI) via assorted jams to a belay stance just below the summit. 2 bolts. 85 feet. **Pitch 6:** Scramble up right to the top. 35 feet. **Descent:** Downclimb an easy groove on the north side to a rappel station. Make a 65-foot rappel to the base of the north face. Scramble down and around the east side of the tower to the base of the south face. **Rack:** Bring at least 15 quickdraws, extra slings, Hexentrics #9 to #11, a set of Stoppers, and double sets of Friends or Camalots.

Geierwand

Geierwand, a 450-foot-high tower on the south side of the west group, presents a wide south face when viewed from the road. The described route is a fine crack and face climb up the narrow west face of the tower. The route is shaded in the morning and sunny in the afternoon.

Finding the tower: Park just past Doupiani Rock in a pullout on the west side of the road. Hike north on a path that passes just west of the tower with Anapafsas Monastery atop. Bend left, and hike around to the base of the west face.

29. Westkante (VI) (5.10a) 5 pitches. Recommended moderate route up the west flank of the tower. Begin below a left-angling dihedral. **Pitch 1:** Easy chimneying and slab climbing up the dihedral to a belay on the left. If you're not used to the rock, use a Camelot #2 or #3 at the exit from the cave. 85 feet. **Pitch 2:** Climb the dihedral crack above to a small roof, step left, and climb over to a bolt. Continue up the open corner above (V). At its top move left on the slab, and climb to a belay. Only 1 bolt, but it's easy to find Friend and nut placements. Medium Hexentrics are useful. 150 feet. **Pitch 3:** Face climb up right then back left up the ridge (VI at the second bolt) to an airy belay. 5 bolts. 100 feet. **Pitch 4:** Steep face climbing (VI) up the narrowing ridge to a belay. 4 bolts. 65 feet. **Pitch 5:** Finish up the lower-angle ridge (IV) to the summit. 2 bolts. 65 feet. You can easily combine Pitches 4 and 5 into a single pitch.
Descent: Three rappels down a chimney system on the north face. Rappel 85 feet from a ringbolt. Next, rappel 100 feet to a ringbolt. Finally, rappel 135 feet to the ground. **Rack:** Quickdraws, set of Stoppers, set of Friends, and two ropes.

Orgelpfeifenwand (Organ Pipe)

This huge rock formation, an east-west trending fin, fronts the road with a wide south face. *Rainbow Warrior,* an excellent crack route, ascends an obvious left-diagonaling crack system on the face's right side. The route is mostly sunny. Avoid during hot weather. Several other long routes are found on the rock. These include *Toccata und Fuge Direkt* (VIII- A0) up the steep south face left of *Rainbow Warrior* and *Aprilschmerz* (VII) on the broad ridge to the right.

Finding the tower: Park just past Doupiani Rock in a pullout on the west side of the road. Hike north on a path that passes just west of the tower with Anapafsas Monastery atop. Past the monastery scramble up a brushy gully to a junction. Hike left onto a terrace below the crack system on the right side of the south face.

30. Regenbogen (Rainbow Warrior) (VII) (5.10d) 5 pitches. Classic crack climb established by Hans Weninger and Bernd Wischhöfer in 1983. A serious and strenuous outing. Retreat is very difficult and involves diagonal rappels. Begin below a left-facing dihedral. **Pitch 1:** Climb the crack in a left-facing corner past a bolt to an off-width section (VI+). Above a possible belay ledge, climb to a piton, then work up the overhanging face to the left (VII) to a bolted belay. 2 bolts. 150 feet. Use double ropes or lots of runners to avoid rope drag. **Pitch 2:** A long pitch. Chimney up the corner (V) to a short crux (V+ A0) until it's possible to face climb (VI-) to a bolted belay above a tree. 6 bolts. 135 feet. **Pitch 3:** Follow the crack system (V-) past a small tree to a bolted belay. 2 bolts. 115 feet. **Pitch 4:** Work up the crack (IV) until it ends, and then stem a groove and face climb (V+) to a bolted belay on the sloping shoulder. 3 bolts. 135 feet. **Pitch 5:** Face climb the final headwall (V+) to easy slabs and the

5 Rappels off back side

Chimney

Gear belay

Off-width

30

summit anchor bolts. 1 bolt. 150 feet. **Descent:** Five rappels down the east chimney separating Orgelpfeifenwand from Wolkenwand to the north. **Rappel 1:** 85 feet from the summit to a notch between the two formations. **Rappel 2:** 65 feet from a tree anchor to a tree anchor. **Rappel 3:** 150 feet from a tree anchor to a tree anchor. **Rappel 4:** 100 feet from a tree anchor to a bolt anchor. **Rappel 5:** 65 feet from a bolt anchor to the ground. The descent is easily down climbed. This is recommended to avoid inconvenient rappels from trees and the possibility of the rope becoming snagged on trees. **Rack:** 10 quickdraws, extra slings, Camalots #1 to #4, Stoppers #4 to #8, and two ropes.

Teufelsturm
(Devil's Tower)

This prominent, 500-foot-high tower with a flat summit sits at the top of a brushy gully right of Metamorphosis Monastery. Several excellent long routes ascend its steep southern face. *Dr. Faust,* the designated route, is perhaps the best trip up the wall and is better protected than *Talkante* to the right. Check the comprehensive guide for topos to the other lines, including *Nordwestweg* (V+), a four-pitch excursion left of *Dr. Faust.*

Finding the tower: Park just past Doupiani Rock in a pullout on the west side of the road. Hike north on a path that passes just west of the tower with Anapafsas Monastery atop. Past the monastery scramble up a brushy gully to a junction. Continue straight up the gully to the toe of the narrow south pillar.

31. Dr. Faust (VII–) (5.10c) 5 pitches. Begin at the toe of the pillar. **Pitch 1:** Face climb up and left (V+) past a couple of bolts to a sloping break. Make crux face moves (VII–) up overhanging rock, and work up left (VI) on the vertical face to a bolted belay. 8 bolts. 100 feet. **Pitch 2:** Climb the easier slab above (VI–) to a bolted belay. 3 bolts. 100 feet. **Pitch 3:** Move left, and follow a groove (V) up right past the right side of a narrow roof. Continue face climbing (VI) to a bolted belay stance. 4 bolts. 100 feet. **Pitch 4:** Steep slab climbing (V) up right leads to a belay below the final rib. 3 bolts. 100 feet. **Pitch 5:** Move up the wall above (V+), and finish up easier rock (IV) to the summit. 1 bolt. 100 feet. **Descent:** Make four rappels down the route. Be careful on the first rappel off the summit since the bolt is placed in flat rock, and the rope can be difficult or impossible to pull! The first rappel is 85 feet to the last belay on top of the pillar. Make three more rappels (100, 100, and 165 feet) to the route base.

Ypsilotérafels (Ypsilotéra Rock)

Ypsilotéra is the tower right of Teufelsturm. Many superb multipitch routes ascend its sunny south face. The crag, sitting high above the rest of the west group, offers excellent climbing in a fairly remote and quiet setting. All the routes are more or less the same, with one difficult pitch and the rest moderately easy. The best routes are *Westkante Direct* for its length and position, *Missing Link* for the difficulty of its first pitch and its excellent protection, and *Himmelsleiter* for its special line. Much of the protection on these routes is by threads around stones and stuck Stoppers between the cobbles. Carry lots of slings and cords for making threads. Descent from all the routes is by four rappels from fixed anchors down the face.

32. Westkante (VI–) (5.9) 5 pitches. Begin by scrambling up the gully to the right of the toe of the southwest buttress to the base of a pointed pillar. Scramble up to a belay stance on the left side of the pillar. **Pitch 1:** Traverse left (III+) for 35 feet past a bolt to a bolted belay stance. **Pitch 2:** Route crux. Face climb steep rock (VI–) past a bolt. Continue straight up (IV–) past two more bolts to a bolted belay. 3 bolts. 115 feet. **Pitch 3:** Fun climbing (IV) up the exposed wall to a bolted belay. 2 bolts. 115 feet. **Pitch 4:** Easier slab climbing (spot of IV but mostly III) leads to belay anchor just below the top. 1 bolt. 100 feet. **Pitch 5:** Easy scrambling to the summit. **Descent:** Four rappels down the wall directly right of the route. There is no route here, only the rappel line with eyebolts. **Rappel 1:** 50 feet from an eyebolt. **Rappel 2:** 100 feet from an eyebolt. **Rappel 3:** 110 feet from an eyebolt. **Rappel 4:** 125 feet from an eyebolt to the route base. Alternatively, you can make three rappels down *Danae* at 50 feet, 150 feet, and 165 feet from the second belay to the ground.

33. Westkante Direct (VI–) (5.9) A fine 2-pitch direct start that adds 250 feet to *Westkante*. Begin at the toe of the southwest buttress opposite the base of Teufelsturm. **Pitch 1:** Pick your way up lichen-covered rock past some bolts to a bolted belay. **Pitch 2:** Continue face climbing to the first belay

stance on *Westkante*. Finish up *Westkante* to the summit.

34. Himmelsleiter (VI) (5.10a) 3 pitches. Classic face route put up by Heinz Lothar Stutte and O. Scheda in 1982. Scramble up the gully below the face to a ledge with trees below the route. **Pitch 1:** Climb steep rock (V+) to a couple cruxes (VI– and VI), and finish at a sloping bolted belay. 4 bolts. 115 feet. **Pitch 2:** Work up a groove (V+) above the belay, and climb (IV) past the right side of an obvious roof. Face climb left of a water streak (III) to a bolted belay. 3 bolts. 135 feet. **Pitch 3:** Continue straight up (IV) to the summit anchors. 2 bolts. 135 feet. **Descent:** Make four double-rope rappels down *Westkante*.

35. Danae (VII–) (5.10c) 4 pitches. A well-protected, harder line established by Aris Theodoropoulos and D. Karalis in 1997. Start just right of *Himmelsleiter*. **Pitch 1:** Climb up (V–) to a bolt and easily traverse right to another bolt. Face climb directly up from here (crux VII–) past 6 bolts to a bolted anchor. 8 bolts. 120 feet. **Pitch 2:** Cruise up fun rock (V) to a bolted belay. 9 bolts. 135 feet. **Pitch 3:** Face climb (V) along a dark streak to a bolted belay. 6 bolts. 115 feet. **Pitch 4:** Easy slab climbing to the summit anchors. 2 bolts. 80 feet. **Descent:** Make three double-rope rappels down the route: 50 feet, 150 feet, and 165 feet from the second belay to the ground.

Monifels and St. Barbara-Turm

Monifels, a 200-foot-high fin topped by the ruins of an ancient monastery, and its neighboring tower St. Barbara-Turm are dwarfed by massive Varlaamturm behind it. A couple of the easier classic routes ascend these towers. Other good routes are also found, including *Wallfahrt* (VI+) on the west ridge of Monifels and *Widerspenstige Zahmung* (VIII-), a direct line up the crack system on the south face of St. Barbara-Turm. Check the comprehensive guide for topos.

Finding the towers: Drive up the scenic road past the parking area for Anapafsas Monastery. Look for a small pullout on the left side of the road. Park and follow a short climber's path to the base of the rocks.

36. Talweg (V-) (5.6) 3 pitches. 100 feet. Begin below an obvious chimney below the east ridge of Monifels. **Pitch 1:** Work up the chimney (III) past some bushes, and belay from a bolt on a ledge. **Pitch 2:** Jam a fist crack (V-) in a right-facing corner until it's possible to chimney inside it. Finish up an off-width (V-) to a small bolted belay stance. 1 bolt. **Pitch 3:** Climb an easy groove crack up left, and carefully edge up the ruined monastery walls to the top. **Descent:** Make a 100-foot, double-rope rappel from summit anchors to the ground. **Rack:** Bring a selection of medium to large Friends and nuts.

37. Ostkante (V- A0) (5.9 A0) 5 pitches. An interesting classic climb up St. Barbara-Turm. Begin at the same place as *Talweg.* **Pitch 1:** Climb the chimney (III-) up and right to a belay on the left side of a long sloping ledge. **Pitch 2:** Traverse right along the airy ledge to a bolted belay. 115 feet. **Pitch 3:** Finish the traverse to a belay on the far right side of the ledge. **Pitch 4:** Do a shoulder stand on your partner to clip a bolt, and climb (V-) up the exposed ridge to a bolted belay below a final headwall. **Pitch 5:** Climb steep slab (V-) to the rock summit. **Descent:** Locate anchors on the south side of the summit, and make a 135-foot rappel to the ground.

Nixenherz

This small crag sits just above the north side of the road before Roussanou Monastery. A few good sport routes ascend its south face. Park in a pullout on the north side of the road just before the deep valley northwest of the monastery. Follow a short trail to the cliff base. Descent is by rappelling from the anchors on top or walking off. Routes are described left to right.

38. Nixenkante (VIII) (5.11d) Established by Vangelis Batsios and Christos Batalogiannis in 1998. Begin below the blunt left edge of the face. Clamber onto a flake, and step right onto the face. Pinch pebbles up the edge and over a couple boulders to a cliff-top anchor. 8 bolts to 1-bolt anchor. 60 feet.

39. Dynamis (IX) (5.12d) A face problem right of *Nixenkante*. Climb the thin, technical face to an anchor by the crack splitting the summit. 7 bolts to 1-bolt anchor. 60 feet.

40. Zerrissenes Herz (VI) (5.10a) Climb the obvious crack system. 8 bolts to 1-bolt anchor. 60 feet.

Heiliggeistwächter

This is the smaller subsidiary tower immediately west of Heiliger Geist. Several classic routes ascend to its rounded summit. Descent is by rappel off the east side. From the summit, face east toward the huge wall of Heiliger Geist. Look for a short path that drops down to a ledge with trees. By the left side is a ringbolt for the first short rappel to a double ringbolt anchor. Make a two-rope, 150-foot rappel to the ground.

Finding the cliff: Drive through Kastraki until you're below Doupiani Rock. Turn right onto the only street here, and drive through the north part of the village until the road reaches a T junction below the southwest flank of Heiliger Geist. Turn left, and park at a convenient pullout. Find one of several trails that cross the meadows below the high cliff, and hike northeast to the base of the obvious south ridge of Heiliggeistwächter. The routes on the opposite side of the tower are accessed by parking farther north up the road and following a trail to the base.

41. Sudwestkante (VI-) (5.9) 6 pitches. This route ascends the broad southwest ridge facing Kastraki. **Pitch 1:** An easy scrambling pitch to a bolt anchor. 130 feet. **Pitch 2:** A long easy pitch (III) up the ridge to a bolt anchor. 130 feet. **Pitch 3:** Climb the ridge (III) to a bolted belay. 65 feet. **Pitch 4:** Climb up right to a steeper headwall, and edge up (V+) to a bolted stance. 2 bolts. 65 feet. **Pitch 5:** Work up the wide ridge (V) on steep rock to a bolted belay. 2 bolts. 65 feet. **Pitch 6:** Continue up the narrowing ridge (V) to easier climbing (IV) to the summit anchors. 2 bolts. 130 feet. **Descent:** Three rappels down the east side. **Rappel 1:** Summit to anchors on a ledge on the east face. **Rappel 2:** Rappel 135 feet from an eyebolt to another bolt. **Rappel 3:** Rappel 35 feet to the ground. Obviously this can be done in one long rappel with double ropes.

Paleokranies Kaukasier Kumariesturm Heiliger Geist Heiliggeistwächter Kastraki

2 or 3 rappels

41

42. Nordostweg (V+) (5.8) 4 pitches. A route up the shady northeast face. Begin at the lower toe of the face. **Pitch 1:** Climb the slab up left (IV+) to a belay. 3 bolts. 135 feet. **Pitch 2:** Work straight up the steepening face (IV) to a bolted belay. 1 bolt. 115 feet. **Pitch 3:** Move up the back and foot chimney (IV) above to some steep face climbing (V+) to a bolted belay under a roof. 4 bolts. 115 feet. **Pitch 4:** Traverse left, and face climb to a groove that leads to a tree belay just below the top. **Descent:** Scramble over the summit and locate the rappel anchors on the left side. Make a couple double-rope rappels to the ground. **Rack:** Quickdraws, extra slings, and some medium to large Friends for Pitches 3 and 4.

43. Schmale Wand (V) (5.7) 3 pitches. An airy route left of *Nordostweg* that's not as hard as it looks at first glance. Begin uphill left of *Nordostweg*. **Pitch 1:** Climb a slab (V-) to a bolted belay. 4 bolts. 135 feet. **Pitch 2:** Move directly up the face (V) left of a chimney to a bolted belay stance. 4 bolts. 150 feet. **Pitch 3:** More face climbing (V) straight up to a tree belay on a ledge. 3 bolts. 135 feet. **Descent:** Scramble over the summit, and locate the rappel anchors on the left side. Make a couple of double-rope rappels to the ground. **Rack:** Quickdraws and some extra slings and cords.

Heiliger Geist (Holy Ghost)

Heiliger Geist, "The Holy Ghost" in English, is one of the most beautiful and elegant formations at Metéora. It also boasts some of the area's best long routes, including the spectacular *Traumpfeiler* or *Pillar of Dreams,* a nine-pitch, 825-foot-long route up the north pillar of the rock. This classic line is the must-do route for every Metéora climber. It simply has it all—fun climbing on steep exposed rock, adequate protection, good belay stances and ledges, and a superb top-out on the rounded summit. You can also scope out the formation and your routes easily by driving up the scenic drive to the parking area below Roussanou Monastery.

Finding the cliff: Drive through Kastraki until you're below Doupiani Rock. Turn right onto the only street you reach, and drive through the north part of the village until the road reaches a T junction below the southwest flank of Heiliger Geist. Turn left, and park at a convenient pullout. Find one of several trails that cross the meadows below the high cliff, and hike northeast around the Heiliggeistwächter, a subsidary pinnacle next to Heiliger Geist. Continue hiking around to the north side of the formation to access the routes.

Descent for all routes is by rappel. After noting your ascent in the summit register, scramble southwest from the summit, and follow cairns to a cairn above *Weg des Wassers (Way of the Water)* and the rappel anchor. From a small ringbolt rappel 35 feet to another set of rappel ringbolts on the left side of a groove. Make two 135-foot rappels from here to a large terrace with a hermitage and some painted crosses on the rock. On your right, while facing the rappel, is a path that descends to the base of the rock, passing under the *Corner of Madness.* At a col the path divides. The left fork goes to the base of the *Traumpfeiler* and *Heiliger Geist* routes. The right fork takes you to the back streets of Kastraki.

44. Action Directe (VIII+ A1) (5.12a A1) 7 pitches. An exposed and difficult route up a black streak on the vertical northwest

face of the Holy Ghost. It was bolted and redpointed by local climbers Christos Batalogiannis and Vangelis Batsios in 1995. Park at a pullout on the north side of Kastraki, and hike a short distance uphill to the base of the face. Begin just right of a large boulder. **Pitch 1:** Face climbing (VI+) up the black streak. 8 bolts. 115 feet. **Pitch 2:** Difficult climbing (VIII-) continues up the slightly overhanging streak. 12 bolts. 85 feet. **Pitch 3:** Vertical face climbing (VII). 11 bolts. 150 feet.

Pitch 4: More steep face climbing (VII+) leads to a horizontal ledge and a bolted belay. 10 bolts. 150 feet. **Pitch 5:** Crux. Pull out the bulge above (VIII+ A0 or A2), and pebble pinch up the groove above to a belay. 11 bolts. 85 feet. **Pitch 6:** Stem up the easier groove above (IV+) to a bolt belay. 2 bolts. 135 feet. **Pitch 7:** Cruise the low-angle gully to the summit. 85 feet. **Descent:** See above description.

45. Heiliger Geist (VIII) (5.11d) 10 pitches. First ascent by Heinz Lothar Stutte and C. Haines in 1986. A steep, classic face route up the right side of the east pillar. Be prepared for some serious runout climbing. All the belays have bolt anchors. Begin below the slabby toe of the buttress right of the deep cave. **Pitch 1:** Climb out right (II) and then back left (V-) up the slab. 2 bolts. 135 feet. **Pitch 2:** Work up the steepening slab right of the cave (IV and V) to a traverse left. Climb straight up (VII-) to a belay up left of a hole and below a groove. 4 bolts. 135 feet. **Pitch 3:** Steep climbing (VII) leads into the groove. Work up the groove (VI) to a belay. 6 bolts. 65 feet. **Pitch 4:** Climb above the belay, and face climb up left on exposed cobbles (VII) to a belay stance at a break. 4 bolts. 85 feet. **Pitch 5:** Move up the airy bulge above the belay (VIII-), and continue up the steep wall above (VI- and VI) to a blunt prow to a belay up left. 5 bolts. 100 feet. **Pitch 6:** Climb up left (VI-) and then up vertical rock (V) to a belay at the base of a groove. 3 bolts. 85 feet. **Pitch 7:** Move up the obvious crack/groove (IV+) protected with Stoppers until it ends. Slab climb up right to a belay. 100 feet. **Pitch 8:** Easier edging up slabby rock (IV-) leads to a belay stance. 1 bolt. 85 feet. **Pitch 9:** Traverse right onto the prow of the buttress, and work directly up the exposed edge (V+) to a good belay ledge. 1 bolt. 115 feet. **Pitch 10:** Climb a short corner (V+), and then wander up the wall above (V-) to the summit anchors. 2 bolts. 135 feet. **Descent:** See above description. **Rack:** Bring 12 quickdraws, #4 to #10 Stoppers, some small to medium Friends, and at least six slings and cords.

46. Traumpfeiler (*Pillar of Dreams*) (VI) (5.9) 9 pitches. First ascent by Heinz Lothar Stutte and Helmet Mägdefrau in 1981. A must-do, excellent, classic route up the east pillar of Heiliger Geist. It's also a serious line with steep face climbing, chimneying, some off-width moves, and difficult retreat. The route gets sun in the morning and shade in the afternoon. Large ringbolts protect the route and provide belay anchors. Reach the start by parking on the roadside opposite the cliff and hiking cross-country on paths to the

cliff base left of a deep recess. Begin just uphill from the left toe of the pillar. **Pitch 1:** Climb up and make a left traverse (5.5), then move up left (5.7+) to a belay with bolts. 3 bolts. 115 feet. **Pitch 2:** Face climb (V) to a rightward traverse to a bolted belay. 3 bolts. 115 feet. **Pitch 3:** Face moves (5.8) to a chimney to a belay below a crack. 2 bolts. 65 feet. **Pitch 4:** An awkward off-width crack (5.7) that gets easier. 50 feet. **Pitch 5:** Face climb up left (V) to a belay below a crack. 2 bolts. 50 feet. **Pitch 6:** Follow a thin crack (5.6) up left. Protect with Stoppers. 50 feet. **Pitch 7:** Slab climb up a streak (IV-) to a bolted belay on the upper pillar. 3 bolts. 130 feet. **Pitch 8:** Work up right on a ramp to a traverse. Face climb the prow above (5.5) to a good belay ledge. 2 bolts. 115 feet. **Pitch 9:** Steep face climbing (5.8) up the prow to a belay on the shoulder below the summit. 2 bolts. 130 feet. **Descent:** See above description. **Rack:** Bring #5 to #9 Stoppers, some small to medium Friends, a few runners, a dozen quickdraws, and two ropes.

47. Athena (VII+ A1) (5.11a/b A1) 6 pitches. First ascent by Aris Theodoropoulos, Dimitris Sotirakis, and V. Karoubis in 1994. A superb direct line up a water gully on the wall right of *Corner of Madness.* Very sustained climbing that is well protected with bolts at the cruxes. **Pitch 1:** Steep and thin face climbing (VII+) to a bolt belay. 15 bolts. 150 feet. **Pitch 2:** Climb easier rock (V+) up a groove to a bolted belay. 5 bolts. 135 feet. **Pitch 3:** Continue up the shallow groove on slabby rock (V-) to a bolted belay below the upper headwall. 3 bolts. 150 feet. **Pitch 4:** Easily traverse left (II) to another belay stance. 50 feet. **Pitch 5:** Sustained and difficult cobble climbing (VII-) leads to the route crux (VIII+/IX- or A1). Above is a bolted belay. 14 bolts. 100 feet. **Pitch 6:** Work up much easier rock above (VI+) to a slab finish and a belay just below the summit. **Descent:** See above description.

48. Wahnsinnsverschneidung (*Corner of Madness*) (VII) (5.10d) 6 pitches. An excellent, strenuous, and sustained crack, the prettiest in Metéora, up the prominent corner system on the southeast face of Heiliger Geist. The crux can be aided, reducing the grade to 5.10-. Hike uphill from *Athena* to the base of the obvious right-facing dihedral. **Pitch 1:** Climb up into the corner (5.7), and stem up (5.8) to a belay. Be extremely careful to the first piton and then the first bolt since the slippery rock is very water polished. 5 bolts. 115 feet. **Pitch 2:** Hand jam up the corner (5.8), then stem (5.9) to a belay. 3 bolts. 115 feet. **Pitch 3:** Layback the crack (5.10-). 1 bolt. 50 feet. **Pitch 4:** The crux lead with pumpy crack climbing. Layback up the wide crack (5.10+) on your left to a belay stance at the top of the corner. Protect with a #4 Camalot. Or aid up bolts (A1) in a small dihedral. 14 bolts. 115 feet. **Pitch 5:** Steep face climbing leads to a short rightward traverse (5.10-). Work up a groove (5.7+) to anchors. 4 bolts. 85 feet. **Pitch 6:** A hand crack (5.7+) leads to stemming to a squeeze chimney (5.5) to the summit. 3 bolts. 115 feet. **Descent:** See above description. **Rack:** #4 to #10 Stoppers, a set of Friends or Camalots (include a #4 Camalot), #9 to #11 Hexentrics, 15 quickdraws, and two ropes.

Alphasporn

This long, finlike formation offers a steep, triangular yellow face on its north flank that faces the scenic drive just before the Roussanou Monastery. *Orchidea,* the described route, is a difficult but well-protected *directissima* up a black watermark that splits the middle of the wall. Local hardmen Christos Batalogiannis and Vangelis Batsios established the line in 1995.

Finding the cliff: Park on the scenic road just before it makes a sharp left turn toward Roussanou Monastery. Follow a path into the valley below, and work your way up to the base of the face.

49. Orchidea (VIII+ A1 or VII+ A1) (5.12a A1 or 5.11a/b A1) 4 pitches. Begin below the center of the face. **Pitch 1:** Continuous climbing (VI+) leads straight up a steep, lichen- and moss-covered slab to a bolted belay stance. 10 bolts. 135 feet. **Pitch 2:** Difficult but well-protected face climbing (VIII+/IX-) up the vertical wall to a bolted belay. Some holds might be loose. 18 bolts. 135 feet. **Pitch 3:** Work up the slightly overhanging wall (VII+ A1 or VIII+) to a belay on a ridge just above the face. 13 bolts. 100 feet. **Pitch 4:** Climb low-angle rock (IV-) and up an obvious gully (II) to the ridge crest. 150 feet. Arriving at the col above the gully, the summit is on your right and the summit register is atop another summit on your left. Belay here for the regular descent. Third class down 65 feet to the first rappel anchors. **Descent:** Make five double-rope rappels from bolt anchors down the wall left of the north face. Or you can rappel the route, but a small pendulum is necessary to catch the second belay.

Sourloti

Sourloti is a huge blocky tower that looms over the east side of Kastraki. Several excellent routes ascend its exposed south face, including the megaclassic *Hypotenuse*.

Finding the cliff: Hike east from Kastraki on the left side of a narrow valley between Sourloti and Pixari. The trail quickly skirts the base of Sourloti's south face. Follow it until you're below the right side of the face. Scramble up left along the right side of a pillar to a low-angle area above it. The first belay is left of the top of the pillar.

Descent off all the described routes is by two rappels. The first anchors are on the east side of the formation above the gap between Sourloti and Modi. Locate the first bolt anchors, and make an 85-foot rappel to anchors at the base of a chimney. The second rappel descends 150 feet to the ground.

50. Sophocles (VII) (5.10d) 6 pitches. First ascent by Aris Theodoropoulos and Dimitris Bakalis in 1996. This excellent, well-protected route ascends the far right margin of the south face. Begin by hiking up the valley between Sourloti and Pixari until it's possible to hike up left to the base of the right side of the face. **Pitch 1:** Climb up left (III) and then straight up the steep slab (V-) to a bolted belay. 2 bolts. 135 feet. **Pitch 2:** Move up and right on easy rock (III) to a bolted belay. 100 feet. **Pitch 3:** Face climbing (VII) just left of the right side of the face. 7 bolts. 150 feet. **Pitch 4:** Straight up the steep slab (VI+). 6 bolts. 150 feet. **Pitch 5:** Climb up past the *Hypotenuse* traverse (VI) and then up a vertical wall (VII-). 7 bolts. 100 feet. **Pitch 6:** Crux climbing up and over a bulge (VII) to a steep slab finish (IV). 5 bolts. 100 feet.

51. Hypotenuse (VI) (5.10a) 6 pitches. Sepp Eichinger, Hans Weninger, Heinz Lothar Stutte, and Dietrich Hasse established the line in 1981. This superb route, weaving a wandering line up the south wall, finishes atop the far right margin of the face. Begin by hiking up to the base of the right side of the face, and either climb a left-facing dihedral (III) or scramble up the right side of a pillar to a low-angle

area. Locate a belay stance to the left. **Pitch 1:** Climb up left on easy cobbled rock (II) to a bolted belay. 115 feet. **Pitch 2:** Climb to a bolt (V), and then work up right to a crux past the next bolt (VI-). Belay from a bolt. 2 bolts. 135 feet. **Pitch 3:** Move up right (IV) to a bolt in a water streak. Climb straight up (VI) to a bolted belay. 2 bolts. 150 feet. **Pitch 4:** Traverse up and right (VI) to a bolted belay. 8 bolts. 100 feet. **Pitch 5:** Traverse right across *Sophocles* to a groove (VI-), and follow it

(V+) past a large stone until it's possible to make a short traverse right to a bolted belay. 5 bolts. 115 feet. **Pitch 6:** Traverse right to a bolt, and then climb easier slabs (III) up right to the summit. 1 bolt. 135 feet. **Rack:** Bring at least 15 quickdraws, a few long runners, and two ropes.

52. Linie des Fallenden Tropfens (VI) (5.10a) 6 pitches. First ascent by Heinz Lothar Stutte and Dietrich Hasse in 1985. A direct line up the right side of the south face. Begin at the same belay as

Hypotenuse. **Pitch 1:** Climb straight up using big cobbles (III+) to a bolted belay. 85 feet. **Pitch 2:** Face climbing (VI) to a bolted belay. 4 bolts. 100 feet. **Pitch 3:** Continue straight up (VI), joining *Hypotenuse's* 3rd pitch, to a bolted belay. 3 bolts. 150 feet. **Pitch 4:** Climb directly above the belay (V+), then back left (VI-) to a bolted belay. 3 bolts. 85 feet. **Pitch 5:** Work up the right side of a vertical, dark streak (VI). Above, move back left (V+) to a bolted belay. 5 bolts. 100 feet. **Pitch 6:** Jam a fist crack (V) to the summit. 50 feet. **Descent:** Four rappels (50 feet, 165 feet, 150 feet, 165 feet) down the route. **Rack:** A dozen quickdraws, some long runners, a large Camelot (#3.5 or #4) for the last pitch crux, and two ropes.

53. Thessalische Schallmauer (VIII-) (5.11b/c) 10 pitches. A great route up the big west face. Start below a prominent dihedral. **Pitch 1:** Climb the dihedral (IV+) to anchors. 115 feet. **Pitch 2:** Traverse right past a couple pitons, then climb straight up (V+) to a belay ledge. 115 feet. **Pitch 3:** Climb an overhang and then up a steep slab (V+) past 5 bolts to a belay on the left. 135 feet. **Pitch 4:** Work up and left (VII-) past 6 bolts to a shallow belay cave. 85 feet. **Pitch 5:** Traverse out left along an obvious sloping shelf (VIII-) protected by 7 bolts. Belay below a steep crack. 65 feet. **Pitch 6:** Work up the steep crack and groove (VIII-) past 4 bolts. Near the crack top, angle up right to an exposed belay stance. 65 feet. **Pitch 7:** Climb up and right (VII), finishing in a groove, to a belay stance. 7 bolts. 85 feet. **Pitch 8:** Steep face climbing up left (VII), then straight up to a belay. 65 feet. 4 bolts. **Pitch 9:** Pull cobbles on lower-angle rock (VI+) past 3 bolts to a stance. 65 feet. **Pitch 10:** Climb up left (IV) to the Sourloti summit. 2 bolts. 150 feet. **Descent:** See above descent information. **Rack:** Bring 12 quickdraws, some extra slings, a selection of Stoppers and Friends, and two ropes.

Pixari

Pixari is the huge formation that dominates the southern skyline of Kastraki. The rock's most distinguishing feature is an immense gash that splits its west wall above Kastraki. *Archimedes,* a classic chimney route, ascends the gash. Note the ancient wooden hermitages clinging to Pixari's southwest face

Finding the cliff: Just before entering Kastraki from Kalambáka, look for a narrow road that goes right. Follow it above the town and below slabs and Pixari. Find a place to park just before the road enters the town, and hike southeast to the base of the obvious chimney.

54. Archimedes (V) (5.7) 5 pitches. First ascent by Dietrich Hasse, Heinz Lothar Stutte, and H. Mägdefrau in 1977. A recommended classic chimney and crack climb up the deep chimney on the west wall. Easy but with very exposed climbing and extensive body jamming. Start below the obvious gash. **Pitch 1:** Climb an easy but unprotected (look for some dubious

54

threads on stones) groove (III) to a ring-bolt belay. 135 feet. **Pitch 2:** Enter the chimney by following a crack that turns to a groove (III) and finally into the chimney to the belay ringbolt. This pitch is steeper than the first and is protected by medium Friends and nuts (no bolts). 150 feet. **Pitch 3:** Climb a few moves above the belay, and then scramble up easy rock to the steeper chimney (V) and climb to a 2-ringbolt belay. This pitch has 2 bolts, but if you're not used to the rock or this style of climbing, use some big Camalots (#4 and #5) to protect it. 85 feet. **Pitch 4:** The airy pitch. Start from the belay facing the right wall, and climb the chimney a few feet to some big stones. Turn around here, and face the left wall for the difficulties above. Thrutch up the exposed, overhanging chimney (V), and then body jam to a 1-ringbolt belay. Protection is 2 bolts and some slings for threads. You can use the big Camalots, but they might cause rope drag, so run it out if you dare. 100 feet. **Pitch 5:** Work up the easier wide chimney above (III), and then face climb up the right wall to a gear belay. No bolts on the pitch, so use Camalots #3 to #5 where you can. The ringbolt belay is on the left lip of the chimney just before the top. 150 feet. **Descent:** Scramble east across the top of the formation to rappel anchors above a gap. Make a 115-foot, double-rope rappel to the ground, and scramble southwest back to the base of the formation. **Rack:** Sets of Stoppers, Friends, big Camalots #3 to #5, extra slings, and two ropes.

Other Metéora Routes

Many other excellent climbing routes are at Metéora besides those described in this guidebook. If you get up the described routes, then do some of the following ones. Detailed topos are found in the area guides, and information can be obtained from local climbers.

1. Talweg (VIII- or VI A1) (5.11c or 5.10a A1) This route ascends Fetelias, a blocky tower located in the north group of rocks at Metéora. A beautiful setting with green fields against the snowy Pindos Mountains. This 4-pitch, 475-foot route climbs cracks and slabs.

2. Meteoritenweg (VI-) (5.9) On Bischofmutze, the small tower just south of Glocke. This 5-pitch, 425-foot route is a good afternoon outing, with some demanding route finding.

3. Pindoskante (V) (5.7) An alternative route up Kastrakiturm with 525 feet of nice, easy climbing.

4. Im Western Nicht Neues (VII-) (5.10c) Another beautiful route on Orgelpfeifen-wand. Cracks, slabs, and grooves on this 6-pitch line.

5. Aufschwung (VII-/VII) (5.10c/d) An excellent classic 4-pitch line up the east ridge of Geierwand, opposite from *Westkante*. Two pitches of difficult crack and chimney climbing to exposed face climbing up the ridge.

6. Schweizer Roullet (VI/A1 or IX-/A0) (5.10a A1 or 5.12b/c A0) An impressive 9-pitch route up the 775-foot south face of Varlaamturm, a huge tower next to Ypsilotérafels. The route, towering above the road that leads to the monasteries, follows steep water stripes and grooves. It was opened in 1990 by the masters Heinz Lothar Stutte and Dietrich Hasse, already well into their sixties, and one of their last great first ascents. This demanding line offers overhangs, grooves, chimneys, slabs, cracks, and traverses. Aid off bolts lessens the grade.

7. Hard Test (*Härtetest*) (VI+) (5.10b) Good views, good rock, and good climbing characterize this 4-pitch route up the north ridge of Kumarieskopf, the large tower directly east of Heiliger Geist.

8. Roussanoukante (V+) (5.8) A 4- or 5-pitch classic line up the north ridge of Kaukasier, the next tower left (east) of Kumarieskopf. The route, easily seen from the loop road, offers some typical slab pitches and a finishing pitch up one of Metéora's most beautiful off-width cracks.

9. Südpfeiler (VII) (5.10d) One of Metéora's best crack climbs. This 4- or 5-pitch route ascends the south flank of Metéoraturm, one of the towers east of Heiliger Geist. The second pitch is a spectacular off-width and squeeze chimney.

10. Augenschein (VII-) (5.10c) The spectacular north face of Gammawand, facing the road, is climbed by this interesting 6-pitch route. It begins on the southeast wall and makes four traversing pitches onto the steep north wall, with the fourth pitch featuring a very airy step onto the face. The next couple pitches offer exposed face climbing.

11. Aprilscherz (VII) (5.10d) This fine but serious 7-pitch route works up the mostly hidden southeast wall of Modi. Expect tricky face climbing and steep crack and groove moves.

12. Schlangenweg (VII+ or VI A0) (5.11a/b or 5.10a A0) A 7-pitch line up the southeast flank of the huge formation of Alyssos. It ascends an easy dihedral for two pitches then difficult cracks and faces to the top.

13. Stan and Olli (VII) (5.10d) This 775-foot, 7-pitch route, just right of *Schlangenweg* on the southeast side of Alyssos, offers difficult and continuous climbing up cracks and grooves to the rounded summit and a deserted monastery.

14. Schwarz auf Weiss (VII-) (5.10c) After you've climbed the classic *Hypotenuse* on the broad southeast wall of Sourloti, turn your attention to this stun-ning line. Look at the cliff left of *Hypotenuse,* and you see a black streak splitting the white wall. This is the 7-pitch route—an almost straight line up an amazing wall. It features athletic movements, solid rock, and lots of exposure.

15. Gordischer Knoten (VII-) (5.10c) One of the four routes on The Spindel, an impressive 130-foot stack in the saddle between Sourloti and Pixari southeast of Kastraki. This 2-pitch route, a good afternoon outing, yields well-protected face climbing up the steep pinnacle facing Modi. The other routes are of similar grades and quality. Under the summit register is a hole with a ringbolt for the rappel.

16. Ewiger Weg (*Eternal Way*) (VII-) (5.10c) This route ascends Kleine Heilige, one of the huge towers north of Kalambáka. The 8-pitch route climbs the northeast ridge of the formation, across from Alyssos. Expect a bit of everything: off-width jamming, chimneying, face climbing, traverses, and slabs.

17. Styx (VIII-) (5.11b/c) This 7-pitch route up the 825-foot-high Grosse Heilige, one of the highest formations, is the longest water streak and groove route at Metéora. The route, overlooking Kalambáka, works directly up the groove to a rounded summit. Quickdraws and a few slings are all you need.

18. Geiersturzflug (VII+) (5.11a/b) A fun 3-pitch route up a water streak and groove on the southeast face of Pixari, above a narrow valley between Pixari and Pyramidenspitze.

19. Fundament (VIII+ or VII A1) (5.12a or 5.10d A1) This 3-pitch groove affair has nice balance moves on solid rock on the northwest face of Pyramidenspitze opposite *Geiersturzflug* and Pixari. After the groove do a 150-foot pitch to the peak's distinctive summit.

VARASOVA

■ OVERVIEW

Varasova lifts its ragged crest high above the Gulf of Patras in western Greece. The bulky, three-summited mountain, trending northwest from the gulf, is broken on its abrupt western flank by tiers of sheer cliffs; the rocky southern end of the mountain dips into the waters of the gulf. The mountain, rising to a height of 3,009 feet (917 meters), is composed of a fine, compact gray limestone. The rock, eroded into buttresses, dihedrals, sheer faces, steep slabs, and vertical crack systems, offers superb climbing adventures. Varasova, one of Greece's oldest and most important climbing venues, yields numerous memorable and aesthetic routes that range from one-pitch sport lines to long, multipitch affairs that ascend to the top of the mountain.

The towering mountain of Varasova, at first impression, is an austere and barren landscape that opens its immense and emaciated faces southwestward to the placid gulf waters. The peak offers a dramatic and strange visage, with its spacious ridges and bare rock escarpments. And the whole strange peak is bathed in a warm, clear light that is amazingly keen. The smallest details can be seen from a distance with startling clarity.

Varasova is an atmospheric place that lies far off the tourist track followed by most North Americans. Almost all the climbers here are Greek, hailing from either Athens or Patras. After you turn off the main highway and begin driving down the final road through the peaceful Etoliko Valley to the southern end of the mountain and the gulf, the years seem to unfold backward. Here walks an old man leading a donkey on the margin of the road. There grow olive trees with a scattering of wildflowers below them. And looming above stretch long cliff bands interrupted by slopes of scree and boulders. At the road's end scatters the tiny hamlet of Krioneri and a friendly taverna beside the concrete dock. Just east of the village is a primitive climber's campsite beside the bay and easy access to the cliffs. At night from the campsite at the base of

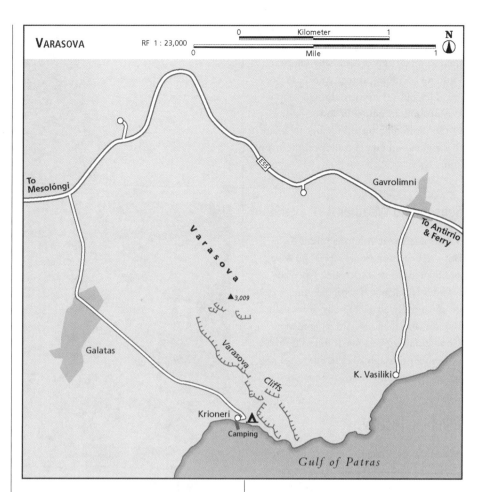

the cliffs and beside the gulf waters, the sparkling lights of Patras, one of Greece's largest cities, twinkle to the south across the narrow strait. Here on the northern shore, though, all is silent and dark.

In ancient Greece Varasova was a natural stronghold that was used to repel seagoing invaders. Nearby sat the Homerian town of Halkia and a small harbor. The mountain was later used from the ninth through the eleventh centuries by Christian hermits who meditated in caves and hermitages on the rocky slopes. They also created a hermit state much like that at Mount Athos, the Holy Mountain.

The limestone at Varasova is perfect for climbing. A diversity of handholds and footholds, including hidden flakes and incut edges, makes the climbing movements both imaginative and thought-provoking. More than one hundred established routes and variations, both sport and adventure routes, currently lace the cliffs. There is room for many more lines to be opened, especially bolted sport climbs.

The cliffs are popular with Greek climbers because the routes span a wide

range of difficulty, from very easy to very hard. Holds and gear placements are often hidden on many routes under vegetation. The Varasova routes are roughly divided into three groups: bolted sport climbs that are mostly difficult; adventure routes that have little or no fixed protection or belay anchors; and instruction routes for beginners and classes, with plentiful bolts for safety.

Rack, Protection, and Descent

Many Varasova routes are well bolted for safety and have fixed belay anchors at the end of each pitch. Where fixed protection is lacking, traditional climbers will find secure nut placements in cracks and flakes. If you want to climb more than just a few sport routes, however, bring a full rack. Most of the multipitch sport routes also require gear placements. A recommended rack includes a full set of Stoppers, a full set of Friends or equivalent camming devices, five or six long runners, ten to twelve quickdraws, and two 165-foot (50-

meter) ropes. A helmet is recommended since falling rock does occur. Goats live on the mountain and occasionally knock loose rocks off, so protect your head.

Descent off most routes is by rappel. It is possible to rappel or lower off most of the more difficult routes, but there are five established rappel routes off the main cliff area.

Season and Weather

Varasova is a year-round climbing area. But the best months are April and May and September and October, when the weather is warm and settled. Summer days on this southwest-facing cliff are usually too hot, and shade is hard to come by. Good climbing weather is found from November through March, but it can also be cold, rainy, and windy.

Climbing History

Although the ancient Greeks undoubtedly scrambled up lower-angle slabs on the mountain, Varasova's technical climbing history began with the ascent of several long routes in the late 1950s. Parties, including the famed Italian alpinist Walter Bonatti, occasionally visited in the 1960s, but it wasn't until the 1970s that modern free climbing was introduced to Varasova. Dimitris Korres created several aesthetic lines, including the classic *African Woman*. In 1979 the area's first guidebook, authored by Korres, was published. That same year English hardman Pete Livesey free climbed *Batman* before a group of astonished Greek climbers. The first Greek free ascent of *Batman* in 1984 by Christoforos Agnoglou, D. Titopoulos, and Dimitris Korres began a new era in both Greek and Varasova rock climbing, with an emphasis on harder sport routes pushed up the featureless walls between crack systems. Some of these routes include *Christoforos Agnoglou* (5.11d), *Mykonos* (5.12a/b), *Spider* (5.13a), and *Psycho* (5.13+), Varasova's hardest route established by Yannis Aliyannis in 1994. In 1996 Aris Theodoropoulos, Thomas Mihailidis, and G. Voutiropoulos opened *Luminous Path*

Aivazidis Dimitrios leads pitch 1 of *Sultana* (IX-) (5.12c/d).

(5.11), a 2,000-foot, seventeen-pitch line to the top of the mountain. Through the 1990s various climbers, including Theodoropoulos, have been establishing and equipping sport routes of all grades.

Getting Around

The easiest way to get to Varasova from Athens (Athínai) is, of course, by car. Most rental car companies in Athens will escort you outside the city so you don't have to deal with traffic jams and difficult route finding. Greece, like other European countries, has different road signage than Americans are used to. Look for the signs pointing toward the towns in the direction you want to go rather than highway or route numbers. Make sure you write down the place names in Greek letters also; otherwise, you won't be able to read the signs.

Varasova lies 145 miles (240 kilometers) west of Athens on the north shore of the Gulf of Patras and across the strait from the large city of Patras (Pátra). The fast way is to drive the big coastal highway between Athens and Patras and then take the ferry across to Andirio. The scenic, off-the-beaten-track way winds through the mountains and along the north shore of the Gulf of Corinth. Specific directions for both routes are below in "Trip Planning Information."

If you don't have a rental car, you can take the bus from the Athens station to Messolongi or Agrinio. Get off the bus at Evinohori, and catch a taxi or local bus to Varasova, about 6 miles (10 kilometers) away.

Camping, Accommodations, and Services

There are few accommodation choices in the immediate vicinity of Varasova. Most climbers camp in the grassy meadow between the cliffs and the shore. The free, primitive site has no toilet facilities, but clean water emerges from the spring at the cliff base. Toilets are located in the *taverna* down the beach. Ask permission to use the facilities or, if they aren't open, use proper disposal and no-trace techniques. Rooms are for rent in Krioneri, and there are hotels in Messolongi and Andirio for those with a car.

You'll find basic services in Krioneri: Bratsos Taverna and a few shops that are open in the summer. The *taverna* serves excellent meals. Ask for a peek in the freezer to see what fresh seafood and fish is available. The nearby town of Galatas, 2 miles (3 kilometers) to the northwest, also has a store, gas station, and some interesting *tavernas*. Messolongi, 6 miles (10 kilometers) away, offers all services.

Cultural Experiences and Rest Days

Varasova lies well off the usual tourist track. Out here is the real Greece, with rugged mountains, ancient ruins, and hospitable people. The nearest must-see attraction is the magical and mysterious ruins of Delphi on the abrupt slopes of Mount Parnassos overlooking the Gulf of Corinth and east of Varasova. The ancient Greeks called Delphi the navel of the earth, the place where two eagles met after being released by Zeus at opposite ends of the world. Here they erected the Sanctuary of Apollo above precipitous cliffs and the powerful Delphic oracle, a priestess who breathed poisonous fumes from a vent and made prophetic utterances that were translated into poetry by a priest. Delphi is a special place to visit for at least a day. The nearby campground offers excellent night views of the surrounding countryside.

Mount Parnassos, the centerpiece of Parnassos National Park, offers some superb hiking across wildflower-strewn meadows in spring and some alpine climbing on its upper flanks. The charming village of Arahova, one of Greece's highest settlements, has some pleasant hotels and shops. South of Arahova is the Moni Osiou Louka monastery, a World Heritage Site, adorned with beautiful Byzantine frescoes.

On the coast east of Varasova is the low-key resort of Galaxidi. This popular seaside destination for Greek vacationers also has the fine Church of Agios Nicholaos and the thirteenth-century nunnery Moni Metamorfosis. Andirio, the ferry link with Patras, and Nafpaktos are both interesting towns that you could prowl around for an afternoon.

Messolongi figured prominently in the Greek War of Independence in the 1820s. The strategically placed town was the western center of resistance to the Turkish rulers. The great English poet Lord Byron came here in 1824 to lend his name and money to the resistance. He contracted a fever, however, and died in a few months. Still Byron became a hero to the independence movement, and most Greek towns have a street named for him. A couple points of interest here include a statue of Byron, under which his heart is buried, and a museum about the revolution.

Besides visiting these few places, it's both fun and informative to drive your rental car around the area's back roads. Some marvelous and beautiful sights—including lofty mountains, deep valleys, and picturesque villages seldom visited by Americans—are out there.

Trip Planning Information

General description: Single and multi-pitch routes on a massive, southwest-facing limestone cliff alongside the Gulf of Patras.

Location: West coast of Greece on the north shore of the Gulf of Patras, 145 miles (240 kilometers) west of Athens.

Camping and accommodations: Free primitive camping is available in a meadow between the cliffs and the sea. Don't camp directly below the cliffs because of rockfall. The closer your tent is to the sea, the safer you will be. Also park your car between the cliff and your tent for more protection. Clean water emerges from a spring at the cliff base. There are no toilets at the camping area. The best thing is to walk to the nearby taverna and ask permission to use the facilities; otherwise, use proper hygiene and dig a cat hole. Other accommodations are rooms in Krioneri and hotels in Messolongi. Some of the nearby rooms have no hot water or heat in winter. Most rooms have enough beds for four people.

Climbing season: Year-round. The best months are April and May and September and October. Summers can be hot. The winter months can be cold, windy, and rainy.

Restrictions and access issues: None.

Guidebooks: *Varasova* by Aris Theodoropoulos, and *Varassova Climbing Guide* by Yannis Aliyannis. Brief information about visiting and climbing at Varasova is on the Internet at the Greek climbing Web site www.oreivatein.com.

Services and shops: Bratsos Taverna (Tel: 26310 41125) by the dock west of the cliff is open year-round. It serves clams, octopus, fish, steaks, and salads. Galatas, 3 kilometers away, has stores, gas stations, and several *tavernas*. The Hera Taverna (Tel: 26310 41282) near the church offers cheap and tasty Greek food like *souvlaki*. Several grocery stores are near the village's

Africana Sector

Corner

Batman Sector

Pirgos Sector

Public Sector

two squares. Messolongi, 10 kilometers away, offers all services. Climbing instruction and guiding is available through Aris Theodoropoulos's EOS Acharnon climbing school.

Emergency services: Dial 112 for emergency services. The nearest hospital is Messolongi Hospital (Tel: 26310 22268).

Nearby climbing areas: Several climbing areas are across the Gulf of Patras around Patras. The best is the sport area of Kalogria, with one hundred routes on good limestone. Mount Giona, above the small village of Sikia in central Greece, offers several faces, including the 3,900-foot Plaka Sikias, the tallest cliff in Greece. Near the village are more than seventy-five sport routes. Also in central Greece is Metéora, as well as sport climbing around Trikala.

Nearby attractions: To the east of Varasova, above the north coast of the Gulf of Corinth, lies the magical site of Delphi. Ancient Delphi, the site of the famed Oracle of Delphi, is an atmospheric

place with a stunning natural setting and well-preserved ruins, including the Temple of Apollo. Nearby is alpine Mount Parnassos in Parnassos National Park, with hiking, climbing, and skiing. A string of small resort towns lie along the gulf shore between Varasova and Delphi. The best is Galaxidi. Check out its Church of Agios Nicholaos and the thirteenth-century Moni Metamorfosis monastery. West of Varasova is Messolongi, where English poet Lord Byron died of fever in 1824 during the War of Independence. His heart is buried under his statue in the Garden of the Heroes.

Finding the cliff: Varasova is 145 miles (240 kilometers) west of Athens and opposite Patras on the north shore of the Gulf of Patras. As in most of Europe, highways are not often numbered. Rely instead on signs that point toward the towns where you are going.

Directions are given from Athens. The fastest approach is via the expressway from Athens to Patras. From Omonia Circle in downtown Athens, follow Agiou

Konstantinou Street. Drive to Kavalas Street, and follow the E95 highway and signs toward Corinth. Just past Corinth (Kórinthos), go right (west) onto highway E65, and drive 75 miles (126 kilometers) to Rio, just east of Patras (Pátra), and follow signs to the ferry. The ferry runs often (every fifteen minutes) and is very cheap. Take the ferry across the gulf to Andirio (Antirrio). Drive west on the E55/E951 highway for another 18 miles (30 kilometers) toward Messolongi (Mesolóngi). Make a left turn at the highway junction posted for Galatas and Krioneri, just before a bridge over the Evinos River. Follow this narrow road southeast for 3.5 miles (6 kilometers) until the road's end at Krioneri and the gulf. The obvious cliffs are to the east (left).

It's also possible to come by bus from the Kiffisou bus station in Athens. Take the bus heading to either Messolongi or Agrinio, and ask the driver to drop you off at Evinohori, where you can catch a taxi for the last 6 miles (10 kilometers).

Routes are described from left to right.

Africana Sector

1. Luminous Path (*Sentero Luminoso*) (5.11d) No topo. 17 pitches. This 2,000-foot route, one of the longest at Varasova, was established by Aris Theodoropoulos, Tomas Mihailidis, and G. Voutiropoulos in 1996. This excellent line offers continuous face climbing on perfect limestone. The route is divided into an upper and a lower section. You can climb the lower seven pitches to the broken area and rappel off. A fit party requires at least ten hours to climb the entire route. All the belay stances are bolted, and bolts are found on every pitch. **Descent:** Make fourteen rappels down the route, or hike off via the summit trail (two hours). Clean well water is in a glade atop the mountain. **Approach:** A thirty-minute hike up the summit trail to the base of the route. **Rack:** Sets of Stoppers and Friends, extra runners, 12 to 15 quickdraws, two 165-foot (50-meter) ropes, helmets.

2. Dalton (VII-/VII) (5.10c/d) 5 pitches. 590 feet. A popular line up good limestone. All belays are bolted. **Pitch 1:** Face climbing (5.10c). 8 bolts. **Pitch 2:** Face climbing (5.10c). 3 bolts. **Pitch 3:** Route crux up overhanging stone above the belay (5.10d). 7 bolts. **Pitch 4:** Face climbing (5.10a). 4 bolts. **Pitch 5:** 5.7 face climbing to the top. **Descent:** Rappel down *African Woman*. **Rack:** Sets of Stoppers and Friends, 10 to 12 quickdraws, two 165-foot (50-meter) ropes.

3. Afrikana (*African Woman*) (VI-/VI) (5.9) 5 pitches. 650 feet. Recommended. This historic classic is one of the cliff's most popular outings. All belays are bolted. Begin just right of *Dalton*. **Pitch 1:** Follow a crack and corner system up right (5.5) to a belay stance. 1 bolt. 100 feet. **Pitch 2:** Climb the obvious crack and groove system (5.8) to a bolted belay. 4 bolts. 115 feet. **Pitch 3:** Crux pitch. Steep face climbing (5.9) to a corner (5.8). 4 bolts. 130 feet. **Pitch 4:** Face climb (5.7) to a crack (5.8). 5 bolts. 100 feet. **Pitch 5:** Work up an easier corner (5.5) to a tree belay. 3 bolts. 115 feet. **Descent:** Rappel down the route from here, or do another pitch (5.6) to the cliff top and rappel. **Rack:** Sets of Stoppers and Friends, 12

quickdraws, two 165-foot (50-meter) ropes, helmet.

4. Christoforos Agnoglou (VIII) (5.11d) 4 pitches. 525 feet. This bold, spectacular route, named for one of Greece's leading climbers who was killed in the Alps in 1987, ascends the blank wall right of *African Woman*. All the belay stations are bolted. **Pitch 1:** Edge up a steep slab (5.10b) to a bolted belay. 6 bolts. 100 feet. **Pitch 2:** Steep face climbing (5.10d) to a bolted belay. 12 bolts. 115 feet. **Pitch 3:** Crux face climbing up edges and smears (5.11d) to a bolted belay. 12 bolts. 130 feet. **Pitch 4:** More face climbing (5.11c) to a bolted belay. 13 bolts. 100 feet. **Descent:** Four rappels down the route. **Rack:** Medium Stoppers, small to medium Friends, runners for threads, 15 quickdraws, and two 165-foot (50-meter) ropes.

5. Mykonos (VIII+) (5.12a/b) 2 pitches. 260 feet. A harder and blanker version of route #4. Aris Theodoropoulos says, "Don't forget your eyeglasses for this one!" Both pitches are bolt-protected, vertical face climbing with bolted belay stances. **Descent:** Rappel the route. **Rack:** 12 to 15 quickdraws, two 165-foot (50-meter) ropes.

6. Bow (*Toxo*) (V/V+) (5.7+) 6 pitches. 720 feet. A 1975 classic that follows a bow-shaped dihedral. The route can be vegetated in spring and summer. Some fixed pitons are found on the route. **Pitch 1:** Climb the easy ramp up right (5.4) to a fixed belay. 100 feet. **Pitch 2:** Continue up the bow (5.5) to a fixed belay. 100 feet. **Pitch 3:** Steeper climbing up the dihedral (5.7) leads to a fixed belay. 130 feet. **Pitch 4:** Work up and right on vertical face climbing past a spot of 5.7+ climbing to a belay stance. 100 feet. **Pitch 5:** Easier climbing goes out right (5.5) and then up to a belay. **Pitch 6:** Climb loose, fractured rock to the cliff top (5.4). 100 feet. **Descent:** Scramble up left to the *African Woman* rappels or down right to the *Pirgos* rappels. **Rack:** Sets of Stoppers and Friends, slings for threads, 12 quickdraws, two 165-foot (50-meter) ropes, helmets.

The beautiful gray slab below *Bow* offers several sport routes. Most are 5.8 or 5.9. The following route is one of the best.

7. Danae (VI-) (5.8) 1 pitch. 130 feet. Fun climbing up the bolted slab leads to a 2-bolt belay and rappel station.

8. Fanatic (VII-/VII) (5.10c/d) 3 pitches. 450 feet. A popular and good climb up the wall right of *Bow*. All belays are fixed. Begin down right of *Danae* above the cliff access trail. **Pitch 1:** Climb a corner (5.5) to a roof. Pull over (5.10a), and continue to a bolted belay. 3 bolts. 130 feet. **Pitch 2:** Vertical face climbing (5.10d crux) to a bolted belay. 5 bolts. 115 feet. **Pitch 3:** Face climb up right (5.10c) to a bolted belay. 3 bolts. 130 feet. **Descent:** Rappel the route. **Rack:** Stoppers, Friends, slings, 12 quickdraws, two 165-foot (50-meter) ropes.

9. Gonia (*Corner*) (VI-) (5.8) No topo. 6 pitches. 600 feet. Another classic Varasova line up a long corner system. It is vegetated in spots but a worthy and fun route. If the belays were bolted, it would improve the route's character by making it possible to rappel from the top of Pitch 4 and avoid the upper looseness. Locate the base of the obvious left-facing corner system above the access trail. **Pitch 1:** Climb the corner (5.7) to a belay ledge. 100 feet. **Pitch 2:** Continue up the corner (5.7+) to another belay ledge. 100 feet. **Pitch 3:** Climb the corner (5.7), and work around a roof (5.8-) to a belay. 115 feet. **Pitch 4:** Finish up the left-facing corner, and pull over a roof (5.8) to a belay stance. 115 feet. **Pitch 5:** Climb easy fractured rock to a belay. 100 feet. **Pitch 6:** More easy rock (5.5) leads to the cliff top. 100 feet. **Descent:** Scramble up left to the *African Woman* rappels or down right to the *Kalidonis* rappels. **Rack:** Sets of Stoppers and Friends, slings for threads, 12 quickdraws, two 165-foot (50-meter) ropes, helmets.

Camping

Batman Sector

10. Simfonia (*Agreement*) (IX-) (5.12c) 2 pitches. A bolted sport route. **Pitch 1:** Crux climbing over the roof to the bolted belay above. **Pitch 2:** Hard face climbing to the roof above, then move left and swing over the roof (A0) to a bolted belay above. **Descent:** Rappel the route.

11. Carcass (IX/IX+) (5.12d/13a) 2 pitches. A good but difficult sport route. **Pitch 1:** Face moves to an overhang. Athletic climbing (5.12d) leads to a thin face and the bolted belay. **Pitch 2:** Face

climbing to the right side of a roof. Pull over, and move up right to a bolted belay. **Descent:** Rappel the route.

12. Is It the Sun or Is It the Moon? (IX-) (5.12c) 1 pitch. Begin just left of *Batman* at the base of the left-leaning crack system. Thin and tricky face climbing leads to a 2-bolt belay.

13. Butterfly (*Petaluda*) (VIII-/VIII) (5.11b/c) 2 or 3 pitches. Usually only the first pitch is climbed. Begin left of *Batman*. Face climb up and left along some bolted water streaks to a 2-bolt belay. Rappel.

14. Batman (VII) (5.10d) 2 pitches. Recommended. The first pitch of this athletic route is exceedingly popular and somewhat polished. The route begins beside the road. The name is painted at the base. **Pitch 1:** Climb up right along a series of holes with some long reaches (5.10d) to a long, vertical hole. Move up right to a roof, and exit right (5.10c) to a bolted belay above. Rappel from here. **Pitch 2:** Climb above the belay (5.10c) to higher anchors.

Pirgos Sector

15. Tower (IV+/V+) (5.8) 5 pitches. 500 feet. A very popular moderate excursion up chimneys and cracks in a large, broken, right-facing dihedral system. Begin below the obvious dihedral that goes up the right side of a pillar or tower. **Pitch 1:** Climb cracks and a chimney (IV+) to a bolted ledge belay. 4 bolts. 80 feet. **Pitch 2:** Continue up the corner (IV+) to a belay. 2 bolts. 80 feet. **Pitch 3:** A short lead up the final corner (V-) to the top of the tower. 1 bolt. 50 feet. **Pitch 4:** Face climb the vertical wall (V) above the tower to a fixed belay stance. 4 bolts. 100 feet. **Pitch 5:** Climb easier rock to the final belay. 85 feet. **Descent:** Make three rappels down the route from fixed anchors: 130 feet, 100 feet, and 80 feet. **Rack:** Bring Stoppers, Friends, quickdraws, and two ropes.

16. Rock'n'Roll (VIII-) (5.11c) 3 pitches. 400 feet. An outstanding route with clean, continuous climbing. Start below a whitish face just right of *Tower's* start.

Pitch 1: Steep face climbing (VI+) to thin corners to a belay ledge with a chained bolt anchor. 7 bolts. 115 feet. **Pitch 2:** Work past a small roof, and follow a curving corner. Climb the steep crux (VIII-) to vertical rock and a belay stance with bolt anchors below a shallow corner. 10 bolts. 100 feet. **Pitch 3:** Work up the corner (VI+) to easier rock (V) and a chained bolt anchor. 7 bolts. 130 feet. **Descent:** Make three rappels down the route from bolt anchors. **Rack:** A small selection of small to medium gear and 12 to 15 quickdraws.

17. Skala (*Staircase*) (VI-) (5.8) 4 pitches. 400 feet. Also called *Pirgos.* Another popular moderate line up a right-facing dihedral system. Begin below an obvious chimney and dihedral system. **Pitch 1:** Climb cracks and chimneys (IV+) to a bolted belay ledge. 1 bolt. 100 feet. **Pitch 2:** Continue up cracks (V+) to a belay stance. 1 bolt. 85 feet. **Pitch 3:** Work up the steep corner above (VI-) to a belay ledge. 2 bolts. 115 feet. **Pitch 4:** Climb broken rock (IV) up and left to the top-

bolted belay on *Tower.* 100 feet. **Descent:** Make three rappels down *Tower.* **Rack:** Stoppers, Friends, quickdraws, and two ropes.

18. Remali (*Bum*) (VII-) (5.10c R) 4 pitches. 430 feet. A demanding line up the center of the face with some runout and difficult-to-protect sections. **Pitch 1:** Face climb up steep limestone to a bolted belay. 2 bolts. 100 feet. **Pitch 2:** Thin face climbing (5.10c) up a narrow right-facing corner system to a bolted belay. 2 bolts. 85 feet. **Pitch 3:** Move up left and then straight up the vertical wall (VI+) to a bolted belay stance. 100 feet. **Pitch 4:** Climb easier rock (V) to the top of the wall. **Descent:** Scramble left and rappel down *Tower,* or make two double-rope rappels down *Scorpion* from the top of Pitch 3. **Rack:** Bring a selection of Stoppers, TCUs, Friends, runners, 12 quickdraws, and two ropes.

19. Skorpios (*Scorpion*) (IX) (5.12d/13a) 2 pitches. 230 feet. A difficult and exposed route opened by J. Aligianis in 1996 up the blankest part of the wall. **Pitch 1:** Face climb up steep and pumpy rock to a high crux. Belay from eyebolts. 11 bolts. 115 feet. **Pitch 2:** Continue up the vertical to overhanging stone above to another crux below the bolt anchors. 11 bolts. 115 feet. **Descent:** Rappel the route. **Rack:** 15 quickdraws.

20. Heavy Metal (VII-) (5.10b) 3 pitches. 430 feet. Recommended classic up the right margin of the face. **Pitch 1:** Work up the vertical face to a corner system (5.10b) to a bolted belay. 8 bolts. 100 feet. **Pitch 2:** Climb a right-facing corner, then move up right and up another corner (5.10b) to a bolted belay. 4 bolts. 115 feet. **Pitch 3:** Climb cracks and corners (5.8) to a bolted belay atop the cliff. 1 bolt. 130 feet. **Descent:** Rappel the route with double ropes. **Rack:** Stoppers, Friends, 12 quickdraws, and two ropes.

21. Geraki (*Hawk*) (VII+ A0 or IX) (5.11a A0 or 5.13a) 3 pitches. Another recommended route. **Pitch 1:** Climb easy rock and continue up a blank face (VII) to a

bolted belay in a groove. 5 bolts. 85 feet. **Pitch 2:** Work up steep rock (VII) to a distinctive white crack. Make a couple aid moves (A0) or free climb (5.13a) past the crux and finish (VII+) to a bolted belay. 8 bolts. 100 feet. **Pitch 3:** Move up right, and climb a face and corner (VI) to easier rock. 4 bolts. 115 feet. **Descent:** Rappel down *Heavy Metal*. **Rack:** Stoppers, Friends, 12 quickdraws, and two ropes.

22. O Xin Agilin (VII) (5.10c/d) 2 pitches. 200 feet. A very good route with thin, thought-provoking cruxes. **Pitch 1:** Climb broken rock and then directly up a smooth face (VII) to a bolted belay. 5 bolts. 85 feet. **Pitch 2:** Continue straight up the face above (VI+) right of the big dihedral to a bolted belay station. 5 bolts. 115 feet. **Descent:** Rappel the route. **Rack:** A small selection of Stoppers and Friends and 12 quickdraws.

23. Kalidonis (*Kalidonische Pfeiler*) (V+) (5.7) 2 pitches. 200 feet. A popular training route with good moves and protection. **Pitch 1:** Climb broken rock and

then climb up right (V) on a steep slab. Above, follow a crack system up left (IV+) to a bolted belay. 3 bolts. 85 feet. **Pitch 2:** Climb directly above the belay, and then move right and climb steep rock (V-) to a small roof (V+), then up left to a bolted belay. 5 bolts. 115 feet. **Descent:** Rappel the route. **Rack:** Selection of Stoppers, Friends, and 12 quickdraws.

24. Mikrula (*Little One*) (VI/VI+) (5.10a) 2 pitches. An excellent and beautiful route up the right side of the buttress. Sustained climbing. **Pitch 1:** Climb a right-facing dihedral (IV) to the top of a pillar. Thin face climbing (VI-) past a couple bolts leads to a thin corner and a 2-bolt belay. 85 feet. **Pitch 2:** Vertical face climbing (VI) up right leads to a crack. Traverse up left along the crack, and finish up the crux headwall (VI+) to a 2-bolt chain anchor. 7 bolts. 100 feet. **Descent:** Make two double-rope rappels down the route. **Rack:** Friends, Stoppers, 12 quickdraws, two 165-foot (50-meter) ropes.

Phyco Sector

25. Apalousa (VII) (5.10c/d) 3 pitches. Great climbing up the right margin of the face. Begin uphill and right of the broken corner of *Mikrula*. **Pitch 1:** Climb up left along a ramp and then over a roof (VI-). Continue up slightly overhanging rock (VII-) to a 2-bolt chain anchor. 8 bolts. 65 feet. **Pitch 2:** Edge up very thin face moves on vertical rock (VII-) to exposed face climbing along a crack to a 2-bolt chain belay. 5 bolts. 65 feet. **Pitch 3:** Follow a crack system (VI+) to the top 2-bolt belay station. 4 bolts. 45 feet. **Descent:** Make two double-rope rappels down the route. **Rack:** A few Stoppers and Friends, 12 quickdraws, and two 165-foot (50-meter) ropes.

26. Sultana *(Sultan's Wife)* (IX-) (5.12c/d) 3 pitches, with the first pitch a popular sport route. Begin just right of *Apalousa* below the buttress prow. **Pitch 1:** Swing up strenuous jugs and pockets on the overhanging wall (5.10c) to a 2-bolt belay and lower off. 8 bolts. 65 feet. **Pitch 2:** One of the hardest pitches at Varasova. Thin edging and pumpy moves (5.12d) up the overhanging wall. 8 bolts to 2-bolt belay. 85 feet. **Pitch 3:** Face climb (VII-) into a corner to a 2-bolt anchor. 4 bolts. 45 feet. **Descent:** Make two double-rope rappels down the route. **Rack:** 12 quickdraws and two 165-foot (50-meter) ropes.

27. Natasa (VII-) (5.10b/c) 3 pitches. 330 feet. Excellent and popular line up the big dihedral. **Pitch 1:** Edge up a slab right of the dihedral past 4 bolts to a short headwall (5.6). Belay on a shelf from eyebolts. 100 feet. **Pitch 2:** Work past 5 bolts up the steep pumpy face (5.10c) just right of the dihedral to an eyebolt belay stance. 115 feet. **Pitch 3:** Vertical face climbing with 5 bolts to a small roof (5.10b) to a belay stance with eyebolts above the cliff. 115 feet. **Descent:** Rappel the route. **Rack:** Stoppers, Friends, 12 quickdraws, two 165-foot (50-meter) ropes.

28. Phyco *(Psicho)* (IX+) (5.13b) 2 pitches. One of the area's hardest climbs. First pitch is good alone. **Pitch 1:** Fun climbing (5.5) directly up a 2-bolt slab to a 2-eyebolt belay. 100 feet. **Pitch 2:**

Crank up the overhanging face (5.13b) past 8 bolts to a 2-bolt chain anchor. 85 feet. **Descent:** Rappel the route. **Rack:** 12 quickdraws.

29. Adolescence (VII-) (5.10c) 5 pitches. Start at the toe of a buttress. **Pitch 1:** A long pitch up a face and slab (5.8) to a small ledge. 2 bolts. 135 feet. **Pitch 2:** Climb up right to a thin face (5.10c). Continue up right (5.6) to a belay on the left side of a ledge. 2 bolts. 115 feet. **Pitch 3:** Traverse up left (5.9) to a stance in a cave. 75 feet. **Pitch 4:** Climb the steep face above (5.10b) to a big bulge. Traverse

out left to a belay stance. 115 feet. **Pitch 5:** Work up easier rock above to the top. **Descent:** Scramble off the top and down to the *Pirgos* rappels, and make three rappels. **Rack:** Stoppers, Friends, 14 quickdraws, two 165-foot (50-meter) ropes.

30. Rilken (VII-) (5.10c) 6 pitches. Begin below a right-facing corner. **Pitch 1:** Climb the corner (5.5) to a stance. 85 feet. **Pitch 2:** Work up right along a right-slanting corner. Surmount a headwall (5.8+), and climb to a stance below a roof. **Pitch 3:** Climb up right below a roof and corner to a ledge. Scramble left on the ledge to a belay. **Pitch 4:** Climb up left from the ledge, then up a face (5.9) to a belay stance. **Pitch 5:** Work up the crack and corner above (5.10c) to a belay ledge above the face. 2 bolts. **Pitch 6:** Easy rock (5.5) to the buttress top. **Descent:** Scramble off the top and down to the Pirgos rappels, and make three rappels. **Rack:** Stoppers, Friends, extra slings, 10 quickdraws, two 165-foot (50-meter) ropes.

31. Allergy (*Alergia*) (VII) (5.10c/d) 5 pitches. 550 feet. Excellent and serious. **Pitch 1:** Climb a slab and over a steep wall (5.10c) to a belay under a headwall.

100 feet. **Pitch 2:** Climb a corner up right (5.8+) to a stance. 90 feet. **Pitch 3:** Scale a short easy corner up and left to a broken ledge. **Pitch 4:** From the left side of the ledge, work up the overhanging bolted face above (5.10d) and move right under a bulge to a belay up right. **Pitch 5:** Climb up left on easier rock (5.6) to the top of the buttress. **Descent:** Scramble off the top and down to the Pirgos rappels, and make three rappels. **Rack:** Stoppers, Friends, extra slings, 10 quickdraws, two 165-foot (50-meter) ropes.

32. Flower's Way (*Dromos Louloudion*) (V-) (5.7) 4 pitches. Good moderate up the

right side of the face. Start below a right-angling corner. **Pitch 1:** Climb slabs to the corner, then up right to a belay at its top. 100 feet. **Pitch 2:** Good moves directly up the steep slab (5.7) to a small stance. 50 feet. **Pitch 3:** Angle up right across a slab (5.6) to a belay below a headwall. 85 feet. **Pitch 4:** Climb up right and then left up a face (5.6) to the top. **Descent:** Scramble off the top and down west to the Pirgos rappels, or from the top of Pitch 3, scramble right to the top of *Public* and make two rappels down. **Rack:** Stoppers, Friends, extra slings, 10 quickdraws, two 165-foot (50-meter) ropes.

Camping

Trail

31 32

33 34 35 36 37

38 39 40

Public Sector

This sector lies on the far right side of the lower cliff band and rises directly out of the water. The start of the routes, established for guiding and schools, are reached by traversing out a wide ledge system. Bolts are found on all the routes, but bring Stoppers, TCUs, and Friends to adequately protect the routes. Also wear helmets because of loose rock. Descent is by rappelling the routes.

33. Public (IV+,V) (5.7) 3 pitches. 300 feet.

34. Loufa (IV+,V) (5.7) 3 pitches. 300 feet.

35. Relax (IV, IV+) (5.6) 3 pitches. 300 feet.

36. Anastasia (IV, IV+) (5.6) 3 pitches. 300 feet.

37. Widow (IV) (5.5) 3 pitches. 300 feet.

38. Alkistis (V-) (5.6) 2 pitches. 130 feet. Descend by scrambling left and down climbing lower-angle rock back to the traversing ledge.

39. Schooling Ridge (IV) (5.5) 2 pitches. 200 feet. Descend by scrambling left and down climbing lower-angle rock back to the traversing ledge.

40. Classic Ridge (IV) (5.5) No topo. 4,000 feet. This classic mountaineering route, established in 1967, ascends the obvious skyline ridge that rises from the gulf. Best climbed in approach shoes. The walk-off descent to Krioneri takes a couple hours.

Germany

Legend:
- Climbing region
- River
- International boundary
- National capital
- Expressway
- Major road

0   50   100   150 Kilometers
0   50   100 Miles

DENMARK

North Sea

Baltic Sea

Bornholm (Den.)

Rügen

Flensburg

Kiel

Rostock

Lübeck

Bremerhaven

Hamburg

Bremen

Elbe

NETHERLANDS

Osnabrück

GERMANY

Mittellandkanal

Potsdam

Berlin

POLAND

Oder

Münster

Weser

Hannover

Magdeburg

Elbe

Neisse

Göttingen

Halle

Leipzig

Cottbus

Duisburg

Dortmund

Essen

Düsseldorf

Kassel

Erfurt

Jena

Dresden

Cologne

Bonn

Werra

Gera

Chemnitz

BELGIUM

Gießen

LUX.

Wiesbaden

Frankfurt

Moselle

Main

FRANKENJURA

Bamberg

Bayreuth

CZECH REPUBLIC

Würzburg

Forchheim

Mannheim

Heidelberg

Nürnberg

Saarbrücken

Rhine

Karlsruhe

Regensburg

Stuttgart

Neckar

Danube

Ingolstadt

Isar

FRANCE

Ulm

Augsburg

Inn

Freiburg

Munich

AUSTRIA

Konstanz

Lake Constance

Garmisch-Partenkirchen

Rhine

SWITZERLAND

FRANKENJURA

■ OVERVIEW

Undulating hills interrupted by gentle valleys characterize the *Fränkische Schweiz* or Frankish Switzerland region within an inverted triangle bounded on its three corners by Nürnberg, Bamberg, and Bayreuth in Germany's Bavaria province. The area, called the Frankenjura by climbers, is filled with fields, pastures, and villages alongside meandering rivers on the valley floors. Dense forests blanket the hillsides, hiding many of this cragging mecca's cliffs behind a veil of leafy greenery. Driving into the region, passing tawny wheat fields, dark wooded vales, and whitewashed Bavarian villages adorned with windowsill boxes spilling with red geraniums, you wonder where the cliffs are hidden. And then you spot one, an alabaster limestone outcrop rearing out of the trees. More rock appears down the valley, a buttress jutting above the narrow road and a white edge crowning a distant hill. You've finally arrived in the vast Frankenjura, one of Europe's legendary climbing areas.

Many American climbers are under the misguided impression that the Frankenjura is an elite rock climber's gymnasium. This is true, but the rest of the story is that the Frankenjura is one of Europe's premier areas with thousands of routes of all grades. The area, the best in Germany, is extremely popular not only with Germans but also with Austrian, Italian, and Swiss climbers. At the climber's campground in Wolfsberg, you'll make friends from Australia, Malaysia, Norway, Sweden, Great Britain, and South Africa. Strangely enough Americans seldom visit the area—partly because in the past it's been difficult to obtain area information—so when you do visit, you're a bit of an oddity.

The cliffs are composed of a Jurassic-age limestone deposited 175 million years ago on the bottom of a shallow sea. The excellent limestone, with abundant edges and pockets, is made for climbing; some sections are so riddled with holes that the stone resembles Swiss cheese. The charac-

ter and quality of the limestone varies from cliff to cliff. The weathered surface ranges from vertical to overhanging, with only a few slabs. A plethora of holds cover the rock, including pockets, huecos, jugs, flakes, nubbins, and spidery cracks. Climbing can be either very fingery and subtly technical or pumpy and thuggish. The beta for a single route might include blocky edges, shallow dishes, a few laybacks off flakes, a fingertip undercling, throws to good pockets, a kneebar rest, and a couple finishing slopers. And then there are the faces that appear completely blank, at least to mortal climbers. Case in point is the overhanging prow of *Action Directe,* one of the world's most savage routes.

The crags often hide behind a wall of trees, with their rounded tops poking above the forest. The cliffs and woods give the Frankenjura a New England–like atmosphere, with moss covering unclimbed rock and dampness lingering in the air. So what makes the Frankenjura so popular and so special? Stand beneath any

crag, and the reasons are apparent: excellent stone, many cliffs, a wide range of routes and difficulties, easy access, plentiful bolts, and gorgeous scenery. Is anything left out? Oh right, the requisite nearby cafe for a traditional coffee and cake, *café und kuchen,* in the afternoon or a cheap stein of the best beer in the world.

At the Frankenjura you're tempted to climb every day. Wherever you go, good routes surround you. The cliffs are everywhere—tucked into the forest, rimming the valleys, overlooking picturesque Bavarian villages, or sitting beside roads. Bernhard Thum's comprehensive guidebook lists 419 separate crags and thousands of routes. Some cliffs yield only a few lines, whereas others offer dozens spread along their length.

With so many crags to pick from, it's difficult to decide which are the best ones. This guide details a diverse selection of areas recommended by a variety of German climbers. The Frankenjura is rich and varied in its climbing and scenery, so no matter where you go, you'll have a

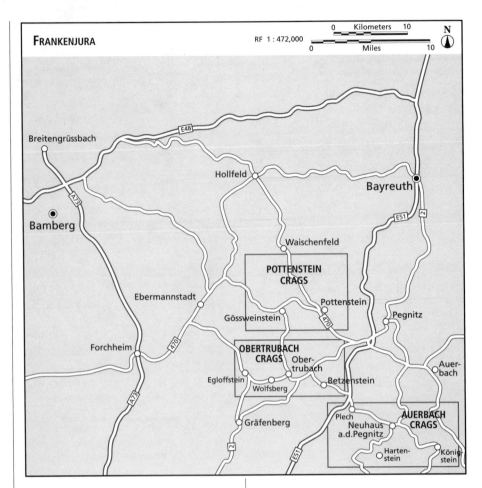

great experience. After visiting the described areas, ask other climbers for their favorite spots, or peruse the hefty local guide for off-the-beaten-track crags. There are few poor crags at the Frank, so don't waste too much time if you end up at one. In a typical day here, it's easy to visit as many as five different cliffs, work on a chosen project, or spend the day ticking all the routes on a single crag. Some routes, especially the classics, are polished, but not as shiny as those in France and Britain.

Rack, Protection, and Descent

Protection on almost all cliffs is excellent. Stainless steel bolts protect most of the routes, and few are runout or dangerous. The one thing that disturbs American climbers is that most of the lower-off stations sport only a single, beefy bolt. Rest assured, however, these are usually glued in place and are very safe. The older and easier routes are often sparsely protected, whereas the newer ones are sewn up with plentiful bolts. Pick and choose your routes. If one doesn't look safe, then move on to another one. The first bolt is sometimes high above the ground, making a stick clip or a bold head useful.

German UIAA grades are translated into Yosemite Decimal System (YDS) grades. As always, take the translated grades with a grain of salt, as an exact conversion is impossible.

A Frankenjura trip requires a small rack with twelve to fifteen quickdraws and a 200-foot (60-meter) rope, although a shorter 165-foot (50-meter) rope is fine for all but a few routes. A small rack of Stoppers and some small to medium Friends is helpful.

Descent off all cliffs is by lowering from fixed anchors.

Climbing History

Most German climbers, until the 1970s, followed an alpinist tradition that began in the Alps. Routes were free climbed whenever possible and then aided for speed. The vaunted seventh grade (UIAA VII) was deemed impossible by the guidelines

Franzsha Schwarz on *Göttner Ged.-Weg* (8) (5.11d) at Bärenschlucht.

of the UIAA mountaineering clubs. The climber's goal was simply to reach the summit, by whatever means, and rock climbing was only training for the mountains. Exceptions to this ethic were found in Germany's Elbsandstein, a rigorous sandstone area near Dresden with hard climbs.

Sandstone outcrops that rise above the rolling hills of the Pfalz along the French border was West Germany's main cragging area. Climbers followed tradi-

tional ethics here and viewed free climbing as a foreign idea not applicable to their little cliffs. But in the mid-1970s, that bias changed as young West German climbers journeyed to Elbsandstein, with its stout free ethic, and to America, particularly Yosemite Valley, then the center of world climbing. They returned to the Pfalz with new ethics and began freeing old aid lines. Local conservatives saw the new order as a threat to established rules, and conflict was inevitable. Bolts were chopped from new routes and oil and grease smeared on holds. But by the late 1970s, climbers resolved these conflicts and embraced modern free-climbing techniques. Those hardmen included Reinhard Karl, Richard Mühe, and Kurt Albert. Albert learned about free climbing at Elbsandstein and began climbing his routes all free, without pulling on gear, and trying to ascend from ground to anchors without a fall. When the route was led free from the ground, he painted a red dot at the base—the birth of today's redpoint (*rotpunkt*) ascent.

The combination of strict Elbsandstein climbing ethics and the skills, strength, technique, and determination of American climbers pushed the German climbing scene to new heights. In 1978 the UIAA was forced to acknowledge the existence of the elusive seventh grade after Reinhard Karl and Helmut Kiene climbed *Pumprisse* in Austria. The following year in the Pfalz, a young Wolfgang Güllich ascended *Superlative,* Germany's first 8 or 5.11d route. The young climbers, however, still chafed at traditional restrictions in the Pfalz, and debates between the two factions led to compromises. Sport climbing was tolerated, but most good climbers migrated away from the Pfalz to the fierce limestone cliffs at the Frankenjura, where the rules were looser and the stone steeper.

The 1980s saw the Frank surpass the Pfalz in western Germany and become the center of German climbing. Easy routes that followed cracks were climbed in the Frankenjura as early as the 1930s, but it was the late 1970s that saw the area transformed into an outdoor gymnasium. Kurt Albert, one of the foremost activists, climbed hard routes like *Osterweg* and *Exorzist,* both 5.11c, in 1977, as well as others in the late 1970s. By 1981 a few routes in the magical 5.12 realm were bolted and redpointed, but only by the two best German climbers: Kurt Albert and Wolfgang Güllich.

The next big jump in standards came in 1981 after an international climbing meet that attracted the world's top rock jocks, including Ron Kauk, Ron Fawcett, and Jean-Claude Droyer. John Bacher stayed for some extra climbing and established the now-classic *Chasin' the Trane* (9)

(5.12d) at Krottenseer Turm, naming the route for a jazz song by John Coltrane. It was not only Germany's hardest climb but also the hardest route in Europe. The impressed locals set to work on the route, and Güllich redpointed the second ascent only days later.

In 1982 Kurt Albert did *Magnet,* the nation's first 9+ or 5.13a, with Güllich repeating it the next year. At the same time Wolfgang "Flipper" Fietz, a boulderer, established classic boulder problems at the Frankenjura and toproped lots of short, hard routes since he was afraid of heights and falling. Many of his toprope problems later became Güllich routes. Through the 1980s the Frankenjura was one of Europe's hardest climbing areas, with lots of 5.12 and 5.13 routes. Englishman Jerry Moffatt established *The Face,* Germany's first route grade 10- or 5.13b, and shortly afterward Güllich put up his own 10-, *Mr. Magnesia.* In 1986 Güllich's route *Ghettoblaster* on Rabenfels became the first 10+ (5.13d/14a) route in Germany. The next year he climbed *Wall Street,* one of the world's first 5.14b routes, on steep rock next to *Chasin' the Trane.* Not long afterward someone enlarged a key finger hole, so Güllich filled it in and reclimbed the route without it.

In the 1980s Wolfgang Güllich simply became one of the world's best rock climbers, ruling the German climbing scene until his untimely death in a car accident in 1992. His modesty, generosity, and amazing climbing skills are legendary. The development of Frankenjura's elevated standards is directly attributable to Güllich's prodigious ability and motivation.

In 1991 Güllich was in the best climbing shape of his life. He worked out intensively by hanging from the tips of his fingers, doing no-feet problems up campus boards, and developing amazing grip strength. That summer he began working on a project that his friend Milan Sykora had bolted on a small, obscure crag called Waldkopf deep in the Frankenjura woods. The route ascended an overhanging, 45-degree, 40-foot-high prow using flat fingertip edges, rounded shallow dishes, strenuous pinches, and thin sidepulls. After

working the route for eleven days over ten weeks, Güllich attempted it again on September 14. For an intense seventy seconds, he attacked the prow and stuck the final dyno to the anchors. The route, named *Action Directe,* set a new standard in world climbing as Güllich graded it the mythical 11 (5.14c). The route still looms in the upper stratosphere of the number grades and has seen only a handful of repeats—a fitting triumph for this great climber.

Getting Around

The size and complexity of the Frankenjura makes getting around problematic. A car is essential to make the most of your tour, and car rental is expensive in Germany. It's best to share expenses to lower hire costs. Hitchhiking is difficult. Without a car you can often scam rides to the crags from other climbers in the campground. And if all else fails, lots of great climbing is within walking distance of the two main climber camping areas at Wolfsberg and Bärenschlucht.

Although this book and the other area guides have useful maps that show the road layout as well as the locations of the crags, it's worth purchasing the detailed walking map—the Wanderkart—for the *Naturpark Fränkische Schweiz.* Besides climbing the area is extremely popular with hikers as the hills are crisscrossed by numerous trails. If you have the detailed map, it's easier to navigate around the many roads, villages, and cliffs. The roads are in excellent condition, and most junctions are well marked, making route finding by car a snap. Parking is usually at designated roadside pullouts, which can sometimes be a problem on busy days at small pullouts. You might have to park farther away from the area if the lot is full. Do not park on the road shoulder.

Despite having this guide in hand along with crag access directions and a map, some cliffs will be hard to find, and some will be downright elusive. Count on it! It's not uncommon to stand before a wall of trees and wonder where the heck is the crag. It's best to poke your head into the woods and have a look around. More often than not, once your eyes become accustomed to the dark gloom, then you'll spot the cliff. Fortunately, most of the cliffs are within a five-minute hike of the parking areas, with many actually just off the road. The longest approaches take fifteen minutes, but with the gentle terrain, there is little elevation gain to the cliff bases.

The roads in the Frankenjura are paved, in good condition, and well signed, especially when compared with other countries. Traveling on the German autobahns is efficient, fast, and free. No tolls are charged, and on weekends there are few trucks. Contrary to popular belief, there are speed restrictions on the autobahns. Don't get carried away by punching your rental Fiat up to 130 mph. Restrictions and fines occur at road construction and major turns. To survive the autobahn use the left lane only for passing, and never pass on the right. It's amazing how quickly a screaming BMW with lights flashing will force you into the slower right lane. Also remember that *links* is left, *rechts* is right, and an *ausfaht* is an exit.

Seasons and Weather

May through September is the best time to visit the Frankenjura, with generally pleasant temperatures. Climbing conditions, however, vary with the weather. Sunny days can be hot, but dense foliage shades most crags. Likewise, if it's cool, there are plenty of cliffs that catch the sun.

There's a reason why lots of vegetation covers the hills here, so plan on rain during your visit. It can rain long and hard, soaking the rock and muddying the approach trails. The cliffs, however, are quick to dry when it warms up. Remember that many cliffs are tucked in recessed valleys, and their overhanging flanks are often dry except after days of heavy rain. The spring months tend to be rainy and cool, giving less than ideal climbing conditions. Many of the cliffs also seep after prolonged rainy spells and in springtime. September and October are predictably the best months for dry weather, although it starts chilling at night by mid-October. Winters are cold and hard, with lots of snow, overcast skies, and

The grave of Wolfgang Güllich, one of Germany's greatest climbers, in Obertrubach.

short, dreary days—better to head south to Spain instead.

Camping, Accommodations, and Services

There are no official public campgrounds in the Frankenjura; instead, most climbers stay in the excellent private sites scattered throughout the region. The local tourist offices can recommend campgrounds. Some climbers, especially the eastern

Europeans from Poland, Slovakia, and Czech Republic, bivouac in the woods, which is a free but frowned-upon option. Most climbers stay in two different sites: Gastof Eichler in the village of Wolfsberg west of Obertrubach and Campingplatz Bärenschlucht just west of Pottenstein.

Gastof Eichler is the best climber's campground. The spacious and inexpensive area, with room for one hundred tents, sits alongside a twisting stream on the valley floor. The now-retired Maria

"Oma" Eichler, well known as *die Kletteroma* or the climbing grandmother, ran the site for years. Now her daughter Martha and grandson Johannes do the daily duties. Amenities include a restaurant with excellent desserts and a small shop that sells beers, some groceries, and local guidebooks.

Campingplatz Bärenschlucht stretches across a meadow below the popular crag Bärenschluchtwände. The site caters to families and caravans, making it not as colorful as Gastof Eichler. Still, some prefer it because it's close to the main sectors.

Many other accommodations are available for noncampers. These include the ubiquitous *gasthaus* found in almost every village. Some are bunkhouses that cater to climbers. Other choices include small inns and hotels, hostels, and self-catering cottages and apartments. Look for the words *zimmer frei* (room free) for vacancies. Precise details and phone numbers can be obtained from any local tourism office.

Almost all of the Frankenjura villages have at least a small grocer, but selection is limited. The larger towns have supermarkets like Aldi and Norma, with fresh produce and good prices. Remember that stores close on Sundays and by 6:00 P.M. during the week, so plan your shopping accordingly.

Food and Drink

Germany is great for eating and drinking, those two all-important cultural experiences. Food in the supermarkets is generally inexpensive, with lots of fresh fruit and vegetables available. Hearty German bread, a meal in itself, is best bought in bakeries. Remember that most shops close at 6:00 P.M., so don't go climbing and expect to buy dinner fixings at the end of the day. They're also closed on Sundays.

Lots of small cafes serve superb food with plentiful portions, although you might quickly tire of the standard German fare of schnitzel, wurst, sauerkraut, and potatoes. Cafes are an important part of the social scene, so there are often several within walking distance of the crag for an afternoon ritual coffee and cake. The bakeries are unbelievable, with a huge variety of sweet delectables that soften the hardest palette. One of the best is Café Müller Bäkerei in Obertrubach. German bread is perhaps the best in the world. A hearty, round loaf wrapped in paper stays fresh for days.

If you're on a budget, remember that many frugal climbers survive for a couple weeks of cragging on a diet of heavy bread laden with cheese and lots of beer or *bier,* the staple of Bavarian life. In Germany beer is considered a food and isn't taxed like other alcoholic beverages. The Frankenjura is famed for the quality of its brews as well as the sheer quantity of local microbrews—more than any other German region. Every village has its own special beer. There is nothing quite like finishing a happy day of cragging by hoisting a few steins with new friends at a beer house. German beers have descriptive names that reflect the taste, ingredients, and color. Some words are *weizen, pils, helles, bristall, dunkles,* and *bock,* along with just plain *bier.* You usually order beer by the type, rather than by brewery name. Back in A.D. 100, Tacitus, a Roman, traveled through Germany and noted in *Germania* that "it rains a lot and the Germans drink lots of beer." Today you'll find that not much changed over the last two millennia. It still rains a lot, and the natives still drink lots of beer.

Cultural Experiences and Rest Days

The Frankenjura region, called *Fränkische Schweiz,* offers a wealth of things to do and see besides rock climbing. Many visiting climbers stop by Wolfgang Güllich's grave in the cemetery behind the church at Obertrubach. Look for a distinctive headstone befitting a great climber, and you'll find it. The region is famed for great hiking, with trails that lace the hills and dales. Detailed hiking guides and maps are available from visitor centers. Likewise, the roads are great for road biking. But you really need to explore the nearby stunning historic cities of Bamberg and Bayreuth.

Bamberg, on the Frankenjura's west side, is considered one of Europe's most beautiful cities. The thriving city, a designated UNESCO World Heritage Site, is a treasure trove of historic architecture. Numerous seventeenth-century buildings, designed by the leading architects of the day, are splendid baroque masterpieces. Places of note include Altes Rathaus spanning the Regnitz River and the nearby Klein Venedig (Little Venice) area of houses lining the riverbank; the Dom, a magnificent Romanesque-Gothic cathedral overlooking the city; the church at the old Kloster St. Michael monastery; and the Fränkisches Brauereimuseum, a brewery museum. The city also offers lots of great cafes and pubs.

Bayreuth, the city that anchors the northeast corner of the Frankenjura, is famous for the annual Wagner Festival that celebrates resident composer Richard Wagner. It takes an average of seven years to garner tickets to the thirty-day event. Bayreuth is another great place to roam about and gawk at the spectacular baroque and rococo architecture along its streets. Beer drinkers will undoubtedly want to tour the Brauerei-und-Büttnerei Museum, which the Guinness Book of World Records calls the world's largest beer museum.

Nürnberg (Nuremberg), the Frankenjura's southern city, is Bavaria's second-largest city after Munich. It was the unofficial capital of the Holy Roman Empire and then one of the Nazi centers in the early twentieth century. By the end of World War II, the city was reduced to ashes and rubble, and was the site of the War Crimes Tribunal. A good walking tour explores the old part of town. Also a visit to the Germanisches National Museum is worthwhile, with many paintings, sculptures, and archeological and historical exhibits.

Trip Planning Information

General description: Excellent limestone sport climbing on numerous small cliffs scattered across forests and valleys.

Location: South-central Germany in northern Bavaria. The Frankenjura lies within a triangle formed by Nürnberg, Bamberg, and Bayreuth. The nearest major airport is in Munich.

Camping and accommodations: Many campgrounds, most catering to the family crowd, are found in the Frankenjura, but the best climber's campsite is Gasthof Eichler. The campground, between Wolfsberg and Untertrubach, sits within an easy drive of the best crags. It's a good place to meet climbers and find partners. The campground offers tent sites, showers and toilets, cooking sheds for rainy evenings, a restaurant with meals and home-baked cakes, and a small kiosk. Climbing guidebooks are also for sale here.

Another popular campground is the Bärenschlucht just west of Pottenstein. A couple of hostels are also found nearby in Gössweinstein and Pottenstein.

For information about campgrounds, hostels, hotels, and guesthouses, ask at the tourist office in larger villages like Pottenstein.

Climbing season: Spring, summer, and fall. The Frankenjura offers better summer climbing than France or Italy. Expect warm days. It can be hot and humid. In September days are cool and nights can be cold. Snow can fall in October. The many cliffs and their varied directions, as well as the thick forest cover, make it easy to find sun or shade.

Restrictions and access issues: Many German climbing areas have restrictions to preserve and protect the natural environment. Fortunately, the Frankenjura has fewer than others. Some cliffs, such as Rabenfels, are closed because of nesting falcons and birds of prey. The closure is from February 1 until July 15, although if the birds are not nesting, the ban is lifted. Look for signs in the crag area announcing the closure and dates.

The cliffs are divided into three zones, with various cliff sectors closed because of rare vegetation. Zone 1 areas are closed to all climbing. Zone 2 areas maintain the status quo. Zone 3 areas are open to climbing and new routes.

Many cliffs are on private land but the landowners allow climbers access. Environmentalists have talked about closing the entire Frankenjura to climbing, saying that chalk, bolts, and climbers are disturbing and damaging the natural environment. Do your part to maintain access by minimizing your impact whenever possible, picking up rubbish, following climber's trails, and not climbing on restricted zones or closed cliffs.

Guidebooks: *Topoführer Nördlicher Frankenjura* by Bernhard Thum is a topo guide. *Kletterführer Frankenjura Band 1* and *Band 2* by Sebastian Schwertner is a complete two-volume topo guide. All three guides are available for purchase at the Gasthof Eichler campground. A bouldering guide is also available.

Services and shops: Climbing shops are in Nürnberg, Erlangen, and Pottenstein. All services in the larger cities and towns.

Limited services in the villages. For the best pastries in the Frankenjura, stop at Café Müller Bäkerei in Obertrubach, just east of the Gasthof Eichler campground.

Emergency services: Call 112 for emergency services or 110 for police (*polizei*). Hospitals are in the nearby cities.

Nearby climbing areas: After climbing the described crags, check out other excellent Frankenjura cliffs. These include sunny Richard Wagner Fels near Obertrubach; Klagemauer, a hard bouldering crag; Hohe Reute, good moderate cliff by the big antenna; Leupoldsteiner Wand, hidden in the woods by Leupoldstein; Roter Fels, big crag by the road; Zimmerbergwände, a nice wooded area; Külochfels, a brilliant cliff with a longish approach; Vordere and Hintere Stadelhofener Wände, two very fine crags; Obere Gossweinsteiner Wände, great cliff by the village of Gössweinstein; Marientaler Wand, superb cliffs above Pottenstein; Holzgauer Wand, some hard lines; Röthefels, a long cliff with moderate

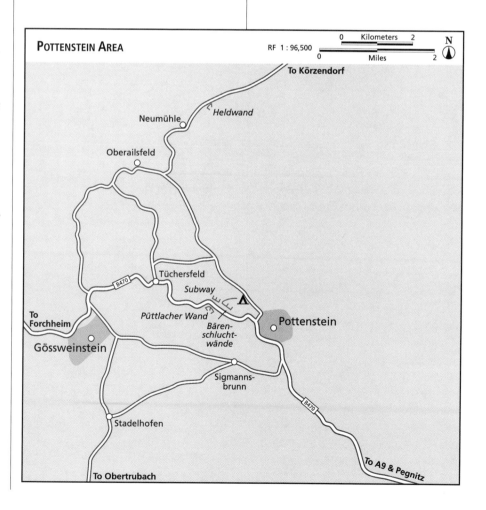

lines; and Rodenstein, a long cliff with great routes.

There are also other good nearby areas. The southern Frankenjura, south of Nürnberg, has several crags, including Kastlwand, Runn, and Schnellneck. The Donautal area in Baden-Württemberg is a lovely valley along the Danube River with limestone cliffs. Donaudurchbruch, a 300-foot cliff, rises out of the Danube and offers good multipitch lines amidst spectacular scenery. Konstein is another Danube Valley cliff. The Fichtelgebirge, an hour east of the Frankenjura, is one of the best granite areas in central Europe.

Nearby attractions: Many historic and cultural attractions are in Nürnberg, Bamberg, Bayreuth, and other towns. If you have limited time, go to Bamberg. The beautiful city, a World Heritage Site, is decorated with stunning buildings from baroque fantasies to gothic nightmares. Nürnberg, famous for the war crimes trials after World War II, was flattened by Allied bombs and then laboriously rebuilt. It's interesting, but definitely not on the same scale as Bamberg. Bayreuth is famous as the home of composer Richard Wagner. Forchheim, on the west side of the Frankenjura, is a lovely town easily explored on foot.

Finding the area: The Frankenjura is north of Nürnberg in south-central Germany. Munich, 102 miles or 170 kilo-meters to the south, is the closest major city with an international airport. It's an hour-and-a-half drive or two-hour train ride from Munich to Nürnberg. Frankfurt is 140 miles or 230 kilometers to the northeast. Allow at least a couple of hours to drive, depending on the traffic, to the Frankenjura.

The easiest access to the main climbing areas from Nürnberg is to drive north on the A9 toward Berlin. Take exit 46 for Plech, Neuhaus, and Betzenstein. Take exit 45 for Obertrubach and Gastof Eichler. Take exit 44 for Pottenstein and Pegnitz. Make sure you pick up a detailed area map to find all the roads to the cliffs.

Bärenschluchtwände

This south-facing cliff, up to 65 feet high, looms above the right side of the Familie Bayer Campingplatz campground west of the village of Pottenstein on the north flank of a narrow valley. The popular cliff offers hard routes up edges and pockets. It's easy to access, often sunny, and dries quickly after rain.

Finding the cliff: Bärenschluchtwände forms a wall along the north side of the Bärenschlucht campground west of Pottenstein. From Pottenstein drive west on highway B470 in the direction of Gössweinstein for 2 kilometers. At the campground turn right (north) onto the road that splits the campground, and park on the dirt right shoulder of the narrow road between the two camping areas. Walk up the road to the cliff and go right onto a short, obvious path along the cliff base. Watch for stinging nettles! Car to cliff base is two minutes. (Parking area GPS: N49° 46.711' E11° 23.171'. Elevation: 1,134 feet.)

Routes are described from left to right.

1. Mai Pen Rai (7) (5.11a) No topo. On the far left side of the cliff. 5 bolts to 1-bolt anchor.

2. Tabula Rasa (7+/8-) No topo. 5 bolts to 1-bolt anchor.

3. Moni's Blackout (7) (5.11a) No topo. Good route. 6 bolts to 1-bolt anchor.

4. Abendspaziergang (8/8+) (5.12a) No topo. 6 bolts to 1-bolt anchor.

5. Bärendreck (8+) (5.12a) Up left off the ledge. 4 bolts to 1-bolt anchor.

6. Metallica (9+) (5.13a/b) Climb easy rock onto a ledge to start. 4 bolts to 2-bolt anchor.

7. Center Court (10-) (5.13c) Established by Wolfgang Güllich. Climb easy rock onto a ledge to start. 4 bolts to 1-bolt anchor.

8. Desaster (10+) (5.13d) Great climb. Up the black streak. Thin and continuous. 6 bolts to 2-bolt anchor.

9. Project (Unknown) 8 bolts to 1-bolt anchor.

10. Bärentöter *(Beerkiller)* (9+) (5.13a/b) Recommended. Start up a thin, left-facing corner, then work up left from the top of the corner. 5 bolts to 1-bolt anchor.

11. Göttner Ged.-Weg (8) (5.11d) Excellent. Start up #10 but angle up right on the steep face after bolt 2.

12. Geierblick (8) (5.11d) Up the outside of a pillar to an overhanging finish. 4 bolts to 1-bolt anchor.

13. Caduta Sassi (9) (5.12d) Go right from a shallow right-facing corner. Sometimes seeps. 6 bolts to 1-bolt anchor.

14. Roter Baron (9-) (5.12b/c) Superb climb. 6 bolts to 1-bolt anchor.

15. Kreuzhang (6+) (5.10b) Climb past the first two bolts of *Roter Baron* or the crack to its right. From the ledge swing up left across the headwall to the last bolt of *Caduta Sassi* and then its anchors. 6 bolts to 1-bolt anchor.

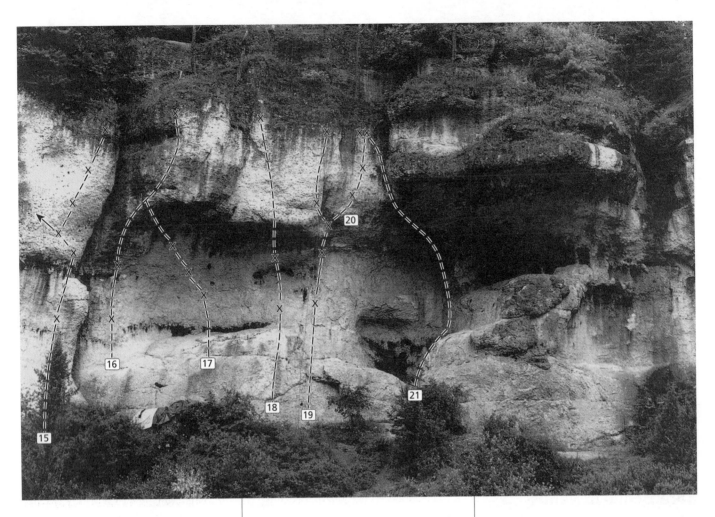

16. Herkules (9/9+) (5.13a) A famous classic route. Herculean moves up and over the left side of a roof. 6 bolts to 1–bolt anchor.

17. Project

18. Skywalk (10-) (5.13c) Up left then out the left side of a roof. 3 bolts to 1-bolt anchor.

19. Amboss (10-) (5.13c) Over a roof to a seam. 4 bolts to 1-bolt anchor.

20. Dr. Jekyl and Mr. Hyde (10+) (5.13d) Climb #19 to bolt 3 then up right. 5 bolts to 1-bolt anchor.

21. Bückling (9-) (5.12b/c) Face climbing below the crack on the left side of the big roof. 3 bolts to 1-bolt anchor.

22. Rauchende Bolts (9) (5.12d)
Excellent. A face to the left side of a bulge. Pull up right on the bulge to a white face. 4 bolts to 1-bolt anchor.

23. Pharao (10) (5.13c) A roof and crux headwall. 6 bolts to 1-bolt anchor.

24. Grand Slam (10-) (5.13c) Climb a corner to a grassy ledge, then directly up the face. 6 bolts to 1-bolt anchor.

25. Nachtwächter (9-) (5.12b/c) Corner to a break then up the wall above. 6 bolts to 1-bolt anchor.

26. Drive-By Shooting (10+/11-) (5.14a) Up the steep face left of the round hole. 6 bolts to 1-bolt anchor.

27. Im Auge des Zyklopen (9/9+) (5.12d) Past the left edge of the hole. 8 bolts to 1-bolt anchor.

More routes are on the white face right of the hole, but these are seldom climbed. The best one is *Sysiphos* (10-) (5.13b/c), farther right on the next cliff section. This route starts off a ledge and climbs past four bolts to an anchor.

Subway

Subway is a small, 25-foot-high roadside cliff tucked into the west side of a short side canyon just left (west) of Bären-schluchtwände. This overhanging crag offers up a few powerful routes up thin edges and small pockets.

Finding the cliff: Drive to Bären-schluchtwände and park on the gravel right shoulder of the road that heads north up the canyon between the two parts of the campground. Walk up the road 300 feet to the cliff on the left side of the canyon. Approach hike is a minute.

Routes described from left to right.

1. Chantre (8-) (5.11c) 2 bolts to 1-bolt lowering anchor.

2. Im Rausch der Tiefe (9+/10-) (5.13b) Begin on the ledge. Climb up left then straight up. 5 bolts to 1-bolt lowering anchor.

3. Small Talk (10+) (5.14a) Recommended. Start same place as #2. Crimp up the steep wall. 4 bolts to 1-bolt lowering anchor.

4. Subway (10) (5.13d) Short, continuous, and good. 5 bolts to 1-bolt lowering anchor.

5. Hot Knives (10/10+) (5.13d) Short and bouldery. 4 bolts to 1-bolt lowering anchor.

6. Unknown (9) (5.12d) On the far right side. 3 bolts to 1-bolt lowering anchor.

Püttlacher Wand

Püttlacher Wand is an excellent, north-facing cliff directly above the B470 highway and the west side of Bärenschlucht campground. The open cliff is sometimes noisy from traffic, but almost all the routes are excellent and worth climbing. It's a good crag for warm days since it's usually shaded. The cliff gets wet when it rains but is quick to dry.

Finding the cliff: Püttlacher Wand towers above the highway just west of Bärenschlucht campground and west of Pottenstein. From Pottenstein drive west on highway B470 in the direction of Gossweinstein. After a couple of kilometers, pass the campground. The obvious cliff towers above the road on the south (left). Park just past the cliff at a pullout on the north (right) side of the highway. Cross the highway, and climb the road bank to a trail that leads east to the cliff base. (Parking lot GPS: N49° 46.775' E11°

22.870'. Elevation: 1,113 feet.)

Routes described from left to right. Hike east to the far left end of the cliff for the first routes.

1. Smör (9) (5.12d) Long and excellent. Go left at bolt 4. 10 bolts to 1-bolt anchor.

2. Das Geschenk (9) (5.12d) Classic. 8 bolts to 1-bolt anchor on ledge up right.

3. The End (9) (5.12d) Recommended. Climb *Das Geschenk* until the final headwall. Go direct to anchors instead of right. 9 bolts to 1-bolt anchor.

4. Riesenslalom Direkt (10) (5.13c) 5 bolts to 1-bolt anchor.

5. Treibjagd (9-) (5.12b/c) Long and sustained. Crux is thin moves above the overhang. 7 bolts to 1-bolt anchor at ledge.

6. Angfang und Ende (9-) (5.12b/c) A low and a high crux keep it interesting. 7 bolts to 1-bolt anchor.

7. Anche per te (8+) (5.12a) White wall to roof. 6 bolts to 1-bolt anchor.

8. Graue Eminenz (9) (5.12d) Superb climbing. Begin on *Anche*, but go right at bolt 2 up the white wall to a crux roof. 7 bolts to 1-bolt anchor.

9. Unknown (9?) (5.12c?) No topo. Start just right of *Graue Eminenz*. Climb up right past the low double roofs to a small upper roof. 5 bolts to 1-bolt anchor.

10. Cool bleim, Chef (8-) (5.11c) Good vertical route right of roofs. 5 bolts to 1-bolt anchor.

11. Abseitsfalle (8-) (5.11c) Excellent and popular. Good warm-up. Vertical face climbing left of a crack system. 5 bolts to 1-bolt anchor.

12. Ikebana (8) (5.11d) Another great route. Up the steep wall right of the crack system. 5 bolts to 1-bolt anchor.

13. Frankenschocker (9-) (5.12b/c) 4 bolts to *Ikebana*'s 1-bolt anchor.

The next routes are on the cliff's right face, almost directly above the parking area. All the routes are excellent. Routes listed from left to right.

14. Red Bull (8-/8) (5.11d) On the left side of the face. 8 bolts to 1-bolt anchor.

15. Intensivstation (9/9+) (5.12d) At the small roof above *Red Bull's* bolt 3, climb straight up. 8 bolts to 1-bolt anchor.

16. Schütze Ged.-Weg (8+) (5.12a) A good but wandering line up the cliff. Begin off block at the middle of the cliff base. 11 bolts to 1-bolt anchor above a high, square roof.

17. K.B. (8+) (5.12a) Long pitch to an anchor at a triangular roof. 11 bolts to 1-bolt anchor.

18. Station 53 (8) (5.11d) Good pumpy pitch with a juggy bulge. 8 bolts to 1-bolt anchor.

19. Tiramisu (9-) (5.12b/c) Up right and over the middle of the roof (crux). 6 bolts to 1-bolt anchor.

20. Unknown (9-) (5.12b/c) Over roofs on the far right side of the face. 7 bolts to 1-bolt anchor.

Heldwand

Heldwand is a superb, north-facing cliff in a pastoral valley north of Pottenstein. The popular face, reached by a two-minute hike, offers a good selection of hard vertical routes. A crack system divides the cliff into two sectors.

Finding the cliff: The cliff is north of Pottenstein. Drive on one of several roads to Oberailsfeld, northwest of Pottenstein. Turn and drive northeast in the direction of Kirchahorn and Feizendorf. Just past the village of Neumühle, look for a right turn and the Heldwand surrounded by trees. Turn right, drive 100 feet, and park in a small lot on the left. The obvious cliff

is reached by a short trail. Routes are listed from left to right.

1. Mutter Theresa (8+) (5.12a) No topo. 5 bolts to 1-bolt anchor.

2. Hans Dampf (8+) (5.12a) No topo. 3 bolts to 1-bolt anchor.

3. Club de toten Dichter (8+) (5.12a) 3 bolts to 1-bolt anchor.

4. Tapferes Schneiderlein (8) (5.11d) 3 bolts to 1-bolt anchor.

5. Heldbräu (8-) (5.11c) 4 bolts to 1-bolt anchor.

6. Lonestar (9-) (5.12b/c) 7 bolts to 1-bolt anchor.

7. Götz von B. (9-) (5.12b/c) 7 bolts to 1-bolt anchor.

8. Gunther Priem U 42 (9-/9) (5.12c) 5 bolts to 1-bolt anchor.

9. Lara Croft (8-/8) (5.11c/d) The first route right of the crack system. 5 bolts to 1-bolt anchor.

10. Flash Gordon (8+/9-) (5.12b) 4 bolts to 1-bolt anchor.

11. Lord Helmchen (8) (5.11d) 5 bolts to 1-bolt anchor.

12. Nicht ohne meine Bürste (7-) (5.10c/d) 5 bolts to 1-bolt anchor.

13. Profilneurose (7+) (5.11b) On the far right side. 5 bolts to 1-bolt anchor.

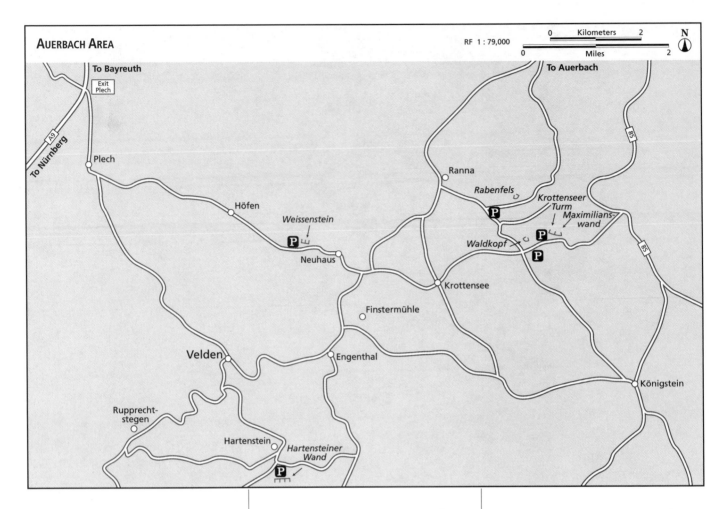

RF 1 : 79,000

Weissenstein

Weissenstein, in the Auerbach area, is the best roadside crag in the Frankenjura. This small, southwest-facing cliff offers excellent routes on its two walls. The open, 50-foot-high right wall curls like an overhanging wave, whereas the left face is shaded and vertical. The rock is riddled with pockets and buckets. It's good in the evening, although it can be very busy then. It's also good on warm mornings since it's shaded. The right side is usually dry on rainy days.

Finding the cliff: From the A9 autobahn take exit #46 (Plech exit), and drive southeast through Plech. Take the turn toward Hofen and Neuhaus, and drive southeast through Hofen. Park at an obvious parking area on the left (north), almost next to the cliff on the road before Neuhaus. (Parking lot GPS: N49° 38.073' E11° 31.871'. Elevation: 1,379 feet.)

Routes are described from left to right.

The first three routes are on a short, north-facing wall on the far left side of the cliff. No topos.

1. Schlingenweg (5-) (5.6) On the far left side of the cliff. 1 bolt and 3 threads/slings to 1-bolt anchor.

2. Beamtenleiter (5) (5.7) 2 bolts and 1 thread/sling to 1-bolt anchor.

3. Mondnavigation (5+) (5.8) 2 bolts and 1 thread/sling to 1-bolt anchor.

The next cliff section is split by vertical cracks into three distinct buttresses.

4. Trepperl (7-) (5.10c/d) 2 bolts to 1-bolt anchor.

5. 7 Up (7) (5.11a) 2 bolts to 1-bolt anchor.

6. R1 or Nullnummer (6-) (5.9) Start up the overhanging crack. 1 bolt to 1-bolt anchor.

7. Eieruhr (6+) (5.10b) 3 bolts to 1-bolt anchor.

8. Don't Worry, Be Happy (6-) (5.9) 2 bolts to 1-bolt anchor.

9. R2 or Muffengang (6-) (5.9) 3 bolts to 1-bolt anchor.

10. R3 (4) (5.5) Easy crack climb. 4 bolts to 1-bolt anchor.

11. Boulderwandl (5+) (5.8) Fun route. 3 bolts to 1-bolt anchor.

12. Annelore (6-) (5.9) 3 bolts to 1-bolt anchor.

13. Chimney Route (5.8) Up the chimney that divides two faces. 5 bolts to 1-bolt anchor.

14. R7 (7-) (5.10c/d) No topo. Left side of pillar on the right side of face. 4 bolts to 1-bolt anchor.

15. Akku (7+) (5.11b) Left side of face. 3 bolts to 1-bolt anchor.

16. Verlobungsweg (7-) (5.10c/d) 3 bolts and 2 threads/slings to 1-bolt anchor. A

direct finish, *Direktausstieg* (7-) (5.10c/d), goes directly above bolt 3 to a 1-bolt anchor.

17. R9 (6+) (5.10b) Recommended. Start in the crack on the right side of the face. Caution! Bolt 1 is 20 feet up. 3 bolts to 1-bolt anchor.

18. Mon Marie (6) (5.10a) Good and well protected. Start right of crack. Bolt 1 is 7 feet off the ground. 7 bolts to 1-bolt anchor.

19. Buchenleiter (6) (5.10a) No topo. Fun pocket route on right side of face. 4 bolts and 1 thread/sling to 1-bolt anchor.

20. Rechte Kante (4) (5.5) No topo. Easy line up the far right edge. Start up *Buchenleiter,* then up right. 4 bolts to 1-bolt anchor.

The next routes are on the buttress right of a 15-foot-wide, broken gap between the two buttresses. The first two routes are on a wall immediately right of the gap and have no topos.

21. Für Zwietsch (4) (5.5) 2 bolts to 1-bolt anchor.

22. Maral (Unknown) Over a slight bulge. 2 bolts to 1-bolt anchor (same as *Für Zwietsch*).

All the following routes on the right buttress are excellent and worth climbing.

23. Affäre (7) (5.11a) No topo. Start right of a tree for this Güllich route. 3 bolts to 1-bolt anchor.

24. Baggi ned (8+) (5.12a) No topo. 3 bolts to 1-bolt anchor.

25. Zwickmühle (8+) (5.12a) Climb to bolt 1 and then up left. 3 bolts to 1-bolt anchor.

26. Ensafter (8+) (5.12a) A 1980 Kurt Albert route. 5 bolts and 1 piton to 1-bolt anchor.

27. Saftpresse (8) (5.11d) Climb *Ensafter* to bolt 4, and then go up right. 6 bolts to 1-bolt anchor.

28. Strohdach (9-) (5.12b/c) First free ascent by American John Bacher in 1981. 4 bolts to 1-bolt anchor.

29. Krampfhammer (9) (5.12d) Recommended. 4 bolts to 1-bolt anchor.

30. Dampfhammer (8) (5.11d) Excellent. 5 bolts to 1-bolt anchor.

31. Alles oder Nichts (9) (5.12d) No topo. A traversing route that climbs to bolt 2 and then up left in a diagonal line to *Ensafter*'s anchors. 7 bolts to 1-bolt anchor.

32. Wilde 13 (8-) (5.11c) Climb up right after bolt 4. 5 bolts to 1-bolt anchor.

33. Wilde 13 Direkt (8-) (5.11c) A direct finish to *Wilde 13*. Go up left at bolt 4. 5 bolts to 1-bolt anchor.

34. Panische Zeiten (7+) (5.11b) Up left after bolt 3. 5 bolts to 1-bolt anchor (same anchor as *Wilde 13*).

35. Direkter Ausstieg (8-) (5.11c) On the far right side of the wall. Climb *Panische Zeiten* to bolt 3 and then up right to anchor. 4 bolts to 1-bolt anchor.

36. The End (5.10?) Same start as *Direkter Ausstieg* but up right at bolt 1 and finish up around the edge of the face. 4 bolts to 1-bolt anchor.

Krottenseer Turm and Maximilianswand

Krottenseer Turm and Maximilianswand, a couple of cliffs hidden in the forest, offer a wide assortment of routes, including several famous climbs. The best known are Güllich's testpiece *Wall Street* (11-) and John Bacher's landmark free ascent of *Chasin' the Trane* (9) (5.12d). The mostly west-facing crags are a bunch of blocky towers with steep faces riddled with pockets. The northwest face of Krottenseer Turm, facing the parking area, is the tallest at 60 feet. The others range from 35 to 50 feet high.

Finding the cliffs: The cliffs are hidden in the woods on a narrow dirt road east of the village of Krottensee. It might take a bit of searching to find the parking the first time. The GPS coordinates below will help.

From the A9 autobahn take exit #46 (Plech exit), and drive southeast through Plech. Take the turn toward Hofen and Neuhaus, and drive southeast to Neuhaus, passing Weissenstein cliff. Drive through Neuhaus, and follow signs east to Krottensee. Follow the narrow road in the direction of Maximiliansgrotte, and enter the forest. The dirt road passes the cave Maximiliansgrotte and its tourist parking lot and continues past a remote intersection toward Sackdilling. About a kilometer from a parking area on the right, look for a small parking area on the left (north) side of the road. The cliff is up right in the trees and invisible from the parking area. Walk on a good trail through the forest for 500 feet to the cliff base. If you have the detailed map "Naturpark Fränkische Schweize Blatt Süd," the parking area is at coordinates I-4 where it says "Steinernen Stadt." (Parking lot GPS: N49° 38.133' E11° 36.779'. Elevation: 1,636 feet.)

Krottenseer Turm is a freestanding tower. The best routes are on the northwest face above the approach trail. There are also several linkups of different routes that are not described. Routes are listed from left to right when facing the cliff.

1. Wüsterman (10+) (5.14a) Up the black streak on the left side of the face. 4 bolts to 1-bolt anchor.

2. Ira Technokratie (9+/10-) (5.13b/c) Boulder up easy rock to bolt 1 then up a black groove to anchors. 4 bolts to tied-off holes and rope anchor.

3. Wall Street (11-) (5.14b) One of the Frankenjura's famous hard routes—put up by Güllich, of course. Face climb left of a black streak to a rounded bulge crux with powerful pulls on small pockets. 5 bolts to 1-bolt anchor.

4. Chasin' the Trane (9) (5.12d) Classic 1981 John Bacher route. The name refers to a John Coltrane song. Face climb to a shallow corner, then right up corners and cracks to anchors. 6 bolts to 1-bolt anchor.

5. Hitchhike the Plane (9+) (5.13a/b) An overhanging rounded face on the right side of the wall. 5 bolts to 1-bolt anchor.

6. Westwand (8-) (5.11c) Start off a big boulder on the right side of the face. Climb a rounded prow to a ledge anchor. 5 bolts to 1-ringbolt anchor (same anchor as *Hitchhike the Plane*).

Another eight routes are on the southwest face of the formation. Consult the area guide for information on these routes. The best is *Südwestkante* (8-) (5.11c), just right of *Westwand* on the left side of the face.

Maximilianswand, the cliff band right of Krottenseer Turm, is a group of huge blocks separated by chimneys and gullies along the crest of a rounded ridgeline. The cliffs, mostly facing southwest, are in the woods above the road. Many excellent and popular routes of varying grades are found here. To approach the cliff hike to Krottenseer Turm, and continue up the slight hill right to the first routes. Routes are described from left to right when approaching the cliff.

7. Bad Brain (10-) (5.13c) On the first good rock past Krottenseer Turm. It ascends a steep wall just left of a chimney. 4 bolts to 1-bolt anchor.

8. Blindes Huhn (6+) (5.10b) Popular. Face right of a chimney. 3 bolts to 1-bolt anchor.

9. Zwiespalt (7) (5.11a) The center of the face. 4 bolts to 1-bolt anchor.

10. Schnitzel on Seitz (8-) (5.11c) Thin, technical face climbing up outside edge of an overhanging prow. 5 bolts to 1-bolt anchor.

11. Westkante (6-) (5.9) Recommended. Begin on the far right side of the face. Climb a leaning corner and over a small roof. Head up right on the slab right of a prow. 3 bolts to 1-bolt anchor.

Around the corner from *Westkante* is a slab. The next routes are on a face right of

the slab. They are the easiest routes here. No topos.

12. Linker Plattenriss (3+) (5.4) *Riss* is German for crack. Climb a broken crack system. 1 bolt to 1-bolt anchor. Bring some nuts.

13. Rechter Plattenriss (3) (5.4) Climb the easy, right-angling crack and corner. Bring nuts and Friends.

14. Sonnenkönig (6-) (5.9) Begin right of the crack. Climb up left across the crack to a thread. Continue straight up to anchor above a roof. 2 bolts and 1 thread to 1-bolt anchor.

15. Schiefer Riss (5) (5.7) An easy crack on the outside of the buttress. Bring nuts and Friends.

Walk around the buttress to its other side to this face with several good routes.

16. Bodum (7+) (5.11b) Good thin climbing up the face right of the crack to a ledge. 4 bolts to 1-bolt anchor above the ledge.

17. Luisenkreutz (6) (5.10a) Face climb to a bolt left of small roof then up a headwall to a ledge. 1 bolt and 1 piton to 1-bolt anchor.

18. Spätlese (6+) (5.10b) Good climb. Begin up a shallow corner to a roof. Out the right side to the crack then up right to the top. 2 bolts to 1-bolt anchor.

19. Luisenband (6-) (5.9) Climb the left-angling crack system to *Bodum's* anchor.

20. Kreutzigung (8+) (5.12a) Begin at the base of the crack. Difficult pockets over a bulge. 3 bolts to 1-bolt anchor on a ledge.

21. Ansbacher Weg (7+) (5.11b) Steep face climbing up the right margin of the face. 4 bolts to 1-bolt anchor on a ledge.

This next face is just right of a breakdown area. It's very popular and clean with some good routes.

22. Lang hi (6+) (5.10b) Pockets and edges up the face left of a tree on a shelf. 4 bolts to 1-bolt anchor.

23. Sudriss (7-) (5.10c/d) Up a thin right-facing corner to a streak. 5 bolts to 1-bolt anchor.

24. Abheber (7+) (5.11b) Over some bulges to a steep finish.

25. Direkte Gratwanderung (7+) (5.11b) Climb a face with 2 bolts then up right. 4 bolts to 1-bolt anchor.

26. Gratwanderung (7) (5.11a) No topo. Climb a moderate slab to bolt 3 on *Direkte Gratwanderung* and finish up it. 2 bolts to 1-bolt anchor.

27. Straight Edge (10+) (5.14a) Technical and sustained movements up the overhanging wall left of the obvious prow on the right side of the face. 5 bolts to 2-bolt anchor.

The next routes are at the far southeast edge of the cliff band and are on the sides of a semidetached tower. The first four routes are on the northwest face.

28. Wimmersberger Ged.-Weg (7-) (5.10c/d) Good climbing. Climb a pillar to a chimney to a bolt. Edge up right across the face to top. 3 bolts to 1-bolt anchor.

29. Anakonda (8+) (5.12a) Recommended. Thin face moves lead 20 feet up and over a roof to bolt 1. Continue to bolt 3 on *Wimmersberger Ged.-Weg*, and finish up it. 3 bolts to 1-bolt anchor.

30. Free Will (8+) (5.12a) Same start as *Anakonda* but work up right from bolt 1, and finish up the exposed prow. 1 bolt to 1-bolt anchor.

31. Wilde Spiele (9-) (5.12b/c) Superb bouldery route put up by Australian Kim Carrigan in 1986. Small pockets and edges up the outside face. 2 bolts to 1-bolt anchor below a horizontal crack.

32. Amazonenpfeiler (8+) (5.12a) Excellent. On the opposite side of the block. Face climb up a seam. 3 bolts to 1-bolt anchor.

33. Another Excess (9) (5.12d) Up the right side of the block's face. 2 bolts to 2-bolt anchor.

Rabenfels

Rabenfels or Raven's Cliff is a unique tower that juts above a wooded valley a few kilometers north of Maximilianswand. The tower, hidden from prying eyes, offers a feast of superb routes on its south-facing walls. It's somewhat hard to find at first but well worth the effort. The cliff is usually closed from spring until mid-July for nesting falcons. The closure dates are posted on a sign below the cliff.

Finding the cliff: Drive 2 kilometers north from Neuhaus in the direction of Ranna and Auerbach. At post 25.5, just south of Ranna and the small St. Magdalena Church, make a right turn onto a narrow tar road that heads south. Follow it to a crossroads marked HOHEN TANNA, and drive another 600 feet to another crossroads marked RABENFELS, with an open field on your right and the forest on your left. This road is 1.1 kilometers south of the main road. Park in a lot here, and walk east along a one-lane dirt road for almost 1 kilometer until you are below the obvious tower. A short path threads through the forest to the cliff base. Do not park on the road near the crag; there is no parking area, and the road is very narrow. (GPS on the road below the formation: N49° 38.562' E11° 35.949'. Elevation: 1,364 feet.)

Routes are described from left to right.

1. Ghetto Blaster (10/10+) (5.13d) No topo. First ascent by Wolfgang Güllich. Up the overhanging west face of the formation. 8 bolts to anchor.

2. Westside Story (10-) (5.13c) Another Güllich testpiece right of *Ghetto Blaster*. 6 bolts to anchor.

3. Robert Lukas Ged.-Weg (6+) (5.10b) 2 pitches. **Pitch 1:** Climb a broken crack system then up left to a belay. 7 bolts and 1 piton to 1-bolt anchor. **Pitch 2:** Climb up and traverse left, and finish up *Ghetto Blaster*. 4 bolts to anchor.

4. Open End (7+/8-) (5.11b) Straight up at bolt 5. 9 bolts to 1-bolt anchor below the roof.

5. Direkt Ausstieg (8) (5.11d) Over the final roof above *Open End*.

6. Richard Holzberger Ged.-Weg (7) (5.11a) First climbed in 1950. 11 bolts to 1-bolt anchor below the roof.

7. Katalysator (8-) (5.11c) No topo. 8 bolts to 1-bolt anchor.

8. Auerbacher Ged.-Weg (8) (5.11d) No topo. 5 bolts to 1-bolt anchor.

9. Stairway to Heaven (9-) (5.12b/c) No topo. 4 bolts to 1-bolt anchor.

Waldkopf

This small cliff, tucked far back in the woods north of the road, has a severely overhanging west face. *Action Directe*, one of the world's hardest rock climbs, ascends a prow on this short face. The cliff is difficult to find at first, but if you are persistent, you will find the right path.

Finding the cliff: From the A9 autobahn take exit #46 (Plech exit), and drive southeast through Plech. Take the turn toward Hofen and Neuhaus, and drive southeast to Neuhaus, passing Weissenstein cliff. Drive through Neuhaus, and follow signs east to Krottensee. Follow the narrow road in the direction of Maximiliansgrotte, and enter the forest. The dirt road passes the cave Maximiliansgrotte and its tourist parking lot and continues to a remote intersection. A left turn here goes toward Rabenfels, and the main road goes straight to Sackdilling. Drive about 0.3 kilometer toward Sackdilling to a small parking area on the right under trees.

The crag is not far from here but is hard to find, so plan on getting lost the first time. Cross the road to the north, and follow a trail that parallels the road left or northwest to a junction, continue a short distance to the next junction, and go right uphill to Waldkopf. Hiking time is less than ten minutes. (GPS at parking area: N 49° 38.032' E 11° 36.181'. GPS at cliff base: N 49° 38.096' E 11° 36.146'. Elevation: 1,565 feet.)

Routes described from left to right.

1. Action Directe (11) (5.14c) A stunning line climbed by Wolfgang Güllich in 1991. First American ascent by Dave Graham in 2001. Rounded pockets and edges up the overhanging west face. 5 bolts to 1-bolt anchor.

2. Feiste Fäuste (9) (5.12d) The crack right of *Action Directe*. 2 bolts and 3 pitons to 1-bolt anchor.

3. Teddy's Wampe (9+) (5.13a/b) Begin at the crack. Climb to bolt 1, and then work up right past 3 bolts then straight up. 5 bolts to 1-bolt anchor.

4. Slim Line (10–) (5.13c) Another Güllich line. 4 bolts to 1-bolt anchor.

5. Mawis Wampe (10–) (5.13c) Up face on the right.

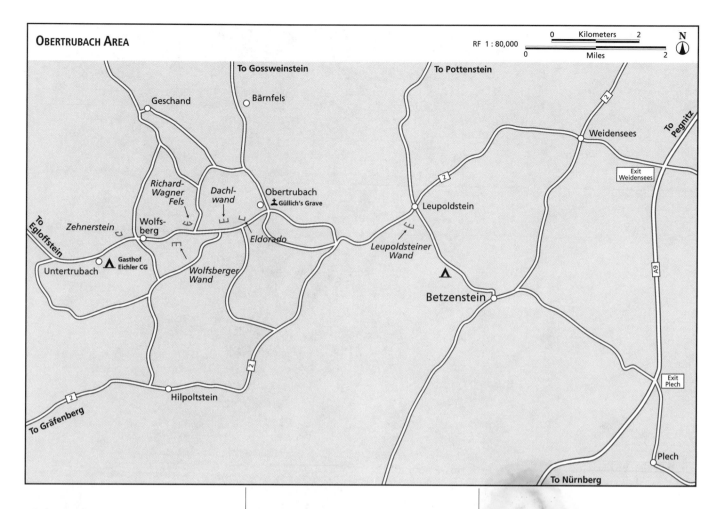

RF 1 : 80,000

To Gossweinstein

To Pottenstein

Geschand

Bärnfels

Weidensees

To Pegnitz

Richard-
Wagner
Fels

Dachl-
wand

Obertrubach

Güllich's Grave

Leupoldstein

Exit
Weidensees

Zehnerstein

Wolfs-
berg

Eldorado

Leupoldsteiner
Wand

To
Egloffstein

Gasthof
Eichler CG

Untertrubach

Wolfsberger
Wand

Betzenstein

Hilpoltstein

To Gräfenberg

Exit
Plech

Plech

To Nürnberg

Eldorado

Eldorado is a short, steeply overhanging wall perched above a roadside parking area and a playground for your kids or climbing partners! The crag, with excellent power routes, is used as a training and warm-up wall. The south-facing cliff is also dry in rain, making it a good alternative for bad-weather spells.

Finding the cliff: Drive west from Obertrubach in the direction of Wolfsberg and Gastof Eichler campground. The obvious crag, parking area, and playground on the north side of the road are about 600 feet west of the village. Scramble up a short path to the base of the cliff. (Parking lot GPS: N 49° 41.476' E 11° 20.478' Elevation: 1,470 feet.)

Routes are described from left to right.

1. Sudtirol, mio amore (9) (5.12d) 2 bolts to 1-bolt anchor.

2. Stone Love (10+) (5.14a) First redpoint by Brit Jerry Moffat in 1988. 4 bolts to 1-bolt anchor.

3. Raubritter (10+) (5.14a) 3 bolts to 1-bolt anchor.

4. Nightmare (10) (5.13d) 3 bolts to 1-bolt anchor.

5. Ekel (9+) (5.13a/b) First by Moffat in 1983. 3 bolts to 1-bolt anchor.

6. No More Babysitting for Neurotic Girls Today (9-) (5.12b/c) First ascent by Wolfgang Güllich in 1983. A long name for a shortie. 2 bolts to 1-bolt anchor.

7. Unbehagen (8) (5.11d) Güllich again in 1983. 2 bolts to 1-bolt anchor.

Dachlwand

Dachlwand is a good south-facing cliff above a farmhouse and the road just west of Obertrubach. The slightly overhanging cliff is open and sunny. Most routes are hard, fingery, and technical. The upper part of the cliff is a steep dark bulge. Anchors are on the lower-angle rock above the bulge.

Finding the cliff: The cliff is just down the road from Eldorado on the north (right) side of the road between Obertrubach and Wolfsberg. Drive west from Obertrubach in the direction of Wolfsberg. After about 2,300 feet, look for a small parking area on the far left side of a roadside farmhouse on the north (right) side of the road. The trail begins here. The cliff is up right above the farmhouse. Walk a couple of minutes up the path to the cliff base. (Parking lot GPS: N 49° 41.426' E 11° 20.157' Elevation: 1,331 feet.)

Routes are described from left to right.

1. Schiefes Dach (8-) (5.11c) A long girdle traverse. Begin on the far left side of the cliff, and follow a diagonal break up right to the far right side of the cliff. 13 bolts to 1-bolt anchor.

2. Oberer Dachweg (3+) (5.5) Easiest route on the cliff. Begin at the far left side. Climb up and over the edge of the roof, then make a long traverse up right, clipping anchors for pro as you go. Belay from whatever anchors you feel comfortable with. Rappel to the ground.

3. Iced Earth (8) (5.11d) Watch for loose rock! 4 bolts to 1-bolt anchor.

4. Bauer Olaf (9) (5.12d) 5 bolts to 1-bolt anchor.

5. Power of Love (9-) (5.12b/c) Recommended. A Kurt Albert route from 1985. Crux bulge at the top. 4 bolts to 1-bolt anchor.

6. Bilbo Baggins (8-) (5.11c) What's a climbing area without a Bilbo route? 6 bolts to 1-bolt anchor.

7. Gollum (8) (5.11d) White face to bulge crux. 5 bolts to 1-bolt anchor.

8. Rainer's erstes Mal (8/8+) (5.11d/12a) 7 bolts to 1-bolt anchor.

9. Golenes Dach (8+/9-) (5.12b) Start on *Rainer's erstes Mal* but go right at bolt 2 and up steep bulges to a high crux. 9 bolts to 1-bolt anchor.

10. Damokles' Schwert (9) (5.12d) Join *Golenes Dach* for its two upper bolts and then right at the last bolt. 7 bolts to 1-bolt anchor.

11. Chaka Khan (9-) (5.12b/c) On the far right side of the cliff. 5 bolts to 1-bolt anchor.

Zehnerstein

Zehnerstein, rising above trees on the north side of the valley near Gastof Eichler, is easily identified by a giant piton driven into its summit. The popular formation, a narrow fin, yields some excellent and fun climbs. Most of the routes end at anchors below the summit, but it's good fun to stand atop its pinnacle.

Finding the cliff: Drive west from Wolfsberg in the direction of Hammerbühl and Untertrubach. Park just west of Wolfsberg in a long pullout on the north side of the road. From the parking area walk west up a narrow road toward the backs of several houses. Behind the first house look for a path that goes right into the woods. Follow the path for 100 yards to the cliff base. The last section is steep. Hiking time is five minutes. (Parking lot GPS: N 49° 41.258' E 11° 18.318'. Elevation: 1,262 feet.)

Routes are described from left to right, beginning at the uphill, west face of the crag. The most uphill sector, not described here, has a few good crack and easier face routes.

Westwand

This west-facing wall offers a good selection of popular midgrade routes. The first three routes climb to a midheight ledge system.

1. Oma Eichler (6) (5.10a) 2 pitches. **Pitch 1:** Up the left side of the face. 2 bolts to 1-bolt anchor. **Pitch 2:** The second route from the left edge. 3 bolts to 1-bolt anchor below the summit.

2. Solleder Ge. Weg (6) (5.10a) Climb #1 to the ledge. Climb the crack on the left margin of the face. 3 bolts to 1-bolt anchor.

3. Kauperriss (6-) (5.9) 2 pitches. Begin just right of #1. **Pitch 1:** A crack system to a face. 4 bolts to 1-bolt anchor on ledge (same belay as #1). **Pitch 2:** Climb the steep face directly above the belay. 3 bolts to 1-bolt anchor.

4. Lineal (7-) (5.10c/d) Climb #3 to its first belay. Work up and over a roof to a steep finish. 3 bolts to 1-bolt anchor.

5. Gerade Westwand (4) Recommended. Also called *Südwestkante*. It's the easiest route to the top. Climb Pitch 1 of either #1 or #3 to the belay ledge. Continue up right, following the easiest line along a groove to anchors on the summit of the rock.

6. Neuer alter Hut (7-) (5.10c/d) Good climbing. Begin just left from the toe of the narrow face that divides the formation. Face climb directly up to anchors. 4 bolts and 1 sling to 2-bolt anchor.

The next routes ascend the spectacular, narrow south face of Zehnerstein. All are very good and recommended.

7. Umleitung (8-) (5.11c) Start at the toe of the face. Climb a short corner then up steep rock left of a big hole and bulge to anchors atop the cliff. 10 bolts to 1-bolt anchor.

8. Erinnerungsweg (9-) (5.12b/c) Begin just right of #7. Climb the steep face to a big hole. Exit out the left side over a bulge, and continue up #7 above to anchors. 11 bolts to 1-bolt anchor.

9. Buchnerpfeiler (9-) (5.12b/c) Climb #8 to the hole, then pull over the big bulge above and crank the exposed prow to an anchor below the summit. 10 bolts to 1-bolt anchor.

10. Toni Schmid-Ged.-Weg (8-) (5.11c) Climb #8 to the hole, and then work up right along an incipient crack system to the top. 11 bolts to 1-bolt anchor.

11. Andi (8-) (5.11c) Excellent and airy. Begin on the left side of the south face. Work up left along a crack past 3 bolts. Climb overhang up right of crack system. 9 bolts to 1-bolt anchor.

12. Affenschaukel (8-) (5.11c) No topo. First ascent by Kurt Albert in 1979. Begin on the right side of the narrow south face. Climb up left and onto prow. 7 bolts to 1-bolt anchor.

13. Seifertriss (6+) (5.10b) First climbed in 1929 with some aid. Same start as *Affenschaukel*, but at bolt 4 continue up the crack above. 7 bolts to 1-bolt anchor.

14. Satisfaction (8+) (5.12a) 3-star line up a steep face. 5 bolts to 1-bolt anchor.

15. Albrecht-Wolf-Jordan-Ged.-Weg (6+) (5.10b) Same starting point as *Satisfaction* but edge up the rib on the right. 3 bolts to 1-bolt anchor.

The last couple of routes are on the pillar on the uphill east side of the formation.

16. Zwei Jahre später (7) (5.11a) 6 bolts to 1-bolt anchor.

17. Himmelsleiter (5+) (5.8) Crack to face. Bring some nuts for the crack. 3 bolts to 1-bolt anchor.

Hartensteiner Wand

Hartensteiner Wand is a superb, north-facing cliff on a wooded hillside above the village of Hartenstein. The shady cliff is good in summer heat. You'll find a wide range of grades on the mostly well-protected, bolted routes. Some Stoppers and Friends are useful on a few routes that are sparsely bolted.

Finding the cliff: Locate the village of Hartenstein in the southeast part of the Frankenjura on your map. Drive from the Plech exit on the A9 south to Plech and then southeast to Velden. Look for a small road that heads south again and up to Hartenstein. Turn off the main road in Hartenstein center, near the church, and drive southeast to a sign that marks a right turn to the Sportsplatz and cemetery. Park at the cemetery by a small chapel or at the Sportsplatz to the west. A one-minute hike through the woods leads to the cliff. (Parking lot GPS: N 49° 35.565' E 11° 31.429'. Elevation: 1,706 feet.)

Routes are described from right to left.

1. Friedhofsriss, aka Westriss (5) (5.7) A crack-and-groove route on the right side of the main buttress. 1 bolt to 1-bolt anchor.

2. Nürnberger Weg, aka Nordwestkante (6+) (5.10b) Start up *Friedhofsriss,* and traverse left onto the route. 2 bolts to 1-bolt anchor.

3. Direckte Nordwestkante, aka Direkteinstieg (8-) (5.11c) Over a bulge. 5 bolts to 1-bolt anchor.

4. Grufty (7+) (5.11b) Recommended classic route over bulges. 4 bolts to 1-bolt anchor.

5. Mama's Boy Direkt (7-) (5.10c/d) 3 bolts to 1-bolt anchor.

6. Trimmpfad (6+) (5.10b R) Head up right from bolt 1. 3 bolts to 1-bolt anchor.

7. Surprise (7) (5.11a) Good route. Shares bolt 1 with *Trimmpfad.* 5 bolts to 1-bolt anchor.

8. Neustadter Riss, aka Nordriss (6-) (5.9) Crack route. 2 bolts to 1-bolt anchor. Bring some Friends.

9. Kletterspatzenweg, aka Donnerwetter
(6) (5.10a) Recommended. Crux bulge at
the top. 5 bolts and 1 sling to 1-bolt
anchor.

10. Abkürzer (6) (5.10a R) Good climbing up the center of the wall. 3 bolts to 1-
bolt anchor.

11. Igor (6) (5.10a) 3 bolts and 1 fixed
sling to 1-bolt anchor.

12. Tante Gretl (6+) (5.10b R) First bolt
is high. 3 bolts to 1-bolt anchor.

13. Die Hundertjährige (6–) (5.9 R)
Traverse up left at bolt 1. 4 bolts to 1-bolt
anchor.

14. Die Hunderteinjährige (7) (5.11a)
Recommended. 5 bolts to 1-bolt anchor.

15. Riss (6+) (5.10b) Crack on the left
side of a flake. 3 bolts to 1-bolt anchor.

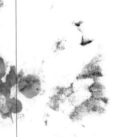

16. Pleasure Line (8-) (5.11c) 4 bolts to 1-bolt anchor.

17. Mann oder Memme (8-) (5.11c) 3 bolts to 1-bolt anchor.

18. Norem (8+) (5.12a) 4 bolts to 1-bolt anchor.

19. Pimpanella (7+) (5.11b) 4 bolts to 1-bolt anchor.

20. Blue Bolt (7+) (5.11b) 3 bolts to 1-bolt anchor (same anchor as *Pimpanella*).

21. Kurzer Riss (4) (5.5) A crack route.

22. Ziech oder Fliech (6) (5.10a) 3 bolts to 1-bolt anchor.

23. Hummelstaner Weg (5+) (5.8) 3 bolts to 1-bolt anchor.

24. Aprilscherz (7–) (5.10c/d) 3 bolts to 1-bolt anchor.

25. 5 vor 12 (8–) (5.11c) 5 bolts to 1-bolt anchor.

26. Flop (7) (5.11a) 3 bolts to 1-bolt anchor.

27. Geschweifter Riss (5–) (5.7) First climbed in 1960 with aid. 2 bolts to 1-bolt anchor. Need gear on this one.

28. Grabsteinweg (6) (5.10a) 3 bolts and 1 fixed sling to 1-bolt anchor.

Norway

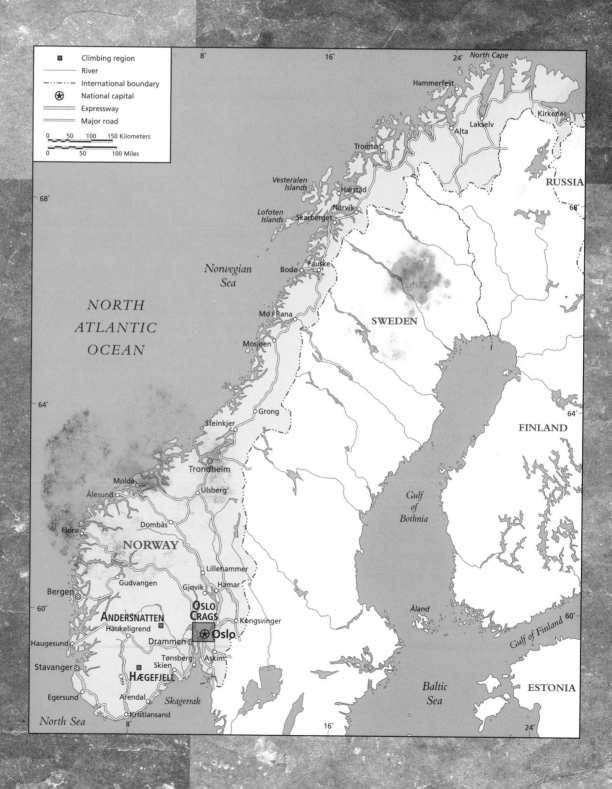

Legend:
- Climbing region
- River
- International boundary
- National capital
- Expressway
- Major road

0   50   100   150 Kilometers
0   50   100 Miles

North Cape

Hammerfest

Kirkenes

Lakselv
Alta

Tromsø

RUSSIA

Vesteralen
Islands

Harstad

Narvik

Lofoten
Islands

Skarberget

*Norwegian
Sea*

Bodø
Fauske

SWEDEN

Mo i Rana

Mosjøen

**NORTH
ATLANTIC
OCEAN**

Grong

FINLAND

Steinkjer

Trondheim

*Gulf
of
Bothnia*

Molde

Ulsberg

Ålesund

Florø

Dombås

NORWAY

Lillehammer

Gudvangen

Gjøvik
Hamar

Bergen

**OSLO
CRAGS**

Åland

ANDERSNATTEN
Haukeligrend

Køngsvinger

Drammen

⊛ **Oslo**

Haugesund

Tønsberg
Skien

Askim

Stavanger

*Baltic
Sea*

ESTONIA

HÆGEFJELL

Egersund

Arendal

Skagerrak

Kristiansand

North Sea

OSLO CRAGS

■ OVERVIEW

Oslo, the capital of Norway, straddles the head of Oslofjord, a 50-mile-long fjord that opens south into the North Sea. It's a lovely, modern city set amid high wooded hills, broad lake-studded valleys, and the sight and smell of the ever-present fjord. Many compact granite and volcanic crags nestle among the city's hills, offering an excellent and rich assortment of sport and traditional routes. The cliffs lie in relatively unspoiled natural areas around Oslo that reflect the Norwegian love of nature.

These cliffs include Kolsås, one of the oldest and most popular climbing areas in Norway. Kolsås is composed of several horizontal cliff bands that line a mountain flank above southeast Oslo. The uppermost cliff, just below the summit, is laced with a selection of classic moderate routes. Thick forests in other parts of the city and its suburbs hide other crags, including Hauktjern and Damtjern, both described in this guide, as well as Løkenhavna, Fjell, and Sørkedalen.

These crags offer mostly hard, bolt-protected routes up vertical to slightly overhanging stone. Almost all the Oslo routes are single-pitch affairs, although some cliffs do have multipitch lines. The harder sport climbs tend to be technical and crimpy since they often ascend vertical granite terrain. To clip the chains on many of these, you need strong fingers and an aggressive attitude. Most of the crags are easy to access, well protected, and have assorted grades, although the sport areas tend to have mostly hard climbs. Be advised that the YDS grades included in this guide are translated from Norwegian grades, so some discrepancies exist. Take the YDS grades with a grain of salt, because they may not always be accurate to your experience.

The Oslo area was shaped by many glacial periods, with immense glaciers blanketing the region. They scraped, smoothed, and quarried the granite bedrock as well as the younger volcanic layers into characteristic glaciated U-shaped valleys, leaving steep walls along valley

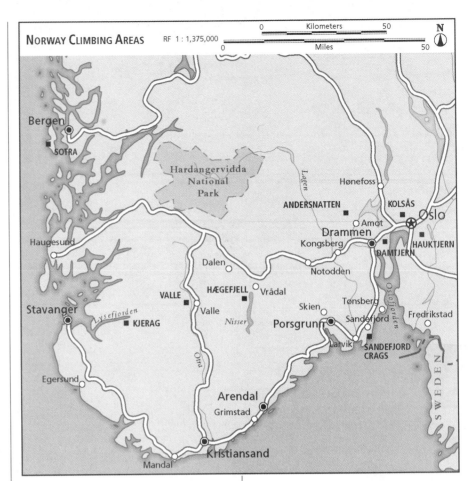

sides. If you examine the cliffs closely, you can still see scraped incisions made by the moving ice. The deep lakes and tarns that floor the area valleys are also characteristic of glaciated topography.

Rack, Protection, and Descent

Hauktjern and Damtjern are both sport crags, whereas Kolsås is a traditional cliff. Bring a rack of a dozen quickdraws and a 165-foot (50-meter) rope to climb the sport routes. Most routes are securely bolted with weather-resistant, stainless steel bolts and feature double-bolt lowering anchors or stout anchor trees atop the cliff. Both areas, however, do have gear routes that require a set of cams and wired nuts. Descent off almost all the routes at Hauktjern and Damtjern is by lowering from bolt anchors.

Bring a full rack of gear including sets of wires, TCUs, and cams to climb at Øvre Sydstup on Kolsås. Some bolt anchors for belaying and rappelling are found atop the popular cliff area, but no

bolts are found on the climbs themselves. Descent off the cliff top is walking down the hiking trail.

Seasons and Weather

Oslo lies at a latitude of 60 degrees north, roughly the same as Anchorage, Alaska. The climate is correspondingly similar. Summers are short with long days, and winters are long with short days. The best time to visit is May through September when the days are warm and long. Expect that it will rain, but not as much as it does in Bergen on the west coast. Summer temperatures range from the 50s to the 70s. July, the warmest month, averages a daily high temperature of 65 degrees. In midsummer the sun shines well past 10:00 P.M., courtesy of the city's northern latitude.

May and September are also pleasant times, although it can sometimes be damp in May, the Norwegian springtime. May highs average 55 degrees. September brings cool but sunny days and long shadows. By October the daily high averages

45 degrees, and the weather begins the march toward the cold winter. Snow can fall at any time, although good days do occur. Oslo locals swear they find decent climbing weather on sunny days in the cold heart of winter, although if you visit then, you'll more likely be strapping on cross-country skis.

Climbing History

Norway, a land of mountains and cliffs, has a long history of technical rock climbing that dates to the beginning of the twentieth century. Climbing began at the classic crag Kolsås, Oslo's oldest climbing area at that time, and the cliff became a gathering place for the era's best Norwegian climbers. Lots of climbers learned rope handling on the cliff in the 1920s and 1930s before venturing to other areas and the nation's high mountains.

Modern climbing techniques, including piton protection, were introduced to Norway in the 1930s by Arne Næss, a philosophy professor and famed mountaineer.

Sport climbing with rappel-bolted routes up previously unclimbable faces began around Oslo in the 1980s. Local climber Marius Morstad, the father of modern Norwegian sport climbing, bolted and climbed hard routes at previously unclimbed crags like Damtjern and Hauktjern. Damtjern was developed mostly in the late 1980s. Morstad climbed the hard classic *Stive dempere* in 1986, and *Marathon,* one of the area's hardest routes, was established by Per Hustad in 1988. Climbing began at Hauktjern more than one hundred years ago with the ascent of some easy lines, but most new route activity occurred in the late 1980s and early 1990s.

Getting Around

Unlike most climbing areas in this book, you can climb in the Oslo area without hiring a car, relying instead on public transportation and taxis, although it is easier and quicker to get around with a rental car. The city's public transport system relies on buses, trams, and an underground rail system, almost all of which begin at the *Bussterminalen,* bus terminal, next to *Oslo Sentralstasjon,* the main train station. Ask at the terminal for information on the various bus routes that go near the crags.

It's easy to hire a car to get around, especially if you plan on traveling to other climbing areas in Norway and Sweden. Daily rental charges are higher than in other parts of Europe but usually include unlimited mileage, a collision damage waiver, and vehicle insurance. As in the rest of Europe, make your reservation from the United States for the best rates and special deals.

When you enter Oslo on any major highway, you pay a hefty toll for that privilege. On-street parking is a problem in downtown Oslo but less so in outlying areas. Park your car in a pay-and-display lot if you need to leave it for more than an hour. Free parking is found at the trailheads

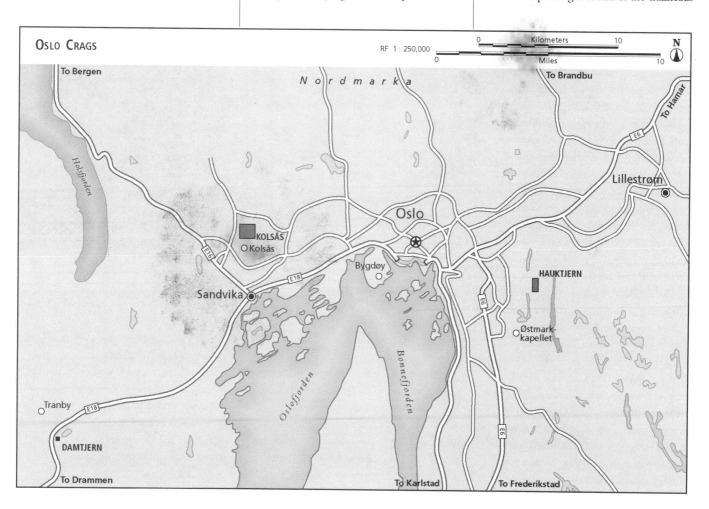

for all the cliffs. Watch your speed when driving, especially on the highways. There are many automatic traffic control cameras that take your picture for a ticket if you exceed the limit. The general highway speed limit is 50 mph (80 kph), unless otherwise posted. Watch for moose (elg) if you are driving in the mountains. They're not afraid of cars and cause a lot of accidents and damage, just like they do in New England.

Camping, Accommodations, and Services

Accommodations are perhaps the greatest budget breaker for a climbing trip to Norway since Oslo is considered both Europe's and the world's most expensive city. So unless you track down a long-lost Norwegian relative who will put you up on the living-room futon, you'll need to set aside a tall stack of kroner to pay for your accommodations—none of which are exactly cheap. Oslo offers a wide range of hotels, along with private rooms, *pensjonater* or boardinghouses, hostels, and campgrounds.

Hotels are, of course, very expensive. Expect to pay 700 to 900 kroner, or more than $100 per night. Many hotels, however, offer substantial savings on weekends in July and August, when most Norwegians abandon the city for the mountains and beaches. Most offer a buffet-style breakfast. The ideal way to find the best rates and specials, to eliminate a lot of phone calls, and to secure a reservation is to visit the *Norges Informasjonssenter* (Norwegian Information Center) down by the harbor. They will make a reservation for a small booking fee.

Several boardinghouses and hostels as well as rooms in private homes are found in the Oslo area and offer the budget climber more choices. Consider this, because you'll need all your extra kroner to buy a nightly bottle of øl or ale. All offer adequate accommodations, without the frills and costs of the higher-scale establishments. Two good hostels, Oslo Haraldsheim and KRUK-KRUM Sleep-In, are recommended. Oslo Haraldsheim, 5 kilometers northeast of the city center,

Chris Fossli on *Marathon* (9) (5.13d) at Damtjern.

offers 270 beds in 71 rooms. It's inexpensive, clean, includes breakfast, has self-catering facilities, and is easily accessed by public transport.

If you have a car and want to save money, it's easy to camp outside the city. More than twenty campgrounds are within a 50-kilometer range of Oslo, and Ekeberg Camping sits a scant 3 kilometers east of Oslo city center. Another good site is Langøyene Camping on one of the small islands offshore from Oslo. Most

campgrounds also rent cabins and cottages. Norway has a long history of public camping almost anywhere, as long as you ask permission from the landowner and respect the privilege. If you need any help or suggestions with Oslo accommodations, don't hesitate to contact Tyrili Klatreklubb, one of the local climbing gyms. The folks there are happy to point you in the right direction.

Food and Drink

Norway is expensive, and dining out in Norway is really expensive. Norwegian restaurants are notoriously pricey, so even most locals content themselves with eating out only on special occasions—otherwise, you'll need a second mortgage to pick up the tab for your pals. Most budget travelers exist by eating picnic-style and meals they cook themselves on a camp stove.

Even without an unlimited budget, however, you can eat very well in Norway. Fresh fish is plentiful and excellent, especially cod and salmon, which come any way you desire, including steamed, grilled, poached, and stuffed. Meat eaters can sample lots of great dishes made with exotic cuts from reindeer and moose. But it's easy to spend $50 for an average meal here, and that's without drinks, so pick your restaurant carefully.

That said, you can eat well without decimating the family fortune. Look for great self-serve buffet breakfasts dished up in most hostels and hotels, as well as the famous Norwegian *koldtbord* (cold table), which offers a fixed price for all-you-can-eat servings of pickled herring, salmon, meatballs, soup, bread, and crackers. Breakfast (*frokost*) is usually hearty bread, preserves, butter, cheese, eggs, and cold sliced meat and fish, washed down by unlimited coffee. Most restaurants offer daily lunch specials. Then there is the usual mélange of fast food joints, like the ubiquitous McDonald's and Burger King, pizzerias, and cafeterias. There's even a taco stand in the train station. Many grocery and department stores have cafeterias. Out on the Oslo streets you'll find *gatekjøkken* or street vendors selling pizza slices and the popular grilled *pølser,* a long hot dog overhanging a small bun. If you're driving back from a Sunday climbing trip and stop in a small town for a snack, a *pølser* and a Coke at the service station might be your only dining option.

Another way to save cash is to make half of your meals yourself. You can eat very well and cheaply by visiting the nearest Meny supermarket. Lots of fresh vegetables and fruits are available, along with good cheeses and meats.

Norway is famous for its strong black coffee, which is served everywhere. Its hearty coffee is a relief to anyone who has traveled in southern Europe where coffee is served in *petit* cups. Beer, on the other hand, is, like everything else here, very expensive. You can relax in the autumn sunshine at an open-air cafe at Aker Brygge fronting the Oslo harbor and sip perhaps the most expensive beer or *øl* in the world. That glass of amber brew, filled with bubbles rising to a frothy head, just emptied your wallet of 56 kroner or $8.00. And the six-pack you bought a few days ago—well, it set you back only twenty-five bucks. Yes, beer, the German staff of life, costs that much here . . . awwwkkk! Be sure to try a small glass of *aquavit,* a 40 percent proof liquor often used as a beer chaser.

If you're invited to someone's house for a meal, remember to thank the host by saying "Takk for matten," pronounced *tock for MAT-ten,* meaning "thanks for the food."

Cultural Experiences and Rest Days

Oslo, one of Europe's smallest capitals, is not an electrifying city like Paris or Florence, which zaps you with stunning architecture, astounding museums, and glorious boulevards. Instead, this sedate and thoroughly modern city grows on you, revealing bits and pieces of itself as you walk around. Its monuments are small and unassertive; the streets are busy, but not hectic. The skyline is unobtrusive against Nordmarka, a low mountain range north of the city. Oslo is a city one would characterize as comfortable, pleasant, civilized, clean, safe, and even quiet. Spend a week here, and you will quickly agree that Oslo is one of Europe's most beautiful and livable cities.

Oslo may be small in population but it's huge in size, encompassing more than 175 square miles, of which half consists of parks and open space. Forests, mountains, and the sea are ever present here, rising beyond blocks of apartments and wooden houses. A mountain trail, cross-country ski track, sandy beach, and granite cliff is never more than a twenty-minute ride away from you wherever you roam in Oslo.

The heart of Oslo is a broad street called Karl Johans Gate, named for King Karl Johan XIV, who ruled both Norway and Sweden in the nineteenth century. (*Gate,* pronounced *GAH-tuh,* means street in Norwegian.) The street runs southeast from the *Slottet* or Royal Palace to Oslo Sentralstasjon, the train station. Lining the street are restaurants, shops, a cathedral, the National Theater, the Parliament building, and Oslo University. The palace itself is, like the city, an unassuming edifice that embraces the common man. No iron-barred fence or stone wall encloses the palace, and no machine gun–armed soldiers patrol the perimeter. Instead, anyone can approach the palace, follow paths across its shady lawns, and picnic next to the flowery gardens.

Oslo boasts some superb museums, including the National Gallery, Munch Museum, Museum of Contemporary Art, Norwegian Folk Museum, and the Viking Ships Museum. The National Gallery houses an excellent collection of Nordic artists, including J. C. Dahl, Christian Krohg, Theodor Kittlesen, and Norway's most famous painter, Edvard Munch. Munch, pronounced *monk,* rendered his most famous painting, *The Scream,* on a seaside levee at Asgårdstrand south of Oslo. After viewing the Munch gallery, you'll want to walk across town to the Munch Museum and its huge collection of paintings, sketches, and drawings bequeathed to the city after his death in 1944. Kon-Tiki Museum and Fram (Explorer's Museum) are also well worth a visit.

Across the harbor on leafy Bygdøy Peninsula are five museums. The largest is the excellent Norwegian Folk Museum with 153 reconstructed buildings from across Norway, including a stave church from Gol, as well as fascinating exhibits from everyday Norwegian life. Nearby is Vikingskiphuset, the Viking Ship Museum. Inside the building sit three full-size Viking burial ships that were interred with royalty more than 1,100 years ago along the west shore of the Oslofjord. Excavated between 1867 and 1904, the ships yielded a trove of artifacts that richly detail the

Chris Fossli belays Henrik Bollingmo on *Catalonia* (6+) (5.10b/c) at Hauktjern crags.

age of the Vikings. The last arty place every Oslo visitor must see is seventy-nine-acre Frogner Park and its amazing garden of 212 bronze sculptures created by Gustav Vigeland. The compelling sculptures represent the stages of life, culminating in a 40-foot-high tower of writhing beings.

After you've climbed, visited museums, and walked all over downtown Oslo, you need to drive southwest along the indented shoreline of Oslofjord. The rocky coast, bordered by forested hills, offers lots of interesting towns, places, and lovely scenery. These include the Viking burial mounds at Borre; the Munch cottage at Asgårdstrand; and Tønsberg, considered the oldest town in Norway. Tønsberg, founded by Harald Hårgagre in 871, was prominent in Viking times and then in the Middle Ages, when its safe harbor made it a trading center. Little remains from those exciting times, but it's still worth a walkabout. Points of interest include the reno-

vated harbor front at Tønsberg Brygge and the old castle ruins of Slottsfjellet above the city, which were burned by the Swedes in 1536. Farther down the coast is the old whaling town of Sandefjord. It's worth stopping for a peek at Gaia, a replica Viking ship, that moors in the harbor. A couple of long, peninsular fingers of glacier-scraped granite, including aptly named World's End, poke south from here into the fjord. Drive out to the blunt tips for some scenic views of the sea lapping against humped bedrock granite and the concrete ruins of old German fortifications from World War II. Good bouldering and climbing is found on the area's small cliffs. The best is Oksåsen, with five sectors and more than seventy routes. Inland are even more cliffs, mostly unknown and unclimbed, that huddle against dark ponds and crown high ridges. It's all enough to keep you amused and interested for a few weeks.

Trip Planning Information

General description: Sport and traditional climbing on a variety of granite and volcanic cliffs.

Location: Around Oslo in south-central Norway.

Camping and accommodations: Lots of hotels, hostels, and rooms are found in the Oslo area, along with many campgrounds in the vicinity. Check at the *Norges Informasjonssenter* (Norwegian Information Center) by the city harbor for suggestions and reservations. Be warned that lodging is the most expensive part of your *Norsk* experience.

Climbing season: May through September is the best season. The summer months have lots of light and warm temperatures. October can be good too, but the weather begins to cool. Locals climb on the sunny cliffs on warm winter days, but that is a hit-or-miss proposition.

Restrictions and access issues: None. There is open access to all area cliffs. Remember to follow proper cliff etiquette by following access trails, not cutting down or damaging trees and vegetation at the base or on cliff faces, and picking up any and all trash.

Guidebooks: The main Oslo climbing guide is *Fører for Oslo,* published by Kolsås Klatreklubb. It's available at Oslo climbing shops and gyms, including Tyrili Klatreklubb. Also the Norwegian Web site www.steepstone.com offers many topos to Oslo sport crags.

Services and shops: All services are found in Oslo. There are also several climbing shops and gyms.

Emergency services: For emergency services dial 113. For police dial 112.

Nearby climbing areas: This guide includes three of the best Oslo crags. Many others are found, including Vardåsen, Fjell, Hellerud, Løkenhavna, Sørkedalen, and Fetsund. Sørkedalen is one of Oslo's best sport crags for hard routes. Find topos and directions in Norwegian to these crags at www.steep stone.com. Look under *førere* for guides. Other nearby cliffs are Andersnatten and crags near Drammen and Sandefjord.

Nearby attractions: There is no shortage of things to do and see around Oslo. Some highlights include Akershus Slott og Festning, a renovated thirteenth-century castle; the Museum of Contemporary Art (Museet for Santidskunst); the National Gallery of Art (Nasjonalgalleriet); Kon-Tiki Museet, a museum detailing Thor Heyerdahl's crossing of the Pacific; Vikingskiphuset, the famous Viking Ship Museum on Bygdøy Peninsula; Frogner Park, with 212 sculptures by artist Gustav Vigeland; and the Munch Museum, with many paintings, drawings, and prints by the famous artist.

Obtain maps, free information, and accommodation suggestions at the *Norges*

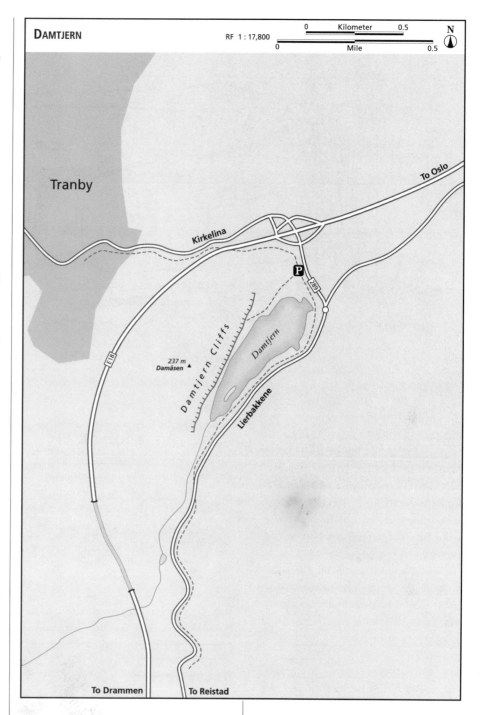

Informasjonssenter, the main tourist information office in Oslo. The center is housed in an old train station on the west side of the waterfront in downtown Oslo. Purchase the useful Oslo Card here, which gives free admittance to all museums, unlimited free travel on the city transport system, and free on-street parking at metered spaces, as well as discounts in shops and restaurants. The card can be bought for periods of twenty-four, forty-eight, or seventy-two hours.

Finding the areas: Detailed directions to each of the three described climbing areas are found under each respective area.

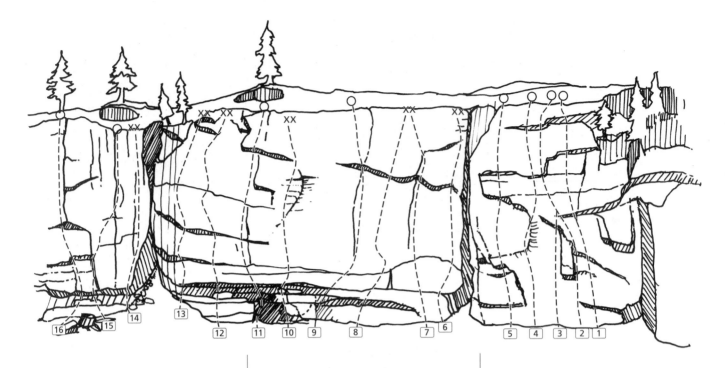

Damtjern

The long cliff Damtjern looms above the west shore of Lake Damtjern, nestled among rounded hills just off the E18 southwest of Oslo. The lake, its edges fringed with lily pads, drops darkly and deeply below the rocky shoreline. A dense fir and pine forest crowds the shoreline, hiding much of the cliff behind a wall of greenery.

The southeast-facing cliff, composed of durable Drammen granite, is mostly vertical, although some routes are slightly overhanging. The abrupt cliff, cleaved and chiseled by a passing glacier, is creased by shallow crack systems. The climbing is mostly on bolted faces up to 70 feet high, using edges, crimps, sidepulls, slopers, and horizontal cracks. A few vertical crack climbs are also found.

An access path skirts the cliff base from the north (right) to its south end. A couple of high ledges require scrambling. The narrow ledge section under *Marathon* is extremely exposed and dangerous. Use caution and a rope if necessary when traversing this ledge, which is 50 feet above the lake. "If you fall—jump!" says local climber Chris Fossli. "The water is very deep. People have been killed who fell off the ledge and landed on the rocks below." One climber, however, plunged 40 feet off the right side of the ledge and landed in

trees and soft ground. He walked away with only scratches.

Finding the cliff: Drive about 25 kilometers southwest from Oslo on the E18 highway toward Drammen. Exit onto RV289 toward Tranby and Liertoppen, going under the highway. Park on the right shoulder of the road (289) after 500 feet near a gate. (Parking lot GPS: N59° 48.376' E10° 17.315'.)

Follow a path southwest through the forest on the north side of the lake to a good, wide trail. Walk south past a red cottage, and continue on a rougher path to the right side of the cliff. Walking time from car to cliff is a little more than five minutes.

Baker Sector

This is the cliff's right-hand sector, with the first routes beginning just right of where the access trail reaches the cliff. Two more routes—*Fange i egen kropp* (7+) and *Diva* (7+) are right of route #1. Routes are described from right to left.

1. Begin . . . End (8-) (5.12a/b) 7 bolts to 2-bolt anchor.

2. Sikre perioder (7+) (5.11d) Up a shallow left-facing corner to a thin roof to a vertical wall. 7 bolts to 2-bolt anchor.

3. Bland edle stener og lekre jenter (8) (5.12b/c) Thin face start. 7 bolts to 2-bolt anchor.

4. Baker for smed (7-/7) (5.11a/b) Recommended. 7 bolts to 2-bolt anchor.

5. Batman (7+) (5.11d) First route right of crack system where the trail reaches the cliff. 7 bolts to 2-bolt anchor.

6. Snikene kommer (7) (5.11b) Left of crack system. 7 bolts to 2-bolt anchor.

7. Kaptein Jazz (7+/8-) (5.11d/12a) Excellent route up vertical wall. 7 bolts to 2-bolt anchor.

8. Fluge på veggan (8-) (5.12a/b) Roof start. 8 bolts to 2-bolt anchor (same as *Kaptein Jazz*).

9. Dala Rambo (8-) (5.12a/b) 7 bolts to 2-bolt anchor.

10. Damios (8) (5.12b/c) Over tiered roofs then up wall right of a black streak. 6 bolts to 2-bolt anchor under a tree at the cliff top.

11. Algene kommer (7+) (5.11c/d) Pull over the big roof to start, then motor up and right. 8 bolts to 2-bolt anchor.

12. Trivsel uten snuten (6+) (5.10b) Over the left side of the long, low roof to start, then up steep rock between two streaks. 7 bolts to 2-bolt anchor.

13. Project Just right of the mossy crack in a narrow right-facing corner. 7 bolts to 2-bolt anchor.

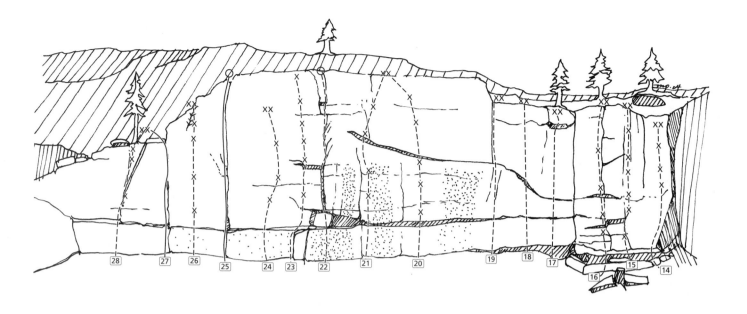

Vegglus Sector

This sector in the midsection of the cliff has mostly vertical face routes and a couple good crack lines. Routes are described from right to left.

14. Project Left of corner.

15. Harakiri Sviskerud (7-/7) (5.11a/b) Bolted line along a thin crack system to a 2-bolt anchor.

16. Kykkeliky (7) (5.11b) Start just left of #15. Face climb directly up to and along a thin crack to a 2-bolt anchor.

17. Sørken by Night (7-) (5.11a) Bolt and gear route over a small roof to a 2-bolt anchor below a tree.

18. Project (7?) Face climb with bolts to a 2-bolt anchor.

19. Hardt arbeid (7) (5.11b/c) Over the roof, then up to a thin crack. Bolts and gear.

20. Pansatt øye (7+) (5.11d) 5 bolts to 2-bolt anchor.

21. Shrekk sprekk (7+) (5.11d) Follow a couple thin crack systems up right. 4 bolts to 2-bolt anchor. **Rack:** Some small to medium Friends and large Stoppers.

22. Klidøl'n (5+) (5.8) Work up a shallow left-facing corner, and continue up the crack system above. **Rack:** Bring small to medium gear.

23. Vegglus (7+) (5.11d) Excellent! Face climb to the left side of a thin roof, then up the vertical face. 4 bolts to 1-bolt anchor.

24. Revejakta (9-) (5.13b/c) First ascent by Håkon Hansen in 1988. Good thin and sustained face climbing. 4 bolts to 2-bolt anchor.

25. Kontoristen (7+) (5.11d) Great thin crack route to a ledge. **Rack:** Small to medium Friends and Stoppers.

26. Permafrost (8-/8) (5.12b/c) 4 bolts to 2-bolt anchor on leaning ledge.

27. Cool Hand Luke (6+) (5.10a) Short crack climb. **Rack:** Small to medium gear.

28. Totalisten (7) (5.11b/c) Short route to ledge. 4 bolts to 2-bolt anchor.

29. Gemini (6+) (5.10a) 2 bolts.

30. Bare bull (8-) (5.12a/b) Thin face right of a crack. 4 bolts to 2-bolt anchor.

31. Odin Margin (6+) (5.10a) Great crack route. Bring Stoppers and small to medium Friends.

32. Fingra fra kinten (7) (5.11b) Excellent thin crack to 2-bolt anchor on ledge.

33. Sloppy Joe (6+) (5.10a) Fun route. 3 bolts to 2-bolt anchor on ledge (#32's anchors).

· LAKE ·

34. Naken lunsj (8-) (5.12a) 4 bolts to 2-bolt anchor.

35. Rogalandsmafiaen (7+/8-) (5.11d/12a) 4 bolts to 2-bolt anchor.

36. Den første musejakta (8-) (5.12a) 3 bolts to 2-bolt anchor.

37. Susis sovepose (8) (5.12b/c) Best route on this cliff sector. 4 bolts to a tree anchor.

38. Svenskedødaren (8) (5.12b/c) 4 bolts to 2-bolt anchor.

39. Matrimonimo (8) (5.12b/c) 3 bolts to 2-bolt anchor.

40. Sorgentri (6+) (5.10a) Left-angling crack.

Marathon Sector

This stunning cliff section, rising above a narrow ledge halfway up the cliff, offers numerous hard lines up the slightly over-hanging wall. The routes are accessed from the right by bouldering over a rock step and then traversing across the ledge. A bolt belay anchor is in the middle of the ledge and can be clipped for safety. Use caution since the ledge is very exposed, and a fall could be fatal.

41. Rå makt (8-) (5.12a) Start off the right side of the ledge, and end direct up the final headwall.

42. Sonic Youth (8+) (5.12d/13a) Begin on #41, and veer left at the top.

43. Vestlandsfanden (9) (5.13b/c) Smooth face. 5 bolts to 2-bolt anchor.

44. Stive dempere (8+) (5.12d/13a) Recommended. Start off the ledge just left of a streak.

45. Draumkvedet (9/9+) (5.13d/14a) Project.

46. Marathon (9) (5.13d) First ascent by Per Hustad in 1988. Excellent hard route directly up the slightly overhanging face. Belay from the bolt on the ledge. 5 bolts to 2-bolt anchor.

47. Project

48. Røya (7+) (5.11d) Grooves and cracks left of *Marathon*.

49. Styrkebeltet (8 A0) (5.12c/d A0) Finish to anchors just above a small roof.

50. Roya (8+) (5.12d/13a) End at #49's anchors.

51. Ayatollah (9-) (5.13c) Up good steep rock to anchors above the left side of the narrow roof.

52. Project

Microkosmos Sector, the next cliff section down and left from the ledge and *Marathon,* offers a dozen good, long routes not described here. Most are 5.12s up vertical stone. Check the comprehensive guide for topos and ratings.

Kolsås

Øvre Sydstup (Upper South Wall)

Kolsås lifts its distinctive bulky shape above the valleys, hills, and suburbs of southwest Oslo. Several cliff bands line the mountain, but the best and most popular climbing is on Øvre Sydstup or the Upper South Wall, the highest cliff that lies just below the rounded summit. The cliffs on Kolsås, one of Oslo's oldest climbing areas, offer more than 200 routes. A steep but good trail winds up the mountain's south flank to its summit and the cliff top. The hike is worth the effort not only for the superb climbing, but also for the stunning views of Oslo, with its square white buildings tucked among rounded hills and the undulating coastline of the Oslofjord.

Kolsås is an unusual mountain composed of many different rock types, including slate, conglomerate, basalt, sandstone, and a rare rhombeporphyry. Volcanic activity formed many of the mountain's alternating cliff bands. Nedra Sydstup was formed by a thick layer of lava that cooled into black basalt. The top of the mountain is composed of porphyry, with its characteristic feldspar crystals. A total of fourteen separate lava flows were deposited before prolonged periods of erosion and glaciation dissected and smoothed the mountain, erasing most of the lava flows. After the last ice age, only one layer of rhombeporphyry and one layer of basalt remained on Kolsås. Øvre Sydstup is composed of the unique rhombeporphyry.

The rock offers lots of edges and cracks and has good friction qualities. The cliff is a traditional area, whereas the others on Kolsås are bolted. Most of the routes follow crack systems that protect well with wired nuts and small cams. The top of the cliff, a popular viewpoint, has several bolt anchors for setting up topropes and belays or rappelling to the cliff base.

Finding the cliff: Øvre Sydstup is visible atop Kolsås from the E18 highway, which runs southwest from Oslo toward Drammen. Kolsås is in the suburb of Bærum, about 14 kilometers west of Oslo center. The easiest way to the cliff is to

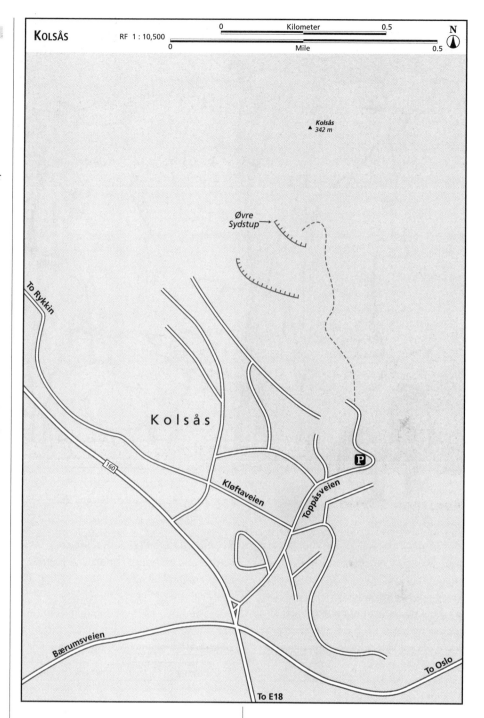

drive southwest from downtown Oslo on the four-lane E18 highway. Exit right onto the E16, and drive northwest through a tunnel. After the tunnel take the next exit onto Bærumsveien (*veien* means "street"). Exit right, labeled KIRKURUA and BUKKESTUA, and drive uphill on Bærumsveien to an intersection with a traffic light and roundabout. The cliff, Øvre Sydstup, is visible from here, just below the summit of Kolsås. Turn left onto Brynsveien, take an immediate right onto Toppåsveien, and drive uphill to a

small parking lot on the left. You can also park on the right shoulder of the road next to the start of the access trail.

If you don't have a car, take the subway to Hauger Stasjon just north of the roundabout. Ask at Oslo Centralstasjon to find the right train.

From the parking area cross the street, and hike uphill through the forest on the 2-mile-long, blue-marked trail (*turvei*) to the summit of Kolsås and the cliff top. Hiking time is about thirty minutes.

To reach the base of the cliff, rappel from fixed bolt anchors (two sets) to the base. A doubled 200-foot (60-meter) rope barely reaches the ground. Be careful not to rappel off the end of the rope; better yet, use two ropes. You can also easily hike down the left side when facing out to the base of *Hollywood*.

Routes are listed from right to left at the cliff base.

1. Kjokkentrappa *(The Kitchen Stairs)* (5) (5.7) Excellent and recommended. Up a crack to *Gårdsplassen (The Yard)*, a big ledge on the right side of the crag. Easy to toprope.

2. Juristen *(The Lawyer)* (3+) (5.4) Another good climb. A left-leaning crack right of *Hollywood*.

3. Hollywood (4+) (5.5) A must-do, megaclassic Norwegian route and perhaps the most climbed route in *Norge*. Climb a short chimney (4+) and then narrow ledges and thin cracks in the middle of the big slab. Work up a beautiful crack on the right to a 2-bolt anchor atop the cliff.

4. Gunnerg (4+) (5.5) Climb *Hollywood* to the thin horizontal seams in the slab. Then follow a crack up left (3+) to a chimney and the top.

5. Bloodway (6+) (5.10b) Climb up easy to moderate rock to a prominent thin crack through a headwall. Use gear (medium Friends) for anchors at the top.

6. Sunset Boulevard (7) (5.11a) Difficult friction climbing. Not very well protected but a good toprope.

7. Beverly Hills (7-) (5.10c/d) Up Y cracks on the left side of the great slab.

8. Birkeland's Renne *(Birkeland's Chimney)* (3) (5.3) Up a chimney to a crack to the top of a pillar. Climb small steps up right to a slab (3), then up a slab to the left (3-) behind a block, and finish up a chimney.

9. Devil's Cochet (6+) (5.10b/c) Start in a big dihedral. Climb up the dihedral 20 feet, then left to a crack. Climb the crack (6) past a small roof (6+). Easier rock leads to the top.

Hauktjern

Hauktjern, translated "Hawk Lake," is another one of the best and most popular Oslo areas. The east-facing cliffs, stretching above the long, narrow lake, offer more than 150 routes, including many moderate climbs. The area consists of several cliffs that range from 35 to 110 feet high. The cliffs, composed of a solid billion-year-old gneiss, offer sharp holds, crimps, and thin edges on mostly vertical to slightly over-hanging walls. The easier routes ascend slabs. A few good crack climbs are also found. The area, reached by a delightful hike through woods, has a good atmos-phere next to the idyllic lake with lots of solitude and silence, although it is busy with climbers on weekends.

Finding the cliff: Hauktjern is in Østmarka on the southeast side of Oslo. From downtown Oslo drive the E6 south. Exit at signs to Abildso and Boler, and go over the highway to Østensjøveien. Follow the street northeast past a lake to an inter-section with a stoplight roundabout, and turn right toward Boler on Eterveien. At the top of a hill, go left when the road dead-ends against General Ruges Veien. Follow the road northeast to a right turn to Østmarkveien, and go uphill a short distance (about 1 kilometer). Park at a large parking area on the right.

The cliff lies about 2.5 kilometers northeast from the parking lot. Hiking time is thirty minutes. Follow a wide trail (used for cross-country skiing in winter) for a short distance on the west side of Ulsrudvannet Lake and then through woods to a junction. Take the second left (the first wide cross-country ski trail bor-dered with street lights to the left) toward Mariholtet and Haugdrud. Follow the trail under a stone bridge, and drop down a hill to the north end of Nøklevann, a long

lake. Following signs to Sarabråten, hike around the lake's end and its northeast shore and then up a hill to Sarabråten ruins (an old stop on the original Stockholm-to-Oslo road). Turn left here on a lesser trail marked HAUKTJERN and then DRONNIGVEIEN. At the top of the

hill, you get a glimpse north to the cliffs. Follow the trail uphill to a junction in a saddle with a monument on the right. Go straight through the junction, then down a short hill to the lake. Turn left, and follow the climber's path along the shoreline to the base of the cliff and the first routes.

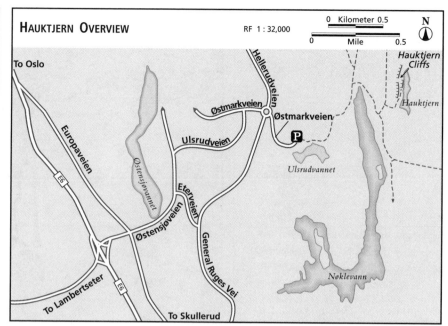

HAUKTJERN OVERVIEW   RF 1 : 32,000

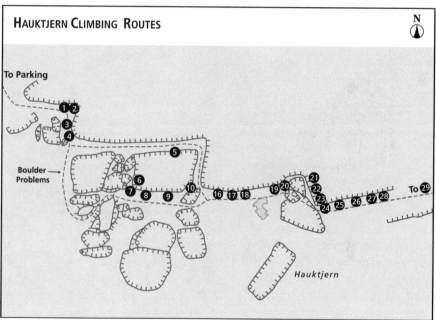

HAUKTJERN CLIMBING ROUTES

These first four routes are by an obvious dihedral on the second set of cliffs encountered after the access trail reaches the cliff. Routes are described from left to right.

1. Sånn-ja (7-) (5.10d/11a) Fun but pumpy line up flakes and laybacks along left-angling crack system left of a dihedral. 4 bolts to 2-bolt anchor. Wires may be used to supplement bolts. First bolt is a spinner.

2. Olavsrisset *(Olav's Crack)* (5+) (5.8+) Excellent classic established in 1976. Jam and stem up double cracks in the perfect dihedral to a 2-bolt anchor. **Rack:** Stoppers and Friends.

3. Arveprinsen (7-) (5.10d/11a) The face just right of the corner. Natural gear.

4. Halvveis (5) (5.7) One of the easier routes here. Edge up a slab to anchors. 3 bolts to 2-bolt anchor. The short bolt-protected headwall above the anchors is 8 (5.12c).

The following route is in the narrow corridor that begins just right of #4. Other routes are on the steep left wall and on the opposite slab.

5. Zappfes smørbrød (4–) (5.4) No topo. A fun, easy route up the obvious crack system up the slab on the corridor's right side to a 2-bolt anchor. A few Stoppers protect the route. Other routes are found on the slab and are easily toproped from the anchors.

These routes ascend the south and east faces of a freestanding pillar that faces the lake. Routes are described from left to right.

6. Lærlingen (7–) (5.10d/11a) South face of freestanding pillar and left of the outside arête. 6 bolts to 2-bolt anchor.

7. Pu på hjørnet (8/8+) (5.12d/13a) Joins *Lærlingen* after bolt #3. 7 bolts to 2-bolt anchor.

8. Sadomaoisten (8+) (5.13a/b) On the left side of the pillar's east face. 7 bolts to 2-bolt anchor.

9. Senterpartiert (7) (5.11b) Follow staple bolts up the face center. 6 bolts to 2-bolt anchor.

10. Venstre (7–) (5.10d/11a) Recommended. 7 bolts to 2-bolt anchor.

11. Høyre (7–) (5.10d/11a) Far right side of the face. The anchors are missing because of a loose block at the top. Traverse left to lower off anchors. 9 bolts to 2-bolt anchor.

The following routes are in the corridor that starts right of the pillar.

12. Speaker's Corner (4+) (5.5) No topo. Crack up the big dihedral on the right at the end of the corridor.

13. Kolibrien (6–) (5.9) No topo. Good route. Mixed gear and bolt route up the right-hand wall of the corridor. 3 bolts to 2-bolt anchor. **Rack:** TCUs and Stoppers protect the upper part of route.

14. Måken Jonathan (7–) (5.10d) Popular line up the outside edge of the corridor. 5 bolts to 2-bolt anchor.

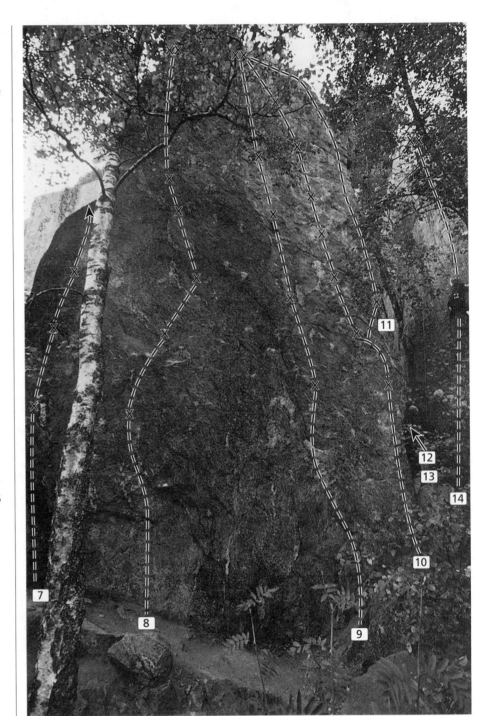

This wide wall, facing the lake, offers an excellent selection of harder routes. Routes are described left to right beginning at the corridor's left edge.

15. Du skrattade, du skal dö (8/8+) (5.12c/d) No topo. 8 bolts to 2-bolt anchor.

16. Vråtter (8) (5.12b/c) Excellent and recommended. Laybacking moves up a right-angling thin crack to a corner finish. 9 bolts to 2-bolt anchor.

17. Gammel jomfru (9-) (5.13b) 9 bolts to 2-bolt anchor.

18. Normalveien (8+/9-) (5.13b) The "Normal Way." Recommended. 8 bolts to 2-bolt anchor.

19. A muerte (8+) (5.13a) 9 bolts to 2-bolt anchor.

20. Prosessen (7+/8-) (5.12d/13a) Edge of an arête to a ledge to a face finish. 11 bolts to 2-bolt anchor.

Routes are up a narrow, south-facing slab right of the dihedral.

21. Sjelefred (6) (5.10a) Long line up the slab just right of the crack. 8 bolts to 2-bolt anchor.

22. Forsvinningsnummeret (6) (5.10a) Fun and popular. 5 bolts to 2-bolt anchor.

23. Paglia Orba (7-) (5.10d/11a) Bolts and gear to *Nesa* anchor.

The following are on the steep face right of the slab.

24. Nesa (6+) (5.10b) Begin on the far left side of the face around right from the slab. Climb a crack then left around a roof. Finish up a blunt arête. 4 bolts to 2-bolt anchor. **Rack:** Stoppers and small to medium Friends.

25. Viskøse fingre (7-) (5.10c) Crack up a corner to a traverse under a long, right-angling roof.

26. Bruk hidet bedre (8) (5.12b/c) 8 bolts to 2-bolt chain anchors.

27. Det gyldne snitt (8-) (5.12a/b) Thin, right-angling crack climb. **Rack:** Wires, TCUs, and small Friends.

28. Barske Glæder (8-) (5.12a/b)

The last route is a brilliant crack and corner climb on the cliff band (right of #28) that drops directly from the trail to the lake. Walk north from #28, and locate the top of an obvious right-facing dihedral. Fix a rope from bolts, and rappel to a large boulder in the lake at the dihedral base.

29. Catalonia (6+) (5.10b/c) No topo. Layback up the perfect dihedral. **Rack:** Wired nuts and small to medium cams.

ANDERSNATTEN

■ OVERVIEW

Andersnatten, in the Eggedal Valley west of Oslo, is an immense peak rimmed by glacier-scraped walls. The mountain towers above the wide U-shaped valley below, which cradles farms with white houses and red barns and the long Lake Soneren. Rounded peaks, also smoothed by glaciers, surround Andersnatten's abrupt cliffed rampart. Dense forests of pine, spruce, and fir blanket the mountain slopes below timberline, spilling down to green valley pastures.

The mountain's prominent southeast-facing cliff, Sørøstveggen, offers most of the climbing on Andersnatten, although Sørvestveggan, a smaller cliff seen from the lake at the parking area, has a couple routes. Sørøstveggen ranges in height from 200 feet on its slabby left side to more than 600 feet on the right.

The most distinctive cliff features are the immense slabs along the base of the wall and a long white stripe that divides the left-hand slabs from the steeper right side. The cliff is composed of a compact, solid gneiss, although it is shattered and broken in places. More than twenty routes ascend the cliff, but many are seldom climbed and are now overgrown with vegetation. Most of the routes on the left side are steep slab climbs, whereas the more difficult routes on the bigger right-hand wall are vertical crack and face climbs. The right side also has more loose rock. Use caution when climbing.

The most popular route and the only long one described in this guide on this immense face is *Den Hvite Stripa* or *The White Stripe*. This six-pitch route is a beautiful, classic, face-climbing line up the white stripe. In winter water on the stripe freezes into a technical ice route.

Andersnatten naturally figures in many local fairy tales since the massive mountain dominates the surrounding landscape. In the old days the mountain was considered bad fortune and associated with the devil and evil. The famed Norwegian artist Theodor Kittlesen, who

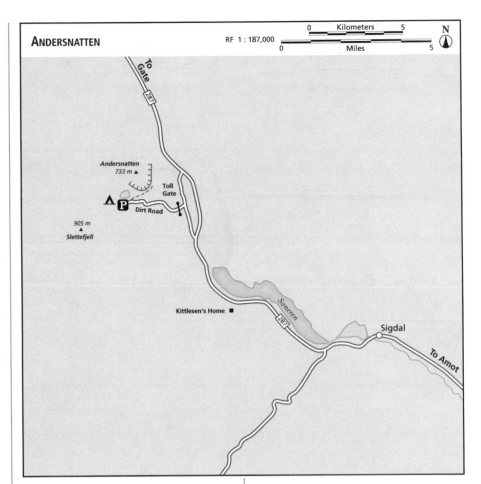

lived and painted by Lake Soneren southeast of the the peak, re-created some of these folk myths in his paintings and drawings. One local legend directly relates to Andersnatten's most prominent climbing feature: the white stripe. Anders, a tough mountain man, once skied to the top of the mountain, where he met a big bad troll who blocked his descent route. Since he had no other escape, Anders turned his tips downward and skied over the cliff, leaving a white stripe down the east face as a mark of his plunge. Geologists, however, use a more pedestrian explanation, saying that the stripe formed from running water that seeps off the summit wetland.

Rack, Protection, and Descent

Most routes require a general rack with a set of Friends, set of TCUs, set of wired nuts, set of brass nuts, a dozen quickdraws, two ropes, and helmets. Fixed bolt anchors and bolt protection are found on many of

the climbs. Some of the old bolts found on routes are unsafe, having deteriorated in the severe weather here. Use caution, and never trust a single bolt at a belay. Most routes are adequately protected, although the lower slabs are sparsely protected.

The usual descent is two rappels from anchors on the left side of the wall. Go south along the cliff top, keeping close to the cliff edge. If you can find the top of *Byger* on the left side of the face, you can make two 150-foot rappels to the cliff base. If you continue farther south, look for a natural scrambling way down where the wall is at its lowest angle. You'll have to make a single rappel from a tree to easier rock below. Be extremely careful on the descent if the rock is wet or it's raining.

Seasons and Weather

Andersnatten lies at a relatively high elevation, so it is subject to severe weather. The climbing season basically runs from May until the end of September or early

Anderstatten rises behind a farmhouse near Lake Soneren.

October, depending on when the snow begins to fly. The season starts when the snow has melted back, especially on the cliff top, and the wall dries out. Be prepared for rain in summer, although it is often dry and warm.

Climbing History

Andersnatten, along with Kolsås in Oslo, is one of the most important cliffs in the history of Norwegian climbing. In 1943 *Sydøstveggen,* the first route on Andersnatten, was climbed by Einer Hoff Hansen and Egmont Nørregaard. Although seldom climbed now, this traversing route was a superb bit of climbing for the time. Most of the routes were established in the 1980s, including *Den Hvite Stripa* (VI) (5.10a/b). This classic Norwegian line was established by Marius Morstad and Ralph Høibakk in 1982.

Camping, Accommodations, and Services

Andersnatten is in a rural region of mountains, forests, small farms, and villages, so services and accommodation choices are limited. Check in Amot and Sigdal, the closest towns, for accommodations. Both towns also offer basic services, including gas, groceries, and restaurants. The area is an easy drive from Oslo, so you can also stay there and drive over for the day.

Excellent free but primitive camping is found by the small lake at the road's end below the cliff. A pit toilet is also here. Bring your own water, or use other water purification techniques.

Cultural Experiences and Rest Days

Andersnatten lies directly west of Oslo in the Eggedal region of the Sigdal Kommune in the county of Buskerud. This

area is famous for its stunning natural beauty, with broad valleys and high, rounded mountains. This beauty has long been an inspiration for Norwegian artists, including Christian Skredsvig and Theodor Kittlesen. Kittlesen, who lived at his home Lauvlia beside Lake Soneren, painted evocative landscapes of the area, including many of Andersnatten, his favorite mountain, as well his famous paintings of trolls. His house is open for tours. Also stop by the Sigdal and Eggedal Museum in Prestfoss on the east end of Lake Soneren. This unique museum re-creates Norway's historic and cultural past with various exhibitions, living history programs, folk music, and traditional foods.

Trip Planning Information

General description: Andersnatten's southeast face is an excellent, easily accessible wall with slab and face routes, including the Norwegian classic *Den Hvite Stripa.*

Location: West of Oslo in Eggedal.

Camping and accommodations: Excellent free camping is found by the lake at the end of the road. Bring water. Other accommodations are found in nearby towns, including Amot. The cliff is easily reached from Oslo on a day trip, so you can avoid camping.

Climbing season: May through September. The routes might be wet early in the season, depending on the previous winter's snowfall. *Den Hvite Stripa* is also a great technical ice climb in winter.

Restrictions and access issues: None. The access road to the parking lot is private. Pay a toll at a self-serve kiosk before driving up.

Guidebooks: *Oslo Climbing Guide,* available at Oslo climbing shops and gyms, including Tyrili Klatresenter in Oslo (Tel: 22 67 28 44) (www.gekkoklatring.no/).

Services and shops: Services, including food and lodging, are found in nearby local villages. Amot and Sigdal are the nearest towns.

Emergency services: For emergency services dial 113. For police dial 112. The nearest hospitals (*sykehus*) are in Drammen and Hønefoss.

Nearby climbing areas: The nearest developed cliffs are the many sport and traditional crags around Oslo to the east.

Nearby attractions: The Eggedal and Sigdal area is known for its beautiful mountain scenery and history. Visit the Theodor Kittlesen Home Lauvlia, Sigdal and Eggedal Museum, Christian Skredsvig Home Hagan, Folk Music Center, and Eggedal Mølle.

Finding the area: From Oslo drive southwest on E18 to Drammen, and exit west onto E134; alternately, exit onto highway 283 on the north side of Drammen. Continue west toward Hokksund, and look for signs toward Amot and highway 35. Go north on highway 35 to Amot, and turn northeast onto highway 287 toward Eggedal past Soneren Lake. Just before

Chris Fossli and Einer Hoff Hansen on *Den Hvite Stripa* (6) (5.10a).

Hole Bridge (*brua*), turn left onto a narrow road. Drive 1 kilometer through farms, and turn left. Pay a fee at a self-serve pay station to travel the private road. Follow the dirt road uphill to a parking lot on the south side of the mountain. Driving time from Oslo is one and a half to two hours.

To reach the cliff base, follow a trail that begins on the north side of the park-ing area. It passes left of the only cabin at the lake. The start might be hard to find. Follow the trail uphill for about a mile through the forest to the base of the east face. It's easy to lose the track, so keep a keen eye out for turns and switchbacks. If you hike north up the slope, you will reach the face. Hiking time is twenty to thirty minutes.

1. Den Hvite Stripa *(The White Stripe)* (6)
(5.10a) 6 pitches. 820 feet. Three to five
hours. Classic route up the obvious white
stripe. The lower section is adequately
protected with bolts but does feel runout
at times. Begin by descending from the
trail high point below the south side of
the face to the base of the white stripe.
Scramble up easy slabs until you find a
belay. **Pitch 1:** Face climb (5.9) up the
stripe past bolts to a belay stance under
the long arching roof. 130 feet. **Pitch 2:**
Step over the roof, and climb up left
(5.9+) along the stripe, using bolts for pro
to a bolted belay stance. 130 feet. **Pitch 3:**
More excellent, bolted climbing (5.10a/b)
continues up the stripe, passing a horizontal break to a small angling belay ledge.
115 feet. **Pitch 4:** The wall steepens above
here, and the route begins to wander. Pay
attention to keep on route by following
the easiest course. Climb up right away
from the stripe along a ramp system, then
up some thin corners (5.8). Work back
left under the big roof, and climb over
it on the left. Climb up right to a
belay under another long narrow roof. 130
feet. **Pitch 5:** Traverse left under the roof
and then over it. Face climb (5.8) up and
move left again under another narrow
roof, then back right along a crack system
to a belay on a high ledge. 150 feet. **Pitch
6:** Follow a crack system alongside the
stripe (5.7), then up right along a ramp to
easy climbing and the cliff top right of the
stripe. 130 feet.

Left of *Den Hvite Stripa* are several other routes. Scramble up the easy slab at the bottom of the face to start all the routes. From left to right these are:

2. Friendly (V+) (5.8) 2 pitches. Good route. The route climbs the far left side of the wall. **Pitch 1:** Climb an obvious right-facing dihedral to a belay shelf with a pine tree anchor (tie off with a sling). **Pitch 2:** Face climb up and left to a short corner to the cliff top. **Descent:** Make two 150-foot rappels down *Byger*. **Rack:** A selection of Friends, Stoppers, and slings.

3. Byger (VI-) (5.9) 2 pitches. Fun moderate route on clean rock. Begin about 25 feet right of *Friendly*. **Pitch 1:** Face climb to a thin corner and then up left across a slanting crack to the belay tree on *Friendly's* ledge. **Pitch 2:** Climb up and right along a leaning corner to a right-

facing corner on the right side of a long roof. Belay from a tree up left. **Descent:** Make two 150-foot rappels from trees to the route base. **Rack:** Small Friends and TCUS along with wired nuts.

4. Salatbar (VI) (5.9+) 3 pitches. Start about 60 feet right of *Byger* and right of a dihedral. **Pitch 1:** Climb the right-facing dihedral to the base of three short corners. Climb the left-hand corner to a belay stance. **Pitch 2:** Work up a crack to a steep section, and face climb (VI) to a belay. **Pitch 3:** Climb a corner, then work up between two roofs and belay on the cliff top. **Descent:** Make two 150-foot rappels down *Byger*. **Rack:** RPs, TCUs, Friends, and Stoppers.

5. Sikringskost (VI) (5.9+) 2 pitches. The route starts about 100 feet right of *Salatbar* by some clumps of grass on the light-

colored slab. **Pitch 1:** Face climb up to a thin, right-facing corner (VI). Above, move up right and belay under a slanting roof. **Pitch 2:** Continue up right under the roof system and then up a right-facing corner (V+) at its end. Pass the left side of a long, narrow roof, scale a short headwall and slab, and then go up right to the top of the cliff. **Descent:** Make two 150-foot rappels down *Byger*. **Rack:** TCUs, Friends, and Stoppers.

More routes are found on the steep face right of *Den Hvite Stripa*. Topos for these are found in the Oslo climbing guidebook. A newer bolted sport route ascends the steep slab left of *Den Hvite Stripa* in four or five long pitches. Ask at the Tyrili Klatresenter in Oslo for beta and information on these and other new routes.

HÆGEFJELL

■ OVERVIEW

Hægefjell, lying in the mountainous Nissedal region of south-central Norway, is a rounded dome with an immense south-facing wall composed of steep slabs and faces stained with vertical water streaks. Other well-defined features on this long, almost 2,000-foot-high wall include cracks systems, huge dihedrals, and flakes. The cliff overlooks a wide valley dotted with shallow lakes, ringed by evergreen forests, and flanked by glacier-scraped mountains. Moose, called *elg* in Norwegian, wade through the lakes and marshes. Giant boulders, fallen from the cliff, scatter along the road/trail below the western half of the wall. Chris Fossli, a leading Norwegian climber, describes 3,350-foot-high (1,021-meter) Hægefjell and the surrounding Nissedal area as a "mini-Yosemite"—an apt description for one of southern Norway's best and most beautiful climbing areas.

Hægefjell, one of several cliffs in the area, is very popular with Scandinavian climbers because of its perfect granite, easy access, short approach, and wide assortment of classic routes that range in difficulty from moderate to difficult. This is not a beginner's area, nor is it for the sport climber. But if your pleasure is long, elegant routes on stellar granite, then this is the place for you. It's also a great place to experience solitude and beauty on a big wall in a wilderness setting. Besides long routes, the area also offers excellent bouldering on large granite blocks found below the cliff face. The best boulders are along the closed road west of the parking area.

The compact, hard granite was smoothed, shaped, and quarried by thick ice sheets that have periodically blanketed Norway. The rock is characterized by few crack systems, numerous handholds from crimps to jugs, smooth vertical faces, steep friction slabs, and arching, blocky roofs.

This guide describes four of the best classic routes on Hægefjell. Other recommended routes include *Sternschnuppe* (5.8),

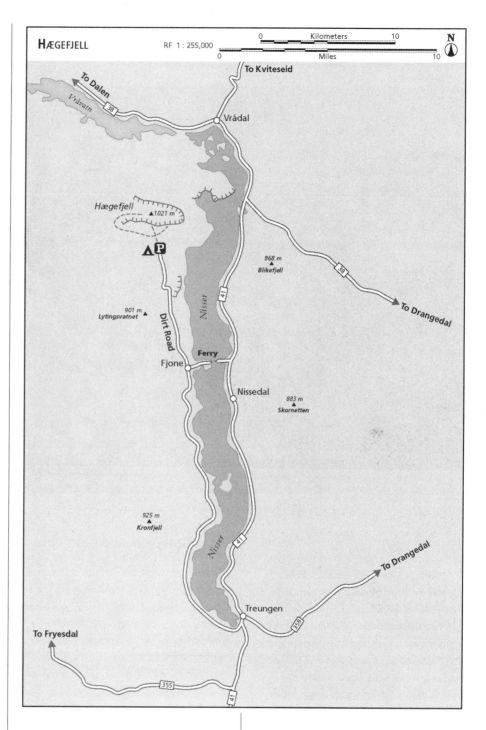

Tyrion (5.11a), *Banana Split around the Corner* (5.10d), *Slow Motion* (5.11a A1), *Hoph Zing* (5.10a), and *Feuervogel* (5.10d). *Sternschnuppe* ascends slabs and cracks left of *Via Lara*. *Tyrion* is an older classic that winds up the central wall. *Banana Split* is a good 7-pitch line up the cliff left of *Tyrion*. *Hoph Zing* offers fine climbing on its 8 pitches just right of *Mot Sola*. The route, established by Marius Olsen, Kjetil Grimsæth, and Marius Grimsæth in 2000, has bolted belay/rappel stations, making

for a quick descent. *Feuervogel* is a 7-pitch line up the sweeping slab on the far left side of the wall. Topos and route descriptions in Norwegian for these and other Hægefjell routes are found at the Web site www.steepstone.com/forere/nissedal.

Other nearby Nissedal cliffs include Langfjell, Nipen, and Baremlandsfjellet. These and other cliffs in the area are rarely climbed compared with Hægefjell but offer many opportunities for superb first ascents in a remote setting. Langfjell, a

Hægefjell towers above glacial ponds near Lake Nisser.

magnificent slab above the west shore of Lake Nisser, is divided into three pillars, with most routes on the South Pillar. Nipen, with only one established route, has great potential and deserves more interest from climbers. Baremlandsfjellet is a pretty sunlit slab and is the first cliff to dry after winter. *Spionführer* is the most popular route here. Topos and route descriptions in Norwegian are found at www.steepstone.com/forere/nissedal.

Despite its somewhat benign appearance, objective dangers are found at Hægefjell. Loose blocks and flakes occur on some routes, although the described routes see a lot of traffic and are cleaned up. Use extreme care, especially in the early summer season after winter freezing and thawing has loosened rocks. It's a good idea to carry and wear a helmet to protect your head from loose pieces dislodged by the leader. Harsh and wet weather conditions can cause the rock to deteriorate or loosen up.

Rack, Protection, and Descent

Rack information is listed in the route descriptions. Keep in mind that the specified gear is only a suggestion of what you might need. Scope out your proposed route, then decide for yourself what you need to carry to safely protect yourself and your partner. Every climber protects routes differently, depending on individual skill and ability. The error is never in taking too much gear, but in taking too little.

All of the described routes are done traditional style, with few bolts or fixed pitons. Natural protection, however, is generally adequate since they usually follow crack systems. Some of the newer and harder routes have bolt-protected sections and bolted belay stations. Always back up fixed gear whenever possible, since freeze-thaw cycles can loosen it.

A standard Hægefjell rack includes sets of Stoppers, TCUs, and Friends or their camming equivalents. Carry some quickdraws as well as a half-dozen longer slings for tying off blocks, threading chockstones, and alleviating rope drag on long pitches. A 165-foot (50-meter) rope is adequate for most routes, although a 200-foot (60-meter) rope allows you to run some pitches together.

Descent off almost all the routes is by walking west from the dome's summit down slabs until you join the hiker's summit trail. Follow this west and down to the closed road, which you then follow east to the parking area. Alternatively, you can hike above the south face, descending slabs until you reach the marked summit path to the west.

Seasons and Weather

The climbing season here runs from June through September. The summer months offer generally good weather with many sunny, warm days. The south-facing cliff also dries quickly after rain. It's possible to climb here in May, depending on how much snowmelt is still running down the face. October also offers good climbing days, but it can also be cold and snow can fall.

Climbing History

Like most Norwegian mountains local hunters undoubtedly scrambled to the bald, rounded summit of Hægefjell. The name itself means Hæge's Mountain (Hæge is a woman's name). Like the big slabs at Valle to the west, Hægefjell was first visited by German climbers who opened the classic *sva* or slab and *riss* or crack routes on the big wall in the early 1980s. Some of the newer routes were established between 2000 and 2002 by Marius Olsen, Kjetil Grimsæth, and Marius Grimsæth.

Getting Around

You'll need a car to get out to this fairly remote climbing area. If you're coming from Oslo, it's easiest to follow highway E134, a major road across southern Norway. At Brunkeberg turn south onto highway 41, which you follow to Nissedal. Here catch a ferry across Lake Nisser to its west shore. A toll dirt road heads north to the cliff. Pay at a self-pay kiosk near the road's start past the ferry drop-off point. Allow four to five hours to drive to Hægefjell from Oslo.

Camping, Accommodations, and Services

The best place to camp is at one of the primitive camping areas scattered in the woods at the road's end near the cliff. At the nearby parking area next to the river are pit toilets and a camp-fee pay station. It's peaceful and quiet out here, far from any towns, and the night sky is a velvet carpet shimmering with stars. The campground can be very busy, particularly on weekends, with climbers from across Scandinavia and northern Europe sharing a friendly camaraderie. If you want more quiet, you can walk farther west to more private sites along the river.

Climbers who don't have camping gear or want more luxury stay at the Reime Family campsite (Reimefamiliens camping) on the west side of Nisser. Here you can tent, rent snug cottages (*hytt*), or stay in a traditional turf hut called a *gammen* with electricity and a fireplace.

Cultural Experiences and Rest Days

Most foreign visitors forego a visit to southern Norway, preferring instead to explore Oslo and then jump a train to the central fjords and Bergen. But the climber who doesn't care to follow the proven tourist track can explore this vast swath of wild mountains and forested valleys and discover some fine scenery and few people. This region, much in the county of Telemark, is surprisingly rural and wild once you leave the coastline to the east. This is a country to explore by driving. Lots of roads, both highways and narrow lanes, twist through the mountains.

Besides the lovely scenery there are some interesting places to visit on your driving explorations. The magnificent Heddal Stave Church (*stavkirke*), the largest surviving one in Norway, lies just west of Notodden. The church, initially built between 1147 and 1249, is open for tours. The 800-year-old stone church at Seljord is also worth a look, as is the small stave church at Eidsborg just north of Dalen. Next to the church is the West Telemark Museum, an old farm with exhibits displaying craft traditions and folk art. Grimdalstunet, just south of Dalen, was the home of the great Norwegian sculptress Anne Grimdalen. The old farm has ten authentic historic houses and a sculpture exhibition.

Telemark also offers lots of outdoor opportunities. These include canoeing on the lakes, hiking up valleys and mountains, wildlife observation of moose (*elg*) and beaver (*bever*), excellent fishing, and mountain biking. Stop by one of the tourist offices in Treungen, Seljord, or Vrådal for maps and information.

Trip Planning Information

General description: Hægefjell, a granite wall in the Nissedal region of southern Norway, is one of the country's best areas for climbing long, multipitch routes.

Location: South-central Norway. Hægefjell is located above the west shore of Lake Nisser, west of Porsgrunn and between Oslo and Stavanger. Allow four hours to drive there from Oslo.

Camping and accommodations: An excellent campsite is found at the parking area below Hægefjell with sites scattered in the nearby woods. This idyllic camping place is both peaceful and quiet. On weekends you'll find groups of climbers from all over Scandinavia camping here. Pay an overnight fee at the small building by the parking lot. Use the pit toilets. Other campgrounds and cottages are found along the road south of the ferry on the west side of Lake Nisser. A recommended place is the Reime Family campsite, which also offers *gammen* or traditional turf huts for rent.

Climbing season: June through September. The wall can be wet from snowmelt in May. October often offers climbable days, but it can also be cold and rainy.

Restrictions and access issues: None. The road and campsite are private. Pay the road toll at a kiosk near its start. A camping fee is payable at a small building at the end of the road.

Guidebooks: The best guide available is on the Internet at www.steepstone .com/forere/nissedal. The site has topos in Norwegian to many of the routes as well as surrounding crags. An old guidebook in German may or may not be found. Nissedal maps are "Bandak #1513 I" and "Figresvathet #1513 II," which are available in many Norwegian bookstores.

Services and shops: Nothing close to the cliffs. The closest shops and restaurants would be in Treungen and Vrådal.

Emergency services: For an ambulance dial 113. For police dial 112.

Nearby climbing areas: Many cliffs are

found in the surrounding area. Most are unclimbed and offer the opportunity for many superb first ascents. Nearby cliffs include Langfjell, Nipen, and Baremlandsfjellet. Many cliffs are found on the mountains flanking the southern end of Lake Nisser.

Nearby attractions: Points of interest include Norsk Skieventyr (Ski Museum) in Morgedal, Seljord Kirke (church), and Heddal Stavkirke (Stave Church) in Notodden. For more information contact Nissedal Tourist Information in Treungen (Tel: 35 04 57 00); Seljord Tourist Information in Seljord (Tel: 35 06 59 88) or www.seljordportalen.no; and Vrådal Tourist Service in Vrådal (Tel: 35 05 63 70) or www.vraadal.com.

Finding the cliff: There are several ways to get to Nissedal from Oslo. One of the fastest ways is to drive southwest from Oslo on the mostly four-lane E18 highway past Drammen and Sandefjord. At Porsgrunn and Skein exit onto highway 35, and drive north toward Porsgrunn. After a few kilometers, past the harbor and

some factories, turn left (west) onto highway 356, and drive 46 kilometers to highway 38. This highway can also be reached by continuing southwest on E18 and exiting onto highway 38. Follow route 38 for 24 kilometers to its intersection with highway 356. Either way you go, drive northwest from that junction for 8 kilometers to Prestestranda and then another 12 kilometers to the intersection of routes 38 and 358. Turn left (west) onto highway 358, and drive 28 kilometers to Treungen at the southern end of Lake Nisser. Drive north from Treungen on highway 41 along the east side of the lake for 21 kilometers to a left turn marked with a ferry sign. Alternatively, you can drive 40 kilometers up the narrow winding road along the west side of the lake to Hægefjell. Although you don't have to pay the ferry toll to drive to the cliff, the road is very time-consuming and slow. If you miss the last ferry, you can drive this route to Treungen. The narrow road winds past many towering, mostly unclimbed cliffs.

To reach Hægefjell and the other cliffs from the east and highway 41, cross

Lake Nisser at its narrowest part on a small ferry. The ferry, holding only a couple of cars, follows an underwater cable. It runs hourly between 8:00 A.M. and 6:00 P.M. The cost is 50 Norwegian kroner. After crossing the lake drive west to a marked gravel road, which runs 13 kilometers north to Hægefjell's parking area and the end of the road. This is a toll road with a 50-kroner fee payable at a small, self-serve, roadside kiosk just north of the road's start. Good swimming holes for warm days are found on polished bedrock alongside the road.

Park at the obvious parking lot at a water diversion station on the Horgevikåa River at the end of the road. Hægefjell looms to the north. Cross the river, and hike left through a gate. Follow a closed dirt road to access the routes on the west side of the wall, or right on a climber's path that winds through the marshy forest to the east side routes. Look for obvious paths that head off this track to the route bases.

Routes are described from right to left when facing the cliff from the south.

1. Via Lara (4)(5.7) 8 or 9 pitches. Maybe the best long beginner's route in Norway. The climb is extremely well protected and follows many perfect hand cracks up a slabby face on the southeast flank of Hægefjell. There are no bolts on the route. The route is very popular on weekends, with many climbers from around Scandinavia coming to climb this classic line.

To find the start hike up right from the parking area on narrow paths until you reach the cliff base. Walk along the base for about 1,600 feet until you reach an alcove with a belay tree. The slabs drop away to the right below here. The ground is well trampled at the start, so you should be able to identify the route.

The first pitch is somewhat runout. Above, follow the obvious crack systems to the top of the wall. One of the only route-finding problems is high on the route—a rightward traverse to another crack system—but it follows a natural line so you shouldn't get lost. **Descent:** The crux of the climb for many! It's a long walk back to the car from the top-out. After finishing scramble to the top of the dome, and follow cairns down the back side of the mountain to a closed road to the west. Follow the road east below Hægefjell's south face to the parking area. Allow two hours to descend and hike back. **Rack:** Sets of Stoppers, TCUs, and Friends to #3.5. A 200-foot (60-meter) rope is useful. Also a helmet.

2. Texas Ranger (7 A0) (5.11a A0) 7
pitches. This excellent route ascends the
steep central part of the wall. Pitches 5
and 6 can be combined with a long rope.
Begin by scrambling up left on a left-
angling ramp for 450 feet to a belay ledge.
Pitch 1: Climb up and left across a slab
(4+) (5.5) and then back right to a 2-bolt
belay stance below a small roof. 200 feet.
Pitch 2: Climb above the belay between
two roofs, and traverse left (6+) (5.10d).
Climb a corner above (6-) (5.10a) to a
short loose traverse right to a belay ledge
atop a pillar. 150 feet. **Pitch 3:** Work up a
short corner and then face climb (7-)
(5.11a) past 2 bolts and a piton to a bolt
out left. Downclimb (A0) 12 feet, then
face climb up left past some loose blocks
to a belay on a shelf in a cave. 165 feet.
Pitch 4: Climb the right side of the
chimney above and then up the chimney
(5) (5.8) to a loose block. Continue above
to a belay shelf. 130 feet. **Pitch 5:** Face
climb up left (4) (5.5) around the left side
of a huge roof and then up an easy slab to
a belay ledge. 150 feet. **Pitch 6:** A short
pitch up right (6-) (5.10a) to a belay. 50
feet. **Pitch 7:** Slab climb directly up (5)
(5.7) or up right past a couple bolts, and
finish up a low-angle, easy slab to the top
of the rock. **Rack:** Bring sets of Stoppers,
Friends, and TCUs; 12 quickdraws; selection of long runners; and a 200-foot (60-
meter) rope.

3. Mot Sola (*Toward the Sun*) (6–) (5.10a)
6 or 7 pitches. A wonderful steep route up
perfect granite. Highly recommended.
Begin by scrambling up left on an easy
slab to a left-angling ramp. Set up the first
belay at the top of the ramp. Pitches 1 and
2 can be combined into a 200-foot pitch.
Pitch 1: Climb the large open book (5.5)
to a belay stance atop a block. **Pitch 2:**
Continue up the dihedral (5.10a) until it's
possible to exit right and climb to a huge,
flat belay ledge with 2 bolts. 135 feet.
Pitch 3: Work up the dihedral above until
you step left (5.9+) into another corner.
Climb to a 1-bolt belay stance. 135 feet.
Pitch 4: Work back right above the corners, and finish up an easy chimney to a
belay stance with 1 bolt. 165 feet. **Pitch
5:** Continue up cracks (5.10a) past the left
side of an arching roof system. Work up a
chimney past a block (5.7), and then move
up right across an exposed slab to a 1-bolt
belay. 115 feet. **Pitch 6:** Climb up right
past the left side of a roof (5.9) to a bolt
(don't belay here because you will have
lots of rope drag on the last pitch).
Continue to a stance with 1 bolt. 50 feet.
Pitch 7: Work up the corner above (5.8)
to a narrow shelf. Belay above in a groove.
165 feet. Stay roped up, and scramble up
and left across the large, vegetated ledge,
then up easy slabs to the shoulder of the
dome. **Rack:** Sets of of Stoppers, TCUs,
and Friends; 200-foot (60-meter) rope;
and a helmet. It's possible to retreat off the
route with two ropes.

4. Hegar (6+) (5.10c) 7 pitches. Excellent, classic long route. Allow three to six hours to climb. The route ascends slabs and a prominent right-facing dihedral system on the left-center part of the wall. Start by scrambling up easy slabs (3rd class) for about 500 feet to a good belay from gear on a stance below the steepening wall. **Pitch 1:** Climb up left over big flakes to a small shelf. Work above up a tricky, awkwardly protected slab crux (5.10c). Don't fall—you might hit the shelf! Continue up left to a belay stance below a big dihedral. 115 feet. **Pitch 2:** Climb the dihedral above to a short traverse (5.8) right, and layback and jam up the right-facing dihedral to a good belay on a ledge. 165 feet. **Pitch 3:** Strenuous laybacking (5.10c) up the big, right-leaning dihedral leads to a precarious exit and a good belay stance above the lip. This pitch is sometimes wet. 165 feet. **Pitch 4:** Climb up left in a left-angling dihedral until the crack widens to an off-width. You have two choices here. For the preferred alternative step left, and jam a nice-looking crack (5.7) on the left to a belay stance in the dihedral. Or you can thrutch up the off-width crack, but it's poorly protected and glassy smooth. 165 feet. **Pitch 5:** Climb an easy pitch up the low-angle dihedral until it steepens, and belay. 165 feet. **Pitch 6:** Jam the steep corner crack above (5.8) until you can exit right. Move back left to a large belay ledge. 165 feet. **Pitch 7:** Climb up and left (5.5) across a slab to a belay. 165 feet. Continue scrambling up left onto the shoulder of the dome for the walk-off descent route. **Rack:** Sets of Stoppers, TCUs, and Friends. Some extra-large sizes are useful. A 200-foot (60-meter) rope is useful but not essential. Use a helmet, particularly if a party is above.

APPENDIX A: REFERENCES

UNITED KINGDOM

Cornish Rock, Rowland Edwards and Tim Dennel

Llanberis Pass, Iwan Arfon Jones (The Climber's Club, 1994).

North Wales: 100 Classic Climbs

North Wales Limestone

On Peak Rock (British Mountaineering Council).

Owgen and Carneddau (The Climber's Club).

Peak Gritstone East, Chris Craggs and Alan James (Rockfax, 2001).

Rockclimbing in Snowdonia, Paul Williams (Constable).

Scrambles in Snowdonia

Slate: A Climber's Guide

Southwest Climbs, Pat Littlejohn (Diadem Books, 1991).

Stanage Topo, Malc Baxter (British Mountaineering Council, 1993).

West Cornwall (The Climber's Club, 2001).

Western Grit, Chris Craggs and Alan James (Rockfax, 2003).

FRANCE

Aiguines: River Gauche, Phillipe Bugada

Buoux, P. Duret, B. Fara, and S. Jaulin (1995).

Buoux Kletterfuhrer, M. Heinkel, Kletterverlag (1992).

Escalade les Calanques, Gilles Bernard, Daniel Gorgeon, Christophe Kern, and Bernard Privat (Editions Aztec, 1997).

Grimper au Verdon, Bernard Gorgeon and Daniel Taupin

Grimper dans les Hautes Alpes

Orpierre et Val de Meouge (1995)

Rock Climbs in the Verdon, Rick Newcombe

BELGIUM

Freÿr, Marc Bott and Pierre Masschelein (2002).

Selected Rock Climbs in Belgium and Luxembourg, Chris Craggs (Cicerone Press).

SPAIN

Andalusian Rock Climbs, Chris Craggs (Cicerone Press, 1992).

Costa Blanca, Mallorca, El Chorro, Alan James and Mark Glaister (Rockfax, 2001).

Costa Blanca Rock, Chris Craggs (Cicerone Press, 1997).

El Chorro-Escalade en Málaga, Javier Romero Rubiols (2003).

Escaladas en le Medio y Alto Vinalopo (1995).

Guia de Escalada del Peñon de Ifach, Roy de Valera (1989).

Guia de Escalada del Puig Campana, Carlos Tudela (1995).

Sella Escalada, Ignacio Sanchez (1999).

ITALY

Arco Falesie, Diego Depretto and Margareth Eisendle (1999).

Arrampicata Sportiva a Cortina d'Ampezzo, Roberto Casanova (Cierre Edizioni).

Klettern in Groden Dolomiten, Mauro Bernardi (Athesia Touristik, 2002).

SWITZERLAND

Plaisir West, Jürg von Känel (Filidor, 2001); www.filador.ch.

Schweiz-Extrem, (Filidor); www.filador.ch.

GREECE

Kálymnos Rock Climbing Guide, Aris Theodoropoulos (2003); www.oreivatein.com.

Meteora Klettern, Heinz Lothar Stutte and Dietrich Hasse (2000).

Meteora Klettern und Wandern, Heinz Lothar Stutte and Dietrich Hasse (1986).

Varasova, Aris Theodoropoulos (Alpine Club of Acharnes, 1996).

Varassova Climbing Guide, Yannis Aliyannis (1997); www.oreivatein.com.

GERMANY

Kletterführer Frankenjura Band 1, Sebastian Schwertner (2001).

Kletterführer Frankenjura Band 2, Sebastian Schwertner (2002).

Topoführer Nördlicher Frankenjura, Bernhard Thum (1998).

NORWAY

Fører For Oslo (Kolsås Klatreklubb).

Oslo Climbing Guide

APPENDIX B: CONTACT INFORMATION

Belgium

Freÿr

Calling from the United States: Dial 011+ 32 + local number (LN) (without initial 0). Calling from Europe: Dial 00 + 32 + LN (without initial 0).

Alpi Rando (climbing shop)
74 Rue Caussin
5500 Anseremme, Dinant
Tel: 082 22 77 17

Club Alpin Belge (CAB)
129, av. Albert ler
5000 Namur
Tel: 081 22 40 84

Dinant Visitor Center
www.dinant.be

Le Chamonix Café
Chaussée des Alpinistes 20
5500 Dinant
Tel: 082 22 20 52

France

Buoux

Calling from the United States: Dial 011 + 33 + local number (LN) (without initial 0). Calling from Europe: Dial 00 + 33 + LN (without initial 0).

Auberge de Jeunesse (hostel)
Saignon
Tel: 04 90 74 39 34

Auberge du Lubéron
8 Place Faubourg du Ballet, Apt
Tel: 04 90 74 12 50

Camping Le Lubéron
Route de Saignon
Tel: 04 90 74 12 19

Camping Municipal Les Cedres
Route de Rustrel, 84400 Apt
Tel: 04 90 74 14 61

Fleurs de Soleil (Independent B&Bs)
www.fleurs-soleil.tm.fr

Gites de France
www.gites-de-france.fr/eng/

Hôtel du Palais
Place Gabriel Péri, Apt
Tel: 04 90 04 89 32

Hôtel L'Aptois
289 Cours Lauze de Perret, Apt
Tel: 04 90 74 64 79

Les Peirelles (B&B)
Muriel and Didier Andreis, proprieters
84560 Ménerbes
Tel: 04 90 72 23 42

Tourist Office/Office de Tourisme
20 Ave Philippe de Girard, Apt
Tel: 04 90 74 03 18
E-mail: tourisme.apt@avignon.pacwan.net

Céüse

Calling from the United States: Dial 011 + 33 + local number (LN) (without initial 0). Calling from Europe: Dial 00 + 33 + LN (without initial 0).

Camping Les Guérins
Sigoyer
Tel: 04 92 57 83 91
E-mail: camping.les.guérins@wanadoo.fr

Hôtel Gaillard
05400 Céüse
Tel: 04 92 57 80 42

Hôtel Muret
05130 Sigoyer
Tel: 04 92 57 83 02

La Grange aux Loups (gîte)
Les Guérins
05130 Sigoyer
Tel: 04 92 57 95 30

Le pré des Roses camping
Sigoyer
Tel: 04 92 57 81 66

Vertige (climbing shop)
Place Jean Marcellin
05000 Gap
Tel: 04 92 51 91 78

Le Calanques

Calling from the United States: Dial 011 + 33 + local number (LN) (without initial 0). Calling from Europe: Dial 00 + 33 + LN (without initial 0).

Alpina (shop)
6 rue Lafon
13006 Marseille
Tel: 04 91 54 35 16

Bonneveine (camping)
Marseille
Tel: 04 91 73 26 99

La Gardiole Youth Hostel
Cassis
Tel: 04 42 01 01 72

La Montagne (shop)
85 rue d'Italie
13006 Marseille
Tel: 04 91 42 18 36

Les Cigales (camping)
Route de Marseille
13260 Cassis
Tel: 04 42 01 02 72

Les Vagues (camping)
Marseille
Tel: 04 91 76 73 30

Les Trois Mousquetons (shop)
17 rue Jacques de la Roque
13,100 Aix en Provence
Tel: 04 42 21 93 98

Orpierre

Calling from the United States: Dial 011 + 33 + local number (LN) (without initial 0). Calling from Europe: Dial 00 + 33 + LN (without initial 0).

Camping des Princes D'Orange
05700 Orpierre
Tel: 04 92 66 22 53
Fax: 04 92 66 31 08

Gîte Etape de Saint-Avons (gîte)
05700 Orpierre
Tel: 04 92 66 23 68

Gîte Les Drailles (gîte)
05700 Orpierre
Tel: 04 92 66 31 20

Hotel le Céans
Les Bégües
05700 Orpierre
Tel: 04 92 66 24 22

Tourist Office/Office de Tourisme
05700 Orpierre
Tel: 04 92 66 30 45
E-mail: ot.orpierre@wanadoo.fr

Vertige Sport (shop)
05700 Orpierre
Tel: 04 92 66 28 50

Verdon Gorge

Calling from the United States: Dial 011 +
33 + local number (LN) (without initial 0).
Calling from Europe: Dial 00 + 33 + LN
(without initial 0).

Auberge de Jeunesses
Tel: 04 92 77 38 72

Auberge des Crêtes
La-Palud-sur-Verdon
04120 Castellane
Tel: 04 92 77 38 47

Bureau des Guides du Verdon
Rue Principale
04120 La-Palud-sur-Verdon
Camping Municipal
Tel: 04 92 77 38 13

Camping de Bourbon
Tel: 04 92 77 38 17

Hôtel des Gorges
Tel: 04 92 77 38 26

Hôtel Le Panoramic
Tel: 04 92 77 35 07

Hôtel Le Provence
La-Palud-sur-Verdon
Tel: 04 92 77 36 50

La Palud Office de Tourisme
E-mail: maisondesgorges@wanadoo.fr
www.lapaludsurverdon.com.

L'Arc-en-Ciel (gîte)
Place de l'Eglise
04120 La-Palud-sur-Verdon
Tel: 04 92 77 37 40

L'Étable (gîte)
Tel: 04 92 77 30 63

Le Perroquet Vert (shop)
Rue Grande
04120 La-Palud-sur-Verdon
Tel: 04 92 77 33 39

Le Wapiti
Tel: 04 92 77 30 02

Refuge de la Maline (Club Alpin Francais)
Chalet-refuge CAF, la Maline
04120 La-Palud-sur-Verdon
Tel: 04 92 77 38 05

Germany

Frankenjura

Calling from the United States: Dial 011
+ 49 + area code (AC) (without initial 0)
+ local number (LN).
Calling from Europe: Dial 00 + 49 + AC
(without initial 0) + LN.

Alpinsport (shop)
Bessemerstrasse 20
90411 Nürnberg
Tel: 09 11 55 01 55

Bäckerei Müller (best bakery)
Obertrubach
Tel: 0 92 45 4 47

Bärenschlucht (camping)
Weidmannsgesees 12
91278 Pottenstein
Tel: 0 92 43206

Gasthof Eichler (camping/guesthouse)
Wolfsberg 43
91286 Obertrubach
Tel: 49 (0) 92 45 383
Fax: 49 (0) 92 45 9116
www.gasthof-eichler.de

Mountain Sport (shop)
Bamberger Str. 62
91301 Forchheim
Tel: 09 191 1 44 18

Roland's Alpin Laden (shop)
Nürnberger Strasse 100
96050 Bamberg
Tel: 09 51 2 57 67

Great Britain

Cornwall

Calling from the United States: Dial 011+
44 + area code (AC) (without initial 0) +
local number (LN).
Calling from Europe: Dial 00 + 44 + AC
(without initial 0) + LN.

Cornwall Tourist Board
Pydar House, Pydar Street
Truro TR1 2XZ
Tel: 01872 274057

Lands End Youth Hostel
Letcha Vean St., Just-in-Penwith, Cornwall
TR19 7NT
Tel: 01736 788437

Kelynack Caravan and Camping Park
Kelynack, St. Just, Penzance, Cornwall
TR19 7RE
Tel/Fax: 01736 787633
E-mail: steve@kelynackholidays.co.uk

Penzance Tourist Office
Tel: 01736 362207

St. Ives Tourist Office
Tel: 01736 796297

Sea View Caravan and Camping Park
Sennen, Cornwall, TR19 7AD
Tel: 01736 871266

Secret Garden Caravan and Camping Park
Bosavern House
St. Just in Penwith, Penzance, Cornwall
TR19 7RD
Tel: 01736 788301
E-mail: info@bosavern.com

Trevedra Farm Caravan and Camping Site
Trevedra Farm
Sennen, Penzance
Tel: (01736) 871818

Gritstone Edges

Calling from the United States: Dial 011+
44 + area code (AC) (without initial 0) +
local number (LN).
Calling from Europe: Dial 00 + 44 + AC
(without initial 0) + LN.

Bakewell Youth Hostel
Bakewell
Tel: 01629 812313
Fax: 01629 812313
E-mail: bakewell@yha.org.uk

Bretton Youth Hostel
Tel: 01142 884541 (bookings)
E-mail: reservations@yha.org.uk

Eric Byne Memorial Campsite
Near the Robin Hood Pub, A619, west of
Baslow
Tel: 01246 582277

Hathersage Youth Hostel
Tel: 01433 650493
Fax: 01433 650493

Hitch 'n' Hike (2 shops)
Mytham Bridge, near Bamford
Hope Valley, Derbyshire S33 0AL
Tel: 01433 651013

8 Castleton Road, Hope
Hope Valley, Derbyshire
Tel: 01433 623331

North Lees Campsite (Stanage)
Tel: 01433 650838

Outside (shop)
Main Road, Hathersage S32 1BB
Tel: 01433 651936

Rock + Run (shop)
98 Devonshire Street
Sheffield S1 4GY
Tel: 01142 756429

Tourist Information Centres
Bakewell, Old Market Hall, Bridge Street
Tel: 01629 813227

Buxton, The Crescent
Tel: 01298 25106

Chesterfield, Peacock Information Centre,
Lower Pavement
Tel: 01246 207777

Leek, Market Place
Tel: 01538 483741

Sheffield, The Peace Gardens
Tel: 01142 734672

North Wales

Calling from the United States Dial 011+
44 + area code (AC) (without initial 0) +
local number (LN).
Calling from Europe: Dial 00 + 44 + AC
(without initial 0) + LN.

Dolgan (camping)
Capel Curig
Snowdonia LL24 0DS
Tel: 01690 720228

Eric Jones's Cafe and Accommodation
(camping and B&B)
Bwlch-y-Moch
Tremadog, Gwynedd LL49 9SN
Tel: 01766 512199
E-mail: info@ericjones-tremadog.c.uk

Garth Farm (camping)
Capel Curig
Tel: 0190 701571

Gwern Gaf Isaf Farm (camping)
Capel Curig
Snowdonia LL24 0E4
Tel: 01690 720276

Gwern y Gof Uchaf (camping)
Capel Curig
Snowdonia LL24 0EU
Tel: 01690 720294

Pete's Eats
40 High Street
Llanberis LL55 4EU
Tel: 02186 870117
www.petes-eats.co.uk

Greece

Kálymnos

Calling from the United States: Dial 011
+ 30 + local number (LN).
Calling from Europe: Dial 00 + 30 + LN.

Antonopoulos Pantelis (hotel)
Tel: 22430 47215

Hotel Panorama
Tel: 22430 23138

Irene's Apartments (hotel)
Myrties
Tel: 22430 48634
E-mail: ireneaprtm@klm.forthnet.gr

Koralli Studios (hotel)
Tel: 22430 47095

Massouri Holidays (hotel)
Tel: 22430 47628
Fax: 47627

Myrsina Hotel
Tel: 22430 47238

Stephanos Gerakios (hotel)
Kantouni
Tel: 22430 47036

Studios Lambrinos
Massouri
Tel: 22430 22110 or 47231 (ask for Maria)
E-mail: lambrinos@oreivatein.com

Metéora

Calling from the United States: Dial 011
+ 30 + local number (LN).
Calling from Europe: Dial 00 + 30 + LN.

Camping the Cave
Kastraki
Tel: 24320 24802

Camping Vrachos
Kastraki
Tel: 24320 23774 or 22293

Divani (hotel)
Kalambáka
Tel: 24320 22584
(a favorite with tour groups)

Dupiani House (hotel)
Kastraki
Tel: 24320 75326

Hotel France
Patrice Papastatis
Kastraki
Tel: 24320 24186

Hotel Kastráki
Kastraki
Tel: 24320 75336

Hotel Metéora
Kalambáka
Tel: 24320 22367

Hotel Spanias
Kastraki
Tel: 24320 75966

Hotel Sydney
Kastraki
Tel: 24320 23079

Koka Roka Rooms (hotel)
Kalambáka
Tel: 24320 24554

Papastathis Rooms (hotel)
Kastraki
Tel: 24320 77782 or 75326

Pension Patavalis (hotel)
Kastraki
Tel: 24320 22801

Sideris Konstantinos (shop)
Patriarxou Dimitriou 26
Kalambáka

Trekking Hellas (guide)
11, Rodou Str.
Kalambáka
Tel: 04320 75214
E-mail: trekking@forthnet.gr

Tsikeli Rooms (hotel)
Kastraki
Tel: 24320 22438

Varasova

Calling from the United States: Dial 011 + 30 + local number (LN).
Calling from Europe: Dial 00 + 30 + LN.

Bratsos Tavern (food)
Tel: 26310 41225 or 41125

Filoxenia Motel
Krioneri
Tel: 26310 41350 or 41326 or 22886

Glyka Rooms
Krioneri
Tel: 26310 41342 or 23761

Motel Kirkinezos
Krioneri
Tel: 26310 41300 or 25794 or 41104

Mourkos Motel
Tel: 26310 41216 or 39214

Plis Fotios
Krioneri
Tel: 26310 41122 or 41411

Italy

Arco

Calling from the United States: Dial 011 + 39 + local number (LN) (without initial 0).
Calling from Europe: Dial 00 + 39 + LN (without initial 0).

Caffè Trentino
Arco
Tel: 0464 516212

Camping Arco (camping)
Tel: 0464 517491

Camping Daino (camping)
Viale Daino 17
38070 Pietramurata
Tel: 0464 507451

Gobbisport Mountain Equipment (gear)
Via Segantini 72
38062 Arco
Tel: 0464 532500
www.gobbisport.com

Guesthouse (condos)
Tel: 0464 514111
E-mail: hmg@guesthouse-arco.com

Red Point Mountain Equipment (gear)
Viale Santoni 15/B
38062 Arco
Tel: 0464 519668

Vertical World Sport (gear)
Via Segantini 41
38062 Arco
Tel: 0464 510202

Viale Daino 17
38070 Pietramurata
Tel: 0464 507082

Zoo Camping (camping)
38062 Arco
Tel: 0464 516232

Dolomites

Calling from the United States: Dial 011 + 39 + local number (LN).
Calling from Europe: Dial 00 + 39 + LN.

Bob Culp Climbing School (guides)
6882 Audubon Avenue
Niwot, CO 80503
(303) 652-2823
www.bobculp.com

Gruppo Guide Alpine Cortina (guides)
P.tta S. Francesco, 5
Tel: 0436 4740
Via C. Battisti, 42
32043 Cortina d'Ampezzo
Tel: 0436 868505

K2 Sport Cortina (shop)
Via C. Battisti, 2
32043 Cortina d'Ampezzo
Tel: 0436 863706

Rifugio Bai de Dones
Tel: 0436 860688

Rifugio Cinque Torri
Tel: 0436 2902

Rifugio Scoiattoli
Tel: 0436 867939

Tourist Board of Val di Fassa
I-38032 Canazei
Tel: 0462 602466
www.fassa.com

Norway

Oslo Crags

Calling from the United States: Dial 011 + 47 + local number (LN).
Calling from Europe: Dial 00 + 47 + LN.

Bogstad Camping
Ankerveien 117
Tel: 22 50 76 80
(lakeside camping 15 kilometers northwest of Oslo center)

Ekeberg Camping
Ekebergveien 65, Oslo
Tel: 22 19 85 68
(campground 3 kilometers east of Oslo center)

KFUK-KFUM Sleep-In (hostel)
Møllergata 1, Oslo
Tel: 22 20 83 97
(cheap central hostel)

Kolsås Klatreklubb (climbing gym)
Maridalsveien 17, 0175 Oslo
Tel: 22 11 28 90
E-mail: kolsaas1@online.no

Langøyene Camping
Langøyene, Oslo
Tel: 22 11 53 21
(popular campground on an offshore island)

Norges Informasjonssenter
(Norwegian Information Center)
Vestbaneplassen 1, Oslo
Tel: 22 83 00 50

Oslo Haraldsheim (hostel)
Haraldsheimveien 4, Grefsen
Tel: 22 22 29 65
Fax: 22 11 10 25
(a very good HI Hostel 5 kilometers northeast of Oslo center)

Tyrili Klatreklubb (climbing gym)
Sverresgate 4, Oslo
Tel: 22 67 28 44
Fax: 22 67 40 10

Spain

Costa Blanca

Calling from the United States: Dial 011 + 34 + local number (LN).
Calling from Europe: Dial 00 + 34 + LN.

Clan Natura Trek Shop
C/Foglietti, 15 03007
Alicante
Tel: 965 131 614

Intersport (shop)
C/Mercado, 3
Benidorm
Tel: 965 857 720

K2 Esports (shop)
Alicante
Tel: 965 206 562

The Orange House
Finestrat
Alicante
Tel: 0034 96 587 8251
www.theorangehouse.net

Zero 95 (shop)
Avda. Gabriel Miro, 22
Calpe
Tel: 965 830 589

El Chorro

Calling from the United States: Dial 011 + 34 + local number (LN).
Calling from Europe: Dial 00 + 34 + LN.

Decathalon (shop)
Centro Cial la Rosaleda
Avda. Simon Bolivar 1, Local 8-40
2901 Málaga

Deportes La Trucha (shop)
Calle Carreteria 100
29008 Málaga
Tel: 952 212 203

Finca la Campana
El Chorro
Tel: 626 963 942
E-mail: el-chorro@el-chorro.com
www.el-chorro.com

Gargantua Hotel
El Chorro
Tel: 524 951 19 (Spanish only)

Intersport Málaga (shop)
Centro Comercial Larios
Avda. Aurora s/n 29001 Málaga
Tel: 952 369 436

La Almona Chica
El Chorro
Tel: 952 119 872
E-mail: sumitch@teleline.es

La pension de Isabel
El Chorro
Tel: 952 495 004

Switzerland

Grimsel Valley

Calling from the United States: Dial 011 + 33 + local number (LN).
Calling from Europe: Dial 00 + 33 + LN.

Camping Aareschlucht
Innertkirchen
Tel: 971 53 32

Hotel Grimsel Hospiz
Tel: 982 46 21

Hotel Handeck
Handegg
Tel: 982 36 11

Hotel Meiringen
CH-3860 Meiringen
Tel: 972 12 12
www.hotel-meiringen.ch

Hotel Urweid
Guttannen
Tel: 971 26 82

Kletterhalle Haslital (climbing gym)
Meiringen
Tel: 971 39 00
E-mail: kletterhalle@alpenregion.ch

Vertical Sport (shop)
Florastr. 12 3800 Interlaken
www.verticalsport.ch

Cyber-Traveling

U.S. State Department offers country information, travel advisories and warnings, and country updates.
www.travel.state.gov

Centers for Disease Control and Prevention is the definitive source for online traveler's health information and advisories.
www.cdc.gov

Travel Health Online has health listings, concerns, advisories, suggested immunizations, and local health care providers for more than 220 countries.
www.tripprep.com/index.html

European Car Rentals

ACE Rent-a-Car
Tel: 011 30 1 968 0700
Rentals in Greece only.

Acropolis Rent-a-Car
Tel: 011 30 1 931 9682
Rentals in Greece only.

Alamo
Tel: (800) 522-9696
www.alamo.com
Rentals in ten countries.

Auto Europe
Tel: (888) 223-5555
www.autoeurope.com
Rentals in twenty-five countries.

Avis Rent-a-Car
Tel: (800) 331-1084
www.avis.com
Rentals and minileases.

Budget Rent-a-Car
Tel: (800) 472-3325
www.drivebudget.com
Rentals in most countries.

DER Tours
Tel: (888) 337-7350
www.dertravel.com
Rentals in twenty-one countries. Long-term Renault leases.

Dollar Rent-a-Car
Tel: (800) 800-6000
www.dollarcar.com
Rentals in twenty-two countries.

Europe by Car
Tel: (800) 223-1516
www.europebycar.com
Long-term rentals in Europe and Britain.

Hertz Rent-a-Car
(800) 634-3001
www.hertz.com
Rentals in all of Europe.

Kemwel Holiday Autos
Tel: (800) 678-0678
www.kemwel.com
Rentals in most of Europe.

National Car Rental
Tel: (800) 227-7368
www.nationalcar.com
Rentals in most of Europe.

Payless Car Rental
Tel: (800) 729-5377
www.paylesscar.com
Rentals in Greece.

Renault Eurodrive
Tel: (800) 221-1052
www.renaultusa.com
Rentals in thirty-three countries. Long-term rentals.

Rent-A-Wreck
Tel: (800) 535-1391
www.rentawreck.com
Rentals in Norway and Sweden.

Thrifty Car Rental
Tel: (800) 847-4389
www.thrifty.com
Rentals in ten countries.

ABOUT THE AUTHOR

Stewart M. Green is a freelance photographer and writer based in Colorado. He travels the world working on projects for The Globe Pequot Press and other publications and has written many books for Globe Pequot, including the popular *Rock Climbing Colorado, Rock Climbing Utah, Rock Climbing New England, Rock Climbing Arizona, Scenic Driving California,* and *Scenic Driving New England.* He is currently working on a collection of essays about the climbing life. Stewart has over thirty years of experience as a professional photographer and is one of the world's leading climbing photographers. In addition to books, his work appears in many catalogues, advertisements, and national publications. Online galleries of some of his favorite images can be viewed at www.stewartgreen.com.

Stewart Green at Passo Falzarego in the Dolomites, Italy.